THE U.S.
MARINE
CORPS
STORY

THE U.S. MARINE CORPS STORY

THIRD REVISED EDITION

J. ROBERT MOSKIN

Little, Brown and Company
Boston   Toronto   London

THIRD REVISED EDITION

LIBRARY OF CONGRESS CATALOGING-IN-PUBLICATION DATA

Moskin, J. Robert.
    The U.S. Marine Corps story / by J. Robert Moskin. — 3rd rev.
updated ed.
        p.   cm.
    Originally published: New York : McGraw Hill, 1977.
    ISBN 0-316-58559-9 (hc)
    ISBN 0-316-58558-0 (pb)
    1. United States.   Marine Corps — History.   I. Title.
VE23.M64   1992
359.9′6′0973 — dc20   92–6485

HC: 10   9   8   7   6   5   4   3   2   1
PB: 10   9   8   7   6   5   4   3   2   1

RRD-VA

Published simultaneously in Canada by Little, Brown & Company (Canada)
Limited

PRINTED IN THE UNITED STATES OF AMERICA

Dedicated to the men and women
who lived this story—
and those who died for it

Contents

Foreword

III

Imperialism in the Caribbean
1901–1934

IV

Getting Ready
1919–1941

V

World War II
1941–1949

VI

The Korean War
1946–1953

VII

Tumultuous Times
1953–1965

VIII

The Vietnam War
1954–1975

MAPS

Following Foreword

Foreword

The story of the U.S. Marine Corps is, first of all, the story of men in battle—the story of individual courage—of men who risked everything to do what had to be done. Although no Marine ever started a war, the Marines have been ready when called. Trained to kill, they are, in Stephen Crane's words, members of "a mysterious fraternity born of smoke and the danger of death."

This is also the story of what America is really like: how it has thrust its power outward around the globe—spearheaded repeatedly by United States Marines. It is, obviously, the story of American imperialism. Some of this story is praiseworthy; some of it is ugly. All of it must be told—unvarnished.

The reader will discover here a mainstream of the nation's story. From the Marines who fought at Princeton, New Orleans, Harpers Ferry, Peking, Haiti, Belleau Wood, Iwo Jima, the Chosin Reservoir, Khe Sanh and Kuwait, the reader will gain a fresh understanding of the meaning and uses—and the price—of more than 200 years of American power.

The reader who has been or is now a Marine will find here the true story of the Corps to which he looks with pride. He will see its story whole, in a way he has not before. He will read of Marines who have fought in his country's every war: John Trevett in the Revolution, Presley O'Bannon at Tripoli, Samuel Miller in the War of 1812, Archibald Henderson in the Indian wars, George Terrett in the Mexican War, Louis Fagan in the Civil War, John Quick in the War with Spain, Tony Waller in the Philippine Insurrection, Dan Daly in World War I, William Deane Hawkins and John Basilone in World War II, Chesty Puller in Korea, Lewis Walt in Vietnam. They were men—Marines—worth reading about.

The Marine Corps' story fascinates me because it mirrors the entire violent sweep of American history. When I was an editor with *Look* magazine, assignments enabled me to report on Marines who fought and served at Da Nang, Inchon, Guantanamo, Chapultepec and Okinawa, and across the United States from Parris Island to Camp Pendleton. I had to be impressed with the effectiveness and pride I saw. Those Marines were by no means all supermen; they had to conquer the fear that hides in everyone. But the *esprit* of their Corps, their code of comradeship made them special and drove them, when their country needed them, to move forward in battle where men kill and are killed.

The American Marines were born in 1775—before the nation. The need was there, as it still is today. Elmer Davis, the World War II director of the U.S. Office of War Information, put it baldly: "This will remain the land of the free only so long as it is the home of the brave." The Marines will be needed as long as the nation must be defended.

By the year of American Independence, nearly three million people had stepped onto these western shores of the Atlantic. They multiplied to two hundred million, strode across the continent and manned outposts around the globe. They became the most powerful people on earth, now at the height—and the limit—of their expansion.

What spurred them on? They were propelled by the desire to escape tyrannies and wars, by hunger for freedom and land and economic well-being, and by faith in a self-appointed mission to spread civilization and God's word—in their own image.

The U.S. Marine Corps acquired, over time, the bloody duty of carrying the flag of empire, until this elite professional corps won an unerasable place in America's history and heritage. The Marine Corps both paced and symbolized the global destiny that the nation chose for itself.

This thrust pushed beyond the continent, through the islands of the Caribbean and the Pacific, and grabbed for footholds on the mainland of Asia. There, it met forces that proved unmovable; and the limits of expansion were learned slowly and painfully.

When the original edition of this book was published, United States Marines were still fighting in Vietnam. This is now the fourth edition, and the story of the United States Marines has moved on to include the tragedy of Beirut, the invasions of Grenada and Panama and the massive conflict on the shore of the Persian Gulf.

This is the only totally independent history of this cavalcade. The Marine Corps Combat Correspondents Association has honored it with its Distinguished Service Award, and it is included on the Commandant's Reading List for all Marine leaders. This is the candid, unofficial story of the nation's growth and of the Marines who led the way. And finally, like most stories worth telling, it is a story of love—of love for country and for those who share the battle and the dying.

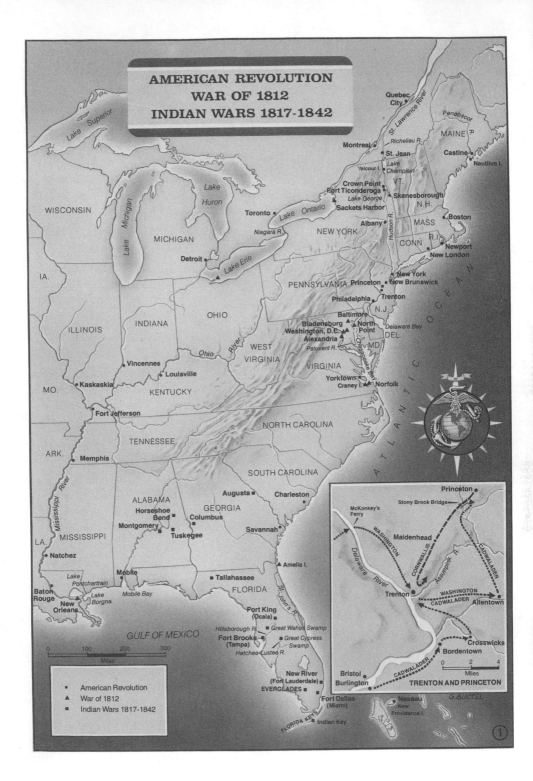

AMERICAN REVOLUTION
WAR OF 1812
INDIAN WARS 1817-1842

Quebec City

Penobscot R.

MAINE

St. Lawrence River

Richelieu R.

Montreal

St. Jean

Castine

Lake Superior

Nautilus I.

Valcour I.

Lake Champlain

VT.

Crown Point

Fort Ticonderoga

Lake George

Skenesborough

N.H.

Lake Huron

Toronto

Lake Ontario

Sackets Harbor

Hudson R.

Albany

MASS.

Boston

R.I.

WISCONSIN

Niagara R.

NEW YORK

CONN.

Newport

New London

Lake Michigan

MICHIGAN

Detroit

Lake Erie

PENNSYLVANIA

New York

Princeton

New Brunswick

IA.

Philadelphia

Trenton

N.J.

Baltimore

Bladensburg

North Point

Washington, D.C.

Delaware Bay

DEL.

ILLINOIS

INDIANA

OHIO

Alexandria

Patuxent R.

MD.

Ohio River

WEST VIRGINIA

Chesapeake Bay

Vincennes

Louisville

VIRGINIA

Yorktown

Norfolk

MO.

Kaskaskia

KENTUCKY

Craney I.

Fort Jefferson

NORTH CAROLINA

ARK.

TENNESSEE

ATLANTIC OCEAN

Memphis

Mississippi River

SOUTH CAROLINA

Augusta

Charleston

ALABAMA

GEORGIA

Horseshoe Bend

Columbus

Montgomery

Tuskegee

Savannah

MISSISSIPPI

Amelia I.

LA.

Natchez

Lake Pontchartrain

Mobile

Tallahassee

Baton Rouge

Lake Borgne

Mobile Bay

FLORIDA

New Orleans

St. John's R.

Fort King (Ocala)

GULF OF MEXICO

Hillsborough R.

Great Wahoo Swamp

Fort Brooke (Tampa)

Great Cypress Swamp

Hatchee-Lustee R.

New River (Fort Lauderdale)

EVERGLADES

Fort Dallas (Miami)

FLORIDA KEYS

Indian Key

Nassau

New Providence I.

0   100   200   300
Miles

- • American Revolution
- ▲ War of 1812
- ■ Indian Wars 1817-1842

Inset map: TRENTON AND PRINCETON

Princeton

McKonkey's Ferry

Stony Brook Bridge

WASHINGTON

Maidenhead

CORNWALLIS

Assunpink R.

CADWALADER

Delaware River

Trenton

WASHINGTON

CADWALADER

Allentown

Crosswicks

Bordentown

Bristol

CADWALADER

Burlington

0   2   4
Miles

G. BUCTEL

①

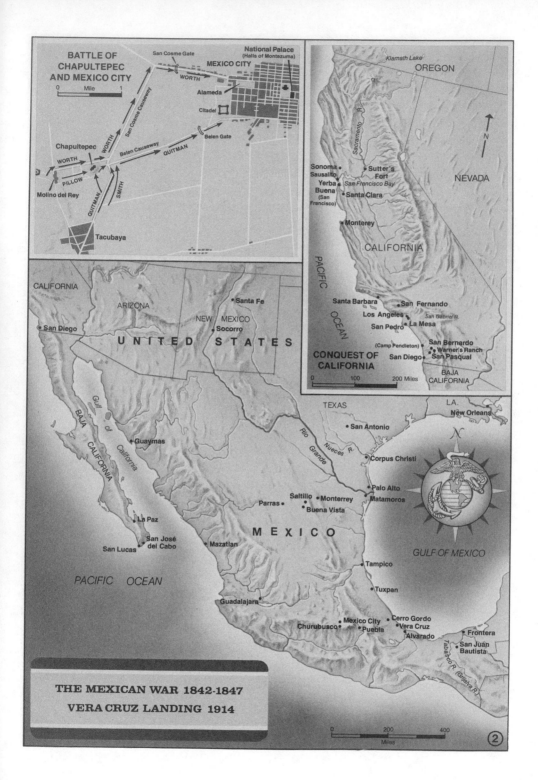

BATTLE OF CHAPULTEPEC AND MEXICO CITY

San Cosme Gate
National Palace
(Halls of Montezuma)
MEXICO CITY
WORTH
Alameda
0 Mile 1
San Cosme Causeway
Citadel
WORTH
Belen Causeway
Belen Gate
Chapultepec
WORTH
QUITMAN
PILLOW
SMITH
Molino del Rey
QUITMAN
Tacubaya

CONQUEST OF CALIFORNIA

Klamath Lake
OREGON
N
Sacramento R.
NEVADA
Sonoma
Sausalito
Sutter's Fort
Yerba Buena (San Francisco)
San Francisco Bay
Santa Clara
Monterey
CALIFORNIA
PACIFIC OCEAN
Santa Barbara
San Fernando
Los Angeles
San Gabriel R.
San Pedro
La Mesa
(Camp Pendleton)
San Bernardo
Warner's Ranch
San Diego
San Pasqual
BAJA CALIFORNIA
0 100 200 Miles

CALIFORNIA
ARIZONA
Santa Fe
NEW MEXICO
San Diego
UNITED STATES
Socorro
Gulf of California
BAJA CALIFORNIA
Guaymas
TEXAS
LA.
New Orleans
San Antonio
Rio Grande
Nueces R.
Corpus Christi
La Paz
San José del Cabo
San Lucas
Mazatlan
Parras
Saltillo
Monterrey
Buena Vista
Palo Alto
Matamoros
MEXICO
N
GULF OF MEXICO
PACIFIC OCEAN
Tampico
Tuxpan
Guadalajara
Churubusco
Mexico City
Cerro Gordo
Puebla
Vera Cruz
Alvarado
Frontera
San Juan Bautista
Tabasco R. (Grijalva R.)

THE MEXICAN WAR 1842-1847
VERA CRUZ LANDING 1914

0 200 400
Miles

②

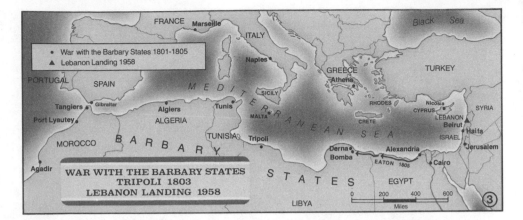

WAR WITH THE BARBARY STATES
TRIPOLI 1803
LEBANON LANDING 1958

- War with the Barbary States 1801-1805
- ▲ Lebanon Landing 1958

THE CIVIL WAR

ACTION
AT FORT FISHER
JAN. 15, 1865

CONFEDERATE
STATES

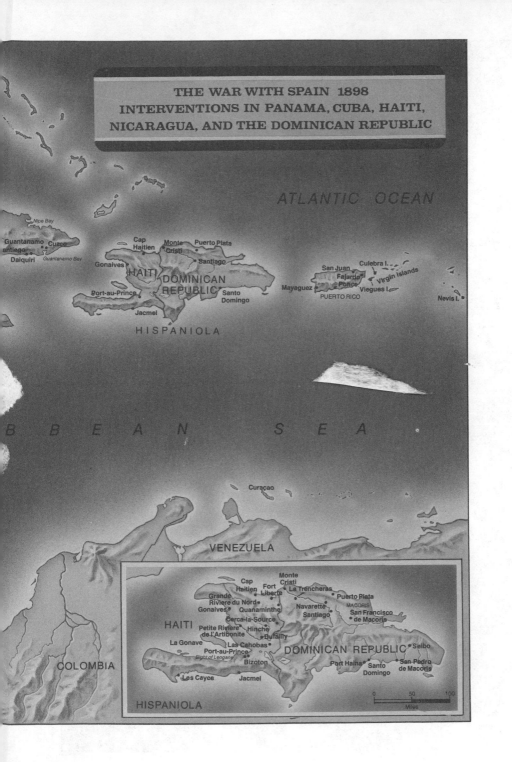

THE WAR WITH SPAIN 1898
INTERVENTIONS IN PANAMA, CUBA, HAITI,
NICARAGUA, AND THE DOMINICAN REPUBLIC

ATLANTIC OCEAN

Nipe Bay
Guantanamo Cuzco
antiego
Daiquiri Guantanamo Bay

Cap   Monte   Puerto Plata
Haitien   Cristi
Gonaives   Santiago
HAITI DOMINICAN
REPUBLIC   Santo
Port-au-Prince   Domingo

Jacmel

HISPANIOLA

San Juan   Culebra I.
Fajardo   Virgin Islands
Mayaguez Ponce
Vieques I.   Nevis I.
PUERTO RICO

C A R I B B E A N   S E A

Curaçao

VENEZUELA

COLOMBIA

HISPANIOLA

Monte
Cap   Fort   Cristi
Haitien Liberte La Trencheras
Grande   Puerto Plata
Riviere du Nord   Navarette MACORIS
Gonaives Quanaminthe   San Francisco
Cerca-la-Source Santiago   de Macoris
HAITI Petite Riviere Hinche
de l'Artibonite Bufailly
La Gonave   Las Cahobas
Port-au-Prince   DOMINICAN REPUBLIC Seibo
Bight of Leogane Bizoton
Les Cayos   Port Haina San Pedro
Jacmel   Santo de Macoris
Domingo

0   50   100
Miles

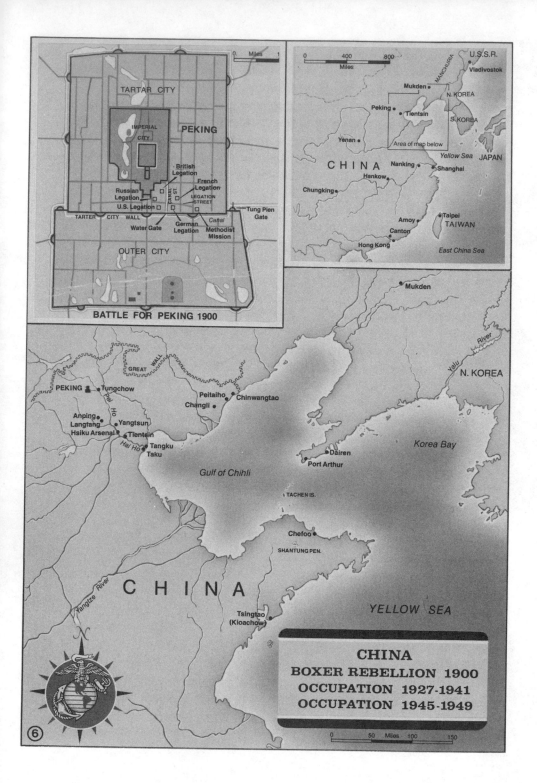

BATTLE FOR PEKING 1900

CHINA
BOXER REBELLION 1900
OCCUPATION 1927-1941
OCCUPATION 1945-1949

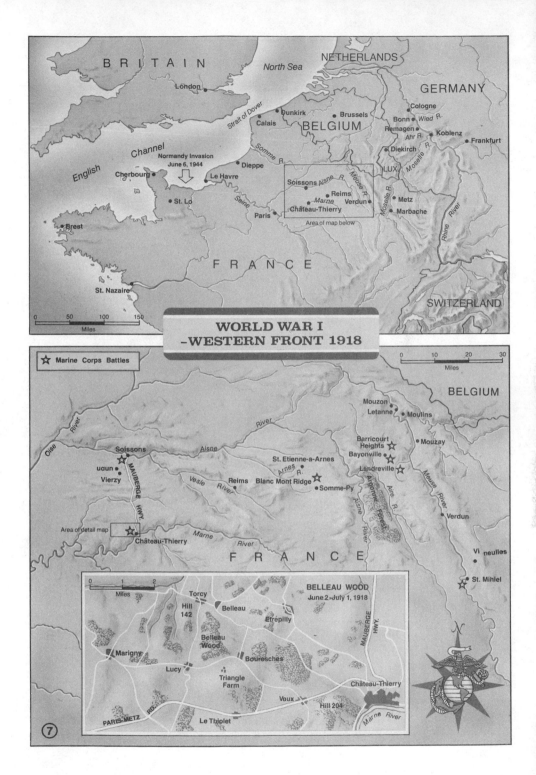

WORLD WAR I —WESTERN FRONT 1918

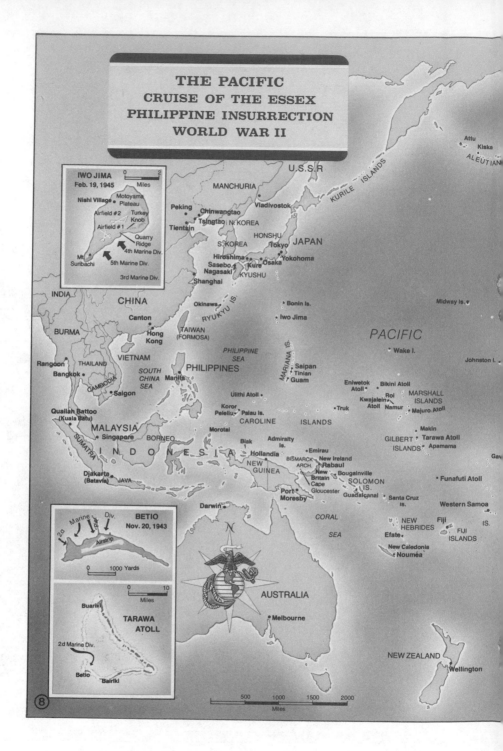

THE PACIFIC
CRUISE OF THE ESSEX
PHILIPPINE INSURRECTION
WORLD WAR II

IWO JIMA
Feb. 19, 1945

0 — 2
Miles

Nishi Village • Motoyama Plateau
Airfield #2 • Turkey Knob
Airfield #1 •
Quarry Ridge
4th Marine Div.
Mt. Suribachi
5th Marine Div.
3rd Marine Div.

BETIO
Nov. 20, 1943

2d Marine Div.
Airstrip

0 — 1000 Yards

0 — 10
Miles

TARAWA ATOLL

Buariki
2d Marine Div.
Betio • Bairiki

U.S.S.R
MANCHURIA
Peking
Chinwangtao
Tsingtao
Tientsin
N. KOREA
HONSHU
S. KOREA
Tokyo
JAPAN
Hiroshima • Yokohoma
Sasebo • Osaka
Nagasaki • Kure
Shanghai • KYUSHU
KURILE ISLANDS
Attu
Kiska
ALEUTIAN
Vladivostok

INDIA
CHINA
Canton
Hong Kong
BURMA
VIETNAM
Rangoon
THAILAND
Bangkok
CAMBODIA
Saigon
SOUTH CHINA SEA
Manila
PHILIPPINES
Qualiah Battoo
(Kuala Batu)
MALAYSIA
Singapore
BORNEO
SUMATRA
INDONESIA
Djakarta (Batavia)
JAVA

Okinawa
RYUKYU IS.
TAIWAN (FORMOSA)
PHILIPPINE SEA
Bonin Is.
Iwo Jima
Midway Is.
PACIFIC
Wake I.
Johnston I.
MARIANA IS.
Saipan
Tinian
Guam
Ulithi Atoll
Koror
Peleliu • Palau Is.
CAROLINE
Morotai
Biak
Admiralty Is.
Hollandia
NEW GUINEA
BISMARCK ARCH.
New Ireland
Rabaul
New Britain
Cape Gloucester
Port Moresby
Darwin
Eniwetok Atoll
Bikini Atoll
Roi
Kwajalein
Atoll Namur
MARSHALL ISLANDS
Truk
Majuro Atoll
Makin
GILBERT ISLANDS
Tarawa Atoll
Apamama
ISLANDS
Bougainville
SOLOMON IS.
Guadalcanal
Santa Cruz Is.
Funafuti Atoll
Emirau
New
Western Samoa
CORAL SEA
NEW HEBRIDES
Efate
New Caledonia
Nouméa
Fiji
FIJI ISLANDS
IS.
Gav

AUSTRALIA
Melbourne

NEW ZEALAND
Wellington

500   1000   1500   2000
Miles

⑧

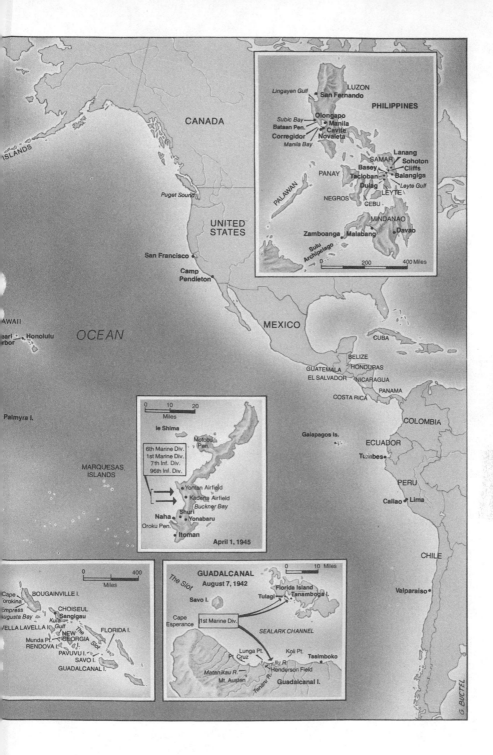

CANADA

ISLANDS

PHILIPPINES

Lingayen Gulf
LUZON
San Fernando

Subic Bay
Olongapo
Bataan Pen.
Manila
Corregidor
Cavite
Novaleta
Manila Bay

Lanang
SAMAR
Sohoton
Basey
Cliffs
Tacloban
Balangiga
PANAY
Dulag
Leyte Gulf
NEGROS
LEYTE
CEBU

MINDANAO

Zamboanga
Malabang
Davao

Sulu
Archipelago

PALAWAN

200   400 Miles

Puget Sound

UNITED
STATES

San Francisco

Camp
Pendleton

MEXICO

CUBA

BELIZE

GUATEMALA
HONDURAS
EL SALVADOR
NICARAGUA
PANAMA
COSTA RICA

COLOMBIA

AWAII
Honolulu
OCEAN
earl
rbor

ECUADOR
Galapagos Is.
Tumbes

Palmyra I.

0   10   20
Miles

Ie Shima

Motobu
Pen.

6th Marine Div.
1st Marine Div.
7th Inf. Div.
96th Inf. Div.

PERU
Callao   Lima

MARQUESAS
ISLANDS

Yontan Airfield
Kadena Airfield
Buckner Bay
Shuri
Naha
Yonabaru
Oroku Pen.
Itoman

April 1, 1945

CHILE

0   400
Miles

Valparaiso

Cape
orokina
BOUGAINVILLE I.
Empress
ugusta Bay
CHOISEUL
Sangigau
Kula
Gulf
ELLA LAVELLA I.
NEW
FLORIDA I.
Munda Pt.
GEORGIA
RENDOVA I.
PAVUVU I.
SAVO I.
GUADALCANAL I.

GUADALCANAL
August 7, 1942

The Slot

Savo I.

Florida Island
Tulagi
Tanamboga I.

0   10 Miles

Cape
Esperance
1st Marine Div.
SEALARK CHANNEL

Lunga Pt.
Koli Pt.
Pt. Cruz
Tasimboko
Matanikau R.
Ilu R.
Henderson Field
Mt. Austen
Guadalcanal I.

G. BUCTEL

KOREA

VIETNAM WAR
MAYAGUEZ INCIDENT

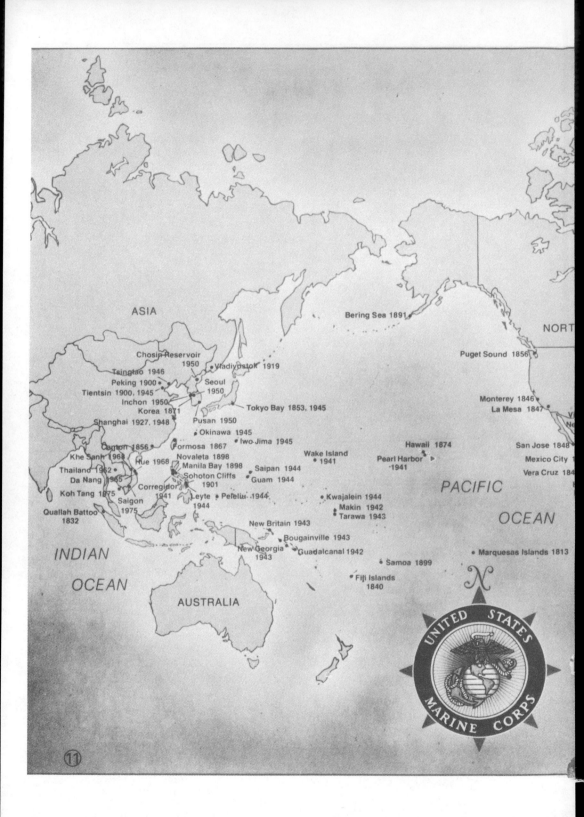

ASIA

Chosin Reservoir
1950
Tsingtao 1946
Peking 1900
Tientsin 1900, 1945
Inchon 1950
Korea 1871
Shanghai 1927, 1948

Vladivostok 1919
Seoul
1950
Tokyo Bay 1853, 1945
Pusan 1950
Okinawa 1945
Iwo Jima 1945

Bering Sea 1891

NORT

Puget Sound 1856

Monterey 1846
La Mesa 1847

Canton 1856
Khe Sanh 1968
Hue 1968
Thailand 1962
Da Nang 1965
Koh Tang 1975
Saigon
1975
Quallah Battoo
1832

Formosa 1867
Novaleta 1898
Manila Bay 1898
Sohoton Cliffs
1901
Corregidor
1941
Leyte
1944
Peleliu 1944

Wake Island
1941

Pearl Harbor
1941

Hawaii 1874

San Jose 1848
Mexico City
Vera Cruz 184

Saipan 1944
Guam 1944

Kwajalein 1944
Makin 1942
Tarawa 1943

PACIFIC

OCEAN

New Britain 1943

Bougainville 1943
New Georgia
1943
Guadalcanal 1942

Samoa 1899

Marquesas Islands 1813

INDIAN

OCEAN

Fiji Islands
1840

AUSTRALIA

N

UNITED STATES

MARINE CORPS

⑪

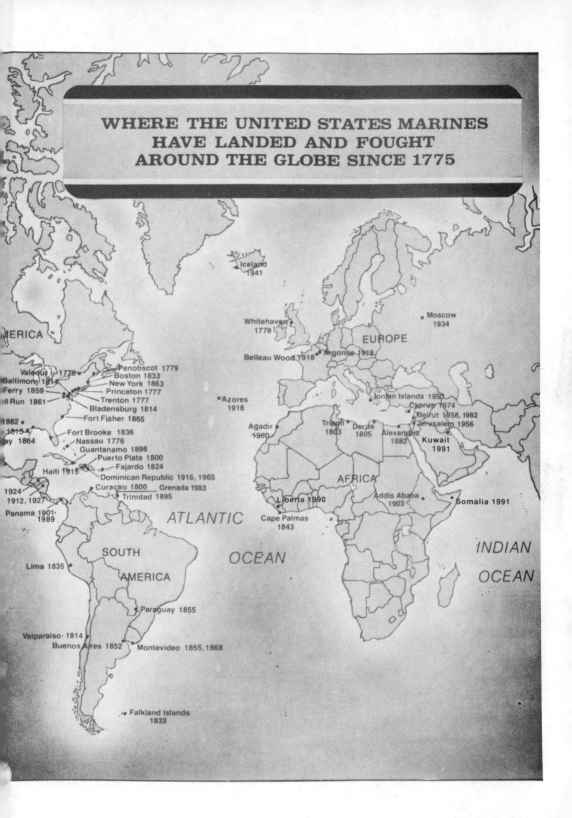

WHERE THE UNITED STATES MARINES HAVE LANDED AND FOUGHT AROUND THE GLOBE SINCE 1775

THE PERSIAN GULF WAR

SEMPER FIDELIS

I
THE
EARLY
YEARS
1775-1902

Archibald Henderson served as Commandant of the
Marine Corps for thirty-eight years,
longer than any other man.
Private Collection, Courtesy of Museums Branch, USMC

Introduction

As Marines tell it, after the fighting of the American Revolution was over and the nation's military forces were disbanded, all that remained was a corps of mules and two battalions of Marines. The Army and the Navy tossed a coin to determine who would take the mules and who, the Marines. The Army, according to the story, won the toss—and took the mules.

The fighting story of the United States Marines sweeps over more than 200 years. The American Marines were created on November 10, 1775, and first landed on March 3, 1776, on New Providence Island in the Bahamas to capture gun powder and cannon from the British. U.S. Marines fought their most recent wartime actions, as of this writing, in the jungles of Panama and Grenada and in the desert of the Persian Gulf, where their skills, firepower, mobility and courage removed the Iraqi invaders from Kuwait.

Marines have fought their country's battles around the globe and spearheaded the United States' expansion across a continent and overseas. They evolved into an elite, professional, amphibious corps, defending Americans' interests and projecting their power.

"The Early Years" covers the first part of the story—from birth to maturity—to the time still within living memory, when the United States Marines fought in France in World War I and served as the cutting edge of American imperialism in the Caribbean and China. The earlier period made possible the modern United States Marines. And the stories of the Marines who fought with Washington at Princeton, on the shores of Tripoli, in the Florida swamps, on the coast of California and into the Halls of Montezuma, in the Civil War and the War with Spain are dramatic tales too often forgotten.

1
The Continental Marines
1775–1784

Their story began on the seacoast—Americans have been an amphibious people from the beginning. The American Revolutionary War started when the colonists gathered to throw the British Army out of Boston seaport. The struggle for independence was shaped by the sea and the wilderness waterways.

In the fall of 1775, seven months after the first gunfire at Lexington and Concord and eight before the Declaration of Independence, George Washington commanded the Continental Army at Boston and, although desperately short of guns and gunpowder, ringed the British troops in an uneasy siege. At Philadelphia, the new-born Continental Navy was organizing its first excursion to sea. On November 10, the Second Continental Congress, in session in Philadelphia, resolved that two battalions of American Marines "be inlisted and commissioned to serve for and during the present war between Great Britain and the colonies."[1] The American Marines were born.

The two battalions were never raised; but on November 28, the Congress commissioned thirty-two-year-old Capt. Samuel Nicholas, a Philadelphia Quaker and innkeeper and a blacksmith's son, as the first Marine officer.

A hundred volunteers, recruited in Rhode Island, arrived at Philadelphia by December 5. One of these was twenty-eight-year-old John Trevett, son of a seafaring family. Trevett was probably signed up in Robert Mullan's Tun Tavern. He believed earnestly in the Revolution. "We are engaged in a good cause," he wrote later in his journal, "and are fighting the Lord's battles."[2]

Commodore Esek Hopkins of Rhode Island, a longtime merchant sea captain, assembled eight ships; and his officers enlisted 234 men to serve in four companies of Marines. Captain Nicholas served aboard the 24-gun flagship *Alfred*. (Also on *Alfred* was a young naval officer, John Paul Jones.) John Trevett was first

[For the location of places in the American Revolution see map No. 1 in the map section.—*Au*.]

25

lieutenant of Marines on the next largest ship, the 20-gun *Columbus*.

The winter ice in Delaware Bay freed the squadron on February 17, 1776; and on March 1, the ships rendezvoused off Great Abaco Island in the Bahamas. Hopkins formed a landing party of Marines and sailors to assault Nassau on New Providence Island, where, he had heard, they would find 600 barrels of gunpowder.

At 2 P.M. on Sunday, March 3, 1776, American Marines landed for the first time. They rowed ashore in whaleboats and landed without opposition two miles east of Fort Montagu. As Lieutenant Trevett led one company to the fort, its defenders fired a few 18-pound shot and surrendered. The invaders spent the night in the fort. At daybreak, Captain Nicholas marched his men the mile to the edge of town; demanded the keys to the second fort, Fort Nassau, and hauled down the British colors. It was as simple as that.

But Nicholas' decision to spend the night at Fort Montagu—and Hopkins' failure to blockade the harbor—had been fatal to the success of the expedition. During the night, the British governor shipped off the bulk of the gunpowder—162 casks—to safety in Florida. The Americans found only 24 casks of powder. They also took 46 cannon, 12 smaller guns and 15 mortars. They sailed on March 17, taking three ships recaptured from the British and Governor Montfort Browne and two other officials as prisoners.

On the return cruise, Hopkins' fleet met the 20-gun *Glasgow* off Block Island. Starting at 2 A.M. on April 6, the American ships engaged the lone frigate for one and a half hours. Among the 11 American dead were four Marines: 2d Lt. John Hood Wilson and 2d Lt. John Fitzpatrick and two enlisted men. Aboard the damaged *Glasgow*, only one man was killed and three wounded, all shot by Marines' muskets.

News of the expedition stirred the Colonies. Commodore Hopkins was congratulated by John Hancock, President of the Continental Congress; and General Washington stopped at New London and honored *Alfred* with a visit. Historians call the gunpowder expedition "the first fight in the records of the Regular Navy." [3]

Throughout the Revolution, many colonists fought as marines aboard ship but were not officially Continental Marines. Some served as soldiers in the Continental Army and others in the navies of the individual states and on privateers.

In the sweltering summer of 1775, a few Americans fought as marines under Col. Benedict Arnold on Lake Champlain. This was part of the crucial fresh-water lifeline, which, if the British could sever it, would divide the Colonies in two. Since there were still no Continental Navy or Marines, Arnold's men served as soldiers in the Continental Army. With two small ships, they controlled the lake and the water route between Montreal and New York.

By the following summer, they had assembled a miniature squadron of ships, row galleys and flat-bottomed gondolas. On October 11, they fought off a British fleet of 53 vessels at Valcour Island and then retreated to Fort Ticonderoga, which Ethan Allen had captured earlier. Although the American fleet was almost totally destroyed, it had stopped the British from advancing down the lake. When Gen. John Burgoyne drove south the next summer, the Americans were mobilized; and on October 12, 1777, Burgoyne surrendered his sword at Saratoga. During the Revolution, American marines fought in no more significant naval campaign than that on Lake Champlain.

The Continental Marines were modeled on the British Marines, who were originally organized in 1664. British Marines led by Marine Maj. John Pitcairn fought the Minute Men on snow-covered Lexington green on the morning of April 19, 1775, and participated in the first shots heard round the world. Two months later, Major Pitcairn was killed in the "Battle of Bunker Hill." British Marines fought Americans hand-to-hand to prevent them from recapturing Savannah in October 1779; the following spring, British Marines helped seize Fort Moultrie in Charleston harbor. And they were in the force that surrendered at Yorktown on October 19, 1781. In 1802, King George III declared the British Marines to be "The Royal Marines."

The Royal Marines and American Marines began as enemies; but over the years after the War of 1812, they became comrades. They were blooded together in the Boxer Rebellion, World War II and Korea. They share many traditions. The Royal Marines wear a badge showing the eastern hemisphere of the globe; U.S. Marines wear one with the western hemisphere.

As did the British Marines, the green-coated Continental Marines provided the Navy with a landing force, kept order aboard warships and in sea battles fired their muskets "from the tops" of the masts and often manned "the great guns." But the Continental Marines could hardly be thought of as a Corps during the Revolution. They were usually recruited to serve in particular ships or squadrons.

On June 25, 1776, Samuel Nicholas, the senior Marine captain who had led the amphibious landing on New Providence, was appointed major of Marines, the highest Marine rank created during the Revolution. He was ordered to organize four more Marine companies for the Continental frigates then being built.

In 1776, the British shoved Washington off Long Island and through Manhattan and chased him across New Jersey. Philadelphia was threatened, and the Marines stationed there and on the ships in the Delaware River were called out to help stem the Redcoated tide. Major Nicholas formed a "battalion" of 131 men from the Marine companies and on December 2 joined Washington's army.

While Congress fled to Baltimore, Washington turned on his tormentors. He crossed back over the ice-littered Delaware on Christmas night and hit the Hessians guarding Trenton. Of the three Continental divisions, only Washington's managed to cross the river. Cadwalader's division, to which Nicholas and his Marines were attached, finally crossed downriver near Bristol, Pennsylvania, the following morning, by which time Washington had recrossed the river.

Washington planned a second bold stroke. He crossed the river once again, as Maj. Gen. Charles Cornwallis advanced swiftly south against him with 8,000 men. On New Year's Day, Washington sent out a force to delay Cornwallis and give the Americans one day of grace. The Pennsylvania riflemen fought at Maidenhead, northeast of Trenton, and then retreated slowly. The Marines were among the troops delaying the British at Assunpink Creek. Washington won the extra day he needed. That severely cold night, he left his campfires burning, slipped around Cornwallis' left flank and marched for Princeton.

Washington detached a brigade, with Nicholas' Marines on the right flank, to hold a stone bridge two miles below Princeton. They marched by the Allentown road; and as the brigade approached the bridge, it ran head on into two British regiments. The British charged with bayonets; the Americans broke. Washington galloped between the opposing forces to rally the Americans. Then, reinforcements arrived; the tide of battle shifted, and

28

the British were routed. Washington's victory at Princeton kept the British out of Philadelphia for the time being. They retreated north. The Marines' first land campaign was over.

Marines also fought on the western frontier beyond the Appalachian Mountains, over the vast territory from New Orleans to the Illinois country. The Commerce Committee of Congress directed twenty-seven-year-old Capt. James Willing to raise a company of Marines, seize British property along the Mississippi River, carry dispatches to New Orleans and return with supplies. On January 10, 1778, he started out from Fort Pitt with a crew of about 35 men in an old boat he named *Rattletrap.*

On their way down the Ohio and Mississippi rivers, Willing and his Marines captured several ships and occupied Natchez. Much of the time Marine Lt. Robert George scouted ahead in a canoe. By the time Willing reached New Orleans, his force had grown to 100 men; and they had swept aside Britain's hold on the Mississippi. In September, they defeated an armed British sloop on Lake Pontchartrain after a hot fight and commanded the lake. Sixty of Willing's men, led by Marine Lts. Robert George and Richard Harrison, marched north to join George Rogers Clark, who was fighting the British-incited Indians in the Illinois country—a struggle that went on long after the American victory at Yorktown. Clark and his men helped make it possible for the nation to expand westward toward the Pacific.

After Esek Hopkins' gunpowder expedition to New Providence in 1776, the Continental Marines participated in one more major amphibious operation during the Revolution. This second landing—on the coast of Maine—was their first in the face of enemy fire and the first in which they tried to hold the ground they seized. The operation was a disaster.

In the spring of 1779, a British force from Halifax built a fort at the mouth of the Penobscot River, near where Castine, Maine, now stands but was then part of Massachusetts. The fort was intended to protect a colony of the many Loyalists who had refused to join the Rebels. Massachusetts assembled a powerful expedition, including three Continental warships. Marine Capt. John Welsh of the frigate *Warren* led the fleet's 300 marines; about half his men were Continental Marines and the rest served in the state navies.

The American warships fought the British for two hours on July 26, 1779, and forced the British ships up the river. Captain

Welsh and the Marines from the Continental sloop *Providence* landed on Nautilus Island, which commands the harbor; routed the 20 British Marines on the island, and installed a three-gun battery.

At dawn on July 28, Captain Welsh and his Marines, together with soldiers under the overall command of Brig. Gen. Solomon Lovell of the Massachusetts militia, assaulted the mainland peninsula where the British were building their fort. The Americans, with the Marines on the right flank, landed under fire at the foot of a steep bluff that rose almost perpendicular from the water. They inched up the cliff and drove back the 300-man guard of British regulars into the main fortifications. The Marines did the heaviest fighting. Captain Welsh and eight Continental Marines were killed in the assault, and Marine Lt. William Hamilton was mortally wounded at the cliff's base.

Although his troops outnumbered the isolated enemy garrison, Brig. Gen. Lovell laid cautious siege to the British fort. On August 13, a British squadron out of New York appeared off the Penobscot. The American commanders panicked and reloaded their force on the transports. They fled upriver. Dudley Saltonstall, in command of the American naval force, ran his ships ashore and set fire to all but three, which were captured. With the British in pursuit, the Americans escaped overland through the forests. Penobscot became a permanent British base for the rest of the war. But the Marines had performed gallantly in battle. For the first time, they had landed from the sea in force against enemy fire.

During the Revolution's hit-and-run naval war, Marines fought in many sea battles. In a Navy so hopelessly outnumbered and outgunned, American ships usually fought alone. The Marines fired from the rigging, where, with muskets and grenades, they picked off British officers and gunners. Sometimes they served as artillerymen. They formed boarding parties to fight hand-to-hand on enemy ships and raiding parties to carry the battle onto enemy shores.

On January 27, 1778, Capt. John Trevett, the Marine who had led a company ashore at New Providence in 1776, participated in a second voyage to that island. This single-ship amphibious operation was one of the more successful raids to which Marines contributed. Its objective was to capture the 16-gun British brig *Mary*. Trevett led 26 Marines ashore after midnight and seized Fort Nassau, which was guarded by only two sentinels. Trevett and his men trained the fort's cannon on the streets of the town and the ships in the harbor and at daybreak hoisted the American flag. They put both forts out of commission and captured *Mary* without a shot fired. They released 30 American prisoners and took off *Mary*, other freed ships and a substantial amount of gunpowder.

Trevett sailed in 1780 under Marine Capt. Gilbert Saltonstall on the first cruise of the 28-gun *Trumbull*, the last of the Continental Navy's original 13 frigates. Off Bermuda on June 1, *Trumbull* battled the 36-gun letter of marque *Watt* in a bruising slugging match at close quarters. The ships were never more than 100 yards apart. The Marines killed or drove below deck *Watt's* Marines. Trevett lost his right eye and three Continental Marine officers and one sergeant were killed. Captain Saltonstall suffered 11 wounds. The fight of *Trumbull* and *Watt* was "one of the most hotly contested engagements fought at sea during the Revolution." [4]

Continental Marines played an important part in all the battles fought in European waters by John Paul Jones, the courageous, violent-tempered little Scot who was the greatest of American sea duelists. On April 22, 1778, he made a raid in *Ranger* at Whitehaven on the Irish Sea. At midnight, a 30-man landing party cast off in two small boats, Jones commanding one and his lieutenant of Marines, Samuel Wallingford, the other. Jones and his party scaled the wall of the fort guarding the southern end of the harbor and spiked its cannon. Their plan was to set fire to the ships in the harbor. But their torches had been extinguished, and at dawn Jones brazenly obtained a fresh light from a public house and set a fire in the hold of a large ship surrounded by nearly 100 other vessels. He held off the townspeople with his pistol while he and his men made their escape.

That same morning, Jones made a second raid, on St. Mary's Isle across Solway Firth, to capture the Earl of Selkirk to use for exchange. But Selkirk was away from home. Lieutenant Wallingford led his men into the house and seized the family silver, which Jones later bought up and returned to the earl.

The next day, Jones' *Ranger* forced a fight with the British 20-gun sloop of war *Drake* off the northeast coast of Ireland. In an hour, the British had 25 men killed or wounded, including the captain, hit by a Marine musket ball. Among Jones' three dead was his Marine commander, Lieutenant Wallingford, shot through the head by a British Marine.

Jones' climactic sea battle came on the afternoon of September 23, 1779, when he commanded an ancient French merchantman renamed *Bonhomme Richard*. Commodore Jones now had a squadron of five warships. They were amply manned by Marines, chiefly Irish infantrymen uniformed in red and white. Twenty-three-year-old Lt. Edward Stack, an officer in the Irish Regiment of the French Army, on leave to fight the British with Jones, was commissioned as an American Marine and commanded the 137 Marines aboard the 42-gun *Bonhomme Richard*. Aboard the second largest ship, the 36-gun frigate *Alliance*, Capt. Matthew Parke led the Marines. *Alliance* was commanded by Pierre Landais, the only Frenchman to be given charge of a Continental naval vessel. He was an experienced officer, but Congress' trust in him would prove a terrible mistake.

Sailing in the North Sea, the Americans sighted a convoy of 41 British merchantmen rounding England's Flamborough Head, escorted by the new 50-gun frigate *Serapis* and the 20-gun sloop of war *Countess of Scarborough*. The merchantmen fled and the British warships sailed confidently for Jones' ships. Landais, failing to obey Jones' signal, kept *Alliance* out of the fray. *Bonhomme Richard* tackled *Serapis*, and the 26-gun frigate *Pallas* took on *Countess of Scarborough*.

Jones stood on the quarterdeck. On the poop were Lt. James O'Kelly and 20 Marines. Marine Lt. Richard Dale commanded the 12-pound guns. In the main top, Lieutenant Stack led four sailors and 15 Marines, whose job was to clear *Serapis'* tops and decks.

At seven o'clock began one of the most dramatic sea fights in history. Jones, at close range, fired a starboard broadside into *Serapis*. His main guns were quickly put out of action by the enemy. But by eight o'clock the Marines cleared *Serapis'* tops; and Jones had the two ships lashed together stern to bow, their guns almost touching as they fired into each other. The Marines in the rigging scrambled from their tops to the enemy's. The aged *Bonhomme Richard* was pierced repeatedly and in danger of sinking.

Jones shifted over a lee quarter-deck 9-pounder and had three guns to fire into the enemy. Stack's Marines in the main top "held out bravely during the whole of the action." [5] Both ships were on fire. The British tried to board *Bonhomme Richard* and were repelled. The British captain asked Jones if he had surrendered. Then came the famous reply: "I have not yet begun to fight!"

The Marines turned the tide. They climbed into *Serapis'* rigging and kept her deck cleared of defenders. A seaman bounced a grenade into *Serapis'* open hatch and blew up the powder among the cannon, killing 20 men. *Alliance* incredibly fired three broadsides at the ships lashed together, damaging *Bonhomme Richard*, killing several men and mortally wounding Marine Lieutenant O'Kelly. But the Americans' fire increased, and at 10:30 the British struck their colors. In the meantime, *Pallas* had more easily conquered *Countess of Scarborough*. When *Serapis* surrendered, *Bonhomme Richard* was afire with five feet of water in her hold. She sank on the morning of the 25th, her flag still flying. In this, the single greatest sea fight of the war, the Marines had helped ensure Jones' victory.

The Continental Marines' final battle was, however, a defeat. In the spring of 1780, the British attacked and conquered Charleston, South Carolina. Continental Marines fought bravely but futilely in its defense. Finally, at Yorktown in October 1781 came victory. On the last day of November 1782, a tentative peace treaty was signed; and in September 1783, the last Continental Marine officer was discharged.

No one knows exactly how many Marines served in the Continental Navy during the Revolution. The best figures suggest that the Marines had, all told, one major, 30 captains and approximately 100 lieutenants and no more than 2,000 enlisted men. By contrast, the British Navy by 1783 had 110,000 seamen and Marines. The Continental Marines did their share on the long road to victory and the establishment of the nation. They fought with a mixture of heroism and amateurishness. They had no traditions, no esprit de corps, no professionalism. They had little sea-fighting experience and less organization. They fought, one might say, as civilians in uniform. The glory of the Corps was yet to come, but the service and honor were there from the beginning.

2
Establishing the Corps
1798–1815

When the Revolution was won, the new nation quickly gave up its military establishment. Americans had reason to fear a standing armed force in tyrannical hands. But ten years after the last Continental Marine had been discharged, fears of a military establishment had given way to the realization that a nation unable to protect itself was prey to every bully. In the next three decades, the United States tackled three bullies: the piratical Barbary states on the north shore of Africa, France and finally England. These three wars were fought in great part on the seas; not until they were over was independence truly won.

In 1794, Congress ordered the building of six naval frigates and the enlistment of seamen and Marines to man them. The nation was bitterly divided over the naval bill, and only three of the ships—*United States, Constitution* and *Constellation*—were launched in 1797. Their Marines were commanded respectively by Capt. Franklin Wharton, a future Commandant of the Corps; Lt. Lemuel Clark, and Lt. Philip Edwards. (The first acting Marine officer on *United States* was Lt. William MacRae.) Each officer enlisted his own detachment. There was no Marine Corps.

The next year, on July 11, 1798, a congressional act provided for "establishing and organizing a Marine Corps" and created the Corps as it is known today. The Marine Corps act provided for 881 men, commanded by a major. Enlistments would be for three years, and the United States Senate would appoint all officers, except when the President acted in the Senate's absence. From the beginning, the principle was established that still holds today: Every Marine is a fighter first and a specialist second. The Marines would keep discipline aboard ship; lead boarding parties and amphibious landings; fight with muskets in short-range naval battles, and, if the captain wished, work some of the ship's long guns. They would also man coastal installations and forts, "or any

[For the location of places in this section see maps No. 1, 5 and 8 in the map section.—*Au.*]

34

other duty ashore, as the President, at his discretion, shall direct." No Negroes, mulattoes or Indians could be enlisted under the original rules; and the foreign-born, even if naturalized, could not make up more than one-fourth of the Corps. (At least three blacks had served in the Continental Marines during the Revolution. The first, John Martin, a former slave, was killed at sea in 1777. As far as is known, these were the first black American Marines; and, officially, they were the last until World War II. There is one reference to an American Indian serving as a Marine private in Nicaragua in 1928.)

On July 12, the day after President John Adams approved the act of Congress creating the Corps, the Secretary of the Navy appointed as Major Commandant the Corps' senior officer; William Ward Burrows, a stocky, forty-year-old lawyer born in Charleston, South Carolina. He commanded the Corps for nearly six years. He set up headquarters in Philadelphia and in 1800 moved it to Washington. He founded the famous Marine Corps Band, which first played in the White House on New Year's Day 1801, and he began building the Marine Barracks at "Eighth and Eye"—the Corps' oldest post. In April 1800, Burrows gained the rank of "Lieutenant Colonel Commandant."

Marines were posted on each of the Navy's 26 vessels; and *Ganges* was the first to put to sea, with Lt. Daniel Carmick and 24 Marines aboard.

By 1798 the United States was engaged in a vicious undeclared war with the French, its former allies, who were impressing American merchant seamen on the high seas and whose privateers were grabbing defenseless ships even in American harbors. American warships fought a series of one-to-one battles at sea. In 1800 the French landed on the Dutch island of Curaçao and threatened to seize American property. Marine 2d Lt. James Middleton led a 70-man party ashore to reinforce the Dutch batteries. The French withdrew from the island.

The United States attempted to hurt the French by aiding the Negroes' fight for freedom on the island of Haiti. The U.S. Navy schooner *Experiment* fought Negroes allied with the French off Haiti; and the frigate *General Greene* blockaded the city of Jacmel on Haiti's southern coast, while anti-French Negroes captured the town. In the spring of 1800, a landing party from *Constitution*—its Marines commanded by Capt. Daniel Carmick—recaptured the British ship *Sandwich* held by the French at Santo Domingo. Carmick and Lt. William Amory then led the Marines ashore through neck-high water, captured the fort and spiked its cannon. Captain Carmick wrote in a letter: "The men went on board like devils."

Although during the decade after 1801 the French seized more than 500 American ships and the British more than 900, by November of that year, the Corps' strength was reduced to 23 officers and 453 enlisted Marines. The Corps remained at about that level for the next six years.

The Barbary states were the Corps' next opponents. The Marine Corps hymn sings the praises of only two actions of the Corps: in the halls of Montezuma and on the shores of Tripoli. But the glory of the "shores of Tripoli" began in disgrace.

The Barbary states—Algiers, Tunis, Morocco and Tripoli— were rapacious little political entities on the North African coast, made up in good part of Moors who had been forced out of Spain and existed as "nations" by preying on unarmed Mediterranean shipping. They were aided by Great Britain, which wanted merchants to use her vessels protected by her Navy. A British-arranged treaty between Algiers and Portugal in 1793 allowed Algerian warships to operate in the Atlantic and led directly to the building of the first U.S. frigates and the creation of the permanent American Navy. In the meanwhile, the U.S. paid the Barbary pirates nearly a million dollars in tribute and ransoms.

By the summer of 1803, the U.S. was strong enough to send an effective squadron under Capt. Edward Preble to the Mediterranean. In October, Preble paraded a show of strength off Morocco, leaving behind to blockade Tripoli the fast frigate *Philadelphia*. On the morning of October 31, Capt. William Bainbridge grounded *Philadelphia* on an uncharted reef. A mosquito fleet of Tripolitan gunboats peppered away at the stranded American giant for four hours. Bainbridge ordered everything—even the guns—thrown overboard to lighten his ship but finally had to strike his flag. Not a man was wounded; 308 Americans, including 43 Marines commanded by 1st Lt. William S. Osborne, were herded ashore and imprisoned for 19 months.

The U.S. Government ordered all possible ships to the Mediterranean; they carried 400 Marines—four-fifths of the enlisted strength of the Corps. The Tripolitans freed *Philadelphia* from the reef and brought her under the guns of the castle. Captain Preble decided to destroy the frigate before the enemy could use her. On the night of February 16, 1804, Navy Lt. Stephen Decatur and 74 volunteers, including eight Marines led by Sgt. Solomon Wren, stole into the harbor in a captured Tripolitan ketch, which they renamed *Intrepid*. Receiving permission to tie up alongside *Philadelphia* in the dark, Decatur and his men boarded the frigate and in 20 minutes killed or captured all the enemy but two and set the ship afire. Then *Intrepid* escaped. Not a man was hurt. British Admiral Horatio Nelson called it "the most bold and daring act of the age." [6]

In the spring of 1805, the Americans launched an overland expedition to overthrow the Pasha of Tripoli and seat his brother Hamet on the throne. This brought on the scene the greatest Marine hero of the Tripolitan war, a young lieutenant from the Blue Ridge Mountains, Presley Neville O'Bannon. The expedition was conceived by William Eaton, a fearless, fiery-tempered Dartmouth graduate who had served since 1797 as consul at Tunis. In November 1804, Eaton sailed for Alexandria, Egypt, to persuade the Pasha's banished brother to lead a force against Tripoli. Eaton traveled in the swift 16-gun brig *Argus*; her captain, Lt. Isaac Hull, would later win fame in the War of 1812. Commanding *Argus'* Marine detachment was twenty-year-old Lieutenant O'Bannon.

Eaton, O'Bannon and 18 men went up the Nile and in February 1805 met Hamet in the desert. He agreed to the scheme. On March 8, they set out with 500 men and 107 camels to conquer Tripoli by marching across the desert along the route that years later would be followed by the mechanized armies of Montgomery and Rommel.

Eaton's expedition became a nightmare. The native drivers mutinied repeatedly and the Arab warriors threatened to desert. Eaton dissuaded them by ordering O'Bannon and his seven Marines to seize the food supply. They marched on. They rested at Bomba for a week; and on April 25, they camped on a hill overlooking Derna, 600 miles from Eaton's starting point and about halfway to Tripoli. The next day, Eaton sent a flag of truce. The governor, with 800 men eager to fight the invaders, sent back the message: "My head or yours!"

Argus, *Hornet* and *Nautilus* bombarded Derna on the morning of April 27. At two o'clock, Eaton ordered a general attack. In the center, O'Bannon led the Marines, 36 Greeks, 24 cannoneers with one gun, and a few Arabs. O'Bannon's attack was stopped cold. Eaton rushed up his reserve. Together, they pressed into the city. Eaton was shot through the left wrist. O'Bannon and his Marines led the charge with the bayonet, racing through the city to the harbor fort in a shower of bullets. At 3:30, O'Bannon raised the American flag over the fort—the first time the Stars and Stripes had been raised in battle in the Eastern Hemisphere.

Among the casualties were three Marine privates; one was wounded, Pvt. John Whitten was killed and Pvt. Edward Steward died later of his wounds.

Eaton organized the defense of the city. On May 13, the Pasha's forces from Tripoli struck and were thrown back in a six-hour struggle. Almost daily skirmishes followed, until on June 10 Hamet totally defeated his brother's men.

The very next day *Constitution* arrived in the harbor with the news that the Americans had made peace with the Pasha. The State Department's agent Tobias Lear had agreed to a treaty that provided a $60,000 ransom for the captives from *Philadelphia*. The prisoners had been freed on June 3, and the treaty signed on the 10th, the very day the Pasha's troops had been decisively beaten. With the American Navy off Tripoli in force and Eaton's army advancing to overthrow the frightened Pasha, the ransom-bought end of the war was disgraceful.

On June 12, the Marines covered Eaton's withdrawal from Derna. Hamet was taken to safety, and Eaton and O'Bannon went home heroes from the shores of Tripoli.

Legend has it that O'Bannon was given Hamet's jeweled sword with its 32⅛-inch blade and that this was the model for the "Mameluke sword" that Marine officers still carry today. The state of Virginia presented O'Bannon a gold sword. But the Marine Corps gave him neither a promotion nor a brevet (an honorary raise in rank); and on March 6, 1807, Lieutenant O'Bannon resigned from the Corps. He went west to Kentucky, married and settled down into obscurity. When he died, he was buried in a small cemetery at Russellville, Logan County; and in 1920, his body was removed to Frankfort, the state capital.

The war with Tripoli ended without honor for the United States. But the war demonstrated that the nation would fight, and it served as a training ground for young naval officers who in a few years would be the captains in the greater struggle with Great Britain. A professional service was begun; men were tested under fire; and this war too produced a few Marine heroes.

The War of 1812 was an affair in which Englishmen fought the descendants of Englishmen only one generation after American independence. The United States had two reasons for going to war on June 18, 1812. Americans were itching to expand; some still dreamt of bringing Canada into the Union, and others hoped to grab fertile lands to the south. They also wanted to stop the impressment of American sailors whom the British Navy claimed were British-born subjects of the king. Thousands of Americans had been seized on the seas.

When the United States declared war, England was busy fighting Napoleon. To those who wanted to expand American borders, it seemed like a good moment to strike. But the United States was unprepared to fight. Its military leadership was incompetent, its militia undependable. It was without a single ship-of-the-line and had only three frigates rated at 44 guns, three with 38 guns, *Essex* with 32 and *Adams* with 28. Only 16 vessels had 21 guns or more. In contrast, the British, when in 1814 their fleet was freed with Napoleon's exile to Elba, had 219 huge ships-of-the-line and 296 swift frigates.

Fortunately, each of the young nation's three 44-gun frigates, although it could never tackle a ship-of-the-line, was superior to any British frigate. And unlike the untried Army, the Navy, as a result of the French and Barbary wars, had the core of a professional service with esprit de corps. Early in this war it won a series of dramatic victories.

In part, these victories were won because the American frigates carried United States Marines, many of whom were backwoodsmen—among the best marksmen in the world. Posted high in the rigging to pick off the officers and gunners on an enemy's decks, their fire was deadly. At the start of the war, according to Theodore Roosevelt's history of the conflict, the Marine Corps had 42 officers and 1,523 men, less than its authorized strength of 46 officers and 1,823 men. Lt. Col. Franklin Wharton, a heavy-jowled, wealthy, forty-five-year-old Philadelphian, had succeeded William Burrows as Commandant in 1804. President Jefferson had appointed him as a matter of seniority. He was most interested in discipline, neatness and the Marine Band. When the rum ration was increased in 1805, he prudently ordered it diluted and issued twice a day to reduce drunkenness; that did not increase his popularity. The War of 1812 would bring him personal disgrace.

The first Marines to see action were the 51 aboard *Constitution*, which on the cloudy afternoon of August 19, 1812, opened fire on the frigate *Guerriere* 750 miles east of Boston. The two ships fought at close range, exchanging broadside for broadside. Despite the heavy seas, the Marines' musket fire was highly effective. The British captain was hit. When the ships locked momentarily, Marine Lt. William S. Bush rallied *Constitution's* boarders and leapt onto the rail. Shot through the head by a British Marine, he fell back dead on *Constitution's* deck. Finally, *Guerriere's* three masts were shot away and she lay rolling wildly, a defenseless hulk. The nation cheered *Constitution's* victory. A British warship had been outsailed, outfought and conquered.

On December 29, *Constitution* met the swifter *Java* off Brazil. The ships closed; and the Marines in the tops, commanded by 1st Lt. John Contee and 2d Lt. William H. Freeman, proved they were sharpshooters that afternoon. Cutlass in hand, *Java's* Captain James Lambert led his boarders and a Marine's bullet wounded him mortally. The slaughter on *Java's* decks was dreadful. She surrendered. The Americans suffered 12 killed, including Marine Thomas Hanson, and 22 wounded; the British had 48 killed and 102 wounded.

On June 1, 1813, *Chesapeake* met *Shannon* outside Boston harbor. Except for the 44 Marines aboard, *Chesapeake's* crew was unexperienced and untried. The ships raced along together firing broadside against broadside at close range. When the British boarded, *Chesapeake's* Capt. James Lawrence, who had been second in command to Decatur when *Intrepid* blew up the captured *Philadelphia*, was shot through the body by a British Marine. Carried below fatally wounded, he gave his famous order: "Don't give up the ship!"

The green American crew panicked. Only the remaining Marines and a handful of sailors held fast and rallied on the forecastle. The British came at them. The Marines fought at bay with clubbed muskets. The British stormed forward and cut down the defenders to the last man. In a fight that lasted just 15 minutes, almost half of *Chesapeake's* crew were casualties. Fourteen Marines, including 1st Lt. James Broom and Cpl. William Dixon, were dead and 18 were wounded. Only one corporal and nine privates remained unscathed.

A year later, the brand-new sloop of war *Wasp* was seizing British merchant prizes in the very mouth of the English Channel. Before dawn on June 28, 1814, she met the British brig-sloop *Reindeer.* In a fierce running battle, *Wasp's* Marines (according to some accounts they were seamen serving as Marines) picked off the British officers. British Capt. William Manners was shot through both thighs; and when he tried to lead his boarders, two more balls from *Wasp's* maintop struck him in the head, killing him. *Wasp's* captain, Master Commandant Johnston Blakely, summoned his 16 Marines, led by Sgt. William D. Barnes, to the point at which the two ships touched. The Americans and British hacked at each other through the portholes. When Manners fell, Blakely gave the command to board. Shouting, the Americans swarmed onto *Reindeer.* In a brief bloody struggle, the British were driven below decks or killed.

These sea fights were four in which Marines played a major role. Several others in which Marines fought, ironically enough, occurred after peace had been signed but before the word could reach the scattered ships at sea. Marine Lt. Levi Twiggs distinguished himself when *President* beat *Endymion* on January 15, 1815, off New York. Twiggs would die in battle 31 years later— still a Marine. On Feburary 20, *Constitution* defeated the two smaller corvettes *Cyane* and *Levant* in a 40-minute battle off Portugal. *Constitution's* 44 Marines, commanded by Capt. Archibald Henderson, were constantly engaged; two were killed and three wounded. Henderson received special mention in the official report of that action. More would be heard of him.

While none of the ocean battles between single ships could be called decisive, the campaigns on Lake Erie and Lake Champlain shaped the outcome of the war. To fight on the lakes, Marines had to be recruited out of the frontier wilderness and soldiers converted into "acting marines."

In the spring of 1813, Oliver Hazard Perry, then twenty-eight years old, took command on Lake Erie. His sole Marine officer was Lt. John Brooks, the son of the governor of Massachusetts. To his force of 12 Marines, Brooks added woodsmen;

41

they served as Marines on Perry's flagship *Lawrence*.

At dawn on Friday, September 10, Perry brought out the little fleet he had built on the lake. The British approached his squadron in tight formation; and for 20 minutes, Perry's flagship took violent punishment. Its sand-strewn decks ran with blood. Of the 102 men aboard who were fit for duty, 83 were killed or wounded. A cannon ball mortally wounded Lieutenant Brooks. Young Perry survived and transferred to fight from *Niagara*. Three more Marines were killed before the British struck their flag and the battle was won. It ended British and Indian attacks on the western frontier and opened the Northwest to expansion.

Exactly a year and a day after Perry's victory came the crucial battle of the war. Napoleon had been defeated on the Continent, and England could now turn her attention to the impudent United States. Regulars from the Duke of Wellington's army, 28,000 strong, were shipped to Canada. The British repeated their plan of the Revolutionary War: to slice down the Lake Champlain-Hudson River valley and split the Americans in two.

On Lake Champlain, the American force had some 200 infantrymen serving as marines. On Sunday, September 11, 1814, the decisive battle was won. Casualties on both sides were heavy. Among the Americans, seven of the acting marines were killed and 10 wounded. But the great invasion by the flower of Wellington's army was defeated. In December, peace was signed.

That Sunday, September 11, 1814, marked high tide for the British. On the Atlantic coast, another expeditionary force, having burned Washington, sailed to attack Baltimore. But by Wednesday night, the Americans had taken the heart out of the enemy.

The attack on Baltimore was preceded by a 16-month campaign to blockade the east coast of the United States. The Secretary of the Navy ordered Commandant Wharton to raise a battalion of Marines to help protect Chesapeake Bay from the mass of British ships assembling there. The naval defense of the bay was assigned to Joshua Barney, a tough fifty-four-year-old veteran of the Revolution. In June 1814, after a number of skirmishes, he was blockaded up the Patuxent River. A few regulars and Marines under Marine Capt. Samuel Miller cooperated with Barney from the shore.

The British had some 4,000 men on hand to invade the United States. President James Madison established an organization under Brig. Gen. Henry Winder that could, if necessary, defend Washington. The British entered the Patuxent on August 17 and two days later landed unopposed at Benedict, Maryland. As the enemy advanced, Barney's men blew up their own boats.

The British started marching the 40 miles to Washington. Barney with 400 of his men joined Brig. Gen. Winder early Monday afternoon, August 22. He found that Captain Miller had arrived from Washington on Sunday noon with 110 Marines and five artillery pieces. Miller reported his men for duty with Barney.

On Wednesday morning, the British army approached Bladensburg, four miles northeast of Washington, where a bridge crossed the Eastern Branch of the Potomac. Winder marched quickly out of Washington, ordering Barney to stay behind and use his guns to guard the Eastern Branch Bridge (now the John Philip Sousa Bridge). At the bridge, Barney met President Madison, stormed over to him and had his assignment changed. The bridge was blown up; and Barney, his sailors and Marines took their guns to the Battle of Bladensburg.

The Americans were drawn up three lines deep along heights on the Washington side of the river, across from Bladensburg. It was nearly 100 degrees under the August sun. Barney placed his battery on a rise in the center, commanding the bridge and the road along which the British would come. To his right stretched 114 Marines and then the 370 flotilla men, all serving as infantry. Barney supervised the battery; Miller and Marine Capt. Alexander Sevier, the infantry.

As the British crossed the bridge, Barney's gunners, with well-aimed 18-pound shot, destroyed the first enemy company to cross. Twice again the British tried to advance up the fire-swept road and were hurled back. Then the enemy extended through the fields to the left and met the sailors and Marines. Miller used his three 12-pounders effectively; the Americans charged—the Marines with bayonets, the sailors with cutlasses—and broke two British regiments.

Barney was now on foot, his horse having been killed. Miller went down in "a shower of musket-balls," badly wounded in the arm and out of action. The British swung wide, forded the river, cut through the remaining militia and overwhelmed the Americans. The sailors and Marines, standing alone against the enemy, retired in order, leaving most of their dead and wounded. Both Barney and Miller were captured.

That evening, the British marched unopposed into Washington. Government officials, the Army and even the Commandant of the Marine Corps had fled. Wharton took Capt. John Crabb and the guard from the Marine Barracks by boat and wagon to Frederick, Maryland. Wharton wrote later, "While the enemy was in the city, I was with the paymaster at Fredricktown. . . . the events of the past days seem as a bad dream."[7] He stayed there until the British went back to their ships. His flight from Washington scandalized the Marine Corps.

The defense of Washington had been a shameful affair. There was more running than fighting. But Barney's sailors and the Marines had given a superb account of themselves. Despite the numbers involved, American casualties were estimated at only 10 to 12 killed and 40 wounded; the Marines alone had 8 killed and 14 wounded. Miller and Sevier were breveted majors.

After two nights in Washington, during which the British burned most of the public buildings, they began withdrawing. On that fateful Sunday, September 11, when the battle on Lake Champlain was being won, the British army showed up in front of Baltimore. Ten thousand Americans had gathered to build earthworks and defend the city. A thousand sailors and Marines were formed into a brigade under Commodore John Rodgers.

Before dawn on Monday, the British landed at North Point, 14 miles from the city. The defenders were pushed back nearly 10 miles but not broken. The British commander, Maj. Gen. Robert Ross, rode forward supervising the attack. A militiaman's bullet struck him in the chest. His death stalled the British; the spark of leadership had been extinguished. The army halted and waited for the navy to turn the American flank. For 24 hours, the ships bombarded Fort McHenry. But when dawn came, the huge Star-Spangled Banner still waved above the fort; and Baltimore was safe. The British army pulled back to its ships. On two of three fronts the invaders had been stopped.

On September 11 (that Sunday again), a party of Marines from the detachment at New Orleans commanded by Maj. Daniel Carmick sailed aboard the schooner *Carolina* to attack the settlement of pirates, led by the infamous brothers Jean and

Pierre Lafitte, on the western side of the Mississippi delta. On September 16, the Marines and the men from the 44th U.S. Infantry landed and destroyed the pirate stronghold. This was one small Gulf Coast prelude to the conflict of arms to come.

Americans' desire to possess the warm and fertile lands to the south was almost irresistible; and long before war was declared officially in Washington, it was a fact on the border between American Georgia and Spanish Florida. They were divided by the St. Mary's River, and one trouble spot was Amelia Island at the river's mouth. Navy ships with Marines aboard aided a force of armed Georgia "patriots" seize the islands on March 17, 1812. A 35-man Marine detachment under Capt. John Williams went ashore and occupied the island. Georgians and Army "volunteers" marched to St. Augustine; and the Marines convoyed wagon trains to the advanced positions, despite Wharton's objections.

On September 12, Captain Williams and about 20 Marines and Georgians, escorting a wagon train into Twelve Mile Swamp, were ambushed by Indians and Negroes who had escaped American slavery. In a furious fight, one Marine was killed and eight were wounded. Williams was hit and died later.

After Maj. Gen. Ross' death at Baltimore, the British command was given to Sir Edward Pakenham, Wellington's wife's brother and a brave if inept soldier. On November 26, 1814, he sailed with 9,000 soldiers from Jamaica for New Orleans. The British hoped to seize the Gulf Coast, New Orleans and the lower Mississippi before the peace treaty was signed.

Only nine days before Pakenham's force arrived off New Orleans, tall, gaunt Maj. Gen. Andrew Jackson rode into the city. He found its 20,000 inhabitants almost defenseless.

Navy Lt. Thomas ap Catesby Jones, commanding five gunboats with 147 sailors and 35 Marines, was ordered to hold Lake Borgne, which is actually not a lake at all but a long arm of the Gulf of Mexico stretching westward to within six miles of where New Orleans then was. Jackson needed time, and Jones' job was to delay the British. They sent a thousand men in 45 barges to meet Jones. On December 14, the battle was joined. Jones and his few men fought gallantly and took a toll of more than 300 British. Jones was severely wounded and captured. Three Marines were killed and two wounded on his "flagship," Gunboat No.

156. The British swept through and touched land at Bayou Bienvenue. New Orleans was in panic. Jackson declared martial law.

But Pakenham moved ponderously, and Jackson slowly gained in strength as more men arrived. On Friday, December 23, 1,700 enemy soldiers were within nine miles of New Orleans. Jackson moved promptly against them. His army consisted of 800 mounted Tennesseans under John Coffee, the best of the Creole militia, the regulars of the 7th Infantry and 56 Marines under Lt. Francis B. de Bellevue. A regiment of Jackson's veteran militia under William Carroll was the reserve.

That night in the darkness, Jackson drove in the surprised British outposts. Enemy reinforcements seized two cannon from the artillerymen and their supporting Marines. Jackson dashed forward, roaring to his men to save the guns. He rallied the Marines until a company of the 7th Infantry came up and dragged off the guns. Slowly, the Americans pushed the British back. Coffee's men fought with long knives against British bayonets. A thick fog rolled in across the blazing battlefield. Men fired blindly in the confusion. Finally, Jackson called a halt. In a couple of hours, the British had lost 247 men and the Americans, 213.

On the next day across the world at Ghent, Belgium, peace was signed. But the men in front of New Orleans did not know the war was over; their battle went on.

Seeing that the British would advance on the city between the river and a cypress swamp, Jackson retreated to the Rodriquez Canal, a mile-long shallow dry ditch—20 feet wide and four deep—that ran at right angles to the British advance, at the narrowest point between river and swamp. There he began to build his line. He posted his 12 guns in batteries. He accepted the services of the Lafittes' controversial pirates and formed a battalion of volunteers under the Creole Maj. Jean B. Plauché. Major Carmick and his Marines joined Plauché.

The British moved within 600 yards of the American army strung out along the canal; and on the morning of December 28, in two columns in close formation and under an umbrella of artillery fire and rockets, the British attacked.

Jackson's artillerymen mowed down the solid advancing columns. The gunners stopped the British infantry; and by noon, Pakenham's army was in retreat. Major Carmick was among the casualities, struck in the forehead by a rocket fragment. Almost two years later, he died, apparently from his wounds.

The British brought up naval guns to blast the Americans out from behind their parapets of cotton bales. An artillery duel opened on New Year's Day, 1815; and the British army was again forced to pull back.

The Marines under Lieutenant de Bellevue were posted on the right of the line, along with the New Orleans Rifles, in support of the three guns of Battery No. 1 and with the 7th Infantry on their left.

Early on January 8, Pakenham marched his men across the open plain directly at the Americans entrenched behind the ditch and breastwork. It was a classic example of military imbecility.

As the fog lifted, the Americans fired on the enemy coming in two great gleaming columns of white and red. The veterans of Wellington's army had beaten the finest in Europe; they advanced confidently.

At the ditch the British halted. They could not be started forward again in the face of the American fire. Pakenham's right arm was shattered. The British retreated out of range to throw off their heavy knapsacks and regroup. Then, supported by the Highlanders of the 93rd Regiment with bagpipes skirling, they surged forward again. Pakenham was killed and two other generals were hit. Many men faltered; but the Highlanders, with incredible bravery, moved within 100 yards of the flaming parapet. Five hundred of their regiment were shot down. They finally broke and fled.

At the other end of the American line, where the British met the regulars, the enemy were routed in 25 minutes. The British advance in the face of murderous fire, against men they could not hit, was blindly heroic and almost insane.

On the field in front of the Rodriquez Canal lay 2,100 British dead and wounded. Five hundred British soldiers had been captured. The Americans had suffered only 71 casualties. The British buried 700 dead. On January 18, prisoners were exchanged; and the British returned to their ships. The next day, the bloody plain was empty.

On February 11, word reached New York that peace had been signed in December.

The Marines in the struggle for New Orleans were few in

number (as they were everywhere in this war), but they were highly commended by Jackson. On Washington's Birthday, Congress passed a resolution: "Resolved, That Congress entertain a high sense of the valor and good conduct of Major Daniel Carmick, of the officers, noncommissioned officers, and Marines under his command, in the defence of the said city, on the late memorable occasion."

But the leading Marine hero of the War of 1812 fought far from the imperiled shores of the United States. He was 1st Lt. John Marshall Gamble, commander of the 32 Marines aboard the frigate *Essex*. Gamble, who had received his commission two years earlier at the age of seventeen, was a handsome daredevil with wild black hair, deep piercing eyes, a high forehead and an air of smiling alertness. He came from a fighting family. His father had been a major in the American Revolution; his three brothers were all to die in the naval service.

The 32-gun *Essex*, under Capt. David Porter, sailed from the Delaware in October 1812 with 319 men aboard. Gamble's Marines included Sgts. Abraham Van Deezer and Pierce G. Small, two corporals, one drummer, one fifer and 25 privates. The frigate was to cut England's ocean trade by intercepting East Indies merchantmen returning home heavily laden. It was fated for one of the great sea adventures of history.

Porter was an exceptional man: daring, able, imaginative, literate, short-tempered and stubborn. He had adopted James Farragut, who went with him on this voyage as an eleven-year-old midshipman. After this cruise, he would take the first name of his adoptive father; as David Farragut, he would become the United States' first admiral.

Porter was supposed to rendezvous with *Constitution*, but her fight with *Java* had forced her to sail north. Before leaving the United States, Porter had won approval of a bold alternative plan. This was to sail *Essex* around Cape Horn into the Pacific and destroy the British whaling fleet, which had been harassing the many American whalers in those waters. Herman Melville was to call this cruise "the strangest and most stirring to be found in the history of the American navy."

In a stormy passage, *Essex* rounded the Cape on March 5. For the first time, U.S. Marines were in the great ocean to fight on shores where so many of them would die in years to come.

Porter seized a number of prizes; and in May, when he took his sixth prize, the 10-gun whaler *Greenwich*, he was beginning to find it difficult to supply prize crews. He wrote in his journal: ". . . for want of sea officers, I put lieutenant Gamble of the Marines in charge of the *Greenwich*. I had much confidence in the discretion of this gentleman; and, to make up for his want of nautical knowledge, I put two expert seamen with him as mates, one of whom is a good navigator." [8]

On the morning of July 12, they sighted three ships. *Essex* quickly took *Charlton*; and *Greenwich* chased the 14-gun *Seringapatam*, the finest British ship in those waters. Chewing tobacco and with a spyglass to his eye, Porter watched Gamble's attack from *Essex*. The enemy tacked and Porter said, "Now, Mr. Gamble, if you'll only stand five minutes and then tack, I'll make you a Prince." Almost as if to Porter's command, Gamble held fast, avoiding raking fire from *Seringapatam*. Porter then said, "Now is your time!" As though he had heard, Gamble tacked, raked the enemy and damaged her badly. Porter put his spyglass under his arm and walked aft with a smile. Gamble was wounded, but the Marine lieutenant had won his naval battle.

By autumn, the American "squadron" had cleared the seas of the British whaling fleet, which Porter figured was worth two and a half million dollars. Hearing that the British were collecting a force to deal with the American raiders, Porter sailed westward to the Marquesas Islands. They arrived on October 23, just about a year after sailing from New York, and established a base on Nukuhiva, which Porter renamed Madison Island. They became involved in the native wars on the island; and in mid-November Porter discovered a plot among some of the many British prisoners who had been captured on the whalers. He counted on his Marines to keep the situation in hand.

On December 9, Porter sailed for the Pacific coast of South America to seek battle with the British warships that had been sent out after him. He left three prizes in charge of Gamble and 22 men so that he would have a base if he found his fight and needed repairs. If Gamble had not heard from Porter after five and a half months, he was to sail for Valparaiso, Chile. Outside that neutral harbor, Porter found his fight and in a brutal battle was forced to surrender to two British ships. Of *Essex's* 255 men, only 76 remained unwounded. Three Marines were missing and one was wounded. Theodore Roosevelt wrote, "throughout the war no ship was so desperately defended as the *Essex*." [9]

Meanwhile, back in the Marquesas Islands, Gamble was having troubles of his own. In mid-April, he started rigging the ships for sea. Mutiny began to build up among the prisoners and the foreign-born members of *Essex*'s crew. On the afternoon of May 7, aboard *Seringapatam*, Gamble was grabbed by a half-dozen men, thrown to the deck, his hands and legs bound. Then he was dropped below deck. The mutineers raised the British flag with a cheer. The officers and eight men—including Marines Benjamin Bispham, Peter Caddington and John Pittenger—did not join them. (Gamble's fourth Marine, John Wetter, had meanwhile drowned while swimming in the surf.)

That night the mutineers sailed *Seringapatam* out of the bay. A prisoner of war who was guarding the captives shot Gamble through the left foot. At sea, the mutineers put Gamble, Midshipman William W. Feltus, Acting Midshipman Clapp and two seamen, William Worth and Richard Sansbury, into a leaking boat. Gamble argued with the mutineers and was finally given two muskets and a keg of cartridges. Clapp bailed; Gamble, in great pain, steered, and the other three rowed. After two hours they reached *Greenwich*.

The next day Gamble transferred supplies to the smaller *Hammond*. The natives attacked a supply party on the beach. Feltus was killed, and Worth and Caddington swam to *Hammond;* the Marine was severely wounded in the head and bleeding profusely. Clapp, Sansbury and Bispham put out in a boat to help the two men. Gamble, alone on *Hammond*, hobbled from gun to gun, firing them at the shore, scaring off the natives.

After setting *Greenwich* afire, the little party aboard *Hammond* sailed from the bay on May 9. Gamble, wounded and feverish, had seven men in his crew. Only Midshipman Clapp and Marine Bispham were in sound health. They had no compass, no spyglass, no maps; only six cartridges were left. They decided to do the one thing they could: run with the tradewinds. On May 23, after sailing for 15 days, they sighted the Hawaiian Islands and made land, exhausted, at Waikiki Bay on May 31.

Two weeks later at sea, *Hammond* was captured by the British *Cherub*, which had helped take *Essex*. Gamble was held aboard *Cherub* until in February at Rio de Janeiro, they learned that the war had ended. Gamble, his health broken, was permitted to sail for home and reached New York two years and ten months after having sailed from that port. He received the recognition he deserved from the Corps. He was commissioned a captain and eventually rose to lieutenant colonel. But he was still suffering from the ravages of his epic cruise in the Pacific, and after a year's illness he died in Brooklyn on September 11, 1836, at the age of forty-six. Captain Porter wrote to the Navy Department of the Marine hero: "No Marine officer in the service ever had such strong claims as Captain Gamble . . . none have been placed in such conspicuous and critical situations, and . . . none could have extricated themselves from them more to their honor."

In the War of 1812, there were never enough Marines to fill their assignments, and their Commandant hardly ranked with the Corps' great leaders. But the men of the Corps—men like Bush on *Constitution*, Brooks on Lake Erie, Carmick, Miller, Sevier, Williams and Gamble—showed the new nation that it could fight.

3
Archibald Henderson and the Indian Wars 1817–1842

Two years after the War of 1812, Marine Capt. Archibald Henderson brought charges against Lt. Col. Franklin Wharton, the Commandant of the Marine Corps, for his conduct during the British assault on Washington. A Navy court decided it did not have jurisdiction because Marines ashore were subject to the Articles of War. So an Army court was convened. But it refused to hear testimony, and President James Monroe approved that decision. Wharton remained as Commandant; but he died in New York City on September 1, 1818, at the age of fifty-one, and was buried in the Old Trinity Church Yard.

Brevet Maj. Anthony Gale, now the senior officer of the Corps, was in line to succeed him. But many Marines—Henderson and Samuel Miller in particular—felt earnestly that Gale was not fit to hold the post. For the next two years, the Corps was torn by the battle among these three men.

Anthony Gale was a tragic figure, the victim of his own weaknesses and the ambitions of stronger men. Irish born, he was commissioned in 1798; and the next year, he had killed Lt. Allen McKenzie, USN, in a duel. He served at sea; and in 1815, while in charge of the Marine Barracks in Philadelphia, a post of distinction, he became involved in a dispute with Commandant Wharton. A court of inquiry cleared him, but he was transferred to a less desirable command in New Orleans. There he began to drink heavily.

When Wharton died, Henderson, next in line after Gale, took charge of the Corps' affairs until a new Commandant could be selected. He and Samuel Miller began politicking for the post. Miller, now forty-three years old and a hero of Bladensburg, was adjutant of the Corps; he was a Headquarters Marine.

Affecting the Corps' politics at the time was one of the most notorious duels in Marine Corps history. In 1816 in the Mediterranean, Commodore Oliver Perry, the hero of Lake Erie, got into an argument with the commander of his Marine detachment, Capt. John Heath, a stout man with little military bearing and an enthusiasm for creature comforts. In his anger, Perry struck Heath. Perry immediately offered to apologize, but other Marine officers urged Heath to demand legal justice. Both men were tried and were sentenced to be reprimanded in private and were restored to duty. The affair became a sensation in the newspapers. Heath, egged on by Marine officers, demanded a duel. The two men finally met on October 19, 1818, near Hoboken, New Jersey, where Burr had killed Hamilton. At a signal, they took five paces and wheeled. Heath fired—and missed. Perry refused to fire.

The following February, a court of inquiry met in Washington to examine the charges against Gale. He was found not guilty and was appointed Lieutenant Commandant of the Marine Corps.

But Gale's troubles were by no means over. He fought a running battle with the Secretary of the Navy over the prerogatives of the Commandant; and on August 29, 1820, he was placed under arrest and a court-martial ordered. Today Gale would be regarded as an alcoholic, and he was not the most competent of men. But clearly vicious headquarters politics were involved.

The outcome was predictable. The court found the Commandant guilty as charged. President Monroe approved its findings; and on October 18, 1820, Gale was cashiered—the only Commandant in the history of the Marine Corps to be so disgraced.

Archibald Henderson, who now became Commandant of the Corps, was a proper Virginian, thirty-seven years old, with a distinguished record in the War of 1812. He had climbed to the top, and he would stay there for 38 years—until his death. His would be the longest term as Commandant in all Marine Corps history. Fortunately for the Corps, he became one of the Marines' great Commandants: able, jealous of the Corps' status and reputation and quick to seize any opportunity to give the Marines a wider role in the nation's destiny.

Morale in the Corps was low when Henderson took over. Its authorized strength was down to 988 officers and men. Its very existence was threatened. The Navy Commissioners wanted the Marines broken up into small detachments. And in 1830, Capt. Lewis Warrington, USN, then a Navy Commissioner, recommended the Corps' abolition. President Andrew Jackson wanted the Corps to be absorbed into the Army. But after congressional hearings, these ideas died. They would come up again—over and over—whenever the nation relaxed in peace.

Exactly what the Marine Corps was to be and what its relationship was to both the Navy and the Army had to be settled. Back in 1812, the Secretary of the Navy had ruled that since a Marine is "for the purpose of performing Naval Services, he is not liable to the orders of any Army officer whatsoever. . . ."[10] But now the Corps' relationship with its parent body, the Navy, also had to be hammered out.

Finally on June 30, 1834, Congress passed "an act for the better organization of the United States 'Marine Corps.'" This was the first major act dealing with the Marines since the 1798 law establishing the Corps. It made the Corps clearly responsible to the Navy except on the "order" of the President. This meant that Marine officers were not responsible to Army officers—and also that the Corps could serve with the Army in many new ways. Just two years later, this possibility would become a reality.

The act of 1834 also set enlistments at four years, made Marine Corps pay parallel to Army pay and Marine rank the same as Army rank. It ruled that no Marine officer shall "exercise command over any navy yard or vessel of the United States." It increased the strength of the Corps to 1,287 officers and men, headed by one "Colonel Commandant." Henderson was promoted to that new rank on July 1.

Two affairs in the early years of Henderson's regime set significant precedents. On March 12, 1824, Brevet Maj. Robert D. Wainwright led a Marine detachment from the Boston Navy Yard to quell a riot in the state prison at Boston. The prison authorities asked the major to fire powder alone at first and, if that did not disperse the prisoners, to fire ball. Wainwright refused. With 30 Marines, he entered the large dining room and tried to reason with the mob of more than 280 prisoners. They refused to surrender. Wainwright told his men to hold up their bullets so that the prisoners could see them, and then load their pieces. Wainwright took out his watch and told the prisoners they had three minutes to leave the room or he would order his men to fire. If the prisoners were willing to risk the first volley, they could have slaughtered the outnumbered Marines before they could reload. For two long minutes, no one moved. Then the prisoners began drifting out; and as the last seconds ran out, the rest broke for the door.

Word of the courage of Wainwright and his men spread throughout the nation. The story, repeated in the widely used McGuffey Readers, was taught to generations of school children, adding to the esteem of the Corps. And the incident became an important precedent for calling on the Corps in moments of civilian disorder.

The second affair was the Marines' most dramatic overseas encounter with pirates in the far-off East Indies. On February 4, 1832, the frigate *Potomac* reached Quallah Battoo on the island of Sumatra to punish the pirates who a year before had killed the mate and two seamen of the merchant ship *Friendship* out of Salem, Massachusetts. At dawn on February 8, a party of 286 sailors and Marines landed a mile north of the town. The Marines with Brevet Capt. Alvin Edson and Lt. George H. Terrett were in the van. They attacked and subdued the nearest fort. Then the party marched through the town. While a division of sailors attacked the main fort, Edson stormed a fort behind the town and killed all who did not flee. Then the entire American force assaulted the center fort—the local rajah's stronghold. After two hours of fighting, the royal magazine exploded. The natives fell back and rallied in the jungle. Two Marines were killed; Edson and another Marine were wounded. As the natives pressed forward, the Marines formed a rear guard for the landing party moving out to the boats. All the houses in the village had been destroyed and the forts wrecked. American power had been brought to the far shores of the Pacific.

In the spring of 1836, Commandant Henderson led the Marines to fight the Indians who had risen to oppose the government's plan to force them to move from their traditional homes, now coveted by white settlers and land speculators, to the wilderness west of the Mississippi River. The scattered Army, numbering only about 4,000 soldiers, needed help. Colonel Henderson volunteered the Marine Corps, and President Jackson accepted with alacrity.

On June 23, Henderson reported 462 men to Maj Gen. Winfield Scott at Columbus, Georgia. They had marched 224 miles across the state in 14 days. The next day, 160 more Marines from New York under Lt. Col. William H. Freeman, reached Milledgeville, Georgia, and headed south to Florida.

The guerrilla war between the southern Indians and the white people stretched far back in time and was filled with hatred.

Andrew Jackson had destroyed the strength of the Creek nation in the famous Battle of Horseshoe Bend on March 27, 1814. Of 1,000 Creek warriors only 70 escaped. Not one surrendered. The survivors joined the Seminole tribe in Spanish Florida. Jackson invaded Spanish Florida in April 1818, and this so-called First Seminole War led to the acquisition of East Florida from Spain. By 1825, Jackson, by intimidation and bribery, had forced treaties on the Seminoles, the Cherokees, the Chickasaws and the Creeks.

In 1829, Jackson, the Indians' great enemy, reached the White House; and the Congress, after prolonged and violent debate, passed a Removal Act. The Chickasaws, the Cherokees and the Choctaws eventually agreed to move west. Jackson was also determined to move out the Creeks and the Seminoles. His policy again led to war. In the Upper Mississippi Valley, Chief Black Hawk threw the Sauk and Fox against the Army. In Florida, Osceola roused his Seminole warriors to resistance. The charismatic son of an English trader and a Creek mother, Osceola would become the Marines' great Indian opponent.

Repeatedly, Osceola attacked U.S. Army units with brilliantly executed tactics. The whole Florida peninsula was shaken by fear.

The tension between the two races was increased by the presence of Negro slaves who had escaped from Southern plantations and joined the Seminoles and Creeks in fighting the white man. Slave hunters wanted them back.

The first Marines to join the Second Seminole War were 57 men under 1st Lt. Nathaniel S. Waldron of *Constitution*. They landed on January 22, 1836, at Fort Brooke, on the site of present-day Tampa. Maj. Gen. Scott led Army soldiers futilely chasing their elusive foe in Florida and then headed north to fight the Creeks, who had risen in Alabama; Henderson and his Marines joined them. The Marines in the Creek country left behind their frock coats and high caps. They wore white fatigues, and most of them were armed with old-fashioned muskets. A few had new Colt rifles.

The Marines conducted company-sized patrols; guarded the mail road from Columbus to Tuskegee, Alabama, and supervised one of the concentration camps in which the Creeks were being collected for removal. In July began the march of the 15,000 Creeks to today's Oklahoma. The Indians called it "the Trail of Tears." The fifth detachment of Creeks was in charge of twenty-six-year-old Marine 2d Lt. John T. Sprague. On September 5, Sprague and his long line of hopeless, humiliated charges started out across Alabama to Memphis, on the Mississippi. In the train were 1,984 Indians, 45 wagons for the children and the sick and 500 ponies. They moved an average of 12 miles a day. By October 27, some 13,000 Indians were congregated at Memphis. Sprague's group was the third to cross the Mississippi. He sent 500 men on their ponies through the huge Mississippi Swamp and arranged for the bulk of his party to go by boat up the Arkansas River directly to Little Rock. On November 22, most of his party arrived at Fort Gibson, the final rendezvous, in what is now Oklahoma. They had traveled 1,225 miles in 96 days, 800 miles by land and 425 by water. Sprague wrote of them, "They were poor, wretchedly, and depravedly poor, many of them without a garment to cover their nakedness. . . ."[11]

The Indians under Sprague's care had been fortunate to have the sympathetic Marine lieutenant in charge. Some of them realized this; they wrote Sprague, thanking him for his kindness. And they added: "You have been with us many moons. . . . You have heard the cries of our women and children . . . our road has been a long one. . . . Tell General Jackson if the white man will let us we will live in peace and friendship. . . . We are men . . . we have women and children, and why should we come like wild horses?"[12] The last piteous cry from a tragic people.

The war with the Creeks had been won, but the Seminoles remained unconquered. Late in that same summer of 1836, Colonel Henderson marched his Marine battalion south; joined Lt. Col. Freeman's battalion, and on October 28 took command at Fort Brooke. The two battalions were reorganized into one regiment of six companies, comprising more than half the strength of the entire Corps. They were joined by 750 Creek volunteers, and Marine officers commanded some of the Creek units. This was the Corps' first experience leading "native troops."

The Army made repeated sorties into the Great Wahoo Swamp without success. The allied Creeks, wearing white turbans to distinguish them from the enemy in battle, led the pursuit. In one such attack, Marine Lt. Andrew Ross, who held the rank of captain in the Creek unit, tried to cross a stream and was shot. He died of his wounds on December 11, the first Marine officer to be killed in action since the end of the War of 1812.

Brig. Gen. Thomas S. Jesup now took over the war. He

organized the Army of the South into two brigades and on January 8, 1837, gave Colonel Henderson command of the Second Brigade, which included the Marines. Lt. Col. Samuel Miller was given responsibility to guard the convoys moving between Tampa Bay and the Army's depots on the military road north to Fort King.

On January 23 near Lake Ahapopka, a detachment including Capt. John Harris' company of mounted Marines ("Horse Marines") fought a large body of Indians. Five days later, Colonel Henderson led a force into the Great Cypress Swamp to find the main concentration of Seminoles. When the Creeks made contact with the Seminoles, Henderson ordered the Marines into the battle. In the dense swamp, the Marines and Creeks engaged the enemy across the Hatchee-Lustee River, a deep, 20-yard-wide stream. Marines and soldiers extended along the river bank to lay in a crossfire. When the enemy's fire slackened, the troops plunged over, swimming or crossing on logs. Captain Harris was one of the first across. The enemy fell back. Marine Pvt. Joel Wright was killed in the crossing and three others were wounded.

Henderson's force pursued the enemy for a half mile through an even more difficult part of the swamp. The Seminoles made repeated stands. Marine Drummer Thomas P. Peterson was killed. But Henderson could never catch up with the enemy's main body. The Battle of the Hatchee-Lustee was the Marines' largest engagement of the war. It led to a conference with the Seminole chiefs and on March 6 an armistice was signed. The Indians agreed to assemble for removal; it looked deceptively as though the war was over.

Six Marines had been killed in action or died later of their wounds. Henderson was promoted to brevet brigadier general, the first Marine to hold general officer rank. Captains William Dulany and Harris were made brevet majors. Henderson returned to Washington in May, and Brevet Lt. Col. Miller was left in command of the troops south of the Hillsborough River. His force included 189 Marines at Tampa Bay, where the Seminoles began to concentrate. Everyone was convinced the war was finished.

Then, at midnight on June 2, in a daring raid at Tampa Bay, Osceola recaptured the more compliant chiefs who had agreed to emigrate and forced them and all their 700 followers to leave the Marine-guarded encampment before dawn. The war began again.

It would go on for five more years.

In July, Miller turned over his command to Brevet Maj. William Dulany. The effort to remove the Seminoles to the West continued. The summer passed without decision; and in October, Osceola offered to parlay under a flag of truce. During the meeting, he was seized and brought in a prisoner. He was taken to Fort Moultrie at Charleston where he died, probably of malaria. He was thirty-three; and as Marine Lt. John Sprague called him, "the master-spirit of the war." [13]

The field command in the fall of 1837 was turned over to Col. Zachary Taylor, who on Christmas Day fought the last big battle of the war at Lake Okeechobee. But it was not decisive; the Indians crept back into the Everglade swamps. The war went on. Many Indians were forceably removed; others holed up in the virtually impenetrable swamps. The Seminoles were really never conquered.

While the Marine regiment served with the Army, other members of the Corps were fighting in Florida with the Navy. For six years, these Marines waged a guerrilla war from the sea and up the rivers leading into the swampy interior. In the summer of 1838, a special naval force was organized in small ships and 140 canoes. This novel unit won the nickname "Mosquito Fleet." It started with 160 sailors and Marines and by 1841 totaled 622 men, including 130 Marines. In November 1839, it was joined by two companies of Marines, led by 1st Lt. George H. Terrett and 2d Lts. Isaac R. Wilson and Robert D. Taylor. Terrett had fought the pirates at Quallah Battoo and would later win renown outside the Halls of Montezuma. They made innumerable patrols into the Everglades before the war ended in July 1842. Nineteen Marines died in this campaign.

In the entire Florida war, a staggering total of 1,466 men of the Regular Army and 61 Marines lost their lives to the enemy and to tropical disease. When it was over, Seminoles remained in the Everglades. The Marine regiment that had been volunteered to fight the Indians marked one of the turning points in Marine Corps history—for the first time, a Marine expeditionary force had fought a sustained campaign ashore to extend the power of the United States. It pointed the way to Belleau Wood, Okinawa and the Chosin Reservoir.

4
The Mexican War
1842–1847

By 1840, the United States had expanded to 17 million people and 26 states. The young nation's thrust outward was transcontinental and global; and more and more often, U.S. Marines participated.

In the summer of 1838, six ships of the Wilkes Exploring Expedition began one of the most remarkable voyages in American history. Into the Pacific with Navy Lt. Charles Wilkes sailed 33 enlisted Marines, led by Quartermaster Sgt. Simeon Stearns. These were the first United States Marines to see Tarawa, Wake and Makin—a century before Pearl Harbor.

By the time the surviving men and ships returned nearly four years later, they had explored the Antarctic, surveyed 208 Pacific islands and 800 miles of the northwest coast of North America and circumnavigated the globe. Landing parties of Marines and sailors fought in the Gilberts. When Marines came back to Tarawa in 1943, they used charts Wilkes had made. They visited Makin Atoll and Wake Atoll in 1841. On to Manila, past Corregidor, then to Singapore, round the Cape of Good Hope and home to New York. Four Marines lost their lives on the expedition, which was a tremendous feat of men and sailing ships.

As the nation stretched its commercial arms around the globe, the Navy became responsible for protecting American interests abroad. Marines were ordered ashore on distant coasts to guard—or avenge the loss of—American lives and property. In 1843, Commodore Matthew Calbraith Perry—Oliver Hazard Perry's younger brother—took a squadron to the African coast. There, he was told that a tribe called the Fishmen, ruled by a giant king named Ben Crack-O, had obscenely tortured and killed the crew of the American schooner *Mary Carver*.

On December 13, Perry went ashore with sailors and Marines commanded by 1st Lt. Jabez C. Rich and 2d Lt. Isaac T. Doughty. (These two young officers would fight on opposing sides 20 years later.) While Perry and Ben Crack-O palavered, Marines stood behind the American delegation. The huge king denied he had had anything to do with the fate of the *Mary Carver's* crew—

[For the location of places in the Mexican War see maps No. 4 and 8 in the map section.—*Au.*]

and then added that the ship's captain had been killed for murdering two tribesmen.

Suddenly, Perry was on his feet, red with anger. The king leaped at Perry and tried to drag the commodore to where he had left an iron spear. Someone jumped on Ben Crack-O, stripping his robe from him. The naked giant strode on with the proud commodore tucked under his arm. Perry shouted for help. The Marines were already moving. A sergeant shot Ben Crack-O; two other Marines bayoneted him. The king fought viciously. He was shot again, stabbed repeatedly and finally overpowered. The Marines fired into the crowd of natives, who scattered immediately. Perry, bruised but not hurt, organized a retreat to the beach, taking the bleeding king with him. The Marines laid down a sharp covering fire. Ben Crack-O died the next day aboard Perry's flagship. Apparently he harbored no grudge; he willed Commodore Perry his seven wives.

In June 1844, 44 Marines and sailors from the sloop of war *St. Louis* went ashore on Whampoa Island near Canton, China, to protect the American compound from an angry mob. The next month, Caleb Cushing signed the Treaty of Wanghia, giving Americans rights equal to those the British had won in the Opium War. The Chinese accepted the doctrine of "extraterritoriality," which gave foreigners the right to try their own citizens. The Marines remained to guard American lives and property.

Closer to home, on October 20, 1842, Commodore Thomas ap Catesby Jones—the gunboat hero at New Orleans back in 1814—landed 150 Marines and seamen from his East Pacific Squadron to seize the Mexican fort at Monterey, California. He erroneously thought war had been declared with Mexico. He had to recall his men; he was four years too early.

Even before the Mexican War began, President James K. Polk had his eye on conquering California and stretching the boundary of Texas, which on July 4, 1845, accepted admittance as a state of the Union. On Thursday night, October 30, Polk held a secret meeting in the White House with Marine 1st Lt. Archibald H. Gillespie, who Secretary of the Navy George Bancroft regarded as "an accomplished and most trustworthy officer." [14] The President wanted California for the United States if war should break out with Mexico, and the Marine officer had been chosen to see that his wishes were carried out. He carried secret instructions to the United States consul at Monterey, Thomas O. Larkin;

dispatches for Commodore John D. Sloat on the Mexican west coast, and personal letters to Army Lt. John C. Frémont, who was exploring the Far West for the Army's Topographical Corps.

Traveling in disguise, Gillespie went via Vera Cruz, Mexico City and Mazatlan—where he located Commodore Sloat—and reached Monterey on April 17, 1846. He delivered his messages to Larkin and then continued north until he met Frémont at the southern tip of Klamath Lake on May 9. Two days later, Polk urged Congress to recognize that "war exists." It did so. And Army Col. Stephen Watts Kearny at Fort Leavenworth, Kansas, was ordered to conquer California.

Frémont and Gillespie rode south into California with rugged companions wearing buckskin and carrying rifles and long hunting knives. Gillespie went ahead to San Francisco Bay and from Commander John B. Montgomery there obtained a keg of powder, 8,000 percussion caps and enough lead to make 9,000 bullets. On June 15, at Sonoma, north of San Francisco Bay, American settlers proclaimed the California "Bear Flag" Republic. Frémont took charge of the military force of the "one-village nation," and Gillespie became his executive officer in charge of training the Bear Flag "army" into effective fighters.

On July 7, Commodore Sloat officially invaded California for the United States, sending Capt. William Mervine, USN, ashore at Monterey with 165 sailors and 85 Marines commanded by Capt. Ward Marston. They raised the American flag over the customs house, and 2d Lt. William A. T. Maddox stayed ashore with a Marine detachment as a garrison—the West Coast's first Marine Corps post.

Two days later, the Bear Flag Republic became American; and 2d Lt. Henry B. Watson landed with 14 Marines to occupy Yerba Buena (San Francisco). When Commodore Robert F. Stockton took over from Sloat, he legitimized Frémont and Gillespie and their 160 mounted irregulars as the "California Battalion of Mounted Riflemen."

Stockton sent the battalion south by ship to San Diego to cut off the Mexicans operating near Los Angeles. It and some 80 Marines raised the American flag at San Diego on July 30. Stockton sent a party, including 1st Lt. Jacob Zeilin and his Marine detachment, ashore to hold Santa Barbara. And the commodore seized San Pedro, the port of Los Angeles.

Stockton entered Los Angeles on August 12 with 360 Marines

and sailors and Frémont and 120 horsemen. Gillespie stayed to hold San Diego with 48 men. Then Stockton dreamt a new dream; he would sail to Acapulco, march to Mexico City and link up with the Army and win the war. First, he named Frémont Military Governor of California and Gillespie as Commandant of the Southern District, the center of Mexican influence.

"Commandant" Gillespie moved up to Los Angeles and tried to rule with an iron hand. Anti-American feeling rose; and on September 25, 400 hard-riding Californians attacked and put Gillespie's small band under siege. After three days, he led his men to a stronger position on a hilltop—but without water. Finally, on September 30, outnumbered 10 to 1, he was permitted by the Mexicans to march out to San Pedro and board a merchant ship. A detachment of the California Battalion, besieged at San Diego, was all that remained of the conquest of southern California.

Stockton struck back. On October 7, Navy Captain Mervine led ashore 310 sailors and Marines, plus Gillespie and his men, to recapture Los Angeles. They failed. That night, swift-striking riders attacked; and the next afternoon, the harassed expedition climbed back in its ships. Late in October, Stockton himself arrived, landed sailors and Marines to hold San Pedro and sent Gillespie down to San Diego with his own men and 20 Marines. The warships' guns could hold the ports. But the Mexicans drove the garrison of 10 Marines out of Santa Barbara.

Then, word arrived that Brevet Brig. Gen. Stephen Kearny, guided by Kit Carson, had reached California after a painful march over mountains and desert. Stockton sent Gillespie and 39 volunteers to meet and reinforce Kearny's troop of 110 men.

At San Pasqual, a hundred Mexicans attacked them. With ammunition wet and useless, the Battle of San Pasqual became a wild struggle between Mexican lances and American sabers. The Americans took the worst of it. Kearny was lanced twice and out of action; Gillespie was badly wounded before the Mexicans rode off. Stockton sent 100 soldiers and 80 Marines under Lieutenant Zeilin to escort Kearny and his men toward San Diego. Years later, the Mexican commander said that only the arrival of the Marines saved Kearny at the end of his historic march.

Then, Stockton set out again to take Los Angeles by marching the 140 miles from San Diego. Seven miles from Los Angeles, the enemy made a stand on bluffs behind the San Gabriel River. With

Zeilin and his Marines holding the right flank, the Americans waded the knee-deep river under fire and charged the enemy. Those in front fled, but the Californian horsemen struck both American flanks. The sailors on the left and the Marines on the right beat them off. The Americans charged up the bluffs, and it was quickly over. One American was killed. It was the Marine Corps' largest battle in California.

The Mexicans made one more stand, at La Mesa, three miles from the white walls of Los Angeles, in what today is Vernon. Three times, the Mexicans charged but the artillery cut them down. At last, the Mexicans rode off into the mountains, leaving the road to Los Angeles open. Again, Gillespie was wounded. On January 10, with the band playing, Stockton and Kearny led their men into Los Angeles. California was finally conquered.

The conquest contained one lesson: If the United States wanted to extend its territory on hostile coasts, it would need amphibious forces to put ashore. California was finally won when the United States could land a force strong enough to hold.

In contrast, the "eastern front" of the Mexican War experienced the first major D-Day in American history, when 70 ships with 12,000 soldiers, sailors and Marines assembled off Vera Cruz, Mexico's largest port, in March 1847. Ready to land in the first wave was a battalion of Marines commanded by Capt. Alvin Edson. This would be the first step to the Halls of Montezuma. Edson and his men pointed the way for the U.S. Marine Corps of the future. For the first time, U.S. Marines were brought together from the shipboard detachments scattered throughout a naval squadron and fought as a unit for a period of time.

The invasion at Vera Cruz was the turning point of the war and the United States' first really important amphibious operation—the largest until World War II. Maj. Gen. Winfield Scott, the head of the U.S. Army and now sixty years old, hurried to land and advance inland before the terrible yellow fever season began on the coast. Captain Edson and his 180 men were assigned to the van of the assault and attached to the First Brigade led by Brig. Gen. William J. Worth, USA.

The morning of March 9 was clear and torridly hot. The men spent hours transferring from ships to specially built "surf boats"—the first American landing craft built to specifications for an amphibious operation. At 6 P.M., gunboats sprayed the landing area at Collado beach with grape; and the surf boats raced for the shore. Edson quickly led his Marines to the crest of the first row of sand dunes and formed a line of skirmishers, ready to fight. But not a shot was fired—the beach was empty. By the next morning, 12,000 men were ashore: and from their landing point south of the city, they completely encircled Vera Cruz with a seven-mile-long line of trenches and strong points. After days of siege, 5,000 enemy soldiers marched out of the city on March 29 and surrendered. Scott rode into Vera Cruz to the strains of "Yankee Doodle." He had executed his invasion and captured Vera Cruz with the loss of only 19 men—one a Marine.

Commodore Matthew Perry created a Naval Brigade of 2,500 sailors and Marines and made several amphibious raids on the Mexican coast. Maj. Gen. Scott, meanwhile, marched swiftly inland from Vera Cruz, and after defeating the Mexican army in the mountain pass at Cerro Gordo on April 18, settled down at Puebla for the summer.

By this time, the enlistments in the Army's old volunteer regiments were running out. Of 3,700 volunteers, those who reenlisted filled only a single company. Scott, down to less than 6,000 men, need replacements. The Secretary of the Navy and Commandant Henderson told President Polk that six companies of Marines were available. Polk gave his permission, and these Marines were organized to fight with the Army. They would write one of the most dramatic chapters in Marine Corps history.

The Marine regiment was commanded by two veterans of the War of 1812: Lt. Col. Samuel E. Watson and Maj. Levi Twiggs. They typified how Commandant Henderson's generation had aged. Both Watson and Twiggs would die in Mexico.

In July, Lt. Col. Watson attached his regiment to a large contingent being taken inland to Scott by Brig. Gen. Franklin Pierce. Watson had brought 314 men to Mexico and been joined by 52 men from the ships in Vera Cruz harbor. The Marines served as the rear guard of Pierce's poorly-disciplined column.

After a march through 200 miles of guerrilla-infested mountains, Pierce finally reached Scott on August 6. These were the last of Scott's replacements; and he now had 14,000 men on his muster rolls, although 2,500 of them were sick with dysentery. Scott prepared to march immediately. The Marines were assigned to the fourth division commanded by Brig. Gen. John A. Quitman. Between Scott's army and Mexico City waited the army of the dictator Antonio Lopez de Santa Anna—30,000 strong.

The assault on Mexico City had two phases. The Marine battalion did not fight in the first, during which Quitman's division was held in reserve. On August 22 Santa Anna asked for an armistice. It lasted exactly two weeks.

On September 7, Scott reopened the war. Worth's Regulars attacked an ancient mill, Molino del Rey, less than a mile west of the Hill of Chapultepec, the strongpoint dominating the plain west of the city. More than 750 Americans were killed or wounded, and that brought Quitman and the Marines to battle.

Since Santa Anna had massed most of his army south of the city, Scott decided to attack from the west. That side was guarded by the Hill of Chapultepec, which rose lone and sheer from the plain, 600 yards long and 200 feet high, surrounded by a 12-foot wall and topped by a gray-walled palace that was now a military school. The Hill was a fearsome objective to assault. But once it was won, the army could move swiftly along two causeways to the so-called gates of Belen and San Cosme—actually blockhouses.

Monday, September 13, 1847, is the most famous date in the Marine Corps' first hundred years. At 8 A.M. the attack started. Quitman's men approached the southern side of Chapultepec under heavy fire. Major Twiggs led a storming party of 120 hand-picked soldiers and Marines, and Marine Capt. John G. Reynolds led 40 Marine and Army volunteers. When enemy gunfire stopped them, Major Twiggs stood up to call to Reynolds and gather his own party. A musket ball killed him.

While other Army units attacked the heavily-defended western slope of the Hill, the Marines struggled up the steep southern side, fighting hand-to-hand with bayonets and clubbed rifles. Cpl. Hugh Graham and five Marine privates were killed. Americans from both sides of the Hill reached the castle simultaneously, and at 9:30 a flag was raised over the fortress of Chapultepec.

While Chapultepec was being stormed, Marine Capt. George H. Terrett led 1st Lt. John D. Simms, 2d Lt. Charles A. Henderson (son of the Commandant) and 36 men to skirt the heights and pursue the retreating enemy northeastward toward the city. Terrett said later he knew "I could not be wrong, so long as the Enemy in large numbers were ahead."[15] Terrett and his Marines raced up the road under heavy fire. Twenty soldiers led by Lt. Ulysses S. Grant joined them as they fought their way up the San Cosme causeway. They were now in front of the army.

Worth's bugles sounded recall. Terrett went back to report to the general. Simms and Henderson plunged ahead with 25 men. The gate was too heavily defended to take frontally so Marine Lieutenants Simms and Jabez C. Rich led seven Marines to attack the strongpoint from the left. Four were hit. Henderson, already wounded in the leg, attacked from the front. Two of his men went down. Together, they seized San Cosme gate. For 15 minutes, they stood against all the fire the Mexicans could mass against them. Then Worth again sounded recall, and the Marines and soldiers withdrew. Six Marines had been killed.

Meanwhile, once Chapultepec fell, Quitman moved his division under fire up the Belen causeway, with the Marine battalion in line just behind the South Carolina regiment that had been assigned the lead. At the Belen gate they were stopped. Marine Pvt. Thomas Kelly was among those killed there. Despite repeated enemy counterattacks, at 1:20 the Marines and soldiers carried the gate by assault. It was dark before Worth established a permanent foothold at the San Cosme gate.

At dawn on September 14, Quitman and Worth prepared to assault the two entrances to the city; but during the night, Santa Anna had abandoned the city. Quitman's men raced through the thronged streets into the Grand Plaza and took possession of the National Palace, where, in ancient days, had stood the Halls of Montezuma. In recognition of the fighting of his soldiers and Marines, Scott named Quitman governor of the City of Mexico; and the Marines were stationed to guard the Palace. It took 36 more hours to clean up the snipers and looters, and then the climactic battle of the war was over. The expansion of the continental United States, except for the Gadsden Purchase and the purchase of Alaska, was completed.

Lt. Col. Watson fell ill and died in Vera Cruz on November 16. In the spring, the veterans were joined by a newly organized Second Marine Battalion of 367 men commanded by Maj. John Harris. By the summer of 1848, both battalions were home again.

In the 1840s, Marine officers and noncoms began wearing scarlet stripes on their dress trousers—to commemorate, tradition came to say, the Marine blood shed at Chapultepec and the Halls of Montezuma.

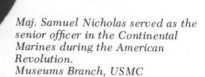

Maj. Samuel Nicholas served as the senior officer in the Continental Marines during the American Revolution.
Museums Branch, USMC

Marines fight in the tops high above the deck of the Continental frigate Alliance *in 1781, as painted by Maj. Charles H. Waterhouse.*
Museums Branch, USMC

Capt. George H. Terrett was a Marine
hero of the battle for Mexico City in
1847 and later joined the Confederate
States Marine Corps.
Private collection; courtesy Museums
Branch, USMC

Marines, in center with white crossed
belts, fight Mexicans in the battle of
Santa Clara, near San Francisco, in
1847. The Marines were led by Capt.
Ward Marston and 2d Lt. Robert
Tansill.
Franklin D. Roosevelt Library

U.S. soldiers and Marines storm the Hill of Chapultepec.
Maj. Levi Twiggs was killed in the assault while leading
the Marines, who dashed ahead to the gates of Mexico City.
Marine Corps Photo, National Archives

On October 18, 1859, U.S. Marines storm the engine
house at Harpers Ferry in which the abolitionist John
Brown and his men had barricaded themselves. Marine
Pvt. Luke Quinn lies mortally wounded in the foreground.
Museums Branch, USMC

In 1864, Maj. Jacob Zeilin, Jr., was
selected over four of his seniors as
Commandant of the Corps. He
became the first Marine to gain
regular general officer rank.
Museums Branch, USMC

*U.S. Marines, on the right, line up for Commodore
Perry's ceremonial landing in Japan near present-day
Yokohama.*
Marine Corps Photo, National Archives

*John Philip Sousa, standing on platform, and the U.S.
Marine Corps Band he made world-famous. Sousa led
the band from 1880 to 1892 and wrote many marches,
including* Semper Fidelis. *Picture was taken about 1890.*
Marine Corps Photo, National Archives

Marine Guard aboard the screw steamer Pensacola,
which participated in Farragut's capture of New Orleans.
This photograph was taken some time after the Civil War.
Official U.S. Navy Photo

Sgt. John H. Quick earned the
Medal of Honor at Guantanamo
Bay, marched with Waller on
Samar and won the Navy Cross for
bringing ammunition to Bouresches
in World War I.
Marine Corps Photo, National
Archives

*Company H, First Marine Battalion, on hike from
Olongapo, Philippine Islands, in 1901.
Marine Corps Photo, National Archives*

Littleton Waller Tazewell Waller
fought in the Boxer Rebellion, led the
disastrous march on Samar, and
battled the Cacos in Haiti. This
full-dress portrait was made during
World War I.
Museums Branch, USMC

Marines at Vera Cruz, Mexico. Left to
right are Capt. Frederick H. Delano,
Sgt. Maj. John H. Quick, Lt. Col.
Wendell C. Neville, Col. John A.
Lejeune and Maj. Smedley D.
Butler. Quick and Neville won the
Medal of Honor; Butler earned two.
Both Neville and Lejeune were to
become Commandant of the Corps.
Marine Corps Photo, National
Archives

Capt. Roy S. Geiger, a pioneer
Marine aviator, won the Navy Cross
in France in 1918 and again on
Guadalcanal. As a lieutenant general,
he commanded the Tenth Army on
Okinawa in World War II.
Museums Branch, USMC

Lt. Alfred A. Cunningham was the
first Marine to report for naval flying
training on May 22, 1912, which is
considered the birth date of Marine
Corps aviation. Cunningham led the
1st Marine Aviation Force to France
in 1918 and was the officer in charge
of the Marine Corps' aviation until
December 1920.
Museums Branch, USMC

5
The Civil War
1857–1865

The old man still stood ramrod stiff. He had been a Marine for 50 years, Commandant for 36. His hair and beard were now white, but the courage he had displayed on the bloody deck of *Constitution* back in 1815 had not faded. Col. Archibald Henderson, at seventy four, was about to face gunfire for the last time.

It was the morning of June 1, 1857. The nation was boiling with tensions that would rapidly build up to the Civil War. The city of Washington was holding a municipal election, and the small police force was trying to keep gangs of toughs away from the citizens lined up to vote. The police were overwhelmed, and the mayor closed the polls and asked President James Buchanan for Marines—the only Federal force in the city—to restore order.

By noon, two companies under the command of Capt. Henry B. Tyler marched to the stucco City Hall and reported to the mayor. Commandant Henderson, still in mufti, followed the detachment. A gang dragged a small brass cannon up Pennsylvania Avenue to 7th and K Streets. Armed only with an umbrella, Henderson went ahead to make certain the mob did not turn the cannon against the Marines. The old gentleman ordered the mob to disperse. Revolvers were fired from the crowd. Brevet Maj. Jacob Zeilin, commanding the first company, sent a platoon forward. The rioters fired pistols and threw rocks at the advancing Marines, who grabbed the gun. One Marine was shot in the face; others were hit by stones. The Marines fired into the crowd, which fled out of range. As Colonel Henderson moved through the ranks to stop the shooting, a man ran to within two feet of the colonel and fired his pistol. His shot missed. A sergeant shot the man in the left arm, and Henderson collared him. The mob continued to fire at the Marines. One was hit. Tyler ordered the Marines to prepare to fire, and the rioters scattered.

The old colonel had acted beyond the call of any duty. It was his last courageous act. On January 6, 1859, he died at home. He was one of the Corps' greatest leaders. The day after he died,

[For the location of places in the Civil War see map No. 3 in the map section.—*Au.*]

another graybeard, Lt. Col. John Harris, was appointed Colonel Commandant of the Corps. Now sixty-eight years old, with 44 years in uniform, he could no longer muster the energy and vision that would be required to lead the Marine Corps through the great civil war that was about to rip the nation apart. Actually, Harris represented what the Corps had become. The dozen years after the Mexican War marked a pause of peace, and the Corps had aged. It was now not ready to meet the challenge of the times.

The Marines stationed in Washington were called out again on Monday afternoon, October 17, 1859. Civil war was now less than two years away, and the Marines were needed. Reports said the slaves in Virginia had risen and seized the Federal arsenal and gun factory at Harpers Ferry, where the Potomac and Shenandoah meet, 55 miles northwest of the capital. President Buchanan ordered out the Marines—one more occasion for the Corps' proud boast: First to Fight.

Eighty five Marines formed at the Navy Yard in their bright blue dress uniforms with fancy blue frock coats, white belts and French fatigue caps. First Lt. Israel Greene, commanding the detachment, wore his light ceremonial sword. (The fact that he did not put on his heavy-duty saber would have its effect on history.) They entrained for Harpers Ferry.

There, Lt. Col. Robert E. Lee, Army hero of the Mexican War, commanded all forces; and cavalry Lt. J. E. B. Stuart served as his aide. A group of white men and Negroes had seized the arsenal and armory, killed a number of local people and held 13 hostages in a small brick building that housed two fire engines. The raiders were led by John Brown of Kansas, who had made a religious crusade of opposing slavery. By that night all but Brown and four of his men were killed or wounded. Escape was impossible; Lt. Col. Lee was concerned to save the hostages. He gave Lieutenant Greene the job of "taking those men out"—don't risk a stray bullet killing a prisoner; use the bayonet.

Early in the morning, Stuart approached the engine house with a white flag. Brown would not surrender; if he were allowed to escape, he would release the prisoners. Stuart gave a signal and Greene ordered his 12-man storming party to batter in the door. Greene plunged through the hole they made in the door. Marine Maj. William W. Russell, paymaster of the Corps, went in after him. The men inside had been reloading, but they shot Pvt. Luke Quinn through the abdomen and Pvt. Mathew Ruppert, in the face. Greene struck Brown in the back of the neck with his light dress sword. It bent double and Brown lived. But the Marines "came rushing in like tigers," and killed two of the raiders. Brown survived to stand trial and rally those who hated slavery.

The Marines' engagement at Harpers Ferry marked the beginning. Before it was over, 600,000 Americans in uniforms of blue and of gray would be killed. Irish-born Luke Quinn was the first.

As civil war approached, the Marine Corps, like the other services, was crippled by resignations. For many, ties of state and region proved stronger than loyalty to country. Very few enlisted Marines quit, but the Corps lost 20 of its 63 officers. They included some of the Corps' finest: George H. Terrett, Jabez C. Rich, John D. Simms and Israel Greene. Three of former Commandant Henderson's sons "went South." Commandant Harris referred to officers who resigned as "those who abandoned the service in its hour of need."[16] Nineteen of the U.S. Marine Corps officers who went South joined the Confederate States Marine Corps.

The Civil War revolutionized the Navy. Sail gave way to steam power; rifled cannon replaced smoothbore guns; explosive shells shattered wooden hulls and hastened the changeover to steel ships. The Navy experimented with mines, turrets, submarines and graduated gunsights.

The U.S. Marine Corps was not prepared for great and rapid change. Under Harris' tired leadership, the Civil War, on the whole, was not to be a time of distinction for the Corps.

Florida seceded on January 10, 1861; and two days later the Warrington Navy Yard at Pensacola, the only major naval base on the Gulf of Mexico, surrendered. The 39 Marines under Capt. Josiah Watson were told to stack arms and later sailed north. But in April, 200 soldiers and 118 Marines under 1st Lt. John C. Cash landed at Fort Pickens in Pensacola Harbor to reinforce a small unit there. The Union held Fort Pickens and neutralized the navy yard throughout the war.

On February 4, the Confederacy was created; and on March 4, Abraham Lincoln took office. The Marine Corps Band played in the line of march of the inauguration parade and again at the Union Ball that night. But the mood in divided Washington was one of tension, not festivity. On April 12, Confederate troops fired on the Federal garrison bottled up in Fort Sumter, controlling the entrance to Charleston, South Carolina. The war began.

The Rebels threatened the great navy yard at Norfolk, Virginia. The 60 Marines there, reinforced by soldiers and 100 more Marines, destroyed the yard, spiked its guns, wrecked its machine shops and set fire to the sail and steam sloop *Merrimack*. The Rebels stormed the burning yard and saved the dry dock and a thousand cannon. The South would raise the sunken hull of *Merrimack* and rebuild her as the mighty ironclad *Virginia*—for a brief moment, the world's most powerful warship.

When the war started, the U.S. Marine Corps had less than 1,800 officers and men; it never exceeded 3,900 men at any time during the conflict. Before the long war was over, 148 U.S. Marines would be killed in battle, 131 would be wounded and 312 would die of disease and other causes. More than 2,000 would desert—mostly during the final stages of the war, when all the services suffered such disloyalty.

In the war's first battle, Brig. Gen. Irvin McDowell led 28,000 raw Union troops to attack the rail junction at Manassas, Virginia, 25 miles southwest of Washington. In his force was a Marine battalion of 12 officers and 353 newly enlisted men commanded by Brevet Maj. John G. Reynolds, who had fought at Chapultepec. The enemy waited north of the junction, across a stream called Bull Run. One of their brigades was commanded by Col. George H. Terrett, late of the U.S. Marine Corps.

The battle finally began early on Sunday morning, July 21. The Marines advanced with Army Capt. Charles Griffin's six-gun "West Point Battery" of artillery, in the van of the main body, to encircle the enemy's left flank. Fording the stream, the Union soldiers and Marines came under heavy fire but pushed the enemy back nearly a mile. The First Virginia Brigade, commanded by Brig. Gen. Thomas J. Jackson, now held "like a stone wall" behind the crest of Henry House Hill. One final Union charge would break the Rebellion. But two Confederate regiments, one led by Col. J. E. B. Stuart, suddenly appeared and wiped out the Union spearhead. The battle continued into the afternoon at a bruising, slam-bang standstill until at 4:40 the Union front collapsed. During the final struggle, the Marines broke three times and finally fled as the rout became universal. Ten Marines had been killed. Later, Commandant Harris wrote to Secretary of the Navy Gideon Welles, "It is the first instance recorded in its history where any portion of its [the Corps'] members turned their backs to the enemy." [17]

The Civil War event with the greatest significance for the Marine Corps' future was the creation of a special amphibious Marine battalion in the autumn of 1861. Commanded by Lt. Col. Reynolds, it never made a combat landing but participated in the great blockade of the Southern coast, which finally strangled the Confederacy. Here the Marine Corps saw most of its action.

On August 28, 1861, 200 Army troops, reinforced by Marines from the naval squadron, seized two forts at Hatteras Inlet on the North Carolina coast. Six hundred Rebel prisoners were taken without a single Union casualty. On the night of September 13, 70 seamen and 20 Marines led by Capt. Edward McF. Reynolds boarded the Rebel schooner *Judah* at the Pensacola navy yard and burned her to the waterline. Marine Pvt. John Smith, the first man to board, was "by a sad mistake" [18] bayoneted and killed by one of his comrades.

In November, the Federal government mounted the largest American amphibious expedition yet attempted. The target was Hilton Head Island on the southern side of Port Royal Sound, South Carolina (near the Marine Corps' present-day Recruit Depot on Parris Island). Fifteen thousand soldiers sailed to make Hilton Head a major base for the Union blockade. With them, aboard the old sidewheeler *Governor*, went Reynolds' battalion of 350 Marines. A hurricane scattered the fleet and battered *Governor*. The Marines were finally saved by jumping into the high-running sea and being picked up by boats from the sailing frigate *Sabine*. The amphibious battalion missed its chance when on November 7 the Army and Navy captured the forts at Hilton Head. But an amphibious organization of Marines had been created in advance of a campaign specifically to serve with the fleet and to assault the enemy from the sea. Here was the seed of the modern Marine Corps.

March 8, 1862, was another kind of day: a day of battle that closed one era of warfare and began a new. That morning, five handsome wooden frigates stood on blockade duty on the broad waters of Hampton Roads, Virginia. Suddenly, shortly after noon, the ironclad *CSS Virginia*, the resurrected *Merrimack*, steamed for the wooden ships. She headed straight at the bow of *Cumberland*; and her first shot killed and wounded nine Marines, commanded by Capt. Charles Heywood and lined up in formation, foolishly exposed, on the foredeck. *Virginia* rammed, and the two ships' guns dueled fiercely. Marines on *Cumberland's* upper deck sent accurate rifle fire at the enemy's ports. Unable to penetrate *Virginia's* iron-sheathed sides, *Cumberland* was sunk. Fourteen of her 46 Marines were killed. *Virginia* bombarded *Congress* at close range until she surrendered. The other three blockading frigates grounded; but with her captain, Franklin Buchanan, wounded, *Virginia* withdrew to her berth.

By one of the strangest coincidences in American naval history, salvation was on the way in the form of *Monitor*, a tiny "cheesebox on a raft." Her commander, Lt. John L. Worden, tied up the little ironclad gunboat alongside the stranded frigate *Minnesota*. At dawn, *Virginia* appeared to destroy *Minnesota* and engaged *Monitor* in a slugging match—the first between armored ships—at close range for four hours. *Virginia* set *Minnesota* afire, and her gunners scored a direct hit on *Monitor's* pilot house and blinded Lieutenant Worden. Then, *Virginia* headed back to the navy yard for repairs. The battle was a stalemate, but the age of iron ships had begun.

On May 9, the Confederate army pulled out from its defensive positions around Norfolk; and Capt. Charles G. Mc-Cawley brought 200 Marines to regarrison the Norfolk Navy Yard. *Monitor*, her sister ironclad *Galena* and the lightly armored floating battery *Naugatuck* moved up the James River and on May 15 at Drewry's Bluff ran into a battalion of Confederate marines commanded by Capt. John D. Simms (of Mexico City). *Galena* was riddled, *Naugatuck's* Parrott gun burst and *Monitor* was hit repeatedly. Aboard *Galena*, Marine Cpl. John F. Mackie fired on the enemy from the exposed deck and rallied the ironclad's crew. His valor that morning earned him the Medal of Honor—the first ever received by a United States Marine. The battle had been a disaster for the Union ships, but Norfolk and its great navy yard were back in U.S. hands.

The truth is that during the Civil War Marines had no consistent function in battle. Many fought as shipboard gun crews and sharpshooters. Some were hastily thrown together as landing battalions, but they had neither the doctrine nor the training for amphibious assaults under fire. When this war ended, their failure to evolve a vital wartime function would threaten the Corps' life.

On the Union's second front in the West, the strategy had two objectives: to close the Gulf ports and to gain control of the Mississippi. On March 7, 1862, *USS Hartford* arrived at the river's mouth, as flagship of the West Gulf Blockading Squadron commanded by sixty-year-old Capt. David G. Farragut—the same Farragut who had sailed as a boy with Porter and Gamble on the cruise of *Essex* back in 1813. His job was to take New Orleans and open the Mississippi. A total of 333 Marines served on 12 of Farragut's largest ships; Capt. John L. Broome commanded the detachment on *Hartford*. On the night of April 24, Farragut fought past the forts defending the lower Mississippi. Young Marine Pvt. Oscar Smith wrote in his diary: "Both sides fired incessantly and shot and shell flew around like hail. Hotly contested by forts and gunboats, we onward went." [19] Pandemonium raged on the river before the forts were finally passed. Farragut's fleet suffered 201 casualties in the hour-long battle; seven Marines died and 19 were wounded. Two days later at New Orleans, Farragut sent ashore a naval lieutenant and 20 Marines to demand the city's surrender. The Marines stood in front of an angry mob at the wharf, while a delegation went to City Hall. The city fathers rejected its demand and the delegates dashed to the safety of the Marines' muskets. Then, Captain Broome took 250 Marines and seized the Customs House and City Hall. Both Norfolk and New Orleans were now recovered; and Farragut prepared to head upriver to meet Maj. Gen. U. S. Grant, who had conquered Memphis and was marching on Vicksburg, 400 miles above New Orleans.

Farragut made two sorties up the river but did not have an adequate landing force to hold. On the night of March 14, 1863, his ships battled past the guns at Port Hudson. The veteran sidewheeler *Mississippi* grounded in range of the Rebel guns; and her executive officer, Lt. George Dewey, USN, was ordered to destroy her. Marine Sgt. Pinkerton R. Vaughn stayed aboard until all the crew had been taken off and the ship set afire. The twenty-four-year-old Marine earned the Medal of Honor that night. Broome won a brevet promotion to lieutenant colonel. On July 4, while Lee was retreating from Gettysburg in the East, Grant finally took Vicksburg. And the Confederacy tottered.

Farragut moved over to Mobile and attacked on August 5, 1864. Despite the enemy's 180 floating mines ("Damn the torpedoes!"), his fleet battled into Mobile Bay and fought and beat the new giant ram *Tennessee*. Her captain was Franklin Buchanan, who had commanded *Virginia*. When he finally surrendered, Brevet Maj. Charles Heywood, who had commanded the Marines aboard *Cumberland*, took aboard a Marine guard. Twenty-four-year-old Heywood became a brevet lieutenant colonel and known as "the boy colonel." Eight enlisted Marines earned the Medal of Honor at Mobile Bay. And Farragut sealed off the Confederacy's final port on the Gulf.

The Marines' most ambitious attempt in this war to land from the sea directly in the face of enemy fire was the attack on Fort Sumter on the night of September 8, 1863, a tragic episode in the long campaign to recapture the port of Charleston. Small boats carried four 100-man volunteer divisions of both sailors and Marines and a fifth division of 125 Marines commanded by Captain McCawley. McCawley's Marines were to cover the assault parties with musket fire and follow them ashore with the bayonet. The operation was a chaotic failure. Boats lost their way. The fort's defenders were not surprised. Two boatloads of Marines commanded by 1st Lt. Percival C. Pope landed with the first wave and suffered 11 casualties before escaping. Men tried to scale the walls but had no ladders. The battle was over in 20 minutes with 127 men, including 31 Marines, casualties or prisoners.

On May 12, 1864, Commandant Harris died in Washington, eight days shy of his seventy-fourth birthday. Secretary of the Navy Welles shattered the tradition of seniority, retired the four senior Marine officers and reached down and named Maj. Jacob Zeilin, Jr., as Commandant. He was an experienced Marine with a distinguished record. He was now fifty-seven; and when this war was over, he would be the first Marine ever to attain regular general officer rank.

As 1864 drew to a close, Grant was battering Lee and Sherman was marching toward Savannah. The Marines had one last chance to pull off a successful amphibious assault. Only Wilmington, North Carolina, on the Cape Fear River, remained open to blockade-runners still squeezing arms and ammunition into the South. If Wilmington could be choked off, the Confederacy would be isolated.

The Union target became Fort Fisher on Federal Point, a skinny peninsula separating the river and the sea. After weeks of fumbling, the Union army hit the beach on January 13, 1865, to attack Fort Fisher's northern face. A Naval Landing Force of 1,600 sailors and Marines would attack its sea side. A Marine battalion of 365 men from the ships and commanded by Marine Capt. Lucian L. Dawson was the force's fourth and final battalion.

The Marines carried muskets and 40 rounds each and were to cover the sailors' assault on the 15th. A company of 43 Marine sharpshooters under 1st Lt. Louis F. Fagan were the first Marines ashore. The naval brigade, with the Marines leading, moved within 1,200 yards of the fort under heavy fire. When the brigade advanced, the fleet lifted its bombardment; and the Rebels reappeared on the parapet to fire down on the sailors and Marines. The brigade was stopped in its tracks; but the Marines pressed forward, inching their way to the corner of the fort near the sea. Then came the order to charge, and sailors and Marines swept on again. The Army had not yet begun to attack, and the Confederates massed all their fire against the lightly armed naval force. Some 350 Union muskets fought 2,000 in the fort. A few Marines reached the eight-foot-high stockade, planted the Stars and Stripes but had to fall back. Sailors and Marines started flooding to the rear. The naval force had been repulsed.

On the beach, a heroic young Marine, Pvt. Henry Wasmuth, saved the life of eighteen-year-old Acting Ensign Robley D. Evans, who would become famous as Admiral "Fighting Bob" Evans. It cost Wasmuth his life; and decades later, the Navy named Destroyer 489 after him. She survived the Japanese attack on Pearl Harbor and later in World War II was lost at sea.

While the Naval Landing Force was being destroyed, the Army finally began its attack. Captain Dawson assembled a force that included 180 Marines and helped cover the Army's left flank. The Army fought for seven hours; on the ramparts the battle was hand-to-hand. At 10 P.M., a victory signal went up from the fort. The greatest amphibious battle of the Civil War had been won, and the Rebellion was at last encircled. On April 3, Richmond, the Confederate capital, fell; and on April 8, Palm Sunday, the Confederacy died at Appomattox village in northern Virginia.

On the night of Good Friday, Abraham Lincoln was shot in the brain by a man bursting with hate. Colonel Zeilin was among the honorary pallbearers, and in the cortege marched a battalion of Marines.

The war was over. The nation was stitched back together with bayonets and bullets. But it was changed forever, and more than a half million young Americans lay in their graves.

6
Sweep Toward Empire
1848–1894

Throughout the half century between the Mexican War and the War with Spain—interrupted by the violence of the Civil War—the Navy and Marine Corps kept open the sea lanes for the produce of a bountiful land and a booming industry. It was a time of production, expansion and confidence.

In the years before the Civil War, the Marine Corps protected American interests and citizens around the world: Buenos Aires (1852); Nicaragua (1853); Montevideo, Uruguay (1855); Paraguay (1855); the Fiji Islands (1855 and 1858); Puget Sound (1856), and the Isthmus of Panama (1856). Most significantly, the Corps joined in two dramatic ventures in East Asia: the opening of Japan and the attack on the forts protecting Canton, China.

On the morning of July 8, 1853, four American warships steamed in a single column up mist-shrouded Tokyo Bay. The ships were cleared for action, their guns shotted, their crews at battle stations. Dignified, portly Commodore Matthew Calbraith Perry knew that he was going where he was not wanted. With him went six Marine officers and some 200 men under the command of Major Zeilin.

The Japanese demanded that Perry withdraw and deal through the Dutch at Nagasaki. He insisted on delivering the letter he carried from President Millard Fillmore to a suitably high official at Tokyo. Finally, the Japanese compromised and permitted a meeting on July 14. Cmdr. Franklin Buchanan of the flagship *Susquehanna* was the first and Major Zeilin the second American to step on shore. A hundred Marines lined the route to the building that had been erected for the reception. In ceremonies that took only half an hour, Perry delivered the President's letter and announced that he would return the next spring to receive the Japanese answer and to negotiate a treaty.

Perry came back to Tokyo Bay on February 13, 1854; and after much discussion, the Japanese agreed to meet with him at Yokohama, then only a small village. On March 8, Perry brought ashore 500 men, including every possible Marine, and opened three weeks of conferences. Perry and the Japanese signed the Treaty of Kanagawa on March 31. It had a monumental effect on Japan. It exposed Japanese minds to Western thought and began the Meiji modernization, which in great part was based on what the Japanese eagerly learned from the West.

During his second visit to Japan, Perry left the sloop of war *Plymouth* at Shanghai. China was then enflamed by the T'ai P'ing Rebellion against the Manchu emperor; and on April 4, 1854, the Imperial Chinese army invaded the foreign trading settlements. A detachment of 60 sailors and Marines landed from *Plymouth* and was joined by British sailors and Marines. They attacked the Chinese soldiers and cleared the foreign settlements.

Trouble erupted at Canton in the fall of 1856, and Marine detachments were repeatedly sent to Canton from U.S. warships lying in the Pearl River below the city. On November 16, an unarmed American boat was fired on from one of the four barrier forts protecting the river approach to Canton. After bombarding the forts, the Navy on November 20 put ashore a landing force of 287 men, including Brevet Capt. John D. Simms and the squadron's 50 Marines. They fought off repeated counterattacks by 1,000 Chinese soldiers and in three days captured all four forts. American casualties totaled seven dead and 22 wounded in action. No Marines were killed but six were wounded.

From Appomattox to the sinking of *Maine*, the United States was at peace for 33 years. The Marine Corps' strength atrophied; its officers aged; at times less than 2,000 men remained in uniform. In 1866, the Congress debated abolishing the Corps entirely but finally rejected the idea. The Corps had to fight for its life.

Brig. Gen. Zeilin retired as Commandant in November 1876 at the age of seventy. President Grant appointed Col. Charles G. McCawley, who had been brevetted at Chapultepec and again in the boat attack on Fort Sumter. He concentrated on recruiting, improving training and promoting officers on their professional qualifications. From 1883 to 1897, all 50 new Marine officers were graduates of the Naval Academy. Of this "Famous Fifty," five became Commandants, 13 more became generals and 15 others made colonel. They dominated the Corps in its most germinal period from 1917 to 1936.

In 1880, McCawley appointed John Philip Sousa as the fourteenth leader of the Marine Band. He led the band for a dozen years and wrote more than a hundred marches. One, *Semper Fidelis*, became the official Marine Corps march. And in 1891 he started the nationwide tours that made the band popular and world-famous.

Earlier when the band was led by Francis M. Scala, White House concerts became traditional and *The Marines' Hymn* came into use. Its origins are murky. There is a tradition that a Marine on duty in Mexico in 1847 wrote the original words to go with the music of the gendarme's song in the opera *Geneviève de Brabant* by Jacques Offenbach.

Commandant McCawley retired in bad health in 1891 and was succeeded by Col. Charles Heywood, who was to become one of the Corps' most able Commandants. He modernized training, established the School of Application and introduced officer schools and regular examinations for officer promotions. After the 1870 breechloading, rifled musket was replaced by the Springfield rifle, model 1884, caliber .45, rifle marksmanship was emphasized and systematized under the direction of Maj. Charles H. Lauchheimer. The Corps adopted the rapid-firing, multi-barreled Gatling gun and the Hotchkiss revolving cannon. When Heywood took office, the Corps had 75 officers and 2,100 enlisted men; when he retired in 1903, it had grown to 278 officers and 7,532 men. Throughout his regime, he had to fight off repeated Navy attempts to replace shipboard Marines with seamen. With the revolutionary changeover from sail to steam, the Marine Corps had to find new purposes to stay afloat. The life-and-death test for the Corps would come in 1898 at Guantanamo Bay, Cuba.

In those years after the Civil War, the Corps was repeatedly called upon to maintain law and order at home and to protect Americans abroad. In 1866, Marines helped the victims of a fire that destroyed much of Portland, Maine. Massive fires in Boston in 1872 and 1873 brought out Marines to prevent looting. In 1870, Marines from the Brooklyn Navy Yard helped revenue officers close illegal stills. In the bitter summer of 1877,

Marine battalions put down labor riots along the East Coast.

Overseas, Marines fought tribesmen on Formosa in 1867; and the next year, small units landed at Osaka and Yokohama to protect foreigners. In July 1882, 70 Marines under Capt. Henry Clay Cochrane and young Lt. Littleton W.T. Waller landed at Alexandria, Egypt, to help the British restore order. Marine detachments helped to rescue the Greeley Arctic Expedition lost off Greenland and to try to stop the slaughter of seals in the Bering Sea.

In Latin America, Marines joined an international landing force at Montevideo in 1868; fought pirates on the Mexican shore; guarded the American consulate at Buenos Aires; made several landings in Nicaragua, and in 1873 and 1885 landed at the city of Panama to protect the trans-isthmus railroad.

On the other side of the globe, Marines saw action in Korea in 1871 after the crew of an American freighter had been massacred and two gunboats had been fired upon in the Han River. On June 10, a force of 651 men, with 109 Marines commanded by Capt. McLane W. Tilton, landed and attacked the Han River forts. In fierce fighting, they captured the three forts and Irishborn Pvt. James Dougherty killed the Korean commander. He was among five Marines who earned the Medal of Honor in hand-to-hand combat in that "weekend war."

7
The Four-Month War With Spain
1898

The War with Spain climaxed the Marines' 19th-century adventures. In this brief war, they proved they could seize and hold advanced bases for the coal-powered Navy. They finished the war a giant step closer to their modern amphibious role.

The trigger for the war was the blowing up of the cruiser *Maine* in Havana harbor on the night of February 15. At 9:40, the ship was rocked by two explosions. First Lt. Albertus W. Catlin, commanding the Marine detachment, groped his way to the deck. Marine Pvt. William F. Anthony, orderly for Capt. Charles D. Sigsbee, *Maine's* commander, made his way below deck despite the havoc, met the captain in the smoke-filled companionway and reported the ship was sinking. *Maine's* entire bow was gone; water rushed in; ammunition was exploding overhead. Among the nearly 250 men killed were 28 Marines.

The American press screamed for vengeance. Congress recognized Cuba's independence from Spain; and on April 25, war was formally declared. Congress enlarged the Marine Corps to an authorized strength of 117 officers and 5,214 enlisted men.

Commandant Heywood assembled men from all East Coast stations into a battalion of 23 officers and 623 enlisted men to fight in Cuba. It encamped at Key West and then sailed to establish a forward naval base at Guantanamo Bay to coal and repair the fleet. On June 10, the First Marine Battalion landed on the eastern side of the bay. Meeting no opposition, four Marine companies pitched a camp of white tents among the palms on a hill above Fisherman's Point. Late the next day, the enemy struck, killing two privates on picket duty. The Spaniards fled before Lt. Col. Robert W. Huntington, an erect, bearded veteran of Bull Run, could counterattack. Two companies pursued; the hidden enemy fired on the Marines at short range. They returned the fire but could not chase the Spaniards through the undergrowth.

During both of the next two nights, the enemy attacked the Marines' camp. To secure their beachhead, two companies marched out on June 14 to destroy the enemy's source of water,

[For the location of places in the Spanish-American war see map No. 5 in the map section.—Au.]

89

the well at Cuzco, six miles to the east. After a difficult march, the Marines and some 50 insurgent Cubans attacked six companies of the Sixth Barcelona Regiment and Cubans defending Cuzco. The cruiser *Dolphin*, which had accompanied the force just offshore, began firing. The Marines were in the ship's line of fire and had to dive for cover. Sgt. John H. Quick, a tall, silent native of West Virginia, improvised a signal flag from his blue polka-dot handkerchief and a stick, and, with his back to the Spanish fire, coolly wigwagged *Dolphin* to cease firing. The enemy concentrated their fire on the lone figure in relief against the sky. *Dolphin* stopped its shelling, and Quick picked up his rifle. The enemy began to retreat. The Marines destroyed Cuzco's well and a signal station. Sergeant Quick received the Medal of Honor and became a national hero. From then on, the Marines were no longer harassed. They stayed until after Santiago fell in July and were pulled out of Guantanamo on August 5.

Those weeks at Guantanamo are usually cited as the first appearance of the kind of amphibious landing forces that would dominate the Corps' second century. This landing heralded a new purpose for the Marines evolving out of the nation's need—which supporters called "manifest destiny" and critics "imperialism."

Far away, the Filipinos were also rebelling against their Spanish conquerors. On April 24, Commodore George Dewey sailed with his squadron from Hong Kong; and at 11:30 P.M. on April 30, the darkened flotilla entered Manila Bay. At daybreak, it passed Manila and closed on the enemy fleet at anchor near Cavite. At 5:42, Dewey gave his famous order to his executive officer: "You may fire when you are ready, Gridley." The Americans destroyed the Spanish ships. First Lt. Dion Williams took a detachment ashore and occupied the arsenal and dockyards of the Cavite Naval Station. Dewey's boldness had made the United States a power in the western Pacific. The cost: seven Americans slightly wounded.

On August 12, the United States and Spain suspended hostilities. The little war had lasted less than four months—but it had transformed the United States into a power on the world stage. Congress doubled the size of the Marine Corps to 225 officers and 6,000 enlisted men. The landing at Guantanamo strengthened the idea of using Marines to seize and hold advanced bases for the Navy. This war pushed the Corps on to a larger role in the great war less than 20 years in the future.

8
On Imperial Duty
1899–1902

After the War with Spain, control of the Philippine Islands, with their 6.7 million people, was America's most violent problem overseas. As part of Dewey's conquest, the exiled Filipino insurgent leader Emilio Aguinaldo had been brought back to the islands from Hong Kong to rally the people against the Spaniards. Aguinaldo demanded Filipino independence and declared himself president of a revolutionary republic. Partly because his men were fighting the U.S. Army, the Senate on February 6, 1899, ratified by a margin of two votes the Treaty of Paris, ending the war with Spain and annexing the Philippines.

The Filipinos rose against the Americans; and into the hot summer rainy season, the U.S. Army pursued Aguinaldo and his guerrilla-style fighters. Two Marine battalions totaling 30 officers and 916 men arrived at Cavite and joined in operations with the Army. In early October, Lt. Col. George F. Elliott, as commander of the First Marine Brigade, led 375 Marines against the enemy at Novaleta, just south of the Cavite Peninsula. The enemy was entrenched. The Marines attacked in the face of heavy fire, pushing the enemy back. Three Marines died and nine were wounded. It was the Corps' first real fight in the insurrection.

Marines secured Cavite and Subic Bay; but then suddenly half the Marines in the Philippines were transferred to China, where the Boxer Rebellion threatened the foreign legations and settlements in Peking and Tientsin.

The Boxer Movement had flared up two years earlier among the peasants in North China. It sought to restore the potency of the feeble regime in Peking and to exterminate the foreigners. The foreigners had been asking for trouble; a number of European nations had occupied, annexed, controlled, grabbed chunks of China. The foreign powers had carved most of China into areas of economic domination. The Chinese could not resist.

As the anti-foreign spirit spread, the xenophobic Boxers butchered Christian missionaries and converts and, racing across North China, approached Peking in May 1900, terrifying the 500 foreigners there.

[For the location of places in this section see maps No. 6 and 8 in the map section.—*Au.*]

Late on the evening of May 31, Capt. John Twiggs Myers, 49 Marines with fixed bayonets and three sailors with a Colt automatic gun led a force of 337 men from six nations up Legation Street in Peking. They had rushed from 17 warships off the Taku bar to the Chinese capital to guard their countries' legations. At Captain Myers' suggestion, the legations organized a common defense. The Boxers cut the railroad and telegraph line, isolating Peking. Myers sent Capt. Newt H. Hall and 20 Marines to protect the people in the Methodist Mission, three-quarters of a mile from the legations. Hall's men dispersed a threatening crowd.

A relief expedition with 2,129 armed men from eight countries left Tientsin on June 10 by railroad for Peking. They never got through. The first train carried half the British contingent and all 112 American sailors and Marines. The Boxers attacked the trains repeatedly and tore up the tracks behind them. Burdened with 264 wounded, the expedition started back downriver to Tientsin, with three Marine sharpshooters at the point.

Meanwhile at Tientsin, the Boxers attacked the foreign settlements in strength. A force of 140 U.S. Marines, the first to arrive from Cavite and led by Maj. Littleton W.T. "Tony" Waller, commandeered a railroad train for Tientsin. They were joined by 440 Russian infantrymen. Twelve miles from the city, they were stopped by a blown-out bridge and had to march toward Tientsin, fighting from village to village. In one two-hour battle, four Marines were killed and nine wounded. The Marines were forced to retreat and leave their dead behind. But bolstered by a British naval detachment and more Russian troops, some 2,000 men started out again for Tientsin and, with the Marines in the van, battled their way to the foreign settlements. Then, they rescued the original expedition, holed up eight miles from Tientsin.

In Peking, the Boxers ranged the city in force, killing, burning and looting. On June 20, the 55-day siege of Peking began. The isolated Legation Quarter, an area three-quarters of a mile square and now jammed with more than 3,000 people, was under constant attack. The Marines and the Germans, whose legations were the southernmost, took and held a section of the Tartar City Wall, on the southern side of the Quarter. By July 3, a quarter of all the foreign military professionals had been killed or wounded. At 3 A.M. that morning, Captain Myers led 14 Marines, 16 Russians and 25 British Marines over the barricade and killed many Chinese in hand-to-hand fighting. Myers was badly wounded in the right leg by a Chinese spear. Two Marines and one Russian were killed.

The Chinese bombarded the Quarter with cannon and pushed their barricades closer and closer. July 13 was a terrible day. The Japanese were shoved back; the British were severely pressed; the Germans saved their area with a bayonet charge, and the Americans fought fiercely on the wall. Two nights later, Pvt. Daniel J. Daly of Glen Cove, New York, volunteered to stay on the wall and hold it alone with his bayoneted rifle all night.

At Tientsin, the allies assembled about 14,000 men to attack the walled city. Col. Robert L. Meade, USMC, commanded the First Marine Regiment, 451 officers and men, and the United States Ninth Infantry—a total of 1,021 men—brought from the Philippines. The Marines were in the heart of the action throughout the day-long attack. The assault went badly; and the Americans, with five Marines dead and 11 wounded, finally withdrew after dark. But early the next morning, the Japanese blew up the city's South Gate and Tientsin fell.

At dawn on August 4, the first units of the International Relief Force marched out of Tientsin to lift the siege of Peking. It included 2,000 Americans, commanded by Maj. Gen. Adna R. Chaffee, USA, and the Marine regiment now led by Maj. William P. Biddle. Major Waller commanded the first battalion of Marines; Capt. Franklin J. Moses, the second battalion, and Capt. Ben H. Fuller, F Company of artillery. At Yangtsun, 25 miles on their way, the Americans and British led the attack and stormed the Chinese earthworks. The march was grueling in the heat of the treeless plain. A bond of friendship between the American Marines and the Royal Welch Fusiliers—begun at the walls of Tientsin—was welded during the ordeal of the march. Years later, at the request of the First Marine Battalion, Sousa honored its British comrades by writing *The Royal Welch Fusiliers* march.

As the relief force approached, the Chinese in Peking tried to overwhelm the legations' defenders. The fighting reached a climax as the allies attacked the city. The Americans, including two companies of Marines, scaled the wall south of the Tung Pien gate. Two privates were hit; 1st Lt. Smedley D. Butler was wounded in the chest but saved by a button on his blouse, and Pvt. Dan Daly earned his first Medal of Honor. Inside the enclave, Myers' Marines cleared obstructions. British Indian troops emerged into Canal Street at 2:30 P.M. on August 13, and the siege was over. In the Quarter, 66 foreigners were dead, 150 wounded. The Empress Dowager Tzü Hsi and her court fled. The allies drove out the Chinese troops and plundered the city. The United States returned its attention and manpower to its festering problem: the Philippine Insurrection.

The return of the First Marine Regiment from China lifted Marine Corps strength in the islands to 1,678. The First Regiment went to Olongapo on Subic Bay and the Second and brigade headquarters were at Cavite. Aguinaldo was captured in March 1901 and took an oath of allegiance to the United States. The spirit went out of the insurgency. Military government ended on July 4, 1901; and Judge William Howard Taft became the Philippines' Civil Governor. But the fighting continued; and in the following year of guerrilla war, the Marine Corps met victory and disaster.

On September 28—just two weeks after Theodore Roosevelt succeeded the assassinated William McKinley in the Presidency— 450 bolo-wielding Filipinos slaughtered the U.S. Ninth Infantry's C Company at Balangiga on the southern end of the island of Samar. The Americans wanted revenge; and hardbitten, stubby Major "Tony" Waller was sent to Samar with a Marine battalion of 14 officers and 300 enlisted men. The Marines conducted daily combat patrols and tracked down rebel bands. The insurgents prepared fortresslike caves and stored supplies in the Sohoton Cliffs, volcanic formations rising 200 feet almost straight up from the river. Waller went after them. On November 15, he took out two columns, one led by Capt. David D. Porter and the other by Capt. Hiram I. Bearss. Waller followed by boat. The Marines scaled the cliffs on rickety bamboo ladders, scattered the enemy and destroyed their camp. Waller commended Porter and Bearss and, among others, Gunnery Sgt. Quick and Acting Cpl. Harry Glenn for conspicuous conduct. Years later, Porter and Bearss were awarded the Medal of Honor for this action.

On December 8, Waller set out on an expedition that became one of the most terrible and dramatic disasters in Marine Corps history. It was an ordeal not against the insurgents but against the jungle. The Army wanted to map routes to string telegraph wire between the strongpoints in southern Samar. Waller took Captains Porter and Bearss, 1st Lt. Alexander S. Williams and 2d Lt. Frank Halford, 50 Marines and a few soldiers from the Seventh Infantry, two native scouts and 33 native carriers. Waller and his Marines started up the Lanang River on December 28 and then climbed into the jungle-covered mountains.

The going was incredibly difficult through the rain-soaked jungle. After several days, the party came to an exhausted halt. Waller decided to press ahead with 2d Lt. Halford and the 13 strongest men. Bearss joined him with a Marine corporal and a Filipino guide. But they became separated from Porter and the main party, whose members were now feverish and crippled. On January 3, Porter, Gunnery Sgt. Quick, six Marines and six Filipinos started back for Lanang. Williams stayed with the rest.

Waller, trudging westward through perpetual rain, finally reached Basey on the west coast on the 6th. He then went back and for nine days searched the jungle for signs of Porter, without success. Porter reached Lanang on the 11th. Williams, with the 31 weakest Marines and 30 Filipinos, slowly followed Porter's path. The men were sick, many unable to move on their own. One by one, those had to be left along the trail to die. Native bearers tried to kill Williams; the Marines protected him with sticks. By the time an Army relief party found them on the 17th, 18 of the Marines had to be carried out on stretchers. Nine were missing; they had gone insane or had died in the jungle.

Events now moved swiftly to another tragic climax. Gunnery Sgt. Quick brought a message from Porter to Waller recommending that the natives who had been mutinous on the march be executed for attacking Williams and refusing to help the desperate Marines. Waller ordered 11 Filipinos shot. When he returned to Cavite, he was charged with murder. Newspapers in the United States were calling him "The Butcher of Samar." A military court was convened in Manila and after an 18-day trial acquitted him.[20] The ugly affair damaged Waller's career. Both in 1910 and 1914, he was a candidate for Commandant but was never selected.

In 1903, most of the Marines in the Philippines were shifted to Olongapo; and the brigade was finally disbanded in 1914. But for years afterward, it was a tradition in the Corps to greet any Marine who had shared the hardships of the march on Samar with the command: "Stand, gentlemen! He served on Samar."

In those first years of the 20th century, the United States Marines saw action from the Caribbean to the Philippines and China. They repeatedly served as America's armed spearhead for the nation which had become entangled in the international rivalries and conflicts that would enmesh all Americans in the decades and generations ahead.

Daniel J. "Fighting Dan" Daly was the only enlisted
Marine ever to win the Medal of Honor for two separate
actions—at Peking and Haiti. He also earned the Navy
Cross and Army Distinguished Service Cross at Belleau
Wood. Commandant Lejeune called Sergeant Daly
"the outstanding Marine of all time."
Museums Branch, USMC

1
Belleau Wood—5 p.m., June 6,1918

Lines of steel-helmeted Marines with bayonets fixed moved forward toward the mile-square French hunting preserve. Its dense underbrush, trees and great boulders made superb cover for doves or the machine-gun nests of the gray-uniformed Germans threatening Paris only 40 miles away. This was Belleau Wood, and the Marine Corps was entering its greatest battle so far.

At 5 P.M. on that sunny spring afternoon—June 6, 1918—three companies of the 3rd Battalion, 5th Marines, led by tall, slim Maj. Benjamin S. Berry, approached the wood from the west, advancing through a quarter-mile-long field of green wheat splashed with red poppies. There had been no pre-assault artillery fire; this was supposed to be a surprise attack. But the Germans in the wood were expecting them. Their massed Maxim machine guns rippled the waist-high grain and chopped gaps in the Marine line.

As the attack started, forty-four-year-old veteran Marine First Sgt. Dan Daly, winner of two Medals of Honor and hero of Peking and Haiti, crouched with his men of the 73rd Machine Gun Company in a grove on the edge of the wheat field. Floyd Gibbons, a war correspondent for the *Chicago Tribune*, described the scene he saw:

> The bullets nipped the tops of the young wheat and ripped the bark from the trees three feet from the ground on which the Marines lay. The minute for the Marine advance was approaching. An old gunnery sergeant commanded the platoon in the absence of the lieutenant, who had been shot and was out of the fight. This old sergeant

[For the location of places in the Western Front in World War I see map No. 7 in the map section.—*Au.*]

was a Marine veteran. His cheeks were bronzed with the wind and sun of the seven seas. The service bar across his left breast showed that he had fought in the Philippines, in Santo Domingo, at the walls of Pekin, and in the streets of Vera Cruz. . . .

As the minute for the advance arrived, he arose from the trees first and jumped out onto the exposed edge of that field that ran with lead, across which he and his men were to charge. Then he turned to give the charge order to the men of his platoon—his mates—the men he loved. He said: "Come on, you sons-o'-bitches! Do you want to live forever?"[1]

The first waves—advancing in well-disciplined but obsolete lines—were slaughtered. The German gunners took a dreadful toll. Many of the men who survived were pinned down in that wheat field; a few struggled to the edge of the wood but could not hold. After dark, they crawled back.

Said the Marines' general, "It was a costly failure bravely attempted."[2]

In the advance, Major Berry was severely wounded in the left forearm. Floyd Gibbons, trying to help him, took three bullets; the third destroyed his left eye. Berry, despite his wounds, rose and rushed forward to his men.

(Before the battle, Gibbons had sent to Paris a dispatch reporting that the Marines were entering combat. Hearing that he had been wounded and apparently killed in action, the censor passed the story unchanged. It was against the rules to identify units in combat, but the censor's sentimentality let the world know that the Marine Corps was in action. By such a fluke came glory.)

On Berry's right, the 3rd Battalion, 6th Marines moved out under Maj. Berton W. Sibley, a short, swarthy forty-one-year-old Vermonter. The young lieutenants shouted, "Follow me!" And the men swept silently across the fields of grass in four waves at right dress into the southern end of Belleau Wood. Men fell. The Germans were aiming low, shooting the Marines in the legs.

On a rise of ground, watching them proudly and trying to keep one eye on Berry's fate was the 6th Regiment's commander, Col. Albertus W. Catlin. A Marine for a quarter of a century, Catlin, from Gowanda, New York, now forty-nine, had commanded the Marines aboard *Maine* when she was sunk and received the Medal of Honor at Vera Cruz in 1914. Suddenly, he went down; a sniper's bullet had pierced his right lung and paralyzed his right side. Still conscious, he ordered a runner to have Lt. Col. Harry Lee come forward and take charge of the attack. Catlin survived an eight-hour ambulance ride to a Paris hospital and was shipped home.

Sibley's battalion reached the wood and entered a roaring hell. German machine guns were placed so that when one was assaulted, the next gun mowed down the attackers. The wood crawled with sharpshooters and was strung with elaborate tangles of barbed wire. With Sibley leading them, the Marines stayed low, hurled their grenades and went forward in rushes, using rifle and bayonet. The fighting was hand-to-hand, wild as a riot. Marines shot the enemy sharpshooters out of the trees. It was a jumbled melee won by sergeants and privates.

Sibley's 82d Company under Capt. Dwight Smith fought its way several hundred yards into the wood. As the Marines advanced, machine guns ripped their forward lines mercilessly. The 83rd Company led by 1st Lt. Alfred H. Noble of Federals-burg, Maryland, also met the German fire. Both companies were forced to swerve from their eastern course to the north. Sibley's two other companies were pinned down by the entrenched machine guns. Second Lt. Louis F. Timmerman, Jr., led his platoon of the 83rd straight through the mile-wide wood; beyond it, they were the target of fire from every side. They dashed back into the wood and captured two machine guns. The platoon charged out again and was decimated; Timmerman was shot in the face. The enemy fire was so intense that he had to pull his six surviving men back into the shelter of the wood. Another small group of Marines joined them, and together they manned the two captured machine guns. Others strengthened the isolated group. One arriving Marine had had his wounds treated by a German medic. Soon, Timmerman had 40 Marines with him; and they fought to hold the ground they had taken. Timmerman won the Distinguished Service Cross.

To Sibley's right, Capt. Randolph T. Zane and his 79th Company of Maj. Thomas Holcomb's 2d Battalion, 6th Marines met murderous enemy fire. In 40 minutes, Lt. Graves B. Erskine's platoon of 58 was reduced to 5. Erskine sent a wounded Marine to find Captain Zane and tell him they could

101

not move forward. An hour later, the wounded man crawled back to report that the captain had said: "Goddammit, continue the advance." They did.[3]

Holcomb's 96th Company stormed the village of Bouresches at the southeast corner of the wood. The company commander, thirty-five-year-old Capt. Donald F. Duncan from Kansas, advanced calmly smoking his pipe; he took a Maxim bullet through the stomach, and then a shell killed him. A bullet momentarily knocked out tall, thin 2d Lt. Clifton B. Cates, the 4th Platoon commander. He recovered, found an abandoned French rifle and with 1st Lt. James F. Robertson led some 30 men into the town. They fought in the streets. Twenty-three Marines held the town for half an hour until others began arriving. The isolated Marines drove off a counterattack.

Word reached the 6th Marines' command post that the men in Bouresches were low on ammunition. By now it was dark, the sky ominous with heavy rain clouds. Two Marines volunteered to take a truck loaded with ammunition through to Bouresches. They raced down the shell-pocked road. Every time a German flare brightened the sky, they stopped the truck and froze. German artillery and machine guns had the road zeroed in. They kept slipping off the road; a wheel broke. Finally, they reached the edge of Bouresches and delivered the ammunition. The two volunteers were 2d Lt. William B. Moore, a young Princeton track and football star, and Regimental Sergeant Major John H. Quick, then almost forty-eight, the tall, silent veteran of Guantanamo, Samar and Vera Cruz. Both men were awarded the Distinguished Service Cross and the Navy Cross.

The night was a torment of confusion. Units were disorganized, their officers unable to form them in the darkness. German shells killed many; and several times, Marines fired on their comrades. Inside Belleau Wood, Sibley's Marines lay on their stomachs, the flank of their line entirely unprotected. But Sibley had no intention of withdrawing. The men dug in for the night, and two companies of the 2d Engineers crept up to reinforce them.

Through that long night, many of the wounded lay where they had fallen. On June 6, 31 officers and 1,056 men of the Marine Brigade were casualties. But the Marines had a foothold in Belleau Wood.

2
The Marine Brigade

When World War I began, nearly four years earlier, the Marines had been busy with brush wars in Haiti, the Dominican Republic and Mexico. But this was to be a totally new dimension of warfare: world-wide, wholesale slaughter. When it was finished, 8.6 million men in uniform would be dead; 21 million, wounded. Of these, 116,000 dead and 243,000 wounded would be Americans.

In the summer of 1914, the pressure cooker of European hostilities had exploded; and when Germany invaded Belgium on August 4, Europe was in flames.

The Germans swept through Belgium, outflanked the French fortifications and plunged down on Paris. But in the desperate Battle of the Marne, the French stopped the Germans outside Paris. The invaders pulled back and dug in behind the Aisne River. They had missed their chance. The Western Front settled into brutal, immobilized trench warfare. The machine gun was lord of the battlefield.

By 1917, four million Allied soldiers faced 2.5 million Germans on the Western Front in an unending war of attrition, devouring hundreds of thousands of lives. The Allies began to falter. The French army, torn with horrendous casualties, mutinied; and revolution in Russia freed more German divisions for the Western Front.

The United States had tried to stay out of it. In 1916, President Woodrow Wilson was reelected on the slogan: "He kept us out of war." But when the crunch came, the United States would not let England and France go under. Five months after his reelection, Wilson asked for a declaration of war.

On April 6, 1917, the United States finally entered the war. Its armed strength was puny compared with that of the grappling giants overseas. The U.S. Regular Army plus the Federalized National Guard on the Mexican border totaled only 208,000 men. The Navy numbered 73,000. American air power consisted of a section of the Army Signal Corps with 130 pilots and 55 planes. Before peace came, four million Americans would enlist or be drafted into the Army and 800,000 would join the Navy. The Marine Corps started with 511 officers and 13,214 enlisted men. By war's end, the Corps, under the slogan "First to Fight," had grown to 2,462 officers and 72,639 enlisted men.

In that April of 1917, the Germans were confident that any American contribution would be too little and too late to make a difference. But the Allies urged the United States to send at least a token force as quickly as possible to shore up the morale of their own bone-weary, discouraged armies.

First to go was Maj. Gen. John J. Pershing, commander of the American Expeditionary Force (AEF). In his small staff that landed at Liverpool on June 8 were two Marine officers: Lt. Col. Robert H. Dunlap and Maj. Logan Feland.

On June 14, the first echelon of the AEF sailed for France. One-fifth of its strength was in the 2,759 men of the 5th Marine Regiment. They sailed in naval transports to circumvent a reluctant Secretary of War and were commanded by Col. Charles A. Doyen, 34 years a Marine.

As most Marines saw it, their main responsibility in the war was to support the Navy of which they were part. But Commandant George Barnett insisted that the Marine Corps was a force-in-readiness, able to share with the Army the first call on the Western Front. A week after *Lusitania* was sunk by a German submarine in May 1915, Col. John A. Lejeune, then Assistant to the Commandant, had said that if the United States were to fight a naval power, the Marine Corps would defend advanced naval bases; but if it faced a non-naval power, the Corps would be "the Advance Guard of the Army . . . first to set foot on hostile soil in order to seize, fortify, and hold a port from which as a base, the Army would prosecute its campaign."[4]

Once the United States declared war, Commandant Barnett pushed for a Marine combat role with the Army and told the Congress, "I do not want the Marine Corps to be considered a police force."[5] On May 22, 1917, the Corps' authorized enlisted strength was increased to 30,000; and three days later, despite Army objections, President Wilson signed an executive order attaching the 5th Marine Regiment to the Army for service in France. The Marines landed at St. Nazaire with the first expeditionary force on June 26; by the evening of July 3, the entire regiment had unloaded its ships and was ashore under canvas.

Then, two disputes raged simultaneously. The first was between Pershing and the European Allies. The AEF commander stubbornly insisted that the Americans fight as a separate army; the Allies wanted to feed them into their own forces in smaller units. The second argument was between Pershing and the Marines. He used the Marines along the line-of-communication as guards and military police; they had to fight for combat assignments.

The 5th Regiment had three commanding officers before it got into action: Col. Charles A. Doyen, Lt. Col. Hiram I. Bearss and Col. Wendell C. Neville. The 6th Regiment of Marines was organized at Quantico, Virginia, and arrived in France between October 5, 1917, and February 6, 1918. Colonel Catlin commanded. He and Neville had been Annapolis classmates.

On October 23, 1917, the two regiments—later joined by the 6th Machine Gun Battalion of Marines—were formed into the 4th Brigade of Marines. Doyen, now a brigadier general, was in command; and the Kentuckian Lt. Col. Feland was his chief of staff. At the outset, the 4th Brigade numbered 258 officers and 8,211 enlisted men; in eight battles it was to suffer 11,968 casualties, of whom 2,461 were killed.

The Marine Brigade and the Army's 3rd Infantry Brigade (the 9th and 23rd Infantry Regiments) plus an artillery brigade were joined together as the 2d U.S. Division—a total of 28,059 men. The Marine and infantry brigades each consisted of two regiments of three rifle battalions and a machine-gun battalion. Doyen, a native of Concord, New Hampshire, commanded the division for its initial two weeks, in October–November, the first Marine ever to lead an Army division. Then he was superseded by Maj. Gen. Omar Bundy, USA.

Pershing insisted that his troops learn to fight in the open, not only in static, defensive trench warfare. His men would move forward.

Most of the men in the ranks were recruits. According to Colonel Catlin, 60 percent of the 6th Marines were college men, many of them athletes. They had a lot to learn: trench digging, conducting and repelling trench raids, hand-grenade throwing, rifle-grenade firing, bayonet skills, the use of the gas mask, how to make barbed wire entanglements. And there was constant marching with a 45-pound pack and marksmanship practice with the Springfield '03. The Marines grew wiser and tougher and meaner.

More Americans were being rushed "over there"; by the end of the year, 50,000 were arriving each month. The 1st Division went into action on October 23, long before the 2d. In mid-March 1918, the Marines went into the line in a "quiet" sector near Verdun; for most, it was their first experience under fire. On April 12, the 74th Company of Marines was severely gassed and had to be evacuated. The 74th, 45th and 84th Companies all had chances to repel German raids on their positions.

The Germans decided to launch a major attack in the West before American weight could be brought to bear. It was now or never. In March, the United States still had only six complete divisions in France, less than 300,000 men. The Germans calculated that the war could be over by midsummer. But they did not give full credit to the willingness of U.S. soldiers and Marines to take punishment in battle and stand firm.

On March 21, the Germans struck their first blow against the British armies in the north. In four days, the Germans advanced 14 miles, the greatest movement on the Western Front since 1914. In this Second Battle of the Somme, the British Fifth Army was practically destroyed before the Germans were stopped. On April 9, they struck a second blow, but in 20 days of vicious fighting they failed to break the British. By April's end, the Allies had suffered 350,000 casualties; the Germans, at least 200,000.

The third German attack hit the French to the south, between Soissons and Reims, on May 27. The Germans took Soissons and reached the north bank of the Marne River at Château-Thierry, 40 miles from Paris. This Third Battle of the Aisne brought the Americans into action.

In this crisis, General Ferdinand Foch was named commander-in-chief of all the allied armies in France. He wanted to fight; and Pershing, putting aside his dream of an American army, threw his 2d and 3rd Divisions into the all-out effort to stop the Germans. On May 31, the 3rd U.S. Division held them at Château-Thierry. Newspapers back home headlined that the Marines had won that battle. But the fact is: no Marine ever claimed he fought in Château-Thierry.

Stopped there at the river, the Germans twisted right toward Vaux and Belleau Wood, still on the north side of the Marne. On May 31, the American 2d Division was brought up the Paris–Metz highway, through crowds of defeated French soldiers and frightened civilians, all pouring rearward, convinced that the war was lost. In Paris, under long-range bombardment for two months, the French government was preparing to evacuate; hundreds of thousands were fleeing. It seemed to the eager young soldiers and Marines of the 2d Division that only they were marching toward the war.

On June 1, Château-Thierry finally fell. The Germans took Vaux and moved into Belleau Wood. The French general commanding the sector placed the 9th U.S. Infantry between the Paris–Metz highway and the Marne, facing Vaux, and urgently called for another regiment. Maj. Gen. Bundy, commanding the 2d Division, ordered Brig. Gen. James G. Harbord, USA, who had taken command of the Marine Brigade when the ill Doyen went home to die, to put in one of his regiments.

Thus did the 6th Marines move up to the left of the 9th Infantry and deploy north from Le Thiolet on the Paris–Metz highway. Major Holcomb's 2d Battalion was on the Marine right, Maj. Maurice E. Shearer's 1st Battalion on the left to the north. The 5th Marines and the 23rd Infantry took positions in support. Bundy and Harbord agreed that the Marine Brigade would fight as a unit north of the highway and the 3rd Infantry Brigade to the south of it, "and on that spur of the moment decision came the alignment and the tremendous consequence, to the glory of the United States Marines, to the fortunes of the two brigades, and to the future of the world."[6]

That evening, the Germans knocked a hole in the French line to the front and left of the Marines. The 23rd Infantry, Maj. Julius S. Turrill's 1st Battalion of the 5th Marines, a part of the 6th Machine Gun Battalion and a company of Engineers rushed over in a forced march of 10 kilometers to plug the wound before it became fatal. By dawn, they were in place; and Harbord put in Maj. Frederic M. Wise's 2d Battalion, 5th Marines to strengthen the defense between Turrill on the left and Shearer on the right. Wise's men were stretched over more than two miles of the line. (Later, Turrill was pulled back in reserve, and the 23rd Infantry filled in.) Now, from the 9th Infantry south of the highway, through the Marines, to the 23rd Infantry, this section of the front—12 miles long—was American.

The Marine line, holding a landscape of grain fields dotted with clumps of woods, was terribly thin. The men were short of ammunition, hot food and water. German shells peppered their positions, taking a toll. The Marines dug in.

By the night of June 2, the Germans held a line from Vaux to Bouresches to Belleau and occupied Belleau Wood. The Americans faced them across rolling farmland from Triangle Farm to Lucy to Hill 142. The Marines' job was, simply stated, "Hold the line at all hazards."[7] Harbord countermanded a French order to dig trenches several hundred yards to the rear; he said, "The Marines will hold where they stand."[8] With bayonets and mess kits, the men dug shallow foxholes, in which a rifleman could lie prone and do his job. There would be no falling back; the Germans were not to pass.

The Germans ordered an advance on Marigny and Lucy and through the wood. Further south, other German divisions were ordered to cross the Marne.

That afternoon of June 3, the German infantry, in extended lines, bayonets fixed, attacked the Marine positions through the wheat fields. Marines were hit; 1st Lt. Lemuel C. Shepherd, Jr., out front, took a machine-gun bullet in the neck. The Marines waited, watching the Germans come on in waves—and then, when they were only 100 yards away, the Marines' deadly rifle fire mowed down the enemy and finally forced the survivors to stop and break through the grain fields for the trees behind them. That charge was the peak of the German drive; the Marines had held.

Wise later wrote:

> If ever there was a miracle in the war, that was it. With a wide front, much of it open, to pick and choose, the German attack had smashed squarely into the center of

those lone two and a half miles we held. Had the same force hit either of our flanks, they could have crumpled us and cleaned us up.

I was in no position to exploit our success. The only thing in the world we could do was stick in our fox holes and hold that line. Out in front of us were Germans in unknown force. Both of our flanks remained unprotected. God alone knew how far back of us any support might be. But the Germans never attacked us again.[9]

The German offensive was finished for the moment, unable to pierce the defense and extended to its utmost in men and supplies. German casualties were enormous. Paris was now out of reach. The German commanders gave the order to dig in on a defensive line including Torcy, Belleau Wood, Le Thiolet and Hill 204 just west of Château-Thierry.

But the French were exhausted; all that night they made their way back through the American lines. One French major ordered Capt. Lloyd Williams, commanding Wise's right-hand company, to withdraw his men. As legend has it, Williams retorted: "Retreat, hell. We just got here." (Wise later claimed he had said the famous words.[10])

By 8 A.M. on June 4, Maj. Gen. Bundy took command of that piece of the Western Front. Now, the 23rd Infantry held the line from the Paris–Metz road north to Triangle Farm; then Holcomb's battalion to Lucy, and Berry's to Hill 142. Artillery, communications and supply were moving up.

The next two days were a standoff; the Germans continued to make local assaults and were thrown back by the Marines' expert fire. Between the two forces fell a rain of rifle and machine-gun fire and shrapnel. The Marines recognized the bravery of the worn-out German troops advancing in close formation to certain death. And shot them down.

The 167th French Division arrived to help out, and Bundy could consolidate. His 3rd Brigade was now on the south; the Marine Brigade to the north. They touched at the Triangle Farm. Each of Bundy's four infantry and Marine regiments held some 2,000 yards of the line, with two battalions up front and one in reserve. Catlin later wrote: "We now stood facing the dark, sullen mystery of Belleau Wood, Berry on the west and Holcomb on the south."[11] It was time for the Americans to attack.

Again, the Germans coiled to strike; but at 3:45 A.M. on June 6, the Americans and French jumped off first. The plan: On the 2d Division's left, the 167th French Division was to attack, while the Marines took Hill 142 to eliminate its flanking fire against the 167th. Then, in the climactic second phase at 5 P.M., the 2d Division was to seize the ridge overlooking the towns of Torcy and Belleau and occupy Belleau Wood and the town of Bouresches at the southeast corner beyond the wood.

But the battle would not go that way.

The Marines had made an important mistake. When the French had pulled back on June 4, they had told the Marines that Belleau Wood was empty of Germans; and the Marines had failed to send out scouting patrols to check for themselves. The French were wrong. The Germans were there—a regiment of German infantry with an interlocking network of machine-gun nests and covered by artillery—the hard-nosed tip of their push toward Paris.

Before dawn, the 1st Battalion, 5th Marines (Turrill) was supposed to hit Hill 142 with the 8th and 23rd Machine Gun Companies and D Company of the 2d Engineers. The 3rd Battalion, 5th Marines (Berry) would move up on Turrill's right. But most of Turrill's command was still scattered on previous assignments. By H-Hour, only Capt. Orlando C. Crowther's 67th Company and Capt. George W. Hamilton's 49th Company were on the mark. In the dark, they went over the top in four waves, and, with bayonets fixed, advanced in ranks into the wheat fields. After 50 yards, the machine guns destroyed them. Hamilton forced his men to their feet and to rush into a small woods. There, they fought the entrenched Germans with steel. Crowther and 1st Sgt. Daniel A. "Beau" Hunter were both killed almost immediately. Hamilton urged his men through the woods and into another field of wheat, where again they came under heavy fire until they could reach the next little woods. Hamilton's men overran their objective by 600 yards. Three Marines actually got into Torcy, where the Germans were concentrated. One of the three, wounded, was sent back for reinforcements. The two others found a hole and continued to fight from it. Two Germans attacked them. All four men died in that hole.

Hamilton had lost all five junior officers, and the 67th Company had only one of its five officers still alive. Hamilton tried to reorganize the two Marine companies; he established strong points and set up a defensive line. Suddenly, the Germans counterattacked, hurling grenades at the few Marines.

Gunnery Sgt. Ernest A. Janson of the 49th Company spotted 12 Germans with automatic rifles crawling toward the Marines. He yelled a warning and killed the first two Germans with his bayonet. The others fled. For his swift stroke that saved his company, the thirty-nine-year-old sergeant from New York City (who served under the name of Charles Hoffman) was the first Marine in World War I to win the Medal of Honor.

Marine Gunner Henry L. Hulbert of the 66th Company was cited for advancing through enemy fire. The Yorkshire-born Hulbert received the Medal of Honor as a private on Samoa in 1899, fighting in the rear guard of a Marine detachment from *Philadelphia*. When the Marines' Colt gun failed, Hulbert, armed only with a rifle, protected several wounded from the attacking natives. Hulbert, now fifty-one, would be killed in October at Blanc Mont while reorganizing his men to meet a German counterattack.

The rest of Turrill's units began showing up and went into action. Capt. Lloyd Williams' 51st Company of Wise's battalion was thrown in on Turrill's left. But both Turrill's flanks hung unprotected, and his men were exhausting their ammunition. His battalion lost nine officers and most of 325 men and by afternoon won Hill 142.

At 5 P.M., with a good three hours of daylight left, the second part of the American offensive began. Berry's and Sibley's battalions went over the top and into a hail of German bullets. They moved forward and entered Belleau Wood.

3
Bois de la Brigade de Marine

As June 7 began, the battlefield was littered with the dead and wounded. The Marine Brigade held a line more or less from Triangle Farm to Bouresches (the Germans still held the railroad station there), through the bottom of Belleau Wood and then north toward Hill 142.

The shelling and firing went on all day. After midnight, the Germans attacked and were stopped cold. At 4 A.M. on June 8, Sibley's battalion attacked and by ten o'clock had been halted with heavy losses. The German defense was too strong.

The battle was deadlocked. And that night south of Belleau Wood, the 1st Battalion, 6th Marines, now led by Maj. John A. "Johnny the Hard" Hughes, moved up to replace Sibley's weary battalion. Sibley had lost 400 men, killed, wounded and missing. Second Lt. Timmerman's platoon, for example, had 19 men left. Every officer of the 82d Company was out of action.

Major Shearer, for the wounded Berry, took over the 3rd Battalion, 5th Marines and replaced Holcomb's men on the right and in Bouresches.

Throughout June 9, an enormous, thundering American and French artillery barrage devastated Belleau Wood. The attractive hunting preserve became a jungle of shattered trees filled with the smell of death.

The Germans counterfired, shelling Lucy and Bouresches and the ground between, and reorganized their defense inside the wood.

At 4:30 A.M. on June 10, Hughes' battalion and some of Maj. Edward B. Cole's 6th Machine Gun Battalion attacked Belleau Wood. At first, the attack went easily; but by 7 A.M., the 75th Company had been stopped by enemy machine guns, and Major

112

Cole was mortally wounded. Brig. Gen. Harbord had seriously underestimated the German strength in the wood.

Next, Harbord ordered Wise's 2d Battalion, 5th Marines to attack the middle of the wood from the west, while Hughes advanced from the south. Wise's units were understrength and tired from days and nights of fighting and shelling. The thirty-nine-year-old New Yorker—a veteran of China, the Philippines and the Caribbean—had lost 25 percent of his men. Wise later insisted Harbord had ordered him to attack the *southern* edge of the wood.[12]

Before dawn on June 11, Wise's battalion moved through the freshly plowed wheat fields and into a thick protective morning mist. As they advanced on Belleau Wood, the men began to fall under heavy fire. The lead companies were shot to pieces. Lloyd Williams was wounded early and died that night. In the wood, it was small-unit, close-range warfare in the underbrush, with isolated platoons against the terror of the interlocking machine-gun fire. Wise wrote later, "Nothing in all our training had foreseen fighting like this. If there was any strategy in it, it was the strategy of the Red Indian. The only thing that drove those Marines through those woods in the face of such resistance as they met was their individual, elemental guts, plus the hardening of the training through which they had gone."[13]

There were no landmarks in the wood; and, unfortunately, these determined Marines were off-target. Rather than heading northeast as expected, they moved directly across the wood's narrow waist. Wise's left-hand companies (Capt. Charles Dunbeck's 43rd and Capt. Lester Wass' 18th) ended up where his right should have been.

At 7 A.M., Brig. Gen. Harbord announced: "The northern end of the Bois de Belleau belongs to the 5th Marines."[14] He was wrong. The Marines had not reached the northern part of the wood. Wise's company commanders were further south than they thought they were—a massive and costly error.

Where they did hit, the Marines smashed the German defenders momentarily and destroyed their southern defense line. One German private, whose company had 30 men left out of 120, wrote in a letter, "We have Americans [Marines] opposite us who are terribly reckless fellows."[15] The Germans began calling them a name in which the Marines took pride: *Teufelhunde*—Devil Dogs.

North of Wise, the Germans established a new defensive line in the wood and poured in reinforcements. They were in front of Wise and on his left flank. And half of Wise's battalion was wiped out. That night, engineers and Marine replacements came up and went directly into the line.

Pershing's headquarters had already announced to the world that the Americans had taken Belleau Wood. So, on June 12, the local commanders needed to make good the news. That afternoon, still believing there would be light resistance, Harbord ordered Wise to make another attack at 5 P.M. This time, the assault was led by the 55th Company of Lt. E. D. Cooke, USA; Dunbeck's 43rd; and Wass' 18th. Again, Hughes' battalion was to hit from the south, as Wise attacked from the west.

Because of the misinformation about the Marines' location, the artillery barrage struck 1,000 yards too far in advance, leaving the German defenders nearest the Marines unharmed. The Germans met the attack with everything they had, including mustard gas. The remaining Marines charged forward yelling. It was brutal no-quarter-given combat with rifle, pistol, bayonet. Pvt. Aloysius Leitner, though mortally wounded, continued fighting and helped capture six Germans operating a machine gun. He won the Army Distinguished Service Cross and the Navy Cross posthumously.

Wise later told this story:

> One squad of his company, Wass told me, had taken a German machine gun camouflaged behind a brush pile in the middle of the woods, that day. The minute they got among the Germans with bayonets, the Germans, who had worked the gun up to that minute and had cut up the Marines pretty badly, surrendered. The Marines took them all prisoners. Not one was killed. And that minute another German machine gun opened up on their flank. They left their prisoners, charged the second gun, and captured it. The minute they got among those Germans with bayonets, every one of them surrendered. And that minute the captured gun crew they had left behind them opened fire on them again. They couldn't play back and forth like this all day. They bayoneted every man of that

Leaders of the Marine Brigade in France in World War I: Maj. Gen. John A. Lejeune and Brig. Gen. Wendell C. Neville.
Museums Branch, USMC

U.S. Marine in France, sketched by Capt. John W. Thomason, Jr., who in his writing and illustrations captured the flavor of the Corps of that era. Collection of Mrs. John W. Thomason, Jr.

Marine Corps women reservists put up recruiting posters in New York City during World War I.
Marine Corps Photo, National Archives

U.S. Marines on review just before the fighting at Belleau Wood.
Brown Brothers

*Marines firing .30-caliber Browning machine gun in the
Meuse-Argonne offensive.
Marine Corps Photo, National Archives.*

*Wounded Marines of the Fourth Brigade
being trucked to a hospital in France.
U.S. Signal Corps Photo, National
Archives*

*Marines march in the giant parade in
Paris on July 4, 1918, after the victory
in Belleau Wood.
Brown Brothers*

Marine on watch on the Rhine River Patrol during the occupation of Germany following the 1918 Armistice.
U.S. Signal Corps Photo, National Archives

Brig. Gen. Smedley D. Butler and mascot "Sergeant Jiggs" were symbols of the post–World War I Marine Corps.
Marine Corps Photo, National Archives.

"Horse Marines" of the Legation Guard in Peking mounted on Mongolian ponies.
Marine Corps Photo, National Archives

"China Marines" watch Chinese refugees streaming to safety across the bridge over Soochow Creek, Shanghai, in 1932.
Marine Corps Photo, National Archives

Capt. Earl H. Ellis was a brilliant planner who helped revolutionize Marine Corps thinking and point the way to the amphibious strategy of World War II in the Pacific. Ellis died mysteriously in the Japanese-held Palau Islands in 1923. Harris and Ewing; photo courtesy Museums Branch, USMC

In early amphibious experiment, Marines unload a 75mm gun from a "Beetle boat" at Culebra, Puerto Rico, in 1923. Museums Branch, USMC

Formation of new F4B-4 fighters fly in echelon over San Diego in 1934. Museums Branch, USMC

Twentieth century Marine Corps rifles: top to bottom, .30-caliber Krag-Jorgensen adopted in 1900; bolt-action Springfield M1903; and Garand M-1 of World War II. National Rifle Association; photo courtesy Museums Branch, USMC

second German gun crew, went back and captured the first gun all over again, and bayoneted every man of that crew before they went on.[16]

Now, the Marines pushed the Germans northward among the rocks and ravines of Belleau Wood. On the right, they shoved the Germans out of the wood; but other elements were still fighting inside. The entire Marine line was bombarded by high-explosive and mustard-gas shells. In the wood, young Capt. Edward C. Fuller, the commander of the 75th Company and the son of the future Commandant, was mortally wounded. At 3 A.M. on June 13, the Germans struck at the wood's eastern side and at Bouresches, where Shearer's sharpshooting battalion stopped them cold.

Early that morning, Turrill's 1st Battalion, 5th Marines was sent in but found that Wise was not where he was supposed to be; the western part of the wood was unexpectedly full of Germans. Holcomb was ordered to relieve Wise's chewed-up battalion. But before he could move up, the Germans opened a vicious mustard-gas attack. Holcomb's battalion suffered 160 gas casualties; Hughes' and Wise's battalions were also gassed. The 74th, 96th and 78th companies had to be evacuated because of the gas that choked men to death. Veteran Gunnery Sgt. Fred W. Stockham of Detroit and the 96th Company gave his gas mask to wounded seventeen-year-old Marine Pvt. Barrett Mattingly of St. Louis, whose mask had been shot away. Stockham was overcome by the poison gas and died on June 22; he was awarded the Medal of Honor.

Finally, on the morning of the 15th, the 17th Company of Capt. Roswell Winans, the young Hoosier who had won the Medal of Honor as an enlisted man in the Dominican Republic, gained a foothold on the western side of the wood. Later that day and into the night, the Marine Brigade was relieved by the 7th Infantry and the French. The front remained under Colonel Neville's command, with Lt. Col. Feland in charge in Belleau Wood.

The bearded, exhausted Marines went to the rear; the Germans in their official reports called them vigorous, self-confident and remarkable marksmen. Two thousand eight hundred replacements filled the holes in their ranks.

In two weeks of battle, the Marine Brigade had taken more

than 50 percent casualties. Holcomb lost 21 officers and 836 men; Sibley, 14 officers and 400 men; Turrill, 16 officers and 544 men; Wise, 19 officers and 615 men.

As the Marines went to the rear to recuperate, a new German battalion came into Belleau Wood, with a second on its right and a third in reserve. They held the northern end of the wood in strength.

The 7th Infantry, untried in battle, was unable to budge the Germans from the wood. Shearer's 3rd Battalion, 5th Marines was brought back to clean out the German resistance, which Harbord continued to underestimate. Shearer attacked at 7 P.M. on June 23, quickly took 130 casualties and bogged down before the German machine guns. It was a badly mangled operation.

Now, the Marine Brigade took over the front again. Shearer's battalion was in the middle of the deadly wood; Ralph S. Keyser, relieving Wise (who had been severely criticized by Harbord and had blown up angrily at the general), was on his left, and Sibley's battalion extended the line to Bouresches on the right. Holcomb, Turrill and Hughes were in reserve.

At 5 P.M. on June 25, following a massive all-day barrage— all too long delayed—Shearer's battalion began to move through the wood. The artillery had knocked out the enemy machine-gun nests. The Marines took heavy casualties, but the Germans were running out of reinforcements and began pulling back to the Belleau–Torcy road north of the wood. One Marine runner, Pvt. Henry P. Lenert, stumbled into a German position and was asked by its captain in English whether there were more troops behind Shearer. The quick-thinking private assured him that the 6th Marines were ready to pass through and attack at dawn. The captain conferred with his officers and then told the young Marine to lead the 82 Germans back to brigade headquarters as his prisoners.

At 7 A.M. on June 26, Capt. Robert Yowell's 16th Company of Shearer's battalion reached the north edge of Belleau Wood; and the battalion commander sent Harbord the message: "Woods now U.S. Marine Corps entirely."[17]

Shearer's men had suffered 250 casualties, killed 150 Germans, taken some 300 prisoners and captured 30 machine guns. That night, they were relieved by Holcomb's battalion. The fighting and the dying were not finished, but Belleau Wood was taken.

The French parliament declared July 4 a national holiday in honor of the Americans fighting on French soil. A gigantic parade was set in Paris, and the 2d Division sent a battalion made up of one company organized out of each regiment. The officers picked the old hands to go to the rose-strewn welcome awaiting them in the capital. There, the Marine Corps flag was hailed with enormous cheers and the cry of *"Vive les Marines!"* But after a night of celebration, the men headed back to the front again. The French premier, Georges Clemenceau, had offered to open his nation's brothels to the Americans; but Pershing turned him down.

The French general commanding the Sixth Army gave the Marines the ultimate compliment and ordered that henceforth the Bois de Belleau would be called the "Bois de la Brigade de Marine." Years later, speaking at the cemetery there, Marshal Foch called it "the cradle of Victory." [18]

The price had been shockingly high: 126 officers and 5,057 enlisted men of the Marine Brigade dead and wounded. During the bloody month of June, the 2d Division had 1,811 battle deaths, of which 1,062 were Marines.

The survivors would never forget. Twenty-two-year-old Gunnery Sgt. Don V. Paradis of the 80th Company, 6th Marines, wrote his family in Detroit, after censorship was lifted:

> I was knocked down by shell concussion and caught in machine gunfire several times but managed to pull through safely. We were in the front lines for sixteen days without any relief and when we did go back it was only into reserve for six days when we came back to the lines again. . . . I am the only sergeant left in our first Platoon that is of the old bunch of course we have all new ones now. . . . We . . . are getting a little real rest and a chance to clean up, which sure means a whole lot as all of us had cooties and had not had a chance to get a real bath. For a month and four days we did not have our clothes off, not even our shoes, only to rub our feet and perhaps wash them with a canteen of water.[19]

General Pershing wrote the 2d Division: "You stood like a wall against the enemy advance on Paris."[20]

The battle had another unhappy aftermath. An envious

rivalry broke out between the Marines and the soldiers of the division. The Army chafed under the glory—and publicity— won by the Marine Brigade. Even the 3rd Brigade's successful July 1 attack on Hill 192 and Vaux, between Bouresches and Château-Thierry, did not compensate. When Clemenceau visited division headquarters, neither Brig. Gen. Harbord nor any of the top Marine officers was invited to meet him. The bitterness simmered for a generation among many of the Army's highest leaders and even helped keep the Marine Corps out of Europe in World War II. But the fortunes of war had shoved the Marines into the battle, and they had stopped the enemy and then driven them out of Belleau Wood.

4
Soissons—Two Days in Hell

On July 15, the Germans—49 divisions strong—lunged again toward Paris, crossed the Marne River between Château-Thierry and Reims and seized a bridgehead four miles deep.

But the military balance had changed. Germany was being drained of fighting men, while the Allies were receiving constant transfusions from America. A million Yanks had reached France, and great numbers of them fought alongside the French to contain the July 15 attack. In 48 hours, the Germans were thrown back across the Marne with dreadful losses to both armies. That was the Germans' last offensive on the Western Front; it would be 22 more years before they marched into Paris.

With this German failure on the south side of their Château-Thierry pocket, General Foch aimed a counterblow at its northern side. His first objective: to cut the Mauberge highway between Château-Thierry and Soissons, over which the Germans were supporting their 40 divisions in the pocket.

Now commanded by Colonel Neville, who had just returned from the hospital, the Marine Brigade moved up as part of the 2d Division to join the counteroffensive. Harbord, promoted to major general, commanded the division; on its left was the First Moroccan Division—a unit of crack assault troops including the tough French Foreign Legion. Further to the left was the U.S. 1st Division. All were part of the French Tenth Army and the spearhead of the Allied counterattack. The Aisne-Marne Offensive now starting would continue till the war was won.

The troops were dumped into the great Retz Forest south of Soissons. The Marines made a silent, confused forced night march to reach the jumpoff point. The forest roads were jammed with men, trucks and guns. Stumbling forward through the rain

125

and moonless black, each man clung the pack of the man in front. Just as the five-minute preparatory barrage began, the last units came up at double time.

At 4:35 A.M. on July 18, the men fixed bayonets; and the three divisions moved forward. In the 2d Division's sector, the 5th Marines, led by Colonel Feland, held the left. The dog-tired Marines met the Germans in the oak forest and advanced northeast for three kilometers against their machine guns. They fought the Germans Indian-style, moving from tree to tree and shooting snipers out of the limbs.

Two sergeants in the 66th Company of the 5th Marines received the Medal of Honor for bravery during this advance. When the company was stopped by a German strongpoint, Serbia-born Sgt. Louis Cukela crawled out on the flank, circled behind the German position, rushed the machine gun and killed or drove off its crew with his bayonet. Picking up German hand grenades, he blasted out the remainder of the strongpoint, destroyed two machine guns and brought in four prisoners. Austrian-born Sgt. Matej Kocak went forward alone, unprotected by covering fire, to wipe out a hidden machine-gun nest. In the face of heavy fire, he attacked the position and scattered the crew with his bayonet. Then he rallied a group of Moroccans who had become separated from their company and led them in destroying another machine-gun nest.

The Moroccan division crushed heavy resistance with bayonets and knives but was delayed enough to expose the Marines' left flank to raking German machine-gun fire. The 17th Marine Company was pressed too far north and with some Moroccans took the town of Chaudun.

As the Marines emerged from the forest, the July morning was hot; and soon the men were racked with thirst. Led now by French tanks, they charged through steaming waist-high wheat fields ablaze with blooming red poppies. At Beaurepaire Farm, the division swung to the southeast. The 3rd Infantry Brigade on the Marines' right was held up until 6 P.M. by a stubborn defense at Vauxcastille, where the fighting was hand-to-hand.

By mid-afternoon, the 2d Division's units were jumbled. Turrill pulled together parts of his 1st Battalion, with some elements of Shearer's 3rd Battalion and the 8th Marine Machine Gun Company, and joined the 23rd Infantry to clean out the village of Vierzy, where the Germans were making a stand.

Marines and infantrymen assaulted the town from different sides, meeting triumphantly in its streets.

At 7 P.M., the 9th Infantry, reinforced by both Turrill's 1st and Keyser's 2d Battalions, pressed forward again. Stopped by German machine guns, Keyser's Marines took a pounding from enemy artillery and suffered heavy casualties. By dark, the Marines and the 3rd Brigade were exhausted, used up.

On the morning of the 19th, Lt. Col. Harry Lee's 6th Marines, most of which had been in reserve, took over the lead. German divisions had been rushed up to halt the offensive at all costs. They would cut up the 6th Marines cruelly.

The Marines moved out, with Hughes' 1st Battalion on the right and Holcomb's 2d Battalion on the left and Sibley's 3rd Battalion in support. Crossing flat, open country, the lead battalions were slaughtered by German artillery, guided by air spotting. The guns knocked out the French tanks. In half an hour, so many Marines had been hit that two of Sibley's companies were sent to fill in.

Sgt. Don V. Paradis remembered:

> What few of us were left fell into these foxholes. We even piled on top of each other to seek cover from that murderous shellfire. I laid there with every muscle in my body twitching, hardly knowing what I was doing. We could hear the wounded calling for help, but very little could be done for them until after dark came.[21]

Of the 196 men in his company, 54 were left.

The Germans finally stopped the Marine advance six miles from its starting point and less than a mile short of its objective, the Mauberge highway. It was hopeless to go on; the lead battalions had lost more than 50 percent of their men. The survivors dug in. French units replaced them during the night; and then, the Marines carried out their wounded.

In two days, the Marine Brigade had lost 2,015 men killed and wounded; the 6th Marines took two-thirds of the losses. But Foch's attack had pushed the Germans back from the Marne to the Vesle River and triggered the general retreat of the German army. It had turned the war around. As the German chancellor said, "The history of the world played out in three days."[22]

The Marines and the rest of the 2d Division moved to the

rear, some companies with only 25 or 30 men left. Maj. Gen. Harbord called them "a victorious remnant."[23]

On July 26, Brig. Gen. John A. Lejeune took over the Brigade. The Louisiana-born Annapolis graduate brought with him as the Brigade's adjutant Lt. Col. Earl H. Ellis, a brilliant officer destined for a strange fate. A few days later, Lejeune, now a major general, assumed command of the 2d Division. Newly promoted Brig. Gen. Neville resumed command of the Marine Brigade for the rest of the war.

The day Lejeune took over the Brigade, he told the men: "I have this day assumed command of the Fourth Brigade, U.S. Marines. To command this brigade is the highest honor that could come to any man. Its renown is imperishable and the skill, endurance and valor of the officers and men have immortalized its name and that of the Marine Corps."[24]

5
St. Mihiel and Blanc Mont Ridge

Between July 25 and September 12, the Marine Brigade had only 15 casualties. The men spent ten days in a quiet sector of the front around Marbache in the Moselle valley and trained for the next round.

The Allies gathered strength. Foch became a Marshal of France and planned a massive offensive along the entire Western Front. Pershing finally got his American army—the U.S. First Army—and, preliminary to Foch's offensive, prepared to wipe out the four-year-old bulge in the line at St. Mihiel, where the Germans had pushed out from the fortress city of Metz on the Moselle River. For two years, there had been little fighting there.

Meanwhile, to the northwest, French and American divisions kept pounding away until, by August 6, exactly two months after the earlier offensive began at Belleau Wood, the line between Reims and Soissons had been hammered straight. The American soldiers carried the heaviest load and took 50,000 casualties.

Still further north, two days later, the British tore open the enemy line. The stricken German High Command called it a "Black Day" for Germany. Germany's leaders decided the war must be ended, and the Kaiser ordered the politicians to sue for peace. Later, some Germans might rant that they had been "stabbed in the back," but in fact they had been broken on the battlefield.

To clip off the St. Mihiel salient between the Meuse and Moselle rivers—the last salient in the Western Front—Pershing had 19 divisions of his own army and six French divisions. Col. William "Billy" Mitchell, USA, commanded 1,400 supporting airplanes.

When the Germans realized that the salient in front of Metz was going to be hit hard, they began pulling back to their Hindenburg Line positions. They had barely started retreating when, at 1 A.M. on September 12, the roaring bombardment of 3,000 guns began; and after four hours, behind a rolling barrage, came the troops.

In the sector of the 2d Division, again at full strength, the 3rd Infantry Brigade led the attack, with the 5th Marines supporting the 9th Infantry on the right and the 6th Marines following the 23rd Infantry on the left. Resistance was slight. At the end of the second day, the Marine Brigade took over the line, fought forward and stood off counterattacks from the Hindenburg Line. Casualties were comparatively light because of the heavy artillery barrage and because the enemy was already falling back when the Marines advanced; the Brigade had 132 dead and 574 wounded. And the persistent St. Mihiel salient had disappeared.

The Germans expected Pershing to go on to Metz; but even before the St. Mihiel attack was finished, reserve troops were moving north to the area between the Meuse River and the Argonne Forest, where Foch wanted to deliver his hardest blow.

The American First Army stood from the Meuse west to the Argonne; the French Fourth Army was west of the forest. Facing the Americans, the Germans had built elaborate defensive positions in great depth; and they controlled the heights on both flanks, the bluffs east of the Meuse and the tree-covered hills of the Argonne on the left. This American sector was at the southern end of the great offensive that Foch opened on September 26 against the main German defensive system from the Meuse all the way to the North Sea.

Although the American First Army outnumbered its opponents eight to one, the enemy's stubborn, shrewd defense and the difficult terrain that Foch had chosen made the Meuse-Argonne battle an epic slugging match. The Germans stayed to fight, and the American soldiers knocked their heads against the enemy's wall in the most bullheaded fashion—at the cost of thousands of lives. Not until the U.S. 2d Division finally took Blanc Mont Ridge to the south on October 5 did the Germans start withdrawing.

Meanwhile, back of the German lines, the generals and

politicians were groping for a way out of the war; and on October 4 they sent President Wilson a cable asking for an armistice. But the young men on both sides continued to die.

At the beginning of the great offensive, the 2d and the 36th U.S. Divisions were turned over to the French Fourth Army, commanded by the distinguished General Henri Gouraud, a French "marine" who had lost an arm at Gallipoli. Pershing was still fighting with Foch to keep the American Army intact, and the release of these two divisions to the French was a compromise.

Lejeune also had to battle French pressure to break up his brigades to support the French divisions. He insisted that the 2d Division fight as a unit and told Gouraud if his division were not divided, it would take Blanc Mont Ridge, which dominated the Arnes Valley in Champagne and was the key to the French Fourth Army's front. Winning the ridge would free the city of Reims. The 2d Division was assigned to take the ridge.

On the cold, starlit night of October 1–2, the Marine Brigade occupied a 2-mile section of the front just north of Somme-Py. The desolate, white-chalk, war-gutted land was ripped by trenches, shellholes, concrete fortifications and tangled wire. In the far distance the towers of Reims were barely visible. The next night, the Marines occupied the so-called Essen Trench, as the Germans withdrew.

At 5:50 A.M., on the gray, misty morning of October 3, the French and Americans attacked. With the Marines on the left and the 3rd Brigade on the right, the two 2d Division brigades were to converge on the pine-covered Blanc Mont Ridge, commanding the scene. The 2d Battalion, 6th Marines led the 4th Brigade's attack, accompanied by a battalion of French tanks. By 8:30, the 2d Battalion captured the German main line of resistance, except for the western slope of Blanc Mont Ridge.

In the assault, two Marines of the 78th Company performed acts of bravery that earned them the Medal of Honor. Chicago-born Pvt. John J. Kelly, running through the American artillery barrage, attacked a machine-gun nest, killed the gunner with a grenade, shot another German with his pistol and brought eight members of the crew back as his prisoners. Cpl. John H. Pruitt, a native of Fayetteville, Arkansas, saw his fellow Marines falling before the fire of two German machine guns, attacked the two guns, destroyed them and killed the two gunners. Then, he

131

captured 40 Germans in a nearby dugout. Shortly afterward, while sniping at the enemy, Pruitt was mortally wounded by shellfire. He died the next day, his twenty-second birthday. Kelly and Pruitt were the last of only six men of the Marine Brigade to win the Medal of Honor in World War I.

Because the French had been unable to move up on the Marines' left, the 1st Battalion, 6th Marines, and the 2d and 3rd Battalions of the 5th Marines had to extend to the left and the 1st Battalion, 5th Marines was ordered to help the French eliminate the machine-gun complex called the "Essen Hook." Capt. LeRoy P. Hunt's 17th Company finally killed and captured the Hook's detachment of 100 Germans. Hunt received the Navy Cross.

The Germans doggedly held the western tip of Blanc Mont Ridge; and later in the afternoon, the French commanders ordered the 2d Division to attack again. The 23rd Infantry advanced another two kilometers; but the 5th Marines, who had been designated to lead the Marine Brigade's attack, received the order too late, and Lejeune postponed their attack until morning. The delay was costly. The Germans heavily reinforced Blanc Mont Ridge during the night.

October 4 was the bloodiest day of the war for the Marines. The 5th Marines led the way and took a beating. Young Maj. Henry L. Larsen of Denver led his 3rd Battalion forward some two kilometers before it was enfiladed from both sides by machine-gun fire and had to retreat. All three battalions of the 5th Marines now came under heavy fire from virtually every side. They hung on, struggling forward, their ranks cut up by shrapnel and machine-gun bullets. Maj. George Hamilton's 1st Battalion fought with bayonets and clubbed rifles. The hardest hit companies were down to two dozen men; the 1st Battalion to hardly more than a hundred. In the day's fighting 1,100 Marines were killed and wounded, most of them from the 5th Marines. The Germans still held part of Blanc Mont Ridge.

At 6 A.M. the next day, Maj. George Shuler's 3rd Battalion, 6th Marines assaulted the German strongpoint on Blanc Mont Ridge and captured 205 of the enemy and 65 machine guns. Catching the Germans in their dugouts, where they had fled from the pre-attack artillery barrage, the battalion suffered no casualties.

That afternoon, the 6th Marines, with the 2d Battalion

leading, tried to move toward St. Etienne-à-Arnes beyond the ridge, but the battalion had only 300 men left, and a strong machine-gun defense stopped them at the edge of the woods southeast of the town.

October 6 saw more heavy fighting, and the 2d Division's depleted frontline units were relieved during that night. Early on the eighth, army units attacked; and the 6th Marines' 76th Company, commanded by Capt. Macon C. Overton, occupied St. Etienne. On Overton's right, the 75th Company was reduced to a handful of enlisted men led by Sgt. Aralzaman C. Marsh. Marsh held his ground against a German counterattack that evening. The last Marine unit, the 3rd Battalion, 6th Marines, with less than 300 men now left, was relieved on October 10. The German armies east of Reims were in retreat to the Aisne River.

The men of the two Marine regiments and the 6th Machine Gun Battalion received their third citation for gallantry from the French, entitling them to wear the green and scarlet cord of the *fourragère* on their left shoulders. In a week of continuous combat, the Marine Brigade had lost 494 dead and 1,864 wounded.

One of the wounded was 1st Sgt. Daly. Lejeune called the wiry little sergeant "the outstanding Marine of all time."[25] Born on November 11, 1873, Daly had been a newsboy in New York City's Park Row and enlisted for the Spanish-American War but saw no action then. The only enlisted Marine ever to win the Medal of Honor for two separate actions—at Peking and Haiti—he was awarded the Navy Cross and Army Distinguished Service Cross for heroism at Belleau Wood, where he put out an ammunition dump fire and singlehandedly captured a machine-gun nest with grenades and an automatic pistol. When Daly arrived home after the Armistice, reporters asked him how he had won his DSC. Daly explained, "I was out there pickin' pansies for my gal in Brooklyn one day," when a car loaded with "brass hats" drove up and they pinned a medal on him. He was the sergeant who had asked his Marines if they wanted to live forever; he died in his bed in Glendale, New York, at age sixty-three.

Now, in France, the 2d Division was ordered to rejoin the American First Army in the Argonne Forest and the final battle of the war.

6
Meuse-Argonne: The Last Battle

The weather turned bitter cold; the rain became sleet. And Germany started to fall apart in the face of irreversible pressure.

In mid-October, the Kaiser fired Gen. Erich Ludendorff, his field commander. In quick order, Bulgaria, Turkey and Austria quit the war. The British broke the German lines near Valenciennes; the German Navy mutinied, and the Germans asked for an armistice. But terms had to be argued out, and the end had to wait for the dramatic 11th hour of the 11th day of the 11th month—at the cost of still more lives. On Sunday morning, November 10, the Kaiser fled to Holland. The next morning, the Western Front fell silent. The carnage stopped. Those still alive now would live—even though the world was safe for absolutely nothing.

But in those final weeks of battle, the Allies kept turning the screw, to make it clear there was no alternative to surrender. On November 1, while the politicians wrangled, the Marine Brigade entered its last battle. During the final 11 days before the Armistice, the brigade would suffer 277 killed and missing and a total of 1,263 casualties.

The vast battle the Marines now joined was already under way between the Argonne Forest and the Meuse River. Across this 15- to 25-mile-wide defile, the Germans manned intricate defenses in depth; above it, they commanded the high ground on both sides and on the watershed spine running up its center. Here, while the Marine Brigade was fighting on Blanc Mont Ridge, half a million Americans and Frenchmen had attacked; and, by October 11, 75,000 men were dead and wounded and thousands more downed by influenza. The need for replacements became urgent.

The 2d Division, rested and retrained and with recruits filling in for the fallen, now was brought to battle with the American First Army's V Corps commanded by Maj. Gen. Charles P. Summerall. V Corps had been fighting up the central spine; and the division was placed in the center of the American drive, as its spearhead.

"The Army that went into action on November 1, 1918, was the greatest America has ever sent to war,"[26] wrote Maj. Gen. Harbord. The 2d Division faced a 2-kilometer-wide sector of the Hindenburg Line called the Kriemhilde Stellung. The division's attack was preceded by explosive and gas shells that ripped the enemy defenses for two hours. The Marines jumped off at 5:30 A.M., "leaning on" a rolling barrage. Overhead, squadrons of planes covered the assault. The day, for a brief change, turned warm and sunny. In the lead were the 1st Battalion, 5th Marines on the right and the 1st Battalion, 6th Marines on the left. The other battalions followed in a column of battalions. Beyond the Marines' right were the 3rd Brigade and then the 89th Division; on their left, the 80th Division. After reaching their first objective, the Marines were to take over the entire division front and advance to the crucial heights of Barricourt.

The Marines fought through a war-pocked landscape, ruined villages, barbed wire mazes and the Germans' protective barrage. On the right, heavy machine-gun fire killed Captain Overton of the 76th Company and Capt. Kirt Green of the 80th. The Marines plunged through the German lines. The divisions on both sides of the 2d were held up, and a specially prepared Marine-infantry battalion under Marine Maj. George A. Stowell came up to protect the Marines' left flank and took the village of Imécourt.

By 8 A.M., as planned, the 2d Battalion of the 5th Marines and the 3rd Battalion of the 6th Marines took over the lead. The former seized Landreville. The latter ran into heavy going at Bayonville, where the Germans, resisting stubbornly, had a second defensive line called the Freya Stellung. Tanks helped the Marines take this position. About noon, the final Marine battalions leapfrogged into the lead and reached Barricourt Heights, their day's objective, by mid-afternoon. That night, the Germans pulled out.

The Marines' progress had been spectacular and decisive,

although against admittedly fall-away defenses. The Germans had been forced to retreat behind the Meuse and to fight only a delaying action in front of the river.

November 2 was a day of rest and probing patrol actions, and then the 3rd Infantry Brigade took over the division lead and advanced 6 miles through heavy rain during that night and the next day and night. The Germans were demoralized by the novel night attacks. The Americans were now racing after the withdrawing enemy. American divisions on the far right crossed the Meuse.

By November 6, the Marine Brigade had its front line along the Meuse. The retreating Germans had destroyed all the bridges, and the 2d Division's crossing was repeatedly postponed. By November 10, the Germans were fleeing with little pretense of trying to stop the Allies; but, to keep open a retreat route, several enemy divisions were holding at the river and on the ridge two to four miles behind it.

The 2d and 89th Divisons were ordered to cross the river and assault the ridge. Enemy artillery and machine guns prevented the Engineers from floating foot bridges across the river at the Marines' main crossing point, a mile northwest of Mouzon. But at a second crossing point, a bit to the south near Letanne, the 2d Engineers, under fire, managed to put one bridge in place. By 11:30 P.M., November 10, the Corps' birthday, the 1st and 2d Battalions of the 5th Marines, under Maj. George W. Hamilton, were over. They took heavy casualties.

After driving the enemy from their immediate front, the Marines waited until a battalion of the 89th Division joined them; and then all three battalions advanced eastward toward Moulins until they learned of the Armistice. Some units did not get the word until 11:45 A.M. By then, the 18th Company was a mile beyond the river.

The two Marine battalions that crossed the Meuse lost 31 killed and 148 wounded—as it proved, unnecessarily.

Gunnery Sgt. Paradis, who fought the entire war without a scratch, figured that of the original 300 men in his 80th Company, only 44 were still there at the Armistice. Of these, 36 had been wounded once or more and returned to the company; 12 had survived every battle.[27]

This climactic six-week battle, which Americans call

Meuse–Argonne, was enormous. Nearly a million Americans were engaged. It was fought by 26 American divisions and seven French divisions. The U.S. First Army suffered 117,000 casualties. The Germans, who used 470,000 men in strongly fortified positions, had 100,000 casualties. Only the arrival of fresh American riflemen in overwhelming numbers had insured the final victory.

Maj. Gen. Lejeune described the final moments of the war for the Marines: "During the last two hours before the Armistice, the enemy's artillery fire was intensified and our artillery sent as good as it received. A few minutes before eleven o'clock, there were tremendous bursts of fire from the two antagonists and then—suddenly—there was complete silence."[28]

That night, the men in the field warmed themselves and dried their clothes over small bonfires and fired rockets and flares into the air all along the front. The lights went on again. Slowly, the earth was covered green once more, marked with the red poppies and the new white gravestones.

7
On Other Wartime Duties

The 4th Brigade was at the heart of the Marine Corps story in World War I, but it was not the entire story by far.

During the war, 78,839 Marines served in the Corps. Of these, 31,871, less than half, served in Europe with the American Expeditionary Force or on shore duty with the Navy. Between May and November, 1918, the Marines suffered 12,179 casualties, including 3,284 deaths, in France.

Every Marine was a volunteer, except for 7,088 who were drafted in the war's last weeks. The Corps' enormous expansion caused the creation of a wartime Marine Corps Reserve with 496 officers and 6,760 enlisted personnel by the war's end. On August 12, 1918, the Secretary of the Navy authorized the Commandant to enroll women as reservists; and the next day, Mrs. Opha M. Johnson became the first woman Marine. In all, 277 women served as enlisted Marines up to the rank of sergeant during the war.

The huge increases in personnel required new facilities. More than 46,000 Marines were trained at the newly developed base at Parris Island, South Carolina, and others at Mare Island, California. Advanced unit training was provided at the new base established in May 1917 at Quantico, Virginia.

Throughout the war, the Corps, led by its energetic Commandant, battled strenuously to expand the 4th Brigade to a division and to send its own artillery units to France. But, in the face of Army and especially Pershing's opposition, it failed. An Advanced Base Force of 7,958 men was kept in readiness but never saw active service. And the Corps did send to France the 5th Brigade commanded by Brig. Gen. Eli K. Cole. Composed of the 11th and 13th Regiments and the 5th Brigade Machine Gun

Battalion, it arrived at Brest on September 24, 1918. It never fought as a brigade, but supplied replacements to the 4th Brigade and performed a variety of other support duties. (One enlisted man in the 11th Regiment, James J. "Gene" Tunney, was assigned to athletic duties and became the AEF's heavyweight boxing champion. He won the world championship in 1926.) Many men of the 5th Brigade reacted to the fragmentation of their unit with an intense and lasting sense of resentment.

Marine officers also led Army units on the Western Front. Colonel Wise commanded the 59th Infantry at St. Mihiel and in the Meuse–Argonne campaign. Lt. Col. Dunlap, who had come to France with Pershing, won the Navy Cross leading the Army's 17th Field Artillery Regiment in the Meuse–Argonne. Colonel Bearss commanded the 102d Regiment of the 26th Division at St. Mihiel. One of the most colorful officers in the Corps, "Hiking Hiram" took his most famous "hike" on the rain-swept night of September 12, 1918, when he led his regiment of New Englanders for 9 kilometers through the fortified forest of Montagne to clip off the salient at Vigneulles.

Exactly two weeks later, Bearss led the 1st Battalion of the 102d 2 kilometers inside the Hindenburg Line in a diversionary attack on the east side of the Meuse River. After desperate hand-to-hand fighting, they took the town of Macheville. The Germans counterattacked and drove them out. Four times the town changed hands; each time Bearss was the first man in and the last out. At dark, he was ordered to withdraw, the feint a success. For this action, he won the Distinguished Service Cross.

In October, while fighting in the Argonne, a shell burst permanently injured Bearss' spine. The short, stocky Hoosier—who had won the Medal of Honor at the Sohoton Cliffs on Samar and served in the Boxer Rebellion, at Vera Cruz and in the Dominican Republic—was retired after 21 years as a fighting Marine with 11 decorations for bravery.

The war also spurred the infant growth of Marine Corps aviation, which had been born on May 22, 1912, when Lt. Alfred A. Cunningham, a thirty-year-old Georgian, was assigned to the Navy's aviation camp at Annapolis. He became Naval Aviator No. 5 and the first Marine to win his wings.

When the United States entered World War I, Marine

aviation consisted of only 39 men. In January 1918, the 1st Marine Aeronautic Company, led by Maj. Francis T. Evans, the fourth Marine flier, started flying antisubmarine patrols in the Azores. And in July, 753 men of the 1st Marine Aviation Force arrived at Brest. Soon, four squadrons (200 officers and 1,000 enlisted men) were serving under the Navy as the Day Wing of the Northern Bombing Group in the area around Dunkirk and Calais. But, until late September, the Marines in France had not a single plane of their own and did most of their flying with British and French squadrons. They participated in 43 joint combat raids and 14 raids that were completely Marine. Marine fliers were also credited with downing 12 enemy planes (although some authorities regard the figure as a high estimate).[29] Major Cunningham commanded the 1st Marine Aviation Force, with Maj. Roy S. Geiger, the fifth Marine aviator, as second in command.

Two Marines earned the Medal of Honor in the air on October 14, 1918: 2d Lt. Ralph Talbot of South Weymouth, Massachusetts, and Gunnery Sgt. Robert G. Robinson of Wayne, Michigan. On a raid over Belgium, motor trouble separated their plane and one other from their formation, which was bombing the Thielt railway junction. Twelve enemy planes attacked them. Robinson shot down one. A bullet shattered his left elbow. His gun jammed; he cleared it with one hand and kept firing. Bullets hit him in the stomach and hip and he collapsed. Talbot then shot down another plane with his front guns. With Robinson unconscious and the motor failing, Talbot dived to escape the enemy planes, crossed the German trenches at a height of 50 feet, landed at the nearest hospital to get help for Robinson and returned to his airdrome. Eleven days later, Talbot, who had just finished his freshman year at Yale University before joining up, crashed on take off and was killed. His observer, 2d Lt. Colgate W. Darden, Jr., was thrown clear and severely hurt; but he survived to become the governor of Virginia.

Marine aviation forces had 47 casualties during the war. Three Marines were killed in action or died of wounds; three were wounded, and 16 died of influenza. By the Armistice, there were 2,462 officers and men in Marine aviation.

The Corps took pride in the fact that, despite its eagerness to fight with the Army in France, it met every call from the Navy for additional men. Marines served on American battleships overseas and on many cruisers. They maintained sizable forces in Cuba, the Dominican Republic and Haiti and manned a variety of ships' detachments and shore stations from Guantanamo to Peking. They took over the Virgin Islands, which were acquired from Denmark just before the declaration of war. And they guarded 75 naval shore establishments in the United States.

Strangely, the Marines' first wartime encounter with the Germans had come not in France but on the Pacific island of Guam. The German cruiser *Cormoran* had been chased into Guam's harbor by the Japanese in 1914 and was interned. On April 7, 1917, the U.S. governor demanded the cruiser's surrender. A cutter racing to warn the Germans on the ship was fired on by U.S. Marines commanded by 1st Lt. Ethelbert Tabot. The Germans blew up their ship and jumped into the bay. Seven were killed; the rest were rescued and escorted by a detachment of Marines to an Army prison camp in Utah.

In June 1918, the Marines participated in another curious adventure. The flagship of the U.S. Asiatic Fleet, *Brooklyn,* was docked at Vladivostok on Russia's Siberian coast. Aboard was a detachment of 75 Marines augmented by 50 Marines from Cavite. On June 29, troops of the Czechoslovak Legion seized control of Vladivostok from the Bolshevik-led Russians. The Legion, made up of 40,000 prisoners and deserters from Austro-Hungary, opposed the Bolsheviks and had made an incredible trek across Russia to Vladivostok—the long way around— hoping to fight with the Allies on the Western Front.

Thirty Marines from *Brooklyn* under Capt. Archie F. Howard, a young Annapolis graduate from Clay Center, Kansas, were sent ashore to protect the American consulate and to join an Allied force of British, Japanese, Chinese and Czechs patrolling the city. Marines also guarded German and Austrian prisoners of war on Russian Island, 5 miles from Vladivostok, and helped patrol the Vladivostok Navy Yard.

The Bolsheviks in Vladivostok constantly expected a revolt among the crew of *Brooklyn* because three times each day a red flag was raised on the warship. It was, in fact, the Navy meal pennant.

141

8
Watch on the Rhine

Six days after the Armistice, the tired 4th Marine Brigade began its long march into Germany with the U.S. Third Army, the American share of the Army of Occupation. The footsore Marines hiked all the way, some 200 miles, 10 hours a day, 50 minutes to the hour. They trudged through the devastated war area, across the Belgian frontier and through Luxembourg. In every Belgian town, the people turned out to cheer their passage. They followed behind the retreating German army. It was a time of armistice, not peace.

The Marines reached the German border at Diekirch on the Sauer River on November 23 and stopped there. Some received fresh uniforms at last. And on December 1, six months to the day after the old-timers had gone into the line at Belleau Wood, they marched peacefully into Germany and down the Ahr Valley. "During each halt the troops were scattered for billeting in the towns and farmhouses. The Germans were reserved but showed no hostility; many of the Americans felt more at home with them than they had with the French."[30] Gunnery Sgt. Paradis felt differently: "I've seen all of this country and people that I want and sure hope they get us out soon. The more I see of them and their pussyfoot ways the worse I dislike them. They try to treat us nice and when I think of the misery and suffering they have caused us I feel like shooting up the whole town."[31]

The Marines led the 2d Division down the Ahr and on December 9 approached the Rhine River, as agreed to by the Armistice. "The men walked silent, remembering the old dead."[32] Some of the men felt the war should have been pushed into the Fatherland; others thanked God it had not.

On Friday the thirteenth, they crossed the Rhine in a driving rain.

The battalion came into a town with paved streets and trolley-cars and tall factory chimneys that did not smoke. Platoon commanders said it was Remagen; those towers to the right would be the bridge. There was a bridge, a great steel structure of high black arches. The battalion filed upon it.[33]

The Marines moved upriver into their sector of the bridgehead east of the Rhine at Koblenz. The bridgehead had a radius of 30 kilometers from the city. The 5th Marines settled in the Wied Valley and the 6th Marines along the Rhine. A few manned the Rhine River Patrol in the American sector; but most were kept occupied drilling, shooting on the rifle ranges, and on maneuvers. They began to eat better. They stayed there for the next seven months, impatient, bored, eager to go home.

In July 1919, the Marines finally began moving out through the French port of Brest, where Brig. Gen. Smedley Butler, who had finally gotten over as commander of the 13th Marines, was running the huge, teeming military Camp Pontanezen. On August 9, the Marine Brigade paraded in the thick summer heat of New York City; with the rest of the 25,000 men of the 2d Division, it marched up Fifth Avenue from Washington Arch to the north end of Central Park Then, it entrained to Quantico and was formally returned to the naval service. On August 12, it was reviewed by President Wilson in Washington. After that, at last, demobilization. The great crusade was over—for now.

World War I was the Marine Corps' first Big Show. It changed the Corps for all time—in size, in capability and in ambition.

The Marines' leadership had by no means been ready for the vast expansion the war made possible. Before the war, the Marines had seen their role as supporting the Navy, manning ships and shore stations and defending advanced bases. Then, suddenly, large numbers of Marines were shipped to France, at the Commandant's insistence, to perform a function identical to the Army's. Their organization, staff system, weapons, uniforms, supply and even drill had to conform with and duplicate the Army's. That was the price of admission the Corps had to pay to the fight in France.

Until August 1916, the Corps had an authorized strength of 10,265. On December 11, 1918, it reached 75,101. This explosive growth—700 percent—forced the Corps to think on a large scale and taught its officers to manage large units of troops. Marine participation with the Army at battalion, regimental and brigade strength related to the future, not the past.

The war also gave the Corps, and especially its junior officers who would be around awhile, experience fighting a powerful foe. Massive warfare with modern weapons provided new and awful lessons that would prove invaluable after Pearl Harbor, only 23 years in the future.

And, finally, the public attention that the Corps received gave it a new certainty. The doubts articulated by Teddy Roosevelt and Captain Fullam were gone. Although by mid-1919 its enlisted strength was reduced to 27,400 and the postwar revulsion against war and killing affected the Corps as much as the other services, the Marine Corps had made a crucial transition to modern warfare and toward a new vision of its function as a major force-in-readiness for the nation.

At Ocotal, Nicaragua, in 1928, a company of mounted
Marines form in front of the house where rebels led by
Augusto Sandino surrounded the Marine garrison in July 1927.
Museums Branch, USMC

III
IMPERIALISM
IN THE
CARIBBEAN
1901-1934

SEMPER FIDELIS

1
The Caribbean Interventions

The Marines were the cutting edge of American imperialism in the Caribbean. U.S. intervention there climaxed between the War with Spain and the beginning of the Good Neighbor Policy in the 1930s. During these three decades much of the Marine Corps served in the Caribbean as an essential weapon of American foreign policy.

This policy had four goals: (1) to control the sea-lanes between the United States and the Panama Canal; (2) to keep other foreign powers—especially the newly muscular Germany—out of the Caribbean; (3) to support American investors in these underdeveloped agricultural countries—what came to be called "Dollar Diplomacy"; and (4) to establish and maintain the local political stability that these strategic and economic purposes required.

The Marines enforced United States policy in a series of "Banana Wars." They extended American power southward, licensed by President Theodore Roosevelt's 1904 corollary to the Monroe Doctrine, in which he proclaimed the United States' unilateral right to intervene in the Western Hemisphere. The Marines kept law and order, suppressed revolts against governments that accepted American aims and prevented the coming to power of independent-minded leaders. The Marines protected American lives, interests and property. They developed public works, education and medical care to help create social stability and economic viability. When ordered to, the Marines went in and supported "our people" and squashed anti-U.S. nationalists. As Maj. Gen. Smedley Butler put it, "Marines are given orders, and they go."[1]

Many who have written about this high-handed chapter in

[For the location of places in the Caribbean see map No. 5 in the map section.—*Au.*]

American history have called the Marines' opponents "bandits." Certainly, many of the thousands killed by the Marines were truly bandits; but often they were peasants fighting to overthrow their governments, whether good or bad, or throw out the American occupiers. In general, they can most fairly be called "rebels," because they opposed the forces in power—both their own countrymen and United States Marines.

During the first three decades of the twentieth century, the United States became a capital-exporting nation to the Caribbean. American financiers built railroads; the United Fruit Company grew to gigantic proportions; mining interests and banks moved in; and sugar plantations were concentrated under American control.

This powerful economic presence spurred the development of some of these small nations; it tended to raise wages; it generated taxes, and it improved communications. But all too frequently, it corrupted public officials, dominated governments for its own benefit, increased dependence on single-crop agriculture and suppressed social reforms.

There was hardly a moment in the first third of this century when U.S. Marines were not ashore on some other nation's territory in the Caribbean. They landed in Panama, Cuba and Mexico; and they made three major interventions: Nicaragua (1912–1913 and 1926–1933); Haiti (1915–1934); and the Dominican Republic (1916–1924). Said one respected historian, "In all three interventions, [the United States] called the tune, and in in all three cases it maintained its troops on foreign soil against the will of the inhabitants of the countries concerned."[2]

If the United States had not used its Marines to ensure law and order and exclude other powers, the Caribbean might have become studded with European naval bases and economic rivalries. But the price the United States paid for its interventions was heavy; they brewed hatreds and nationalist movements that at best insisted on American hands-off and at worst turned eventually to the United States' modern-day rivals for world power.

Sumner Welles, an exceptionally astute American diplomat in Latin America, said of the "constant interference and even . . . armed intervention" in the Caribbean: "No aspect of our earlier inter-American policy has done more harm than this to the welfare of the entire hemisphere."[3]

2
Securing the Canal—Panama

The Marine Corps played a critical role in the complex maneuvering by which the United States built and dominated the Panama Canal.

Marines went ashore on the Isthmus of Panama—then part of Colombia—late in 1901, when Colombian officials refused to run the trains across the isthmus without American protection. Marines had landed there to protect American interests repeatedly since 1860. This time, 245 Marines landed at Panama City on the Pacific coast; and a smaller force landed at Colon on the Caribbean. They served as train guards while Colombian troops and Panamanian Liberals skirmished.

On September 22, 1902, Lt. Col. Benjamin R. Russell arrived at Colon with a Marine battalion of 342 men. While one company stayed in Colon, the remainder went to Panama City, the center of the disturbance. They guarded the trains and managed to keep the peace; and after the Liberals laid down their arms and the Colombians took over the trains, they reembarked on November 17.

Meanwhile, in Washington, the government was encouraging—and New York business interests were financing—the Panamanians to revolt against Colombia. The government of Colombia refused to ratify the treaty that would turn over the French canal-building concession to the Americans. With "remarkable split-second timing,"[4] the cruiser *Nashville* arrived at Colon on November 2, 1903, and a Panamanian revolution started in Panama City. The next morning, 4,000 Colombian troops arrived at Colon by sea. *Nashville's* captain, Cmdr. John Hubbard, refused to let them ride the trains to put down the revolution in Panama City. Hubbard twice sent ashore

151

a landing force and finally persuaded the Colombians to return to their ships.

With the revolution in full swing and the Republic of Panama proclaimed, a Marine battalion arrived in the transport *Dixie* on the evening of the fifth. Maj. John A. Lejeune immediately landed two of his companies at Colon and relieved *Nashville's* landing force. Although the Marines left again in 24 hours, they and the Navy, acting on orders from Washington, had given the revolution enough weight to succeed. The United States instantly recognized the new republic and procured a treaty gaining the rights to the isthmus canal. Years later, the United States paid Colombia $25 million for this imperious interference.

During those unsettled days in 1903, the Navy sent an expeditionary force to Real de Santa Maria and Yaviza, two strategic border points through which Colombia could attack Panama. In mid-December, the sailors were joined by Capt. Smedley D. Butler and a company of Marines. They were reinforced by the Marine detachment from *Boston.*

Lejeune's Marines established a camp ashore and were joined by a battalion under Maj. Louis C. Lucas. On January 3, 1904, the Commandant, Brig. Gen. Elliott, arrived with two more battalions, totaling 635 men, and assumed command of all the Marines in Panama. It was the first time a Commandant had taken charge of troops in the field since Henderson had done so in the Florida Indian war. Organized into a provisional brigade of two regiments commanded by Lt. Cols. Biddle and Waller, the Marines spent their time scouting, mapping the country and studying the defenses of the canal and Panama City. In mid-February, Colombia agreed not to invade Panama; and the brigade began withdrawing to Guantanamo. By the end of March, only Lejeune's 1st Battalion of the 1st Regiment remained in the Canal Zone. He was kept busy protecting his men from tropical and venereal diseases.

The next fall came trouble: the Panamanian army ungratefully threatened to take over the country. The Marine battalion's A Company moved into the hospital on Ancon Hill in the Canal Zone, and the rest of the battalion was held in readiness. Under the threat of action by the Marines, the Panamanian general agreed to retire and his army was disbanded. In 1911, the U.S. Army began to take over the defense of the Canal Zone.

Smedley Butler was present for the dedication of the Canal in 1913, when

> . . . a group of important and pompous army officials boarded a tug to make the first trip. None of the Marines had been invited to join them. I walked down to the Canal to watch the festivities.
>
> By golly! A dugout shot around the bank. It was proudly flying a little Marine flag, and two Marines were paddling like the devil. They went through first, cheered and applauded by the crowd.[5]

The Canal opened for business in August 1914. A couple of hundred Marines stayed in Panama until early that year, with a side trip on expeditionary duty to Nicaragua in 1912. The Marines had served as a force in readiness that helped President Roosevelt make the Panama Canal American.

3
Pacifying Cuba

In Cuba, the Marines made three significant landings but did no actual fighting. The Corps primarily guarded American sugar and mining properties and railroads and freed the Cuban army to fight the opposition.

The United States Army had occupied Cuba at the beginning of 1899 and turned it free three years later. But the Platt Amendment, shoehorned into the new Cuban constitution, reserved for the United States the right to intervene to protect Cuban independence as well as life, individual liberty and property. The provision was broad enough to cover a variety of self-serving American actions.

By the summer of 1906, Cuba was torn by strife between two political factions. Insurrection spread swiftly across the island. American sugar property was destroyed. The "ins" wanted American intervention to protect them against the stronger "outs." The "outs" wanted intervention because they were confident they would win any free elections.

A battalion of Marines, under Maj. Albertus W. Catlin, who had commanded the Marines on *Maine* when she was sunk, was sent to Cuban waters. On September 13, 130 Marines and sailors from the cruiser *Denver* landed at Havana and camped in front of the president's palace. The next morning, the U.S. State Department ordered them back to their ship. During the next few days, elements of Major Catlin's battalion went ashore specifically to protect threatened sugar plantations and to guard the railroads.

President Roosevelt rushed Secretary of War William Howard Taft to Cuba. He arranged a truce, but the turmoil continued, and Taft recommended mobilizing for intervention. An

154

expeditionary force of 5,400 men sailed for Cuba, including a Marine battalion in the transport *Dixie*. The Marine Corps was prepared to contribute two more battalions from its shore stations. Organized as the 1st Marine Regiment under Lt. Col. George Barnett, they were ready to sail in 36 hours but were delayed by the lack of sea transportation.

After the Cuban government of Estrada Palma resigned on September 28, the 2,800-man Provisional Marine Brigade, including 500 men of the 1st Regiment, landed at Havana. During October, the Marines, now commanded by Colonel Waller, patrolled towns and plantations, keeping the peace. By November 1, Army troops had relieved many Marine detachments, and the Corps' strength in Cuba was down to one thousand organized as the 1st Provisional Regiment.

Pacification took longer than expected; but a general election made José Miguel Gomez, leader of the Liberal Party "outs," president on February 1, 1909. Nine days earlier, the last of the Marine regiment left Cuba.

In the following years, Cuban politics sank into inefficiency, graft and corruption. In 1912, a revolt mounted in Oriente Province by Evaristo Estenoz took a strident racial form. It was feared that Estenoz wanted to create a black republic on the eastern end of Cuba, an area spotted with American-owned copper mines, sugar holdings and railroads. The American government started mobilizing again.

The 1st Provisional Marine Regiment of 800 men, now commanded by Col. Lincoln Karmany, quickly arrived at Guantanamo Bay on May 28 and guarded American property and railroads. The Marines freed the Cuban army to fight the rebels, who were burning sugar plantations and railroad property. One American-owned railroad had the gall to send the Marine Corps a bill for tickets for the Marines who had ridden its trains as guards. It was not paid.

On the night of June 9, a detachment of Marines was attacked at El Cuero; but the rebels were repulsed without casualties on either side. In late June, Estenoz was killed in a skirmish; and within another month, the rebellion had been crushed. The Marines began withdrawing to Guantanamo.

The Cubans continued to settle their political differences with guns. Gomez and the Liberals lost power and marched on

Havana. Although many Cuban army garrisons went over to the Liberals, the government mustered enough strength to invade Santa Clara province and captured Gomez on March 7, 1917.

The United States was fast approaching war against Germany, and rebels now rampaging through eastern Cuba threatened to endanger the Allies' sugar supply. The American sugar companies pressed for intervention; and on March 4, a six-company battalion of Marines was carved out of the 1st Brigade in Haiti and shipped to Cuba. Two hundred and twenty Marines occupied Guantanamo City to protect American property and the naval station's water supply. Units from the brigade and from a division of battleships briefly occupied threatened plantations. Several ships' Marine detachments plus the 43rd and 51st Companies from Haiti patrolled Santiago. Later, the 43rd Company was sent to guard the iron mines and ore docks at Daiquiri; and the 55th Company occupied posts at Nipe Bay on the north coast. Under pressure of the war in Europe, the last of the Marines were withdrawn from the Guantanamo district by May 23 and returned to the United States.

Bands of rebels continued to roam the countryside; and, to protect the sugar-producing areas, the 7th Marine Regiment, under Lt. Col. Melville J. Shaw, went to Cuba in August. The 9th Regiment joined it in December, and they were formed into a brigade commanded by Col. James E. Mahoney. By August 1919, only a two-company battalion remained in Cuba. On February 6, 1922, it sailed for Guantanamo Bay.

Two years later, Gerardo Machado became president. He developed into a vicious dictator and in 1933 was ousted by a leftist junta. With United States encouragement, the Cuban army responded by putting into power Fulgencio Batista. He also ruled tyrannically and dominated Cuban political life until Fidel Castro's revolution overthrew him in 1959.

156

4
Back to Vera Cruz

The Marine Corps' invasion of Mexico in 1914 was triggered by an incident reminiscent of an earlier day—an insult to the American flag.

At the time, Mexico was ripped apart by a violent social revolution and savaged by revolutionary generals determined to overthrow a government dominated by business interests and the Catholic Church. Americans had more than $2 billion invested in Mexico; 70,000 Americans lived and worked there. In February, 1913, tough, hard-drinking Gen. Victoriano Huerta deposed the reformer President Francisco Madero and his vice president; and one of Huerta's generals murdered them both. The United States moved Army troops to Galveston and naval ships to ports on both Mexican coasts. The Marine Corps assembled some 2,170 men under Colonel Lincoln Karmany and shipped them to Guantanamo to stand by. But President Taft refused to intervene.

President Woodrow Wilson, who took office the following month, came up with a new principle: the United States would recognize only those Latin American governments that had come to power by constitutional means. Deeply sympathetic to the hopes of the Mexican people, Wilson refused to recognize Huerta's reactionary government, which was fighting a Constitutionalist army led by stubborn, cautious Venustiano Carranza and his regional chiefs Pancho Villa, Emiliano Zapata and Alvaro Obregón, names that were to become part of the folklore. Wilson called Huerta's regime "a government of butchers."[6]

In this atmosphere of tension, on April 6, 1914, a whaleboat from *USS Dolphin* was loading supplies at a dock in the oil refinery port of Tampico, which was then threatened by the

157

revolutionary army. Huerta's men arrested seven sailors and *Dolphin's* paymaster and threw them into jail. They were released in less than an hour, but Rear Adm. Henry T. Mayo demanded that the Mexicans apologize by firing a 21-gun salute to the American flag. Huerta waffled and offered substitute apologies that were deemed unacceptable.

On Monday, April 20, President Wilson asked Congressional approval to use armed force to win respect for the flag. He had already sent a fleet, including seven battleships, to intercept supplies Huerta was receiving from Germany.

The Americans planned a naval demonstration off Tampico. This was changed to a landing at Vera Cruz, Mexico's principal port, when the German ship *Ypiranga* was reported bringing 200 machine guns and large amounts of ammunition there for Huerta. The United States wanted to seize these arms—but to avoid an incident with Germany, it had to be done after they had left the German ship and before they reached Huerta's hands.

Elements of the Marine Corps' 1st Advanced Base Brigade, commanded by Colonel Lejeune, were already in Mexican waters. The 1st Regiment was at New Orleans and the 2d Regiment was at Pensacola. Four rifle companies of the 2d were rushed to Mexico. At the same time, the 4th Regiment of Marines was organized on the West Coast under Col. Joseph H. Pendleton and sent down the west coast of Mexico.

Ypiranga was due at Vera Cruz at 10:30 Tuesday morning, April 21. Rear Adm. Frank F. Fletcher was ordered to land a force of sailors and Marines at 8:30 A.M., take the Customs House and prevent the delivery of the German arms. First ashore were the Marines of the 2d Regiment led by Lt. Col. Wendell C. Neville and Major Butler's battalion that had come up from Panama. Five hundred Marines of the 2d Regiment seized a main pier and the cable station and an electric power plant nearby. When Neville moved his main body a half mile toward the railroad station, the Marines were fired on. They had to fight to take the roundhouse just west of the city. By dark, the Americans controlled the section of the city around the rail yards and the Customs House. During the night, more Marines and sailors landed; and these Marines formed a provisional 3rd Regiment led by Major Catlin, the Fleet Marine Officer.

The next morning, the two Marine regiments advanced

158

house-to-house to clear the city against a determined sniper defense from rooftops and windows. That afternoon, Lt. Col. Charles C. Long's 1st Regiment landed; and Lejeune took command of all the Marines ashore as the 1st Marine Brigade. By the end of the second day, the Americans had been able to clear only half the city; the heavy Spanish-style construction enabled the Mexican defenders to slow their progress.

On the third day, the Marines searched each building for hidden snipers, and the center of the city was occupied. By the fourth day, 7,000 armed Americans were ashore, including 2,469 in the Marine Brigade. Lejeune formed a novel Artillery Battalion from three companies armed with 3-inch field guns. Another regiment of 894 men joined the brigade on April 29, and Colonel Waller, as the senior officer, took over command from Lejeune on May 1. In a flurry of governmental generosity, nine Marines, all officers with the rank of captain or above, received the Medal of Honor.

Ypiranga lay passively at Vera Cruz for several weeks and later unloaded its arms at another Mexican port. Major Butler, in civilian clothes, went on a secret spying mission in Mexico City at Rear Adm. Fletcher's request to check on military strengths and defenses—in case the Mexican refusal to apologize inspired further military action. After the U.S. Army arrived, the Marines manned two-thirds of the outpost line through a row of hot, mosquito-infested sand hills to the beach northwest of the city.

Both factions in the Mexican fighting condemned the American invasion, while in the United States volunteers flooded into recruiting stations. No one knew whether the United States was at war or not.

On July 15, Huerta left Mexico in *Ypiranga*. The demanded apology to the flag was never made, but Huerta had been overthrown. The cost: 19 Americans dead, 71 wounded—and more than 300 Mexicans dead.

Pancho Villa continued to make trouble on the northern border. His March 9, 1916, shooting-up of Columbus, New Mexico, sent Brig. Gen. John J. Pershing and 6,000 Regulars chasing after him into Mexico. By 1917, Carranza had held an election and become Mexico's legitimate President; the last of the American punitive expeditionary force had withdrawn, and Mexico had a new and lasting constitution—the acme of its revolution.

5
Nicaragua

The Marine Corps' first major Caribbean intervention began in Nicaragua on the Central American mainland in 1912. This biggest of the "Banana Wars" ranged over 20 years and reached two climaxes separated by World War I.

The original decision to send in the Marines had two causes: fear of European meddling in a country so close to the Panama Canal; and the desire to protect the American investments that the U.S. government had encouraged in Nicaragua, which was increasingly dominated by the great fruit companies.

As early as 1853, United States Marines had landed in Nicaragua to protect American interests and property, including Cornelius Vanderbilt's railroad between the two oceans. Marines landed again in 1857 and several times in the 1890s. By the time of President Taft's Administration, the brutal dictator José Santos Zelaya was leading Nicaragua into bankruptcy. Conditions grew so bad that the local Conservative party joined with the foreign investors and bankers to oust the dictator. Taft was reluctant to intervene; but when Zelaya shot two American citizens, Secretary of State Philander Knox protested. Not wanting to take on both the Conservatives and the United States, Zelaya resigned.

On May 19, 1910, Marines and sailors landed near Bluefields on the Atlantic coast to guard American property. They were joined by a two-company battalion of Marines from Panama commanded by Major Butler. Now, the Liberal government started to fall apart; the Conservatives marched into Managua, the capital, and two American banks, which had loaned Nicaragua $14 million, set up a national bank and took control of the country's customs.

In 1912, the Conservative president, Adolfo Diaz, faced with strong Liberal opposition, told the Americans that he could not guarantee the protection of American citizens and property and asked the United States to intervene. He figured that an American presence might help his unpopular regime hold power. He was right. The first phase of the Marine intervention in Nicaragua would keep in power the Conservatives, who accepted American economic domination of their country.

Early in August, a small force of U.S. sailors arrived in Managua; and a detachment of Marines and sailors entered Bluefields. On the fourteenth, Butler's battalion of 13 officers and 341 enlisted men landed at Corinto on the Pacific coast and moved into the capital. The Marines' Nicaraguan intervention had begun.

Reinforcements were arriving at Corinto; and Butler, in Managua, had to communicate with them. He sent a detachment of 10 Marines and 40 sailors on a commandeered train. At the town of Leon, armed rebels seized the train and sent the humiliated Americans back to Managua on foot.

Butler angrily set out with 190 officers and men to open the railroad between Managua and Corinto. With him went Marine Lieutenants Alexander A. Vandegrift, Edward A. Ostermann and Richard Tebbs. Near Leon, a rebel leader threatened Butler in a long tirade and drew his pistol. Butler grabbed the gun and with a flourish unloaded it. The watching rebels roared with laughter, and Butler took their leader along as his hostage. At Leon, a hostile mob gathered; a huge woman brandishing a machete approached Butler, screaming at him. Instead of shooting her and starting a battle, Butler chucked her under the chin; she fled. Butler went on to Corinto, conferred with the American naval officers there and returned to Managua.

On September 4, Colonel Pendleton arrived at Corinto with the 1st and 2d Battalions of the 1st Provisional Regiment, a total of 753 Marines. He left one battalion at Corinto and took the other directly to Managua.

Pendleton assigned Butler the job of clearing the railroad from Managua southward through Masaya to Granada. Armed with machine guns and three-inch field pieces, Butler entrained three companies and ran into a pitched battle between government troops and Gen. Benjamin Zeledon's Liberal army near

Masaya. Butler arranged meetings between Zeledon and U.S. Rear Adm. William H. H. Southerland and was finally permitted to pass through the rebel lines. In Masaya, rebel snipers opened up on the train. The Marines returned the fire, some jumping off the train to take cover. Butler raced his train ahead, leaving some Marines behind. Capt. Nelson P. Vulte rounded up most of the men, grabbed a handcar and overtook the train when Butler halted to reorganize his forces. Butler was fit to be tied until Zeledon sent him a note of apology and returned three Marines who had been abandoned in the skirmish. It was here that Marines began calling the sharp-tempered Butler, his eyes bloodshot and sunken from malaria, "Old Gimlet Eye."

Approaching Granada, Butler faced a faction of rebels under Gen. Luis Mena. He ordered Mena to surrender or he would attack Granada; at the last minute, Mena's letter of surrender arrived. He was allowed to go into exile. Pendleton, having heard a rumor that Butler was besieged, rushed to Granada with reinforcements and a load of rations and Red Cross supplies for the inhabitants, who had been starved by the Liberals. "The gratitude of the inhabitants, who had been at the mercy of their vindictive enemies for several weeks, was unbounded and freely and frankly expressed—especially by the women of that city."[7]

Zeledon's army still controlled the 500-foot hill of Coyotepe that dominated both the railroad and Masaya. On the night of October 2, the U.S. Marines and sailors and government troops moved into position to assault the hill. Pendleton had the artillery bombard it throughout the next day. At 5:15 on the morning of October 4, the Americans attacked. Maj. William N. McKelvy's 1st Battalion was in the center and bore the brunt of the fighting; Butler's, consisting of two companies of Marines and one of sailors, was on the left, and a battalion of sailors from *California*, on the right. The Marines and sailors charged up the hill through ineffective rebel fire, and in 40 minutes the battle was over. Most of the rebels fled. Zeledon was killed by his own men while attempting to get away. Seven Marines and sailors were killed.

Masaya fell, and later Leon surrendered to Lt. Col. Long and a force of 1,200 Marines and sailors. The revolution was finished. The bulk of the Marines withdrew from Nicaragua in

January 1913, leaving a strong guard of 105 men at the legation in Managua. The Marines had been the key to keeping Diaz and his unpopular Conservatives in power.

During World War I, the Marine Legation Guard stayed in Managua and became a resented symbol of American imperialism. Nicaraguans recognized that the Marines were there to prevent an anti-American from coming to power. The embarrassing problem was that the anti-American Liberals would win any fair election. Finally, by 1924, a relatively honest election was held, and a coalition government was inaugurated. The Marines were withdrawn on August 4, 1925—but not for long.

By the end of October, both the Conservative president and the Liberal vice president had fled the country, and right-wing General Emiliano Chamorro took over. The United States refused to recognize him.

When rioting broke out, Marines landed again at Bluefields. This time, they guarded a "neutral zone" to keep the warring factions away from American property. In 1926, Chamorro resigned; Adolfo Diaz returned to power, and the United States recognized his government.

Diaz, unable to end the Liberal rebellion, called on the United States for help; but President Calvin Coolidge chose to stay out of the mess. Then the rebels started raiding American fruit, lumber and mining companies, and a U.S. citizen was killed; Americans began talking about the danger of Bolshevism. Coolidge announced that he would protect American lives and property and authorized the sale to President Diaz of 3,000 Krag rifles, 200 Browning machine guns and three million rounds of ammunition.

Marines went ashore at three points on the east coast; and on January 6, 1927, Marines and sailors landed at Corinto and rushed to guard foreigners in the capital. The 2d Battalion, 5th Regiment landed at Bluefields, established a neutral zone there, and, leaving the 51st Company behind, sailed through the Panama Canal for Corinto. On February 1, the Marines led by Lt. Col. James J. Meade took over the defense of Managua. The rest of the 5th Regiment arrived; and on March 7, Brig. Gen. Logan Feland, a veteran of World War I, took command of the 2,000 Marines now in Nicaragua. They garrisoned 14 towns along the railroad. The Marines' second Nicaraguan intervention was in full bloom.

In February, Marine Observation Squadron One, VO-1M, commanded by Maj. Ross E. Rowell, a forty-two-year-old Iowan, arrived with eight officers, 81 enlisted men and six DeHavilland aircraft. During their service in Nicaragua, the Marines would be among the first fliers to dive-bomb an organized enemy, to use air-to-ground communication during combat and to move troops and supplies by air.

The renewed Marine intervention started out hopefully. President Coolidge sent Henry L. Stimson as his personal envoy to work out a peaceful solution. Stimson arranged a fragile truce that would keep Diaz in office until the 1928 elections. Both sides asked for more Marines to keep order. The 11th Regiment led by Col. Randolph C. Berkeley and another Marine air squadron, VO-4M, arrived before Stimson left on May 22. The Marines, now numbering 3,300 men, were organized as the 2d Marine Brigade.

Both Nicaraguan parties turned in large quantities of arms and ammunition, but about 150 Liberals led by Augusto C. Sandino refused to disarm and fled to Nueva Segovia province in the north. They became the core of the guerrillas who would fight the Marines for the next five years, and Sandino became the Marines' ablest opponent. This most renowned and charismatic of the rebel leaders was a slender, frail-looking man, an energetic Liberal partisan and a nationalist. He had worked in the Mexican oil fields and marched with Pancho Villa.

Clashes between Marines and rebel bands continued sporadically. At 2 A.M. on May 16, one large mounted group raided the town of La Paz Centro, and Capt. Richard B. Buchanan and the Marine garrison charged at them down the main street. Buchanan and Pvt. Marvin A. Jackson were killed.

After Stimson's truce went into effect, the Marine brigade was cut back to about a thousand men. The Marines set about creating the Guardia Nacional de Nicaragua, manned by Nicaraguans and with American Marine Col. Robert Y. Rhea and shortly afterward Col. Elias R. Beadle in charge. Recruiting for the Guardia proved extremely difficult.

As Sandino and other rebel leaders began operating near the Honduran border, the Marines worked their way north into rebel territory. In this wild, thinly populated country of coffee plantations and mines, the law was seldom enforced. Capt. Gilbert D. Hatfield and a Marine patrol probed Nueva Segovia and established a base at Ocotal, the province's capital. In July, they were joined by the First Company of the Guardia. The garrison had three Marine officers, two Guardia officers, 38 Marines and 48 Nicaraguan guardsmen. The townspeople, most of them friendly to Sandino, expected trouble.

On the night of July 15, it came. Hatfield, anticipating an attack, had doubled the guard. In small groups, Sandino's men slipped into the town. At 1:15 A.M., a Marine sentry at the walled Spanish house where the Marines were billeted spotted someone moving in the street and fired the first shot. The rebels attacked immediately and surrounded the house. The Guardia in another building could support the Marines only with rifle fire. Three charges were turned back by the Marines. After two hours of fighting, there was a lull; at dawn, the battle started again. The rebels demanded that Hatfield surrender; he replied that Marines did not know how to surrender.

At mid-morning, two Marine DeHavillands arrived overhead and strafed the enemy. Lt. Hayne D. Boyden landed near Ocotal and from a peasant discovered the seriousness of the situation. He raced back to Managua for help. In the second plane, Chief Marine Gunner Michael Wodarczyk, the Polish-born flier known as the "Polish Warhorse," strafed the rebels until his ammunition was gone.

In mid-afternoon, five DeHavillands led by Major Rowell appeared just as the Sandinistas were about to attack again. The planes dive-bombed the town, dropping their 17-pound bombs from heights of 600 and 300 feet, and then strafed for 45 minutes. The rebels fired back. "The ground was strewn with the dead and dying. Houses, in which they had taken refuge, were demolished. Groups were in stampede."[8] This was the Marines' first use of dive-bombing and low-altitude support of ground troops, which would become so basic to Marine Corps aviation in the future. On their way back, the planes bucked a thunderstorm and, out of gas, were forced down at Leon. For this day's work, Rowell won the first Distinguished Flying Cross awarded to a Marine.

Hatfield's men cleaned up the few rebels who stayed to

fight. Fifty-six enemy bodies were recovered; the Marines had one dead and five wounded.

Meanwhile, Brig. Gen. Feland had ordered Maj. Oliver Floyd to take a strong mounted patrol of 225 Marines and Guardias and go after Sandino. But the rebel leader escaped to his mountain fortress called El Chipote; and, with the start of the rainy season, Floyd left a garrison at Jicaro and returned to Managua.

The Marine brigade was further reduced. The Americans were underestimating Sandino; he was crafty, popular, effective. At 1 A.M. on September 19, he struck the Marine detachment in the village of Telpaneca, east of Ocotal, and left two Marines dead.

In those rugged northern mountains, Marine aviation linked together and supplied the scattered garrisons and patrols. Because the DeHavillands were too small for the job, five trimotor Fokker transports, part of the Marines' aviation modernization, were brought in to haul everything from ammunitions to mules.

On October 8, 1927, rebel rifle fire shot down one of two Marine planes patrolling near Quilali. Gunner Wodarczyk piloting the second plane saw the plane crash and burst into flames; he raced off to notify the garrisons at Ocotal and Jicaro. The two downed fliers, 2d Lt. Earl A. Thomas and Sgt. Frank E. Dowdell, forced natives to lead them toward Jicaro and were hiding in a cave when Sandino's men found them.

Within an hour of the crash, 1st Lt. George J. O'Shea at Jicaro rode to the rescue with a detachment of Marines and Guardias. The next morning, a reconnaissance plane dropped a message telling O'Shea that the remains of the downed plane was three miles away on Sapotillal Ridge. It took the men three hours to reach the base of the ridge; as they advanced up the hill, the enemy opened fire. They were caught between two rebel groups and fought their way out of the trap and back to Jicaro. Marines did not reach the crash site for another ten days. Thomas and Dowdell were never seen again.

Meanwhile, on Nicaragua's east coast, the Marines supervised local elections. Because they helped keep the voting honest, the Liberals won easily and became more amenable toward the Marines' presence. In fact, early in 1928, the newly elected Liberals petitioned President Diaz to place a Marine officer in command of the Bluefields police department.

The pursuit of Sandino went on vigorously in the north, with numerous clashes between the Marines and rebel detachments. To finish the affair, Sandino would have to be driven from his fortress on El Chipote. The attempt ended in disaster. First, patrols scouted the area, and planes bombed and strafed El Chipote. Then, on December 19, 1927, one patrol of 140 Marines under Capt. Richard Livingston left Jinotega and 60 men under Guardia 1st Lt. Merton A. Richal left Telpaneca to converge on Sandino's hideout.

On December 30, Livingston's column was ambushed a mile south of Quilali. In 80 minutes, five Marines and two members of the Guardia were dead and 23 Marines including Livingston and two Nicaraguans wounded. On New Year's Day 1928, Richal's patrol, which was approaching Quilali from the north, was hit by dynamite bombs and machine-gun fire. First Sgt. Thomas G. Bruce, a first lieutenant in the Guardia who had won the Navy Cross at Ocotal, was killed instantly. A Guardia sergeant, Policarpo Gutierrez, lost his left arm recovering Bruce's body. Then the enemy charged, and the patrol's point fell back. The Marines' machine gun jammed; a mortar and a 37mm gun went into action. Richal was shot in the face and lost his left eye. Gunnery Sgt. Edward G. Brown organized an attack up Las Cruces Hill and took the crest. There, the Marines dug in to wait for help.

In a few minutes, Marine planes strafed the enemy; and a reinforced rifle platoon, coming out of Quilali to meet Richal, heard of the battle and pushed ahead to the Marines on the hill. The combined force spent the night on Las Cruces, and, after an early-morning air drop of water and nails for stretchers, headed into Quilali.

Sandino took the offensive and laid siege to Quilali. There were some 30 wounded in the town. Despite the absence of an airfield, 1st Lt. Christian F. Schilt, a tall thirty-two-year-old airplane racer from Olney, Illinois, volunteered to fly in medicines and bring out the wounded. The Marines on the ground leveled walls to convert the main street into a landing strip. It was perilously short and ended at the top of a steep cliff. Schilt's Vought O2U-1 Corsair biplane had no brakes, so when it landed, Marines had to act as "wing runners" and grab hold of the wings to slow the rolling plane. Schilt disarmed his plane and left his parachute behind to eliminate all possible weight. On take-offs, the enemy fired their rifles at the unarmed plane. On landings, Schilt had to stall his engines and drop the plane the last ten feet; the lurching aircraft made three great bounces, and, with Marines clinging to its wings, finally rolled to a stop 200 feet from the precipice.

During January 6–8, Schilt made 10 daring flights into Quilali, bringing in 1,400 pounds of medicines and supplies and flying out 18 of the most seriously wounded to Ocotal. On the eighth landing, Schilt's tail-skid assembly was wrecked; and on the ninth, the center section struts bent under the strain. But both times he took off again with two wounded men. For at least three of the wounded, Schilt's courage meant they would live. President Coolidge awarded 1st Lt. Schilt the Medal of Honor on the White House lawn. (The following year, Schilt and Charles A. Lindbergh worked out air routes over Nicaragua for Pan American Airways.)

El Chipote was still the Marines' target. Ground patrols pressed the rebels back into their redoubt, where the Marines' planes could bomb and destroy them. Several hundred rebels were now gathered on the mountain top; and Major Rowell led a four-plane attack there on February 1. Sandino met the low-flying Vought Corsairs with a barrage of rifle and machine-gun fire. After Rowell had dropped his two bombs and fired 200 machine-gun rounds, engine trouble forced him to break off. The other planes continued the attack, dropping four 50-pound and eighteen 17-pound bombs and firing 2,800 machine-gun rounds. When a strong patrol led by Maj. Archibald Young cautiously probed the top of El Chipote, they found that Sandino and most of his men had fled.

The rebels continued to ambush Marine patrols. On February 27, they attacked a 35-man patrol led by 1st Lt. Edward F. O'Day, killing five and wounding seven.

Recognizing the difficulty of suppressing Sandino's rebellion, the Marine Corps was now rebuilding its strength in Nicaragua. In January 1928, the 11th Regiment, commanded by Col. Robert H. Dunlap, a veteran of Samar and France, returned; and Brig. Gen. Feland resumed command of the enlarged brigade. The Marines in the north were heavily reinforced and organized as a special military zone under Dunlap's command. They destroyed rebel camps and supplies. The effect of this buildup was that the rebels avoided tackling the strong patrols and backed further into the eastern interior.

On the east coast, newly arrived Maj. Harold H. Utley listened as a new strategy against Sandino was proposed by Capt. Merritt A. Edson, the commander of the Marine detachment on *USS Denver*. The thirty-year-old, red-headed Vermonter and several other junior officers had worked out a plan using the Coco River, which rose in the mountains near El Chipote and wandered many miles to the Atlantic. Their idea was to throw a defensive screen across the lower section of the river, at the same time send a strong unit upstream into the bowels of Sandino's territory and then crush the rebels between the two forces of Marines. Sandino would either have to sideslip into Honduras or surrender.

Since the Coco basin was unmapped, Edson was instructed, as a first move, to take five Marines from *Denver* and scout as far upriver as possible. The patrol set out on March 8 in a 16-foot flat-bottomed launch powered by a motor salvaged from a Model T Ford. They returned 20 days later with information that Sandino was recruiting men as far east as Bocay, 350 miles upriver from the Atlantic coast, and that a strong force of Marines based in Huaspac, at the junction of the Coco and Huaspac rivers, could block the rebels from getting into the lower stretches of the Coco. Edson went on the sick list with malaria; but by April 14, he, 2d Lt. Jesse S. Cook, Jr., and 37 Marines from *Denver* established a base camp at Huaspac.

The rebels were raiding the gold mines in the area south of Edson's position. Major Utley sent combat patrols after them and gave Edson the job of preventing their escape northward into Honduras. Edson took 32 men in three boats and lay his ambush at Great Falls up the Huaspac River, but the rebels did not appear. So he pushed his men on a hard march through the rain-swept jungle toward Bocay, living on bananas, beans, beef and monkey meat—"the sweetest and most tender of any meat I have ever eaten," said Edson.[9] They reached Bocay, a settlement of 50 thatched huts, on June 2—only to learn that a small group of rebels had passed through the town the previous day. Edson's first Coco River patrol returned to the coast.

After conferring with Feland, Utley sent Edson upriver again on a second Coco River patrol. His goal was to reach

Poteca, where Sandino's forces were reportedly concentrated. Edson started out from Bocay on July 26 with 21 Marines. It rained steadily for five days; the river rose 20 feet and became a raging terror. The Marines lived off the land and fought skirmishes with rebel bands. On August 6, when they were still a day's hike from Poteca, two OL-8 amphibians airdropped rations and mail. One pilot spotted an enemy camp 2 miles upriver, bombed and strafed it and notified Edson. The Marines, advancing in boats and through the jungle, caught the rebel party by surprise. The Marines opened a fire fight on both sides of the river; the rebels, armed with Russian-made rifles and two machine guns, gave them a tough battle. Pvt. Myer Stengel was killed (and later was awarded the Navy Cross) and four Marines were wounded; the rebels had at least 10 dead. Edson won his first Navy Cross that day.

When the Marines finally reached Poteca on August 17, Edson learned that Sandino himself had been with the rebel party the Marines had attacked and had fled after the initial bombing. But Sandino was now locked between Edson in the Coco Valley and the Marines in Nueva Segovia province to the west.

There, a 37-man Marine-Guardia patrol under Capt. Robert S. Hunter, an experienced 15-year veteran, ran into a sizable rebel band near the Bocaycito River. One Marine on point, Private Honyust, was a full-blooded American Indian—a rarity in the pre-World War II Marine Corps. The patrol drove off the enemy's advance elements but then was ambushed along a narrow jungle trail. A corporal was killed, and Hunter was mortally wounded, shot in the chest and shoulder. A young Naval Academy graduate, 2d Lt. Earl S. Piper, took command and organized a perimeter defense on Casa Hill for the night. In the morning, the Marines had to fight a 45-minute battle to break out. Captain Hunter struggled up from his stretcher to join the fight. The next day, Piper's men reached the La Flor coffee plantation and set up a strong defensive position. Hunter died there. It took a week for reinforcements led by Maj. Keller E. Rockey to reach the patrol.

There was a lull in the fighting during the Nicaraguan elections in November 1928. Some 900 Marines and sailors helped the Guardia to limit corruption and intimidation. The

Sandinistas tried to disrupt the voting; but, for the first time, the Liberals won a national election; and Gen. Jose Maria Moncada became president.

The Americans were convinced that Nicaragua could not be left on its own until a trained constabulary was established to enforce the laws. In March 1929, Col. Douglas C. McDougal took command of the Guardia and changed his predecessor's policy. He organized a Guardia battalion and put it in the field against the rebels.

The Marines assigned to train the Guardia had their hands full. There were nine mutinies in the Guardia between 1928 and 1932. On October 5, 1929, at Telpaneca, the Guardias killed their commanding officer, Marine Sgt. Lewis H. Trogler. Marine Sgt. Charles J. Levonski, a second lieutenant in the Guardia, was sent in with additional men. The garrison mutinied again and seized two Americans—Levonski and 2d Lt. James C. Rimes— and fled toward Honduras. Some of the newly arrived Guardias remained loyal and helped the two Americans escape to safety.

Early in 1929, the fighting picked up again. Patrols were ambushed and Marines killed. First Lt. Herman H. Hanneken, who had killed the rebel leader Charlemagne Peralte in Haiti 10 years earlier, captured another guerrilla chief. Hanneken's Marines had pitched camp near a small stream, and the lieutenant sent eight of his men to bathe in the creek. Wary of an ambush, Hanneken told Cpl. Roy Waddle to have four of the men stand guard while the others took their turn in the water. Suddenly, Pvt. Merle W. Rittenour, guarding the trail, saw a man approaching on a mule. The Marines leaped from the water, grabbed Springfield rifles and waited. Half asleep, his head on his chest, the rebel leader Manuel Jiron was surrounded by the Marines and taken prisoner. Since Sandino had gone to Mexico to raise money for his forces, Jiron's capture was a heavy blow to the rebels. But the guerrilla fighting went on.

As the Guardia was able to carry more of the burden, Marines were shipped out of Nicaragua. The last of the 11th Regiment left for the States on August 20, 1929. With only 2,000 Marines left in the country, the anti-guerrilla campaign became less effective than ever. The Marines' thinly spread, heavily equipped patrols did not have mobility enough to catch up with the lightly loaded, elusive rebels. In the spring of 1930, the

Marines tried to deprive them of food by dragging the local population off their farms and into concentration areas. After a couple of months, this unpopular scheme was allowed to die.

Meanwhile, Sandino had returned. Reportedly, he had found financial help in New York. On June 19, Marine planes spotted his camp with about 150 men on top of a fortified hill. The fliers blasted them. A bomb fragment wounded Sandino in the leg, and he retreated into the Coco basin's wilderness to recuperate.

The Marines followed and mounted three expeditions between August 1930 and February 1931 into the jungle area between the Coco and Bocay rivers in far northern Nicaragua. Among the most effective patrol leaders was 1st Lt. Lewis B. Puller, who had won his commission as a jungle fighter in Haiti and was now a captain in the Guardia. Puller—a native of West Point, Virginia; grandson of a Confederate cavalry officer; and cousin of George S. Patton—had attended Virginia Military Institute, and quit to enlist in the Corps in 1918. As a Gendarmerie officer in Haiti, he had led many patrols and survived many ambushes. In Nicaragua, his aggressiveness won him the label "The Tiger of the Mountains." He received his first two Navy Crosses for his fighting there. He would win three more.

Increasingly, the Americans depended on the Guardia to eliminate the rebels. In the beginning of 1931, an effort was made to enlarge the Guardia and use it entirely in the field. Realizing that the Americans, overwhelmed by the Depression at home, were tiring of the occupation, President Moncada agreed, and Marine strength was severely reduced. By June, only one battalion and the aviation units remained.

Then, in three minutes in mid-morning of March 31, an earthquake destroyed most of the city of Managua and killed an estimated 2,000 inhabitants. Two Guardia officers were among the dead. The Marines immediately went to work rescuing the injured, battling fires and taking care of the homeless. First Lt. Evans F. Carlson won the first of his three Navy Crosses for his work in the emergency as Department Commander of Managua. A stream of American aircraft brought in medicine and supplies; Marines flew the first 92 missions.

The rebels continued the sporadic guerrilla war in the northeast. Coming down the Coco River, 150 rebels led by

Pedro Blandon ambushed a Marine-Guardia patrol and killed Capt. Harlan Pefley. Two days later,.Marine aircraft spotted the rebel column; and a patrol attacked and killed Blandon and eight of his men. Responding to this new rebel activity, the garrisons at Bluefields and Puerto Cabezas were increased.

In April 1932, there was a Guardia mutiny at Kisalaya; and the commanding officer, Lt. Charles J. Levonski—who had been taken prisoner by mutineers in 1929—was shot to death.

The Guardia's worst disaster came on April 21, 1932, when the rebels ambushed a Guardia patrol led by 1st Lt. Laurin T. Covington and killed four men. First Lt. Laurence C. Brunton brought a relief column to the rescue. The rebels laid another trap; Covington and Brunton were both killed and the combined patrols, routed. Ten Guardia were killed that day.

On September 20, Lieutenant Puller set out from Jinotega with Company M, his special mobile patrol of about 40 men. While crossing a mountain stream on the twenty-sixth, they were ambushed by rebels firing machine guns and Browning automatic rifles from cover. Guardia Lt. William A. Lee, Puller's second in command, was wounded in the head and right arm. A Marine gunnery sergeant, Lee was an expert shot. While Puller directed the attack, Lee was able to pin down the enemy with a light shoulder-fired Lewis machine gun until the Guardia had climbed the ridges above the trail and could fire on the rebels. The patrol killed 16 guerrillas and suffered two dead and three wounded. To save his wounded, Puller headed back to Jinotega, some 75 miles away. Company M fought through two ambushes and arrived at base safely on the thirtieth. For this patrol, "Chesty" Puller received his second Navy Cross and "Iron Man" Lee, his third.

The Liberals won the election on November 6, 1932, and Juan B. Sacasa became president. Retiring President Moncada planned to drive the final spike in a new railroad line he had built inland 80 miles from Leon to El Sauce. It was heard that Sandino would try to destroy the line and kill Moncada; Puller volunteered to protect him. On December 26, Puller took seven Marines including Lee and 64 Guardias and entrained for El Sauce. At 4:30 P.M., they approached a construction camp a few miles short of El Sauce just as 100 guerrillas were sacking the camp. Machine-gun fire sprayed the boxcar. Mounted rebels encircled the train, firing rifles and throwing dynamite bombs. Puller's men jumped from the train with their guns blazing. Lt. Bennie M. Bunn tossed his pistol to a Guardia and took the man's BAR. He walked directly at the enemy, firing short bursts from the hip. The rebels broke. Bunn later was given the Navy Cross. Now, each force tried to flank the other, and the Guardias decimated the rebels. In 70 minutes, 32 guerrillas were killed. Three days later, Moncada formally opened the line. He promoted Puller to major and Bill Lee to captain in the Guardia on the spot.

On the evening of January 2, 1933, the day after Sacasa was inaugurated, the last elements of the 5th Regiment sailed from Corinto. The second Nicaraguan intervention was over.

The first intervention had brought Nicaragua momentary stability and discouraged European intervention, but the second was less successful. When it ended, Sandino remained at large; and the U.S. occupation had aroused many Latin Americans to a deep fury.

Before the Marines left Nicaragua, a Marine officer, writing about the Guardia, made a dire and accurate prediction: "At best, there is sure to be a shake-up in the Guardia; it will soon become a partisan force, used to further the party in power."[10] In 1934, President Sacasa granted Sandino amnesty, and the Guardia murdered him. Two years later, the Guardia's leader, Anastasio Somoza, backed by his Marine-created force, made himself president and then dictator of Nicaragua. By building native constabularies, the Marines gave strong men a strong weapon.

For the Marine Corps itself, the long, nasty, tough second Nicaraguan campaign taught ground troops and fliers to operate together and introduced such World War II leaders as Edson, Puller, Carlson, Rowell and Schilt to jungle fighting. In another decade, that introduction would pay off.

6
Haiti

The intervention in Haiti was the Marines' longest and perhaps least effective. Certainly, it was one of the most severely criticized. It began at 5:50 P.M. on July 28, 1915, when two companies of Marines and three of sailors landed at the navy yard at Bizoton, three miles from Port-au-Prince, the Haitian capital. It ended 19 years later on August 15, 1934, with the withdrawal of the 1st Marine Brigade.

When the Marines arrived at Bizoton, they marched into chaos. The day before, 162 of 167 political prisoners in the National Penitentiary had been slaughtered on the order of President Vilbrun Gjuillaume Sam. The next morning, an aroused mob stormed the French Legation where President Sam had taken refuge and hacked his body to pieces. Another crowd entered the Dominican Legation and shot to death the prison's commanding officer. That evening, the Marines, led by Capt. George O. Van Orden, landed, marched on the capital, suffered some casualties, placed guards at various foreign legations and took charge of the city.

Haiti, which lies 48 miles east of Cuba and occupies the western third of the island of Hispaniola, had been a French colony. The French had imported more than a million African slaves to work the sugar plantations; the slaves drove out the whites and created the second independent nation in the Western Hemisphere, ruled by a succession of cruel and corrupt military dictators, each in turn replaced in a bloody revolt.

By 1910, the country was heavily indebted to American, French and German bankers. The creditors formed the Banque Nationale, a private bank, to act as the government treasury. By the end of 1914. the government was broke and revenues had

175

shrunk. President Woodrow Wilson wanted a stable government in Haiti and proposed steps to ensure financial recovery. The Haitian Senate laughed.

There were rumors that the Haitian government would seize the Banque Nationale's gold reserve. Such reports were surely believable. Nervously, the National City Bank of New York, which was backing the Haitian bank at the urging of the U.S. Department of State, arranged with the government in Washington to have the gold secretly transferred to New York. Sixty-five Marines under Maj. Charles B. Hatch snatched it. They arrived aboard *USS Machias* on December 17, brought $500,000 in gold on board and left immediately for New York. The 5th Marine Regiment was aboard *USS Hancock* in Haitian waters, standing by in case of trouble.

By March 4, 1915, General Sam had led a "caco" army to Port-au-Prince and had himself named President. "Caco" is an ambiguous term. What it means depends on the eye of the beholder: revolutionary, mercenary, bandit. A caco, usually a poor peasant, was a member of an organized group that, either out of loyalty or for pay, supported a Haitian political or military leader. The cacos were the Marines' enemy in Haiti, and Marine officers like Smedley Butler used the word interchangeably with "bandit." In any case, the cacos were the men who fought the American occupation for two decades.

President Sam brought a brief interlude of quiet to Haiti; but in less than four months, another wave of revolution inundated the country. This one was led by red-headed Dr. Rosalvo Bobo, who typically went to northern Haiti near the Dominican border and gathered caco support. On June 19, the French landed men at Cap Haitien, the nation's second largest city, to protect their citizens; and Rear Adm. William B. Caperton, USN, arrived on July 1 and took charge of the port. President Wilson did not want Germany or anyone else to move in and exploit Haiti's weakness. Europe was already at war, and Germany had repeatedly demonstrated its interest in a foothold in Haiti.

Meanwhile, Bobo's revolution had broken out in Port-au-Prince, and Caperton rushed over on July 28 to try to put out the fire. There, he learned of the massacre in the prison the day before and the mob violence sweeping the capital. He received orders to land troops and promptly did so. It was the beginning of a long stay for the Marines.

Caperton also put out a call for Marines from Guantanamo; and by the next afternoon, the 24th Company arrived and went ashore. Americans and Haitians clashed on July 30, and two sailors were killed. Within 24 hours, five companies of the 2d Marine Regiment left Philadelphia, led by Col. Eli K. Cole, and arrived on August 4. They eased the tension in the capital. Marines landed at Cap Haitien; and in Port-au-Prince, Caperton occupied Fort Nationale and ordered all Haitian soldiers out of the city. Some resisted, and two Haitians were killed.

A struggle for power now raged between Bobo and Philippe Sudre Dartiguenave, the presiding officer of the Haitian Senate who was willing to accept U.S. domination. Bobo's forces, anticipating that the Haitian Congress would elect his opponent, threatened to use guns to prevent that body from meeting. Marines were sent in; they stood by while the legislature elected Dartiguenave as president.

The price for American armed support was a ten-year treaty that put Haiti's customs under U.S. control and provided for a constabulary to be led by American officers. The treaty was renewable for another ten years on demand by either side. It gave the intervention the smell of legitimacy.

Marines kept arriving; by the end of August, the 1st Brigade of Marines had 88 officers and 1,941 men garrisoning ten towns. Colonel Waller now commanded all American forces ashore.

But the cacos in the north, opposing the government shored up by Americans, were far from finished. They skirmished with the Americans at the port of Gonaives early in September. Learning that the Gonaives Marine garrison was besieged, Maj. Smedley D. Butler and Lt. Alexander A. Vandegrift sped there in a small boat; and Butler led the local Marine detachment, the 7th Company, in pushing the cacos out of town. That evening, Butler heard the rebels were burning the railroad, and he turned out the men, still in their underwear. They raced down the street to the railroad and lit into the rebels. "It was the funniest fight I ever saw," Butler reported later.[11] Butler took 50 mounted men and pursued the enemy. He caught up with the rebel general and, as Butler told the story, pulled him off his horse and forced him to surrender.

Butler pushed an aggressive campaign to snuff out the cacos opposition. He wrote much later, "A lot of north Haiti was burned before we got through."[12]

At Cap Haitien, where Colonel Cole commanded the 1st Battalion, 1st Marines,* the cacos began cutting off the food supply and practically encircled the city. Cole tried to persuade their chiefs to put down their weapons but had little success. As a show of force, he sent out strong patrols of Marines. A five-squad patrol commanded by Capt. F. A. Barker was fired on. When two other Marine patrols fought their way through to support Barker, the cacos surrounded the combined Marine force. Cole brought in sailors from *Connecticut* to take over guarding the city while he led out the rest of the Marines to join the fight. The cacos fought well enough to win the Marines' respect but were finally driven off, leaving 40 dead on the field. Ten Marines were wounded.

A disturbance was reported at Petite Riviere de l'Artibonite further south, and half a company of mounted Marines was sent out from St. Marc. In a fight with the cacos on September 26, Sgt. John Platt of the 24th Company was killed—the first Marine to die in action in Haiti. (In front of the Marine barracks at Guantanamo, there is a plaque honoring Sergeant Platt.)

Now, Waller came north with the 11th Company, landed at Fort Liberte and marched to Ouanaminthe near the Dominican border. This area had been the seedbed of many Haitian revolutions, and Waller stationed Marine garrisons at the frontier town and at Fort Liberte.

More Marines were poured into the northern areas that the cacos dominated. Cole and Butler moved their headquarters inland to the town of Grande Riviere du Nord and sent out strong patrols. Butler took a mounted detachment of 40 veteran Marines on a deep reconnaissance into the mountains. After dark on October 24, while his command was leading its horses across a river in a deep ravine near little Fort Dipite, it was ambushed from three sides. Twelve horses were killed. The Marines fought their way to a defensible position a mile away.

---

*U.S. Marine regiments are referred to as 1st Marines, 4th Marines, etc.; Army regiments are referred to as 1st Infantry, etc. Although this form did not come into common use until the 1930s, it is used consistently in this book after World War I. The first permanent Marine Corps regiments were organized in 1913.

Their only machine gun had been lost in the river. Gunnery Sgt. Daniel J. "Fighting Dan" Daly stole back on his own and, under fire, recovered the gun from the back of a dead horse. All night, the cacos kept up a poorly aimed fire; the Marines returned it only when the enemy closed in. At daybreak, squads led by Capt. William P. Upshur, 1st Lt. Edward A. Ostermann and Gunnery Sgt. Daly moved out in three directions and chased off the cacos. Upshur and Ostermann with 13 Marines then took Fort Dipite, and burned it and the houses nearby. Upshur, Ostermann and Daly received the Medal of Honor. It was the hard-boiled sergeant's second; his first had been earned at Peking as a private 15 years before. He would be decorated again in France.

Throughout the next weeks, the Marines pressed after the Haitians; the enemy repeatedly fought and fled. The cacos were driven back into their final retreat, an "impregnable" old French masonry fort called Fort Riviere, on a mountain top south of Grande Riviere du Nord.

During the night of November 17, a strong force of Marines and sailors surrounded the fort. At 7:50 A.M., Major Butler blew a whistle and all units attacked. They took the cacos totally by surprise. Some of the rebels tried to leap the walls and were mowed down by the Marines' automatic Benet rifles. The Marines of the 15th Company, led by Capt. W. W. Low and accompanied by Butler, made their final rush across rocky bare ground and reached the opening in the fort's wall. They found the tunnel was four feet high and three wide; only one man could enter at a time. The Marines flattened themselves against the wall. Sgt. Ross L. Iams said, "Oh, hell, I'm going through," and was the first man in, followed quickly by Butler's diminutive orderly, Pvt. Samuel Gross (real name: Samuel Marguiles). Butler was the third man in. More Marines crawled through; and a wild, hand-to-hand struggle was underway with rifles, bayonets, machetes, clubs and rocks. In 15 minutes, more than 50 cacos were killed. Butler blew up the fort. Iams, Gross and Butler received the Medal of Honor. It was Butler's second; he had earned his first at Vera Cruz the year before. Daly and Butler are the only Marines ever to receive the Medal of Honor for two separate actions.

The ferocity of Waller's campaign in the north was condemned in Washington, and the Marines were ordered to limit their activities to protecting peaceful inhabitants and themselves. Fewer encounters followed, and two years of relative peace began. Still, on January 5, 1916, 75 cacos attacked the Marine provost marshal's building at Port-au-Prince. Seven armed Marines and ten gendarmes armed only with clubs chased off the attackers.

On February 1, Rear Adm. Caperton issued a proclamation that the Gendarmerie d'Haiti would assume all military and police duties and the Marine brigade would be held in support. By autumn, most of the Marines had been withdrawn. Just before the United States entered World War I, three more companies were pulled out to help form the 5th Marines for duty in France. About 600 Marines were left in Haiti.

By the time the Marines had finished this first phase of their Haitian intervention, public opinion in the black republic was vigorously anti-American. The occupation could not be expected to "win the hearts and minds" of the Haitians; and there were enough cases of American incompetence, insensitivity and even brutality to enflame opposition.

To supplant Haiti's inefficient and corrupt political leaders, Americans took over the main executive posts of the government: customs, public works, public sanitation, agriculture and the Gendarmerie d'Haiti. Friction was constant and exacerbated by the division of American rule between civilian appointees of the President of the United States and the Marines.

In the meanwhile, the Marine-officered Gendarmerie was taking over much of the job of keeping the peace. From the beginning, recruitment for the Gendarmerie was difficult because the Haitian police were universally hated. Training was complicated by the language gap: none of the recruits knew English and the Marines knew no Creole and little French.

Smedley Butler had been put in charge of organizing the Gendarmerie on December 3, 1915, with "the imposing rank of major general."[13] A total of 120 Marines served as officers—captains as colonels in the Gendarmerie, first lieutenants as majors, second lieutenants as captains and noncoms as first lieutenants. By the time Washington ratified the treaty with Haiti early in 1916, Butler had in being a constabulary with 1,500 enlisted men garrisoning 117 posts.

The gendarmes' first test came in March, when the cacos made a number of attacks on their new posts in the north. Before dawn on March 3, at Cerca-la-Source near the Dominican border, a Gendarmerie detachment was routed in a surprise attack and abandoned its arms and equipment to the cacos. When Krag-Jörgensen carbines started arriving for the gendarmes, they gave a better account of themselves. And their numbers increased, so that a year later they totaled 2,533 Haitians and 115 Americans.

Tests of 1,200 gendarmes revealed that 95 percent had syphilis, and many had hookworm and other diseases. Partly for this reason, in the early days gendarmes on guard or sentry duty almost invariably fell asleep at their posts. Medical treatment greatly alleviated the problem.

The Gendarmerie worked, under Butler's direction, at cleaning up the cities, overseeing the repair of telegraph lines, improving irrigation projects and taking charge of road building with forced labor. The so-called "corvee system" of forced labor quickly became a source of bitterness. Local officials used the system to get rich, and some gendarmes accepted bribes to excuse men from the road-gang lists. When the Marines had arrived, Haiti had been virtually roadless. Using forced labor, they built and repaired 630 miles of road; and by the end of 1917, an automobile could travel the 180 miles from the capital to Cap Haitien in 14 hours, a trip that had taken three days on horseback.

An effort was made to recruit and train Haitians as officers for the Gendarmerie, but the program failed because all young Haitians of "good families" who signed up found the instruction and duty onerous and unpopular and soon resigned.

When the United States entered World War I, Brig. Gen. Eli K. Cole, who had replaced Waller as Marine brigade commander, faced a new National Assembly extremely hostile to American domination. The legislature refused to accept American proposals for revising the Haitian constitution in order to give renewed legality to the occupation. (Later, it developed that the American version of the new constitution had been drafted by Assistant Secretary of the Navy Franklin D. Roosevelt. This became a political issue; and in the 1920 U.S. election campaign, the Republican Presidential candidate, Warren G. Harding, declared: "If I am elected I will not empower any Assistant Secretary of Navy to draft a constitution for helpless neighbors and jam it down their throats at the point of bayonets borne by United States Marines."[14])

The conflict with the Haitian legislature reached a climax on June 19, 1917, when the National Assembly was pushing through a constitution unacceptable to Washington. Cole instructed Butler, in his capacity as "a Haitian officer," to stop it. Butler rushed to President Dartiguenave and insisted he send his chauffeur to round up two cabinet members. They reluctantly signed a decree dissolving the legislature.

No Haitian would dare take the President's decree to the legislature, so Butler went himself. He was greeted with loud hissing. The gendarmes on duty cocked their rifles. Butler ordered them to put down their weapons. He handed the decree to the presiding officer, who, instead of reading it to the delegates, began a tirade against it. The hall was in an uproar. Tables and chairs were thrown over, deputies shouted and surged forward. The gendarmes again prepared to shoot. Finally, the presiding officer rang a bell for order and read the decree, declared the Assembly dissolved and directed the hall cleared. The gendarmes locked the doors. Butler grabbed the decree and stuffed it in his pocket. He would use it later in a U.S. Senate hearing when his opponents charged that the president's decree had never existed.

The constitution in the form desired by the United States was presented to a plebiscite without public discussion and under Gendarmerie supervision. The Gendarmerie had orders to turn out a large vote in favor of the constitution, but less than 100,000 votes were cast. Only 769 were negative, and even some of those were dubious. The whole procedure was "in essence farcical."[15]

A new era of guerrilla warfare began on October 11, 1917, when the cacos were rising against the corvee or forced-labor system. They attacked the home of Capt. John L. Doxey, commanding the Gendarmerie district of Hinche in the heart of the mountains of central Haiti. The gendarmes easily beat off the attack, killed the cacos' leader and captured their second in command. He implicated three Peralte brothers, who lived near Hinche. Two brothers were arrested and tried by Marine Corps provost courts. One was acquitted; but Charlemagne Peralte was sentenced to five years of hard labor and put to work sweeping the streets of Cap Haitien. This humiliation enflamed European-educated Charlemagne Peralte's hatred of the Gendarmerie and its Marine leaders—a hatred that would last until his death.

On September 3, 1918, Peralte escaped to the hills. Although Col. Alexander S. Williams, now chief of the Gendarmerie, ordered the corvee abolished the following month, Peralte soon gathered several thousand followers and became the most effective caco leader to fight the Marines. Peralte commanded in the north; his assistant, Benoit Batraville, directed the cacos in the center of the country. They operated in scattered groups and attacked Gendarmerie detachments to seize rifles and ammunition. A hundred cacos struck Hinche on October 17, and the gendarmes led by Gendarmerie Lt. Patrick F. Kelly, a courageous Marine first sergeant, killed 35 in an hour's battle. On November 10, the Marine Corps' 143rd birthday, Peralte and some 60 cacos raided the town of Maissade, northwest of Hinche. They burned the Gendarmerie barracks and other buildings, and robbed the city hall.

The fighting went on sporadically; and after the end of the war in Europe, Marine Corps morale in Haiti dropped. Many officers in the wartime-expanded Corps were inexperienced, and enlisted men assigned to the Caribbean felt that they had missed the big show and resented having to stay in service after the Armistice in Europe. Enemy activity increased, and the Marines in Haiti came in for severe criticism.

Cacos ambushed gendarme patrols, killed gendarmes repairing telephone lines, and made a major attack on Cerca-la-Source. There, now-Captain Kelly, the gendarme commander, escaped death when one of his men shielded him from enemy fire. The Haitian who saved him lost an arm and a leg.

Marine Sgt. Nicholas B. Moskoff, a lieutenant in the Gendarmerie, and five of his men were ambushed at Dufailly by a large force of cacos on March 21, 1919. Moskoff was mortally wounded in the spine by the first volley. Taking the wounded Marine with them, his gendarmes fought a two-hour retreating battle. Moskoff's Haitian second-in-command was killed, and the men saw the cacos chop off his head with a machete. Moskoff was the first Gendarmerie officer killed.

The cacos became too strong for the Gendarmerie to handle

alone. In March, 1919, the Marine Brigade, now commanded by Brig. Gen. Albertus W. Catlin, who had been wounded at Belleau Wood, was reinforced from Guantanamo; and the 4th Marine Air Squadron (VO-9M) brought in the first 13 planes. Lt. Lawson H. M. Sanderson was one of the earliest pilots to experiment with low-level glide bombing. Combined Marine-Gendarmerie patrols were constantly in the field. In July, Col. Frederic M. Wise, another Belleau Wood veteran, became the third chief of the Gendarmerie, commanding 2,500 Haitians and 112 Marines serving as officers.

Peralte was getting supplies from Port-au-Prince; and, as his weapons improved, his attacks became more effective and more vicious. On October 7, he and 300 men dared invade the capital itself. Alerted by a warning of the cacos' approach, the Marines and gendarmes drove them from the city. The next day, the gendarmes assaulted Peralte's camp 15 miles from Port-au-Prince and scattered his men.

Twenty-six-year-old Marine Sgt. Herman H. Hanneken, a captain in the Gendarmerie, plotted to capture or kill Peralte. The tall blond Marine had started to become a priest, wandered West, worked as a cowpuncher and finally joined the Corps. He now arranged for two loyal Haitian civilians and a gendarme to denounce the American occupation and establish themselves as caco chiefs at Fort Capois, five hours into the interior from Grande Riviere du Nord. Hanneken's three "secret agents" attracted a large number of followers and were visited by emissaries from Peralte. The leader of the three, a well-to-do Haitian named Jean B. Conze, risked his life repeatedly by coming into town to report to Hanneken. The Marine faked several attacks on Fort Capois and once returned to Grande Riviere du Nord with his arm in a sling, pretending to have been wounded in battle. He then sent off part of his detachment to Cap Haitien and let it be known that his weakened force feared a cacos attack on Grande Riviere du Nord.

Conze urged Peralte to attack the town. Peralte agreed and with a thousand men arrived at Fort Capois on Sunday, October 26, 1919, to plan the assault. They decided to strike on Friday night, October 31. Peralte himself would wait at Mazare a half hour away and, after the expected victory, would enter the town triumphantly.

Marines led by Maj. James J. Meade secretly strengthened the garrison at Grande Riviere de Nord with men and a machine gun during the night before the attack. Hanneken and twenty-three-year-old Marine Cpl. William R. Button, a first lieutenant in the Gendarmerie, their faces blackened and with 20 well-armed gendarmes in dirty, old civilian clothes, went to Mazare.

Peralte did not show up. About 10 P.M., Hanneken's gendarme "deserter," Pvt. Jean Edmond Francois, appeared and reported that Peralte had changed his mind; he would await the outcome of the battle on top of a hill between Fort Capois and Grande Riviere. When the town was taken, Conze, who was leading the attack, would send back to Peralte the code message "General Jean."

Hanneken decided that he, Button and their men would bring Peralte the "good news." Led by Francois, they hiked for three hours and passed Peralte's first outpost with the countersign. Francois, who was well known to the cacos, went ahead to Peralte and was instructed to bring the news-bearing detachment to him. Hanneken's group had to pass six more outposts. Francois led the way, followed by Hanneken armed with two revolvers and Button carrying a Browning automatic rifle. The disguised gendarmes were armed with carbines and carried their ammunition in straw sacks.

They passed the first four outposts successfully but were stopped at the fifth. Hanneken, pretending exhaustion, stepped by the sentry; but the commander of the outpost questioned Button about his BAR, until Button pulled away, saying he had to keep up with his leader.

At the final guardpost, Peralte stood over a fire talking with a woman. Francois dropped back, and Hanneken and Button moved within 15 feet of Peralte. Hanneken said, "All right!" and, as Peralte tried to get away, shot him twice in the chest with his .45. Button cleared the camp with his Browning.

The gendarmes took positions to ward off counterattacks and remained on the hilltop until daybreak. Then they slung Peralte's body on a mule, and, fighting off caco attacks, returned to Grande Riviere du Nord.

Meanwhile, Major Meade and his men had thrown back the caco assault on the town. The next day, the Marines and Hanneken went to Fort Capois to destroy the cacos there.

Hanneken's gendarmes were to hit the fort at daybreak, while the Marines struck from the other side. But long after the appointed hour, the Marines still had not attacked; and caco guards spotted Hanneken's force. His men came under heavy rifle and cannon fire. They crawled on their stomachs without concealment toward the fort. The cacos finally fled before the Marine detachment arrived to prevent their escape. During the next week, more than 300 cacos surrendered to Hanneken.

The two St. Louis-born Marines, Hanneken and Button, were awarded the Medal of Honor for "extraordinary heroism." Young Button died at Cap Haitien of malaria. Hanneken killed another rebel leader the next April, for which he received the Navy Cross; was commissioned in 1920; fought in Nicaragua and World War II, and retired as a brigadier general. A silent, cold-eyed Marine, he was widely known as "Hard Head" and "Haiti" Hanneken.

Peralte's death ended the caco uprising in the north; but his assistant, Benoit Batraville, continued the cacos movement in the mountains of central Haiti. He gathered some 2,500 men, and part of his force raided the town of La Chapelle. With the new year, Col. John H. Russell, now the Marine brigade commander, opened a campaign against him. The Marine brigade numbered 1,344 men and the aviation squadron, and the Gendarmerie, 2,700. Russell and hard-driving Lt. Col. Louis McC. Little, who had fought Aguinaldo and the Boxers, instituted a system of rotating patrols, so that, as one tired, the next would take over and keep constant pressure on the rebels. On the night of January 14, 1920, Batraville boldly sent 300 men to attack Port-au-Prince. Although the assault was especially well executed, half the cacos were killed, wounded or captured.

On April 4, a patrol of Marines and gendarmes led by Marine Sgt. Lawrence Muth, a lieutenant in the Gendarmerie who had come to Haiti with his friend "Chesty" Puller, was ambushed while climbing a narrow trail near Las Cahobas. Muth and Marine Private Stone were hit immediately. The patrol retreated, leaving Muth, whom the men erroneously thought dead, lying at the ambush.

A Marine patrol led by Lt. Col. Little recovered Muth's body. His heart had been cut out and his head severed. The

Marines learned that Batraville had been at the scene of the ambush and had used his machete on Muth.

On May 18, a patrol of 29 Marines led by Capt. Jesse L. Perkins and Sgt. William F. Passmore attacked Batraville's camp. Passmore, with an automatic rifle, was the first man into the camp, followed by Perkins and two other Marines. There stood Batraville. He fired at the sergeant and Passmore shot him. The main body of the patrol, led by 2d Lt. Edgar G. Kirkpatrick, dispersed the remaining enemy. Sgt. Albert A. Taubert saw Batraville trying to get up and killed him with his revolver. Batraville's rifle had belonged to Gunnery Sgt. Dan Daly; it had been taken in the cacos' last attack on Port-au-Prince; Batraville's pistol had been issued to Sergeant Muth. With Batraville's death, the caco movement was destroyed.

The end of World War I had already eliminated the rationale that the Marine occupation was needed to counter the threat of a German invasion of the Caribbean. And with the end of the caco resistance, there was peace in Haiti. But the Marines stayed.

The Marine Corps occupation was severely criticized. The Marines were accused of trying civilians over whom they had no jurisdiction, even under martial law. They were attacked for being unwilling to turn over control of public works in their charge. In some cases, individual Marines dealt with Haitians corruptly and handled them brutally. The prejudice of some against blacks also damaged relations between the Corps and the Haitians. Over the long occupation, there were individual cases of drunkenness, rape, torture to get information and the shooting of escaping prisoners.

A first-hand study by Dr. Carl Kelsey, Professor of Sociology at the University of Pennsylvania, while acknowledging that such criticisms were well-founded, went on to say:

> On the whole I feel that the men of the Marine Corps deserve our respect. . . . there were many more acts of kindness than of cruelty. The good things have not been advertised to the world. Day after day I have talked with officers and men who are bending all their energies towards helping the Haitians. I have seen peasants going

187

out of their way to call on and bring presents to men who have been stationed in their communities.[16]

But Dr. Kelsey was highly critical of the corvee, saying, "In my opinion this was the greatest mistake made by the Marine Corps in Haiti."[17]

In 1921–1922, two investigations were made into the conduct of the Marines in Haiti. A naval court of inquiry, consisting of Marine Maj. Gen. Wendell C. Neville and two admirals, visited the island and concluded that there had been a "small number of isolated crimes or offenses that have been committed by a few individuals." In one terrible and explosive case, a Marine private, a lieutenant in the Gendarmerie, and two other Marines got drunk, made two Haitians dig their own graves and shot them. But the court said that charges of practically indiscriminate killing of natives were not warranted. This finding was attacked as a whitewash, and Haiti was visited by a Select Committee of the U.S. Senate. The Committee took months of testimony and reported that most of the incidents that could be confirmed apparently resulted from the failure of superior officers to keep full control of subordinates, especially when they were patrolling or stationed in remote areas. The Committee felt that there was an important lesson to be learned from the charges of misconduct in the "bandit campaign": "The lesson is the extreme importance in a campaign of this kind for higher command to require daily operations reports to be prepared by patrol leaders. In the early days of the outbreak such reports were not systematically required."[18]

The Senate Committee also condemned the lack of coordination among the various elements of the occupation administration that reported to different departments in Washington. The Committee recommended that one man be given overall responsibility for the entire occupation. As a result, early in 1922, Brig. Gen. John H. Russell, commander of the 1st Marine Brigade, was appointed United States High Commissioner to Haiti with the rank of ambassador. But by then authority would have been better placed in the hands of a civilian administrator.

The Gendarmerie was beginning to overcome its failure to handle the caco revolt and its reputation for exacting tribute from the people. It was able to improve its arms and equipment:

the Marine Corps lent it 4,000 Springfield rifles. And over the next few years, the better Haitian families' opposition to their sons entering the service relaxed. Suitable officer recruits underwent a two-year course of training; and by 1926, 53 Haitian officers were on duty. The Marines instilled in the Gendarmerie their own pride in rifle marksmanship; and in the 1924 Olympic Games, Haiti tied France for second place, outshot only by the United States team.

Most of the 1920s were years of peace in Haiti. The brigade was reduced to little more than 500, and it was used to back up the Gendarmerie.

It was also the era of a romantic Marine Corps story. The Gendarmerie had taken charge of the island of La Gonave in the bay of Port-au-Prince. In 1925, Marine Sgt. Faustin E. Wirkus, a young ex-miner from Pittston, Pa., was made commander of the gendarmes on the island. He was well known for having killed the caco leaders Estraville and Olivier while leading patrols in the Haitian mountains. As the man responsible for the island's 12,000 impoverished inhabitants, Wirkus took a deep interest in their well-being and ruled for almost four years with nearly absolute power. He was widely written about as the "White King of La Gonave."

In 1928, the Gendarmerie's name was changed to the Garde d'Haiti to reflect its military as well as police duties. By then, it had about 200 officers and 2,600 enlisted men, and 46 percent of its officers in the grade of captain and below were Haitian.

The following year, the Marines had to deal with the last major crisis of the Haitian intervention. By now, Louis Borno had been president of Haiti since 1922, and there was a spreading demand for popular elections. But Borno announced that there would be no election in 1930 and that the president would again be chosen by the appointed Council of State, which had replaced the legislature dissolved in 1917 with Smedley Butler's help.

In this atmosphere of political tension, on October 31, 1929, 200 students from the agricultural college outside Port-au-Prince marched on the capital to protest the reduction of the allowance paid them for attending school. The strike spread; and in mid-December, protesting students, now 20,000 strong, were joined by government employees. There were violent clashes with the authorities and arrests. At Cayes, 20 Marines commanded by Capt. Roy C. Swink routed with machine-gun fire 1,500 peasants armed with machetes and clubs. The Marines fired over their heads. The crowd advanced again. The Marines killed six and wounded 28. In other towns, mobs were handled without gunfire. Martial law was invoked and the crisis finally quieted down.

President Herbert Hoover appointed a commission of prominent citizens to examine the United States' Haitian policy. After 17 days in Haiti, the Forbes Commission reported to the President on March 26, 1930. It praised Brig. Gen. Russell's efforts and the material progress that had been achieved. It recommended that the Marine brigade be gradually phased out of Haiti and that all the government services be rapidly turned over to Haitians. Hoover adopted the commission's recommendations. They were popular in both the United States and in Haiti, although many Haitians would have preferred the immediate removal of the Marines.

In May, Borno resigned and left Haiti. In November, elections were held, and the new National Assembly named Stenio Vincent as president. Russell was replaced by a civilian American minister. The Garde d'Haiti's American officers were withdrawn on August 1, 1934; and on the fifteenth, the 1st Marine Brigade departed from Haiti. The long occupation was over. In 1958, a Marine Corps mission came back to Haiti for five years to help the dictator François "Papa Doc" Duvalier strengthen his army.

7
The Dominican Republic

The third major Marine intervention in the Caribbean began in the spring of 1916 while Europe was aflame. President Wilson feared for American security in the area; the government of the Dominican Republic had quit and left the little country, sharing the island of Hispaniola with Haiti, awash with trouble.

The Dominican Republic, known earlier as Santo Domingo, had been torn apart by political fighting for more than 70 years. In 1904, with the country virtually bankrupt, Theodore Roosevelt had forced the Dominicans to allow the United States to collect their customs duties and pay off their creditors. His aggressive action became the model for U.S. imperialism in the Caribbean. In 1911, 750 Marines of the 2d Provisional Regiment sat in their ships off the Dominican coast for two months, while American commissioners tried to arrange political stability and peace.

On May 5, 1916, when political factions were battling in the capital, Santo Domingo city, 150 men of the 6th and 9th Companies of Marines under Capt. Frederic M. "Fritz" Wise came over from Haiti to guard the American and Haitian legations. The next day, the Dominican president resigned. By May 15, a battalion of Marines under Maj. Newt H. Hall (who had been at Peking) and a battalion of sailors entered the city and manned the key points of the capital. There was no resistance, but the Dominicans were angry and sullen.

Marines kept pouring in. Col. Theodore P. Kane arrived with three more companies and took command. By the end of May, 750 Marines were ashore. On the north coast at Puerto Plata, where anti-government rebels ruled, Marine guards of several ships and a naval detachment, all under Maj. Charles B.

191

Hatch, landed in the face of heavy rifle fire on June 1. Naval gunfire drove the Dominicans from their positions; and, with the sailors leading, the Americans took one of the two forts defending the city. Marine Capt. Herbert J. Hirshinger was mortally wounded. The rebels retreated southward. Further west along the northern coast, Marines and sailors led by Captain Wise landed on the morning of May 26 and took Monte Cristi; a counterattack was repulsed later with devastating machine-gun fire.

Col. Joseph H. Pendleton arrived with the 4th Marines from San Diego and took command of all U.S. forces ashore. He landed the regiment at Monte Cristi and prepared to advance up the Zaza River valley 75 miles to Santiago, where the rebels had set up a government. On June 26, leaving 235 Marines at Monte Cristi, he led 837 men toward Santiago. At the same time, the 4th and 9th companies left Puerto Plata to meet Pendleton inland at Navarette and jointly attack Santiago. The United States government was prepared to fight to suppress anti-American power in the Dominican Republic.

Pendleton pushed ahead for 24 miles and early on the second morning faced two fortified ridges called Las Trencheras, a position the Dominicans had long regarded as invulnerable. It was now held by a strong rebel force in two lines across the Marines' route of march. At 8 A.M., the regiment attacked. A battery of artillery bombarded the enemy; a machine-gun company protected the artillery's flank. Under covering fire, the regiment moved up. It was stopped. The two Marine battalions were not working well together. But Maj. Robert H. Dunlap, Pendleton's chief of staff, took command of some of the front-line units and led a bayonet charge which drove the rebels from their first line of trenches. Accurate Marine rifle fire dislodged them from the second trenches near the crest of the second ridge. The 45-minute battle cost the Marines one dead and four wounded. It was the first fight in which the Marines had attacked with modern artillery and machine-gun support.

After Las Trencheras, the going continued to be heavy. Roads were virtually impassable; bridges had to be repaired. Pendleton advanced 10 miles, and that night the rebels attacked the Marine camp and were driven off. On July 3, the Marines charged a large entrenched force of rebels blocking the road at

Guayacanas; one corporal was killed and ten privates were wounded. First Sgt. Roswell Winans and Cpl. Joseph A. Glowin won the Medal of Honor. Glowin of the Artillery Battalion kept firing his Colt machine rifle after he was wounded, and Winans cleared a jammed gun while exposed to enemy fire. Capt. Julian C. Smith led the 6th Company to fight off a rebel attack on the supply train. Pendleton reached Navarette the next day.

Meanwhile, the two companies from Puerto Plata headed for Navarette by railroad. They skirmished with the enemy. Lt. Col. Hiram I. Bearss, the veteran of Samar, brought up the Marine detachment from *New Jersey* and took command of the "railroad battalion."

At Alta Mira, the rebels held a ridge pierced by a railroad tunnel. On a handcar, Bearss led 60 men through the tunnel to cut the enemy's escape; but the rebels fled and avoided the trap. There is a Marine Corps story of Bearss standing atop a trench in a hail of bullets, yelling at a private who stuck up his head: "Get down, you damn fool! You'll get shot."[19]

Bearss joined Pendleton at Navarette on July 4. The next day, a peace delegation came out from Santiago and met with Pendleton. The following afternoon, the Marines peacefully marched into the city. They occupied towns around Santiago and rounded up rebel leaders.

By fall, 47 Marine officers and 1,738 enlisted men were in the Dominican Republic; they were organized as the 2d Brigade. The country's temporary president insisted on holding general elections in November. The Americans opposed the idea because they feared the chief rebel leader, Desiderio Arias, would win and damage American interests.

There were violent clashes between Marines and Dominicans around the capital. The result was that the State Department, with President Wilson's approval, imposed a military government on November 29. The United States would take over the country's entire administration—a step more radical than those taken elsewhere in the Caribbean. The military governor, Capt. Harry S. Knapp, USN, established strict censorship and forbade the traditional carrying of firearms. In protest, Dominican cabinet members and officials refused to serve in the military government. Knapp had to appoint Americans to all the important administrative posts. Pendleton headed the Departments of War, Navy, Interior and Police, and Col. Rufus H. Lane, USMC, ran the Departments of Foreign Relations, Justice and Public Administration.

In the north, east of Santiago, Governor Juan Perez refused to submit to the American occupiers. At San Francisco de Macoris, twenty-nine-year-old 1st Lt. Ernest C. Williams from Broadwell, Illinois, commanded 125 Marines. He feared that the local Dominican garrison would release the hundred prisoners held in the Fortaleza. As soon as he learned of the establishment of military government, Williams decided to seize the fort. Immediately taking with him the dozen Marines available, he rushed its open gate. Before they could reach it, eight of his men were cut down by rifle fire. Williams threw himself against the gate, just as it was being closed, and forced his way in. His pistol jammed. Drummer Schovan jumped in front of him and grabbed the rifle of a Dominican about to fire at the lieutenant point-blank. Williams and his four Marines killed two guards and quickly took control of the prison and prisoners. Williams received the Medal of Honor for his daring.

With many well-armed followers, Governor Perez fled south by train. Several Marine detachments were sent after them; they fought a few skirmishes but could never close with the rebels.

Brig. Gen. Pendleton's 2d Marine Brigade provided muscle for the American military government. The Marines fought a guerrilla war against organized rebel groups and tried to disarm the populace. Disarming proved difficult and unpopular; the Marines made house-to-house searches and used strong-arm methods, trying to neutralize the opposition to their occupation.

During the first half of 1917, a hundred patrols went out after the rebels. "Hiking Hiram" Bearss made a colorful reputation pursuing (with shirttail flying) and fighting a rebel leader known as Chacha. Chacha and three of his men surrendered, but the rest continued the war under Vincentico Evangelista. Late in March, a patrol led by Capt. R. S. Kingsbury was attacked by the rebels; it killed 15 and wounded a number of them, including Evangelista. In June, Evangelista was persuaded by First Sgt. William West to surrender with 200 of his men to Lt. Col. George Thorpe. (Thorpe had been a hero of Novaleta in the Philippines and in 1903 had led 19 Marines on a daring 500-mile trek into Abyssinia to escort the first U.S. diplomatic mission to Addis Ababa.) Shortly after Evangelista surrendered, he was killed "while attempting to escape."[20] With his death, the rebels' strength was broken and the fighting subsided.

But occasional clashes continued, and it was believed that German agents were arming the rebels and fanning the Dominican people's hatred of the American occupation. Once the United States entered World War I, most of the best officers left for France. Many of the Marines who remained were poorly trained and disgruntled with their assignment. At times, Dominican civilians were collected into the towns while the rebels lay waste the countryside. Frequently, the rebels ambushed Marine patrols. Marines succumbed to malaria and dengue fever and sometimes to corruption and misuse of their power. It was hard, boring and often dangerous duty.

One fight in particular became famous in the Marine Corps. Near the town of Manchado, a mounted patrol of four Marines led by Cpl. Bascome Breedon was ambushed while crossing a stream on August 13, 1918. The Marines killed a number of the enemy; but one by one, they were cut down. The last Marine alive, Pvt. Thomas J. Rushforth, had bullet and machete wounds in his body and left hand. A rebel tried to decapitate him, missed and partly severed his right hand. Rushforth escaped in a shower of bullets; one went through his saddle and hip; another pierced his horse's neck. The Marine reached camp covered with blood. He was commended by the Secretary of the Navy but was denied the Medal of Honor because no witnesses to the action were left alive.

At the direction of the Secretary of the Navy, the military government in 1917 had disbanded the Dominican army and organized a native constabulary, the Guardia Nacional Dominicana. The Guardia was regarded as a tool of the oppressors, and no respectable Dominican would serve in it. During the early years, almost all of its officers were Marine Corps officers or noncoms. Training centers were set up at Haina and Santiago. At first, the Guardia guarded the border with Haiti and garrisoned towns; but after the United States entered World War I and Marines were withdrawn to France, the Guardia was sent into the field to help the remaining Marines fight the rebels.

Once the war in Europe was won, the 15th Regiment and the 1st Air Squadron brought the 2d Marine Brigade's strength up to 3,000 men. By the middle of 1919, the 15th and half of the 3rd Regiment began vigorous patrolling in Seibo and Macoris provinces. The Marines' new aggressiveness raised the level of combat. And the guerrilla war entered a new dimension with the addition of primitive Marine air power to the struggle. The aviation squadron's six biplanes dive-bombed and machine-gunned enemy concentrations and became the eyes of the men on the ground seeking to root out the rebels in the jungles and mountains.

The military government achieved many social improvements in the Dominican Republic. Roads were built, public health measures were introduced and education was made available to more children. At first, the high wartime price of sugar provided funds, but the collapse of sugar prices in 1920 brought much of these good works to an end.

By the close of that year, President Wilson had decided to discontinue the American occupation. The size of the brigade was progressively reduced as wartime enlistments ran out and many Marines, resentful that they had not served in France and had been kept in uniform after the Armistice, left for home.

The reduction of Marine strength—as well as the postwar depression and unemployment—encouraged the Dominican opposition to the occupation. As a result, the brigade commander, Brig. Gen. Logan Feland, stepped up patrolling in the fall of 1920. In October 1921, a cordon system was put into operation in the eastern part of the country. Under Col. William C. Harllee, a renowned marksman, Marines surrounded and cordoned off large areas and rounded up every suspicious-seeming adult male. Round-ups were often conducted in the middle of the night and many civilians were pulled in on very little evidence. At the subsequent trials, more than 500 convictions were obtained. But these ruthless tactics aroused such anger among the people that cordoning had to be discontinued.

As the Dominican occupation slipped into its final years, the Marine Brigade commander, Brig. Gen. Harry Lee, also a veteran of the fighting in France, was directed to win the people's friendship and insist that the Marines deal with the Dominicans fairly and sympathetically. Amnesty was offered to anyone who had not committed a serious crime; and by the time the offer of amnesty expired on May 31, 1922, armed opposition was practically eliminated. A number of rebel leaders who surrendered were given suspended sentences on good behavior. Obviously, the Dominicans welcomed peace.

By October 21, 1922, a provisional government had assumed control of the country; and on July 12, 1924, a constitutional government was installed. The 2d Marine Brigade began leaving the Dominican Republic. The final large contingent shipped to San Diego, was reorganized into the 4th Marines and in March 1927 transferred to Shanghai, China. The last Marine company left the Dominican Republic in September 1924.

The Marines left behind a stable and solvent government. But it did not last long; and in 1930, the Guardia, renamed the Policia Nacional Dominicana—which the Marines had helped create—took over the Dominican government. General Rafael Trujillo, who had started his rise in 1919 as a lieutenant in the Guardia, became dictator. He maintained his contacts with Marine Corps officers,[21] especially Col. Richard M. Cutts,[22] the last commandant of the Policia, a U.S. national rifle champion and a White House aide to President Franklin D. Roosevelt. Trujillo became a bestial tyrant; and by 1960, the United States government was encouraging his enemies. He was assassinated on May 30, 1961. Four years later, the Marines landed again.

The eight-year Dominican occupation did its share to build throughout Latin America a heritage of hatred against United States imperialism.

The Marine interventions in the Caribbean never had the full support of the American people. These military actions were always controversial and debated, and opposition increased whenever there were reports of American atrocities and when Latin American resentment reached a fever pitch.

After World War I, the rationalization that the interventions were necessary to protect the Panama Canal and keep European powers away from American shores did not attract much support. In 1929, the United States Senate disavowed Theodore Roosevelt's corollary to the Monroe Doctrine that had assumed a unilaterally declared U.S. right to intervene.

In 1933, President Franklin Roosevelt, using the term "good neighbor" in his inaugural address, moved toward a new

197

hemispheric relationship that emphasized non-intervention, freer trade relations and aid for economic development. The United States agreed at Montevideo that "No state has a right to intervene in the internal or external affairs of another."[23] The next year, the United States deserted the Platt Amendment, which had permitted it to interfere in Cuban affairs; withdrew from Haiti, and began negotiating a treaty with Panama. The era of prolonged interventions was over.

This is not to say that military interference was finished in the Caribbean. The Bay of Pigs disaster in 1961, the Cuban missile crisis in 1962 and the Dominican invasion in 1965 were all danger-filled reminders that the United States still regarded the Caribbean as vital to its national interest. And the Marines continued ready to perform whatever duty their government ordered to protect that vital interest.

8
"An Efficient and Very Mobile Force"

As the nation tiptoed into the world's troubles between the Spanish-American War and World War I, the Marine Corps changed enormously. In those two decades, the Corps swelled from 3,800 men to 13,600 in 1916. Even more important, its mission was transformed from the pre-1898 duty of supplying gunners and guards aboard warships to the embryo of a permanent expeditionary force that could go ashore and seize and hold advanced bases.

Such a metamorphosis had started with the advent of coal-driven ships but it was not made without opposition. Some planners wanted the Corps taken out of the Navy entirely and integrated into the Army; others wanted the Corps removed from naval ships and concentrated exclusively for expeditionary work. The Corps itself fought for both roles: to stay afloat and to defend the newly needed advanced bases.

During this same period, the Corps had three Commandants—and recurring controversy over the post. When Maj. Gen. Commandant Charles Heywood retired on October 3, 1903, President Theodore Roosevelt selected Brig. Gen. George F. Elliott to succeed him. The fifty-six-year-old native of Green County, Alabama, had studied at West Point for two years and was discharged for deficiencies in mathematics and French. Strangely, Jacob Zeilin and Elliott, the only two Commandants to attend the U.S. Military Academy, both flunked out.

Right after leaving West Point in 1870, Elliott was commissioned as a Marine officer and had a long and active career: the railroad strike of 1877, Korea and Peking in 1894, Guantanamo in 1898, the battle of Novaleta in 1899. During his seven years as Commandant, Marines landed throughout the Caribbean as well

199

as in China, Korea and North Africa, and established posts at Hawaii and Midway.

Elliott was party to a nasty feud with Col. Charles H. Lauchheimer, the Adjutant and Inspector of the Corps. As a result, in 1910, President Taft banished Lauchheimer from Washington to the Philippines. The fight was rooted in a tangle of the Corps' high-pressured campaign to keep Marines on battleships, the rivalry between line and staff officers, Elliott's heavy drinking and Lauchheimer's alleged efforts to have him dismissed. Lauchheimer's exile aroused accusations of partisan politics and anti-Semitism. Jewish leaders charged discrimination; the affair grew into a scandal. It was called a second Dreyfus Affair. Lauchheimer, a member of a prominent Jewish family in Baltimore, was an Annapolis graduate and had many political connections in Washington. After Elliott retired in 1911, political pressure brought Lauchheimer back to Washington just before the 1912 election. By 1916, he was a brigadier general. When he died in 1920, while still on active duty after 36 years, his family contributed the Lauchheimer Trophy for marksmanship to the Corps.[24]

Long after Elliott's retirement on his sixty-fourth birthday, the former Commandant—on Thanksgiving Day 1922—sent an inspirational message to the Corps: "I can tell you a text in the Bible that points directly to our Marine Corps—it is in Revelations: 'Be ye faithful unto death. . . .' That is our motto, isn't it? 'Faithful unto death.' "[25]

Picking a successor to Elliott brought more bitterness. The obvious candidate was "Tony" Waller, who had a spectacular record as a fighting Marine. But the uproar over the killing of the Filipinos on Samar and his courtmartial had scarred his reputation. Waller mustered substantial support in Congress, especially among the representatives from his native Virginia; and it was not until February 3, 1911, that President Taft finally appointed Col. William P. Biddle. It was a highly political appointment pressed by Senator Bois Penrose of Pennsylvania.

A member of the notable Philadelphia family, Biddle had served on *Olympia* in the Battle of Manila Bay and in the Philippines and in China during the Boxer Rebellion. While he was Commandant, advanced base forces were organized and the first Marine fliers were trained; but relations between the Navy and the Marine Corps were strained. By the end of 1913, President Wilson's Secretary of the Navy, Josephus Daniels, was determined to alter the Marines' function, concentrate them in fewer stations, relieve them of guard and police duty and give them expeditionary-service training.

When the heavy-set Biddle retired early in 1914, after 30 years' service, Waller again was the center of controversy and again was passed over. Col. George Barnett, the first Naval Academy graduate to become Commandant and a veteran of the Spanish-American War and the Cuban intervention, was appointed Major General Commandant for a four-year term and led the Corps into World War I.

All three of these Commandants shared in the Corps' transformation. As soon as the General Board of the Navy was created in 1900 to advise the Secretary of the Navy, the Marine Corps was designated the best possible force to defend advanced naval bases. And the following year, the Board recommended that the Commandant organize four 104-man companies, each "ready for instant use"[26] on expeditionary service. A battalion was created and trained. In 1908 and 1909, the Congress increased the strength of the Corps to provide men for such assignments. And in 1910, Elliott established an Advanced Base School, first at New London, Connecticut, and later at Philadelphia.

President Roosevelt removed the Marines from shipboard duty with Executive Order No. 969 on November 12, 1908. This was a victory—for the moment—for Navy Capt. William F. Fullam and his adherents, who wanted the Marines taken off American warships. Roosevelt favored transferring the Marine Corps to the Army. The Corps fought back; Waller, Neville, Lauchheimer, Butler and Frank L. Denny organized to defend it. And Admiral Dewey, president of the Navy's General Board, led the fight to keep the Marines in the Navy. Dewey was willing to remove them from the policeman's job afloat but he wanted the Navy to retain control over the Corps.

Roosevelt's vision of the Corps' new mission—"To furnish the first line of the mobile defense of naval bases and naval stations beyond the continental limits of the United States"[27]—was ahead of its time. His Executive Order created a great fight in the Congress. Commandant Elliott reacted to the Secretary of the Navy's order that the Marines be removed immediately from 13 ships by demanding that if they were taken off any Navy ships, they be removed from all. As a result, more than 2,000 Marines were transferred ashore and their shipboard places were filled by sailors. The Marine Corps lobbied vigorously and effectively against the change, and public opinion was marshalled in the Corps' support. Representative Thomas Butler, chairman of the House Naval Affairs Committee and Smedley Butler's father, held hearings. The issue was resolved the following March, when Senator Eugene C. Hale, chairman of the Senate Committee on Naval Affairs, amended the Naval Appropriations Bill to provide that eight percent of the enlisted men on battleships and armored cruisers be Marines. The Senate passed the amendment, 51 to 12, and it survived in conference. Just before Roosevelt left office, he restored the Marines to the warships but left their duty assignments up to the ships' captains. President Taft then immediately gave the Marines back their previous duties aboard ship. Sensing a continuing danger, a group of officers formed the Marine Corps Association to support the Corps.

Meanwhile, the struggle to use the Marines in expeditionary roles went ahead. Among early Marine Corps studies that developed advanced-base doctrines were those by Maj. Henry C. Haines, Maj. Dion Williams, Maj. John H. Russell and Lt. Col. Eli K. Cole. Williams, then a captain in the naval intelligence service, wrote the first report in 1902. He advocated that the Marine Corps should garrison naval stations and should be kept under Navy control. He wrote: "Long experience has shown that the so-called cooperation of the Navy and the Army in a campaign is a myth and that neither will subordinate itself to the other, each having its own work to do in its own way."[28] He urged that the Corps be enlarged to 15,000 men and that all its officers be trained at the Naval Academy. Williams predicted that it would be necessary to establish temporary bases in a naval campaign; and, he said, "The Navy has in the Marine Corps an efficient and very mobile force, ever kept at a high state of discipline. . . ."[29]

Much of Williams' thinking was eventually adopted. By 1914, the Corps had organized two "fixed defense" regiments of 1,250 men, at Philadelphia and Mare Island, California, and had plans to form two "mobile defense" regiments in case of war. The mobile regiments would oppose enemy landings that were beyond the range of the guns of a fixed defense unit guarding an advanced base.

During January 1914, the Marines' Advanced Base Force trained with the Atlantic Fleet at Culebra Island off the east coast of Puerto Rico to test both men and equipment. The Fixed Defense Regiment was commanded by Col. Charles G. Long and the Mobile Regiment by Lt. Col. John A. Lejeune. They worked together as the First Advanced Base Brigade under Colonel Barnett. When Barnett was named Commandant, he turned over the brigade to Lejeune, who took it to the invasion of Vera Cruz.

In the long run, these Culebra exercises were crucial to the future of the Marine Corps. The previous May, Captain Fullam, as inspector for the Navy, had reported that the Marines advanced base force was a failure. He again recommended that the Marine Corps be organized into battalions and removed from naval vessels. Admiral Dewey and the General Board rejected Fullam's recommendations, fearing that if they were followed the Marine Corps would eventually be absorbed by the Army.

The Marines wanted to keep both their shipboard and new advanced base defense missions. To many, the very existence of the Corps seemed threatened by Fullam's ideas. Only much later, with the wisdom of hindsight, did the Corps come to recognize that Captain Fullam was pointing the way to the future.

But first there was World War I to fight. The Naval Appropriations Bill of August 1916 expanded the Navy and, largely as a result of Barnett's, Lejeune's and Lauchheimer's efforts, increased the Marine Corps from about 8,000 to more than 13,000 enlisted men, and from 343 to 600 officers. A Marine Corps Reserve was established, and eight brigadier generals were authorized. Waller, Pendleton, Cole and Lejeune were among those promoted. Jauntily attired in their four-dent "Montana peak" campaign hats, the Marines (as already related in these pages) began getting ready for action in France.

*U.S. Marines guard the border of the International
Settlement in Shanghai in 1937.
Museums Branch, USMC*

SEMPER FIDELIS

IV
GETTING
READY
1919-1941

1
The Lean Years

After World War I, the Marine Corps prepared to fight the next war rather than to re-fight the last one.

This did not happen suddenly. At first, Marines gloried in the Big Show in France. But some of their more prescient leaders began to see who the next enemy would be and what kind of war the Marines would have to fight. Men like Lejeune, Russell and Ellis started to get the Corps ready.

At home, the Corps stumbled into two roadblocks: postwar civilian revulsion against everything military and the Great Depression, which squeezed both fat and muscle from all military budgets. In July 1919, Congress slashed the Marine Corps to 1,093 officers and 27,400 enlisted men; but it was unable to enlist even that number. By 1933, authorized strength had dropped to 15,000 enlisted men. Not until World War II began in 1939 was it raised again to 25,000.

During these lean years, the Marines survived on public relations. The Corps crowed about its heroism in France; and, led by Smedley D. Butler's frenetic enthusiasm, it sent rifle and athletic teams around that nation; staged full-dress recreations of Civil War battles, and started building at Quantico, Virginia, the world's largest football stadium. In both 1921 and 1926, the Corps took on the highly visible job of protecting the U.S. mails against robberies.

Fortunately, the Corps had, for eight years of this period, the leadership of one of the most attractive Commandants in its history: John A. Lejeune, a battle-decorated, popular, forward-looking, publicity-aware general. He wanted the Corps to be known and respected throughout the country, and he fought its battles in the Congressional cloakrooms and the White House.

He understood the uses of political power and laid the foundation for the Corps' amphibious revolution.

Lejeune became Commandant on July 1, 1920, when George Barnett, who had been reappointed in 1918, was retired prematurely and abruptly. He had alienated Navy Secretary Josephus Daniels and Congressman Thomas Butler, father of Smedley Butler and senior member of the House Naval Affairs Committee. Smedley Butler thought Barnett had kept him from leading a regiment into combat in France. His father called Barnett "a rocking chair warrior."[1] During the Lejeune years, Congressman Butler was the Marines' good and powerful friend and until his death in 1928 supplied important help with appropriations.

The congressman's son, a round-shouldered, beak-nosed 130-pounder, was one of the Corps' best-known characters, outspoken, colorful, full of drive and ambition. He wore two Medals of Honor. When Lejeune retired in 1929 to become Superintendent of the Virginia Military Institute, Butler expected to be named Commandant. Although he had helped make Lejeune Commandant, Lejeune strongly recommended as his successor Wendell C. "Buck" Neville, who had led the 5th Marines and the 4th Brigade in France. Neville won the job but died on July 8, 1930. Again, Butler's hopes rose. He was now a major general, the youngest Marine until then to hold that rank and the Corps' ranking general. However, President Herbert Hoover passed over both Butler and Maj. Gen. Logan Feland and chose Brig. Gen. Ben H. Fuller—quiet, sixty-year-old "Uncle Ben," a Marine for 39 years.

Butler was furious, but he had made too many enemies. One incident that had not helped his cause occurred in 1926, during Prohibition days, when Butler preferred charges in San Diego against Col. Alexander S. Williams for turning up at a hotel dance "very drunk."[2] Williams, who as a young lieutenant had been with Waller on the tragic march on Samar, was relieved of his command. Six months later, his car plunged into San Francisco Bay and he drowned. His death was declared accidental, but many people called it suicide and blamed Butler.

After Fuller was named Commandant, Butler made some imprudent public remarks against the Italian Fascist leader, Benito Mussolini. The Italian government protested, and a court-martial was ordered. As his defense lawyer, Butler engaged Henry Leonard, who had saved his life in China. The case was settled with a reprimand before the trial started; but Butler retired in 1931, a very angry man.

Two more Marines became Commandant before Pearl Harbor. John H. Russell, who had won fame in Haiti, took over after Fuller retired for age early in 1934. Although Russell was from the older generation, he played a major part in preparing the Corps for World War II. When he too retired for age at the end of 1936, President Franklin D. Roosevelt reached down and picked a junior man, much as Navy Secretary Welles had done during the Civil War. Roosevelt selected Brig. Gen. Thomas Holcomb, fifty-seven, a descendant of Commodore Joshua Barney, an expert shot and a veteran of the fighting in France. Holcomb was a stern silent man with steel-rimmed glasses and known as a planner and administrator. This time, there were no dramatic resignations; and Holcomb, now a major general, led the Corps into its biggest war.

2
China Marines

In these years of apparent peace, the Marine Corps was surprisingly busy overseas. Marines "intervened" in the Dominican Republic until 1924; in Haiti until 1934, and in Nicaragua, for the second time, from 1927 until 1933, as described in Part IX. In addition, a few Marines landed again at Vladivostok in 1919 and in Honduras in 1924 and 1925.*

The second world-wide war boiled up earliest on the far side of the Pacific, where China, chaotic and crippled, was squeezed between Soviet communism and Japanese imperialism. China became the main stage outside the Caribbean for the Marine Corps: first, in the 1920s when Chiang Kai-shek's Nationalists fought the warlords and Communists for control of the country, and again in the 1930s when the Japanese invaded China. In 1928, more than 5,000 U.S. Marines (a fourth of the Corps)—and in 1937, 2,536 Marines—were stationed in China.

Marine ships' detachments had gone ashore at Hankow and Shanghai in the fall of 1911, and a battalion of 375 men under Maj. Philip M. Bannon went to Peking. China's Manchu Dynasty—shaken by the foreign invasion against the Boxer Rebellion and destroyed by the Revolution of 1911—finally abdicated on February 12, 1912. The Marine legation guard at Peking was kept at more than 500 men until May, when the situation seemed to quiet down.

During China's turmoil, Japan moved in on the wounded giant. Japan had already annexed Korea in 1910; and while

*On December 5, 1929, Marine Capt. Alton N. Parker was the first pilot to fly over large parts of the Antarctic continent. He and three Marine sergeants were members of the Byrd Antarctic Expedition. Master Tech. Sgt. Victor H. Czegka went back with Rear Adm. Richard E. Byrd's second expedition in 1933–1935.

European powers were massacring each other in World War I, Japan scooped up Germany's islands in the Central Pacific, grabbed the German economic monopoly in China's Shantung Province and pressed demands that "effectively envisaged China's subordination to Japan's will."[3] None of the Western powers was prepared to slap down the Japanese. When China bowed to Japan's Twenty-one Demands in 1915, a new era opened in Asia. Japan was hungry for a mainland empire, and its appetite would not be suppressed until after Hiroshima—30 years later.

Inside China, the nationalist leader Sun Yat-sen had himself named the "Provisional President of China" in Canton on May 5, 1921. Less than two months later, the Chinese Communist Party was born at Shanghai—with Moscow's midwifery. But the Peking government and the provincial warlords still dominated most of the vast country. When Sun Yat-sen asked the United States for help and was rejected, he sent a mission headed by Chiang Kai-shek to Moscow.

After Sun Yat-sen died of cancer in 1925, Chiang Kai-shek made himself commander-in-chief of the National Revolutionary Army. In March 1927, aided by an uprising of Communist-organized workers, he captured the great port city of Shanghai and then seized Nanking.

Leading the right wing of Sun Yat-sen's Kuomintang Party, Chiang on April 12 turned on the Shanghai workers' organizations and killed some 300 Communist and labor leaders. Six days later, he organized his own Nationalist government in Nanking. His armies defeated the Communist-led troops, and soon Chiang controlled a one-party dictatorship.

This was a time of riots, panic, disruption of trade. There was fighting between the northern warlords and the southern revolutionaries, between the Kuomintang and the Communists, and between the left and right wings of the Nationalist movement itself. Anti-foreign disorders spread. Foreign warships gathered at Shanghai.

Into this danger-fraught situation came the Marines. Small Marine detachments had gone to Tungchow, Peking, Tientsin, Chinwangtao, Canton and especially Shanghai from 1920 to 1926. (One private first class in the Peking detachment was future U.S. Senator "Mike" Mansfield.) But the major intervention began early in 1927 when the International Settlement at

Shanghai, the great trading center between China and the industrial world, was threatened by civil war and anti-imperialist violence.

On February 4, 1927, four companies of 341 Marines from Guam landed at Shanghai; and a few weeks later arrived 1,228 Marines of the 4th Regiment, commanded by Col. Charles S. "Jumbo" Hill. They stayed aboard ship at the Standard Oil compound five miles below the city.

The 4th was the only Marine regiment on duty continuously between the two world wars. Activated on April 16, 1914, it had fought in the Dominican Republic from 1916 to 1924. It would stay in Shanghai for the next 14 years without ever firing a shot and become famous as the "China Marines." Seven of its China-duty members eventually became Commandants of the Corps: Alexander A. Vandegrift (who commanded the 3rd Battalion in 1927); Clifton B. Cates; Lemuel C. Shepherd, Jr.; Randolph McC. Pate; David M. Shoup; Wallace M. Greene, Jr.; and Robert E. Cushman, Jr. China was a nursery for the Marine Corps leadership of World War II.

When the steel-helmeted Marines marched ashore on March 16, 1927, their job was not to solve China's problems but to help the British and the six other foreign powers present keep the Chinese out of the International Settlement. This area of the city, completely controlled by foreigners, was dotted with white buildings and hotels and clubs for Occidentals only. It was the target of Chinese anti-foreign resentment.

To reinforce the 4th Regiment with men and artillery and aviation elements, Brig. Gen. Smedley Butler arrived on March 25, followed on May 2 by most of the 6th Regiment, commanded by Col. Harold C. Snyder. Butler took charge of all the Marines in China as the 3rd Marine Brigade. When two more battalions arrived, the 3rd Brigade had 238 officers, 18 warrant officers and 4,179 enlisted men. Its Aircraft Squadrons totaled 170 men.

Although the crisis had passed by the time Butler got to Shanghai, he wanted to place the Marines on perimeter defense alongside the British at Soochow Creek, bordering the Settlement, and sent machine-gun-armed truck patrols through it.

In June, with Chiang in control at Shanghai, Butler left the 4th Regiment there and took most of the other Marines north to Tientsin, where he had fought 27 years before. From Tientsin,

Marine pilots flew Jennys on regular reconnaisance patrols over Chiang's army. In a year and a half, three Marine fighter squadrons marked up 3,818 sorties.[4]

The U.S. Army already had 1,800 soldiers at Tientsin and along the railroad to Peking. The Legation Guard in Peking now totaled 516 Marines, including a detachment of 22 men mounted on Mongolian ponies. These "Horse Marines" were trained and equipped like cavalry to protect Americans. In truth, they were used mostly to climax Marine parades with a galloping dash, their sabers flashing.

The Marines, both in Shanghai and up north, were ordered to avoid conflicts with the Chinese. They filled their days with drilling, athletics and parades. The energetic Butler kept his Marines at Tientsin ready to leave instantly for Peking if trouble should start. Trucks with machine guns, ammunition and rations stood by like fire engines to evacuate Americans from Peking.

The day before Christmas, 1927, a tremendous fire broke out in the Standard Oil Plant on the Hai Ho River at Tientsin. A million pounds of candle grease ignited in two huge warehouses. Within minutes, the Marines were on the spot. To prevent a massive explosion, they formed human chains and passed gasoline tins out of an adjoining warehouse. By mid-afternoon, 2,000 Marines were fighting the flames. It took four days to put the fire out.

On July 25, 1928, the United States became the first of the powers to sign a tariff treaty with Chiang Kai-shek's government in Nanking. After Chiang became president of China, the 3rd Marine Brigade was withdrawn in January 1929, leaving 500 Marines in Peking and 1,150 of the 4th Regiment at Shanghai.

Life in Shanghai was comfortable and exotic. Chinese "roomboys" and White Russian girlfriends helped do the chores and counteract the boredom—even on a Marine's pay of $21 a month. He could buy a steak for 30 cents, Scotch for less than a dollar, beer for two cents a quart. It was very good duty.

In September 1931, the Japanese struck. Their army invaded Manchuria and seized most of China's iron ore and much of its coal, electric power and cement. Japan was out to grab land and resources, to erect a buffer state between itself and the Soviet Union and to forestall American economic expansion in

213

Asia. War with flabby, apparently defenseless China seemed a small price to pay for those goals. But the road led elsewhere.

Although the League of Nations objected to Japan's aggression, no one came to China's aid; and Japan ignored the League's protests. The United States declined to join any collective effort to stop Japan, which set up in Manchuria the puppet state of Manchukuo. Chiang Kai-shek, unable to contain Japan, re-opened diplomatic relations with the Soviet Union after a five-year break. In March 1933, Japan walked out of the League of Nations. It was the first step toward world war.

Anti-Japanese tension mounted in Shanghai. In January 1932, the Japanese army attacked Chinese soldiers in the Chapei district of Shanghai across narrow Soochow Creek from the International Settlement. The fighting spread, and the 4th Marines again took to the barricades facing the creek. To help keep the conflict out of the Settlement, they were soon reinforced by 334 Marines from the Philippines; the Marine detachment from the ill-fated *USS Houston,* and the U.S. Army's 31st Infantry. Stray shells fell into the American sector, and the Marines were exposed to fire from both warring sides.

The battle ended when the Chinese pulled out of Chapei on March 3; and by June, the emergency was officially over. The Marines returned to garrison and shipboard duty, and the 31st Infantry, to the Philippines.

But the early 1930s were terrible years for China. Not only did the world-wide Depression wreck its export trade, but drought and famine swept the land. The peasants were milked for taxes to support the vast military establishments, and the countryside was ripe for revolution. In response, Chiang Kai-shek raised a series of military campaigns against the Communists. In October 1934, the Red Army broke through Chiang's lines and began its historic Long March of 6,000 miles to Shensi Province in China's far northwest.

In January 1936, Japan walked out of the Second London Conference on naval strength and in November signed a treaty with Nazi Germany. The following month, some of Chiang's own military colleagues kidnapped and held him until he agreed to end the civil war against the Communists and fight the Japanese. Ironically, the man who saved him from assassination and negotiated for a common front against the Japanese was his Communist enemy, Chou En-lai.

At the Marco Polo Bridge outside Peking on the balmy summer night of July 7, 1937, Japanese and Chinese troops clashed; and the Second Sino-Japanese War began. The Chinese Twenty-ninth Army manned positions in Peking against possible Japanese attacks. A cavalry squad approached; the Chinese at the barricades opened fire. The mounted men were not Japanese but U.S. Marines—the Horse Marines. One Marine was wounded, and the rest ducked into a side street until the mix-up was untangled. That was the only fighting in Peking itself.[5]

After the Japanese marched into Peking on August 8, Chiang Kai-shek and Chou En-lai finally agreed on a united front. The Red Army became the Eighth Route Army of the National Revolutionary Army.

The Japanese fired on American hospitals, churches and schools across China. They sank the gunboat *USS Panay*, patrolling the Yangtze River, and killed three Americans and seriously wounded 11. President Roosevelt had urged a "quarantine" against aggressors, but Americans still sold shiploads of scrap steel to Japan. The Russians were supplying China with war supplies, planes and pilots.

For the China Marines in that summer of '37, training was stepped up: conditioning hikes with heavy packs, rifle practice and weapons drill and parades out to the Race Course. On August 12, when fighting between the Japanese and Chinese approached Shanghai, Col. Charles F. B. Price sent his two battalions of the 4th Marines to the south bank of Soochow Creek. Lt. Col. William H. Rupertus' 1st Battalion and Lt. Col. Roswell Winans' 2d Battalion sandbagged 58 strongpoints and positioned automatic weapons to provide interlocking fields of fire. Capt. Wallace M. Greene, Jr.'s, E Company was formed into a special "riot company" to deal with disorders and looting. Most of its 90 Marines were organized into four-man "fighting teams"—the forerunners of the Marines' four-man fire teams of World War II.

By the fourteenth, "Bloody Saturday," the fighting grew intense. Thousands of Chinese refugees crowded across the creek into the Settlement. Chinese bombs, aimed at the Japanese ships in the Whangpo River, killed some 500 Chinese. Japanese antiaircraft fire sprinkled Marine positions. On August 21, a shell killed one and wounded 18 aboard *USS Augusta*.

Two companies of Marines arrived from Cavite; and the 6th Marines and the headquarters of the 2d Marine Brigade, commanded by Brig. Gen. John C. Beaumont, arrived from San Diego. There were now 2,536 Marines in China. Col. Thomas S. Clarke's 6th Marines—Lt. Col. Alphonse de Carre's 1st Battalion and Lt. Col. Cates' 2d Battalion—rotated with the 4th Marines on the line.

On October 25, when the Japanese established an amphibious beachhead north of Shanghai, the massive battle reached a climax. The Chinese began an orderly retreat; and by the end of the month the fighting was over. In mid-February, the 2d Brigade and 6th Marines left; and once again the 4th Marines were alone on guard in Shanghai.

The Japanese conquered the capital in the infamous "rape of Nanking"; and the National government fled to Chungking, far up the Yangtze River. Within the year, the Japanese occupied Hankow and Canton. The Chinese armies were cut off, except for Russian supplies creeping in through Central Asia.

Duty in Shanghai during this emergency proved especially important to two Vermont-reared Marines who in World War II would command the Corps' first two Raider battalions. Maj. Merritt A. Edson, veteran of the Coco River patrols in Nicaragua, studied Japanese amphibious tactics at close range. And Capt. Evans F. Carlson came back to Shanghai for the third time, specifically to study the Chinese language. He learned a lot more. The American journalist Edgar Snow, whom Carlson had met in China in the 1920s, encouraged him to go and observe the Chinese Communist armies in Yenan. Getting permission from Chairman Mao Tse-tung on December 7, 1937, Carlson was the first foreign military officer to visit the Communist armies. In Shansi Province, he hiked with a small detachment 200 miles through bare, treeless mountains in freezing weather. He studied guerrilla warfare and how the Chinese Communists used surprise and feints, stayed constantly in motion and fought only when they felt strong enough to win. He became an ardent devotee of the smart, tough, spartan guerrillas. Of the Japanese army, he said, "Its effort to conquer Shansi was about as effective as an attempt to plow the ocean."[6] When he returned to Shanghai, Carlson reported what he had learned to Naval Intelligence and wrote to Franklin Roosevelt, as the President

216

had asked him to. FDR had come to know Carlson when he commanded the Marine guard at the Little White House at Warm Springs, Georgia.

The skinny six-foot Marine had talked with Chou En-lai and Mao Tse-tung in Chinese, slept in a Yenan cave and in 1938 traveled for three months in the remote areas of China and Inner Mongolia where the Communists were fighting the Japanese. After that experience, he tried personally to convince Chiang Kai-shek to send more help to the under-equipped Communists; and he began to make public statements warning Americans of war with Japan and trying to rally American support for the hard-pressed Chinese. This intense son of a New England preacher was already widely regarded as a maverick. He returned to the United States, resigned and wrote and made speeches about what he had seen in China. He went back to China as a civilian in 1940, became convinced war with Japan was imminent and rejoined the Corps in April 1941. Sent to England, he studied the methods of the British Commandos, a mission that helped give birth to the Marine Raiders.

Once World War II began in 1939, the Marines in China were increasingly isolated. By the summer of 1940, the British, French and Italians in Shanghai were no longer effective partners there.

Maj. Lewis B. "Chesty" Puller had one potentially dangerous brush with the Japanese in Shanghai. In 1933, he had commanded the 50-man Horse Marines in Peking. One night in 1940 when he was back in China, 80 Japanese soldiers invaded Shanghai's International Settlement and rounded up 200 Chinese. Puller took 22 Marines, hurried to the spot where the Chinese were being held, ordered his men to set up two heavy machine guns and drew his pistol on the Japanese officer. The Japanese left without their prisoners.

In January 1940, the United States finally restricted the shipment of war supplies to Japan. In September, after France fell to Hitler, Japan seized northern Indochina; when Germany attacked the Soviet Union in 1941, Japan took the rest. The United States froze Japanese assets in the States, embargoed petroleum exports to Japan and on November 26 told Japan to get out of China and Indochina. These measures were intended to drain Japan of oil and to halt her conquest of the Asian mainland. In fact, they turned Japan's aggressiveness southward and led directly to the attacks on American, British and Dutch holdings in the Pacific—and the raid on Pearl Harbor.

As the Japanese tightened their hold over China and formally joined the Axis Powers, war between Japan and the United States appeared increasingly likely. Adm. Thomas C. Hart, commander of the American Asiatic Fleet, urged that the 4th Marines be pulled out of China. Finally, on November 10, 1941, orders arrived from Washington to evacuate the regiment. The 1st Battalion sailed for Subic Bay on *President Madison* on November 27, and the rest of the regiment rushed to sail the next day aboard *President Harrison*. The Japanese tried to block the evacuation. But the Marines loaded *President Harrison* by lighter; and at 9 A.M. on the twenty-eighth, the remainder of the regiment formed behind its band and marched down Bubbling Well and Nanking roads to the dock on the Bund. A cheering crowd lined the route. A lighter took the Marines downstream to the ship. At 2 P.M., *Harrison* weighed anchor. It was the end of the pre-war China Marines.

3
Toward a New Mission

While Marines were guarding Soochow Creek and chasing Sandino in Nicaragua, back home something even more important—and more revolutionary—was developing in the Corps.

The story starts with the cloak-and-dagger mystery of Earl H. "Pete" Ellis. Born in the prairie village of Iuka, Kansas, on December 19, 1880, Ellis enlisted as a Marine private in 1900 and became the Corps' most prophetic thinker and planner of his time. He was a lieutenant colonel when he died, May 12, 1923, on Koror in Japan's newly acquired Palau Islands.

After Ellis' death, Commandant Lejeune acknowledged that Ellis had been on a secret military intelligence mission when he disappeared.[7] He was trying to find out whether the Japanese were fortifying their mandated Pacific islands, where no foreigner was welcome.

Even before World War I, during which he won the Navy Cross in France, the young, slim Marine officer had been fascinated with the problems of advanced base defense. He learned Japanese while on two tours of duty in the Philippines and became convinced that the United States would have to fight the next war in Japanese waters. In 1921, he predicted in detail how the Marine Corps would, in the war he saw coming, capture western Pacific bases from Japan. Ellis revolutionized Marine Corps thinking. His brilliant paper, "Advanced Base Operations in Micronesia, 1921," was accepted in toto by the Commandant and became the famous Operations Plan 712. Much of what he foresaw is now history.

In death, Ellis became a legend. To this day, what happened to him is unknown. The official story was that he took a

219

leave of absence from the Corps and went traveling. The Japanese said he became ill in the Palaus and died. It is believed that they murdered him.

What is known for sure is that in 1922 Ellis was hospitalized in Japan for acute alcoholic poisoning. Although ordered home, he decided to complete his mission to penetrate the Japanese-held islands. He walked out of the Yokohama Naval Hospital on the night of October 6 and disappeared. Later, it was learned that he had gone, disguised as a commercial traveler, to the Marshall Islands and after several months made his way on a Japanese ship to the Palaus.

In 1950, Marine Lt. Col. Waite W. Worden unearthed some facts about Ellis' last days on Koror. He had lived with a native girl named Metauie, drank heavily and spent much of his time prowling around Japanese installations. Japanese police in civilian clothes, presuming or knowing Ellis was a spy, shadowed him closely. One morning, according to a native woman who had known him on Koror, he went "crazy drunk," and by 5 P.M. he was dead. Worden commented, "With his apparent unquenchable thirst, and his frantic searches, at times, for something to drink, it would not have been too difficult to poison him."[8]

Gen. Holland M. Smith, who called Ellis "one of our most brilliant strategists," added a haunting footnote:

> The mystery of Ellis' death deepened when a young [sic] chief pharmacist's mate [Lawrence Zembsch, a wartime Navy lieutenant] from the U.S. Naval Hospital in Yokohama volunteered to go to Palau and recovered his body. He cremated the body but returned to Yokohama a mental case, unable to give a coherent story of his trip or any intelligent information about Ellis. His condition improved, and it seemed possible he would regain enough mental equilibrium to tell his story, but both he and his wife died in the ruins when the 1923 Japanese earthquake demolished the hospital.[9]

A Marine Corps historian who probed the Ellis case wrote that Zembsch had reported "that Ellis had been known for what he actually was while he was staying in the Marshalls."[10]

220

What involved Ellis so passionately that it lured him to his death was no less than a vision, still invisible to most everyone, of how the Marine Corps could most effectively meet the new danger to the United States in the Pacific. He was by no means alone in recognizing that the balance of power in the Pacific had shifted and that Japan's new position astride America's sealanes conflicted with U.S. economic and political interests. Ellis' unique contribution was that he knew what the Marine Corps should do about the threat.

He urged that the Corps get ready to assault heavily defended Japanese islands and capture the bases necessary to project American power across the Pacific. He wrote:

> To effect such a landing under the sea and shore conditions obtaining and in the face of enemy resistance required careful training and preparation, to say the least; and this along Marine Corps lines. It is not enough that the troops be skilled infantry men or artillery men of high morale; they must be skilled water men and jungle men who know it can be done—Marines with Marine training.[11]

The Marine Corps was ripe for a new vision of the future. Its leaders were increasingly aware that the Corps' existence could not long hang on—and was, in fact, even endangered by—its heroic performance in World War I. Not only had the Marines' well publicized feats attracted powerful and jealous enemies, but the Corps was vulnerable because its World War I mission and organization had been so totally imitative of the Army. If the Corps existed only to do what the Army could do (even though better perhaps), very soon the powers-that-be might be convinced that the Marine Corps was an unnecessary carbon copy.

Lejeune understood the danger. He knew that the Corps could not survive on memories of Belleau Wood and re-enactments of Civil War battles. In a memorandum to the General Board of the Navy on February 11, 1922, Lejeune declared that it was vital to have "a mobile Marine Corps force adequate to conduct offensive land operations against hostile Naval bases . . . ."[12]

This was revolutionary. Previously, it had been accepted that Marines would be used to *defend* advanced bases for the Navy. Marine advanced base units were essentially coast artillery. But, with Guantanamo and Manila in memory, Lejeune was carrying this mission a giant step forward. He wrote, "The primary war mission of the Marine Corps is to supply a mobile force to accompany the Fleet for operations on shore in support of the fleet. . . ." He added that the Corps should be used "in conjunction with Army operations on shore, when the active naval operations reach such a stage as to permit its temporary detachment from the Navy."[13]

Lejeune's memorandum was a direct reaction to the Washington Disarmament Conference that had ended only five days earlier. At that conference, the world's naval powers set the rules by which they hoped to prevent a naval arms race. They established ratios of capital ships among the big powers, and they froze the status quo of naval bases in the western Pacific. The Americans, Japanese and British were neither to strengthen nor construct naval bases there for 10 years.

Lejeune pointed out to the General Board that, while navies were now limited by agreement, the mobile forces assigned to them were not restricted. He also emphasized the importance of the American island of Guam because the United States had no naval bases between Honolulu and Manila. He saw a future job for the Marine Corps—the one Ellis had predicted.

In 1927, the Joint Board of the Army and Navy gave the Corps the responsibility to "provide and maintain forces for the initial seizure of advanced bases and for such limited auxiliary land operations as are essential to the prosecution of the naval campaign."[14]

Under the pressure of severe Depression austerity, the role of the Marine Corps was reexamined again in 1931–1932. One result was Navy Department General Order No. 241 on December 7, 1933, based on a suggestion from Maj. Gen. John H. Russell, Assistant to the Commandant. The General Order established the Fleet Marine Force—a permanent Marine strike force to be kept in a state of readiness for operations with the fleet. The FMF's mission would be to execute landing operations. By the time the Corps was withdrawn from its Caribbean interventions in 1933, the theoretical revolution was complete.

Simultaneously, the Corps had begun primitive training in advanced base assault. In early 1922, a Marine force led by Lt. Col. Richard M. Cutts joined naval exercises in the Caribbean. Marine officers discovered that they had to learn how to attack a base as well as to defend one. At the end of 1923, a Marine expeditionary force led by Brig. Gen. Eli K. Cole tried to land against a defending force commanded by Col. Dion Williams. Some 3,000 men participated and it was a fiasco. Boats landed on the wrong beach, naval bombardment was inadequate, transports were badly loaded. But the fact that exercises were held and errors were spotted marked progress. After 1,500 Marines joined in joint Army–Navy exercises at Oahu, Hawaii, in 1925, the Marines were too busy in Nicaragua, Haiti and China to participate in fleet exercises again until 1932.

In the meanwhile, work on a viable amphibious assault doctrine had begun in 1931 under Brig. Gen. Randolph C. Berkeley, the first general officer to head the Marine Corps Schools. In January 1933, the Joint Board issued a general doctrine for joint overseas expeditions. The Marine Corps Schools' curriculum was radically revised to eliminate its Army orientation and teach how to defend and seize advanced bases. Specific Pacific islands were used as models. On November 14, 1933, all classes at Quantico were suspended; and staff and students, some 70 officers, devoted all their time to producing a landing operations manual. They worked on the frontier of military knowledge. By the following July, the Navy Department was able to publish a manual. In July, 1935, a board headed by Lt. Col. Charles D. Barrett finished the first edition to be widely distributed. Titled *Tentative Landing Operations Manual,* it became the Bible of amphibious warfare. Eventually adopted by both the Navy and the Army, it underwent repeated revisions, based on new experience, well into World War II.

The manual dealt with all the basic elements of amphibious operations: the nature of the landing force, the allocation of command responsibilities, ship-to-shore movements, survival on the beachhead, fitting naval gunfire support to the need of the landing force, the coordination of close air support, logistics, the combat-loading of transports, the use of landing craft. In all this, the Marine Corps was exploring new ground. Ever since the World War I defeat at Gallipoli, the presumption had been that the defense had all the advantages against amphibious landings. (No attention was paid to the successful 1917 German amphibious assault against the Russians at Riga.) The Marine Corps set out to prove that conclusion was wrong. By December 1941, it had a workable doctrine ready to go.

After World War II, Gen. Alexander A. Vandegrift summed up the importance of what the Marine Corps had achieved:

> Despite its outstanding record as a combat force in the past war, the Marine Corps' far greater contribution to victory was doctrinal: that is, the fact that the basic amphibious doctrines which carried Allied troops over every beachhead of World War II had been largely shaped—often in the face of uninterested and doubting military orthodoxy—by U.S. Marines, and mainly between 1922 and 1935.[15]

During this same period, the Corps focused its attention on still another field of special knowledge—its experience fighting "small wars." In 1922, Maj. Samuel M. Harrington pulled together the Marines' expertise, and his paper was incorporated in the Marine Corps Schools' curriculum. By 1940, the Corps had developed a unique *Small Wars Manual*, which it still used for its pacification program in Vietnam 25 years later.

To prove out their doctrine, strategy and tactics of amphibious landing operations and "small wars," the Marines pressed hard against a scarcity of funds and frustrating bureaucratic opposition. Nothing could be accomplished alone. Marines could never make it ashore without the Navy and naval air. In amphibious assault, the Navy and Marine Corps were extensions of each other. As Adm. Richmond Kelly Turner, who commanded Marine landings throughout World War II, said, "No one service invented amphibious warfare. The Marines contributed much (patterned on Japanese methods) to its development in recent years. But so also did the Navy, including Naval Aviation. Furthermore, beginning in 1940, the Army contributed a great deal."[16]

The first real chance to test the landing operations manual's theories came in 1935. By then, enough Marines were available to make up an expeditionary force. Fleet landing exercises, which took place each winter until Pearl Harbor, attacked the problems and tested the equipment for amphibious assault. Marines practiced daylight and night landings. Naval gunfire support was improved; for example, surface-bursting shells replaced the armor-piercing shells that warships normally carried. Close air support was added. Landing craft were tried out.

The last fleet landing exercise (Flex-7) was held in the Caribbean in February 1941 and included the 1st Marine Division and the 1st Marine Aircraft Group—a larger amphibious force than had been previously assembled. But there were still defects: landing craft were still inadequate; naval gunfire lacked fire control equipment, proper guns and projectiles; and communication between ships and shore was faulty.

Because of the need for a larger base, the Marine Corps obtained a new site for amphibious exercises at New River, North Carolina—the future Camp Lejeune. In June and July 1941, exercises were held there, climaxed with a two-division landing. By now, amphibious training was under hard-driving Maj. Gen. Holland M. Smith.

As the Corps learned the ropes, it also trained Army divisions in amphibious tactics. The 1st Infantry Division later participated in the invasions of Sicily and Omaha Beach; the 3rd Infantry Division landed at Casablanca, Sicily and Anzio; the 7th landed at Attu, Kiska, Kwajalein, Leyte and Okinawa; the 9th Division landed at Algiers, Palermo and Normandy. And the two original Marine divisions fed men trained in amphibious assault into newer Marine divisions. "Officers and men of the Navy, Army and Marine Corps, trained in these exercises, ultimately found their way into every theater of war where amphibious operations were conducted."[17]

Since existing Navy equipment proved unsuitable for lifting men and weapons ashore against hostile fire, efficient landing craft were badly needed.

In the early 1920s, the Marines experimented with a British-designed "Beetle boat" and a Christie amphibian tractor. Both were useless. In 1936, the Marines tried out five different commercial boats as possible landing craft. They even tested fishing boats and boats seized from rum runners; but all had exposed rudders and propellers, and men had to drop as far as 10 feet into the water.

225

The answers started to take shape when Andrew J. Higgins, a New Orleans boat builder, working with the Marine Corps and Navy, modified the shallow-water Eureka boat that he had designed for trappers and oil drillers on the Gulf Coast. In April 1941, Maj. Ernest E. Linsert showed Higgins pictures that Capt. Victor H. Krulak had taken of landing boats the Japanese used at Shanghai in 1937 One type had a ramp in its bow. At his own expense, Higgins put a retractable bow ramp on his 36-foot Eureka boat; this became the precursor of the LCVP of World War II.

At the same time, a lighter to get tanks ashore was developed with similar experiments and failures. Higgins again solved the problem. He designed a 50-foot boat, originally designed in a smaller version for use in South America, to carry a 30-ton tank and land it over a bow ramp. Senator Harry S. Truman's War Investigating Committee had to intercede with the Navy before Higgins' model became the standard LCM.

The crucial amphibian tractor was developed after Maj. Gen. Louis McCarty Little, then commanding the FMF, was shown a picture in a 1937 issue of *Life* magazine of the Alligator created by Donald Roebling, Jr., grandson of the builder of the Brooklyn Bridge. By 1940, Roebling's tractor had been improved to travel 29 mph on land and 9.7 mph in the water. In February 1941, Krulak persuaded Adm. Ernest J. King, commander of the Atlantic Fleet, to ride in an aluminum Alligator at Culebra, Puerto Rico. The vehicle broke a track on a reef and the impatient admiral waded ashore. But in July, Roebling had the first steel-welded Alligator ready; and by the end of World War II, 15,654 LVTs had been built and had become the key to successful amphibious assault.

Simultaneously, Marine aviation learned to provide close air support for amphibious landings. The Marines had practiced air support techniques in the mountains of Nicaragua; but faster planes brought more complex problems and required more reliable communication between air and ground. The toughest problem was to hit the enemy and not friendly troops nearby.

In January 1939, the Navy's General Board declared that Marine aviation's prime mission was the support of the FMF in landing operations and in the field. Marine aviation was still a small organization; when World War II began, the Corps had only 251 planes of all types. At that time, Marine aviation's director was Col. Ralph J. Mitchell, who had won the Distinguished Flying Cross in Nicaragua. Brig. Gen. Roy S. Geiger commanded that 1st Marine Aircraft Wing (MAW) at Quantico, and Brig. Gen. Ross E. Rowell, the 2d MAW, which was based at San Diego and had most of its air group on Hawaii.

When summoned to war, the Marine Corps had certainly not ironed out all the problems of amphibious assault. That would require the test of combat. But the Corps had a mission, a doctrine, a knowledge of tactics, officers and men trained in landing operations and the most essential equipment to get them ashore. The Marines had worked for some 20 years to get ready. They would lead the way across the Pacific.

Marines fighting on Eniwetok Atoll in the
Marshall Islands in February 1944.
U.S. Coast Guard Photo, National Archives

SEMPER FIDELIS

V
WORLD
WAR II
1941-1949

1
December 7, 1941

Sunday morning started sunny and bright. After breakfast, Marine Capt. Leonard Ashwell, the officer of the day, strolled out of the mess hall. He heard the roar of aircraft engines and looked up to the northern sky. He recognized two formations of Japanese torpedo bombers flying eastward from the direction of nearby Barber's Point. Then, down over the mountains came 21 Zero fighters. Ashwell raced to the guardhouse to sound the alarm. The Zeros hit. It was 7:55 A.M. War had come to Ewa Mooring Mast Field, the Marines' airfield four miles west of Pearl Harbor.

The Zeros drove in low, some of them 20 feet above the ground. They strafed the 47 planes of Marine Aircraft Group 21, parked wing tip to wing tip against sabotage, and in repeated passes destroyed or damaged every one.

Marines dashed to their stations and organized a makeshift defense. They tried futilely to get planes into the air. They broke out spare machine guns and wrenched others from wrecked planes. They fought back with rifles and pistols. There were no antiaircraft guns. Lt. Col. Claude A. "Sheriff" Larkin, the group commander and senior Marine aviator in the Pacific, was wounded while driving to the field but took command of his men by 8:05.

Half an hour later, the Japanese swept back from the direction of Pearl Harbor. They concentrated on strafing buildings and hospital tents and men. Master Technical Sgt. Emil S. Peters and Pvt. William C. Turner shot down a Val bomber with the machine gun in the rear cockpit of a parked dive bomber. Turner was mortally wounded. The Zeros attacked a third time, but now the Marine gunners were able to deflect the blow.

[For the location of places in the Pacific in World War II see map No. 8 in the map section.—*Au.*]

Walter Lord in *Day of Infamy* tells: "Up above, Lieutenant Yoshio Shiga raked Ewa with his Zero fighter. He noticed a Marine standing beside a disabled plane and charged down, all guns blazing. The man refused to budge . . . kept firing with a pistol. Shiga still considers him the bravest American he ever met."[1]

Dive bombers came from the direction of Pearl Harbor and bombed and strafed Ewa. They were followed by fighters, which, two and three at a time, strafed the field, protecting the Japanese raiders as they assembled to return to their carriers. The last of the enemy planes headed out to sea at 9:45 A.M. It was all over in less than two hours. At Ewa, four enlisted Marines were dead or fatally wounded, 13 wounded. The field was a junkyard of burning planes.

The Japanese struck Pearl Harbor two minutes after they hit Ewa. The guard bugler turned out the Marines at the Navy Yard. The men of the Marine Barracks and the 1st and 3rd Defense Battalions raced for the armories and gun sheds and fired their rifles at the planes, as warships began exploding. At the Naval Air Station on Ford Island, the Japanese destroyed the seaplanes before the sailors and the 102 Marines there could react. "There was no ready ammunition at any aircraft gun position on the island."[2]

Within six minutes after the attack started, Col. Harry K. Pickett, commander of the 485-man Marine Barracks at the Navy Yard, ordered out his Marines. They had already set up eight machine guns and were getting ammunition. Hundreds of Marines on the barracks' parade ground were issued rifle ammunition. They got 38 machine guns into action and shot down three dive bombers. Nine Marines were wounded. Colonel Pickett ordered 3-inch antiaircraft guns dragged from storage to the parade ground. But all their ammunition was at the Lualualei depot, 27 miles back in the hills. The last Japanese planes had left long before the shells reached Pearl Harbor. The Marines were no more prepared for undeclared war than any other Americans.

The targets of the Japanese were the warships of the United States Pacific Fleet, berthed in Pearl Harbor. The Japanese sank four battleships and damaged four more and three cruisers. Marines helped defend the stricken ships; the cruiser *Helena's*

Marine gunners shot down a plane. When *USS Arizona* blew up, Maj. Alan Shapley of Detroit, a former Annapolis quarterback, was hurled into the water, regained consciousness and saved a Marine from drowning. Among 877 Marines in the ships' detachments, 108 were killed and 49 wounded. In all, 2,280 Americans were killed and 1,109 wounded. The Japanese lost 29 planes, five midget submarines and fewer than 100 men.

The militarists in Tokyo planned to wipe the European powers and the United States out of the western and southern Pacific. In Europe, France had already fallen to the Nazis; the British had their backs against the wall. Japan was poised to conquer Thailand, the Philippines, Borneo, Singapore and, the richest prize of all, Dutch-ruled Java.

The Japanese knew the U.S. Pacific Fleet spent each weekend in Pearl Harbor. They had sent six carriers far north of normal shipping lanes, and, 275 miles north of Pearl Harbor, launched 360 warplanes at the unsuspecting Americans. At that very moment, Japan's envoys in Washington were waiting to confer again with Secretary of State Cordell Hull. By the time they met, Hull already had in hand the first message sent from Ford Island at 7:58: "AIR RAID PEARL HARBOR—THIS IS NO DRILL!!"

The Americans were vulnerable to a sneak attack because their military leaders had stupidly underestimated the Japanese—and defensive preparations were criminally sloppy. Naval historian Samuel Eliot Morison was also critical of the Japanese planners: "On the tactical level, the Pearl Harbor attack was wrongly concentrated on ships rather than permanent installations and oil tanks. On the strategic level it was idiotic. On the high political level it was disastrous."[3] The Japanese neutralized the American fleet for the moment, but they brought down on themselves all the power of the United States.

The Japanese also had one important bit of bad luck. The two U.S. aircraft carriers in the Pacific, *Enterprise* and *Lexington*, were not in Pearl Harbor that Sunday morning. *Enterprise* steamed some 200 miles west of Hawaii, having ferried Marine Fighter Squadron 211's planes to Wake Island. *Lexington* was on her way to Midway Island to deliver Marine Scout Bomber Squadron 231's planes; she turned back to Pearl when she heard of the attack. Ten days later, those 17 Marine planes flew directly from Oahu to Midway, 1,137 miles distant, the longest single-engine landplane massed flight then recorded.

The effect of the hit-and-run Pearl Harbor raid was bad enough, but the disaster was not total. A number of heavy cruisers were also at sea, the carrier *Saratoga* was at San Diego and the battleship *Colorado*, at Bremerton, Washington. The carrier *Yorktown* and three battleships, plus planes and destroyers, were promptly shifted from the Atlantic into the Pacific.

Immediately after the attack, all the Marines in the Pearl Harbor Navy Yard area were pooled to strengthen its defenses and provide an infantry reserve in case of an amphibious landing. By the end of the month, Marines of the defense battalions were being shipped out to reinforce the tiny garrisons at Midway, Johnston Island and Palmyra. The job of reorganizing began at once.

2
"Marines Surrender Hard"

Despite American fears, the Japanese had no intention of landing on Hawaii. They had gobbled up enough of the Pacific and Southeast Asia to choke a python and would need months to digest their kill.

U.S. Marines met the Japanese face to face on the ground only in four places: China, Guam, Wake and the Philippines. The encounters in China and on Guam were quickly finished; Wake and the Philippines took longer.

That morning (December 8 in China), 2d Lt. Richard M. Huizenga was supervising the loading of Marine Corps supplies aboard *President Harrison* on the docks at Chinwangtao, northeast of Tientsin. The raid on Pearl Harbor was already over when a truck driver brought him word of the attack. The lieutenant rushed back to his men at the railhead. He found the 21 Marines surrounded by Japanese soldiers. Chief Marine Gunner William A. Lee, who had won three Navy Crosses in Nicaragua, was organizing a strongpoint and had broken out two machine guns and Thompson submachine guns and BARs. Their situation was hopeless but they were ready to fight. The Japanese captain allowed 2d Lt. Huizenga to communicate with Maj. Luther A. Brown at Tientsin, who ordered him not to resist.

In both Tientsin and Peking, the Japanese surrounded the Marine Barracks and demanded that the Marines surrender. Col. William W. Ashurst, the senior Marine officer at the U.S. Embassy, was given until noon to decide whether to fight or surrender. After communicating with the commander of the U.S. Asiatic Fleet in Manila and with Major Brown at Tientsin, Colonel Ashurst ordered his men, fewer than 200 Marines, to lay down their arms. He hoped that as embassy guards they would

235

be repatriated with the diplomatic personnel. But it was not to be. The Marines were imprisoned in Shanghai.

On the island of Guam, the garrison of 153 Marines was as helpless as the handful of Marines in China. The island lay among the Japanese-held Mariana Islands and had been neutralized by the 1922 disarmament treaty. The 1941 American war plan, Rainbow 5, conceded Guam's capture.

In addition to the Marines, Guam had 271 Navy personnel and a native force of 326 armed with obsolete rifles. Lt. Col. William K. McNulty commanded the Marines; 122 of them were at Sumay barracks on the south side of Apra harbor; the rest were stationed in villages around the island.

At 5:45 A.M. December 8, Guam time, the garrison commander and island governor, Capt. George J. McMillin, USN, was informed of the attack on Pearl Harbor. At 8:27, Japanese bombers from Saipan hit. They immediately sank the minesweeper *Penguin* in Apra harbor. Her guns were Guam's only weapons larger than .30 caliber machine guns. Planes bombed and strafed the island the rest of that day and the next. There was no effective defense.

At 4 A.M. on December 10, 400 Japanese sailors landed at Dungcas Beach, just north of the town of Agaña on Guam's west coast. And 5,500 soldiers landed at Tumon Bay north of the beach and on the southwest coast. When the first enemy sailors reached Agaña, a detachment of native troops commanded by Marine 1st Lt. Charles S. Todd met them in the plaza with rifle and machine-gun fire. They pushed the invaders back twice and lost 17 men, but they could not hold out long.

Captain McMillin saw that the situation was futile. Shortly after 6 A.M., he surrendered to the Japanese naval commander. He sent orders to the Marines at Sumay not to resist, but scattered fighting continued the rest of the day as the Japanese spread out over the island. Nineteen of the garrison were killed and 42 wounded, including four Marines killed and 12 wounded. The surviving Americans were shipped to prison camps in Japan. It would be two and a half years before Marines returned to Guam.

The day after Guam fell, the defenders of Wake Island scored the first American victory of the war. It was heartening but temporary.

At 5 A.M. on December 11, Japanese cruisers, escorting transports loaded with 450 Special Naval Landing Troops, opened fire on Wake. Marine lookouts had spotted the flotilla in the light of the half moon; but Maj. James P. S. Devereux, commanding the Marine defense battalion detachment, held his fire to prevent the enemy from locating his guns prematurely. At 6:15, the new light cruiser *Yubari* and three destroyers closed to 4,500 yards. Now, the Marines opened up. The 5-inch guns of Battery A at Peacock Point, commanded by 1st Lt. Clarence A. Barninger, hit *Yubari* three times; the cruiser turned tail and fled, trailing smoke. On Wilkes Island, Battery L's 5-inch guns, commanded by 2d Lt. John A. McAlister, sank the lead destroyer *Hayate*; she was the first Japanese surface craft sunk by U.S. naval forces in the war. The Marine gun crews were so excited they stopped firing and started cheering. Platoon Sgt. Henry A. Bedell, an old China hand, brought them back to business, bellowing: "Knock it off, you bastards, you get back on the guns. What d'ya think this is, a ball game?"[4]

The keyed-up Marine gunners promptly hit a second destroyer and the lead transport and sent off the other two transports. Their accurate firing then found a light cruiser, and she also turned away. First Lt. Woodrow W. Kessler's Marines at Battery B on Peale Island scored on a destroyer.

The Marine gunners had driven off the invasion force. Four Marine Grumman F4F Wildcats, led by Maj. Paul A. Putnam, of Washington, Iowa, chased the retreating ships, strafed them, dropped 100-pound bombs and scooted home to re-arm. The planes shuttled out; damaged two warships and a transport, and Capt. Henry T. Elrod of Thomasville, Georgia, sank the destroyer *Kisaragi*. There were no survivors.

The battle was an unqualified victory for the Marines. They had sunk two destroyers, damaged a cruiser and several other ships, shot down three Japanese bombers and damaged four more. The enemy lost some 500 men; on Wake, there were no casualties. Historian Morison wrote: "The eleventh day of December 1941 should always be a proud day in the history of the Corps. Never again, in this Pacific War, did coast defense guns beat off an amphibious landing."[5] But the Marines' superb shooting could not save Wake.

The Japanese were determined to take the atoll. A lonely

237

speck 450 miles from the nearest land, it was made up of three islands in the shape of a wishbone open to the northwest. The main island was Wake; Wilkes was at the tip of the southern branch of the wishbone, and Peale at the tip of the northern. The atoll, which had been visited by the Wilkes Exploring Expedition in 1841 and annexed by the United States in 1899, sat astride the Pacific lines of communication of both the United States and Japan—a strategically placed coral aircraft carrier.

When war came, there were on Wake only 388 Marines of the 1st Defense Battalion commanded by small, wiry Major Devereux, who had been an enlisted Marine in Nicaragua and China; Major Putnam's Marine Fighter Squadron 211 of 61 men and 12 blue and gray Wildcats (flown off *Enterprise* on December 4); 68 Navy personnel; five Army communications men; 70 Pan American civilians, and 1,146 civilian contract employees who had been trying to pound Wake's coral boulders into a naval air base. Navy Commander Winfield Scott Cunningham, a lanky aviator, was the atoll commander.

Only the understrength Marines were armed. A total of six 5-inch and a dozen 3-inch guns were emplaced on Peale and Wilkes islands and on Peacock Point at the base of Wake. There were Marines enough to man but six of the 3-inch antiaircraft guns.

After sunrise on Monday (Sunday, December 7 in Hawaii), Pan American's *Philippine Clipper* took off and headed west toward Guam. The Marines were finishing breakfast. Major Devereux was shaving. At 6:50, Army Capt. Henry S. Wilson dashed into the major's tent with an uncoded message that Hawaii was under attack. Devereux told the bugler to sound Call to Arms. Marines grabbed their Springfield '03 rifles and ammunition and World War I-style helmets, piled into trucks and rushed to their batteries. By 7:35, all positions were manned. Aviators had their planes warmed up and dispersed as much as possible; civilians started digging foxholes. The Clipper was recalled and returned. A four-plane patrol went up and swung to the north to scout for enemy planes.

Just before noon, 36 twin-engine bombers, approaching from the south, swooped down out of a rain cloud. The island had no radar; and with the constantly roaring surf, nobody heard or saw the bombers until 15 seconds before the first bombs fell.

In ten furious minutes, the Japanese destroyed seven of the eight Wildcats on the ground; wrecked the Pan Am Station, riddled the Clipper; killed 10 civilians; and killed 23 aviation Marines and wounded 11 more. The enemy fliers flew off intact, waggling their wings to celebrate their success.

An hour later, the Clipper managed to take off for Midway to the northeast. The Marines and some volunteers from Dan Teters' civilian construction crew cared for the wounded, repaired damage, salvaged planes and mined the runway to prevent an airborne landing. The Marines could not get permission to use the contractor's ditchdiggers to bury their communications wires.

For the next two days, Wake was pounded. Only three Wildcats were operational. Lt. David D. Kliewer and Tech. Sgt. William J. Hamilton flew in on the flanks of one enemy raid and shot down a straggling bomber. Captain Elrod shot down two more. The bombers hit guns, ammunition, barracks, radio station and machine shops. They burned the hospital to the ground, killing four Marines, 55 civilians and several corpsmen.

On the third night, December 11, the Japanese made their first attempt to land and were thrown back by the Marine gunners.

At Pearl Harbor, the American naval commanders organized a relief expedition built around three fast-carrier task forces with *Lexington, Enterprise* and *Saratoga.* But the relief expedition was crippled by indecisiveness and excessive caution. Naval officers feared risking their then-irreplaceable carriers.

Bombers clobbered the island almost daily; there was no hiding from the hell they dropped. By December 14, two planes had been wrecked; and VMF-211 was down to one again. Cannibalizing planes, the Marines on the seventeenth had four Wildcats that could do battle.

On Saturday, December 20, a Navy PBY arrived: Wake's first physical contact with the outside world since the island was attacked. The plane brought the plans of the relief expedition, cheering all hands, and took off again early the next morning. Two hours later, the first Japanese carrier dive bombers and fighters appeared. They promised that the Japanese were preparing another landing attempt.

The twenty-first was a bitter day; Battery D on Peale was

virtually destroyed. On the twenty-second, only two Wildcats could fly. Capt. Herbert C. Freuler and 2d Lt. Carl R. Davidson took them up and attacked 33 carrier dive bombers and six Zeros. Davidson dived at one of the bombers; a Zero shot him down. Freuler exploded another Zero. A Zero tailed him and wounded him twice. He escaped and crash-landed his plane on Wake. That wiped out the Marine airpower for good. What was left of VMF-211, less than 20 able-bodied men, joined the Defense Battalion as infantry.

It was now a race between the American relief expedition and the enemy landing force. The Japanese won. *Saratoga* was still 600 miles from Wake; but Rear Adm. Frank Jack Fletcher spent December 22 refueling. Then it was too late.

The Marines spotted the Japanese amphibious force at 2:15 A.M. on December 23, an intensely dark, moonless night. This time, the Japanese came to stay. They brought six heavy cruisers, six destroyers and two carriers. In the landing force were an estimated 1,500 men.

At 2:35, the enemy landed simultaneously on Wilkes and the southern shore of Wake. About 100 men hit Wilkes. There, big, tough Marine Gunner Clarence B. McKinstry, commanding Battery F, began the battle by firing a .50 caliber machine gun at the landing barges. On Wake Island, 1,000 Japanese landed against some 85 Marines on the beach. An unmanned 3-inch gun on a slight rise was the only large weapon that could bear on the two destroyer-transports disembarking their men. Second Lt. Robert M. Hanna quickly gathered a scratch crew, raced to this gun and threw 15 shells into the grounded landing craft. But the enemy scrambled ashore. Devereux sent Major Putnam, Captain Elrod and the VMF-211 Marines between the enemy and Hanna's gun. They fought off several hundred Japanese for six hours, until all but one of the defenders, Marines and civilians, were killed or wounded. Among the dead was Hank Elrod. The thirty-six-year-old flier was the first Marine aviator in World War II to earn the Medal of Honor—awarded for his courage in the air and on the ground.

The Marine Defense Battalion had no infantry component; small detachments, bolstered by a few civilian workers, met repeated enemy attacks and shouting bayonet charges. They fought the enemy with machine guns, rifles and grenades. The

Japanese captured the hospital and tied up the wounded Marines with telephone wire. Maj. George H. Potter, Jr., Devereux's executive officer, and 40 men fought from a defense line that crossed the airstrip. At 5 A.M., a half hour before dawn, Commander Cunningham sent a message to Pearl Harbor: "ENEMY ON ISLAND ISSUE IN DOUBT." The Japanese were firmly established on the atoll. The Marines' thin line was just too thin.

At Pearl, Vice Adm. William S. Pye, temporarily commander of the Pacific Fleet, fearful of losing *Saratoga*, ordered the mismanaged relief expedition back to Hawaii. On *Saratoga*, sailors and Marines were furious; Marine aviators cursed and wept. Wake's last hope was snuffed out.

At 7:30, Cunningham and Devereux, knowing now that no relief could be expected, decided to surrender. Devereux, with Sgt. Donald Malleck carrying a white rag on a mop handle, walked south to meet the nearest Japanese commander. But the fighting continued for hours, and Devereux had to go to each Marine position to bring the battle to a halt. As Morison wrote, "Marines surrender hard."[6]

The final battle was fought on little Wilkes Island, where there were 70 Marines and a number of sailors and civilians. Gunner McKinstry's Marines were forced back to join men from Battery L commanded by 2d Lt. McAlister. From this position, they were able to block the way to the main island.

Capt. Wesley McC. Platt's command post on Wilkes was on the far side of the Japanese landing force. Down near the beach, on that side, the Marine machine gun nearest the landing was able to repel attacks until dawn.

As day broke, Captain Platt led Platoon Sgt. Raymond L. Coulson and eight Marine riflemen against nearly 100 Japanese. They drove the surprised Japanese back toward the McAlister–McKinstry line. McAlister gathered 24 Marines and counterattacked from his side. Platt and McAlister joined forces and together wiped out the rest of the Japanese landing force on Wilkes.

But Platt was now out of communication with Devereux's command post. Under dive bomber attack, he and his Marines marched east toward Wake Island. At 1:30 P.M., Platt saw three men approaching: two Marines and a Japanese officer with a large sword. The Marines were Devereux and Malleck; the major

241

told Platt that the atoll had been surrendered. The battle for Wake was over.

The Japanese made prisoners of 470 officers and men and 1,146 civilians. The American dead were 49 Marines, three sailors and about 70 civilians. Enemy casualties in taking Wake were estimated to total 820 killed and 333 wounded.

The prisoners kept hoping for an American counterattack until they sailed on January 12 for Shanghai. En route, they were half-starved and repeatedly beaten. Two Marine sergeants from VMF-211 and three sailors were beheaded. In Woosung prison camp near Shanghai, the Wake Marines joined Colonel Ashurst and the Marines from North China. They would be there a very long time.

3
Bataan and Corregidor—
"An Example of Courage"

Marine Capt. Francis H. "Joe" Williams and a demolition team spent Christmas Day erasing the Olongapo Naval Station on Subic Bay, the Philippines, from the face of the earth. They blew up and burned everything except the Marine Barracks, which stood too close to the civilian town. Then, the last elements of the 4th Marine Regiment left for the naval base at Mariveles on the tip of the Bataan Peninsula, on their way to Corregidor, "The Rock."

Gen. Douglas MacArthur, commanding the defense of the Philippines, had not asked for the 4th Marines to be assigned to his command until December 20. By then, the Japanese were already advancing on Manila.

The war had come to the Philippines at 3 A.M. December 8 (local time). Marine Lt. Col. William T. Clement, the duty officer at Navy headquarters on the Manila waterfront, brought the message to Adm. Thomas C. Hart, commander of the U.S. Asiatic Fleet, at the Manila Hotel. Clement's radio operator had intercepted the message that told the world of the attack on Pearl Harbor.

The Japanese bombed the Philippines that first day of the war. They caught American air power on the ground at Clark Field, knocked out one third of the fighters and half the bombers. By December 12, they had won control of the air, destroyed the Navy Yard at Cavite and landed on both ends of Luzon, the main Philippine island. The day after Christmas, MacArthur declared Manila an open city, not to be defended, and brought the U.S. forces to the Bataan Peninsula on the northern side of Manila Bay.

The defense of the Philippines was heroic, but the Ameri-

243

cans' resistance there did not affect the enemy's grand strategy. All the Americans and Filipinos had the strength to do, in the end, was to deny the use of Manila Bay to the Japanese Navy for a time. Holding out beyond any realistic hope of relief, their courage and suffering on Bataan and Corregidor became important symbols back home in those defeat-strewn early days of the war.

The 4th Marines had arrived at Olongapo at the end of November with only 44 officers and 728 enlisted men. Since the regiment had been allowed to dwindle by attrition in China, Col. Samuel L. Howard had only two battalions, each short one company and each company short one rifle platoon. The 1st Battalion, soon after arriving in the Philippines, went to Mariveles on the tip of Bataan.

Across Manila Bay, at Cavite, the 1st Separate Marine Battalion, commanded by Lt. Col. John P. Adams, provided antiaircraft defense for the naval base there. After the battalion's 3-inch guns shot down one dive bomber, enemy planes stayed above the guns' range and bombed the base at will. By December 10, it was in flames.

On Christmas Day, while Captain Williams was wrecking the Olongapo Naval Station, Adams' battalion completed the destruction of Cavite. The next night, 411 men from Adams' command were the first Marines to make the seven-and-a-half-mile voyage from Mariveles to Corregidor to man the beach defenses of that island fortress. Most of the 4th Marines joined them during the next two nights; and on New Year's Day, the Separate Battalion became the 3rd Battalion, 4th Marines.

Remaining on Bataan were Batteries A and C and the radar detachment of Adams' battalion. Battery A, commanded by 1st Lt. William F. Hogaboom, and Battery C, commanded by 1st Lt. Willard C. Holdredge, were incorporated into a naval battalion organized to protect Mariveles. The 120 Marines in the two antiaircraft batteries were an infinitesimal part of the 80,000 American and Filipinos bottled up on the 30-mile-long jungle-covered peninsula. In mid-January, 49 Marines were brought back from Corregidor to guard MacArthur's advance headquarters on Bataan.

On the night of January 22–23, a 900-man Japanese amphibious force landed behind the American-Filipino front across

Bataan. This brought the Marines into action. Hogaboom and Holdredge were ordered to take out patrols made up mostly of sailors, with Marines as squad and platoon leaders. They set up blocking positions on a hill above the landing site at Quinauan Point. The next day, Hogaboom—a young Annapolis graduate from Vicksburg who was to die as a POW—led a patrol down. The Americans got a taste of jungle warfare, fighting an enemy they could not see. The Japanese added firepower and Hogaboom retreated to the high ground. Meanwhile, a patrol led by Holdredge surprised the Japanese on Longoskawayan Point and killed a number of them before they pushed Holdredge's men back onto the ridges.

The patrols were reinforced by a machine-gun platoon and an 81mm mortar platoon from the 4th Marines on Corregidor. Holdredge ran into a superior force and was among the many wounded before the Americans could fall back to the ridges.

On the twenty-seventh, a skirmish line of some 200 men, including 60 to 75 Marines, attacked. The fighting was fierce, but they could not dislodge the Japanese. Two days later, a battalion of Philippine Scouts, supported by the Marines' mortars and machine guns, smashed the enemy and wiped out the landing force. That threat to Mariveles was finally eliminated.

Most of the naval battalion joined the 4th Marines on Corregidor in mid-February. On March 12, MacArthur left the Philippines; and on April 3, the Japanese, now greatly strengthened, reopened their offensive on Bataan. The defenders, dazed by the incessant bombardment, suffering from disease and short rations, were driven back. In a week, it was all over. Munitions and fuel dumps at Mariveles were blown up. Small craft took all possible men over to The Rock. And on April 9, 75,000 Americans and Filipinos, including 105 Marines, went on the infamous Death March and into captivity.

The very next day, the siege of Corregidor began. The 4th Marines, armed with Springfields and wearing their World War I-style helmets, dug into their beach-defense positions, strung barbed wire, laid mine fields and placed their guns and communications to meet the inevitable attack.

Overall, Corregidor was three and a half miles long. The western end was a broad area a mile and a half wide, and to the east ran a long, narrow tail. In the middle was the extensively tunneled Malinta Hill, which contained the headquarters for the defenders. The Marines' 1st Battalion guarded Malinta Hill and the island's eastern tail. West of the 1st Battalion was Lt. Col. Adams' 3rd Battalion, and the 2d Battalion covered the rest of the shoreline. About 100 Marines were sent over to bolster the defenses on nearby Caballo Island and tiny El Fraile Island.

The men on the exposed beaches took a beating. The Japanese pounded them from the air and with 105mm guns on Cavite Province. The enemy could spot any movement in daylight. The beach defenders received food after dark and before dawn, mostly rice and a little canned salmon. Water was scarce. The 11,000 men isolated on Corregidor held out for 27 brutal days.

The 4th Marines were joined by personnel from the naval battalion and the sunken ships and by more than 700 Philippine Air Cadets. The regiment, which had started with less than 800 Marines, had, in the end, nearly 4,000 men from all the services, including 72 Marine officers and 1,368 enlisted Marines. Most of the newcomers were in terrible physical shape, gaunt, emaciated. The 275-man naval battalion of sailors from Mariveles and the scuttled submarine tender *Canopus* became the 4th Battalion, 4th Marines. It had only six Marines: now-Major Williams, their commanding officer, and five noncoms. Williams' battalion joined the regimental reserve commanded by Maj. Max W. Schaeffer.

Williams has gone down in Marine Corps history as a special hero. During the bombardment he was "a giant among men at a time when courage was commonplace."[7] "Wherever the bombardment was heaviest, he showed up to see how his men weathered the storm . . . he led rescue parties from 4/4 into the . . . holocausts of flame, choking smoke and exploding ammunition to rescue the wounded."[8]

The 4th Marines were determined to get back at the enemy they had been unable to hit. Their morale was high; almost until the end, they hoped for rescue. As Morison described the scene:

> . . . the toll of casualties rose, and the nervous strain was almost unbearable. A certain number of officers and men gave in under the tension. Some saw hallucinations, others became completely ineffectual and could not per-

form their duties. But the tough and the strongminded held the team together and inspired the rest. Colonel Howard's 4th Marine Regiment . . . lived up to the great traditions of the Corps in the last bitter days. The backbone of Corregidor's beach defense, it set an example of courage for those who began to give under the strain.[9]

The Japanese set their D-Day for the night of May 5. On April 29, the Emperor's birthday, they celebrated by beginning a bombardment that never let up day or night. The water supply in the East Sector was knocked out; wire communications were ruined; casualties mounted. The defensive installations of the 1st Battalion, defending the island's eastern tail, were virtually destroyed. On the night of May 3, the submarine *Spearfish* made the last evacuation from The Rock, taking a few officers and 14 nurses who had been ordered out.

Starting at 10:45 P.M. on May 5, the Japanese poured in the most intensive bombardment yet on the strip of beach between Cavalry and Infantry Points, east of Malinta Hill, where they planned to land. But their barges, carried by a strong incoming tide, actually headed for North Point, almost at the island's tail.

As the first enemy battalion came ashore, the whole area erupted with gunfire. Japanese casualties were high. On the beach, Platoon Sgt. William "Tex" Haynes emptied two pistols at the advancing enemy, then fired a .30 caliber machine gun cradled in his arms until a grenade wounded him severely. A Company's 2d Platoon, commanded by Master Gunnery Sgt. John Mercurio, defended the beach between Cavalry Point and North Point and was overwhelmed.

By midnight, a second battalion landed in the light of the newly risen full moon. Enough Japanese made it ashore to drive onto the hogback that ran down the middle of the island's tail. They seized Denver Battery on high ground behind Cavalry Point and forced a hole in the center of the defenders' line. Marine Gunner Harold M. Ferrell organized a new line on the hogback to protect the rear of the defenders on the beach. Lt. Col. Curtis T. Beecher sent squads one at a time to build up the line Ferrell had begun. These men took severe casualties; the 1,000 yards to the Denver Battery was a deathtrap.

247

By 1:30 A.M., the surviving defenders on the eastern end of the island were isolated. Colonel Howard ordered up Major Schaeffer's two reserve companies. Two platoons of Lieutenant Hogaboom's company got into position; but the third platoon was chopped to pieces. Capt. Robert Chambers, Jr.,'s company was shelled by the guns on Bataan, and only the equivalent of one platoon ran the gauntlet.

Major Schaeffer ordered three counterattacks against the dug-in Japanese, who had set up machine guns at the base of a stone water tower. Schaeffer's reserves drove up the slope and were repeatedly shoved back. Sgt. Major Thomas F. Sweeney and Quartermaster Sgt. John E. Haskin, two oldtimers and close friends, personally attacked the machine gunners. Haskin was killed bringing more grenades up to Sweeney on top of the water tower. Sweeney destroyed one of the guns before he too died.

At 4:30, Colonel Howard ordered up his last reserves, Major Williams' 4th Battalion, which had been waiting in the hot confusion of the Malinta Tunnel. When Williams' men reached the "line," Schaeffer's command had been almost wiped out. Williams took charge. Opposing units slugged it out 30 yards apart. "It was a barroom brawl."[10]

At dawn, Williams moved along the line, telling his Army and Navy officers to be ready to attack at 6:15. Every man was in the line. There were no reserves. The companies on the left pushed the enemy back some 200 yards; but on the right, the men could make no progress. The fighting was at grenade range.

At 9:30, Japanese tanks were unloaded off barges at Cavalry Point; by 10, they were in position, and enemy artillery pounded the area in front of the Japanese line. The Americans began falling back in disorder. At 10:30, Williams ordered the units on the left back to the ruins of a concrete trench in front of the Malinta Tunnel. Casualties were severe. "It was each man for himself."[11] Only Williams, now wounded, and about 150 men made it to the trench. The Japanese were less than 300 yards away, and their tanks were moving to outflank them. At 11:30, Williams was told the decision had been made to surrender at noon.

The order went out to destroy all weapons larger than .45 caliber. The Marines of the 2d and 4rd Battalions, who had never been brought to battle, smashed their rifles on the rocks.

Some veterans were crying openly. Colonel Howard ordered the regimental colors burned. He wept, "My God, and I had to be the first Marine officer ever to surrender a regiment."[12]

Two Marines, Capt. Golland L. Clark, Jr., (who later died aboard a prison ship at Formosa) and 1st Lt. Alan S. Manning, took Lt. Gen. Jonathan M. Wainwright's truce flag to the enemy. At midnight, Wainwright broadcast a surrender message to all the forces in the Philippines.

The total losses of the 4th Marines in the Philippines were 330 killed and 357 wounded. Most of them fell on Corregidor, where 1,283 Marines were taken prisoner. For thousands of Americans and Filipinos, the next three years brought death and brutal mistreatment in Japanese prison camps. Of the 4th Marines, 239 officers and men died in Japanese hands.

4
Going On the Offensive

The final battle for Corregidor was, in reality, a mopping-up operation. The Japanese had already swept on to grab the riches of Southeast Asia, from Java (March 9) to Rangoon, Burma (March 8). They could have left Corregidor's holed-up defenders to starve.

By the time Corregidor surrendered, the Japanese tide had crested. Two great sea battles stopped them. On May 4–8, American and Japanese aircraft carriers fought the Battle of the Coral Sea at the southern end of the Japanese offensive. *Lexington* was lost and *Yorktown* damaged, but the Americans drove off the enemy force advancing against Port Moresby on the southern coast of New Guinea, opposite northern Australia.

Far to the north, the Battle of Midway, June 3–5, finished the last Japanese offensive in the Pacific. The Japanese lost four big carriers; and with its air cover destroyed, the enemy amphibious force heading for Midway turned back. After that victory, the U.S. Navy was ready to go on the attack.

By Pearl Harbor Day, the Marine Corps had grown to two divisions and 65,000 men. It had 13 aviation squadrons and 251 aircraft of all types. Just six days earlier, Admiral Harold R. Stark, the Chief of Naval Operations, had opposed the formation of a third Marine division and the use of dive bombers by the Marines.

In the forefront of the Corps were its static Defense Battalions, each organized on the average with 952 Marines but tailored for the job assigned. The 5th Defense Battalion was on Iceland, where it had arrived with the 1st Provisional Marine Brigade (6th Marines reinforced) in July. The 3rd, 4th and part of the 1st Defense Battalions were in Hawaii. The rest of the 1st was divided over tiny Wake, Johnston and Palmyra islands. The 7th Defense Battalion guarded Samoa far to the south and the 6th, Midway in the north. These islands west of Hawaii now formed America's Pacific frontline.

On January 23, 1942, the 2d Marine Brigade (4,798 Marines) arrived to build Samoa into the main Marine base in the Pacific. With the coming of the 3rd Marine Brigade and MAG-13, 10,000 Marine ground troops were in the Samoan area by the end of May. It became a combat training center and a staging base for future amphibious operations in the Solomon Islands.

At the northern end of the line, Midway, by the end of 1941, was Hawaii's strongest outpost. The isolated two-island atoll, 1,135 miles northwest of Pearl Harbor, had been an American coaling station since 1867.

On the night of December 7, 1941, two Japanese destroyers had shelled Midway's air base to cover their carriers' withdrawal from Hawaii. One round zipped into the Sand Island power plant's air vent and exploded inside the concrete building. First Lt. George H. Cannon, the St. Louis-born commander of Battery H, 6th Defense Battalion, was severely wounded; but he refused to be evacuated until the other wounded had been cared for and Cpl. Harold R. Hazelwood had the switchboard operating again. Cannon died from loss of blood a few minutes after reaching the aid station and was the first Marine in World War II to be awarded the Medal of Honor. Hazelwood was awarded the Navy Cross. In the 23-minute attack, four men were killed and 19 wounded.

In the next three weeks, Midway was reinforced by VMSB-231, which made its historic flight directly from Oahu; by VMF-221, which flew off the deck of *Saratoga* after she had been pulled back from Wake, and by elements of the 4th Defense Battalion.

In May 1942, Adm. Chester W. Nimitz, commander of the U.S. Pacific Fleet expected—because the U.S. had broken the Japanese code—a Japanese attempt to capture Midway and destroy the American fleet. The atoll was sent most of the 3rd Defense Battalion, two rifle companies of the 2d Marine Raider Battalion, five light tanks and vital search radars. The newly organized MAG-22 received dive bombers and fighters, which were soon to prove obsolete for this war; and by the month's

251

end, Midway was jammed with more than 100 Marine, Army and Navy planes.

At 6:16 A.M. on Thursday, June 4, the Midway Marines began their part in the decisive Battle of Midway, which was to become chiefly a struggle between the aircraft of opposing carrier forces. The Japanese fleet sent 108 planes against Midway; and 25 Marine fighter pilots led by Maj. Floyd B. Parks and Capt. John F. Carey tackled the incoming dive bombers. In the opening encounter, the faster, more maneuverable Zeros shot down nine of 12 Marine pilots. A second group of 13 Marine fighters led by Capt. Kirk Armistead followed up the attack. Both groups made their kills; but, in all, 15 of the 25 Marine pilots, including Major Parks, were killed. At 6:30, the enemy carrier planes struck the atoll through heavy antiaircraft fire and did widespread damage in a violent half hour.

Marine dive bombers attacked the Japanese carriers far north of the island after an unsuccessful attempt by Army and Navy planes from Midway. The first Marine striking unit, led by Maj. Lofton R. Henderson, scored no hits; and only half its 16 planes got back to Midway. (Henderson was shot down, and the airfield on Guadalcanal was named in his honor two months later.) Then, 15 B-17s took a crack at the enemy fleet, and failed. A second wave of 11 Marine bombers, led by Maj. Benjamin W. Norris, also missed and lost three aircraft. (Norris did not return from a mission to find the already burning carrier *Hiryu* that evening.) Half of Midway's aircraft were now gone.

But two hours later, carrier planes attacked the four Japanese carriers just as their planes, returned from Midway, were being refueled and rearmed for a second strike. The planes from *Enterprise* and *Yorktown*, taking full advantage of this phenomenal break, knocked out three of the enemy carriers loaded with aircraft. That evening, dive bombers from *Enterprise* mortally wounded the remaining *Hiryu*.

The next morning, 12 Marine bombers from Midway, led by Capt. Marshall A. Tyler, attacked two damaged enemy cruisers. Capt. Richard E. Fleming of St. Paul, Minnesota, his plane in flames, slammed into an after turret of the cruiser *Mikuma*. He was awarded the Medal of Honor.

In the Battle of Midway, the United States lost *Yorktown* and 98 carrier planes. Marine Corps casualties were 49 killed and 53 wounded. Expressing the survivors' bitterness, Lt. Col. Larkin at Ewa protested to President Roosevelt through his son, Maj. James Roosevelt, USMCR, of the fatal inadequacy of the Marines' antiquated aircraft.

The Japanese lost four carriers, some 322 planes and a great portion of their experienced naval pilots. They never recovered. And the United States went on the offensive.

The preliminary steps had already been taken. On March 12, the U.S. Army had landed at Nouméa, New Caledonia, where nickel mines might attract the enemy. Two weeks later, 500 soldiers, the Marines' 4th Defense Battalion and VMF-212 moved up to Efate in the New Hebrides. (At noon on April 18, 16 B-25s led by Lt. Col. James H. Doolittle, USA, bombed Toyko.) And on June 14, the 1st Marine Division reached Wellington, New Zealand.

At the end of May, Admiral Nimitz proposed sending the 1st Marine Raider Battalion to raid and destroy the seaplane base that the Japanese were building at Tulagi in the Solomons. But the tide turned faster than that. The Battle of Midway set the stage for a bigger operation. From now on, the rest of the Marine Corps story in this war would be of attack.

5
First, Carlson's Raiders

Evans Carlson, still the idealist, more than ever the believer in *Gung Ho*, was now 46 years old, gaunt, his face deeply lined, hair grayed. His 2d Raider Battalion was just nine months old. The Raiders were a controversial pet idea of President Roosevelt and Secretary of the Navy Frank Knox. Before the United States entered the war, two young captains, Samuel B. Griffith, II, and Wallace M. Greene, Jr., had been sent to England and Scotland to observe the British Commandos; and on their recommendation, Commandant Holcomb had authorized two raider battalions. Lt. Col. Merritt A. Edson formed one on the East Coast; Lt. Col. Carlson, the other on the West Coast.[13] They were organized to make hit-and-run raids, spearhead amphibious landings and fight as guerrillas behind enemy lines.

The Raiders were all picked men, all hardened to hike 50 miles a day without food and then to fight a battle with automatic weapons and knives. They were tough, with great confidence in themselves and a pride in being Raiders.

Although half of Carlson's battalion had been diverted to Midway, the rest was about to launch the first truly Raider operation. This raid on Makin Atoll in the Gilbert Islands, was planned, allegedly, to distract the enemy from the Guadalcanal landings, although the value and purpose of this bit of bravado are certainly not clear today.

Two big submarines, *Nautilus* and *Argonaut*, slipped out of Pearl Harbor on August 9, 1942, two days after the Marines had landed on Guadalcanal. Crowded in these boats were 222 Marines of A and B Companies, 2d Raider Battalion. It was thought that on Makin the Japanese had only some 43 defenders, but the Marine raid would still have very mixed results.

On the moonless night of August 17, the men, faces blackened, poured into rubber boats. The high seas flooded their outboard motors. Helped by the tide, the Marines paddled for an hour toward the east side of Butaritari, Makin's largest island. As dawn broke, 15 of the boats grounded on the designated beach across the island from Government Wharf; three other boats landed slightly to the north, and one boat, a mile south—as it turned out, behind the enemy. The men in the main element hid their boats, posted guards, made contact with the subs by radio and oiled their soaked weapons. Suddenly, the great advantage of surprise was lost when a Raider accidentally fired his BAR.

The small Japanese garrison quickly manned its machine-gun posts, and its snipers climbed to the bushy tops of the coconut palms. Lt. Merwyn C. Plumley and his A Company crossed the island to the lagoon side, and headed toward the enemy strongpoint two miles south. Carlson had *Nautilus* shell both it and two ships in the lagoon. Machine gunners and snipers worked over the Raiders. Second Lt. Wilfred S. LeFrancois and his men turned back a *banzai* charge. The former enlisted man from Watertown, New York, was hit in the right shoulder by five machine-gun bullets. Constantly in the van, with a shotgun for close-in fighting, Sgt. Clyde Thomason, a reservist from Atlanta, wiped out a Japanese attack before a sniper killed him. He was the only man on Makin—and the first enlisted Marine in the war—to earn the Medal of Honor.

Carlson was everywhere, encouraging his men, coolly smoking his pipe. Machine guns, a flamethrower, snipers slowed the Marine advance; and Carlson had to send in B Company. Just before noon, Japanese planes bombed and strafed the invaders; and two flying boats put ashore 35 more Japanese. The Marines destroyed the planes. Frustrated by the snipers in the coconut groves, Carlson retreated northward to draw the Japanese into more open ground. It worked. The enemy pursued, and the next Japanese bombing raid clobbered them—in the Marines' former positions.

Lt. Oscar F. Peatross and 11 Marines in the boat that had landed far to the south wrecked the Japanese strongpoint and radio station and killed a number of the enemy. After dark, Peatross' eight surviving Raiders returned to their submarine.

Carlson also tried to slip off the island, as the plan required;

but less than half of the men made it. The rest paddled and bailed, boats capsized, men lost their weapons, giant waves threw the exhausted men back onto the beach. Among the 120 Marines now on the atoll, more than a half dozen were wounded. During the rainy night, red-headed Pfc. Jesse Hawkins of Paragould, Arkansas, took two bullets in the chest but drove off an enemy patrol.

In the morning, Maj. James Roosevelt, Carlson's executive officer, plowed through the surf with four boats. Five Marines on *Nautilus* volunteered to bring ashore weapons, ammunition and a line. They were strafed by seaplanes, and only one man reached the beach. There were now 70 Americans left on Makin.

There is a story that a Raider officer set out to surrender the unit but could find no Japanese left on Butaritari to surrender to. The Raiders discovered that the enemy were either dead or had fled to smaller islands. The Raiders armed themselves with Japanese weapons, destroyed arms and installations and counted 86 enemy dead. That second night, with natives' help, the Raiders put their last four boats and a native canoe into the water on the lagoon side and struggled back to the submarines. This time they made it.

In addition to Thomason's Medal of Honor, the Raiders' bravery was recognized when Carlson, LeFrancois, Peatross, Plumley, Roosevelt and 13 others received the Navy Cross.

But 21 Marines were dead, and nine Raiders, still alive, had been left behind. They were captured and moved to Kwajalein. Vice Adm. Koso Abe ordered them executed; and on October 16, they were beheaded. After the war, Abe was hanged on Guam for this atrocity.

Although the Makin raid heartened the folks back home and Carlson's Raiders were widely publicized, the action had another disastrous aftermath. In good part as a result of it, the Japanese recognized their vulnerability and fortified the Gilberts intensely. The Marines found nearly 5,000 dug-in Japanese waiting for them on Tarawa.

6
The Canal

Eight months after Pearl Harbor and two months after the Battle of Midway, the United States began its first amphibious attack in the Pacific. The idea: Adm. Ernest J. King, commander-in-chief, United States Fleet, figured that the Japanese were overextended. The target: Guadalcanal and Tulagi in the enemy-occupied Solomon Islands, less than 600 miles southeast of the huge Japanese base at Rabaul. The instrument: the 1st Marine Division.

This was to be the germinal battle of the Pacific war. Men of all services learned to fight and defeat the Japanese. It was the first advance toward Tokyo and the Marines' longest engagement in World War II.

First, important decisions had to be made. General MacArthur wanted to strike directly at Rabaul, not at the out-islands; but the Navy refused to risk its scarce aircraft carriers. Gen. George C. Marshall, the U.S. Army Chief of Staff, wanted MacArthur in charge of the operation; the Solomons were in his theater. But King insisted on Admiral Nimitz because the Navy would provide the men and ships and planes. The newly organized Joint Chiefs of Staff had to resolve that one and, to give the job to the Navy, shifted the boundary line between the general's and the admiral's theaters of responsibility.

Then, Rear Adm. Richmond Kelly Turner, a tall, able naval aviator with no amphibious experience, was given command of the amphibious force, Task Force 62; the Marines were irritated by that. Finally, the Marine Corps wanted clear-cut command of operations ashore; but the Navy regarded the Marines as a subordinate extension of the fleet. This dispute was not resolved in time for this landing.

The Navy assembled a mass of power: three carriers (*Saratoga, Enterprise* and *Wasp*), two new battleships, heavy and light cruisers, 250 carrier aircraft. The 19,000-man Marine landing force was built on the 1st Marine Division. This was the first time a Marine division had sailed from the United States. It had the 1st and 5th Marines, but its 7th Marines, on duty at Samoa, was replaced by the 2d Marines from the 2d Division at San Diego. Added to the 1st Division were the 1st Raider Battalion, the 1st Parachute Battalion and the 3rd Defense Battalion. In command of the Marines was a veteran of Nicaragua, Vera Cruz, Haiti and China, quiet, persistent Maj. Gen. Alexander A. Vandegrift.

Vandegrift had expected to train his division in New Zealand until early 1943. When he got the word on June 26, he was shocked: Less than five weeks to get ready and he did not even know where Guadalcanal was. He managed to have the landing delayed a week, until August 7. But the Japanese were building an airfield on Guadalcanal, and the landing had to be made before planes from there could attack the invading armada.

When the division's rear echelon, the 1st Marines, arrived at Wellington, New Zealand, on July 11, it had only 11 days to empty and reload its ships for combat. Because of labor problems, the Marines had to do the whole job themselves, round the clock, working through day after day of heavy rains. But under the direction of Lt. Col. Randolph McC. Pate, the division's logistics officer, it was done.

On July 17, Lt. Col. Merrill B. Twining and Maj. William B. McKean flew up to Guadalcanal in an Army B-17 and inspected the landing beaches. No accurate maps existed; the Army took aerial photographs; but, through a succession of foul-ups, they never reached the Marines. The division intelligence officer, Lt. Col. Frank B. Goettge, flew to Australia and hunted down colonial officials, traders, planters, missionaries, shipmasters—anyone who knew Guadalcanal or Tulagi.

The Marines were headed for one of the wettest places on earth: rain-heavy, volcanic islands, jagged, jungle-covered and steaming with tropical heat, stinking with jungle decay. Guadalcanal itself was 90 miles long and 25 wide. North of it, across the 20-mile-wide Sealark Channel, lay Florida Island. Snuggled up against the southern shore of Florida were Tulagi Island with an excellent harbor and the small twin islets of Gavutu-Tanambogo. From coastwatchers' reports, especially those of a lanky British captain, W. F. Martin Clemens, on Guadalcanal, the Marines expected to find only 1,500 Japanese on Tulagi, both troops and laborers, and 2,300 (600 soldiers and 1,700 laborers) on Guadalcanal.

There would be five simultaneous landings. Group X-Ray, led by the 1st and 5th Marines and Vandegrift himself, would land on Guadalcanal's northern coastal plain about three miles east of Lunga Point, where on July 4 a reconnaissance plane had first seen Japanese working on the airstrip. The Marines' prime mission was to seize and hold that airfield.

Brig. Gen. William H. Rupertus, the assistant division commander, would take Group Yoke to the north side of Sealark Channel. Lt. Col. Merritt A. Edson, "Red Mike," would lead his 1st Raider Battalion and other detachments ashore on Tulagi's south coast. Maj. Robert H. Williams would land his 1st Parachute Battalion on Gavutu-Tanambogo; and the 1st Battalion, 2d Marines would sweep the coast of Florida Island behind the off-islands.

Many new recruits filled out the ranks of the division, but the old timers were the reinforcing steel. Samuel B. Griffith, II, who would lead some of them ashore on Tulagi, later described them this way:

> They were a motley bunch. Hundreds were young recruits only recently out of boot training at Parris Island. Others were older; first sergeants yanked off "planks" in Navy yards, sergeants from recruiting duty, gunnery sergeants who had fought in France, perennial privates with disciplinary records a yard long. These were the professionals, the "Old Breed" of United States Marines. Many had fought "Cacos" in Haiti, "bandidos" in Nicaragua, and French, English, Italian and American soldiers and sailors in every bar in Shanghai, Manila, Tsingtao, Tientsin, and Peking.
>
> They were inveterate gamblers and accomplished scroungers, who drank hair tonic in preference to post exchange beer ("horse piss"), cursed with wonderful fluency, and never went to chapel ("the God-box") unless

forced to. Many dipped snuff, smoked rank cigars or chewed tobacco (cigarettes were for women and children). . . . They knew their weapons and they knew their tactics. They knew they were tough and they knew they were good. There were enough of them to leaven the Division and to impart to the thousands of younger men a share both of the unique spirit which they animated and the skills they possessed.[14]

A rehearsal of the hastily assembled force was held in the Fijis from July 28 to 31. Because the site had been badly chosen, only one-third of the Marines participated in the amphibious practice. After the war, Vandegrift called the rehearsal "a complete bust," though in later years he somewhat softened that judgment.[15]

Another nervous note: It would take five days to unload the landing force and its equipment; but Vice Adm. Fletcher, the always cautious commander of the Expeditionary Force, warned that he would permit his big carriers to stay and risk air attack for only two days. In a heated meeting, Vandegrift objected vigorously.

The task forces left the Fijis at dusk on July 31. Bad weather kept the enemy planes at Rabaul grounded, and the 82 ships were not spotted. By the night of August 6, the entire group was west of Guadalcanal. The Marines slept in their green utilities, packs ready, weapons oiled. They had beans for breakfast. At 6:13 A.M., the heavy cruiser *Quincy* opened fire. Ships and carrier dive bombers began pounding the shorelines and quickly silenced the enemy's few guns.

At 6:50, as the sun rose on that overcast Friday morning, the Marines scrambled down the cargo nets and into 475 36-foot Higgins boats (only 116 had ramps). At 9:13, after a four and a half mile trip, the first units of the 1st and 3rd Battalions, 5th Marines came ashore at Red Beach, a 1,600-yard strip of black sand just east of the Tenaru River. The landing went smoothly. The Marines were met only by midday air attacks; and at dark, 11,000 Marines were on Guadalcanal.

On the beach, supplies piled up in a chaos of confusion and congestion. Sweating Marines and sailors stripped to the waist manhandled the crates. Vandegrift felt he could not spare men from the line to clear the beach. The Marines managed the unloading badly, and they would pay later for this failure.

The 1st Battalion, 5th Marines, under the regimental command of Col. LeRoy P. Hunt, who had led the company that took the Essen Hook at Blanc Mont in World War I, moved west and crossed the shallow Lunga River with a tank company at noon Saturday. They squelched some minor opposition and by 3 P.M. were at the enemy's strongpoint at Kukum on Lunga Point. The enemy had fled abruptly. Within the next hour, the 1st Battalion, 1st Marines, whose regimental commander was Col. Clifton B. Cates, another decorated veteran of the fighting in France, occupied the airstrip that was soon named Henderson Field.

Across the Skylark Channel, H-hour was even earlier: 8 A.M. The 1st Battalion, 2d Marines made two landings on Florida Island at H minus 20 minutes to protect the Tulagi force's flank. The Marines on Florida did not have to fire a shot. Edson's Raiders, led at first by Major Griffith, waded through waist-deep water to Tulagi's 600-yard-wide Blue Beach. Many were ·cut bloody on the coral. They entered the jungle, crossed the island's central ridge and moved south along the far shore. The second wave of Raiders, with A Company led by Capt. Lewis W. Walt, a Colorado State University athlete and student-body president, and C Company led by Maj. Kenneth D. Bailey— followed by the 2d Battalion, 5th Marines—covered the near coast. Bailey, a rugged six-foot-three former University of Illinois football end, roused a machine-gun nest in a cave, went in and cleaned it out with a BAR.

Walt and Bailey met the toughest resistance at a deep ravine in front of Hill 281. The Japanese were dug into coral caves and snipers were tied into the coconut palms. That night, they made four *banzai* counterattacks, one even reaching to battalion headquarters. When it was over, one BAR man, Pfc. Edward H. Ahrens, lay in his foxhole shot twice in the chest, bayoneted three times. Around him sprawled 13 enemy bodies. Walt carried him back for help. The dying Marine said, "Captain, they tried to come over me last night, but I don't think they made it." Walt replied, "They didn't, Johnny, they didn't."[16]

At dawn, two battalions of the 2d Marines came ashore and blasted the caves with dynamite attached to long poles. Saturday

261

afternoon, Hill 281 and Tulagi were finally secured with 200 Japanese dead. Edson earned his second Navy Cross, exactly 14 years after his first on the Coco River.

On Gavutu and Tanambogo, the fight was even meaner. Here was the Marines' first true amphibious assault—an attack from the sea against defended beaches. Fletcher's carrier planes destroyed the enemy's seaplane base and its 23 aircraft; and the warships pounded the islands, where the Japanese were hidden in coral caves and dugouts. At noon, the 1st Parachute Battalion, 395 drenched men, landed on Gavutu in three waves—after a seven-mile ride in choppy seas—and met a hail of rifle and machine-gun fire. The first boatloads were decimated on the beach. In two hours, one in 10 Marines was a casualty and most of the rest were pinned down. A squad did overrun Hill 148 and raised a small American flag, which Pfc. Edward Cooke pulled out of his pack.

Enemy automatic fire covered the causeway between the two little islands. After dark, the first landing attempt on Tanambogo was repulsed. Although 30 Marines got ashore, Japanese resistance was so overwhelming that they had to withdraw with heavy losses. On Saturday, the 3rd Battalion, 2d Marines landed on Gavutu but could not force the causeway. At 4:20 PM, I Company and two tanks assaulted Tanambogo. The Japanese destroyed the first tank, jamming its track with an iron bar, and killed all but one of its crew with hand grenades and knives. The second tank, accompanied by 60 Marines, blasted the enemy dugouts until K Company moved up the causeway from Gavutu and met the defenders with bayonets.

That night was filled with close-in fighting; and by late Sunday, the Marines secured the twin islets. On the three smaller islands were 1,500 dead Japanese; Marine casualties were 108 dead and 140 wounded.

From the first afternoon, the Japanese had sent air attacks against the collected American warships. Antiaircraft gunners and carrier pilots, alerted by the intrepid coastwatchers, shot down at least 30 bombers; but they managed to damage a destroyer and set fire to a transport.

Saturday evening, Vice Adm. Fletcher withdrew his three carriers and started south—even earlier than he had warned he would. Vice Adm. Robert L. Ghormley, commander of South

Pacific Forces, approved the move. Turner protested. Vandegrift was alarmed. Nimitz called Fletcher's decision "most unfortunate."[17] Vandegrift later wrote, "Fletcher was running away twelve hours earlier than he had already threatened during our unpleasant meeting."[18]

As the carriers moved off to the southeast, leaving Turner's ships between Guadalcanal and Tulagi without air protection, the Japanese Eighth Fleet was charging, unrecognized, down the wide channel called "The Slot" between the two strings of Solomon Islands. At 1:30 A.M. Sunday, the Japanese struck. "The resulting melee was one of the worst defeats ever suffered by the U.S. Navy."[19] In the brief Battle of Savo Island, three U.S. cruisers and the Australian cruiser *Canberra* were sunk, and the cruiser *Chicago* lost part of its bow. In those dark, shark-infested waters, 1,023 Americans died. No enemy ship was sunk. Much later, Turner wrote, "We took a hell of a beating."[20]

The Japanese failed to go after the sitting-duck transports, which continued to unload frantically off Lunga Point until they left for Nouméa that afternoon. Now, some 16,000 Marines were abandoned in the Solomons with 37 days' supply of food and four days' of ammunition. The rest, including 1,400 of the 2d Marines in the division reserve, had not been unloaded. The Marines ashore felt angry, depressed, cut off, but determined to hold.

The survival of the five battalions on Guadalcanal depended on the airfield. Holding it became Vandegrift's foremost concern—a defensive stance. Because the transports had carried away the bulldozers and other construction equipment, the airstrip had to be made operational as fast as possible with captured equipment and by hand. Col. Pedro A. del Valle's 11th Marines and the 3rd Defense Battalion pulled their guns tight around the strip, and the infantry-trained artillerymen and engineers patrolled the jungle to the south.

The Japanese controlled the air and sea but had little strength on the island. Vandegrift expected them to make amphibious landings of their own. He had the Marines build a defensive front facing the sea from Kukum eastward around Lunga Point to the mouth of the Ilu River. Enemy destroyers and submarines shelled the area at will and high-flying bombers attacked the airfield. Single bombers nicknamed "Washing

Machine Charlie" harassed the Marines all night. Their weapons could not reach the enemy planes.

Obviously, there were questions to ask about the planning of the Guadalcanal operation, so swiftly thrown together and called "Operation Shoestring" by the participants. Although they had met only meager opposition in landing on Guadalcanal, the Marines were left to their own devices, cut to two meals a day, short of all kinds of equipment and dependent on abandoned Japanese rice, trucks, fuel, even cigarettes. After Midway, the strategic opportunity had presented itself before American strength was ready. Between planning and reality was a gap that would take many lives to fill.

Fortunately, the enemy committed his forces to the Solomons piecemeal and chose to bomb and shell the airfield rather than destroy the irreplaceable supplies jammed up on the beachhead.

Henderson Field was declared ready on August 12, but no planes were available. On the night of August 15, four destroyer-transports scooted in with aviation gasoline, ammunition, bombs, ground crews and a Navy Seabee unit (including Ensign George W. Polk, who was killed while a CBS correspondent in Greece in 1948). On the twentieth, 31 planes finally arrived from the escort carrier *Long Island*, standing 200 miles off Guadalcanal. These were the forward echelon of Marine Aircraft Group 23, and the Marines cheered their coming.

The next day, Maj. John L. Smith, commander of VMF-223, scored Henderson Field's first kill—he would finish with 19 planes shot down. Army and Navy planes also began to show up. On September 3, Brig. Gen. Roy S. Geiger, a cold, tough bear of a man who had been one of the earliest Marine fliers, took command of all planes flying out of Henderson. The Seabees and the Marines' 1st Engineer Battalion kept the field operating, mastering the mud and repairing hundreds of bomb and shell craters—a never-ending job.

Meanwhile, the bulk of the Japanese were located beyond the brown-flowing Matanikau River, seven miles west of Lunga Point. A prisoner said they were ready to surrender. Lt. Col. Goettge, the division intelligence officer, took out a 25-man reconnaissance patrol in two lighters. In the moonless dark, on August 12, they waded ashore west of the Matanikau. The

Japanese attacked them on the beach, and only three enlisted Marines escaped. During the next week, three companies of the 5th Marines fought through the stifling jungle in that area, but the enemy did not stay to fight. The three companies killed 65 Japanese and lost four Marines killed and 11 wounded

The first crucial contest for Guadalcanal—the Battle of the Tenaru River—began on the night of August 18, when nearly 1,000 Japanese soldiers landed 22 air miles east of the Lunga River and 500 Special Landing Force troops landed west of the Marines' perimeter. The next day, a Marine combat patrol ran into part of the former unit and in an hour-long fight killed 31 of the 35 men. Now discovered, the Japanese commander decided to attack toward the airfield at once.

At 3:10 A.M., on August 21, after an exchange of rifle fire with the 2d Battalion, 1st Marines, commanded by Lt. Col Edwin A. Pollock, 200 screaming Japanese, bayonets fixed, rushed from the east at the sandbar across the mouth of the slow, scum-green Ilu River, which the Marines' maps mistakenly identified as the Tenaru River. The enemy ran into a single strand of barbed wire and a storm of bullets. Many were killed in the bright moonlight; but, fighting with knives, bayonets and rifle butts, some broke into the battalion's position west of the river before the battalion reserve, G Company, could counterattack and drive them back across the creek. The crocodiles fed on many bodies. The Japanese then waded beyond the breakers and plunged through the surf west of the Ilu's mouth. They came up against the Marines' strength: machine guns and artillery placed to repel an attack from the sea. By dawn, the sandy battlefield was littered with enemy bodies.

At 7 A.M., the 1st Battalion of Cates' 1st Marines crossed the Ilu upstream and in a well-coordinated attack squeezed the Japanese, now concentrated in a coconut grove, onto the point of land on the Ilu's east bank. The Japanese attacked with bayonets, trying to escape toward the east through the surf, along the beach and overland. Fighter pilots from VMF-223 strafed them. At 3 P.M., Vandegrift ordered five light tanks to attack across the sandspit. The tanks pivoted through the coconut grove, chasing the enemy, grinding over their bodies. It was, said Vandegrift, "war without quarter."[21] In two more hours, the Battle of the Tenaru was over. Nearly 800 Japanese were dead, piled up in the grove and on the sandspit; 15 were taken prisoner, and a few escaped into the jungle. Their commander, Col. Kiyono Ichiki, committed suicide. The Marines, with 34 dead and 75 wounded, had won their first big battle on Guadalcanal. "From that time on, United States Marines were invincible."[22]

The Japanese next sent toward Guadalcanal a fleet of three aircraft carriers, eight battleships, six cruisers, 22 destroyers and five transports loaded with troops. On August 24, the "Cactus Air Force" pilots of Henderson Field scored their first major success by shooting down six presumably unbeatable Zeros and 10 bombers. American carrier planes sank a light carrier, a cruiser and a destroyer and shot down 90 planes. The next morning, bombers from Henderson Field sank a transport and a destroyer. The Japanese ships turned back to Rabaul.

On the last day of August, the Japanese high command made a decision to delay their offensive in New Guinea and clean up Guadalcanal first. For the Americans on Guadalcanal, the situation was already desperate, even without the pressure this decision promised. Their needs had to compete against both the North African invasion and MacArthur's campaign in the Southwest Pacific.

To strengthen the perimeter, the 2d Battalion, 5th Marines; the 1st Raider Battalion, and the 1st Parachute Battalion moved over from the north side of Sealark Channel. Before dawn on September 8, 700 men of Edson's Raiders and the Parachute Battalion made an amphibious raid near Tasimboko, 18 miles east of Lunga Point. MAG-23 planes and two destroyer-transports supported their attack. With the paratroopers protecting their flank and rear, the Raiders stormed the village. The Japanese fled into the jungle. Edson destroyed their supply dump and threw their guns into the sea. He brought back in triumph a Japanese general's white dress uniform.

Edson estimated that 4,000 Japanese had been in the area—part of the Kawaguchi Force that had landed during the last two nights of August via the so-called "Tokyo Express." They planned to attack Henderson Field in what would be the second major contest for Guadalcanal—the Battle of Edson's Ridge.

The 1st Marines guarded the east side of the Marine perimeter, the 5th Marines the west side. In between, facing southward for a stretch of four miles, the defensive line was covered only by strongpoints and outposts. Eight hundred Raiders and Paramarines, weakened by battle and malaria, held the center of that thin line. Their positions keyed on a long, kunai grass-covered ridge that ran south from Henderson Field and offered the Japanese the best high-ground approach to the airstrip. Captured enemy documents convinced Edson that they would attack here. On Saturday, September 12, Edson, always meticulous, walked the ground and organized a "cushion defense" in depth. He ordered his men to dig in on the southernmost tip of what was about to become known as Bloody Ridge or Edson's Ridge.

In the dim moonlight that night, the enemy probed the Raider-paratrooper positions. Fighting broke out all along the southern front, and Edson's right flank was pushed back. Early Sunday morning, Edson counterattacked but could not uproot the enemy. His now-exhausted men established a new line on higher ground further back on the ridge.

In the meanwhile, Henderson Field was attracting an extra helping of Japanese air raids; and over the weekend, Navy pilots flew in 60 planes to bolster the plane-short, fuel-short Cactus fliers.

At 9 P.M. Sunday, "Washing Machine Charlie" dropped a green flare; Japanese destroyers in the channel opened up; south of Edson a red rocket rose, and two battalions—screaming "Gas! Gas!"—hit Edson's precarious line.

In the center, Capt. John B. Sweeney's Raider B Company withstood the heaviest assault. But on the west or right flank, the enemy drove a hole between A and B Companies. B Company's right platoon was surrounded and fought its way back 250 yards to join C Company, which was in reserve. Up on the ridge, the rest of B Company held; and Edson called in 105mm howitzer fire to within 200 yards of his men. The Japanese came on, took over some of B Company's foxholes, cut communication lines, threw in a heavy mortar barrage and then attacked the two paratroop companies to the east or left of the Raiders. The paratroopers, fighting hard, were driven back along the ridge, leaving B Company's left flank exposed. B Company, down to 60 men, was now being hit on three sides. Edson had them fall back to make a last-ditch stand with C Company, only 1,500 yards from the airfield. Edson moved among his men, rallying them. C Company exhausted its grenade supply; Major Bailey brought up more and crawled from foxhole to foxhole, handing them out. Despite a severe head wound, he led his men in hand-to-hand combat and in covering B Company's retreat.

Fighting off repeated attacks in the dark, the Marines finally stood on the last spur of the ridge. If the enemy broke through here, Henderson Field would be doomed.

The Japanese attacked again and again and were stopped again and again. The Parachute Battalion counterattacked and took 40 percent casualties. About 30 Japanese sneaked through Edson's line and seized two machine-gun positions from the 1st Engineers just east of the division CP. Three Japanese were killed right in front of Vandegrift. Headquarters troops and artillerymen rushed to plug the gap.

At 4 A.M., the 2d Battalion, 5th Marines strengthened Edson's battered left flank. And with dawn, the corpse-covered ridge was silent. The Marines still held, and the Cactus Air Force rose to bomb and strafe the retreating enemy. On Edson's Ridge, 40 Marines had been killed and 103 wounded—one in every five Marines who fought there. Edson and Bailey received the Medal of Honor.

While Edson was under attack, other Japanese units struck the 3rd Battalion, 1st Marines to the east, near the Ilu River. Six Marine tanks lunged forward without infantry support and only one survived. But by Sunday night, about half the original Japanese force was hacking its way through the jungle, fleeing toward the Matanikau. Henderson Field had been saved.

The 3rd Battalion, 2d Marines was brought over from Tulagi to reinforce the perimeter; and after a long argument between Vandegrift and Turner, 4,262 fresh men of the 7th Marines arrived on September 18 with tanks, ammunition, gasoline and rations. Of the 7th Marines' arrival, Vandegrift wrote, "I knew from previous experience that Turner held certain strategic and tactical ideas which so long as they pertained to naval operations were valid enough. When he got into the work of the generals, however, he should have saved his time. In this instance he favored the quaint notion of sprinkling little groups of the 7th Marines all over Guadalcanal."[23]

Bringing the 7th Marines to Guadalcanal was expensive:

Wasp was sunk; the battleship *North Carolina* was damaged, and the destroyer *O'Brien* was hit and later broke in two. The transports that brought in the 7th Marines took out the 1st Parachute Battalion (which had suffered all told 50 percent casualties), 162 other American wounded and eight Japanese prisoners.

Vandegrift now had 19,200 men. He could build up the southern rim of his perimeter and switch to an "active defense." First, he wanted to destroy a growing Japanese force on the far bank of the Matanikau River to the west.

The newly arrived 1st Battalion, 7th Marines, commanded by jungle-wise, barrel-chested Lt. Col. Lewis B. Puller, now forty-four and still loving a fight, passed through the perimeter on September 23. Puller followed a rugged jungle trail, and late the next day, with B Company in the van, fought a Japanese unit on the slopes of Mount Austen, which dominated the scene south of the Marine beachhead. Puller, the only officer in the battalion to have experienced combat, led in young men new to battle. When Capt. Chester Cockrell was killed and his B Company was mauled, Capt. Zach D. Cox led a charge and drove off the enemy. The Marines suffered seven killed and 25 wounded.

The 2d Battalion, 5th Marines came out in the morning to reinforce Puller; and most of the combined force pressed westward to the Matanikau. On the afternoon of the twenty-sixth, near the river's mouth, Puller's force was stopped by heavy mortar and machine-gun fire; Marine casualties were high.

Vandegrift ordered out the depleted Raider Battalion, now commanded by Lt. Col. Griffith, and sent Colonel Edson up front to take command, with Puller as his executive officer. Edson planned an aggressive two-pronged attack for the next day; but during the night, the Japanese crossed the river and set up on high ground. When the Raiders climbed toward them on Sunday morning, the twenty-seventh, the enemy's fire wounded Griffith in the shoulder, and a machine-gun burst killed Medal of Honor winner Kenneth Bailey.

The message informing Edson that the Raiders had been stopped was garbled; he thought they had crossed the river and closed with the enemy's main body. He ordered the attacks forward at 1:30 P.M. A and B Companies of Puller's battalion,

269

led by Maj. Otho L. Rogers, circled the Japanese position by sea. They landed and advanced to a high ridge 500 yards inland. A mortar round killed Rogers, and the enemy cut off the Marines from the beach. They were trapped.

Overhead, 2d Lt. Dale M. Leslie flying a dive bomber spotted the word "HELP" spelled out with white undershirts. He radioed to Edson; and Puller collected landing craft, boarded the destroyer *Ballard* offshore and rushed to the rescue.

From the ridge, Sgt. Robert D. Raysbrook semaphored to the destroyer that the Marines were cut off. *Ballard* blasted out a path, and the Marines fought their way to the sea. Platoon Sgt. Anthony P. Malanowski, Jr., from Baltimore, covered A Company's withdrawal with a BAR until he was killed.

The Marines set up a perimeter on the beach, and Higgins boats moved in to take them off. The Japanese drove the boats away. Second Lt. Leslie strafed the enemy and herded the landing craft back toward the beach. The Marines flocked on board. Coast Guardsman Douglas A. Munro placed his boat between the Japanese and the Marines and was killed. He was the only Coast Guardsman ever to receive the Medal of Honor. The cost of the "active defense" operation: 60 Marines dead and 100 wounded. It had been a costly failure.

The "Tokyo Express" kept landing troops nearly every night and brought in 150mm howitzers, which threatened Henderson Field from a range the Marines' guns could not reach. Vandegrift had to try again to dislodge the enemy at the Matanikau, but this time the Marines would go in five-battalion strength.

On October 7, Marines led by Col. William J. Whaling, a jungle warfare expert and Olympic marksman, skirmished with an enemy force that had crossed the river inland; and Edson's 5th Marines ran into another Japanese bridgehead near the coast. A mortar section run by the spectacular mortarman, goateed Master Gunnery Sgt. Leland "Lou" Diamond, now fifty-two years old and known throughout the Corps, shared in pounding the enemy. After two days of heavy fighting, the enemy bridgehead was wiped out in hand-to-hand combat. (John Hersey accompanied a Marine patrol during this action and afterwards wrote *Into the Valley*, one of the great books about men in combat.)

The Marines upriver could finally advance on October 9;

they crossed the river and wheeled northward toward the coast in three columns. Whaling led the column on the right; Lt. Col. Herman H. Hanneken, who had killed Charlemagne Peralte in Haiti in 1919, commanded the center column, and Puller led the left-hand column. Whaling and Hanneken reached the coast easily; but Puller ran into a strong enemy force at a deep circular ravine. He called in artillery and mortar fire, and the Marines' machine guns picked off the survivors as they tried to climb out of the ravine to escape. Then, the Marines re-crossed the Matanikau. The cost of the three-day operation: 65 Marines dead and 125 wounded.

By mid-October, both sides were pouring men and arms onto this godforsaken jungle island. The Japanese had put on Guadalcanal about 20,000 men, including the Sendai Division. Vandegrift's force, which had evacuated 800 battle casualties and had 1,960 hospitalized malaria patients, was at just about the same strength. The Marines—and their enemies—were tired, filthy, on short rations, riddled with disease.

On the night of October 11 off Guadalcanal's northwest tip, the U.S. Navy sank one Japanese cruiser and severely damaged another. Two American cruisers were damaged and the destroyer *Duncan* sunk; but this Battle of Cape Esperance was the first tactical victory for the United States in Iron Bottom Sound, as the Sealark Channel was now being called.

Early on October 13, the transports *McCawley* and *Zeilin* brought Vandegrift reinforcements: 2,850 soldiers of the 164th Infantry of the Americal Division and 295 Marines. But otherwise, it was a bad day. Air raids, the 150mm howitzers and a ferocious nighttime naval bombardment chewed up Henderson Field and the new Fighter 1 strip nearby. By the next dawn, most of the gasoline supplies had gone up in flames; 41 more men were dead, and only 42 of the 90 planes could still fly. Air bombing and howitzer shelling continued all day; by mid-afternoon, Henderson Field was useless. The following day, despite all efforts by the Marine fliers, enemy transports put 3,000 soldiers ashore in broad daylight. At night, naval shelling again pounded the Americans. Japan's all-out effort was finally having its effect. The situation ashore had become ominous. Vandegrift demanded that the Navy take control of the sea around Guadalcanal.

Late on the afternoon of the sixteenth, 26 planes of VMF-212 arrived, led by Lt. Col. Harold W. Bauer, Annapolis quarterback in 1930, who had already downed five enemy planes on "visits" to Guadalcanal. The Marine planes came in during an attack by nine Japanese dive bombers. With his fuel tanks almost empty, Bauer went right after the enemy alone and in a virtuoso performance shot down four of the bombers before running out of fuel. Bauer won the Medal of Honor for his spectacular feat; on November 14, he was shot down into the sea and killed. He then had 11 enemy planes to his credit.

The Japanese bombardments heralded a major coordinated attempt to retake Henderson Field. One enemy force of 2,900 men would cross the mouth of the Matanikau. The main body with 5,600 troops set out October 16 on an eight-day, single-file trek through the rugged rain forest south of the airfield. This force was completely unknown to the Marines. Vandegrift only expected the attack from the west; and on the evening of the twenty-third, nine 18-ton tanks tried to penetrate the Marine line there. The Marines destroyed all nine, plus three others before they could attack, and killed hundreds of infantrymen assembled to follow the tanks. The premature western assault failed.

Vandegrift and Commandant Holcomb, who had spent three days on Guadalcanal, flew to conferences at Nouméa with Vice Adm. William F. Halsey, Jr. The aggressive Halsey had replaced Ghormley as commander of the South Pacific Area. (Vandegrift was delighted.) And Brig. Gen. Rupertus became acting commander of the 1st Marine Division.

Late on Saturday, October 24, Puller's understrength 1st Battalion, 7th Marines, guarding the perimeter's southern face east of the Lunga River, began detecting signs of the Japanese main body. It had abandoned its artillery and mortars on the punishing hike through the jungle.

At 9:30 P.M. in a lashing rain, the Japanese swept past a 46-man outpost far in front of Puller's barbed wire. Sgt. Ralph Briggs telephoned a whispered warning to Puller. The Japanese, screaming and throwing grenades, attacked at a spot the Marines named Coffin Corner. With supporting fire from the 2d Battalion, 164th Infantry on the left, Puller's men stopped them. When A Company on the left fired all its ammunition, Puller told Capt. Regan Fuller to hold with the bayonet. The enemy regrouped and came on again, a half dozen times. Twenty-five-year-old Sgt. "Manila John" Basilone mowed them down with his machine guns. He had to send out men to push aside the piled-up bodies to free their field of fire. One Japanese element penetrated the Marine line, seized a mortar position and nearly wiped out a C Company machine-gun nest until Basilone, moving silently, lugged up another gun on his back and fired on the enemy. When ammunition ran low and the re-supply route was cut off, Basilone fought through the Japanese to bring up more.

The big machine-gunner was the first enlisted Marine in World War II to receive the Medal of Honor. One of ten children of an Italian-born tailor, young Basilone had driven a laundry truck in Raritan, New Jersey, and then served as an Army private in the Philippines before joining the Marines. In recommending him for the Medal of Honor, Puller said he had "contributed materially to the defeat and virtually the annihilation of a Japanese regiment."[24]

The 3rd Battalion, 164th Infantry came through the rain and mud and was scattered among Puller's Marines to stand against the fury of the repeated assaults. The soldiers' new M-1 rifles added much-needed firepower to the Marines' older Springfield '03s. As the American fire took its toll, fewer and fewer of the enemy came forward. At dawn, the Japanese pulled back. The perimeter and airfield had again been saved. Puller won his third Navy Cross.

The defenders spent the day, the first fair weather in three days, absorbing blows from Japanese aircraft, destroyers and howitzers. Capt. Joseph J. Foss of VMF-121 shot down four fighters—for the second time in three days.

The Japanese launched a new night attack, throwing themselves at the Americans over and over again, but could not penetrate. To the west, between the perimeter and the Matanikau, another enemy force attacked Hanneken's 2d Battalion, 7th Marines on a ridge parallel to the coast—now called Hanneken's Ridge. F Company was overrun, and the Japanese fired two of its machine guns until they were driven off.

That night, twenty-four-year-old Platoon Sgt. Mitchell Paige from Charleroi, Pennsylvania, won a battlefield commission and became the second enlisted Marine to receive the Medal of Honor in World War II. Paige commanded a machine-gun

273

section in a saddle between E and F Companies. In the darkness and pelting rain, the Japanese stormed the Marines' position; and they battled hand-to-hand until all Paige's men were killed or wounded. Alone, the sergeant fought the gun, killed the oncoming soldiers; and when the gun was destroyed, he moved to his right and brought back another gun and a few riflemen. They opened fire. As dawn came, Paige saw Japanese crawling to an unattended gun; he raced them to it, while the enemy concentrated their fire on him. He won. Three Marines started to bring him belts of ammunition; each in turn was hit. Paige would fire a burst and then move; grenades would hit where he had been. He would fire again. He threw two ammo belts around his shoulders, picked up the hot machine gun and led the riflemen he had collected down the ridge, their bayonets fixed, whooping like Indians. The enemy melted away. And then all was quiet. The battle was over. Paige's arms were blistered from fingertips to elbows. There were more than 100 Japanese bodies in front of his sector. That was the end of the enemy's strongest effort to recapture Henderson Field. Bulldozers shoved 2,000 Japanese corpses into mass graves.

Elsewhere, events had their impact on the grimy Marines hanging on to Guadalcanal. Commandant Holcomb, following· his visit to the battlefield, won endorsements from Halsey, Nimitz and King for the Marines' principle that the landing force commander, once ashore, should be on the same command level as the naval task force commander and free to make his own decisions. This not only ended the dispute between Vandegrift and Turner, but shaped lines of command for future Pacific amphibious operations. And most crucial of all, on October 24, President Roosevelt settled a hot-and-heavy controversy within the Joint Chiefs of Staff and sent each member of the Joint Chiefs a strong message demanding that "every possible weapon"[25] be sent to Guadalcanal. This was not a decision lightly made. German submarines were taking a dreadful toll in the Atlantic, sinking 88 ships in October alone; and the Allied North African invasion was already underway.

As a result of FDR's decision, Guadalcanal began to receive meaningful numbers of new men: the 147th Infantry, the 8th Marines, C and E Companies of Carlson's 2d Raider Battalion and additional Marine and Army artillery, including two batteries of 155mm guns that could finally answer the Japanese 150mms. Air power was bolstered by Marine Aircraft Group 11.

Rear Adm. Turner used the infusion of manpower to start his long-desired second front—a plan Vandegrift continued to oppose. All the ground reinforcements except the 8th Marines were directed to Aola Bay, 40 miles east of the Lunga River.

Vandegrift, his numbers increased, mounted another campaign to the west. The 1st Engineer Battalion bridged the Matanikau on the night of October 31, and Edson's 5th Marines crossed over. The 1st Battalion ran into the main enemy resistance at the base of Point Cruz. The 3rd Battalion was brought up; and the next morning, the 2d Battalion, now led by Maj. Lewis W. Walt, who had been a notable Raider, covered the western side of the enemy pocket. The Marines attacked; and by November 3, the Japanese were wiped out. Second Lt. Paul Moore, Jr. (later to become the Episcopal Bishop of New York), won the Navy Cross and was shot through the chest leading his F Company platoon in driving the enemy into the sea.

The Japanese, whipsawing the Americans, landed troops near Koli Point to the east of the Lunga perimeter. Adm. Isoroku Yamamoto wanted to keep the Americans' attention and forces divided. But other Japanese commanders, worrying about the price of this battle, were suggesting that Guadalcanal be left to wither and Japanese defenses be concentrated closer to Rabaul.

While Edson fought west of the Matanikau, Hanneken took the 2d Battalion, 7th Marines on a forced march 13 miles east of the perimeter. On November 3, the enemy hit his flank and forced the battalion to retreat some five miles to Koli Point. Hanneken called in air strikes, but the first "friendly" planes bombed and strafed the Marines. Vandegrift rushed Puller's 1st Battalion, 7th Marines to the scene by boat and two 164th Infantry battalions overland to envelop Koli Point from the south. And Carlson's Raiders hiked from Aola Bay through the jungle to block any Japanese retreat eastward.

On the eighth, the 7th Marines and 164th Infantry advanced and located the enemy at swampy Gavaga Creek 2,000 yards east of the Metapona River. Puller's battalion met heavy resistance; Puller was wounded. Maj. John Weber took over the battalion, which by now had 25 percent casualties, including half its officers. Hanneken's 2d Battalion circled around to the east side of the Japanese and the 2d Battalion, 164th Infantry faced them on the south. (Across the world, Eisenhower's troops were going ashore in North Africa.)

The battle went on for two days before most of the enemy were able to escape south along Gavaga Creek through a gap in the 164th.

Carlson's Raiders pursued the retreating Japanese. The heroic native scout, Jacob Vouza, who wore the Silver Star that Vandegrift had awarded him, led the way through the jungle. Lt. Col. Carlson put his main party on a parallel trail and then had a smaller group strike the Japanese in the rear. When they whirled to meet their attackers, the larger Raider force would hit their flank. The 400 Raiders hiked 150 miles and fought a dozen guerrilla skirmishes in the jungle. By December 4, they had lost 16 killed and 18 .wounded and figured they had killed 488 Japanese. It was a historic patrol. Carlson won his third Navy Cross.

The Raiders stayed in the vortex of controversy. Some admirals were eager to create more Raider battalions and to use Marines only in small units. The Corps wanted to keep its divisions. An independent-minded maverick, *Gung Ho* Evans Carlson never again commanded troops directly in combat. After Guadalcanal was over, he was made executive officer of the new 1st Raider Regiment commanded by Col. Harry B. Liversedge, who had led the 3rd Raider Battalion. Lt. Col. Alan Shapley took over Carlson's old 2d Battalion and later the 2d Raider Regiment. Early in 1944, all the Raider battalions were converted into the new 4th Marines.

When the Japanese landed nearly 2,000 more troops west of the perimeter, the Marines and soldiers in the Point Cruz area went after them. On one patrol, Cpl. Barney D. Ross, the former boxing champion, won the Silver Star; he killed 22 Japanese and stood guard over three wounded Marines through the night after his unit withdrew.

The Japanese were preparing still another counteroffensive and a showdown. They intended to land their veteran, battle-tried 38th Division, 10,000 men, far west of the Marine perimeter. On Friday, November 13, an enemy naval force came into Iron Bottom Sound to knock out Henderson Field before the troop transports showed up. During that star-filled night, they sank the cruisers *Atlanta* and *Juneau* and four destroyers, killing

Rear Admirals Daniel J. Callaghan and Norman Scott. But the enemy naval bombardment force never reached the airfield. A wild, running sea battle raged for three nights; and American fliers sank seven of the 11 troop transports coming down The Slot.

This hard-fought and crucial Naval Battle of Guadalcanal prevented the enemy from landing their troops under cover of darkness. At first light on the fifteenth, the four surviving transports were run aground at the landing beaches. American guns, planes and ships attacked the 2,000 soldiers and reduced the transports to hulks.

This was the climax of the struggle for Guadalcanal. The Japanese could no longer sufficiently reinforce their troops. "The Japanese never again advanced and the Allies never stopped."[26] FDR called it "the turning point in this war."[27]

Now, the 1st Marine Division could be relieved from its over-long stint on the island. It had done its job. Doing it, the division had lost 650 dead, 31 missing and 1,278 wounded. Thousands of men had been stricken by malaria and other jungle diseases. The Marines were exhausted. On December 9, they started shipping out to Australia. Many were too weak to climb the transports' cargo nets.

On that same day, Vandegrift passed the command of the troops on Guadalcanal to Maj. Gen. Alexander M. Patch, USA. More Army units landed, including two regiments of the Americal Division and Maj. Gen. J. Lawton Collins' 25th Division. In the first week of January, the 6th Marines arrived to complete, with the 2d and 8th Marines, the 2d Marine Division. Brig. Gen. Alphonse De Carre served as division commander; Maj. Gen. John Marston, who had led the Marines to Iceland in July 1941 and was senior to Patch, remained in New Zealand.

By January 7, 1943, Guadalcanal held about 50,000 Americans, including the 2d Marine Division's 14,733. The Japanese had there an estimated 25,000 weary men, and the U.S. fliers were making it extremely difficult for them to add fresh soldiers. Henderson's air strength was built up to a level unimaginable in the early Operation Shoestring days. On January 15, Major Foss bagged three more Zeros, bringing his total of kills to 26, one more than Eddie Rickenbacker's World War I score. By the end of the month, VMF-121 had downed 164 planes at a cost of 20 pilots, including ace Lt. William P. Marontate (13 kills).

Maj. Gen. Patch began his campaign to push the enemy off Guadalcanal by assaulting their positions on and around Mount Austen, three miles south of Henderson Field. In an intense jungle battle, the enemy strongpoint was isolated and its defenders reduced to starvation. After a final convulsive Japanese counterattack on January 21, it was destroyed.

Patch ordered an advance in the greatest strength yet against the enemy to the west. His command was now designated the XIV Corps. The Army units moved out on January 10; and the 2d Marine Division's 2d and 8th Regiments attacked three days later on the right flank, between the 25th Infantry Division and the sea. The enemy, shrewdly dug in, met the Marines with crossfire down the long axis of successive valleys and ravines. On January 15, the fresh 6th Marines took over for the 2d, which was long overdue to leave Guadalcanal for New Zealand. In five days, the 6th and the 8th Marines, with gunfire support from naval ships offshore, advanced 1,500 yards and killed more than 600 Japanese. They took two prisoners.

The Americans pressed westward. The 6th Marines along the coast had heavy going; but the Japanese, though still full of fight, were falling back now. Pursuing the enemy toward Cape Esperance, the Americans reached the Poha River on January 25. Then, aerial reconnaissance warned of a large naval concentration at Rabaul; and Patch and Halsey feared the Japanese would attempt again to retake the island. Patch pulled back troops and left the 147th Infantry to continue the pressure, with the 6th Marines in support.

But, unknown to the American commanders, Japan's Imperial War Council had on January 4 decided to evacuate Guadalcanal. The Japanese would keep the island under air attack from a new airfield being built at Munda Point on New Georgia Island, 175 miles northwest of Henderson Field. Munda became the new focal point for both the Tokyo Express and the Guadalcanal fliers.

On Guadalcanal, the Japanese put up a determined rearguard stand at the Bonegi River from January 30 to February 2, And 12,000 soldiers, most of them wounded and weakened by disease, were evacuated by the night of February 7. They escaped completely undetected by the American generals—an incredible performance.

After precisely six months of battle, the Guadalcanal campaign was over. President Roosevelt draped the Medal of Honor around Vandegrift's neck.

The tenacious Japanese had lost some 23,000 dead in battle and from disease, including 600 of their best naval pilots. Total American ground forces lost in combat were 1,598 killed and 4,709 wounded, of which 1,152 dead and 2,799 wounded were Marines. In addition, Marine aviation units had 55 dead, 85 missing and 127 wounded.

The contribution of Marine fliers to the defense of Guadalcanal was incalculable. The pilots and their gunners climbed from a primitive, often shell-pocked field day after day to do combat in all kinds of weather and against all odds. Before the island was secured, four fliers besides Lt. Col. Bauer had earned the Medal of Honor: 1st Lt. Jefferson J. DeBlanc, Capt. Joseph J. Foss, Maj. Robert E. Galer and Maj. John L. Smith. Foss had shot down 26 planes, Smith 19, Marion E. Carl 18½, Galer 13, Marontate 13, Bauer 11, DeBlanc 9. The battle for Guadalcanal was truly three dimensional.

Rear Adm. Raizo Tanaka, a most able opponent, wrote later, "There is no question that Japan's doom was Guadalcanal."[28] Other Japanese commanders would have cause to speak similarly of other battles in the months to come—Tanaka was only the first.

The island was an unattractive piece of geography— malarial, harborless, soon to be left behind. Some disputed the value of the sacrifice it cost. But the United States had to start attacking somewhere, and the Japanese decision to resist so insistently made the price almost inevitable.

Guadalcanal had been a brutal experience; it would be the Marines' longest battle of the war. Some of the higher commanders believed the Marines should have been relieved much sooner, but there had been no one to replace them. The Guadalcanal Marines became battle-hardened veterans of jungle warfare and aerial combat, and they spread their knowledge through the rapidly expanding Corps.

Strategically, the battle for Guadalcanal diverted Japanese strength; saved New Guinea from being overrun; sped up MacArthur's advance through New Guinea and the Philippines, and gave the United States a springboard from which to go after the enemy through the Central Pacific.

7
Isolating Rabaul

Now, the objective was Rabaul, the massive base on the eastern end of New Britain Island. As long as the enemy there could send out planes and ships to smash Allied landing operations, MacArthur could not advance along the northern coast of New Guinea and Nimitz could not pierce the Bismarck Archipelago and break out into the Central Pacific.

MacArthur wanted to conquer Rabaul, but the Allies at the Quebec Conference in August 1943 accepted the Joint Chiefs of Staff's recommendation to neutralize it. The Conference also fixed the grand Pacific strategy that would attack Japan both over the New Guinea–Philippine route (MacArthur) and through the Central Pacific islands (Nimitz).

To pulverize Rabaul, rather than to occupy it, required a series of landings and an enormous amount of bombing; but it cost much less in lives and materiel than a frontal assault. In the 10-month campaign to neutralize Rabaul, Marines participated in the air and on the ground. Three amphibious operations were particularly important: New Georgia, Bougainville and Cape Gloucester.

But first, the Japanese air war against Guadalcanal had to be controlled. The job was made easier when in February 1943 Marines began to switch to the gull-winged F4U Vought Corsairs, which could fly faster than any Japanese plane. On the afternoon of April 7, 76 fighters from Henderson Field shot down 39 of 160 attacking planes. First Lt. James E. Swett, a lanky twenty-two-year-old from San Mateo, California, earned the Medal of Honor and became an instant hero when he knocked off seven dive bombers in 15 minutes on his virgin combat flight. Swett, flying a Wildcat, shot down the first three over The Canal; then, he was hit by an American antiaircraft shell. He flew over Florida Island and shot down four more bombers before a Japanese rear gunner winged him. Swett killed the gunner and then ran out of ammunition. He crash-landed in the water, breaking his nose.

On June 30, Swett, now a captain, shot down three planes and on July 11 over Rendova added two more. That day, his wingman, 1st Lt. Harold E. Segal of New York City, scored three kills—the first when he shot a Zero off Swett's tail. Segal finished the war with 12 planes to his credit; but on July 11, both Swett and he ended in the drink. Segal was picked up by a destroyer; Swett spent 12 hours in the ocean off Japanese-held New Georgia before he was rescued by natives in a canoe and taken to a Navy patrol boat.

In the meanwhile, on April 18, in a carefully planned coup of inestimable value, Army P-38s shot down over Bougainville a twin-engine bomber carrying Fleet Adm. Isoroku Yamamoto, Commander in Chief, Combined Fleet, and erased Japan's most formidable naval mind.

The air assault on Guadalcanal climaxed in June, when the enemy took unacceptable losses—107 of 120 planes on June 16, for example—and gave up their daylight raids. The air action began to shift to the skies over Rabaul.

The first significant amphibious advance up the Solomons was to seize the Japanese air base at Munda Point on the northern end of New Georgia Island. The New Georgia operation was badly planned. It required five amphibious landings, 30,000 soldiers and Marines and more than a month of treacherous fighting. It wasted American lives.

The campaign started prematurely. On June 21, O and P Companies of the 4th Raider Battalion landed at Segi Point, at the southern end of New Georgia, and rescued Coastwatcher Donald G. Kennedy, whom the Japanese were hunting down. The Raiders then set out to destroy a 3-inch coastal gun at Viru Harbor before an Army force tried to land there. Led by Lt. Col. Michael S. Currin, the Raiders paddled eight miles through the moonless night and then plunged into the jungle. After four days struggling through mangrove swamps and across rivers, they overwhelmed the Japanese encampment on both sides of Viru Harbor. Eight Marines were killed in the final assault.

281

At the northern end of New Georgia, Army troops and the 9th Marine Defense Battalion landed on Rendova Island, across the lagoon from Munda Point, on June 30. Of the planes that rose to oppose the landing, 101 were shot down. On July 5, Army troops crossed over to Zanana Beach on New Georgia proper; and Marine Col. Harry B. Liversedge took two battalions of the 37th Infantry Division plus Lt. Col. Griffith's 1st Raider Battalion ashore as a blocking force at Rice Anchorage behind Munda Point. That night, in the naval Battle of Kula Gulf, the cruiser *Helena* and two Japanese destroyers were sunk.

Colonel Liversedge, a veteran of France and an Olympic shot-putter, known as "Harry the Horse" because of his 6'4" height, led his 2,600 men southwest toward Bairoko Harbor to cut off Munda's defenders from both reinforcement and escape. Soldiers and Marines fought through the thick rain-sodden jungle along a route scouted by a daring Raider patrol led by Capt. Clay A. Boyd. Liversedge's men ferried their equipment across the flooded Tamakau River on rafts made of ponchos and branches. After a brief fire fight with a Japanese patrol, Griffith's Raiders swept forward as swiftly as possible. On July 8, they killed 50 Japanese; but 400 Japanese attacked Liversedge's perimeter at Triri and pushed back its defenders until the Raiders hit the enemy rear.

The next day, the Raiders attacked again and were beaten back. On the morning of the tenth, the Raiders, without food for 24 hours, dispersed the enemy at the village of Enogai and seized their 140mm coastal guns. Late that afternoon, an Army company brought up food that had been airdropped at Triri. The hungry and angry Marines dined on K-rations and Japanese canned fish, rice and sake. Japanese casualties were estimated at 350; since advancing from Triri, the Marines had lost 51 dead and 74 wounded.

When Currin's 4th Raider Battalion (short 200 men) arrived on July 18, Liversedge set out to attack Bairoko Harbor, the next Japanese-held indentation on the coast toward Munda. On the twentieth, he sent the Marines along the coast and the soldiers straight across the intervening Dragons Peninsula.

An air strike Liversedge had requested never came, and the Marines were met by well-placed automatic weapons hidden in log and coral bunkers and by snipers in trees with light Nambu machine guns. After 20 minutes of furious combat, Griffith threw in his only reserve platoon and took pillbox after pillbox with heavy casualties. Griffith messaged Liversedge: "I have committed the works."[29] Liversedge sent up Currin's battalion, and the Marines inched forward a yard at a time. The Japanese began bombarding them with 90mm shells. The Raiders, always without artillery, had no weapons to reply. A screaming attack pushed the Marines back; D Company, 1st Battalion counterattacked and sent the enemy reeling. Q Company, 4th Battalion followed with a direct assault but was butchered and forced to retreat. Liversedge desperately needed help, but the Army battalion that was supposed to attack the enemy's flank had been held up in the jungle by strong resistance. By now, the Raiders had suffered 30 percent casualties; and, after reconnoitering the front lines, Griffith recommended that Liversedge withdraw. The Marines, only 300 yards from Bairoko, their objective, were exhausted from seven hours of battle, low on ammunition, out of water and burdened by 200 wounded. The next day, they struggled back to Enogai, carrying their dead and wounded. When the 25th Division finally entered Bairoko, it had been evacuated. The Raider battalions were returned to Guadalcanal; less than half of their 933 survivors were judged still effective for combat.

The whole operation had been mismanaged. The Japanese simply reinforced Munda over another route; Liversedge's trail block had not even cut the main Munda–Bairoko trail. The Americans' courageous fighting hardly justified the effort and the cost: 128 Marines dead and 307 wounded.

After a long, botched campaign, the Army, helped by Marine tanks, seized the Munda airfield on August 5. Historian Morison wrote, "We certainly took it the hard way."[30] But the Japanese had lost 358 planes trying to hold Munda; and VMF-123 and -124 were soon flying from the field.

The next move in the Solomons, 10 days later, was a bit smarter: Halsey leapfrogged heavily defended Kolombangara Island just north of New Georgia and took lightly defended Vella Lavella instead. The Allies should have learned a crucial lesson from this: Bypass enemy strongpoints and hit them where they ain't.

American air power continued drumming away at Rabaul.

The most spectacular Marine flier that fall was Maj. Gregory Boyington, who shot down five planes on his first mission on September 16. He was called "Pappy" because he was all of thirty-one years old. He designed and led fighter-sweeps, daring the Japanese pilots to come up and fight. His Black Sheep Squadron, VMF-214, downed 57 enemy planes in its first month of combat. Boyington earned the Medal of Honor and became the Marine Corps' top ace with 28 kills—counting the six planes he had destroyed earlier with the Flying Tigers in China. When he was shot down, badly wounded, over Rabaul on January 3, 1944, he parachuted into the sea, was picked up by a Japanese submarine and imprisoned until the end of the war.

These months also saw command changes important to the Marines. In July 1943, Turner was succeeded by Rear Adm. Theodore S. Wilkinson as commander of Amphibious Forces, South Pacific Area. Turner moved over to the Fifth Fleet in the Central Pacific. And now-Lieutenant General Vandegrift took command of the I Marine Amphibious Corps, responsible for all Marine amphibious units in the South Pacific. Vandegrift had a hand in planning the next operation before turning over the job on September 15 to Maj. Gen. Charles D. Barrett, an expert Marine planner. But when Barrett was killed in a fall at Nouméa, Vandegrift was recalled and completed the planning. On November 9, Maj. Gen. Roy S. Geiger took over I MAC; Vandegrift finally headed home to become Commandant of the Corps.

By the fall of 1943, three Marine divisions were in the Pacific. The 1st was preparing for Cape Gloucester on New Britain; the 2d for Tarawa in the Gilbert Islands, and the 3rd for Bougainville.

Bougainville was the final giant step up the Solomons to acquire an airfield that would bring the Allies within land-based fighter range of Rabaul. To deceive the Japanese, feints were sent against the Treasury Islands by the 8th New Zealand Brigade Group and against Choiseul Island by the Marines. Thirty-year-old Lt. Col. Victor H. Krulak took 656 men of the 2d Parachute Battalion ashore on Choiseul just after midnight on October 28. Krulak—a small, wiry man and like all Annapolis coxswains nicknamed "Brute"—had the unusual assignment of raising a rumpus so that the Japanese would think his landing was the beginning of the next big operation. In truth, the main American landing was to strike north of Bougainville's Empress Augusta Bay. Krulak's "Paramarines" landed on Choiseul and hiked south toward the enemy's barge base at Sangigai. They killed only seven of a 10-man Japanese unit so that the survivors could carry word of the landing back to the enemy commanders. Then, the Marines hit Sangigai from two sides. When E Company attacked along the coast, the Japanese fled into the hills and ran right into the rest of Krulak's force. In an hour-long hand-to-hand fight, four Marines were killed and 12 wounded; Krulak was wounded in the arm and face.

Maj. Warner T. Bigger led an 87-man patrol north to the Warrior River and bombarded an enemy supply base with mortar fire. The Japanese landed from barges to cut off Bigger's return and fought the patrol on the river bank. It was rescued by landing craft under cover of two PT boats, one commanded by Lt. John F. Kennedy, USNR, who had previously had his *PT 109* rammed by a Japanese destroyer. When one of the landing craft began to sink, Kennedy's boat, *PT 59*, took aboard some of the Marines, including three seriously wounded. Cpl. Edward J. Schnell of Wilmette, Illinois, critically wounded with a bullet in his chest, died in Kennedy's bunk. The next night, the rest of Krulak's parachutists were withdrawn from Choiseul.

The site of the main landing midway up Bougainville's west coast—210 miles from Rabaul—was the most uninviting on the 125-mile-long island. The narrow beaches were backed by brackish lagoons and swamps; and further inland, the Marines faced dense jungle more impenetrable than Guadalcanal's. Intelligence estimated that 17,000 Japanese were at the southern end of the island; 5,000 at the northern tip, but only 300 at Cape Torokina, where the "hit-'em-where-they-ain't" landing was contemplated.

The 3rd Marine Division was commanded by Maj. Gen. Allen H. Turnage, a veteran of France, Haiti and China, and composed of the 3rd, 9th and 21st Marines, with the artillery of the 12th Marines, the engineers of the 19th Marines and Seabees. To it were added the 2d and 3rd Raider Battalions and the 3rd Defense Battalion. The division had not been in combat, but many of its men were experienced and most had had jungle warfare training at Samoa and Guadalcanal. The assault would be made by two landing teams: the 3rd Marines plus the 2d Raider Battalion and the 9th Marines plus the 3rd Raider Battalion. When the division was entirely ashore, the 37th Infantry Division would land.

On the bright morning of November 1, the Marines landed on 12 beaches from Cape Torokina northward. The rough surf wrecked 86 of the 9th Marines' landing craft. On the extreme right, the 1st Battalion, 3rd Marines, met the strongest resistance; its boats were caught in a crossfire from Cape Torokina and Puruata Island just offshore. The enemy's single 75mm gun sank four of the landing craft.

As the Marines reached the beach, machine guns, mortars and rifle fire opened up from solid log and sand bunkers. The gunfire of four destroyers had accomplished little. The landing became a shambles. One of the first men ashore, Sgt. Robert A. Owens, twenty-three years old from Greenville, South Carolina, alone charged the fire port of the destructive 75mm gun, which had by now hit 14 boats. Owens drove the crew out through the rear of the bunker and silenced the gun before he was killed. His Medal of Honor citation recognized his act as "indomitable and aggressive in the face of almost certain death."

Working expertly, the Marines knocked out Cape Torokina's 25 bunkers. Enemy air attacks strafed the narrow beaches; cargo piled up. There were now 14,000 men ashore. The Marines spent the rain-filled night huddled three to a foxhole, one man always awake. Infiltrators were disposed of with bayonets and knives.

That night, in the naval battle of Empress Augusta Bay, U.S. Navy Task Force 29 successfully protected the beachhead and sank a cruiser and a destroyer.

The Marines had two jobs ashore: to build an airfield and to expand and strengthen the perimeter. The 2d Raiders, aided by 29 dogs of the 1st Marine War Dog Platoon, pushed inland up the Mission Trail. In the muck of the swampland, the amphibian tractor (LVT) proved invaluable. By November 5, the perimeter was 10,000 yards along the beach and 5,000 yards deep.

Two days later, the northern flank of the beachhead was attacked by a counterlanding of 475 men. One enemy detachment met a patrol led by Lt. Orville Freeman and wounded the future Secretary of Agriculture. By the next day, the Japanese force had been eliminated in close-range fighting.

On the seventh and eighth, a strong enemy force hit a trail block the Raiders had set up inland west of the junction of the Piva and Numa Numa trails; the seesaw battle ended shortly after noon on the ninth when the superior firepower of four Raider companies finally prevailed. The Raiders occupied the Piva–Numa Numa junction and dug in. They had lost 12 killed and 30 wounded. Two battalions of the 9th Marines now moved through the Raider positions and occupied Piva Village. And the Army's 148th Regimental Combat Team arrived and took over the northern half of the beachhead perimeter. By November 13, there were 33,861 soldiers and Marines ashore.

An airfield site was selected 1,500 yards inland beyond the Marine perimeter; and the 2d Battalion, 21st Marines was sent forward to hold the area. But the enemy got there first and ambushed E Company in a coconut grove.

The Japanese set up strong blocks on both the Numa Numa and the East-West trails in front of the Marines. The 2d and 3rd Battalions, 3rd Marines moved up the trails until Lt. William Kay, an expert scout known as "The Fox," found a 400-foot jungle hill from which the entire area could be dominated. First Lt. Steve J. Cibik and his platoon occupied the height late on November 20 and the next morning hurled back three enemy attacks.

When the Marines moved forward again, they ran into heavy going. This became known as the Battle of Piva Forks. On Wednesday, November 24, Thanksgiving Day back home, the two battalions of the 3rd Marines attacked across the east branch of the Piva River. After a 20-minute artillery barrage, the 2d Battalion advanced only 250 yards through the jungle before it took 70 casualties. Flamethrowers destroyed the enemy bunkers. The 3rd Battalion on the left side of the trail stopped a flank attack in hand-to-hand fighting. By the time the Marines reached their objectives, they counted 1,071 enemy bodies and had 115 casualties themselves. Back at the beachhead, a shipment of Thanksgiving turkeys arrived; the cooks roasted them and sent a share to the units up front.

The 1st Battalion, 9th Marines attacked down Cibik Ridge

and tried to capture a small 20-foot-high knoll where about 70 Japanese were dug in with an ample supply of grenades. The Marines never did take the crest of "Grenade Hill" until the enemy withdrew. Then, the Marines held the high ground from which the enemy could threaten the beachhead.

Under command of Maj. Richard Fagan, the newly arrived 1st Parachute Battalion and M Company of the 3rd Raider Battalion were sent to raid Koiari, 10 miles down the coast from Cape Torokina, in the early hours of November 29. They landed in the middle of a Japanese supply dump. An officer, expecting Japanese boats and carrying only a sword, greeted them at the beach. Surprise was mutual; the officer was killed. When the enemy recovered, they hit the beachhead with mortar shells, grenades and machine-gun fire and rushed the Marines. Casualties mounted. Fagan radioed a request that his outnumbered unit be pulled out. Enemy artillery repulsed two rescue attempts by landing craft. Three U.S. destroyers were rushed to the scene, and the ships and 155mm guns at Cape Torokina lay a box of fire around the beleaguered Marines. Behind that shield, the landing craft raced to the beach and took off the men. The detachment, which totaled 614 men, had 15 killed, 99 wounded and seven missing. The raid had been a bloody failure.

The final move to anchor the perimeter required the seizure of a large hill mass where the enemy made a strong stand on a spur of Hill 1000 that the Marines came to call Hellzapoppin Ridge. It took until December 18 before the Japanese were finally dislodged by the 21st Marines, working with effective Marine close air support.

By the end of January 1944, the Marines were withdrawn; they had lost 423 killed and 1,418 wounded on Bougainville. For this price an air base had been bought 210 miles from Rabaul. The high-risk venture had paid off. From the strip at Torokina, VMF-216 had flown close support missions at Hellzapoppin Ridge; and by the end of the year, the Piva bomber field was functioning. Now, fighter aircraft could escort bombers all the way to Rabaul.

On March 9, a force of some 12,000 Japanese soldiers came over the mountains and attacked the Torokina perimeter, determined to push the American XIV Corps' two Army divisions and the 3rd Marine Defense Battalion into the sea. The enemy made six major assaults in the next two weeks and 6,843 Japanese died in the futile attempt. The enemy, having lost control of sea and air, never tried again.

American air power continued to wallop Rabaul; and by February, mastery of the sky had been won over that hard-hit base. Marine 1st Lt. Robert M. Hanson, the Corps' third leading ace in the war with 25 kills, was shot down. The Japanese lost nearly 400 planes defending Rabaul; and on February 20, they pulled back the remainder to Truk. That altered the strategic situation critically. Although planes from Bougainville kept bombing Rabaul, the great Japanese base was already impotent.

MacArthur wanted to occupy Cape Gloucester on the western end of New Britain Island, 350 jungle miles from Rabaul, to protect his flank as he moved up along New Guinea's coast. After the war, Historian Morison judged: "General MacArthur believed that Cape Gloucester must be taken . . . . The wisdom of hindsight makes it seem superfluous."[31] For the 1st Marine Division alone, this "waste of time and effort"[32] would cost 310 killed and 1,083 wounded, plus weeks of battling jungle, rain and disease.

After the Army landed in Marine amphibian tractors at the Aware Peninsula on the southern New Britain coast, the 1st Marine Division assaulted Cape Gloucester the day after Christmas 1943. The now hard-nosed division was commanded by Maj. Gen. Rupertus and refreshed from its Melbourne fling. The Marines were armed with the semiautomatic M-1 rifle, which had replaced the bolt-action Springfield '03; and most of the officers and noncoms were Guadalcanal veterans. To the frustration of Intelligence, these experienced Marines were loath to take prisoners.

The 1st and 3rd Battalions of Col. Julian N. Frisbie's 7th Marines went in east of the cape, followed by the 3rd Battalion, 1st Marines. On the other side of the cape, Lt. Col. James M. Masters, Sr.,'s 2d Battalion, 1st Marines (Masters' Bastards) landed on a black volcanic beach near Tauali to set up a jungle trail block.

The main landing on the east side went easily, although the Japanese resisted the lead company's advance toward the airfield. By that night, 11,000 men were ashore; and the immediate

289

beachhead was secure. Once again, 1st Division Marines lay in the moonless jungle dark and monsoon rains, waiting for the Japanese to attack.

They hit the center of the perimeter, and a disorganized battle raged in the rain-soaked pitch-black darkness. The Marines were attacked again and again over the next few days, but the strength of the assaults steadily diminished.

Meanwhile, Col. William J. Whaling's 1st Marines moved cautiously toward the cape's airfields. Men and tanks had to eliminate the Japanese from solid beach defenses at Hell's Point. By the evening of December 29, the 1st Battalion, 1st Marines reached the airfield; and three battalions looped a perimeter around the strips. The Japanese waited in the hills south of the airfield and the next day fought Lt. Col. Lewis W. Walt's 2d Battalion, 5th Marines on Razorback Hill, which dominated the field. Finally, the 3rd Battalion, 1st Marines, took the summit. At noon on the last day of 1943, Maj. Gen. Rupertus formally raised the American flag on Cape Gloucester. MacArthur sent his congratulations: "Your gallant division has maintained the immortal record of the Marine Corps and covered itself with glory."[33]

On the other side of the peninsula, the Tauali trail block was hit four times; and on January 5, 1944, the battalion there started moving over to join the main force.

On January 2, the 3rd Battalion, 7th Marines started south of Target Hill through the wet, stinking jungle eastward toward Borgen Bay. At a 20-foot-wide sluggish jungle stream, the Marines met enemy fire; and the 3rd Battalion, 5th Marines joined on their right. The Marines could not see the enemy hidden across the stream in foxholes and log bunkers. Each Marine who tried to cross was picked off. The stream became a deathtrap known as Suicide Creek.

Before dawn the next morning, the Japanese attacked the eastern end of the perimeter at Target Hill. They took 102 casualties beating their heads against the Marine line there.

As the battle of Suicide Creek continued, the Marines finally crossed on the enemy's flanks but could not dislodge them. First Lt. Elisha Atkins, a Harvard Phi Beta Kappa student and football player known to the men as "Tommy Harvard," led his machine-gun platoon across. The men were hit by automatic fire and forced back into the creek. Atkins, hit three times, ordered his men to leave him there. On the Marines' side of the creek, Pfc. Luther J. Raschke of Harvard, Illinois, crept to the edge of the stream, while three Marines covered him, and called to Atkins: "Tommy Harvard, Tommy Harvard." They finally found the lieutenant, weak from the loss of blood, and carried him to safety. Raschke was awarded a Silver Star.[34] Atkins survived to become a doctor and professor of medicine at Yale.

Maj. Gen. Rupertus sent Lt. Col. Puller, the 7th Marines' executive officer, to get the 3rd Battalion moving. Engineers of the 17th Marines rushed a corduroy road across the coastal swamp and late that afternoon three Sherman tanks lumbered up. The Engineers cut down Suicide Creek's 12-foot-high bank with an unprotected bulldozer. Snipers shot two drivers, Cpl. John E. Capito and Staff Sgt. Keary Lane, before Pfc. Randall Johnson, crouching out of the line of fire and moving the controls with a shovel and an axe handle, opened the way for the tanks and half-tracks. Then, the tank-infantry teams went about the business of eradicating the Japanese. And the assault battalions broke through and pushed forward a thousand yards. At Suicide Creek and Target Hill, 41 Marines were killed and 218 wounded. Still ahead were an estimated 1,300 Japanese.

The Marines set out to find Aogiri Ridge, hidden in the jungle, where Intelligence knew the Japanese were entrenched. As the three assault battalions approached, enemy fire stopped them. The commander and executive officer of the 3rd Battalion, 5th Marines, were both wounded; and Puller took over that battalion also until Lt. Col. Walt could come up and take command. (It was Navy Cross No. 4 for "Chesty" Puller.)

The enemy did not waste manpower this time but waited for Walt's Marines to penetrate the thick jungle. In 24 hours, 15 Marines were killed and 161 wounded as the Japanese beat back repeated Marine attacks. By January 9, the attackers were running out of strength. A 37mm gun was dragged up. Walt called for volunteers, and he and his runner put their shoulders to one wheel and helped push the gun up Aogiri Ridge, stopping every few feet to fire. As more Marines joined them and were hit, others took their places and the line surged forward.

Walt's men clung to the forward slope and crest of the ridge, ten yards from the enemy. At 1:15 A.M. on the tenth, they were hit by four screaming bayonet attacks through a driving rain. Walt called in artillery within 50 yards of his own lines. Finally, a fifth charge was beaten down; and with first light, the fight was over. Aogiri Ridge would be known as Walt's Ridge.

Lt. Col. Henry W. Buse, Jr., now commanding the 3rd Battalion, 7th Marines, was assigned the job of taking the final Marine objective—Hill 660. Capt. Joseph W. Buckley, a Marine since 1915, led a detachment with two tanks and two half tracks to block the coastal trail behind the hill. Buse's Marines had to sling their rifles and pull themselves up Hill 660's steep muddy face. It took them two days to seize the hill; and when they did, Buckley's gunners picked off the fleeing enemy soldiers on the beach and in the surf.

On January 16, a last counterattack was destroyed; and the battle for Cape Gloucester was finally won. The remaining Japanese, starving and sick, started pulling out of western New Britain on the long, killing march to the east. The Marines pursued them with a number of overland expeditions and a shore-to-shore landing by the 5th Marines, now commanded by Col. Oliver P. Smith, on the Willaumez Peninsula on March 6. The Marines lost 17 killed and 114 wounded there. On April 24, the exhausted 1st Marine Division began to be relieved by the 40th Infantry Division.

The 1st Division convinced itself it was going back to the interrupted pleasures of Melbourne but was shipped instead to Pavuvu, the largest of the Russell Islands—a haven of rotten coconuts, coral, rats, land crabs and rain, rain, rain. Pavuvu was a hell of mud and boredom and loneliness. The only U.S.O. show to reach the Marines there arrived because Bob Hope insisted on squeezing in a morning performance for them. Maj. Gen. Rupertus, in Washington for conferences, finally won agreement that 4,860 of his men with 24 months overseas would be rotated home. Those who stayed behind, after six months or so, began to get ready for Peleliu.

The ring around Rabaul was already closed by the time the 1st Division left New Britain. The 3rd New Zealand Division landed on the Green Islands on February 15. Elements of the 1st Cavalry Division hit Los Negros Island two weeks later and ran into tough opposition before securing the Admiralty Islands and magnificent Seeadler Harbor. And on March 20, Emirau was occupied without resistance by the newly reformed 4th Marines, made up of former Raider units. At Rabaul, planes no longer rose to fight; in the harbor rested only the hulks of sunken ships.

In April, MacArthur's troops leapfrogged ahead to Hollandia, New Guinea. Marine ground forces in the South Pacific were returned to Admiral Nimitz's command for the drive up the Central Pacific. Most Marine air units went into MacArthur's Southwest Pacific command. No longer would Marines ashore have their own close air support—except briefly at Peleliu and Iwo Jima—until both drives toward Japan met again on Okinawa. In the meantime, Marine fliers did a close-support job for the Army in the Philippines.

But the fighting in the Central Pacific islands had already begun.

8
Tarawa

"Hawk" was a lean, six-foot Texan from El Paso, the twenty-nine-year-old commander of the Scout-Sniper Platoon of the 2d Marines. "The bravest man I have ever known," wrote Robert Sherrod, a *Time* correspondent who landed with the Marines at Tarawa. First Lt. William Deane Hawkins was a natural leader. He had worked his way through the Texas College of Mines as a ranch hand and bellhop and was rejected for Army and Navy flight training because he had been badly scarred by scalding water as an infant. Enlisting in the Marine Corps, he had shipped overseas as a private first class, landed on Tulagi as a sergeant and been commissioned a month later. After he was dead, Tarawa's assault commander said quietly, "It's not often that you can credit a first lieutenant with winning a battle, but Hawkins came as near to it as any man could."[35]

At 8:55 A.M. on Saturday, November 20, 1943—15 minutes ahead of the first assault wave—Hawkins led five men up the seaplane ramp at the tip of the 550-yard-long pier jutting out from Tarawa. They raced along the pier, and Hawkins signaled the rest of the men in the LCVP to follow. The Japanese began firing at them, hitting the gasoline drums stored on the pier. Hawkins waved the men back, and with his four scouts and 2d Lt. Alan G. Leslie, Jr., began fighting down the length of the pier. Leslie's flamethrower burned two shacks in which machine gunners waited to enfilade the approaching landing craft. The scouts cleared the pier.

Then, Hawkins' platoon of 34 expert fighters moved toward shore in three amtracs (LVTs); and behind them roared the assault waves of the 2d Marine Division, hardened veterans of Guadalcanal, into one of the most desperate battles in Marine Corps history.

The assault on Tarawa launched the advance onto the Central Pacific island stepping-stones toward Japan. The landing—three weeks after the 3rd Marine Division assaulted Bougainville—was part of a three-pronged invasion of the Japanese-held Gilbert Islands. The 165th Regimental Combat Team of the Army's 27th Infantry Division, a New York National Guard unit, was sent north to take Makin, which Carlson had raided earlier. The V Marine Amphibious Corps Reconnaissance Company occupied Apamama south of Tarawa Atoll—and the 2d Marine Division attacked Tarawa. The Army's 6,470 soldiers needed three days to defeat the 300 Japanese troops on Makin and lost only 66 dead, but Tarawa was a 76-hour slaughterhouse.

The American commanders knew it would be tough. Tarawa was a triangular coral atoll of islands and reefs, 12 miles across and 18 miles long. On the island of Betio, at the southwest corner of the atoll, the Japanese had built a small airfield. Betio was three miles long and 600 yards across at its widest point. Since Carlson's Raiders had struck Makin, the Japanese had made Betio a fortress they considered impregnable, fringed with a forest of 200 guns and manned with 2,600 first-class troops and 2,200 laborers. "Corregidor was an open town by comparison."[36] The Japanese boasted that a million Americans could not take Betio in a hundred years.

The Americans insisted on assaulting Betio because they wanted its airfield from which to step up the island chain into the Marshall Islands. At Tarawa, 1,113 Marines and attached Navy personnel were killed and 2,290 wounded. The battle teetered on the beaches; only the determination of individual Marines pushed it forward.

The price for Tarawa was so high because the planners (1) assigned too few Marines to take it; (2) vetoed the proposal to land artillery on the adjoining island to bombard Betio before the invasion; (3) gambled on the long shot that the water over the coral reef surrounding Betio would be at least 3.5 feet deep, enough to float the LCVPs; and (4) had too few amphibian tractors in case the water was shallower—as it proved to be.

Before the landing craft started for the three beaches on the northern or lagoon side of Betio, warships and carrier planes laid down the greatest naval barrage ever to pound so small a target. Shells and bombs knocked out enemy guns and communications, but it was not enough. And when the landing was delayed by 40 minutes, the naval gunfire was lifted because smoke concealed the landing craft. The defenders were handed a precious half hour to shift men to the lagoon side.

Then, three waves of the 2d and 3rd Battalions, 2d Marines and the 2d Battalion, 8th Marines, mostly battle dressed in mottled green dungarees and helmet covers, headed for the beaches in 93 amtracs able to crawl over the coral reef. On the east (Beach Red 3)—toward the middle of the island—Maj. Henry P. "Jim" Crowe's 3d Battalion, 8th Marines touched shore at 9:10 A.M. On the west (Red 1), elements of Maj. John F. Schoettel's 3rd Battalion, 2d Marines made it seven minutes later, despite heavy casualties. Schoettel himself could not get ashore; at 9:59, he radioed that the issue was in doubt. Told to land his reserve, he replied, "We have nothing left to land."[37]

In the center of the assault at Red 2, resistance was toughest and initial losses were heaviest. The 2d Battalion, 2d Marines reached the beach at 9:22. A machine gun killed its tall, popular commander, Lt. Col. Herbert R. Amey, Jr., when his LVT was stopped by barbed wire and he started to wade in the last 50 yards. Lt. Col. Walter I. Jordan, an observer from the 4th Marine Division, took over Amey's badly shot up battalion.

The Marines found the narrow beaches backed by a coconut log seawall about four feet high. Starting within 15 feet of the wall, the Japanese commander, Rear Adm. Keiji Shibasaki, had cleverly sited machine guns and artillery to throw back any assault. The first three waves of Marines were pinned to the beaches between the water and the log wall. If a Marine raised himself to fire his weapon, he risked immediate death. Two amtracs of Crowe's battalion found a breach in the wall near the base of the long pier, dashed through and unloaded their Marines near the airstrip. But the flanking fire was unbearable and they had to reboard and scoot back to the beach.

In another amtrac, all but five Marines were killed on the reef. One survivor, Staff Sgt. William J. Bordelon, Jr., of the division engineers, the 18th Marines, scrambled to the beach with Sgt. Elden H. Beers of Deer Park, Washington, and Pvt. Jack G. Ashworth, Jr., of Los Angeles. They hurriedly made up demolition charges, and the wiry Bordelon went over the sea wall and destroyed two pillboxes. He was shot in the left arm. As he went out alone again and attacked a third pillbox, he was hit by machine-gun fire. Severely wounded, he picked up a rifle and covered Marines scaling the seawall. An enemy grenade ripped Beers' stomach. Bordelon heard cries for help from the blood-stained water, went back and dragged ashore one of his demolition men and another Marine who had been hit while trying to rescue the wounded engineer. Repeatedly refusing medical aid, Bordelon destroyed a fourth pillbox with a rifle grenade and then was killed instantly. Twenty-two-year-old Bordelon, who had enlisted at San Antonio, Texas, right after Pearl Harbor, was awarded the Medal of Honor posthumously.

After the third wave, the Marines were forced to use LCVPs because of the shortage of amtracs; and the landing craft grounded at the outer edge of the coral reef. The men had to wade in. They were destroyed in the water. Junior officers and noncoms kept the survivors going.

Ten Sherman medium tanks and a number of light tanks got ashore in the fifth wave. The 2d Tank Battalion commander, Lt. Col. Alexander B. Swenceski, badly wounded, dragged himself up on a pile of bodies to keep from drowning and lay there until the next day.

Col. David M. Shoup, thirty-nine years old from Battle Ground, Indiana, commanded the assault. When the commander of the 2d Marines had fallen ill just before the invasion, tough, able Dave Shoup had been spot-promoted to colonel and replaced him. By 11 A.M., Shoup, along with Maj. Thomas A. Culhane, Jr.; Lt. Col. Presley M. Rixey, commander of the 1st Battalion, 10th Marines of the division artillery, and a sergeant with a radio on his back, waded to the side of the pier. Although wounded in the leg, Shoup directed the battle from there, under fire in waist-deep water.

He had the warships bombard the eastern end of the island and brought Maj. Wood B. Kyle's 1st Battalion, 2d Marines toward the center beach with orders to move westward and help the men on Red 1. He sent half of Maj. Robert H. Ruud's 3rd Battalion, 8th Marines to support Crowe on Red 3. Ruud's men waded in, under fire, for 700 yards—an incredible ordeal; some drowned in water over their heads; others were killed by the enemy. Only 100 of Ruud's first wave, 30 percent, reached Betio. Signaling frantically, Shoup drew the second wave toward the pier; but they found little shelter there and casualties mounted.

The third wave was practically wiped out. Few of the fourth wave landed; the rest were held off under heavy fire.

By noon, the assault had stalled; masses of sweating Marines hugged the 20-foot-wide beaches, unable to advance or retreat. Rifles and grenades were of little use against the dug-in enemy, and flamethrowers were scarce. Reinforcements could not get in. Landing craft were stuck on the reef full of dead and wounded. Small groups of Marines charged over the log wall and tried to move forward to kill the enemy and destroy his bunkers and machine guns. Half of the bravest were shot down.

On Red 1, at the western end of Betio, a 500-yard cove exposed the Marines to a murderous crossfire. I and K Companies of 3rd Battalion, 2d Marines charged over the barricade and lost half their men in two hours. L Company was grounded 500 yards offshore, and 35 percent of its men were hit in the water. L Company's commander, Maj. Michael P. Ryan, and assorted survivors formed a small separate beachhead at the island's western tip, 600 yards from the main landing.

Six Sherman tanks were led in over the reef by Marines walking ahead of them with flags. The tanks' commander found so many dead and wounded Marines on the beach that he could not maneuver. He took the tanks back into the water, and they rumbled toward the western end of the island. Four tanks drowned in potholes; the two surviving tanks were hit but reached Ryan's beachhead and helped protect his flank. Ryan's force managed to advance 500 yards but had to pull back to a tighter perimeter when dark came.

On Red 2, in the center, Jordan used flamethrowers and TNT charges; and one company crawled about 100 yards inland. East of the long pier, large, red-mustached Crowe, of Boston, Kentucky, who had been an enlisted Marine for 14 years and won a Silver Star on Guadalcanal, also pushed ahead about 100 yards. Of four tanks that tried to support Crowe's Marines, three were destroyed, one by a friendly dive bomber. Some of Crowe's men reached the triangle between the airfield's runway and taxistrips; but on their left flank near the water, they were stopped by a strongpoint near the base of the short Burns-Philp Wharf.

Hawkins' Scout-Sniper Platoon was up over the seawall all day, destroying bunkers. His 34 men killed ten times their number of Japanese. Hawkins himself rode an amtrac and personally cleaned out six machine-gun nests. He took two bullets in his shoulders but kept fighting.

About noon, Shoup came ashore and set up a command post 15 feet inland, in the shadow of a huge coconut log bunker still crowded with scores of Japanese. Marines covered the entrances to contain them. Shoup sent Col. Evans Carlson, the former Raider who was with him as a 4th Division observer, out to the command ship, the battleship *Maryland,* to hurry more men, water, ammunition and guns to the pier. Destroyers and planes gave close support all day long.

At 1:31, Maj. Gen. Julian C. Smith, commander of the 2d Division, radioed Maj. Gen. Holland M. Smith, commander of the V Marine Amphibious Corps, who was on Rear Adm. Richmond K. Turner's flagship at Makin. He asked for the release of the corps reserve, the 6th Marines, who were standing by off Tarawa to support either invasion. When Turner swiftly approved the request, Julian Smith ordered the 1st Battalion, 8th Marines, his own last division reserve, to land; but communications failed, and the battalion waited in its boats throughout the long night.

By nightfall, some 5,000 Marines were ashore on the edge of Betio; 1,500 had been killed or wounded. The survivors were struggling for a toehold, refusing to be pushed back into the sea.

That night, the smell of death pervaded the beachheads. The Marines, expecting the customary Japanese night attacks, prepared for the worst. They dug foxholes in the sand and over the seawall. Reinforcements were boated to the far end of the long pier and then worked their way under and alongside the log cribwork to the beach. The artillerymen of the 10th Marines lugged pieces of their 75mm pack howitzers ashore on their backs. Brig. Gen. Leo D. Hermle, the assistant division commander, organized carrying parties on the pier to bring ammunition and water through the enemy fire.

On Betio, unlike the defense of Edson's Ridge on Guadalcanal, there was no room to fall back and regroup, no possibility of a defense in depth—nothing but a very thin line of Marines.

Miraculously, the Japanese did not attack. The pre-invasion bombardment had shredded their wire communications; Rear Adm. Shibasaki could not pull together his scattered and hard-hit forces. Had he attacked that first night, he might have driven the Marines off Betio. Because he did not, he lost the battle.

At dawn, Hawkins and his scouts resumed their deadly work clearing out enemy bunkers. Hawkins led his men against a strongpoint covered by five machine guns. He crawled forward under heavy fire, shot point-blank into the bunker's ports and hurled in grenades. Wounded in the chest and hand, he, again, stayed in the fight and destroyed three more pillboxes before an explosive machine-gun bullet severed an artery in his shoulder. He was dying when his scouts carried him to the rear.

His Medal of Honor citation said, "His relentless fighting spirit in the face of formidable opposition and his exceptionally daring tactics served as an inspiration to his comrades during the most crucial phase of the battle." Betio's airfield was later named Hawkins Field.

Shoup's plan for the second day was for the 1st Battalion, 8th Marines to land and fight westward to strengthen the Red 1 beachhead. Then, Ryan would clean up the western end of the island. In the center, Kyle and Jordan would cut the island in two. And east on Red 3, Crowe, a private in France in World War I, would smash the strongpoint at the Burns-Philp Wharf.

At 6:15 A.M., the first waves of Maj. Lawrence C. Hays, Jr.'s 1st Battalion, 8th Marines finally began wading the 500 yards to shore. They were hit by flanking machine-gun fire and decimated. The carnage in the water was worse than on the first day. Weary, bearded Marines ashore attacked to suppress the enemy fire, which came from bunkers, trees, privies the Japanese had built over the water and the hulk of a Japanese freighter. By 8 A.M., half the men of Hays' battalion had reached the beach and struggled westward to help Ryan. But they had lost most of their flamethrowers and demolitions and without them could make little progress against the bunkers.

In the center, A and B Companies of Kyle's battalion fought to the south coast and took the Japanese entrenchments, which had been set up to repel an attack from the sea. Lt. Col. Jordan with these men and some from the 2d Battalion, 2d Marines— no more than 135 Marines—formed a precarious perimeter there. The enemy counterattacked, and the Marines took heavy casualties. Kyle's C Company fought off a Japanese attack and joined them. Kyle assumed command of this isolated band,

and Jordan reverted to his "observer status" with high praise from Shoup.

At the eastern end of the main perimeter on the lagoon, Crowe's battalion could not advance against the enemy pillboxes but at dusk managed to take the wharf and extend a line to the middle of the airfield triangle.

By late afternoon, Ryan's Marines had overrun three 80mm coastal guns and established a line across the island, 200 yards in from Betio's western beaches. Their advance cheered the Marines' commanders and allowed Col. Maurice G. Holmes to land his 6th Marines. Holmes sent his 2d Battalion around to Bairiki, the island just east of Betio, where it landed without resistance. By 6:35 P.M., Maj. William K. Jones brought the 1st Battalion, 6th Marines ashore on Betio's western beaches in rubber boats towed by LCVPs.

Everywhere, small groups of Marines inched forward from shell craters, ruined buildings, from behind fallen trees and piles of battle debris. In the blazing heat, they hurled grenades and blocks of TNT into bunkers; and flamethrower operators dashed forward and sprayed the interiors with liquid fire.

Shortly after noon, momentum had been created. The fighting was intense, but the hope of victory seemed real for the first time. The water over the reef deepened and some LCVPs could get to the beach. At 5:06 P.M., Shoup radioed: "Casualties many. Percentage dead not known. Combat efficiency—we are winning."[38] Three hours later, the veteran Col. Merritt A. Edson, now the 2d Division's chief of staff, arrived and took overall command ashore. Shoup concentrated his attention on his own combat team trying to join the northern and western beachheads.

By the end of the second day, the main perimeter stretched about 400 yards on either side of the long pier in the middle of the landing areas. Kyle's force held on the south coast, and the entire western side of Betio was in Marine hands.

On the third morning, Jones' battalion led by three light tanks, pushed along the south shore to link up with Kyle's men. On Betio's north side, Crowe and Ruud attacked the strongpoint east of the wharf with tanks, flamethrowers and mortars. Marines climbed its sandpiled sides. The Japanese charged them to protect this key position. One man broke their attack: 1st Lt.

Alexander Bonnyman, Jr., of Atlanta, executive officer of the 8th Marines' 2d Battalion Shore Party. The previous days, Bonnyman had fought heroically on the long pier and ashore. He had crawled 40 yards in front of the Marine position to place charges in the entrance of a bombproof. Now, he stormed the bastion, directed the placement of demolition charges and seized the top of the bunker. As the enemy poured out, he turned his flamethrower on them. Then, standing on the bunker, he fought off their counterattack and led his men down before he was mortally wounded. Bulldozers sealed up the bunker, and the Marines burst forward 400 yards without further casualties. Bonnyman's was the third and last posthumous Medal of Honor earned on Tarawa, where only Colonel Shoup was awarded the highest medal and lived to wear it.

At 11 A.M., Lt. Col. Kenneth F. McLeod's 3rd Battalion, 6th Marines landed on the western beaches and followed Jones' battalion along the south coast. Julian Smith came ashore; on the way in, his LVT driver was hit, and the general had to transfer to another amtrac. By afternoon, Jones' battalion and elements of 2d and 3rd Battalions, 8th Marines had formed a line across the island near the eastern end of the airfield. At 7:30 P.M., the Japanese counterattacked and briefly drove a hole between Jones' A and B Companies. The enemy threw themselves against the Marine line again and again into the night. The Marines fought them off with grenades and rifle fire; artillery shelled as close as 75 yards in front of the Marines' positions, and destroyers fired from the lagoon. By 5 A.M. of the fourth day, the enemy's spasmodic attacks had been shattered; within 50 yards of the Marines lay 200 Japanese bodies.

Now, on D-Day plus three, two jobs remained: to wipe out the western strongpoint between Red 1 and 2 and to sweep the island's eastern tail. The 3rd Battalion, 2d Marines and the 1st Battalion, 8th Marines with a new supply of flamethrowers eliminated the pocket to the west by 1:15 P.M. The 6th Marines, with tanks and flamethrowers, reached the eastern tip by 1:10. Betio was secured. Marines and Seabees were already repairing the airstrip for which so many had died.

Of the 4,836 Japanese soldiers and Korean laborers on Betio, only 146 were taken prisoner; of those, 17 were Japanese. The rest were killed. The mopping up continued for two days. The stench of rotting bodies was terrible.

Lt. Col. Raymond L. Murray's 2d Battalion, 6th Marines was sent up the atoll's other islands. The Marines found no resistance until they reached Buariki, the northern-most large island, on November 26. There, 175 Japanese made a last-ditch stand. The next morning, the Marines killed all but two whom they took prisoner. The battalion had 32 killed and 59 wounded in this last round.

The bloodiness of the battle for Tarawa shocked the nation. Some protested the judgment of frontally assaulting so strongly defended an island and questioned whether Tarawa should have been bypassed, as were Rabaul and Truk, infinitely bigger enemy bases. Others felt the amphibious lessons learned were worth the price; they would save lives later in this island war.[39] There is no way to settle that argument. It is only possible to quote Maj. Gen. Holland M. Smith, true believer in amphibious assault and commander of all the Marines in the Gilberts invasions:

> Was Tarawa worth it? My answer is unqualified: No. From the very beginning the decision of the Joint Chiefs to seize Tarawa was a mistake and from their initial mistake grew the terrible drama of errors, errors of omission rather than commission, resulting in these needless casualties. . . . Tarawa should have been by-passed. Its capture—a mission executed by Marines under direct orders from the high command—was a terrible waste of life and effort . . . . The futile sacrifice of Marines on that strategically useless coral strand makes me sad today as it did then . . . . In the strategical scheme of the Central Pacific offensive, it taught me that the instrument of high policy known as the Joint Chiefs of Staff was not infallible. Tarawa was a mistake.[40]

Whatever the strategical correctness of this battle, anyone reading the story of Tarawa must wonder what drove individual Marines forward against such a fierce and concentrated defense. Every man was scared, and many did cower in the meager shelter of seawall or shell holes; but as Colonel Shoup wrote after the battle, "A surprising number . . . displayed a fearless eagerness to go to the extreme for their country and fellow men."[41]

Robert Sherrod explained best the mystery of courage: "The Marines fought almost solely on *esprit de corps*, I was certain. It was inconceivable to most Marines that they should let another Marine down, or that they could be responsible for dimming the bright reputation of their corps. The Marines simply assumed that they were the world's best fighting men."[42]

9
The Marshalls: Swift Victory

Tarawa, in Holland Smith's acerbic view, again offered the decision makers a lesson they should have learned at Munda Point: Leapfrog the enemy's strongpoints. Leave his island garrisons to rot. And no more cruel primitivism of Marines walking helplessly through the sea into the face of unanswerable gunfire.

It was now 1944, two years after Pearl Harbor; and new American fleets and forces had been built. The nation's bull-like strength was beginning to press against Japan. Nazi Germany was still Enemy Number One, and the invasion of Normandy was being mounted; but since the Battle of Midway, it had been only a matter of time—and mass (and good men dead)—before the attackers of Pearl Harbor were driven to their knees.

The question was "How?" The Allies planned to approach Japan from three directions: the China–Burma–India push to open the Burma Road and the two fists of the American cross-Pacific offensive—MacArthur's the left and Nimitz's the right. The long-range plan was to bomb Japan itself from the mainland of China. MacArthur, the Supreme Commander of Allied Forces in the Southwest Pacific Area, took the southern route: over the land masses of New Guinea and the Philippines. He was determined to keep his pledge to return to the Philippines. Nimitz ran the direct line over the Central Pacific islands. MacArthur used land-based air power; Nimitz depended on carrier-based air, the powerful new weapon that gave the Navy enormous mobility in choosing its amphibious targets.

In a raging interservice squabble, Army and Navy wrestled for priorities over manpower and equipment. Slowly, despite MacArthur's most vigorous and reasoned objections, the Navy's

Pacific strategy won the support of the Army Air Forces, which hungered for bomber attacks directly from the Marianas against Japan. The new B-29 Superfortress could dump 10,000 pounds of bombs on a target 1,500 miles away.

In the end, Japan would be crushed from the air. The men on the ground and in the ships made that possible; and for them, it was a brutal war. With Japan's soldiers trained to die (even at their own hands) rather than surrender, there could be no cheap victory.

On January 1, 1944, Vandegrift of Guadalcanal succeeded Holcomb of Belleau Wood as Commandant of the Marine Corps. Now, the Corps had 390,000 men and women, five divisions and four air wings. The Women's Reserve was activated on February 13, 1943, and by June 1944 had enrolled its full strength of 1,000 officers and 18,000 enlisted women. They were led by Col. Ruth Cheney Streeter.

Rupertus' 1st Division was fighting at Cape Gloucester; Julian Smith's 2d Division was in Hawaii licking its Tarawan wounds; Turnage's 3rd Division was shipping out from Bougainville; Harry Schmidt's 4th Division was moving from San Diego to Kwajalein, and Keller E. Rockey's 5th Division was shaping up at Camp Pendleton, California. The Marine Corps had grown big—too big, some complained. Vandegrift said candidly, "I know that General Holcomb had won permission to establish the 5th Division practically over General Marshall's dead body."[43]

Army, Navy and Marines teamed up to cross the Central Pacific quickly. By Washington's Birthday, they would control the vast Marshall Island chain. The first major target in the Marshalls was Kwajalein Atoll, the world's largest atoll with 93 islands and a lagoon 60 by 30 miles. Seven hundred miles northwest of Tarawa, it lay in the very heart of the Marshalls; and Nimitz chose it boldly.

The Japanese had held the Marshalls for a quarter of a century; Kwajalein was their administrative and communications center, and they were completing a bomber strip there. The American commanders expected Kwajalein's defenses to be even more impenetrable than Tarawa's. But the American (including Marine) planners were wrong. "Contrary to American fears, the enemy had not, before the outbreak of World War II, been

building up his Pacific military bases as mighty fortresses."[44]
Instead, Japan had been spending its resources on an aggressive
battle fleet. And that fleet did not intend to defend the Marshalls.
As soon as U.S. fliers won mastery over the skies, Kwajalein was
isolated and could be freely and massively bombed.

At the northern end of the atoll were the twin islands of Roi
and Namur, linked by both a sandspit and a man-made causeway. Holland Smith planned that the 4th Marine Division
would grab the twins and the Army's 7th Division would
capture Kwajalein Island at the atoll's southern end, 44 miles
away. The brand-new 4th Marine Division, although it had not
yet been in combat together, was spiced with combat veterans
and former Raiders.

The American expeditionary force used the costly know-
how from Tarawa: Naval gunfire would be vastly increased and
improved. Before the main amphibious assault, lesser islands
nearby would be seized so that artillery could be emplaced on
them. (Julian Smith had wanted to do that at Betio.) For the first
time, Naval Underwater Demolition Teams would swim in and
check out the beach defenses in advance. Finally, the troop-
carrying LVTs would be escorted by heavily armed armored
amtracs.

As Kwajalein was attacked, Capt. James L. Jones' V Amphibious Corps Reconnaissance Company, which had taken
Apamama in the Gilberts, and an Army battalion easily seized
Majuro Atoll, 265 miles to the southeast. On January 31, 1944,
they raised the American flag for the first time over territory that
had been Japan's before Pearl Harbor.

That same morning, the 25th Marines landed on five small
islands near Kwajalein Atoll's Roi and Namur islands. Controlling both sea and air, Rear Adm. Richard L. Conolly moved his
battleships in close and won from the Marines the appreciative
nickname "Close-in Conolly." The seas were rough and the
landings sloppy; but by the end of the day, the 14th Marines'
howitzers were registered to add their 5,000 rounds to the
bombardment of Roi-Namur. The landings cost the 25th Marines 24 dead and 40 wounded.

The next morning, February 1, the 23rd Marines struck Roi
and the 24th Marines, Namur. Because it had been difficult to
reassemble the LVTs, these main assaults were a shambles.

Fortunately, when the 23rd landed on Roi at 11:33 A.M., resistance was light; and by 6 P.M., organized opposition in the rubble was finished. Col. Louis R. Jones, the 23rd's commander, called Roi a "pip." Namur was not.

There, anti-tank ditches prevented the 24th Marines' amtracs from moving inland; and resistance stiffened. Riflemen and demolition teams destroyed the enemy pillboxes. At about one o'clock, Namur was rocked by three tremendous explosions. A pilot overhead thought the entire island had blown up. A Marine demolition team had exploded an enemy storehouse of heavy munitions and torpedo warheads. Twenty Marines were killed and 100 wounded.

When the 2d and 3rd Battalions re-opened the offensive, five light tanks led the way. Japanese swarmed over them and were shot down. As fierce fighting continued, Maj. Gen. Schmidt, the 4th Division's commander, who had served in China and Nicaragua, took command ashore. He ordered the 23rd's 3rd Battalion over to support the 24th Marines and brought Sherman tanks from Roi across the sandspit. The tanks cleared Namur's most northerly point, but the day ended with the Marines still embattled.

During the night, Japanese popped out of their holes to harass the Marines; and at dawn, the Japanese counterattacked. Fighting raged for 25 minutes before the attack was eradicated. All morning, Lt. Col. Aquilla J. Dyess of the 24th's 1st Battalion led his men forward. Standing on the parapet of an antitank ditch, directing a flanking attack against the last enemy position, he was killed by machine-gun fire. The Marine officer from Augusta, Georgia, was awarded the Medal of Honor. Shortly after noon, the assault battalions met at Namur's northern point; and at 2:18 P.M., the island was declared secured.

At the southern end of the atoll, the 32d and 184th Regiments of the Army's 7th Division also landed on February 1. Their amphibious assault was superbly executed, but it took the soldiers four days to secure crescent-shaped Kwajalein Island. Holland Smith was impatient. The Army fought in a different, slower style than did the Marines. The Marines plunged ahead, leaving by-passed strongpoints to be stamped out by following units. "In contrast to the Marines, the Army was taught not to advance until all possible fire had been brought to bear on the path ahead of the troops. This took time."[45] Which technique cost fewer American lives was continually debated.

The 25th Marines and the Army's 17th Infantry cleaned up the atoll's lesser islets; they made 30 landings and had to fight on ten of the islands. By February 7, the entire atoll was in American hands. The 4th Marine Division figured it had defeated 3,563 of the enemy; its own losses were 313 killed and 502 wounded.

The victory at Kwajalein had been so surprisingly swift that the next offensive, against Eniwetok Atoll, 326 miles northwest of Roi, was moved up from its planned date of May 1 to February 17.

At dawn that day, the aircraft carriers of Vice Adm. Raymond A. Spruance's Fifth Fleet hurled a swarm of warplanes against the great Japanese base of Truk—the so-called Gibralter of the Pacific. In two days, the Navy pilots shot up more than 200 of 365 planes, destroyed some 40 naval and merchant ships and almost killed "Pappy" Boyington and six other American pilot-prisoners who were being transferred to Japan through Truk at that moment. The dramatically successful carrier raid neutralized Truk, demoralized the government in Tokyo and left the Japanese unable to offer significant air opposition in the Central Pacific.

Eniwetok was another vast atoll, 40 islands with a lagoon 21 by 17 miles. The 10,000 troops for this Army-Marine expedition were commanded by Marine Brig. Gen. Thomas E. Watson. Although the reinforced 22d Marines, led by Col. John T. Walker, had come from 18 months of garrison duty on Samoa, this orphan regiment was well trained; and its rifle squads were effectively organized into fire teams of three or four men to give them greater flexibility in combat.

Walker's Marines would tackle Engebi, a triangular island where the Japanese had built an airfield at the north end of the atoll. The Army, with some help from the Marines, would assault Eniwetok Island and Parry Island, which were believed to be lightly held. Intelligence discovered that the Japanese had brought in 2,586 troops from Manchuria in great secrecy; their presence encouraged the Americans to strike as soon as possible.

Paralleling the tactics so effective at Kwajalein, the battleships closed in tight; and the Marines seized five islets near

Engebi on windy, overcast February 17. Not a single enemy ship or plane challenged the invasion.

The next morning, the 22d Marines assaulted Engebi's lagoon-side beaches. Most of the island's 1,200 defenders concentrated in a large coconut grove. At some points, they were dug into defensive "spider webs." Each of these was centered on a camouflaged underground core from which radiated tunnels usually lined with oil drums laid end to end. The Japanese hid in these webs and jumped up to shoot the advancing Marines from behind. The Marines quickly learned to toss in smoke grenades; and, as the smoke revealed the outline of the spider web, they destroyed it with demolitions.

The fighting was fierce; but by 3 P.M., Engebi was declared secured. A thousand of the enemy were dead; only 19 surrendered. The 22d Marines had lost 64 killed, 81 missing and 158 wounded.

On February 19, the 106th Infantry of the 27th Infantry Division stormed Eniwetok Island. Maj. Clair W. Shisler's 3rd Battalion, 22d Marines, in reserve aboard ship, came ashore by 3:15 P.M., and began attacking side by side with the 1st Battalion of the 106th. Flamethrowers seared the log emplacements in the dense underbrush. After dark, the 106th continued its attack; but the Marines, following their doctrine, dug in for the night. "On the Marines' 400-yard front, there was no shooting, but on the adjoining front GIs shot at anything that moved, including Marines. . . . Fortunately, God loves the Marines, and apart from a few wounds the main results were unpleasantness and foul language."[46] The next day, Eniwetok Island was secured.

Heavy bombardment softened up Parry Island, just northeast of Eniwetok Island. For three days, ships and planes and howitzers on the nearby islands all hurled shells onto this island of no more than 200 acres. At 9 A.M. on February 22, the 22d Marines' 1st and 2d Battalions landed with the 3rd Battalion again in reserve. Parry was bitterly defended. The 2d Battalion needed help from tanks and bulldozers before it secured the northern end at 2 P.M. The 1st Battalion was met at the shoreline by machine guns and mortars and hand-to-hand fighting. The Japanese had three light tanks, and Shermans had to wipe them out. The 3rd Battalion came ashore under fire; and at 1:30, it and the 1st Battalion started moving south. They secured Parry the next morning after overcoming determined resistance from the dug-in enemy.

The Japanese had planned their Marshalls defense as a delaying action, but the Americans had not been delayed. Eniwetok Atoll was conquered three months ahead of the original plan. The Marines there lost 254 killed and 555 wounded; the 106th Infantry had 94 killed and 311 wounded. Only 66 of the enemy surrendered.

During the following weeks, the 22d Marines made 29 additional landings among the Marshall Islands, sweeping out enemy pockets. They killed 2,564 Japanese of a total garrison estimated at 13,000 men; the rest were left to starve, and the enemy-held islands were kept neutralized by the 4th Marine Base Defense Aircraft Wing for the remainder of the war.

In March, the Joint Chiefs of Staff took a fresh look at the Pacific war and decided on new priorities and a new timetable. They pretty much gave up on bombing Japan from China because air base defense would depend on Chiang Kai-shek's dubious capabilities. MacArthur was ordered to invade the Philippines by mid-November. Nimitz was ordered to bypass Truk, invade the Marianas on June 15 and then take the Palaus to protect MacArthur's flank into the Philippines. By February 15, 1945, attacks were to be launched against both Formosa and Luzon.

The Joint Chiefs at the same time divided up the military strength left behind in the backwash of the South Pacific area. MacArthur's force was increased from six to 12 Army divisions and Nimitz now had four Marine and six Army divisions.

These were major decisions. With the help of Nimitz's fleet and using Army Engineer Amphibian Brigades, MacArthur landed at Hollandia, New Guinea, on April 22 and captured three airfields at Lake Sentani. By the end of July, he would reach the western tip of New Guinea, with the Philippines ahead. In the Central Pacific, the swift seizure of the Marshalls and the decision to bypass Truk freed great striking power for the Marianas.

Both MacArthur's and Nimitz's drives were galloping ahead. The nervousness of the Guadalcanal days was gone; the nation had confidence in victory. American power now being assembled against Japan was invincible.

10
The Marianas: Decisive Battle

June 1944 was a momentous month. Eisenhower's army stormed across the English Channel; in the Pacific, the U.S. Navy fought the war's greatest carrier battle, and Marines and soldiers leapt forward a thousand miles to a new kind of target. The Marines landed this time not primarily to seize advanced naval bases or air bases to support the fleet—but to capture something significantly different: bases for strategic airpower. From the Marianas, B-29s could reach Japan itself.

These 15 volcanic islands were larger than coral atolls and provided plenty of room for artillery sites and a cave-buried defense-in-depth. Only the four largest and southernmost islands—Guam, Rota, Tinian and Saipan—were of military importance. All but Guam had been Japanese since World War I. The Marines' first objective would be Saipan. It was 13 miles long; and Garapan, a town of 10,000 people on its west coast, was Japan's Central Pacific capital. On Saipan's southern end was Aslito Airfield, 1,200 miles from Tokyo. Three miles to the south lay Tinian with three new airfields.

The U.S. Joint Expeditionary Force steaming toward the Marianas compared to the North African landing force in size: 535 ships and 127,571 troops. They were commanded by Vice Adm. Turner, his fifth big amphibious operation. "He had learned more about this specialized brand of warfare than anyone else ever had, or probably ever would."[47] The troops were commanded by the sixty-two-year-old Alabamian, Lt. Gen. Holland M. Smith. "Howlin' Mad," a veteran of 38 years in the Corps with duty in France and the Caribbean, was the hard-driving, bad-tempered father of modern amphibious warfare. He directly commanded the Northern Landing Force (the V

Amphibious Corps) of the 2d and the 4th Marine Divisions, headed for Saipan and Tinian. Maj. Gen. Roy S. Geiger led the Southern Landing Force (the III Amphibious Corps), targeted for Guam and consisting of the 3rd Marine Division and the 1st Provisional Marine Brigade. Said Lt. Gen. Smith, "The Marine Corps had come of age."[48]

In reserve were two Army divisions, the 27th and 77th, although Smith, dissatisfied with the performance of elements of the 27th on Makin and Eniwetok, accepted that division reluctantly.

The enemy intended to defend. U.S. submarines had prevented the Japanese garrison, reinforced out of Manchuria, from being fully manned or equipped; but on Saipan alone, Lt. Gen. Yoshitsugu Saito commanded nearly 32,000 men, far more than U.S. Intelligence expected to find there. And the Japanese were eager to challenge the American armada itself; their Mobile Fleet was hurrying up to save Saipan. The U.S. naval commanders welcomed this threat; they hoped for a second Battle of Midway.

Vice Adm. Marc A. Mitscher's fast carriers bombed enemy airfields from the Bonins to the Marshalls and wiped out all the planes they could find in the Marianas themselves. Battleships bombarded Saipan and Tinian; and Navy underwater demolition teams daringly cleared paths for the Marines' amtracs and tanks.

The Marine divisions that would assault the Marianas had been changed considerably since the Marshalls operation. The old 12-man rifle squad, on the recommendation of a board headed by Lt. Col. Samuel B. Griffith II, was now enlarged by one man and divided into three four-man fire teams—each team consisting of one BAR-man and three riflemen—plus the squad leader. The fire-team leaders were trained for independent command in combat. The division's BARs had been increased from 558 to 853. Flamethrowers had been increased from 24 to 243 portable ones plus 24 long-range Ronsons that could be mounted on light Satan tanks. The tank battalion now had 46 medium Sherman tanks instead of 54 light tanks. The number of pack howitzers had been reduced and mortars increased. And for an amphibious operation, a 535-man amphibian tractor battalion was added. Although the basic division had been tightened from 19,965 to 17,465 men, its firepower had been greatly strengthened.[49]

D-Day at Saipan, June 15, was cool and clear. On a two-division front almost four miles long, eight veteran battalions of Marines headed for the beaches on the southern half of Saipan's west coast. Naval gunfire blasted the beaches, and carrier planes strafed to within 100 yards ahead of the landing craft. First in went 24 LCI-G gunboats firing rockets and 40mm guns. Then came the lead wave of 96 amtracs—LVTs—loaded with Marines and escorted by 68 armored amtracs—LVT(A)s—, each with a howitzer and a machine gun. The amtracs took severe losses crossing the reef and lagoon and on the beaches. The first Marines landed at 8:43 A.M. and at once came under intense fire. In 20 minutes, 8,000 Marines were ashore. They were fighting from the moment they jumped out of their amtracs.

On the left flank, the 6th and 8th Marines landed 900 yards too far north and suffered heavy casualties. All four assault battalion commanders, including Tarawa veterans Lt. Cols. Henry P. Crowe and Raymond L. Murray, were wounded early in the fighting. Japanese long-range artillery and mortars and machine guns behind the beach were deadly. The 6th Marines were stopped 400 yards beyond the beach; by midday 35 percent of the regiment had been killed or wounded.

Both assault battalions of the 8th Marines landed on one beach, and the confusion delayed the seizure of Afetna Point in the center of the beachhead. They needed help from the regiment's reserve battalion and even the division reserve, the 1st Battalion, 29th Marines. The enemy artillery was ferocious; more than a third of the 8th Regiment were casualties.

Further south, a few men of the 23rd Marines powered ahead to the ridge line a mile behind the beach; but others were stopped almost at the water's edge. By the day's end, the regiment had cleared the shattered village of Charan Kanoa, where the bougainvillea were blazing red, and clung to a beachhead some 800 yards deep.

To the south on the far right flank, the 25th Marines, heavy with former Raiders, received brutal enfilading fire from Agingan Point south of the beachhead. The 1st Battalion was held within a dozen yards of the beach. At 9:30 A.M., the Japanese hit the battalion's open flank; naval gunfire and air strikes broke up the attacks. When the enemy tried a second time, the 4th Tank Battalion's Shermans wiped out two Japanese companies. The 25th Marines made it to the ridge line, but an enemy force isolated on the tip of Agingan Point continued to fight.

Sunset found 20,000 Marines holding only half the planned beachhead. An estimated 2,000 men had been killed or wounded by the well-hidden enemy; preinvasion air and naval gunfire support had once again proven inadequate. The Japanese still held Afetna Point in the middle of the beachhead and shelled the Marines from the ridge above the coastal plain. Because of the unexpectedly strong resistance and the submarine-sighted approach of the Japanese fleet, the landing on Guam, set for June 18, was postponed.

The first night ashore was filled with enemy counterattacks; and at dawn, the 2d Division protected against attacks from the north while the 4th Division fought its way across to Magicienne Bay on Saipan's east coast to split the island. Early on the second day, June 16, the 2d Battalion, 8th Marines mopped up Afetna Point. But a lone enemy soldier, spotting the Marines from the smokestack of the ruined Charan Kanoa sugar refinery, enabled the Japanese artillery to work over the beachhead with devastating accuracy.

The 4th Division's first attempt to bisect the island failed. The 25th Marines, plus the 3rd Battalion, 24th Marines, led by Lt. Col. Alexander A. Vandegrift, Jr., inched to within half a mile of Aslito Airfield. In those first two days, the 4th Division took 2,200 casualties. Holland Smith decided to land the 27th Infantry Division, starting with the 165th Infantry.

At 3:30 A.M. on June 17, 500 of Lt. Gen. Saito's troops roared down the coastal plain and hit the 2d Marine Division hard. The attack, headed by 44 tanks, erupted into a vicious battle against the 1st Battalion, 6th Marines commanded by twenty-seven-year-old Lt. Col. William K. Jones, who had led it at Tarawa. The Marines fought back with all the firepower they had; mostly infantrymen fought tanks. Pvt. Robert S. Reed of Cabot, Arkansas, hit four tanks with his bazooka and then climbed on a fifth and dropped in a grenade. Sgt. Alex B. Smith of Lake Providence, Louisiana, knocked out three tanks. Pfc. Charlie D. Merritt of Greenville, South Carolina, and Pfc. Herbert J.

Hodges of Anchorage, Kentucky, hit seven tanks with their bazooka. Only a dozen of the Japanese tanks survived; more than 300 enemy soldiers were killed; and by 7 A.M., the assault was squashed.

Despite its losses, the 2d Division attacked to the north and east. On the eighteenth, the 24th and 25th Marines fought through to Magicienne Bay on the east coast; and the 165th Infantry occupied Aslito Airfield, which was renamed Isely Field. The enemy still held the hilly jungle southeast of Aslito, and his main force was concentrated in the north behind a line that ran from south of Garapan across to Magicienne Bay, which the Marines called Magazine Bay. The Japanese understood their problem perfectly; the Emperor sent a message: "Although the frontline officers and troops are fighting splendidly, if Saipan is lost, air raids on Tokyo will take place often; therefore you will hold Saipan."[50]

This was the battle situation for the 78,000 Americans ashore when the U.S. Navy entered "the greatest carrier action of all time"[51]: The Battle of the Philippine Sea. Mitscher's 98,618-man Task Force 58 destroyed the enemy planes on Guam early on June 19, just before Japanese carriers hurled four massive air attacks against the American fleet west of the Marianas. The young American fliers triumphed. In two days, they shot down 476 Japanese planes in "the Great Marianas Turkey Shoot"; only 50 U.S. planes were lost in combat. Submarines sank two large Japanese carriers and U.S. carrier pilots destroyed a third. The Japanese were left with 35 carrier planes operational. But the second-day strike required a perilous night recovery, and Mitscher won every pilot's everlasting love; he ignored the menace from enemy submarines and planes and ordered all the lights of the task force turned on. Although 80 planes were lost, most of their crews were saved. The final toll over the two days was 76 American fliers dead.

Task Force 58 failed to destroy the Japanese fleet, but it had won mastery of both the sea and air and made possible the conquest of the Marianas. "And victory in the Marianas made an American victory over Japan inevitable."[52]

The Japanese in the Marianas were now sealed off without hope, but they fought on. Holland Smith and Maj. Gen. Ralph C. Smith, USA, commander of the 27th Division, got into a

*Marines charge ashore on
Guadalcanal in the first offensive
action of the Pacific war.
Wide World Photos*

*Guadalcanal was a tropical hell of rain and malaria. After
winning their longest battle of World War II, Marines
camped in coconut groves like this.
Sgt. Mundell, USMC Photo*

Lt. Col. Evans F. Carlson learned guerrilla tactics observing the Chinese Communists in Yenan. He led the 2d Raider Battalion in the Makin raid and on Guadalcanal. U.S. Navy Photo

Maj. Gregory "Pappy" Boyington, the leading Marine Corps ace of World War II with twenty-eight kills, briefs the fliers of his Black Sheep Squadron for an attack against Rabaul. Shortly after this picture was taken, Boyington was shot down over Rabaul and imprisoned by the Japanese for the rest of the war. USMC Photo

Capt. Joseph J. Foss was the Marine Corps' No. 2 ace with twenty-six kills. After the war, he was elected governor of South Dakota. Official U.S. Navy Photo

These weary 1st Division Marines are
coming out of twenty-three days in
the front lines on Cape Gloucester.
Brenner, USMC Photo

At Tarawa in November 1943, 2d
Division Marines who survived the
deadly waters off Betio Island crouch
on the narrow beach behind the
seawall and begin to attack inland
against heavy Japanese resistance.
USMC Photo

Marine reinforcements wade ashore beneath Betio's long
pier which the "Hawk" and his men cleared in the
initial assault on Tarawa Atoll.
USMC Photo

First Marines to reach the beach on Saipan take cover behind a sand dune and wait for next waves to join them.
Sgt. James Burns, USMC Photo

1st Division Marines fight in the crazy-quilt Umurbrogol ridges on Peleliu in September 1944.
Pfc. John Smith, USMC Photo

First waves of the Marines' 4th and 5th Divisions assault
Iwo Jima at 9 A.M. on February 19, 1945. In the
background looms Mount Suribachi.
Navy Dept. Photo, National Archives

Men of the 28th Marines, whose job
it was to take Suribachi, disgorge
from landing craft onto Iwo Jima.
Photo by George Burns

Marines under fire from Suribachi
cling to the black volanic ash of Iwo
Jima's beach on D-Day.
Louis Lowery, Leatherneck Magazine

Badly shocked by a Japanese mortar shell, a Marine is helped to an aid station on Iwo Jima.
Staff Sgt. Cornelius, USMC Photo.

The first flag raising on Iwo Jima by men of E Company, 28th Marines on the rim of Mount Suribachi's crater on February 23, 1945.
Louis Lowery, Leatherneck Magazine

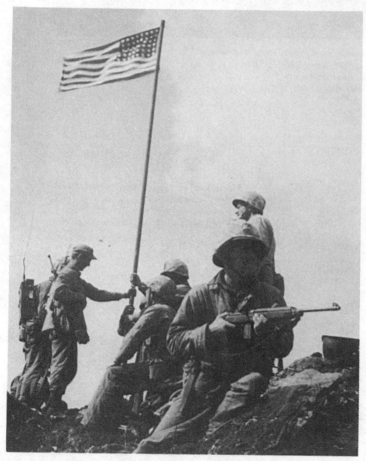

The most famous war photograph ever taken:
AP Photographer Joe Rosenthal's picture of the raising
atop Suribachi of the larger flag from LST 779. This
photograph became the model of the giant U.S. Marine
Corps Memorial at Arlington National Cemetery.
Wide World Photos

Two Marines attack Japanese caves
on Iwo Jima with flamethrowers.
Navy Dept. Photo, National Archives

Marines manhandle crates of supplies
out of landing craft and up Iwo's beach.
U.S. Coast Guard Photo

A chaplain celebrates Mass for Marines on Iwo Jima
while the fighting continues.
U.S. Office of War Information Photo, National Archives

Marines killed in the first wave lie in
the sands of Iwo Jima.
Joe Rosenthal, Wide World Photos

1st Division Marines and flamethrowing
tank advance on Okinawa.
USMC Photo

dispute over orders to the 105th Infantry, which was assigned to clean up the enemy dug in on Nafutan Point at the island's southeast corner. Both Smiths had issued orders; therefore, Holland Smith charged, Ralph Smith had contravened an order from his Marine superior.

Opening the second phase of the Saipan invasion, the two Marine divisions pivoted in a great turning movement northward against the enemy defense line across the island's waist. Their full-scale attack began at 6 A.M. on June 22. By now, the Landing Force had taken 6,165 casualties—2,514 in the 2d Marine Division, 3,628 in the 4th Division and 320 in the 27th Infantry Division. But the two Marine divisions were still powerful offensive weapons.

On the far left, the 6th Marines took the summit of 1,133-foot-high Mount Tipo Pale. The 8th Marines tackled Mount Tapotchau, the extinct volcano that dominated the center of the island. To the 2d Division's right, the 4th Division's 24th Marines fought along Magicienne Bay; and the 25th Marines' 3rd Battalion led the advance nearly 2,000 yards, until it was stopped by the Japanese entrenched in caves. The battalion's commander, Lt. Col. Justice M. Chambers of Huntington, West Virginia, a former Edson Raider who wore pistols on his hip and in his armpit, and Lt. Col. Evans Carlson, now on the 4th Division staff, tried to carry to safety Pfc. Vito Cassaro, Chambers' radioman, who had been hit by machine-gun fire. Carlson took a burst in his right arm and left thigh. The great Raider leader had seen his last combat.

Holland Smith kept the pressure on. The Americans now faced Lt. Gen. Saito's main line of resistance where he had 15,000 men. That evening, Holland Smith ordered the 27th Division to pass through the 25th Marines and all three divisions to attack the next morning. He also brought north two battalions from the 105th Infantry as a reserve for the 27th. Ralph Smith ordered the remaining 2d Battalion, 105th Infantry to mop up at Nafutan Point, where 1,000 Japanese soldiers and civilians still held out. But that battalion was in corps reserve. And Holland Smith later objected that Ralph Smith had again issued an order to a unit not under his tactical control. The dispute between the Marine and Army Smiths was heating up.

On June 23, the 106th Infantry arrived late at the line-of-departure. The Army attack was delayed and exposed the flanks of the Marine divisions on either side. The 106th and 165th were unable to advance in the center of the line, where the steep ridges were honeycombed with strongly defended caves. The front looked like a sagging "U" with the 27th Division in the bottom.

In the south, the 2d Battalion, 105th Infantry was hours late in launching its attack at Nafutan Point and then made no progress.

That night, the 27th Division was hit by two tank-led counterattacks. On the rugged slopes of Mount Tapotchau, Pfc. Harold G. Epperson of Akron, Ohio, a machine gunner with the 1st Battalion, 6th Marines, helped break up an enemy counterattack and killed several Japanese. Suddenly, a Japanese soldier, assumed to be dead, hurled a grenade into Epperson's position. He dived on the grenade and died to save his fellow Marines. He was awarded the Medal of Honor.

Holland Smith was angered at the 27th Division's failure to move swiftly enough; and Ralph Smith agreed with him. Early on the twenty-fourth, Holland Smith sent Ralph Smith a message beginning "Commanding General is highly displeased with the failure of the 27th Division . . . "[53] and demanding that the Army move forward. The 27th Division was faced with advancing up heavily fortified "Death Valley" exposed to fire from the sheer sides of Mount Tapotchau on its left and from heavily wooded "Purple Heart Ridge" on its right. The 106th and 165th could make virtually no progress and took casualties. That evening, Ralph Smith was replaced by Maj. Gen. Sanderford Jarman, USA.

Holland Smith called the relief of Ralph Smith "one of the most disagreeable tasks I have ever been forced to perform."[54] When Holland Smith posed the problem to Admirals Turner and Spruance aboard *Indianapolis,* they both agreed to, and Spruance, the overall commander, directed Ralph Smith's replacement by Jarman. In making his case against Ralph Smith, Holland Smith cited the two earlier conflicts over orders but stressed the Army division's "defective performance."[55]

Historians of the incident have said: "The corps commander [Holland] Smith had reason to be dissatisfied . . . The 27th

Division had been slow to take Nafutan Point and had retarded the advance of the two marine divisions. A far more patient corps commander than Holland M. Smith might reasonably have concluded that a command shake up within the division was necessary. Holland Smith was not a patient man."[56]

The relief exploded into bitter controversy. Lt. Gen. Robert C. Richardson, Jr., top Army officer in the Central Pacific, was furious and convened a board of Army officers to investigate what was regarded as an insult to the Army. The board, headed by Lt. Gen. Simon B. Buckner, Jr., decided that Holland Smith had overreacted, although he had had the legal authority to relieve Ralph Smith. In Washington, General Marshall's advisors concurred that the 27th Division's performance had been deficient but felt that its commander's relief had been an act of bad judgment. Lt. Gen. Richardson came to Saipan and held a heated argument with Holland Smith. To cool things off, the War Department transferred Ralph Smith to Europe. After the Saipan operation, Holland Smith assumed command of the Fleet Marine Force, Pacific, which had no control over Army divisions.

Meanwhile, the battle of the Smiths broke out in the press and created a prolonged public ruckus. In Marines' eyes, Ralph Smith had failed either to force his division's advance or to replace his subordinate commanders. So the general responsible for the success of the Saipan operation replaced him, despite the storm he well knew would follow.[57] But the interservice bitterness aroused by the incident would fester for a very long time.

The battle for Saipan could not wait. On June 25, the 8th Marines; the 1st Battalion, 29th Marines, and the Division Scout Company captured the summit of rugged Mount Tapotchau. On the right, the 4th Division easily overran Kagman Peninsula north of Magicienne Bay. And after Maj. Gen. Jarman replaced the commander of his 106th Regiment, it seized all but the northern tip of Purple Heart Ridge. On the twenty-sixth, the 2d Battation, 105th Infantry secured Nafutan Point in the south. But there, 500 enemy soldiers and sailors, some in American uniforms, crashed through the Army's trap and stormed across Aslito Airfield, until the survivors were wiped out by the 25th and 14th Marines.

In the north, the American attack pressed inexorably forward against dogged opposition. Holland Smith described the fighting:

> Although they resisted from caves and hideouts in the ridges, and tried to harass us at night from by-passed pockets, we dug them out and smoked them out in hand-to-hand combat. With flame throwers and hand grenades, the Marines ferreted the Japanese out of their holes and killed them. Patrols covered the terrain yard by yard, combing thick vegetation and rocky fastnesses for snipers. It was war such as nobody had fought before: a subterranean campaign in which men climbed, crawled, clubbed, shot, burned and bayonetted each other to death.[58]

By June 30, central Saipan was under U.S. control. The 2d Marine Division had taken 4,488 casualties since the landing; the 4th Division, 4,454, and the 27th Division, 1,836. The Japanese withdrew to their final defensive line across the northern part of the island.

The three American divisions began their climactic offensive on July 2. The 2d Marines went into the ruins of Garapan and had a taste of street fighting. On the Fourth of July, they cleaned up Mutcho Point above Garapan; and the 6th and 8th Marines reached the coast at Tanapag Harbor. Then, the 2d Division was squeezed out of the front to rest up for the coming invasion of Tinian. The 27th and 4th Divisions charged up the narrower end of Saipan. Holland Smith assigned the 27th, now commanded by Maj. Gen. George W. Griner, USA, to tackle the west coast, centered on the village of Makunsha, and aimed the 4th Division at Marpi Point, Saipan's northern tip. When the 27th Division ran into a heavily defended area called Paradise Valley, inland from Makunsha, the 2d Marines had to be fitted back into the line. Lt. Gen. Saito, wounded and headquartered in a cave in a Paradise Valley hillside, ordered a final *banzai* attack and committed *hara-kiri*. In a nearby cave, Vice Adm. Chuichi Nagumo, who had led the raid on Pearl Harbor and was now commander of the no longer existing Central Pacific Area Fleet, shot himself in the head.

At 4 A.M. on July 7, Saito's survivors carried out his last order and made a desperate, savage attack that had no possible purpose but to kill Americans. An estimated 3,000 screaming Japanese came stampeding down the west coast plain against the 105th Infantry and shattered both the 1st and 2d Battalions. The attack plunged on to hit the 3rd Battalion, 10th Marines. The foremost battery, Battery H, cut its fuses so that its shells exploded 50 yards from the muzzles of its 105mm howitzers. The battery's survivors finally pulled back into an abandoned Japanese machinery dump. The enemy killed the artillery battalion's commander, Maj. William L. Crouch. The battalion's other batteries also formed a defense, aided by elements of the 1st Battalion, 106th Infantry, and a few men from the 4th Battalion, 10th Marines. One of them, Pfc. Harold C. Agerholm of Racine, Wisconsin, grabbed an abandoned ambulance Jeep and under heavy fire singlehandedly loaded and evacuated 45 wounded Marines over three hours before he was mortally wounded by a Japanese sniper. He was awarded the Medal of Honor.

When the attack lost enough steam to be stopped, the 106th Infantry counterattacked and retook the Marine positions. By 6 P.M., most of the ground lost, and now covered with Japanese dead, had been regained. The two crushed battalions of the 105th had suffered 406 killed and 512 wounded; the 3rd Battalion, 10th Marines lost 45 killed and 82 wounded.

Holland Smith brought the 2d Division back into the line, and the American attack was resumed against tough pockets of resistance. By 4:15 P.M. on July 9, the 4th Division reached the northern coast; and Vice Adm. Turner declared Saipan secured.

There was one final tragedy. Hundreds of frightened Japanese civilians committed suicide by leaping from the cliffs above Marpi Point. Some were forced to their deaths by Japanese soldiers. Nine thousand Japanese civilians and 3,000 native Chamorros were interned.

The bloody three and a half week battle for Saipan had cost 3,426 American dead and 13,099 wounded. Enemy dead were estimated at more than 32,800. It was a costly struggle, but as a Japanese admiral said after the war was over, "Our war was lost with the loss of Saipan."[59] Holland Smith agreed; he termed it "the decisive battle of the Pacific offensive."[60]

On July 18, the day the fall of Saipan was announced to the

Japanese people, Premier Gen. Hideki Tojo and his cabinet resigned; and Gen. Kuniaki Koiso formed a new government. But no Japanese political leader dared to propose peace. On November 24, 100 Army B-29s rose from Saipan to strike Tokyo for the first time since Doolittle's raid in 1942.

Even before Saipan was secured, Tinian was bombarded across the three-mile channel to the south. This handsome island, checkerboarded with sugar cane fields, was 12 miles long by 5 wide at its center and protected by steep coral cliffs and 9,000 Japanese soldiers and sailors. To assault it would require not a ship-to-shore but a more unusual shore-to-shore movement. Despite that difference, Holland Smith would call the Tinian invasion "the perfect amphibious operation in the Pacific war."[61]

Tinian was superbly suited for major airfields. The Japanese had a large field with two airstrips on Ushi Point at the northern end of the island and one at Gurguan Point on the west side and were finishing still another behind Tinian Town on the southwest coast. From the Ushi field on August 6, 1945, the B-29 "Enola Gay" would carry the atomic bomb to Hiroshima.

The Japanese had to expect an invasion of Tinian; so, to gain tactical surprise, the American commanders decided to gamble and land on two narrow beaches, one only 60 yards wide and the other 160 yards, on the northwest coast below Ushi Point. These obscure beaches were within range of Saipan's artillery and appeared too small for a big assault force. Evans Carlson called them "the enemy's back door."[62]

By mid-July 1944, 13 battalions of Marine and Army artillery were pounding Tinian. Naval gunfire, carrier planes and P-47s from Isely Field also hit airfields, roads and Tinian Town itself. A new weapon joined the air bombardment: napalm powder was added to aircraft fuel and the inflammable mixture dropped in fuel tanks on woods and cane fields. As Holland Smith wrote later: "We were resolved that there would be no repetition of our Tarawa and Saipan experiences, where we suffered from lack of preliminary preparation and lost heavily in consequence."[63]

When Smith assumed command of the Fleet Marine Force, Pacific on July 12, Maj. Gen. Harry Schmidt, who had led the

4th Division on Saipan, took over the V Amphibious Corps and Maj. Gen. Clifton B. Cates headed Schmidt's division. Maj. Gen. Thomas E. Watson continued in command of the 2d Division. Smith retained overall command of the Expeditionary Troops; but on July 20, he sailed to oversee the invasion of Guam.

On the two nights before the Tinian invasion, men of the V Corps Amphibious Reconnaissance Battalion under Capt. James L. Jones, Lt. Col. William K. Jones' brother, went in with naval UDT "frogmen" to scout the beaches' approaches and exits. Swimming in from their rubber boats, they found the larger beach (White 2) framed by coral barriers, leaving merely a 70-yard-wide passage free for 16 LVTs. The smaller beach (White 1) could accommodate only eight LVTs at a time. Beyond the beaches were cliffs six to ten feet high. To widen the access for vehicles, the Seabees devised an ingenious portable ramp that would carry the weight of a 30-ton medium tank.

Because of the tight landing conditions, the individual Marine went ashore without a pack. He stuffed his pockets with emergency rations, a spoon, an extra pair of socks and a bottle of insect repellant. Over his cartridge belt he folded his poncho.

The landing force had 533 amtracs, including 68 armored amphibians and 10 amtracs with the special portable ramps, and 130 DUKWs, plus a variety of other landing craft. The plan was for the 4th Division to assault the narrow White beaches directly from Saipan. The 2d Division would feint in front of Tinian Town and then follow the 4th Division ashore over the White beaches. The 27th Infantry Division would stay in reserve on Saipan, ready to go on four hours' notice.

The 2d Division's realistic demonstration sent empty landing craft within 400 yards of the shore and held in place the Japanese troops defending Tinian Town. But hidden 6-inch guns smashed the battleship *Colorado*, killing 43 and wounding 176, including 41 Marine casualties.

At 7:47 A.M. on July 24, eight amtracs landed Company E, 24th Marines on narrow White Beach 1. The Marines destroyed a small beach defense detachment and moved rapidly inland to make room for the rest of the 2d Battalion. By 8:46, both the 2d and 1st Battalions, 24th Marines were ashore.

White Beach 2 was more heavily defended. Until antiboat mines could be cleared, the first Marines had to avoid the beach and climb the nearby rocky ledges. The 25th Marines were ashore at 9:30; and by dark, both regiments held a beachhead 4,000 yards wide and 1,500 deep. Four artillery battalions of the 10th and 14th Marines were also landed. Ashore then were 15,600 Marines with 48 medium tanks and 15 light tanks armed with Ronson flamethrowers. Marine casualties on J-Day numbered only 15 killed and 225 wounded. There were 438 Japanese dead. The Marines had achieved tactical surprise over beaches the Japanese had regarded as impassable.

Maj. Gen. Cates expected a counterattack to throw the Marines back into the sea as soon as the enemy could readjust to the shock of the landing's location. He brought ashore his division reserve, the 23rd Marines, and ordered the men to dig in and string barbed wire along the entire perimeter. They placed machine guns to provide interlocking fire and bazookas to cover possible tank approaches.

Cates' preparations were well taken. The Marines faced a night of hard fighting. At 2 A.M., 600 Japanese naval troops counterattacked on the left flank; in three hours of fierce battle in the moonless dark, the 24th Marines slaughtered 476. Japanese soldiers broke through between the 24th and 25th Marines, and the 14th Marines wiped them out. On the right or south, the Japanese attacked at 3:30. Six light tanks in the lead were met by a wall of fire; five were swiftly destroyed. But the enemy infantrymen kept coming, until by dawn 267 Japanese bodies lay among the 23rd Marines' foxholes. The night's battle had killed 1,241 of the enemy and, as Cates said, "broke the Jap's back."[64]

The second day, the 8th Marines came ashore and with the 24th Marines occupied part of Ushi Airfield. The 23rd Marines pushed southward. In the center, the 25th Marines took 290-foot Mt. Maga in a double envelopment. The entire second-day operation went well with light American casualties.

On July 26, the 8th Marines cleared the rest of Ushi Airfield, and P-47s were flying from it two days later. By the end of the twenty-sixth, the two Marine divisions now ashore were stretched across the width of Tinian. They rolled steadily southward over the gentle landscape against minor resistance and overran the airstrip at Gurguan Point.

The Marines pushed through stifling cane fields that hid

nests of Japanese. As the 24th Marines approached Tinian Town on July 30, enemy machine gunners and riflemen concealed in coastal caves north of the town stopped them. The Marines called up tanks and armored amtracs offshore; flamethrowers seared the caves, and combat engineers then sealed them with demolition charges. The now-classic Marine tank-infantry team worked well.

The Marines found Tinian Town flattened and deserted. They encountered only one Japanese soldier. The town's defenses had been laid out to meet an assault from the sea, and the enemy commanders recognized that they could not deal with a tank-reinforced land attack.

On July 31, the Marines assaulted the southern end of the island preceded by a mighty bombardment from artillery, warships and 126 aircraft. The Japanese waited for the Marines there on a high plateau fronted with cliffs and jungle.

On the east coast, the cliff before the plateau rose almost vertically, and the 2d and 6th Marines halted at its base. Further inland, the 8th Marines, now opposed at every step, grabbed a foothold on the plateau. To the west, the 23rd Marines met heavy mortar and machine-gun fire but fought to the plateau's top. On the western end of the line, the 24th Marines found the road to the high ground heavily mined.

That night, the enemy tried to throw the 8th Marines back off the plateau; but Col. Clarence R. Wallace was determined his regiment would hold. The Japanese hit the 2d Battalion again and again. Maj. William C. Chamberlain, the 2d Battalion's executive officer, called simply "Let's go!" and led the Marines to wipe out the Japanese. The two battalions of the 8th Marines held.

At 5:15 A.M. on August 1, 1,600 well-armed soldiers and sailors charged the Marines atop the plateau. This was the major effort for the Japanese. In one hour, the Marines suffered 74 casualties, killed 200 Japanese and stopped the attack. The enemy made an orderly retreat into the cliffs and woods to the southeast.

That morning, after the 3rd Battalion, 6th Marines replaced the battered 2d Battalion, 8th Marines on the plateau, the advance was held up by crowds of civilians who approached waving white cloths. Nearly 8,500 civilians, Japanese and Korean, emerged from their caves and surrendered during the next five days.

At 6:55 P.M., Maj. Gen. Schmidt declared the island secured. Organized resistance was over, but many die-hard Japanese were still prepared to kill Marines. Just before dawn on August 2, hundreds of the enemy attacked the 6th Marines; Lt. Col. John W. Easley, the 3rd Battalion's commander, was killed. More assaults followed for the next three days as the enemy tried to take Marines with them into death. The final mopping up was given over to the 8th Marines under the command of Brig. Gen. Edson, the 2d Division's assistant commander.

Overall, the conquest of Tinian cost the 2d Marine Division 105 killed and 653 wounded and the 4th Division 212 killed and 897 wounded. About 5,000 Japanese troops were killed.

Success on Tinian was the result of boldness fortified by luck. The overwhelming preinvasion bombardment and the decision to land on unexpected beaches cut down casualties and knocked the island's defenders off balance. They never recovered enough to stand effectively against the Marines' superior manpower and firepower.

The third phase of the Marianas campaign was the recapture of Guam, the American possession that the Japanese had scooped up so easily at the very beginning of the war. They made Guam a much tougher nut to crack than Tinian. In 21 days of fighting, Guam cost 1,744 Americans dead and 6,540 wounded.

Lying about 100 miles south of Saipan, Guam was shaped like a sock hanging on a line. The heel on the west coast contained the island's main treasure: Apra Harbor, a large anchorage. The Marines planned to land north and south of the heel, double-envelop Apra Harbor and grab the airfield on Orote Peninsula, which forms the harbor's south side.

There were twice as many Japanese troops on Guam as on Tinian, and their leaders figured pretty well where the Marines would land. Being much larger (30 miles long and 4 to 8 miles wide) and more rugged than both Saipan and Tinian, Guam gave the defenders more room to maneuver and made it difficult to root them out of the densely covered volcanic hills. Finally, the Japanese gained extra time to dig in by forcing a month's delay of the invasion—from June 18 to July 21—first by sending their battle fleet at the Marianas and then by defending Saipan so doggedly.

But the Japanese could not take all the credit. The American commanders landed on obvious and strongly defended beaches, and the northern landing site was backed by a palisade of coral ridges from which the enemy could pepper the Marines on the beaches and contest every step taken inland. And once the Japanese fled to the north, the Americans pursued them into the jungle.

The Marines of Maj. Gen. Geiger's III Amphibious Corps sweated out the delayed invasion for an average of 50 days on crowded transports under the broiling sun. Geiger had 20,328 men of the 3rd Marine Division—the 3rd, 9th and 21st Marines, veterans of Bougainville—and 9,886 men of the new 1st Provisional Marine Brigade made up of the reactivated 4th and the 22d Marines, which had fought at Eniwetok. Maj. Gen. Turnage still commanded the division; and Brig. Gen. Lemuel C. Shepherd, Jr., led the brigade. In charge of the corps artillery was Brig. Gen. Pedro A. del Valle. It was an experienced team.

The invasion delay was used to pound Guam with weeks of intense naval and air bombardment on "a scale and length of time never before seen in World War II."[65] But, as always, many enemy installations escaped destruction. Starting on July 14, UDTs swam in to clear the approaches to the invasion beaches; they destroyed 900 log cribs and wire cages filled with coral. On the reef, they left a sign: "Welcome Marines!"[66]

Also waiting for the Marines were 18,500 Japanese soldiers and sailors under the operational command of Lt. Gen. Takeshi Takashina. They were concentrated around Apra Harbor and the island's airfields, including the strip built on the former Marine Barracks' golf course on Orote Peninsula. During the time gained by the delay in W-Day, the Japanese had energetically strengthened their beach defenses and dug a system of trenches and foxholes across the neck of Orote Peninsula. Many of the island's 21,500 native civilians were put to work as forced labor.

The preinvasion bombing told the Japanese where to expect the landing. The 3rd Division would assault a 2,500-yard front between Adelup Point and Asan Point, north of Apra Harbor and south of Agaña, the island's capital. Simultaneously, the 1st

Provisional Marine Brigade would land five miles further south, below Orote Penisula. The brigade's job was to capture the peninsula—fast.

Early on July 21, the transports' loudspeakers blared out *The Marines' Hymn* as the men climbed into their amtracs. Leading the assault were LCI(G) rocket-armed gunboats followed by LVT(A)s firing 37mm guns and then 360 troop-carrying LVTs. When the first Marines were within 100 yards of the beaches, they were hit by artillery and mortars. Naval gunfire and planes roared in and squelched this damaging fire. By 8:33 A.M., Marines were ashore on all the beaches—back on Guam after two and a half years.

The ring of ridges behind the northern beaches was strongly defended. On the far left, Japanese manned guns and mortars above the beach and caused heavy casualties among the 3rd Marines on the beach and the reef. They could advance neither up nor around sheer, 300-foot-high Chonito Cliff that came right down to the sea, until tanks and flamethrowers fired squarely into the enemy's caves. By afternoon, Chonito Cliff and Adelup Point had been cleared. Then, the 3rd Marines faced a ridge, 400 feet high, jungle covered and protected by mortars and machine guns. The assault by Capt. Geary R. Bundschu's A Company finally reached the crest, but the captain was among those killed, and the company could not hold Bundschu Ridge.

In the center, the 21st Marines' 2d and 3rd Battalions fought up two defiles through which flowed branches of the Asan River. The 2d struggled through a series of ridges in what became known as the battle for Banzai Ridge. F Company's Marines assaulted a 100-foot cliff frontally, pulling themselves up, clinging to bushes in the tropical heat. The right-hand platoon was nearly decimated. E Company also climbed up, but the long confinement on shipboard had weakened the men. The few who made it dug in under machine-gun fire from the next ridge less than 50 yards away.

On the right flank of the northern beaches, the 9th Marines took 231 casualties and secured a beachhead 1,500 yards deep. There were many gaps in the division's 400-yard perimeter; the enemy still held most of the high ground. In all, W-Day cost the 3rd Division 105 men killed, 526 wounded and 56 missing in action.

336

On the southern beaches, the 1st Brigade ran a gauntlet of fire registered on the beach; and the 22d Marines on the left took severe losses. Once through that, the 22d advanced into the ruins of Agat village and to high ground 1,000 yards inland. On the right, the 4th Marines seized Bangi Point; fought up Hill 40, and reached the foot of Mount Alifan. Brig. Gen. Shepherd now had a beachhead 4,500 yards long and 2,000 yards deep, at the cost of 350 casualties. He brought the 305th Infantry wading in from his reserve.

That first night, the Japanese counterattacked the brigade in force. All along the southern beachhead, brilliant star shells exposed the enemy to the dug-in Marines. Japanese carrying demolition charges infiltrated the perimeter and were killed. Light tanks probed the Marine lines; four were swiftly knocked out. The Japanese attacks reduced one A Company rifle platoon to four men. At dawn, the infiltrators were mopped up. The counterattack cost the enemy 600 dead; the brigade suffered some 50 killed and twice that number wounded.

On the northern front that same night, the Japanese tried to push the Marines off the high ground. The 21st Marines had heavy casualties but clung to the edge of its cliff. The Japanese attempted to take back Chonito Cliff and Adelup Point from the 3rd Marines. Pfc. Luther Skaggs, Jr., of Henderson, Kentucky, his leg shattered by a Japanese grenade, improvised a tourniquet and fired his rifle and hurled grenades at the enemy for eight more hours. Then, Skaggs, the first Marine to earn the Medal of Honor on Guam, coolly crawled out of his foxhole and continued to battle until the enemy were exterminated.

On the second day, the 9th Marines occupied the ruins of the former U.S. Navy Yard at Piti; that made the unloading of supplies easier. The 3rd Battalion assaulted the mine-littered offshore islet of Cabras. And the 3rd Marines fought desperately to reach the top of Bundschu Ridge, a natural fortress for the enemy; but mortar and machine-gun fire drove them back again. In this battle, Pfc. Leonard F. Mason of Middlesboro, Kentucky, alone attacked two machine guns. Japanese riflemen on higher ground shot him repeatedly; but Mason moved around the machine-gun position, and, although mortally wounded, killed five Japanese with his BAR and wiped out the position.[67]

The second night, the enemy again charged the 21st Marines and were slaughtered. These aggressive night attacks were devouring the best of the enemy's troops, and Lt. Gen. Takashina began planning an all-out counterattack while he still had the strength. On July 23, the 3rd Marines found that the Japanese had withdrawn from Bundschu Ridge, leaving behind deadly nests of riflemen and machine gunners. The Marines worked steadily forward on the high ground.

On the southern front, the 4th Marines fought up the slopes of Mount Alifan and took Magpo Point on the right end of the beachhead. On the left, the 22d Marines tried to pry open the base of Orote Peninsula and ran into trouble. Enemy artillery was registered on the ground over which the Marines had to advance, and the regiment suffered more than 100 casualties.

On July 24, the day Tinian was invaded, the 22d Marines advanced between the sea and the rice paddies at the peninsula's base and then spread out on a two-battalion front. Shermans destroyed five tanks and pounded concrete and coconut log bunkers. Enemy guns hidden in Orote's cliffs also joined the battle until two LCI(G)s closed in offshore and stifled their fire. Meanwhile, the 2d Battalion crossed the peninsula and advanced along its northern coast.

The 22d Marines spent July 25 trying to seal off the peninsula, and the 4th Marines came into line on the 22d's left. The 77th Infantry Division, Geiger's reserve, probed the foothills of the mass called Mt. Tenjo. And patrols of the 9th Marines and the 22d Marines linked the two beachheads along Apra Harbor's shore.

That night, Lt. Gen. Takashina launched the most massive counterattack of the war to date. The Marines were overextended; "their front line resembled a sieve."[68] All along the five-mile front on the northern beachhead, vulnerable gaps separated the Marine units. The enemy pounded the entire perimeter. In the sector of the 1st Battalion, 21st Marines, the Japanese annihilated 50 men of B Company and dashed through that hole. Many of the attackers were loaded down with explosives and land mines that blew up with roar after roar. The Japanese hit Marine tanks in the rear and the battalion's mortar platoon, 200 yards behind the front line.

The sake-flushed Japanese struck hardest against Lt. Col. Robert E. Cushman's 2d Battalion, 9th Marines, which was attached to the 3rd Marines on Fonte Hill. The battalion withstood seven major attacks, climaxed before dawn on July 26 by waves of Japanese charging, screaming, into close-quarter combat. Half of Cushman's men were killed or wounded. With first light, Shermans got into the fight and smashed the final attack; the battalion was barely able to hold on.

Capt. Louis H. Wilson, Jr., of Brandon, Mississippi, the twenty-four-year-old commander of the battalion's F Company, had been wounded three times the previous day. When the Japanese counterattacked, he left the medical aid station and rejoined his men. At one point in the battle, he dashed 50 yards in front of his line to rescue a wounded Marine. All night, he led his men in hand-to-hand fighting. Then, he took a 17-man patrol up a critical nearby slope against intense fire that cut down 13 of the men. He and the four surviving Marines seized the critical high ground. Wilson received the Medal of Honor.

Twenty-five men of the division's Reconnaissance Company tried futilely to cover the 800-yard gap between the 21st and 9th Marines. Many infiltrators flooded through, and some reached the command post of the 3rd Battalion, 21st Marines at Hill 460. Headquarters troops fought them off until L Company, 9th Marines sneaked up, hurling grenades, and wiped them out.

More than 50 Japanese attacked the division hospital 200 yards from the beach. Patients were hastily evacuated, and hospital personnel and 41 walking wounded formed a defense. Two Pioneer companies and a motley of rear-echelon men rushed over; and by noon, the hospital was back in operation. During the mopping up, Lt. Col. Hector de Zayas, commander of the 2d Battalion, 3rd Marines, was killed.

On Orote Peninsula, 500 drunken Japanese soldiers joined in the general counterattack. They charged the 22d Marines, screaming. Most of them were blown up by artillery and the rest were killed in hand-to-hand fighting.

The Japanese lost an estimated 3,200 men in the night's counterattack; the Marines had a total of 600 killed and wounded. Lt. Gen. Takashina had shot his bolt and failed. From now on, he could only wage a battle of attrition.

At 7 A.M. on July 26, the 4th and 22d Marines jumped off to assault Orote. Both regiments advanced to the main enemy defense line, where they were stopped cold and had to pull back to safety and dig in for the night.

The next morning, the 4th Marines, supported by tanks,

again battered the Japanese defenses. A sniper killed the 4th Marines' executive officer, Lt. Col. Samuel D. Puller ("Chesty" Puller's younger brother). The 22d Marines advanced against vicious automatic weapons fire. Tank-infantry teams kept pressing forward; by dark, the 22d Marines were on the high ground overlooking the former Marine Barracks.

On July 28, the 22d Marines took the town of Sumay, the barracks ruins and the cliffs along the harbor. But the 4th Marines ran into a defense-in-depth of pillboxes and minefields. There was no way around them. E and I Companies led a frontal assault, smashed through with help from Marine and Army tanks and reached positions just shy of the former Marine rifle range. The next morning, the Marines swept on to the tip of the peninsula. Retaking Orote Peninsula had cost 115 Marines killed, 38 missing and 721 wounded.

At 3:30 P.M. on July 29 at the charred ruins of the Marine Barracks, "To the Colors" was blown on a captured Japanese bugle; and the American flag was officially raised on Guam for the first time since December 10, 1941.

Meanwhile, the 77th Infantry Division was patrolling all of southern Guam; and the 3rd Division after a deadly contest had occupied the Fonte Plateau. On July 28, units from the separate beachheads met at Mt. Tenjo. But the main body of Japanese survivors was already filtering up to the northern jungles. In the flight, Lt. Gen. Takashina was killed by a Marine tank's machine gun. By now, an estimated 9,000 Japanese had been killed; only 50 prisoners had been taken. There were still plenty of the enemy alive on Guam.

On July 31, the 3rd Division, with the 77th Division on its right, drove into the rain-soaked hill country of northern Guam. The 3rd Marines entered the rubble of the capital of Agaña. The 9th Marines took Tiyan airfield. At the edge of the northern plateau, the 77th Division secured the village of Barrigada and 640-foot Mt. Barrigada.

The enemy fought with well-laid ambushes, mines and roadblocks. The thick northern jungle hid the Japanese and kept the American units out of touch with each other. As a result, one tank-led Army patrol powered through two roadblocks and attacked a third, which, unfortunately, was held by the 2d Battalion, 9th Marines. Seven Marines were wounded before the tanks' guns could be stopped.

With the 1st Battalion, 9th Marines on August 3, Pfc. Frank P. Witek of Derby, Connecticut, was caught in an ambush, stood up and killed eight Japanese at point-blank range with his BAR to enable his platoon to take cover. As the men pulled back, Witek stayed with a badly wounded Marine until stretcher bearers arrived and then covered their retreat. After that, Witek raced ahead again, throwing grenades and firing at the enemy. He destroyed a machine-gun emplacement and killed eight more Japanese before he was killed. He was awarded the Medal of Honor.

Throughout the fighting on Guam, the Marines experimented with the use of several platoons of war dogs. These were mostly Doberman pinschers, trained to kill on command, dig Japanese out of their caves, spot snipers, carry messages under fire and provide night security. Four of the dogs and two of the handlers were killed in action.

The 77th Division was now prepared to attack 840-foot Mt. Santa Rosa, near the east coast, where the Japanese had constructed their last-stand positions. The Marine division drove directly north in the center of the island and the 1st Marine Brigade came up on the western side.

At noon on August 7, the Army opened its final offensive. Tanks and riflemen were quickly enveloped in a raging battle. The Marines found less resistance in their zones. VMF-225 flew combat air patrols from Orote airfield. The next day, the 77th Division found Mt. Santa Rosa undefended. In the jungle fighting, there was a discouraging number of incidents of Americans firing on Americans. And Marine patrols found groups of Guamanians whom the Japanese had used as laborers and then beheaded.

The 1st Brigade reached the northwestern coast, and the 9th Marines advanced to Pati Point at the northeastern corner of the island. On August 10, Maj. Gen Geiger announced that all organized resistance had ended. Guam was American once more.

Although the island was officially secured and the enemy was unable to fight effectively, thousands of Japanese were still alive on Guam. Many died of starvation; the rest were eliminated over months of guerrilla warfare. Guam was rapidly converted into a major naval and training base, and two great B-29 airfields were carved out of the northern jungle.

The Marianas campaign had brought American air power within striking distance of the Japanese homeland. It had also drawn out the enemy fleet and destroyed its naval aviation. The enemy made the Americans pay dearly for their achievements. For the Marine Corps alone, casualties in the Central Pacific campaign from Tarawa through the Marianas had totalled 6,902 dead and 19,471 wounded—the equivalent of much more than an entire Marine division.

11
Peleliu and the Philippines

Peleliu was another bad mistake. Out in the middle of nowhere—one of the Palau Islands some 500 miles east of the Philippines—it cost the United States 1,794 dead and 7,800 wounded. It was not worth it. Adm. William F. Halsey, Jr., had recommended a last-minute cancellation of the invasion. When his carrier sweeps discovered that Japanese air power in the central Philippines was "a hollow shell,"[69] he judged the Peleliu operation unnecessary. He recalled, "I feared another Tarawa—and I was right."[70]

After the war, historian Samuel Eliot Morison said of the Palaus: "Admiral Halsey had the right idea; they should have been bypassed."[71] They were not isolated and neutralized because Admiral Nimitz was committed to protect the flank of General MacArthur's move into the Philippines and Nimitz saw the Palaus* as a staging point for the invasion of Leyte. As a result, the Marines assaulted Peleliu. But it was of little purpose. Eight days later, the Army landed on Ulithi Atoll and won a real anchorage—with no lives lost.

The 28,484 men of the 1st Marine Division (reinforced) fought on Peleliu—"one of the bloodiest battles of the war"[72]— because MacArthur had won his fight to return to the Philippines. He had consistently opposed the Central Pacific campaign. He even took his case to the public and was quoted on page one of *The New York Times*: "Island hopping . . . is not my idea of how to end the war as soon and as cheaply as possible."[73] Admiral King called MacArthur's strategy "absurd."[74]

*Lt. Col. Earl H. Ellis had died on Koror Island in the Palaus in 1923. See page 219.

On March 12, 1944, the Joint Chiefs of Staff finally reached a compromise: MacArthur would head for the Philippines and Nimitz into the Marianas. And in July at Honolulu, MacArthur convinced President Roosevelt and Admiral Nimitz that unless he returned to the Philippines all Asia would "lose faith in American honor."[75] The decision intensified Army-Navy rivalry and therefore increased the pressure for speed on the Marines' offensive timetable and consequently the number of their casualties. It also permitted MacArthur to engage in massive battles throughout the Philippines, which he insisted on liberating island after island.

The Japanese helped the general win support for his return to the Philippines. That summer, their armies struck southward in China, pushed the 14th U.S. Army Air Force back from its airfields nearest Japan and cut off Chiang Kai-shek from the Chinese coast, where the Allies might have landed without fighting.

So, Peleliu. Maj. Gen. William H. Rupertus, the 1st Marine Division's commander, predicted that, although this would be a hard fight, it would take only two or three days. His misjudgment would make the Marines bitter.

Of course, Rupertus and the other planners for Peleliu did not know that the Japanese would change their style of defense so radically and successfully. But the enemy had learned an important lesson from the prolonged fighting on Saipan and from a defensive experiment they had made on Biak Island. On Peleliu, instead of trying to shove the Marines off the beaches, the Japanese burrowed into caves in the Umurbrogol ridges, the central spine of the island; and the Americans felt compelled to dig them out. This cost time and lives, which was exactly what the enemy wanted—they would do it again on Iwo Jima and Okinawa. The days of the wasteful beach-and-*banzai* defense were over.

Peleliu, shaped like a horse's skull facing northeast, was only six miles long and two across at its widest; but it was known to hold 10,200 first-class Japanese troops, some of them proud veterans of Manchuria. They constructed a tough defense-in-depth. They mined the beaches, sank underwater obstacles and dug huge antitank ditches, all covered by interlocking fields of fire. And in the central mess of coral ridges and boulders, they created an elaborate network of caves and tunnels, well armed and stocked. There, they were prepared to fight to the death. And they did.

At 8:32 on Friday morning, September 15, 1944, the 1st Marine Division, straight from its miserable rest area on Pavuvu, assaulted Peleliu's western beaches. At the same time, in Europe, the Americans took Aachen, the first major German city to fall, and paratroopers dropped on Arnhem; and in the Southwest Pacific, MacArthur's soldiers landed at Morotai. Back home, for once, the Marines were virtually forgotten.

Col. Lewis B. "Chesty" Puller landed his 1st Marines on the left flank to attack the Umurbrogol ridges just north of Peleliu's airfield.

Col. Harold D. "Bucky" Harris landed his 5th Marines in the center to plunge straight across the island and capture the airfield.

Col. Herman H. "Haiti" Hanneken took his 7th Marines into the beaches on the right to clean up the island's wide southern end.

The only division reserve was the 2d Battalion of the 7th Marines—with the Army's 81st Infantry Division a floating reserve on eight hours' call. The odds did not favor the Marines—9,000 infantrymen (plus a lot of firepower, of course) against 10,000 heavily fortified Japanese.

Colonel Puller did not like the smell of the whole operation—knocking heads with a well-prepared enemy and too few men in back-up. But the commanders in charge pointed reassuringly to the three days of preliminary bombardment. And Maj. Gen. Rupertus did not want Army troops on Peleliu if he could help it.

Enemy guns and mortars on the high ground were zeroed in on Peleliu's broad reef and white coral sand beaches. At both ends of the proposed beachhead, the Japanese had enfilading fire. A chaplain who went in with the assault wrote: "How we got through the murderous mortar fire which the Japs were laying down on the reef we'll never know. The bursts were everywhere and our men were being hit, left and right."[76] The Japanese destroyed 26 LVTs, disabled many more and hit every one of the 30 tanks unloaded with the fourth wave.

Puller's K Company, commanded by Capt. George P. Hunt,

landed on the extreme left flank against vicious raking fire. K Company "was destined to execute a classic example of a small-unit attack on a fortified position."[77] That is official language to describe one hell of a fight.

Hunt wrote much later:

> Among the 235 of Company K were every type, tall and short, stocky and thin, fair and dark, but unifying them into one driving spirit was an unshakable loyalty to each other, a unity far deeper than mere comradeship, and governed by a stern, silent code of mutual respect which could not be broken by a man in battle without his incurring the humiliating contempt of former friends. This was a force that would never allow them to let each other down and that would impel them to perform acts of bravery which, in the normal circumstances of peace, would seem incredible.[78]

(Of the eight Medals of Honor earned by Marines on Peleliu, six were awarded to men who covered grenades with their bodies to save their comrades.)

K Company's objective was a point of coral 30 feet high, jutting out into the sea at the north end of the entire beachhead and infested with Japanese machine guns and antitank guns. The 3rd Platoon on the left landed 100 yards south of The Point and fought northward to within 50 yards of it. The 2d Platoon made about 75 yards straight ahead westward, ran into a 10-foot-deep tank trap and took heavy fire from an unexpected ridge 40 feet high on its right front; the ridge was honeycombed with Japanese caves. The 2d Platoon was surrounded in the tank trap; the machine-gun section kept off the Japanese. Each platoon was quickly shaved down to squad strength. To close the gap between them, Captain Hunt sent in his reserve 1st Platoon, which had to fight through five concrete pillboxes to reach The Point.

Since the enemy guns were oriented to the beach, Hunt's Marines hit The Point from the rear and by 10:15 seized the crest. An enemy 47mm gun was still firing below them. The 1st Platoon leader, 2d Lt. William A. Willis, a New Yorker, eased himself down the cliff and lobbed in a smoke grenade. Then, a

Corporal Anderson fired in a rifle grenade that ignited the gun's ammunition. As the Japanese raced out in flames, the bullets in their belts popping, the Marines killed them.

Hunt could locate only 32 survivors from his 1st and 3rd Platoons to form an isolated perimeter defense atop The Point. They set up a captured machine gun. When evening finally came after a long day of battle, Willis said to the captain, "Anyway, there's one thing to be said for our situation. We'll be able to kill some more of the bastards."[79]

South of the ridge that had stopped Hunt's 2d Platoon, the rest of Puller's 3rd Battalion ran into trouble. A Company of the 1st Battalion hurried up to help, took heavy casualties and stormed the ridge's southern slopes. On Puller's right, Harris' 5th Marines quickly moved to the near side of the airfield and set up a defensive line, expecting a tank attack. For 15 minutes, K Company of the 5th Marines was the exposed right flank of the entire invasion because Hanneken's 7th Marines had hit underwater obstacles and mines and fierce fire from the promontory south of the beach and from a nameless islet nearby. Many Marines had to wade in.

There was an exceptional amount of confusion between the 5th and 7th Marines, although this was an experienced division with many veterans of Guadalcanal and Cape Gloucester. Part of the 3rd Battalion, 7th Marines landed on the beach of the 3rd Battalion, 5th Marines. Sherman tanks sent to help I Company of the 7th Marines destroy a large blockhouse attached themselves to I Company, 5th Marines by mistake. And the 3rd Battalion, 5th Marines, its commander hit and evacuated, pushed dangerously far forward because it thought the 3rd Battalion, 7th Marines was ahead of it, when actually that unit was 200 yards to the rear. Headquarters personnel had to plug the hole. Partly because of such foul-ups, L Company, 5th Marines was the only element to cross the whole island on D-Day.

When, at 5 P.M., the commander of the 3rd Battalion, 5th Marines was wounded and his executive officer killed, Lt. Col. Lewis W. Walt, the 5th Marines' executive officer, took command. He made a personal reconnaissance accompanied only by his runner, located his scattered companies and built a perimeter near the airfield.

Late that afternoon, the Japanese counterattacked. They did

not rush out in a wild *banzai* charge but advanced carefully, taking advantage of cover. A dozen enemy tanks clanged across the airfield and struck the junction of the 1st and 5th Marines in the woods southwest of the field. Having anticipated exactly this, Colonel Harris had heavy machine guns, 37mm antitank guns and three tanks in place. The Shermans' first armor-piercing shells tore right through the light Japanese tanks and exploded harmlessly; but when the tankers switched to high explosive ammunition and four more Shermans joined in, most of the Japanese tanks were destroyed.

The amphibious assault failed to meet its D-Day objectives. The Marines managed only to advance about 300 yards in the confused fighting on the northern beaches and to shove a narrow wedge across the island. For this, they suffered 210 dead and 910 wounded, not counting the many cases of heat prostration and combat fatigue.

During the night, small units of Japanese attacked the Marines isolated on The Point. Hunt's men used grenades to avoid revealing their positions. Mortars pounded the Marines; then came furious fire fights. The Marines' ranks thinned. By morning, Hunt had 18 men and one machine gun left. Because the division command post ashore could not communicate with the 1st Marines, Brig. Gen. Oliver P. Smith, the assistant division commander, did not know how precarious their situation was.

On the second day, the Marines fought the dogged enemy and a torturous shortage of water. Drinking water had been floated ashore in oil drums that had not been properly cleaned; the men retched. Their tongues grew too swollen to talk or swallow.

On the right, the 7th Marines with flamethrowers and bazookas pulverized pillboxes and concrete gun emplacements. Nineteen-year-old Cleveland-born Pfc. Arthur J. Jackson charged a large pillbox, poured in automatic fire, hurled grenades and explosives and killed all 35 Japanese soldiers inside. Under heavy fire, Jackson stormed one gun position after the other. His one-man assault wiped out 12 pillboxes and 50 Japanese. He received the Medal of Honor and a battlefield commission.

Slowed down by the lack of water, the 7th Marines did not clear the strongly-defended twin bulges at the southern end of the island until D plus three; they counted 2,609 enemy dead but took not a single prisoner. They lost 47 killed, 414 wounded and 36 missing.

In the center, the 5th Marines were bedeviled by American planes and artillery; the 2d Battalion alone had 34 casualties from "friendlies." The regiment went on to secure the swampy eastern peninsula of the island by D plus six.

On D plus one, the 1st Marines captured the stubborn ridge; and B Company linked up with Hunt's isolated survivors on The Point. That night 500 Japanese tried to retake The Point. The outnumbered Marines fought them off for four hours with automatic weapons, mortars and grenades. Their firepower decided the issue. When K Company was relieved by I Company the next morning, Hunt (who won the Navy Cross, as did Willis) had only 78 of the 235 men he had led ashore.

Now, most of the enemy were holed up in the crumbled mass of coral, rubble, crags and gulches known as the Umurbrogol ridges. These stark, crazy hills, none more than a few hundred feet high, were porous with hundreds of connected caves, some of which held two men, others large enough for artillery and 150mm mortars and even a battalion of men. The Japanese commander, Col. Kunio Nakagawa, was tied by telephone and suboceanic cable with higher headquarters on Babelthaup Island to the north, a fact not discovered until the battle was over.

The 1st and 5th Marines assaulted Umurbrogol's slopes. They could not dig in to escape the Japanese mortars. There was no front line, just small groups of Marines fighting and attacking in every direction. The heat was scorching, 110 degrees; the coral ridges were shadeless. In the first three days, Puller's regiment had 1,236 casualties—nearly half its strength.

On Monday, September 18, the 2d Battalion, 7th Marines had to relieve the depleted, exhausted 1st Battalion, 1st Marines. The 2d Battalions of the 1st and 7th Marines fought up Hill 210 in the blazing heat and took the crest. Not many made it to the top.

Cpl. Russell Davis, a scout with the 1st Marines, later described it:

As the riflemen climbed higher they grew fewer, until only a handful of men still climbed in the lead squads.

These were the pick of the bunch—the few men who would go forward, no matter what was ahead. There were only a few. Of the thousands who land with a division and the hundreds who go up with a company of the line, there are only a few who manage to live and have enough courage to go through anything. They are the bone structure of a fighting outfit. All the rest is so much weight and sometimes merely flab. There aren't more than a few dozen in every thousand men, even in the Marines. They clawed and clubbed and stabbed their way up. The rest of us watched.

Watching them go up, Buck, the old rifleman, said, "Take a look at that sight and remember it. Those are riflemen, boy, and there ain't many like them. I was one once."[80]

The rugged fighting, terrible heat and lack of water all took their toll. Casualties were shockingly high, corpsmen and stretcher bearers gave out and rear echelon troops had to help. The Negro Marines of the 16th Field Depot won particular praise in this dangerous service.

September 19, the fighting was intense. The 1st Marines' 2d Battalion assaulted the Five Sisters, five ridges separated by steep cliffs, while C Company attacked the rear of Hill 100, later called Walt Ridge. F and G Companies' survivors had to be consolidated into one understrength company. Fighting upward in fast squad rushes, C Company surprised the enemy, but then was hit by fire from the next ridge 50 yards away. The men stayed, isolated, calling for help, and fought on the crest all night. The company commander, Capt. Everett P. Pope of Milton, Massachusetts, had only 15 men left. By dawn, they had exhausted their ammunition and were using bayonets, chunks of coral, broken ammunition boxes and their fists to fight off the counterattacks. When the enemy brought up machine guns, the Marines finally had to retreat.[81]

Puller sent both his 1st and 2d Battalions against Hill 100, throwing cooks, wiremen and supply handlers into the line. The attackers fell back with severe losses. The 7th Marines' 1st and 3rd Battalions had to relieve them. For two days, they flung themselves at the hill, gaining a few yards and being forced to retreat, each assault costing lives. These "fruitless frontal assaults"[82] were draining the division. Experienced platoon leaders and sergeants were virtually gone. The men attacked again and again, but there were not enough of them to hold. One sergeant, trying to rally his exhausted remnant, said, "Let's get killed up on that high ground there. It ain't good to get it down here."[83] The men went.

In that first week, while the 1st Marines were attacking the ridges, the 5th Marines had taken the airfield; and the 7th Marines had painfully seized all the island to the south. But the Japanese still held the ridges overlooking the airfield. The cost to date: 3,946 Marine casualties. The 1st Marines had 56 percent casualties; in the nine rifle platoons of Maj. Raymond G. Davis' 1st Battalion, not one original platoon leader and only 74 of the original nearly 500 riflemen were left. Puller's regiment had 1,672 casualties—"the highest regimental losses in the history of the Corps."[84] Said a sergeant, "This ain't a regiment. We're just survivors."[85]

That first week raised serious questions about the Marine doctrine that pounding straight ahead as fast as possible conserved American lives. Marines advanced with infinite courage when ordered to, but these bullheaded tactics against a skillful enemy who could not retreat and would not surrender simply did not work. Finally, somebody had to call a halt to the slaughter and start looking for a smarter way to invade the Umurbrogol ridges.

On September 21, Maj. Gen. Roy S. Geiger, commander of the III Amphibious Corps, ordered the 1st Marines replaced immediately by the 321st Infantry of the 81st Infantry Division. Rupertus stubbornly protested that the 1st Marines could finish the job; but the enlisted Marines welcomed the soldiers.

A tactical change was needed; and at 7 A.M. on September 24, the second phase of the battle opened. The 321st Infantry drove up the narrow west coast plain to isolate the Umurbrogol hill mass from the north while the 7th Marines continued the pressure on the central ridges. The 321st found a trail to the east coast just north of the enemy bastion and seized strongly-defended Hill 100, which dominated the trail.

The 5th Marines dashed up to the northern end of the island and in tough, yard-by-yard, cave-by-cave fighting with flamethrowers and tanks cleared the Amiangal ridges there. On September 28, its 3rd Battalion took Ngesebus Island just north of Peleliu in a shore-to-shore landing well supported by naval gunfire, artillery and Corsairs of Maj. Robert F. "Cowboy" Stout's newly arrived VMF-114. The rest of the 5th Marines cleaned up most of the resistance on northern Peleliu by September 29. The 1st Division had a total of 5,044 casualties.

Now, the Marines had to concentrate on the Umurbrogol. The 7th Marines attacking those central ridges were hampered by typhoon rains, dysentery and a shortage of rations. But by the end of October 3, despite heavy casualties, they captured two important hills, Walt and Boyd Ridges. Col. Joseph F. Hankins, the division Provost Marshal, was killed by a sniper in a cave above Dead Man's Curve on the west road; he was the highest ranking officer killed on Peleliu.

The next afternoon, Marines of L Company, 7th Marines climbing Hill 120 were caught in a crossfire. A platoon led by 2d Lt. James E. Dunn of Duluth, Minnesota, was wiped out. Bullets broke Dunn's hold on the cliffside, and he fell to his death. Capt. James V. "Jamo" Shanley tried to rescue the wounded; a mortar shell wounded him mortally. Second Lt. Harold J. Collis rushed out to aid him and was killed at his side. (Shanley, who had earned a Navy Cross on Cape Gloucester, was awarded his second posthumously.) Three hours after the 48 Marines had started to climb that ridge, 11 were left.

By the end of October 5, the 7th Marines were finished; the 1st Battalion had 100 men still able to fight and the 2d Battalion was down to 30 percent effective. The 5th Marines, descendants of the Marines of Belleau Wood, came down from the north to replace them.

Colonel Harris finally changed the Marines' style of assaulting the Umurbrogol. Although division headquarters objected and called for faster results, Harris insisted that his men advance deliberately, trying to save lives. It worked. Attacking the north side of the pocket, Harris' tired, under-strength 5th Regiment seized Wattie Ridge, Baldy Ridge, Hill 120 and finally Hill 140, which dominated the area. By October 11, the Marines held the high ground on the northern side of the Umurbrogol.

When the 5th Marines were relieved by the 321st Infantry

on the morning of October 15—one month after D-Day—1,150 Japanese still held an area of 400 yards by 500 yards. Except for some heavy fighting by the 5th Marines south of the pocket, where the enemy had reoccupied caves, the 1st Marine Division's offensive action on Peleliu was over. The Marines returned to Pavuvu. It looked a lot better now.

The 1st Division had 1,124 killed, 5,024 wounded and 117 missing—a total of 6,265 casualties. The 81st Infantry Division had 277 killed and 1,008 wounded on Peleliu. The Japanese had an estimated 10,200 killed and 302 taken prisoner. The Army took over the battle, supported by VMF-114 and VMF(N)-541, and methodically squeezed the pocket until organized resistance ceased on November 27. Peleliu had been a brutal and unnecessary battle. The Marines had led the way to a pointless victory at a dreadful cost.

Although Marines fought and died on Peleliu in support of the Philippine invasion, the only Marines to fight in the Philippines themselves were 1,500 men of the V Amphibious Corps Artillery commanded by Brig. Gen. Thomas E. Bourke and the fliers of the 1st Marine Aircraft Wing.

The artillerymen went to Leyte by a fluke. Back during the Marianas operation, they had exchanged places with Army artillery units; and the mix-up had never been straightened out. The Marine gunners landed north of Dulag on Leyte on October 23 (A-Day plus three) and supported the Army's advance. On December 6, when Japanese paratroopers jumped onto Buri airfield, Capt. Eugene S. Roane, Jr., organized the Marine defense there in a battle that lasted for five days. On December 13, the Marine artillerymen were pulled out of Leyte.

The arrival of the Marine fliers in the Philippines was the result of a frightening new development in the war: the kamikaze. The truth is that Marine aviation had been unable to perform its primary role: supporting the Marine Corps' amphibious assaults. There were two reasons for this: First, as the Central Pacific campaign advanced in giant steps beyond the range of land-based fighter planes, the Navy was reluctant to turn over escort aircraft carriers to the Marines. Secondly, the Marines failed to make a determined fight to get onto carriers for close support missions. The leaders of Marine aviation were more attracted to the glories of aerial combat than to the mundane work of supplying close air support to Marines on the ground. Said a respected historian of Marine aviation, "High-ranking Marine officers—aviators and nonaviators alike—showed a remarkable lack of foresight in failing to insist that their flyers be put on escort carriers at this time [1943]. . . . [T]he top Marine aviators . . . were too deeply interested in shooting enemy planes out of the wild blue yonder, so they lost sight of their primary mission."[86] In fact, in June 1943, the requirement that Marine pilots meet carrier qualifications was actually dropped—with Marine Corps agreement. No pilot could become an ace in close support, and no Marine won the Medal of Honor in the air after January 1944. Once in the vast Central Pacific where air support had to be carrier-based, the war left the Marine fliers behind.

One rear-area unit, VMF-422, met tragedy. Led by Maj. John S. MacLaughlin, Jr., 23 Corsairs left Tarawa on January 25, 1944, on a 700-mile flight to Funafuti. Only one pilot, Lt. John E. Hansen, made it. The rest hit bad weather and ran out of fuel. Twelve pilots landed in the sea and got into one-man life rafts surrounded by sharks. After two days, a destroyer picked them up. The flight lost 22 aircraft and six pilots.

By mid-1944, the Marine Corps had five air wings and 112,626 aviation personnel, including 10,457 pilots. Admiral King thought the whole program too large; in view of how Marine air was used, he was right. Commandant Vandegrift proposed a deal: one wing be dropped but Marine pilots be put onto escort carriers. King agreed if Admiral Nimitz concurred. So Vandegrift went out to sell Nimitz.

But it was the unexpected and terrifying appearance of the desperate Japanese kamikaze suicide planes at Leyte that brought Marine aviation back into the war. The kamikazes threatened the American aircraft carriers and applied enormous pressure on the Army's land-based fighters. Admiral Halsey suggested to General MacArthur that he bring up MAG-12 from the Solomons. As a result, Marines provided air support to Army ground troops, not to Marines.

For the most part, Army divisional and regimental commanders were exceedingly dubious about the value and safety of close air support. And they were especially wary of the Marine system, unlike Army and Navy doctrine, of managing close air support by direct radio communication between the attacking aircraft and ground liaison parties with the frontline troops.

On October 20, 1944, the first Marine flier in the Philippines was Maj. Gen. Ralph J. Mitchell, commanding general of the 1st Marine Aircraft Wing. When the Japanese Navy was destroyed as an offensive force in the great naval Battle of Leyte Gulf on October 23–26, planes from lost and damaged American carriers tried to land at the primitive Tacloban, Leyte, airfield. Mitchell, a pilot since 1921, grabbed a pair of signal flags and brought in the Navy planes himself.

On December 3, 66 Corsairs of MAG-12 and 12 Hellcats of VMF(N)-541 arrived at Tacloban to help stop the kamikazes and the flow of Japanese reinforcements into western Leyte. The Marines destroyed at least 22 Japanese ships and 67 aircraft, but they never flew the close-support missions they had trained for.

MacArthur next sailed to the Lingayen Gulf north of Manila; and on January 6 alone, kamikazes hit 16 ships of his invasion fleet. The Army landed unopposed on January 9; and two days later, Col. Clayton C. Jerome, commander of MAG-32, and two other Marines went ashore and laid out an airfield on a rice paddy near Mangaldan. It became headquarters for MAG-24 and -32; and by the end of January, 3,472 Marines and 174 Douglas Dauntless dive bombers were operating there.

The Marine fliers experienced their most dramatic Philippine adventure when MacArthur ordered the 1st Cavalry Division to dash down to Manila, free the American prisoners interned in the Santo Tomás University and seize the Malacanan Palace. Marine Capt. Francis R. B. "Frisco" Godolphin visited 1st Cavalry headquarters and found the division G-2, Lt. Col. Robert F. Goheen, who had been a student of his at Princeton University. With a bit of old-school-tie cooperation, they arranged for MAG-24 and -32 to support the race to Manila. Starting at dawn on February 1, Marine air liaison parties accompanied the soldiers; and Marines flew a nine-plane dawn to dusk screen for the division. Marine dive bombers scouted and bombed ahead of the column, helped it skirt delaying battles, bombed roadblocks and rode shotgun on its exposed left flank. The 1st Cavalry sped into Manila on the evening of February 3 and freed 3,700 Santo Tomás internees. It was a

355

daring feat, and the division's commanding general praised the Marine fliers close support; as he said, "They will try anything once."[87]

Marines also flew close support missions for guerrilla forces in the Philippines. Late in February, for example, six Marines were put ashore 50 miles behind enemy lines in northwestern Luzon. They called in Marine planes to support the attack of Col. Russell W. Volckmann's guerrillas on the port of San Fernando. They used Nicaragua-style cloth panels to mark the friendly front lines. Army P-51 Mustangs and Marine Corsairs dropped fragmentation bombs 200 yards in front of the guerrillas. When the enemy rallied, five Marine dive bombers strafed and bombed the Japanese and drove them from the ridge above the city.

Having won the enthusiastic support of the 1st Cavalry Division, the Marines convinced the commander of the 6th Infantry Division to use them to dive-bomb the heavily defended Japanese Shimbu line in the mountains northeast of Manila. They also blasted Nichols Field, Corregidor and the hulks of ships that provided the enemy cover in Manila harbor. In April, when heavy rains washed out the rice paddy field at Mangaldan, MAG-24 and -32 moved south to Clark Field. On Luzon, the two air groups flew 8,842 combat missions.

Not satisfied with having gained a strategic base on Leyte and Luzon, MacArthur insisted on freeing all the bypassed Philippine Islands. MAG-12, -14 and -32 gave direct support to the 41st Infantry Division taking the Zamboanga Peninsula on the large southern island of Mindanao. Even before the invasion, 16 Marine Corsairs flew from a guerrilla-controlled grass airstrip on the enemy-held island. Later, the Marines established a field at San Roque, naming it for Lt. Col. Paul Moret. From Moret Field, Marines flew direct support missions for approximately 50 landings on Panay, Cebu, Negros, Mindanao and the islands of the Sulu Archipelago. In April, MAG-24 established a field at Malabang and named it for Capt. John A. Titcomb, who had been killed on Luzon.

In the Philippines, Marine aviation lost 100 men killed in action, 127 wounded and 50 dead from accidents and other causes. Marine fliers got their chance at last to prove the value of their concept of close air support. But to fly support missions for Marines, they would still have to win a place on carriers.

This began to happen when at Pearl Harbor in August 1944 Commandant Vandegrift and Admiral Nimitz agreed that Marine squadrons would be assigned to escort carriers for close support missions, and Aircraft, FMF Pacific was established with 1,620 Marine planes of all types. The following month, the process accelerated when Vandegrift exiled the old-timer Maj. Gen. Ross E. Rowell to Lima, Peru, to help train the Peruvian air force and gave Maj. Gen. Francis P. Mulcahy the top Marine aviation job in the Pacific.

On October 21, 1944, the day after MacArthur landed on Leyte, Marine Carrier Groups, Aircraft, FMF Pacific became a tactical command under Col. Albert D. Cooley. By May 1945, Marines were aboard four escort carriers, each with 18 fighter planes and 12 torpedo bombers. The long-range plan was for Marines to have eight escort carriers in time for the invasion of Japan. But in the meanwhile, the invasion of Iwo Jima was covered almost entirely by Navy pilots.

Before the Marines got their own escort carriers, eight Marine fighter squadrons flew from four large attack carriers during the first six months of 1945. Fifty-four Marine pilots of VMF-124 and -213 went aboard *Essex* and flew combat strikes against Okinawa, Tokyo and Southeast Asian airfields at Cam Ranh Bay and Bien Hoa and Tan Son Nhut at Saigon. On January 12, 500 American carrier planes, including a few Marines, shot up Saigon and sunk 14 warships and 33 merchant ships. Marine Lt. Joseph O. Lynch was one of four pilots shot down and saved by the French; pilots captured by the Japanese were shot.

At Iwo Jima, the Navy's attack carriers launched prelanding strikes by 600 planes. Among them were 24 Marine Corsairs commanded by Lt. Col. William A. Millington of VMF-124. Marines flew some close support missions there from the large carriers until February 22, when the job was turned over to the Navy's escort carrier planes and Army P-51s. Marine close air support for Marines had not yet come into its own.

12
Iwo Jima—"The Toughest Yet"

Lt. Gen. Tadamichi Kuribayashi was fifty-four years old, five feet nine, over 200 pounds and had a pot belly. As a young man, he had been for two years a military attaché in the United States and he respected American power. This smart, tough cavalryman, former commander of the Emperor's Imperial Guards, would transform the invasion of Iwo Jima into the costliest battle in Marine Corps history.

The Americans decided to assault Iwo Jima because it was halfway between the Marianas and Tokyo—about 670 miles from each. It could provide an emergency landing field for B-29s fire-bombing Tokyo and a base for shorter-range fighters escorting the giant Superfortresses. Iwo Jima was a sulfurous flyspeck (its name means Sulfur Island), volcanic, ugly, waterless, stinking—but strategic.

Three divisions of Marines (controversially minus one regiment) would try to seize it. This time, there would be more Marine casualties than Japanese. Of the 80 Marines who received the Medal of Honor in World War II, 22 earned it here.

Lt. Gen. Kuribayashi appreciated Iwo Jima's strategic value. The island was actually part of the Prefecture of Tokyo; and he wrote his son, "this island is the gateway to Japan."[88] He had 23,000 well-armed troops, 361 artillery pieces and 22 tanks. (The tanks were commanded by Lt. Col. Takeichi Nishi, who had won an equestrian jumping gold medal riding Uranus in the 1932 Olympic Games at Los Angeles.) Kuribayashi shipped out the traditionalist officers who insisted on meeting the Americans flamboyantly on the beaches. He went underground and "fortified Iwo to near perfection."[89] He would make the American Marines come to him and buy every rocky inch with blood. "Iwo

358

was in effect all beachhead. It was an amphibious assault that lasted for thirty-six days."[90]

Kuribayashi knew that he was doomed. The Japanese Navy had been shattered; its air power crushed. Japan was cut off from the raw materials and oil of Southeast Asia (which had been the original reason for the war). American fleets and planes roamed almost at will; Tokyo itself was being bombed; the war was rushing to its climax. Kuribayashi would have to fight without hope of reinforcement or salvation.

Coming against him from Saipan was a tremendous force of Americans: 800 ships and 220,000 men. B-24s out of the Marianas struck Iwo Jima for 74 consecutive days before the invasion. But Intelligence saw that the Japanese defense lines, blockhouses and pillboxes were growing stronger. Lt. Gen. Holland Smith, present rather superfluously in his last combat assignment as Commanding General, Expeditionary Troops, expected that one in four of the 60,000 assault troops would be killed or wounded.

In a brutal, deadly way, Iwo Jima was what the Marine Corps was all about: young men—Tony Stein, John Basilone, Doug Jacobson, Jack Lummus—assaulting a defended objective from the sea and then advancing in the face of death and disfigurement, exhausted beyond reason, seeing their leaders and buddies dying around them, but moving forward. Like it or not, a lot of American history converged on this desolate little island.

Iwo Jima was only five miles long, porkchop-shaped with the thick end, two and a half miles wide, toward the north. It smelled like rotten eggs. Nothing lived there but wading birds and the waiting Japanese. At the southern end was the steep cone of the extinct 550-foot volcano, Mount Suribachi. In the center was a flat area where the Japanese had two airfields. Toward the north the land rose to the Motoyama Plateau, level enough in the middle, but cut hideously by gorges and ravines plunging down to both coasts. At the very north was a morass of cliffs and ridges that the defenders had perforated with caves, beautifully camouflaged gun emplacements and 11 miles of tunnels. Japanese like Kuribayashi had learned.

The invasion started with arguments and bitterness. The Marines wanted the Navy to produce ten days of pre-invasion

359

bombardment; they got three. The Navy said it had to conserve ammunition for the forthcoming invasion of Okinawa. The Marines accused the Navy of sending carrier Task Force 58 scooting off to bomb Japan on February 16–17, 1945, because of all the attention the Army's B-29s were winning, when it should have stayed and saved Marine lives at Iwo Jima. (TF 58 now included eight Marine air squadrons—144 Corsairs and 216 Marine pilots.) Admiral Spruance insisted the carrier attacks would prevent Japan-based aircraft from interfering with the Iwo Jima landing. The arguments were complex; the fact was simple: The Marines assaulted Iwo Jima with less than optimal gunfire preparation.

On D-Day minus two, the Japanese made a mistake. Contrary to orders, artillery opened up on 12 LCI gunboats covering the UDT reconnaissance of Iwo Jima, hitting all the boats but exposing the hidden batteries to naval gunfire. The Navy took full advantage of this expensive break.

Monday morning, February 19, was lovely: cool, clear, calm. The Marines ate the now traditional D-Day steak-and-eggs breakfast and went to work. In 482 amtracs, behind a heavy naval bombardment and a final rolling barrage, they roared toward Iwo Jima's ugly southeastern beaches to meet a determined, highly disciplined enemy. They landed on loose black gravel-like volcanic ash in which men sank to their ankles and vehicles were immobilized.

The 4th and 5th Marine Divisions made the initial assault with four regiments; the two from the 5th Division on the left (south); the 4th Division's two on the right. At the extreme south, ex-Raider Col. Harry B. "The Horse" Liversedge's 28th Marines were to take Suribachi and cross the island's narrow neck. On Liversedge's right, Col. Thomas A. Wornham's 27th Marines headed for Airfield No. 1. Maj. Gen. Keller E. Rockey's 5th Division had not yet been in battle as a unit, but its ranks included many combat veterans. Rockey himself had won the Navy Cross at Belleau Wood.

The experienced 4th Division was commanded by Maj. Gen. Clifton B. Cates, who had commanded the 1st Marines on Guadalcanal. Its two assault regiments were Col. Walter W. Wensinger's 23rd and Col. John R. Lanigan's 25th. Lanigan's Marines had to seize the quarry at the far right or north end of the invasion beaches.

In reserve were Col. Walter I. Jordan's 24th Marines and Col. Chester B. Graham's 26th Marines, plus the veteran 3rd Marine Division commanded by Maj. Gen. Graves B. Erskine. At forty-seven, Erskine was one of the youngest generals in the Corps and one of the toughest. His 3rd Division would not fight on D-Day but would make up for it later.

The plan of Maj. Gen. Harry Schmidt, in command of the V Amphibious Corps, was simple. Take the airfields as fast as possible; grab Suribachi to the south, and then combine all forces and drive north. The operation was scheduled for 14 days. But it would consume a month of fighting and 5,931 Marines killed and 17,372 wounded—one Marine casualty for each Japanese on the island. Kuribayashi knew his business.

When the amtracs were 400 yards from the beaches, 24 Marine Corsairs and 24 Navy Hellcats led by Lt. Col. William A. Millington of VMF-124, flying off *Essex*, strafed the beaches. But the enemy waited below ground.

The first Marines hit the beach at 8:59 A.M. and faced a sloping terrace pushed eight to 15 feet high by the sea and wind. The rise blocked their fields of fire. Men and vehicles floundered in the volcanic ash. Foxholes filled up as soon as they were dug. Within 15 minutes, the Marines started receiving heavy mortar fire, then machine-gun and rifle fire from an invisible enemy. Now, the landing beaches were ablaze. Unlike Tarawa (or Omaha Beach), there was not even a seawall to hide behind.

All eight assault battalions were ashore in 90 minutes. At 10 A.M., the first 16 tanks landed; three immediately struck mines. The beaches were littered with the mangled and the dead. "They had died as amphibious creatures die: not far inland, not far from the sea."[91]

Cpl. Tony Stein of Dayton, Ohio, and A Company, 28th Marines, had improvised a hand-held machine gun from a wrecked Navy fighter's gun and in those early moments attacked pillbox after pillbox, killing 20 Japanese. Eight times under intense fire, he struggled barefoot to the beach for more ammunition. Each time, he dragged back a wounded Marine. The twenty-four-year-old veteran of Guadalcanal and Bougainville received the Medal of Honor.

The commander of B Company, 28th Marines, Capt. Dwayne E. Mears, armed only with a pistol, attacked pillboxes until he was killed; and by 10:35, Lt. Frank J. Wright and four men of B Company's 1st Platoon had crossed the 700 yards of the island's narrow southern neck. Half an hour later, Lt. Wesley C. Bates and six men of the 2d Platoon joined them. The 28th's 1st Battalion took heavy casualties, and Colonel Liversedge brought up his 3rd Battalion from reserve. At 3:45, the 2d and 3rd Battalions tried futilely to attack Mount Suribachi against gun fire pouring down from the "Hot Rock." They needed armor, but most of the tanks could not get off the beach. At 5 P.M., the 2d Battalion attacked the mountain alone, advanced 150 yards and then had to fall back.

To the right of the hard-hit 28th, the 27th Marines reached the southern end of Airfield No. 1. Gunnery Sgt. John Basilone, who had been the first enlisted Marine to earn the Medal of Honor on Guadalcanal and had turned down a commission, led his machine-gun platoon past the end of the airfield and raced toward the island's west coast. He climbed a blockhouse and destroyed it with grenades and demolitions and then under fire guided a tank through a minefield. About 10:30, a mortar shell mortally wounded Basilone and four of his men. This time, they gave "Manila John" a Navy Cross posthumously.

By mid-afternoon, the 27th had seized the cliffs overlooking the west coast; and the 26th Marines landed to reinforce them. The Negro drivers of the Army's 471st Amphibian Truck Company brought the 13th Marines' guns ashore, and they started adding artillery support.

Further north, the 23rd Marines were stopped within 250 yards of the water with many casualties on the congested beach. Capt. John J. Kalen, commander of A Company, bled to death there. First Lt. William E. Worsham took command, tried to lead an end run around a strongpoint and was killed. The mortar platoon leader, 1st Lt. Frank S. Doyoe, Jr., took over and was hit in the left shoulder. First Lt. Arthur W. Zimmerman now led the men toward the airfield and brought up a tank that smashed a huge blockhouse. He was A Company's fourth commander.

In the first wave, Sgt. Darrell S. Cole of Flat River, Missouri, led his machine-gun section of B Company up the sloping beach toward Airfield No. 1 and, under fire, destroyed two positions with grenades and a third with his machine gun. His unit was pinned down by grenades and knee mortars. Cole advanced, hurled his last grenade at a pillbox, went back for more and wiped out the strongpoint before a grenade killed him. He was awarded the Medal of Honor.

The situation on the beach became desperate as the surf rose and the wounded began piling up. By nightfall, the 23rd had fought to the edge of the airfield. Two battalions of the 24th Marines were landed to stiffen the center of the beachhead.

At the extreme north, Colonel Lanigan's 25th Marines landed below a strongly fortified cliff. The right flank battalion, the 3rd, led by Lt. Col. Justice M. Chambers, veteran of Tulagi and Saipan, took a terrible beating and lost many of its officers trying to capture Quarry Ridge. The 2d Battalion headed for the high ground above the quarry, from which the Japanese were firing on the beaches. After an eight-hour battle, the two battalions captured the heights; but the 3rd Battalion had only about 150 men left. The 1st Battalion, 24th Marines had to replace them.

D-Day was bloody and frustrating. Few Marines ever saw a live Japanese; not a single prisoner was taken. By the day's end, 30,000 Marines were ashore and Suribachi was isolated; but the first-day objectives had nowhere been reached. Although the confusion on the beachhead made exact casualty figures impossible to calculate, an estimated 548 Marines had been killed and 1,775 wounded.

The Marines dug in expecting the customary *banzai* counterattack. But if they had not absorbed the significance of the defense of Saipan, Biak and Peleliu, Kuribayashi had. All night, the Japanese rained artillery and mortar shells on the crowded, chaotic beachhead, content to kill more Marines at little cost to themselves.

On the second day, the enemy continued to blast the beachhead from the high ground to the north. Pfc. Jacklyn H. Lucas of Plymouth, North Carolina, and three other Marines of C Company, 26th Marines were ambushed in a ravine. Two grenades landed among them. Lucas, hurling himself over the other men, fell on one grenade and pulled the second under him. He absorbed the explosions with his body. Only seventeen years and six days old, Lucas was the youngest Marine ever awarded the Medal of Honor.

To the south, the gray sides of Suribachi held 1,600 Japanese, dug into well-concealed pillboxes, bunkers, caves and spider holes. That morning in a light rain, the 2d and 3rd Battalions of the 28th Marines again plunged toward the base of the volcano. Each strongpoint had to be attacked with flame-throwers followed by Marines with grenades and demolitions. At nightfall, they had advanced some 200 yards and closed off 40 caves.

By noon on Wednesday, the 1st and 3rd Battalions reached the base of Suribachi. Tony Stein was wounded in the shoulder by shrapnel and sent to the beach; he would be back. Along the east coast, the 2d Battalion ran into fierce mortar fire; but the survivors kept moving into the face of death. Pfc. Donald J. Ruhl, twenty-one, of Columbus, Montana, fought aggressively for two days and then smothered a grenade with his body to save the life of Sgt. Henry O. Hansen of Somerville, Massachusetts. By evening, the 28th Marines formed a semicircle around Suribachi. A cold rain began to fall. Fifty kamikazes hit the American invasion fleet, badly damaged the carrier *Saratoga* and sank the escort carrier *Bismarck Sea*.

On Thursday, Suribachi was surrounded. The rain turned the ground into mush and clogged the Marines' weapons. Hundreds of Japanese still hid in the caves on the mountainsides. On Friday, February 23, a four-man patrol led by Sgt. Sherman B. Watson of the 2d Battalion scaled the volcano; they found machine guns but no Japanese. Two other patrols scouted the slopes, but none drew enemy fire.

First Lt. Harold G. Schrier, a tall, slim, ex-Raider, was sent with 40 men from E Company to secure the crest. The battalion commander, Lt. Col. Chandler W. Johnson, gave Schrier a small American flag that the battalion adjutant, 2d Lt. G. Greeley Wells, had brought ashore in his map case. The route was steep, and sometimes the men had to climb on their hands and knees. In half an hour, they reached the crater's rim; the caves inside were silent. The Marines found a 20-foot piece of pipe, lashed the flag to it and thrust the end of the pipe into the soft ground near the north rim. It was 10:20 A.M. As the flag went up, Marines below shouted and the bells and whistles of the ships of the fleet sounded out. At the base of Suribachi, Secretary of the Navy James V. Forrestal watched the flag go up and said to Lt. Gen. Smith: "Holland, the raising of that flag on Suribachi means a Marine Corps for the next 500 years."[92]

Sgt. Louis R. Lowery photographed the flag-raising for *Leatherneck* magazine. Two Japanese charged out of a cave, and BAR-man Pfc. James A. Robeson shot one. Before the other was killed, he threw a grenade. Lowery leapt over the crater's rim and slid 50 feet down the mountain; his camera was smashed but his negatives were safe.

Six men raised that first flag: 1st Lt. Schrier; Platoon Sgt. Ernest I. Thomas, Jr.; Sergeant Hansen (whose life Pfc. Ruhl had saved); Cpl. Charles W. Lindberg; Pfc. James R. Michels, and Pvt. Louis Charlo, a Crow Indian. Of these six, Hansen, Thomas and Charlo would be killed on Iwo Jima—Thomas on March 3, his twentieth birthday—and Lindberg and Michels would be wounded. Only Schrier got through Iwo Jima safely.

Lt. Col. Johnson figured someone would grab that historic flag; he wanted it saved. So he had 2d Lt. Wells get a larger one from *LST 779*. As it was raised on top of Suribachi, Associated Press photographer Joe Rosenthal, who was on his fourth invasion with the Marines, made the picture that became the most famous war photograph ever taken and was later reproduced as a postage stamp and as a giant statue at Arlington National Cemetery.

The men in Rosenthal's photograph were by happenstance a cross section of the nation: left to right, Pfc. Ira H. Hayes of Bapchule, Arizona; Pfc. Franklin R. Sousely of Flemingsburg, Kentucky; Sgt. Michael Strank of Conemaugh, Pennsylvania; Pharmacist's Mate Second Class John H. Bradley of Appleton, Wisconsin; Pfc. Rene A. Gagnon of Manchester, New Hampshire, and Cpl. Harlon H. Block of Weslaco, Texas. (Sousely, Strank and Block were all to die in action on Iwo Jima.)

On Suribachi, the 28th Marines and the 5th Engineer Battalion set about destroying 165 concrete pillboxes and sealing 200 caves. The 28th Marines had 115 killed and 375 wounded, in addition to the 385 casualties it suffered on D-Day itself.

Meanwhile, seven badly hurt battalions were moving north against Lt. Gen. Kuribayashi's main force. Guns on the high ground dominated the Marines, who fought through the rough crazy-quilt terrain taking heavy casualties. By the end of Tuesday, the Marines controlled Airfield No. 1 and nearly one third of the island.

On Wednesday, the 3rd Division's 21st Marines, veterans of

Bougainville and Guam, came ashore to help take Airfield No. 2. In the first 58 hours, the landing force had 4,500 casualties. There were uncountable acts of individual heroism. Northeast of Airfield No. 1, Sgt. Ross F. Gray of A Company, 25th Marines crawled forward alone with a satchel charge. Three riflemen covered him. He hurled the explosives, ran back, got another charge and blasted another emplacement. The Marine from Marvel Valley, Alabama, singlehandedly killed more than 25 Japanese, destroyed six positions and opened the path for his men. Nearby, the commander of G Company, 24th Marines, Capt. Joseph J. McCarthy, a big ex-Chicago fireman and Silver Star winner on Saipan, led a squad across open ground under fire, blasted a pillbox with grenades, killed two Japanese, charged and destroyed another pillbox and then called to his company which swarmed over the ridge in front of the airfield. Both Gray and McCarthy received the Medal of Honor.

The nights were filled with mortar and artillery fire, local counterattacks and repeated attempts to infiltrate the the Marine lines. By Thursday, the sleepless Marines were exhausted, living on K rations and water in the cold, heavy rain. The 26th Marines were severely mauled and had to pull back. The 21st Marines took a pounding. A machine-gun bullet entered Lt. Col. Chambers' collarbone and lung; awarded the Medal of Honor, he was the third battalion commander of the 25th Marines to fall in three days.

Friday and Saturday, the Marines could make little progress. Although 2,000 Seabees started repairing Airfield No. 1, the second field further north was ringed with hundreds of pillboxes; and enemy artillery was sited to fire straight down the open ground of the runways. Here was the Japanese main defense line. Cpl. Hershel W. Williams of Quiet Dell, West Virginia, received the Medal of Honor for destroying a series of pillboxes with his flamethrower in four hours of intense battle. But there were always more strongpoints. The Americans massed all possible artillery, tanks and naval gunfire on the Japanese positions. It did not seem to make a dent.

Eventually, a dozen tanks reached the fringes of Airfield No. 2; and in the center, Col. Hartnoll J. Withers' 21st Marines attacked the field. K Company's commander, Capt. Rodney L. Heinze, was killed on the edge of the runway. On his right, I

Company's commander, Capt. Clayton S. Rockmore, took a bullet in the throat and was killed. Quickly, lieutenants were hit and sergeants took over the companies. Then, 1st Lt. Raoul J. Archambault, who had been decorated on both Bougainville and Guam, rallied the remaining men of the two companies. They knew the tall, lean Archambault and followed him in a wild charge across the runways. The first dozen Marines onto the ridge beyond the airfield were thrown back; Lt. Dominick J. Grossi led them right back up again and this time they held. They fought the Japanese in ankle-deep sand with rifle butts, bayonets, knives. The survivors opened a gap in the main enemy line.

On the right of the 21st Marines, the 24th had an equally tough fight. They ran into a major Japanese defense point on a ridge called Charlie-Dog. The Japanese opened a mortar barrage and drove them off the ridge. Lt. Col. Alexander A. Vandegrift, Jr., the commander of the 3rd Battalion, was wounded in both legs. By now, after six days of battle, the Marines had 7,758 casualties.

As the second phase of the battle for Iwo Jima opened against the main Japanese defenses on the northern Motoyama Plateau, the Marine commanders were under pressure to finish the struggle quickly. The Pacific Fleet had to be freed for the invasion of Okinawa only five weeks in the future.

On Saturday, the 9th Marines came ashore; only the 3rd Marines remained in reserve. Maj. Gen. Schmidt organized a three-division front. In the center, the 9th and 21st Marines of Erskine's 3rd Division entered an inferno of bunkers and caves and fissures of evil-smelling sulfur fumes. The 5th Division advanced along the west coast on the left, fighting over one ridge after another. On the right, the 4th Division faced "the most extensive and powerful defenses on the island"[93]: Hill 382, the highest point on northern Iwo Jima and bristling with artillery, antitank guns and machine guns; Turkey Knob, a small knoll that contained a vast Japanese communications center of reinforced concrete; and a depression known as the Amphitheater. The Marines called the complex the Meat Grinder.

The main effort had to be right up the middle. Col. Howard N. Kenyon's fresh 9th Marines pounded away at the Japanese center. In the first two days, 20 of the tanks supporting them

367

were knocked out. Against heavy enemy fire, the 9th Marines slowly overwhelmed Hills Peter and Oboe. Pvt. Wilson D. Watson, twenty-four, of Tuscumbia, Alabama, led his squad forward with a BAR and grenades. On Tuesday morning, February 27, he held the crest of a hill alone for 15 minutes and, firing from the hip, killed 60 Japanese. He was not scratched.[94]

By the end of that day (D plus eight), the 3rd Division had massed more artillery, broken out on the Motoyama Plateau and cut through the main line of resistance. But at 3 A.M. on March 4, Lt. Gen. Kuribayashi counterattacked; and the 9th Marines took severe casualties. The 21st Marines relieved the 9th and reached the high ground overlooking unfinished Airfield No. 3.

Killed with the 21st was Sgt. Reid Carlos Chamberlain who had fought with the old 4th Marines on Bataan and Corregidor and, although wounded, had escaped and joined the guerrillas on Mindanao. Commissioned in the U.S. Army, he eventually returned to the States by submarine and plane and received the Distinguished Service Cross. But he resigned his Army commission and rejoined the Marines as a corporal. While running messages to the front lines north of Iwo Jima's Airfield No. 2, Chamberlain was shot in the head.

After blasting through the center of the main Japanese line with flamethrowers and bazookas, the 3rd Division had to wait for the divisions on both sides to catch up. The 5th Division pushing up the west coast ran into some of the heaviest fighting on Iwo Jima. On February 28, the 27th Marines assaulted Hill 362A in hand-to-hand fighting. The next day, the 28th Marines, the men who had conquered Suribachi, took over the attack. A Company went around the right side of the hill and came under heavy fire. Cpl. Tony Stein, back in action, led 20 men to clear the ridge. Only seven returned; Stein was among the dead. On this day Sergeant Hansen, Sergeant Strank and Corporal Block were all killed in front of Hill 362A. But by the day's end, the 28th Marines had occupied the deadly height. Liversedge was awarded his second Navy Cross.

Now the regiment attacked Nishi Ridge, which extended from the plateau almost to the sea. It took until March 3 to capture the ridge, and for the 26th Marines, fighting through deep gorges, to battle to the top of Hill 362B. On March 3 alone, the 26th Marines took 281 casualties. Five Marines of the 5th

Division won the Medal of Honor that day. One of them was Sgt. William G. Harrell of Rio Grande City, Texas, and A Company, 28th Marines. He battled a night attack until a grenade tore off his left hand. He continued to fight and pushed away another grenade, which exploded, killing his attacker and severing Harrell's right hand. As the 5th Division grew depleted by the fierce struggle, headquarters and weapons company men had to fill in on the line.

On the east side of the American offensive north of Quarry Ridge, the 4th Division ground into the Meat Grinder. Progress was terribly slow. On February 26 and 27, the 23rd Marines battled up Hill 382. The 1st Battalion hit the reverse slope; and Sgt. Fritz G. Truan, a famous rodeo cowboy leading A Company's assault platoon, was killed. The 3rd Battalion was reduced to company strength. Nineteen-year-old Pfc. Douglas T. Jacobson of Port Washington, New York, with the 3rd Battalion, grabbed a bazooka and killed the crew of a 20mm gun; then he destroyed two machine-gun positions, a tank, two pillboxes and a blockhouse. Jacobson kept going on his one-man attack and killed 75 Japanese and captured 16 positions on Hill 382. Marines compared him to Sergeant York in World War I. He was awarded the Medal of Honor. (After the war, Doug Jacobson accompanied Tony Stein's body home to Dayton, Ohio, for burial. Jacobson stayed in the Corps, served in North China and retired as a major.)

The 3rd Battalion fought at the hilltop hand-to-hand and was beaten off. The 25th Marines tried to envelop Turkey Knob and failed. By March 1, the 24th Marines had to replace the remnant of the 23rd, and Schmidt and Erskine asked for the 3rd Marines, who were still in transports off Iwo Jima, to be brought to battle. Vice Adm. Turner turned them down on the grounds that there were enough Marines ashore. The argument over that decision grew long and heated. The V Amphibious Corps operations officer (who was to command the Marine Brigade in Korea) said the decision was wrong and increased casualties.

March 2 was a day of desperate fighting. E Company of the 24th Marines tried to outflank Hill 382 from the right; all its officers except 2d Lt. Richard Reich were killed or seriously wounded; but joined by F Company, it finally took the hill. The Japanese still fought from pillboxes and caves.

369

There was no letup. The 24th Marines drove ahead north and east of Hill 382; and the 25th Marines kept beating against Turkey Knob, where the Japanese destroyed them with mortar and rocket fire. Exhausted squads and fire teams attacked enemy strongpoints. Most of the Marines' experienced leaders had been wiped out; less well trained individual replacements were filling the assault ranks and morale was plummeting. On March 3, the 23rd Marines relieved the 25th Marines and attacked the blockhouse on Turkey Knob with flamethrowers and demolition teams. But at day's end the enemy still held it. The 4th Division was now down to 50 percent of combat strength.

The toll had been so gruesomely severe that Maj. Gen. Schmidt had to declare Monday, March 5—two weeks after D-Day—a day of rest, regroupment and replacement. There would be no attacks.

On the next day, the whole brutal process started again with a tremendous artillery barrage that had little effect. Maj. Gen. Erskine tried a new tactic to take Hill 362C. At 5 A.M. on March 7, the 21st Marines and the 3rd Battalion, 9th Marines, jumped off in the dark to surprise the enemy. (In Europe on this day, American GIs seized the Remagen bridge over the Rhine River.) Moving silently through a light rain, the Marines caught the Japanese asleep. But with daylight, they discovered that they had captured the wrong hill. Their real objective was still 250 yards in front of them, and surprise had been lost. Now, in vicious battle, trapped in a labyrinth of crags, E and F Companies were all but annihilated; of E Company seven men survived, of F Company, five. The 3rd Battalion, 9th Marines finally took Hill 362C, and the Marines at last held much of the high ground on the Motoyama Plateau.

Trying to link up with the 3rd Battalion that afternoon, B Company, 9th Marines was cut off. Second Lt. John H. Leims of Chicago crawled out 400 yards across fire-swept terrain and brought his men back. After dark, he crawled out alone twice more under machine-gun fire and carried in wounded Marines.[95]

The 9th and 21st Regiments split Iwo Jima and reached the northeastern coast on March 9. But Lt. Gen. Kuribayashi still held a square mile of the island; he would defend it to the death.

The 5th Division on the right also had trouble making forward progress when the attack began again on March 6. The next day, H Company of the 26th Marines took a 30-foot knoll just north of Nishi Village. Suddenly, the entire hill exploded. The Japanese had blown up their own command post and caused 43 Marine casualties.

As the 27th Marines approached the sea, the Japanese defended every crevice. On March 8, tall, slim 1st Lt. Jack Lummus, of Ennis, Texas, an All-America football end from Baylor University who had signed with the New York Giants, led E Company's assault on a final jumble of rocks. Knocked down by a grenade explosion, he rose and under fire rushed a gun emplacement. A second grenade shattered his shoulder; he attacked a second pillbox and killed all its occupants. Lummus called to his platoon to follow him, and he wiped out a third position. A land mine blew off both his legs, but he still yelled to his men to attack, and they plunged in a wild charge to the ridge above the sea. Lummus died later that day and was awarded the Medal of Honor.

Lt. Gen. Kuribayashi was now holed up in a pocket on a long ridgeline above a deep gorge near Kitano Point, the island's northern tip. By March 9, the 5th Division was battling in sight of the sea toward that ridge over some of the worst ground on Iwo Jima. Progress was measured in feet, not yards. That day, the commander of the 1st Battalion, 27th Marines, Lt. Col. Justin G. Duryea, and the commander of the 2d Battalion, Maj. John W. A. Antonelli, were both wounded when Duryea's runner stepped on the detonater of a 6-inch naval shell buried in the ground. The explosion tore off Duryea's left arm at the elbow and smashed his left knee. Antonelli's eyes were damaged and his eardrum broken, but he walked out of the division hospital and returned to his battalion.

On the eastern side of the renewed offensive, the 4th Division bypassed Turkey Knob and the Amphitheater and worked an anvil-and-hammer tactic with the enemy in between; the 23rd and 24th Marines were the hammer while the tank-supported 25th Marines to the south served as the defensive anvil. By dark on March 8, the division was down to 40 percent combat efficiency and had lost many experienced officers and noncoms. Then at 11 P.M., some thousand Japanese Navy personnel, cut off from Kuribayashi's control, counterattacked the junction of the 23rd and 24th Marines in Iwo Jima's only *banzai* attack. The fighting went on all night; at daybreak, 800 Japanese bodies were found. The night's attack cost the Marines 90 killed and 257 wounded, but it eliminated most of the enemy force holding the eastern part of the island.

On March 9, more than 300 B-29s from the Marianas dumped 1,665 tons of fire bombs on wind-swept Tokyo. This most destructive bombing mission of the war destroyed 16 square miles of the Japanese capital and killed nearly 84,000 people.

On March 10, the 23rd Marines gained 700 yards, "an enormous amount of ground . . . by Iwo standards";[96] and patrols reached the east coast near Tachiiwa Point. The 25th Marines completely surrounded Turkey Knob. Japanese resistance on eastern Iwo Jima was virtually finished.

Now, the job was to clean up fiercely defended pockets that no longer had any central command direction. The Japanese stayed in their pillboxes and caves and made the Marines pay. There were few Marines left who had landed on D-Day; and the replacements, although willing, were new to battle and often felt they were working and fighting with strangers. By March 16, the 3rd Division at terrific cost cleaned up the strongpoint known as Cushman's Pocket and reached Kitano Point.

The 5th Division still faced Lt. Gen. Kuribayashi's final stronghold in the gorge at the northwestern end of the island. Here, artillery was useless. Each Japanese had to be killed at close range by flamethrowing tanks and riflemen. Pvt. Franklin E. Sigler of Glen Ridge, New Jersey, took over his rifle squad and led it against a gun position that had held up his company for days. He wiped out the gun's crew with grenades and in a one-man assault continued the attack. Although severely wounded, he directed fire on the Japanese caves and carried three wounded squad members to safety. He received the Medal of Honor.

Although Iwo Jima was officially declared secured at 6 P.M. on March 16, the next day (D plus 26) the Marines fought in the 700-yard-long gorge that had many rock outcroppings and all its approaches covered by well-hidden machine-gun and rifle fire. On March 21, the Marines in the gorge finally destroyed the enemy command post with four tons of explosives. But Lt. Gen. Kuribayashi had already moved out to another cave nearer the sea. By March 24, the enemy pocket was squeezed into an area

50 by 50 yards. Then, the exhausted Marines sealed the remaining caves. The general's body was never found.

Still, on March 26, some 200 Japanese on the western coast attacked Marine and Army units and an Army field hospital. Seabees, Army Air Corps and medical personnel and the Negro troops of the Corps Shore Party, who "conducted themselves with marked coolness and courage,"[97] broke the enemy attack. But it had killed 53 Americans and wounded 119. Pvt. James M. Whitlock and Pvt. James Davis of the all-Negro 26th Depot Company won the Bronze Star. And 1st Lt. Harry L. Martin of Bucyrus, Ohio, who rallied his men of the 5th Pioneer Battalion and killed four Japanese before he died, was the last Marine to earn the Medal of Honor on Iwo Jima.

As Admiral Nimitz said after the battle was won, "Among the Americans who served on Iwo Island uncommon valor was a common virtue."[98]

In April and May, 1,600 more Japanese were killed on the island.

The total of Marine casualties on Iwo Jima was 25,851. (Navy doctors and corpsmen suffered 738 dead and wounded with the Marines.) The enormous number of casualties was severely criticized back home.

Iwo Jima swiftly began serving the purpose for which so many had been sacrificed. The Seabees changed the face of the island; and before the end of the war, 2,500 Superfortresses made emergency landings on Iwo Jima. Army fighter planes started arriving on March 6, and VMTB-242 arrived from Tinian on March 9. By that summer, Japanese air power was so reduced that B-29s did not need fighter escorts; but still, 1,191 escort sorties and 3,081 strikes against targets in Japan were flown from Iwo Jima.

While the battle for Iwo Jima was still going on, Secretary Forrestal spoke of his "tremendous admiration and reverence for the guy who walks up the beaches and takes enemy positions with a rifle and grenades or his bare hands."[99] As other analysts put it: "to a greater degree than was necessary, taking Iwo Jima was like throwing human flesh against reinforced concrete."[100]

Said Holland Smith, "Iwo Jima was the most savage and the most costly battle in the history of the Marine Corps. Indeed, it has few parallels in military annals."[101]

13
The Last Battle:Okinawa

On the ships of the armada steaming north from Ulithi, the Marines lightened the pre-invasion tension with songs built on bad puns: "After Rabaul Is Over," "Tarawa Boom-de-ay" and "Goodbye, Mama, I'm Off to Okinawa."

Easter Sunday 1945 promised to be one more bloody island steppingstone to Japan. The Marines could not know that Okinawa would be their last big battle in World War II. They only knew they were going to hit a beach within 350 miles of the enemy's homeland; it had to be rough.

The war seemed endless. Many of the Marines had already made one amphibious assault; some had made three. The war in Europe was being fought inside Hitler's Germany; the atomic bomb was still an untested secret; the Russians were not yet ready to attack the Japanese. Most military planners were convinced that the Allies would have to invade Japan itself and that the Japanese would fight to the last man.

The battle for Okinawa—rejoining MacArthur's and Nimitz's campaigns—would be the Pacific's biggest: 548,000 Americans of all the services taking part before it was over. Initially, the United States Tenth Army would land with a front of four divisions—two Army and two Marine—led by ill-starred Lt. Gen. Simon Bolivar Buckner, Jr., a Confederate general's son who had just spent four years in Alaska and was destined to die on Okinawa watching the Marines advance.

The Americans were headed for a number of surprises. Most astonishingly, the Japanese would not defend the invasion beaches at all—or the two airfields immediately behind them. Secondly, the invaders would fight for 82 days and suffer 75,000 casualties to secure the island; Lt. Gen. Mitsuru Ushijima's

Thirty-second Army would do its job superbly, eating up the clock of war. And, finally, more U.S. Navy men would die in battle than either soldiers or Marines, because bombers and some 1,900 kamikaze suicide planes would clobber the fleet offshore, sinking 36 ships (including 12 destroyers) and damaging 368 more—"The greatest material and personnel damage in the history of the United States Navy."[102] And in the air, 763 U.S. aircraft would be lost. If the Americans had not been able to mass overwhelming power—in the tradition of Grant and Sherman—this would have been a disaster at the very gates of Japan.

But Okinawa was a climactic victory. The Japanese were already tightly squeezed. The Battle of Leyte Gulf the previous October had given the United States control of the western Pacific. American submarines were sinking most of Japan's merchant shipping and cutting off its essential supplies. American bombers had been pounding Japan's great cities since November. And Japan's air power was stomped on so heavily that it did not effectively contest the Okinawa landing.

Before the invasion, the Navy's fast carriers went in close and bombed Japan's airfields. Marine squadrons were on board. From *Bennington*, Maj. Herman Hansen led Corsairs of VMF-112 against Kyushu's airfields; and Maj. Thomas E. Mobley, Jr., took VMF-123 over Hiroshima and Kure. From *Bunker Hill*, Maj. Herbert H. Long's Corsairs of VMF-451 helped punish the enemy carrier *Ryuho*. When *Franklin* was hit by two bombs 55 miles off Japan's coast on March 19—causing the worst naval inferno of the carrier war—among *Franklin's* 772 dead were 65 Marines of VMF-452 and VMF-214 ("Pappy" Boyington's old squadron). In the same fight, *Wasp* was also knocked out of the war with 302 casualties. Although the price was horrendously high, the U.S. carrier offensive cut down mass kamikaze attacks against the fleet off Okinawa until the troops were well ashore.

To meet the American juggernaut, the Japanese on Okinawa itself did the only thing they could. They dug into the rocky southern end of the island and waited. Lt. Gen. Ushijima commanded some 100,000 men, one-fifth of them Okinawans drafted into service. He dragged out the battle, hoping the kamikazes could destroy the U.S. fleet, isolate the Tenth Army and disrupt the invasion of Japan. The Japanese even threw in their last naval trump, the giant battleship *Yamato*, with fuel enough for only a one-way voyage, in the attempt to sink American ships.

Skinny and 60 miles long, Okinawa, the largest of the Ryukyu Islands, was to be the main advance base for the invasion of Japan. After the smothering heat of the South Pacific, the Americans at first would find it cool and climatically comfortable. The small neat farms, villages with red-tiled roofs, rolling countryside and umbrella-topped pines were attractive. The hills were dappled with large womb-shaped family tombs, many of which the Japanese converted into machine-gun strong-points.

Most of Okinawa's 500,000 peaceful people, ruled by Japan since 1875, lived on the southern third of the island. North of the two-mile-wide Ishikawa Isthmus bottleneck, the island was barren, wild and mountainous. The stubby northern Motobu Peninsula gave Okinawa its greatest width of 18 miles and pointed toward the island of Ie Shima, three and a half miles to the west.

South of the narrow isthmus rose a series of cross-island ridges, ideal for defense. The Japanese, using them effectively, dug caves and tunnels and entrenched mortars in the reverse slopes. To the south were the main towns: Naha, the capital and port on the west, and Shuri, the ancient citadel in the center. The Japanese had built three airfields on the west coast. The east coast offered two vast bays. The U.S. Navy wanted to assault the east coast and grab these inviting anchorages, but the Army and Marines argued for the rapid capture of the airfields. Winds and tides gave the final decision to the western Hagushi beaches north of Naha.

Heading into this final battle, the Marine Corps had 421,600 men and women in uniform. (By comparison, the Corps had started World War I with less than 14,000 Marines and at its end had 75,101.) There were now six Marine divisions organized equally into two corps. Each division's table of organization called for 856 officers and 16,069 enlisted men, plus assorted support and artillery units. Marine aviation in the Pacific had four wings, containing 16 air groups and 70 tactical squadrons. In addition, 44 squadrons were preparing to go overseas on new escort carriers. Women Reservists numbered 18,365— proudly freeing the equivalent of one division of men for combat. And 16,000 Navy doctors and corpsmen were assigned to the Marines. Much of this power would be brought to bear on Okinawa.

Before L-Day (the invasion of Iwo Jima, being planned at the same time, was designated D-Day), Maj. James L. Jones' Amphibious Reconnaissance Battalion invaded Keise Shima, five miles off Naha, on the night of March 27. They found no Japanese, and the Army set up 24 155mm guns to fire on southern Okinawa. The Army's 77th Division seized nine islands of Kerama Retto, killing 975 Japanese and giving the Navy an anchorage 15 miles west of Naha.

Starting on the twenty-sixth, kamikazes hit the invasion fleet. Coming in underneath the radar at dawn and dusk, they crashed six ships before L-Day, including Adm. Raymond A. Spruance's flagship *Indianapolis*; and near misses damaged 10 more.

The Navy blasted Okinawa with 27,226 rounds, 5-inch and larger, before the main landing. For the most part, this was wasted; the naval gunfire could have been better used on Iwo Jima. Minesweepers destroyed 257 mines; UDT swimmers blew up 2,700 posts embedded in the reef off the west coast landing area. Carrier aircraft flew 3,095 sorties against the island; and by March 29, Okinawa's air strength had been eliminated.

Sunday, April 1—Easter and April Fool's Day—dawned clear and calm and a pleasant 75 degrees. Five hundred carrier planes, including four Marine squadrons from *Bennington* and *Bunker Hill*, strafed and napalmed the landing beaches. Ten battleships, 9 cruisers, 23 destroyers and 177 gunboats pounded the beaches with 3,800 tons of shells. The 96th Infantry Division landed at the southern end of the beachhead, with the 7th Infantry Division on its left. They were the assault element of the Army's XXIV Corps commanded by the veteran Maj. Gen. John R. Hodge, USA.

Two Marine divisions landed to the Army's left, north of the Bishi River. They were organized into the III Amphibious Corps under Maj. Gen. Roy S. Geiger. The 5th and 7th Marines of the oldest Marine division, the 1st, landed on the right, with the 1st Marines in reserve. The 1st Division was led by Maj. Gen. Pedro A. del Valle, the Puerto Rico-born Naval Academy graduate who had commanded the artillery on Guadalcanal and Guam.

The Marines' newest division, the 6th, attacked on the far

northern end of the front, with the 22d and 4th Marines in assault and the 29th Marines (the last regiment formed in the war) in reserve. Some of the 6th Division were veterans starting their second Pacific tour. The division was commanded by Maj. Gen. Lemuel·C. Shepherd, Jr., the VMI graduate who had been wounded three times in France and served on Cape Gloucester and Guam.

The 2d Marine Division, the III Corps' floating reserve, made a diversionary feint at the southeastern side of the island to immobilize the defenders. Ironically, the 2d Division, which never landed, suffered the most casualties on L-Day when kamikazes hit two transports and killed 16 and wounded 37 Marines. The kamikaze threat sent the division back to Saipan.

The assault troops stormed the western beaches and climbed the seawall that they had feared would be worse than Tarawa's. Several Marine units landed on the wrong beaches; but the first wave was ashore by 8:32 A.M., and all eight Marine battalions, by 9 A.M. There were few casualties. By 1 P.M., the 4th Marines had secured Yontan Airfield and were plunging ahead with their tanks against light opposition. The 1st Marine Division also met only minor resistance from Japanese service troops and Okinawan home guards and advanced swiftly. The Army captured Kadena Airfield. By the end of L-Day, the Americans had carved out a beachhead four miles wide and two miles deep. The absence of opposition amazed and relieved everyone from generals to privates. In less than eight hours, 50,000 men had been landed with only 28 killed, 27 missing and 104 wounded in the four assault divisions. It looked deceptively easy.

On Monday, the 4th Marines, running into heavier resistance, killed 250 Japanese and advanced another 1,000 yards. The 1st Division still met only light opposition. The Marines' 6th Engineer Battalion repaired enough of Yontan Airfield so that afternoon the first artillery spotter plane landed, and by April 8, four-engine transports were evacuating the wounded to Guam.

While the 1st Marine Division cleaned up, the 6th Marine Division wheeled north toward the Ishikawa Isthmus; and the Army divisions swung south. On L-Day plus two, they bisected the island. No one yet knew where the main body of Japanese was holed up.

It was not all a cakewalk. The terrain grew more rugged toward the north. On the second day, L Company, 22d Marines, ran into trouble. As it entered a deep ravine, the whole hillside blazed with enemy fire. The company commander, Capt. Nelson C. Dale, was severely wounded; six Marines fell, and a machine-gun team was destroyed before it could fire a shot. Lt. Daniel B. Brewster's 2d Platoon was isolated. Six Marines were killed trying to reach it before Sgt. Otis Thorpe got through. Pfc. Anthony Caso crawled back to report the location of the enemy guns. Several corpsmen were killed trying to help the wounded. Lt. Marvin D. Perskie now led the company to save the men up front. The Marines dashed forward, blasting caves and killing the enemy. Only ten of Brewster's platoon walked out.

Tuesday night, the 6th Division was anchored at the base of the isthmus—12 days ahead of schedule—and by Thursday, held a line across the northern end of the isthmus. Ishikawa had a magnificent beach; the Marines swam, roasted pigs and chickens and "liberated" horses to carry their mortars and ammunition. The 1st Division occupied the Katchin Peninsula on the east coast. But the Army to the south started to encounter strong enemy outposts and massed artillery fire and had to throw back a counterattack. By the end of the first week, the XXIV Corps had been stopped.

On April 10, the Army's 27th Division landed; and there were 160,000 American troops on Okinawa. But the 2d Marine Division, veterans of Guadalcanal and Tarawa, was shipped back to Saipan, "a move which turned out to be unwise."[103] American Intelligence was seriously underestimating the enemy's strength.

Off the east coast, Major Jones' reconnaissance battalion scouted six islands guarding Nagagusuku Wan (later to be called Buckner Bay). Elements of the 27th Division wiped out the defenders on Tsugen Shima there and opened up the east coast for the unloading of supplies. By April 11, a half million tons of cargo had been put ashore on Okinawa.

On L-Day plus one, Maj. Gen. Francis P. Mulcahy, USMC, set up the command post for the Tenth Army's land-based Tactical Air Force. MAG-31 began operating from Yontan; and MAG-33, from Kadena. Marine aviators got back into the Marine war at Okinawa. They flew some close support for the ground forces—their prime intended mission—but mostly they battled

379

the intense and continuous air counteroffensive that the Japanese hurled against the American and British warships.

The first major kamikaze raid—the war's largest—struck on April 6 and 7 with 699 planes, of which 355 were suiciders. They sank six ships and seriously damaged 10. On April 7, VMF-311—flying Corsairs with the new 20mm cannon instead of .50 caliber machine guns—scored the Marines' first kamikaze kill.

That same day, the battleship *Yamato*, venturing toward Okinawa without air cover, was sunk by the carrier fliers. It was a Navy show; but one Marine, Lt. Kenneth E. Huntington, raced through antiaircraft fire and stuck his bomb on *Yamato's* forward turret.

In Tokyo on that same April 7, Gen. Kuniaki Koiso resigned as prime minister and the aged Adm. Kantaro Suzuki was chosen to replace him and find a way out of the war. Wrote historian Samuel Eliot Morison: "It is a sad reflection that this costly operation [Okinawa], and everything that followed until 16 August, was unnecessary from any point of view but that of keeping 'face' for the military leaders who had started the war."[104]

The next major kamikaze raid came on April 12 and 13 with 185 suicide planes. Major Hansen shot down three kamikazes to become an ace and win the Navy Cross. Lt. John M. Callahan destroyed three enemy fighters in five minutes. And Maj. Archie G. Donahue got five kills to bring his total for the war to 14.

In the big raid of April 15 and 16 with 165 enemy planes, Lt. William E. Eldridge shot down four suiciders and Capt. Floyd C. Kirkpatrick and Lt. Selva E. McGinty, three each. At dusk on April 22, 80 Japanese planes attacked the ships on the radar picket line; and Navy and Marine pilots shot down 54. Maj. Jefferson D. Dorroh destroyed six planes and Maj. George C. Axtell, Jr., and Lt. Jeremiah J. O'Keefe got five each.

Meanwhile, on the ground the 6th Marine Division discovered that the enemy force in the north had chosen to make its stand in the mountains of the Motobu Peninsula up the west coast. On April 8, the 29th Marines attacked the peninsula and found the enemy concentrated in a complex cave system centered around 1,200-foot Mount Yaetake. The terrain was so rugged and mines and roadblocks so numerous that tanks were useless. The 4th Marines joined the 29th in the most strenuous kind of mountain fighting.

Battling at short range and blowing up caves and pillboxes, the 4th Marines attacked the Yaetake hill mass early on April 14. To the Marines the enemy seemed like phantoms; hidden from sight, they picked off the officers and anyone with a map or a pistol. The next day, small, tough Col. William J. Whaling, the expert jungle fighter from Guadalcanal and Cape Gloucester, took over the 29th Marines from Col. Victor F. Bleasdale, a highly-decorated veteran who had received the Navy Cross and a battlefield commission long ago in France.

The Marines attacked Mount Yaetake from three sides. The 1st Battalion, 22d Marines filled the gap between the 4th and 29th Marines and reached Yaetake's western slopes. A twenty-year-old squad leader in the 4th Marines, Cpl. Richard E. Bush of Glasgow, Kentucky, led his men through artillery fire to seize a crucial ridge. Seriously wounded, Bush was dragged behind rocks with other wounded men. A grenade landed among them. Bush pulled it to him as it exploded. Amazingly, he lived; he was the only Marine to win the Medal of Honor on Motobu.

On the 16th, the 4th Marines' A and C Companies reached Yaetake's crest; and the Japanese threw them back. The Marines took the crest again. Fighting at close quarters, neither side could hold the summit. Finally, supporting fire enabled the Marines to stay. All available men, including Lt. Col. Fred D. Beans, the ex-Raider commanding the 1st Battalion, carried ammunition and water up to the assault troops just in time to meet a *banzai* attack. Seventy-five Japanese were annihilated; and by dark, the Marines held the mountain permanently.

When the 29th and 4th Marines reached the north coast on April 20, organized resistance on the peninsula was finished. The battle had cost the Marines 213 dead and 757 wounded.

On April 16, the 77th Infantry Division had assaulted Ie Shima, where the Japanese had three runways, and for six days fought 7,000 troops concealed in caves and bunkers. Ernie Pyle, the widely loved Hoosier war correspondent, was killed there on April 18 by a machine-gun burst. Pyle had gone ashore with the Marines on L-Day and had written this impression of the Marines on Okinawa:

> In peacetime, when the Marine Corps was a small outfit, with its campaigns high-lighted, everybody was a volunteer and you could understand why they felt so superior. But with the war the Marine Corps had grown by

hundreds of thousands of men. It became an outfit of ordinary people—some big, some little, some even draftees. It had changed, in fact, until marines looked to me exactly like a company of soldiers in Europe. Yet that Marine Corps spirit still remained. I never did find out what perpetuated it. The men were not necessarily better trained, nor were they any better equipped; often they were not so well supplied as other troops. But a marine still considered himself a better soldier than anybody else, even though nine-tenths of them didn't want to be soldiers at all. . . . No, marines don't thirst for battles. I've read and heard enough about them to have no doubts whatever about the things they can do when they have to. They are o.k. for my money, in battle or out.[105]

On April 21, the 77th Division captured the dead-volcano peak of Ie Shima; and the 22d Marines reached the northern tip of Okinawa.

In the meanwhile, on Friday, April 13, the men were told of the death of President Roosevelt. Many were deeply shaken. On Sunday, services were held throughout the vast invasion force. One young lieutenant, who had gone ashore with the 1st Marines on L-Day, wrote home to Doylestown, Pennsylvania: "By far the most serious event of the two weeks was the news of the death of President Roosevelt. The shock threw us all off balance and we spent all day yesterday in argument and meditation over the possible and probable future. We feel, quite naturally, more isolated than usual."[106]

On April 19, after days of preparatory bombardment, the three divisions of the XXIV Army Corps attacked down the width of the island, four miles north of Naha. The infantry-tank advance was supported by 324 pieces of artillery and 650 Navy and Marine planes with rockets, bombs, napalm and strafing. The Japanese defense was keyed on Shuri Ridge and dug into underground caves connected by elaborate tunnels. The attack failed to break through.

The Army fought for five days, measuring its progress in yards. Lt. Gen. Ushijima, under enormous pressure, pulled back to his inner ring of defenses around Shuri. He had anticipated such a move and built his defenses in concentric rings bristling with interlocking automatic weapons and artillery.

The failure of the April 19 attack and the heavy casualties in the following days raised doubts about Buckner's bulldog straight-ahead tactics. Commandant Vandegrift—who had recently been made the first four-star general on active duty in the Marine Corps—visited Okinawa on April 21; and he and Maj. Gen. Geiger tried to convince Buckner to bring back the 2d Marine Division and land it behind the enemy. Vandegrift promised to have it underway from Saipan in six hours. Vice Adm. Richmond K. Turner and Maj. Gen. Hodge supported his idea. But Buckner and the Tenth Army staff argued that a landing on the southeast coast might be another Anzio.

The American press became critical. Homer Bigart on Okinawa wrote, "Our tactics were ultraconservative. Instead of an end run, we persisted in frontal attacks."[107] And David Lawrence called it "a worse example of military incompetence than Pearl Harbor."[108] But the generals and admirals, fearing another Smith versus Smith scandal, did not oppose Buckner openly.

So the "slugging match" continued. And on May 1, the 1st Marine Division replaced the unfortunate 27th Infantry Division, which went north and released the 6th Marine Division for battle.

One sidelight: As they had previously in this war, the Marines had in their ranks Navajo Indians and used them to talk over the telephone in their own language so messages could not be intercepted by the enemy. They made possible swift, secret communication.

The arrival of the 1st Division before the Shuri defenses opened the second phase of the campaign for the Marines. With the Army, they now faced the main body of Japanese. Shuri was the core of the Japanese defenses, which were anchored at Naha on the west and Yonabaru on the east. Shuri itself was protected on three sides by cave-riddled ridges.

The 1st Division went into action on the west coast near the Machinato Airfield. In a driving rain, the Marines fought toward the Asa River but repeatedly had to pull back under heavy fire. In this battle, nineteen-year-old Corpsman Robert E. Bush of South Bend, Washington, with the 5th Marines, was giving plasma to a wounded Marine officer on a ridge crest when the enemy counterattacked. Holding the plasma bottle high with one hand, Bush fired his pistol at the oncoming enemy until his ammunition ran out. He was seriously wounded and lost his right eye, but he picked up a discarded carbine and shot six more Japanese charging over the hill.[109]

The enemy planned a major counterattack for the night of May 3–4, coordinated with a 159-plane kamikaze raid. The kamikazes did severe damage. In fighting them off, Lt. Thomas A. Gribbin II and Lt. Melvin S. Jarvis each received the Navy Cross for chasing suiciders through antiaircraft fire and shooting them down before they could reach their destroyer targets.

The enemy counterattack started when the Japanese stole up both coasts by barge to get in behind the American lines. Seven hundred men skirting the west coast landed by mistake too close to the 1st Marines and were destroyed. Those who landed elsewhere on the west coast were hunted down by the 1st Reconnaissance Company and war dog platoons. The east coast counterlanding penetrated the Army's lines but finally was smashed with 400 enemy killed. On May 5, the 1st Marines were dug in on commanding ground above the Asa River. All across the front, the Japanese had at least 6,200 dead. They had also lost 59 artillery pieces. The defeat of the counterattack had been "decisive."[110]

With the 1st Marines on May 7, Pvt. Dale M. Hansen of Wisner, Nebraska, coolly destroyed a pillbox with his bazooka; and when enemy fire wrecked his weapon, he grabbed a rifle, leaped across the crest of a ridge, shot four Japanese to death and beat off two others with the rifle butt. Then, he rampaged on to wipe out a mortar position and kill eight more Japanese. With the 5th Marines that same day, Pfc. Albert E. Schwab, a husky flamethrower operator from Tulsa, Oklahoma, advanced straight up a ridge under fire and burned out a machine-gun position that had his company pinned down. When a second machine gun opened fire, Schwab continued his attack and, although mortally wounded by the machine-gun's fire, destroyed the gun before he died.[111]

May 8 was V-E Day in Europe. But for the men on Okinawa, it was another day of fighting in a cold rain. As the only celebration of the war's end in Europe, at noon all the artillery and ships fired at the enemy.

The 6th Division moved in on the right of the 1st, and the 22d Marines replaced the 7th Marines on the high bluff overlooking the Asa River. On May 9, the 1st Marines started to clear the enemy off Hill 60; and the 5th Marines attacked the stubborn Awacha Pocket. In this fight, Maj. Paul H. Douglas, the future United States Senator from Illinois, was seriously wounded in the arm when serving as a stretcher bearer. The fifty-three-year-old economics professor had enlisted as a private and won the Bronze Star on Peleliu.

Late that night, the 6th Engineer Battalion threw a footbridge over the Asa River; and four companies of the 22d Marines scurried across the bridge and waded the river under fire. Then a two-man Japanese suicide team with satchel charges rushed the bridge and destroyed it and themselves. The Marines tried to enlarge their bridgehead south of the Asa but in six hours of fighting could advance only 150 yards. Although more companies waded the river, the Marines were unable to crack the enemy line. Badly needed tanks could not cross the muddy stream.

Teamwork of tanks and infantry was indispensable throughout the struggle for Okinawa. The Tenth Army lost 153 tanks during the campaign. It has been judged that "the tank-infantry team on Okinawa reached the apex of its development for the entire Pacific War."[112] Tanks and flamethrower tanks (nicknamed Zippos after the cigarette lighter) destroyed caves and bunkers at short range, while infantrymen and engineers removed mines and prevented the enemy from laying satchel charges on the tanks. When the tanks crushed a target, the riflemen cleaned it out and held the ground. Lt. Gen. Buckner called this technique of attacking fortified caves the "blowtorch and corkscrew" method: flamethrowers were the blowtorch and demolitions were the corkscrew.

South of the Asa River, C Company, 22d Marines was devastated in a two-day effort to take a small fortified coral hill called Charlie. After a brutal fight starting on May 10, one platoon was cut off. The company commander, Capt. Warren F. Lloyd, took Sgt. Joe Passanante's squad and rushed a machine-gun-armed tomb; in five minutes, half the squad was down. But the survivors seized the top of the little hill; it cost C Company's 256 men, 35 killed and 68 wounded. (Captain Lloyd, twenty-four years old, came from a Marine family; his father, three brothers and brother-in-law were all Marines.)

May 10 also saw one of the war's most spectacular Marine air feats. Capt. Kenneth L. Reusser and his wingman, 1st Lt. Robert R. Klingman, of VMF-312, were flying on combat air patrol over Ie Shima when they intercepted a Nick fighter at 38,000 feet. Using the last of his ammunition, Reusser shot up the enemy's left wing and tail. Klingman's guns froze at the high altitude, but he made three attacks at the enemy plane. On the first, his Corsair's propeller almost cut off the Nick's rudder and sawed into the rear gunner's cockpit. The second pass severed the rudder and ripped the right stabilizers; the final approach cut off the stabilizer. The Nick went into a spin and lost both its wings. Klingman landed his plane at Kadena out of gas and on its belly.

On May 10 and 11, the Japanese attacked the American fleet with 217 planes, including 104 kamikazes. They knocked the carrier *Bunker Hill* out of the war; among the 389 men killed were 29 Marines. In this fight, Marine pilots shot down four enemy planes; one went to Capt. James E. Swett, who ended the war with 15½ kills. Now, the only Marine fast carrier pilots left were on *Bennington*. When she sailed for Leyte Gulf in June, that ended World War II for the Marine squadrons on the fast carriers.

The Marines finally went into action from the escort carriers (CVEs) that Commandant Vandegrift had won for them. On the morning of May 10, 30 Marine planes flew the first strike, a close support mission, off *Block Island*. The second Marine CVE, *Gilbert Islands*, arrived on May 21. *Cape Gloucester* and *Vella Gulf* reached the Pacific war zone after the long battle for Okinawa was finished. "The CVEs were badly used during their brief taste of the Pacific war. . . . The boss of all the escort carriers at Okinawa, Rear Admiral Calvin T. Durgin, frowned upon the idea of the Marine specialization which had been agreed upon."[113] He would rarely assign the Marine squadrons to close combat support, for which these pilots had been specially trained.

The general American offensive that opened on May 11 began two weeks of bloody fighting. East to west across the island, the 96th Division fought for the hill mass called Conical

Hill; the 77th Division pounded at the Shuri heights in the center; the 1st Marine Division attacked toward Shuri up the crucial Wana Draw, and the 6th Marine Division faced its greatest test against Sugar Loaf Hill. The goal of the entire effort was to smash the enemy's Shuri defense line.

Under fire in the dark, the 6th Engineers assembled a Bailey bridge over the Asa River. At 11 A.M., Lt. Col. Robert L. Denig, Jr.,'s Marine tanks rumbled across and helped the 22d Marines leap ahead, take the high ground overlooking Naha and send patrols through the capital's suburbs to the banks of the Asato River. Inland, the 1st Division seized vital Dakeshi Ridge and finally cleaned up the Awacha Pocket.

By May 14, the Tenth Army reached the enemy's main line of resistance. The Marines could not break through the defenses west of Wana and northeast of Naha. Eighteen Marine tanks were knocked out and the infantry units took heavy losses.

The 22d Marines had come up against a steep, rectangular mound 300 yards long and 50 feet high; someone named it Sugar Loaf Hill. In front of it was open ground, murderous to cross. Sugar Loaf was actually the spearhead of a triangular group of three hills that formed the western anchor of the Shuri defense line. Sugar Loaf was backed on the southeast by Half Moon Hill, which rose to Shuri, and on the southwest by The Horseshoe. The complex blocked the way both left to Shuri and right to Naha. All three hills were laced with caves and tunnels and covered by interlocking fire. Any troops attempting to flank Sugar Loaf would be met by mortars hidden on the other two hills and by fire from Shuri heights.

When the 22d Marines reached Sugar Loaf on May 12, they had no clue to its importance. G Company led the first attack. Two platoons were pinned down; and Capt. Owen T. Stebbins, the company commander, and Lt. Dale W. Bair led the 40 men of the remaining platoon charging to the hill. One hundred yards later, only 12 men were still on their feet; both Stebbins' legs were chopped up by machine-gun bullets. Bair was hit in the left arm; but he rallied 25 Marines; and, led by tanks, they reached Sugar Loaf's top. While the men gathered up their wounded, Bair, six feet two and 225 pounds, stood on the crest with a light machine gun in his good arm, blasting any Japanese who fired on his men.

For two days, the 22d Marines repeatedly took Sugar Loaf and repeatedly were driven off. On May 14, the 22d was down to 62 percent of combat efficiency. But the division had been brought to a complete halt, and the regiment was ordered to take Sugar Loaf that day at any cost. F and G Companies tried and failed. At 5 P.M., they were sent forward again, supported by E Company's fire. By 7:30, three of their four tanks had been destroyed; of the 150 men who had started the assault, only 44 could still fight. They clung to the base of the hill under mortar fire; grenades rolled down on them. Maj. Henry A. Courtney, Jr., the 2d Battalion's twenty-eight-year-old executive officer from Duluth, Minnesota, led the men around the hill under heavy fire. He blasted out caves as he went; and, at 11 P.M., reinforced by 26 men and an LVT load of grenades, they stormed the crest, hurling their grenades. At midnight, Courtney saw the enemy gathering for a *banzai* attack less than 100 yards away. He instantly led an attack, killed many of the enemy and forced the rest back into their caves. While organizing the crest's defense and helping his wounded, Courtney was killed by an enemy mortar burst. He was awarded the Medal of Honor for "great personal valor."

At 2:30 A.M., K Company went up to support Courtney's 25 remaining men. Near the top, Cpl. Donald Golar, a red-headed former San Francisco longshoreman, fired his light machine gun until his ammunition was gone. Of the dozen Marines near him, only he and two riflemen were left. Golar emptied his pistol at the Japanese and then flung it at them. He hurled grenades taken from fallen Marines and fired a dead Marine's BAR until it jammed. He and Pvt. Donald Kelly started carrying wounded Marines to safety, when Golar was killed.

By 8 A.M., Courtney's last eight men were ordered off the hill. First Lt. George E. Murphy, who had played end for Notre Dame, led a platoon from D Company up Sugar Loaf. The platoon was decimated when the enemy charged the crest. Murphy was hit in the back by a mortar fragment. He turned around and emptied his pistol at the Japanese before he fell dead. By noon, the few survivors of K Company and the 11 left from Murphy's platoon were taken off Sugar Loaf.

For two days, the 29th Marines, on the 22d's left, hurled themselves at Half Moon Hill under fire from Shuri's heights. Japanese howitzers knocked out several tanks. Lt. Col. Jean W.

Moreau, commander of the 1st Battalion, was severely wounded by an artillery shell. Cpl. John A. Spazzaferro was hit by six bullets before he withdrew with the last two men of his 14-man squad. His platoon leader, Lt. Edgar C. Greene, who called Spazzaferro "the toughest guy I ever saw,"[114] was shot in the side and fell by the railroad track that ran between Half Moon and Sugar Loaf. Greene saw the corporal still firing his Tommy gun despite his wounds. Then Spazzaferro collapsed 10 feet from Greene. Four Japanese approached; Greene played dead. One Japanese took Greene's wristwatch but withdrew his hand from Greene's pocket covered with blood. After the Japanese had moved on, Greene called "Spazz!" and was relieved to see the tough corporal grin. The two men lay there until tanks rescued them the next day.

By the end of May 16, I Company, 22d Marines, reached the top of Sugar Loaf with the help of tanks; but when counterattacks forced the 29th Marines off the north slope of Half Moon, I Company, depleted by casualties, was in danger and had to come back from Sugar Loaf. The 6th Marine Division regarded May 16 as its bitterest day on Okinawa; casualties were high. The 22d Marines was down to 40 percent combat efficiency, and the 29th Marines took over the attack on Sugar Loaf. By now the entire Tenth Army had 3,963 killed, 18,258 wounded and 302 missing. Okinawa, which had seemed so easy at first, had changed into a brutal battle.

A young lieutenant in a 1st Marines' rifle company, which had four of its seven officers out of action since coming south, wrote home: "You can be as reckless as possible and never get hit—or be too careful and get blown to bits. I take the middle way—going in the open when I have to and staying in my holes the rest of the time."[115]

On May 17, Maj. Gen. Shepherd organized an attack by Colonel Whaling's 29th Marines on all three hills at once. E Company reached Sugar Loaf's crest four times and each time was driven off. The company had 160 men killed and wounded. But by now the enemy had also been badly hurt. Lt. Col. William G. Robb's 2d Battalion attacked Sugar Loaf again the next morning. Capt. Howard L. Mabie of D Company designed a skillful, tank-led double envelopment; and although six tanks were disabled, the battalion secured Sugar Loaf at last.

The Marines had turned the corner; but in nine days, the 6th

Division had a total of 2,662 battle casualties and 1,289 "non-battle" casualties from combat fatigue and exhaustion. The cost had been "tremendous."[116]

On May 19, Col. Alan Shapley's 4th Marines replaced the 29th. Bringing the rested 4th Marines out of reserve was crucial. G Company seized the western end of Half Moon; E Company enveloped its eastern flank. And before the day was out, the 3rd Battalion had taken the north slope of The Horseshoe and that night held it against a fierce counterattack.

While the 6th Division had been battling into the Sugar Loaf complex, the 1st Division on its left was fighting forward under the guns on the Shuri hill mass. The 1st Division and the 77th Infantry Division came up against the Wana defenses just northwest of Shuri. Behind Wana Ridge was a steep gorge, the Wana Draw, through which flowed the southern branch of the Asa River. Heavily fortified Hill 55 guarded the western entrance to the draw. Eastward toward Shuri, Wana Draw narrowed under steep dominating cliffs, 200 to 300 feet high.

For days, the 5th Marines tried to penetrate Wana Draw. The 7th Marines fought up the western nose of Wana Ridge. Tanks and howitzers pounded the high ground. The 1st Battalion was reduced to a single company, and the 3rd Battalion lost 12 officers in its rifle companies. In five days before Wana Ridge, the 7th Marines suffered 51 killed and missing, 387 wounded and 91 "non-battle" casualties. On May 19, the 1st Marines replaced that battered regiment.

The 1st Marines attacked the northern slope of Wana Ridge and after a tough grenade battle seized the ridge top, except for the summit of 110 Meter Hill at the ridge's eastern end. By May 20, the 5th Marines had taken Hill 55 at the western end of Wana Draw and were striking into the draw. But as long as the enemy held 110 Meter Hill, it was impossible to stay in Wana Draw or approach Shuri itself.

On the night of May 21, the rains began; and the battle became deadlocked in an oozing sea of mud. The mud clogged weapons, immobilized vehicles, infected wounds and fouled food and clothes.

Up to this time, the XXIV Corps to the east of the Marines had hammered at Shuri's defenses. The 77th Division in the center, measuring its gains in yards, finally pushed into the outskirts of Shuri. On the far left, the 96th Division took Conical Hill and turned the enemy's eastern flank. On May 22, Maj. Gen. Hodge put in the 7th Division, which seized the high ground south of the east coast port of Yonabaru in a surprise night attack. But then the rains made the roads impassable; and the Army, like the Marines, bogged down. The rain continued for nine days; the whole front became a swamp—stalemated.

Two battalions of the 4th Marines waded the ankle-deep Asato River on May 23; but the next day, the rains had made the Asato a chest-high torrent. Finally, the 4th and 22d Marines crossed over and burst into the ruins of Naha, fighting Japanese holed up in shells of buildings and in the tombs on the ridges.

Under the full moon on the night of May 24, as part of a mass air attack, the Japanese sent a suicide force to cripple Yontan and Kadena Airfields. One enemy plane got through and made a wheels-up landing on the Yontan runway. Some 10 soldiers poured out, threw grenades and explosives and sprayed the area with small arms fire. Two Marines were killed and 18 wounded, probably mostly by wild friendly fire. The raiders destroyed eight planes, damaged 26 others and blew up 70,000 gallons of gasoline before they were killed. It was a flamboyant gesture.

By May 28, the rains finally stopped; and slowly the Americans began to close in on Shuri. On Tuesday, May 29, at 7:30 A.M., the 5th Marines assaulted Shuri Ridge despite heavy mortar fire and took the crest. Lt. Col. Charles W. Shelburne of the 1st Battalion asked permission to attack Shuri Castle, which was 800 yards to the east in the 77th Infantry Division's zone. Maj. Gen. del Valle approved the move at once, estimating that the 77th Division would need two more days of hard fighting to reach the castle. Capt. Julian D. Dusenbury led his A Company through the mud into the ruins of the castle at 10:15. Dusenbury, who came from Claussen, South Carolina, hoisted over the parapet the Confederate flag he carried in his helmet. Buckner must have smiled, but del Valle promptly sent over the 1st Division flag that had flown on Guadalcanal, New Britain and Peleliu. The Army was more than annoyed at the Marines. But the deadly Wana Draw had been bypassed, and the ancient Okinawan citadel was now in American hands.

In the end, the castle had fallen so swiftly because Lt. Gen.

Ushijima, with his flanks crushed, had started pulling his main force out of the Shuri defense line to the far southern tip of the island. He left behind a tough rear guard that delayed the Americans. Artillery and naval gunfire pounded the retreating Japanese. Ushijima set up his headquarters inside Hill 89, 11 miles south of Shuri. It would take three more weeks of fighting to secure Okinawa.

The rains began again, and the Tenth Army's pursuit bogged down in the mud until, on the last day of May, the weather broke out into welcomed sunshine; and Marines and soldiers occupied the city of Shuri. By now, the Tenth Army had captured all but a few square miles of Okinawa and killed an estimated 62,500 Japanese. Lt. Gen. Buckner's army had lost 5,655 killed and missing and 23,909 wounded. The Marines' ranks were filled with individual replacements; and the inexperienced men seriously diluted the level of combat effectiveness and the sense of teamwork. The replacement system was simply not effective when casualties were as heavy as they were in this prolonged battle.

While the Army and the 1st Marine Division pushed southward after Ushijima, the 6th Marine Division attacked the Oroku Peninsula across the Kokuba estuary south of Naha. The peninsula was the site of Naha's airfield, and its high ground dominated Naha harbor. The 4th Marines led the shore-to-shore amphibious assault early on June 4.

Fortunately, the Japanese had decided to defend the center of the peninsula, not the beaches. The 4th Marines encountered only mud, mines and scattered machine-gun fire as they raced from their LVTs 300 yards to high ground. The 29th Marines followed them ashore. The 6th Reconnaissance Company landed on Ono Yama, the island in the middle of the estuary, and protected the engineers while they built a 340-foot Bailey bridge from Naha to the island and then to the peninsula.

On June 5, Okinawa was whipped by a severe typhoon that damaged more American ships than any kamikaze attack. By the next day, the Marines on Oroku Peninsula began running into defenses supported by machine guns and 20mm cannon. The Japanese, led by Rear Adm. Minoru Ota, who had fought the Marine Raiders on New Georgia, were dug into the hills. The Marines slowly encircled them and then closed in on their caves.

To prevent the Japanese from escaping, the 22d Marines blocked the base of the peninsula.

The fight in the center of the peninsula was vicious, and the 4th Marines' casualties mounted. The 29th Marines could make little progress in hard fighting. Pvt. Robert M. McTureous, Jr., of Altoona, Florida, a replacement who had been with H Company only seven days, saw stretcher bearers hit by machine-gun fire while they carried out the wounded. Filling his shirt with grenades, the 138-pound McTureous charged in a furious one-man attack and smashed grenades into the cave entrances from which came the heaviest fire. He returned for another supply of grenades and went out again and silenced "a large number of hostile guns." He was seriously wounded in the stomach but crawled back 200 yards to the Marines' lines before calling for help. He died four days later and was awarded the Medal of Honor posthumously.

By June 9, the Japanese were pressed into a small pocket; and the next night, the survivors tried to break out of the trap. Tanks and eight battalions of Marines pounded them; and by June 12, the last enemy strongpoint was taken. The survivors began fleeing. First Lt. Spencer V. Silverthorne, a Williams College graduate who had served as a language officer since Bougainville, working under fire, persuaded 56 Japanese to surrender. Pfc. Harry M. Tuttle, an interpreter, found as he said, "Their greatest fear was of maltreatment at the hands of their captors."[117] Fear rather than dishonor was clearly the reason that many Japanese fought to the death or committed suicide when cornered.

By the fourteenth, organized resistance on Oroku Peninsula was declared at an end. More than 4,000 Japanese had been killed in the 10-day battle. The Marines had 1,608 casualties and 30 tanks disabled.

Meanwhile, the XXIV Corps and the 1st Marine Division were slogging southward from the Naha-Yonabaru Valley toward the island's highest hill mass. Tanks and trucks were mired in the rain and mud until the skies cleared on June 7. Toward the south, resistance stiffened. On June 10, the 7th Marines waded 400 yards across the mouth of the muddy Mukue River, scaled a seawall and stormed through the heavily mined ruins of the town of Itoman. Directly to the east, the 1st Battalion, 1st

Marines had to take Yuza Hill. C Company attacked in the face of machine-gun and artillery fire and lost 70 of its 175 men; all of the company's officers were killed or wounded. The battalion took the hill by noon; but there were so many replacements that, as one Marine said, "nobody knew anybody else."[118]

A small-plane strip was leveled north of Itoman; and in the next dozen days, VMO-3 and VMO-7 flew out 641 wounded. The eight-minute flight to the hospital replaced the long rough ride in an ambulance Jeep and saved lives.

Now the 7th Marines faced the defenders of Kunishi Ridge, "the most frantic, bewildering and costly close-in battle on the southern tip of Okinawa."[119] This coral ridge ran northwest to southwest for 1,500 yards and formed the western anchor of the enemy's last heavily defended line. Both slopes of Kunishi Ridge were full of caves, fortified tombs and weapon emplacements. Between the 7th Marines and the ridge lay a broad valley of grasslands and rice paddies, giving the defenders unobstructed lanes of fire and the attackers little cover.

Col. Edward W. Snedeker proposed a night attack; and at 3:30 A.M. on June 12, his 7th Marines tried to cross the valley. C and F Companies, leading the assault, achieved complete surprise and seized a piece of the ridge's crest. B and G Companies, sent to reinforce them in daylight, were stopped. The lead companies were isolated and badly in need of ammunition, rations and medical supplies.

Darkness allowed the rest of the attackers to reach the height. By the next dawn, the 7th Marines were on the ridge and the Japanese were in it. Enemy snipers were deadly. One marksman killed or wounded 22 Marines before he was located and dispatched. The isolated Marines had to be supplied by tanks and air drops. Sherman tanks shuttled back and forth, carrying up supplies and reinforcements and taking down the badly wounded. Some of the wounded had to be strapped to the tanks' sides, with sandbags protecting them against enemy fire. Twenty-one tanks were destroyed or damaged; the Marines fought from cave to cave for four days.

The 2d Battalion, 1st Marines assaulted Kunishi Ridge at 3 A.M. on June 14. Flares, shot up by mistake, exposed the men to the enemy. Two platoons from E Company and one from G Company made the crest but were cut off by heavy enemy fire.

Casualties mounted rapidly and tanks came up to support the men. Even water had to be carried up by the tanks.

First Lt. Marcus H. Jaffe, who had recently taken over command of G Company, wrote home:

> I have taken the company up against two objectives. The first we cracked with only light casualties. The second was a bitch all the way around. The attack was planned badly from above, supply and evacuation was almost an impossibility, and we had some damn bad luck when a f——d up Army M7 began firing its 105 into the troops. . . . The two assault platoons did a great job in working up to and securing their objective—then the tide turned and not a thing seemed to go right. I know now that in the prosecution of war on this scale—with the terrible potential to kill possessed by our weapons—the inadequacies of the human mind and body cannot prevent needless slaughter. Fortunately for my peace of mind (though the sorrow will exist for others) the personnel of this company and battalion has changed so much in the past month that very few of the dead are good friends of mine.[120]

Three days later, he wrote that of the 21 officers who had started out in his battalion's line companies, only six were left.

After dark on June 15, the 2d Battalion, 5th Marines relieved the shot-up 1st Marines; and the 7th Marines were also thrown into the battle. By the end of June 16, Kunishi Ridge was painstakingly cleaned out; it cost the Marines 1,150 casualties.

The 6th Marine Division, freed from the Oroku Peninsula, now joined the battle in the south. The 22d Marines promptly attacked and seized Mezado Ridge beyond Kunishi Ridge near the west coast. There was no reserve division to relieve the exhausted Marines. Later, Maj. Gen. Geiger recommended that a Marine corps be built of three divisions so one could always be rested.

Some worn-out Marines finally received relief when Col. Clarence R. Wallace's 8th Marines of the 2d Division entered the lines. The regiment had been brought back from Saipan at the end of May and had occupied two islands north of Okinawa without opposition. On June 18, as the Tenth Army was facing a weakening defense, the 8th Marines demonstrated the value of fresh troops and advanced 1,400 yards. Early that morning, Lt. Gen. Buckner came forward to watch the 8th Marines go into action. At the regimental observation post, a Japanese shell drove a piece of coral into Buckner's chest, wounding him mortally.

Admiral Nimitz immediately gave Maj. Gen. Geiger command of the Tenth Army. The veteran Marine aviator became for a few days the first Marine officer to command a field army. He was promoted to lieutenant general and led the Tenth Army in the final days of the battle for Okinawa. On June 23, Gen. Joseph W. Stilwell, USA, who had commanded U.S. forces in the China-Burma-India Theater, took over from Geiger, who was named commanding general, Fleet Marine Force, Pacific.

Before Stilwell arrived, the Tenth Army pressed the remaining Japanese into three small pockets. On the west, the 5th and 8th Marines reached the sea at the bottom of the island on June 19. While the 22d Marines were eliminating resistance at Mezado Ridge, its commander, Col. Harold C. Roberts, was killed by a sniper. Pfc. Nicholas Woloshuk, Jr., picked off the man who shot him. Roberts was awarded his third Navy Cross. The big native New Yorker had earned his first at Belleau Wood, where he served as a Navy corpsman with the Marines, and after being commissioned in the Marine Corps, had won his second in 1928 on Nicaragua's Coco River.

The 29th Marines on the extreme western flank reached the tip of Okinawa on June 20, but the 4th Marines still had to battle the enemy in the Kiyamu hill mass. June 21 was the final day of the organized campaign, and the Marines spent it in heavy fighting. In the rifle platoons, there were few Marines left who had landed on Easter Sunday.

At 1:05 P.M. on June 21, Lt. Gen. Geiger declared Okinawa secured, although the Army was still crushing a Japanese last-ditch stand. At noon on June 22, Lt. Gen. Ushijima committed *hara-kiri* on a cliff overlooking the sea.

Even on that day, the kamikazes struck Okinawa again. Capt. Robert Baird of VMF(N)-533 downed two and became the first Marine night fighter ace of the war. A suicider was also shot down by Capt. Kenneth A. Walsh, who had won the Medal of Honor in the Solomons and had not had a kill since 1943. This raised Walsh's wartime total to 21 and placed him fourth among the Marine Corps' 125 aces after Boyington (28), Foss (26) and the late Robert M. Hanson (25).

By the end of the campaign, a fourth Marine Aircraft Group, MAG-14, had been brought up to Okinawa. And early in June, Maj. Gen. Louis E. Woods had taken over as commander of the 2d MAW from Maj. Gen. Mulcahy. In all of the Okinawa battle, 700 Marine planes had participated. Eighty-six pilots and 11 crewmen were killed in combat flights; 24 aviation Marines were killed on the ground, and 156 were wounded.

After organized resistance ended, General Stilwell ordered southern Okinawa mopped up. The Americans finally counted 107,539 enemy dead on Okinawa. Intelligence judged that total enemy casualties numbered 142,000, of which 42,000 were Okinawan civilians; but all such figures were only guesses.

American casualties could be counted more accurately. The Tenth Army had 7,613 killed and missing and 31,807 wounded or injured in action. In addition, it had 26,221 "non-battle" casualties. This latter category consisted chiefly of neuropsychiatric cases. Said the official Army history of the campaign, "The most important cause of this was unquestionably the great amount of enemy artillery and mortar fire, the heaviest concentrations experienced in the Pacific war. Another cause of men's nerves giving way was the unending close-in battle with a fanatical foe. The rate of psychiatric cases was probably higher on Okinawa than in any previous operation in the Pacific."[121] This was stark commentary on the failure to provide for the relief of combat troops during the long Okinawan battle.

The Marine Corps (and its attached naval medical personnel) had a total of 20,020 casualties at Okinawa, of which 3,561 were battle deaths. The Navy had 4,907 killed in action, more than either of the other services.

The invasion of Japan itself was still ahead. The 6th Marine Division shipped out of Naha for Guam to get ready for this next fearsome operation. And rumors swept the 1st Division that it was going to Hawaii. As the division historian recorded:

> It had been nearly two years [from the time the Division left Melbourne] since some of the men had tasted a civilian environment. For a great majority it had been

something over a year. There was the desire to tie up, if possible, alongside a woman. But there were other desires, too—to flick a light switch, to see road signs and civilian cars, to watch children at play, to be able to spend money, to drink a *cold* beer, or "a good glass of milk."[122]

But to everyone's horror the division was sent up to make camp on Okinawa's Motobu Peninsula. The division had been fighting the Japanese longer than any other American division. Now, it expected to fight in the streets of Tokyo.

14
The End of the War

The Pacific war pounded to a finish. Japan's naval power had been smashed; but its armies of 4.7 million men had not been conquered, and 1.5 million soldiers waited to defend Japan itself. American Intelligence figured that to invade Japan would cost a very minimum of 100,000 Americans killed and wounded.

Two invasions were planned against Japan. The first, named Olympic, would attack the southern home island, of Kyushu on November 1, 1945. The second, called Coronet, would land on Honshu's Tokyo Plain in March 1946. The great offensive was approaching its climax.

All six Marine divisions were to penetrate Japan. Maj. Gen. Harry Schmidt's V Amphibious Corps, with the 2d, 3rd and 5th Marine Divisions and three air wings, would join ten Army divisions attacking the southern end of Kyushu. A grand total of 815,548 troops would participate in the operation. The Japanese were estimated to have 450,000 troops on the island; and they had still hoarded 11,000 planes, including 5,000 kamikazes. The later assault on Honshu would be made by 11 Army divisions and the III Marine Amphibious Corps, now led by Maj. Gen Keller E. Rockey. The commander of the entire invasion would be General of the Army MacArthur.

Not all American military leaders were convinced that these invasions of Japan were necessary. In the main, the U.S. Army's generals believed that the Japanese army must be defeated and the home islands occupied. The naval members of the Joint Chiefs of Staff predicted that sea and air power would strangle Japan. Said Fleet Admiral William D. Leahy, Chief of Staff to Presidents Roosevelt and Truman, "I believed that a completely blockaded Japan would then fall by its own weight."[123]

399

That July, American air and sea power, striking day and night, lay siege to Japan. B-29s averaged 1,200 sorties a week. B-24s escorted by Marine Corsairs attacked from Okinawa.

But the political front outraced the military. On July 15, President Truman met with Stalin and Churchill at Potsdam, outside Berlin. And on the twenty-fourth he ordered the Army Air Forces to drop an atomic bomb on Japan on the first day after August 3 that weather conditions permitted.

The next step was to offer the Japanese the chance to surrender unconditionally without either invasion or atomic destruction. On July 26, the United States, the United Kingdom and the Republic of China issued the Potsdam Declaration. It promised that the Japanese people would not be enslaved, but it insisted that Japan be disarmed and occupied and its war-making power be destroyed. Two days later, Prime Minister Suzuki announced that Japan would continue to fight.

Events rushed ahead. On August 6, the B-29 "Enola Gay" rose from North Field, Tinian, and at 8:15 A.M. exploded its single atomic bomb over the city of Hiroshima. Bombing attacks against Japan by 550 B-29s and carrier aircraft followed. On August 8, the Soviet Union declared war on Japan and started to roll into Manchuria, Sakhalin Island and Korea. On August 9, a second atomic bomb swallowed Nagasaki in a mushroom-shaped cloud. On August 10, Japan asked for peace on the terms of the Potsdam Declaration, with the sole condition that the Emperor retain his throne. Three days of discussion followed; and then, Truman announced that the Emperor could stay, subject to the Supreme Commander of the Allied Powers. On August 14, Emperor Hirohito made the decision to surrender. At 6:15 A.M. on August 15, Fleet Admiral Nimitz ordered all offensive operations against Japan stopped at once. His message concluded with the warning: "Beware of Treachery." The war was done.

The cavalcade that had started for the Marines at Ewa and Pearl Harbor, at Wake and Corregidor was over. The hatred and the gut-churning fear could now subside. The dead would be remembered and then in time forgotten. The maimed would try to splice their lives together. Those who had fought and survived, the heroes and the cowards, would lie awake with their memories. The captains would savour their good fortune and regret their mistakes. And hundreds of thousands of men would feel only joy that the killing was finished, that they lived and could go home.

On the day that Emperor Hirohito surrendered, the 5,400 men of the 4th Marines loaded into transports at Guam and sailed the next evening for Japan. The Marines prepared their weapons, just in case; but Lt. Col. Fred D. Beans, now the regiment's commander, ordered them to lock their weapons, not to put a bullet in the chamber and not to fire unless fired upon.

The reborn 4th Marines, the regiment that had been forced to surrender at the war's beginning, was chosen to lead the Navy into Japan. Reinforced, it became the keystone of the Fleet Landing Force, which also included a provisional regiment of 2,000 Marines from 33 ships of the Third Fleet, a naval regiment of 956 sailors and a British battalion of 450 Royal Marines and sailors. The Fleet Landing Force was commanded by Marine Brig. Gen. William T. Clement, who had served in Shanghai with the old 4th Marines and under orders had escaped from Corregidor by submarine. Later, he had fought on Guam and Okinawa.

Clement's job was to occupy the Yokosuka naval base and airfield on the west side of the mouth of Tokyo Bay, while the Army's 11th Airborne Division landed at Atsugi Airdrome 14 miles southwest of Tokyo. Maj. Frank Carney led the 2d Battalion, 4th Marines ashore across the bay on Futtsu Cape at 5:58 A.M. on August 30 and claimed to be "the first American combat troops to set foot in Japan."[124]

There was no opposition; the Japanese cooperated completely. The 4th Marines moved inland from Yokosuka to establish a perimeter, and its patrols linked up with the 11th Airborne Division. By mid-afternoon, MacArthur, Nimitz and Halsey were all ashore.

The formal surrender ceremonies were held on Sunday, September 2, aboard the battleship *Missouri* in Tokyo Bay—in front of the 31-starred flag that Commodore Perry had carried into Tokyo Bay in 1853. From *Missouri's* flagstaff flew the flag that had flown over The Capitol in Washington on Sunday, December 7, 1941.

Lt. Gen. Geiger represented the Corps at the surrender; but

if any Marines expected to be the first to march in the streets of Tokyo, they were disappointed. That honor went to the 1st Cavalry Division, which had been the first into Manila.

MAG-31 commanded by Col. John C. Munn arrived from Okinawa at Yokosuka on September 7. Before Lt. Col. Beans relieved Brig. Gen. Clement, he witnessed a ceremony in which 120 released prisoners of war from the old 4th Marines received the colors of the new 4th Marines. Clement shook hands with Marines he had last seen on Corregidor.

By January 1946, the 1st and 2d Battalions, 4th Marines sailed for the United States and the headquarters detachment joined the 6th Marine Division at Tsingtao, China. The 3rd Battalion remained at Yokosuka as a guard battalion.

In the meanwhile, Maj. Gen. Schmidt's V Amphibious Corps occupied Kyushu with the 2d and 5th Marine Divisions. The 32d Infantry Division substituted for the 3rd Marine Division in order to leave one full Marine division in the Marianas. The 5th Marine Division began arriving at Sasebo on September 22. The next day, the 2d Marine Division landed at Nagasaki and curtained off the city's atom bomb–devastated section.

In December, the 5th Marine Division returned to the United States. By July 1946, the 2d Division turned over its responsibilities to the 24th Infantry Division and ended its involvement with Japan that had begun on Guadalcanal.

On September 4, Marines returned to Wake Island, scene of their heroic defense at the war's beginning. The first man ashore was Col. Walter L. J. Bayler, who had become known as "the last man off Wake Island." Brig. Gen. Lawson H. M. Sanderson, commanding general of the 4th Marine Aircraft Wing, received the surrender of 1,262 Japanese military and naval personnel. Another 1,288 had died of starvation, and 600 had been killed by American bombs. An unknown number of Americans were found buried in two common graves.

Other bypassed Japanese islands were also occupied. At Truk, 38,355 Japanese surrendered to Marine Brig. Gen. Robert Blake; and in the Ryukyus, 105,000 surrendered to General Stilwell.

The day before the 4th Marines landed at Yokosuka, special

naval rescue teams, with medical personnel and Marine security detachments, raced ahead to reach the prisoners of war in the many large camps in the Tokyo-Yokohama area. On August 29, the first 739 POWs, including those from the Shinagawa hospital camp, were taken on board the hospital ship *Benevolence.*

Weeks more were required before all the prisoners could be rescued from Manchuria, Korea, China, Formosa and other parts of Japan. Among thousands of Allies, 2,270 Marines had been captured by the Japanese. They were held in 33 camps throughout East Asia. Only 1,756 ever returned to the United States. The rest died or were killed in captivity.

In addition, the Germans captured four Marines in Europe, where they were working with the French underground for the Office of Strategic Services. Maj. Peter J. Ortiz (two Navy Crosses), Sgt. John P. Bodnar and Sgt. Jack R. Risler surrendered to the Gestapo south of Lake Geneva rather than have the local populace suffer reprisals. Another member of the unit, Sgt. Frederick J. Brunner, swam a river and escaped to a Resistance group. The Germans' fourth Marine prisoner, 2d Lt. Walter W. Taylor, was captured near Nice after he was knocked out by a grenade explosion.

Maj. Pierre Julien "Peter" Ortiz, the New York–born son of an editor of Paris *Vogue,* had been a prisoner of the Germans for 16 months before the United States entered the war. He received a direct Marine commission and was wounded in North Africa. In 1943, he parachuted into occupied France for the Office of Strategic Services (OSS) and helped sabotage German installations and free Allied prisoners, for which he received the first of his Navy Crosses. In 1944, he and five other Marines parachuted back into Europe. When the Germans threatened to shoot hostages until Major Ortiz surrendered, he gave himself up. Beaten and placed in solitary confinement, he tried to escape repeatedly and was finally liberated by Allied troops. Two movies were made about his exploits.

Few Marines served in Europe. Thirty landed with the Army in French North Africa on November 8, 1942, as part of Operation Torch; two were killed, and one was wounded. Three hundred six Marines participated in D-Day at Normandy, including four officers on Eisenhower's staff and enlisted men who acted as riflemen on shipboard and exploded floating mines in their ships' paths. Others worked 5-inch batteries during the North African and Normandy landings. And there was a Marine Barracks at

Londonderry, Northern Ireland. On August 29, 1944, Marine detachments from *Augusta* and *Philadelphia* landed on the islands of Ratonneau and If near Marseille and disarmed 700 Germans.

Among the Marines who served with the OSS, Capt. John Hamilton, who was actually the movie actor Sterling Hayden, jumped into Yugoslavia with Gunnery Sgt. John Harnicker and a Navy radio operator. Working with partisans, they provided for the rescue of Allied pilots downed in enemy-held territory. And Capt. Walter R. Mansfield, a demolitions expert, parachuted into Yugoslavia to help Tito's partisans blow up rails and bridges. Late in 1944, Mansfield dropped into China with Cpls. John Owens and Cedric Poland and ambushed Japanese truck convoys and troop detachments with Chinese guerrillas. Another Marine who worked with the Chinese guerrillas was Lt. Robert H. Barrow, who later played a dramatic part in the Korean war and in 1979 became Commandant of the Corps.

Most Marines imprisoned by the Japanese were captured early in the war; the rest were chiefly fliers who were shot down. "Pappy" Boyington, the war's leading Marine ace, was downed over Rabaul and imprisoned near Tokyo. He was repeatedly beaten, and the Japanese never reported his existence. Marine Lt. Donald Carlson, shot down over Tokyo, was kept in solitary confinement for 40 days and had all his teeth knocked out. Both men were liberated at the end of the war.

The first Marines captured at Peking and Tientsin were put in Woosung Prison near Shanghai, where Col. William W. Ashurst, commander of the Peking Embassy Guard, became the senior officer prisoner. Chief Marine Gunner William A. Lee, who wore three Navy Crosses, had his teeth kicked out but survived to retire in 1950 as a colonel. The Marines captured on Guam were eventually taken to Osaka. Eighty Marines and sailors regarded as "uncooperative" were made to shovel coal and iron ore in a steel mill. They lost an average of 45 pounds apiece. Others worked in rice paddies and as stevedores.

When the Marines captured on Wake were removed to Japanese camps and Woosung Prison, they had to leave behind 300 civilian construction workers and 100 servicemen and civilians too ill to be moved. On the night of October 7, 1943, nearly 100 American civilians on Wake were executed by machine gun on the beach. After the war, Rear Adm. Shigematsu Sakaibara and several officers were hanged for this crime.

A few Marines managed to escape their captors. In March 1942, four enlisted Marines escaped from Woosung, but they were recaptured a month later. In October 1944, Marine Cpl. Jerold Story, one of the four, and a British and an American naval officer escaped from Shanghai's Ward Road Gaol and made their way to Chungking and freedom.

While 901 prisoners were being moved by train from Shanghai to Peking on the night of May 9, 1945, two Wake Marines, 1st Lt. John F. Kinney and 1st Lt. John A. McAlister, and two North China Marines, 1st Lt. Richard M. Huizenga and 1st Lt. James D. McBrayer—and Lewis S. Bishop, a former Flying Tiger pilot—jumped out of a window. Chinese guerrillas found them and turned them over to Nationalist troops. The group participated in many local patriotic rallies and, when asked to sing their national anthem, obliged by singing *The Marines' Hymn*. In time, all five returned safely to the United States.

When the cruiser *Houston* was sunk off Java on March 1, 1942, only 368 men of 1,064 men aboard—and 24 of 74 Marines—survived. The Japanese put them to work unloading transports; taken to Burma, they were forced to work building a railroad. Some ended up as stevedores in Saigon.

The largest group of Marine prisoners was captured in the Philippines: 105 Marines on Bataan and 1,283 on Corregidor. Of these, 490 men never survived their wounds, malnutrition, beatings and disease or were executed, killed by American bombs or massacred at the Puerto Princesa prison camp.

In April 1942, thousands of Americans and Filipinos made the 85-mile Bataan Death March. When Corregidor fell on May 6, nearly half the prisoners who made up a military police unit to keep order with moral and physical persuasion were Marines.

Of the prisoners from the Philippines, 40 to 50 men of all services died daily in prison camps near Cabanatuan, 75 miles north of Manila. A thousand of the prisoners were shipped to the Davao Penal Colony, a huge plantation on Mindanao. There, a dozen men, including Capt. Austin C. Shofner and 1st Lts. Jack Hawkins and Michiel Dobervich of the 4th Marines, escaped in April 1943 and reached the guerrilla forces of Col. Wendell W. Fertig, USA. They helped raid Japanese garrisons for six months and then were taken to Australia by submarine.

One hundred and forty American prisoners, including 23 Marines, were murdered at the Puerto Princesa prison camp on

Palawan Island in the Philippines on December 14, 1944. The Japanese killed them with burning gasoline and machine-gun fire; those who tried to flee were picked off in the water by rifle fire. One Marine and four other men escaped.

One day earlier, 1,619 prisoners in Manila were herded into the hold of a Japanese ship. They were jammed in so tightly that some went berserk and killed one another. Others died of suffocation, including Lt. Col. John P. Adams, commander of the 3rd Battalion, 4th Marines. Fifteen prisoners died that first night. U.S. Navy planes bombed the convoy, and a number of prisoners were killed and wounded. The ship limped into Subic Bay; planes attacked again, killing many prisoners. Many drowned swimming to shore. In all, 419 were killed, including 21 Marines. Ashore at Olongapo, the 15 prisoners in the worst condition were beheaded. They included Lt. Col. Samuel W. Freeny, executive officer of the 1st Battalion, 4th Marines.

The remaining POWs were taken to Formosa, where 400 were killed when their unmarked ship was bombed. The survivors were moved to Moji on Kyushu; en route, 30 to 40 prisoners died each day. Only 470 reached Moji, and 300 of them died in the next month. The rest went to prison camps in Korea.

In all, 184 men of the 4th Marines were killed by American fliers and submariners who had no idea that they were attacking ships carrying American prisoners. Some unmarked prison camps in Japan were also bombed by American planes.

Most of the prisoners of the Japanese endured inhumane treatment. They were underfed, overworked, humiliated, denied medical care, beaten, tortured, killed. When they could, many Marines and other POWs tried to sabotage the Japanese war effort by wrecking machines and tools, adding water to oil drums and slowing their work to a snail's pace. Frequently, they were painfully punished for their efforts. A few Japanese guards gave prisoners extra food and medicine, but they were the exception. The POWs survived on hope and group discipline and faith in an ultimate American victory.

15
North China:
Bitter Taste of the Future

Fifty-three thousand Marines went into North China in the autumn of 1945 to ensure the surrender of the Japanese armies—and stayed to wrestle the Chinese Communists.

In Europe at the end of World War II, a reasonably clear line was drawn between Communist and non-Communist blocs; but no such line could be fixed in Asia. Generalissimo Chiang Kai-shek's Nationalist government, which the United States recognized and supported, and the armies of the Chinese Communist revolutionary movement battled for four more years. The Marines, as the amphibious tip of American sea power, remained in China until practically the end of that struggle. At the same time in southeast Asia, nationalist and communist factions were fighting against the resurrection of Western colonialism. The turmoil there would go on for decades, its outcome shaping the westward expansion of United States power.

The Joint Chiefs of Staff wanted to see Chiang's armies established throughout China and particularly in industrial Manchuria, which the Russians had already overrun. The Marines were sent to disarm and replace the Japanese garrisons in North China's ports and communications centers, to begin repatriating the Japanese and to prevent great quantities of Japanese arms from falling into Communist hands. On V-J Day, the Nationalists controlled only southeast China; and until they could be brought north, the Marines would attempt to fill the strategic vacuum in North China. The Communists, who had 170,000 regular troops there, were prepared to take over all North China if they could; but, as one Marine officer later wrote candidly, "the presence of the Marines frustrated this."[125]

407

The civil war that the Marines encountered in China was massive. Nationalist armies numbered three million men and the Communists', one million. Naively, the Marines were charged with both supporting the Nationalists and retaining their own neutrality. As a result, they became the first Americans to do battle with Chairman Mao Tse-tung's forces.

Maj. Gen. Keller E. Rockey's III Amphibious Corps was assigned to China. Many of its officers and senior noncoms had served in China between World Wars I and II. On September 30, the 1st Marine Division landed at Tangku and moved to the Tientsin–Peking region. And on October 11, the 6th Marine Division landed at Tsingtao on the Shantung Peninsula. They all came under the command of Lt. Gen. Albert C. Wedemeyer, USA, commander of United States forces in China.

Before either landing, the pattern was already stenciled. On September 20, an advance party led by Brig. Gen. William A. Worton, Rockey's chief of staff, and Col. Charles C. Brown, the corps G-2, arrived at Shanghai. Both Worton and Brown had served in China. When the party flew up to Tientsin, no one knew what opposition might be offered by the Japanese—or by the Chinese Communists.

Worton conferred with the Japanese commanders in Tientsin and Peking. And he was visited by Gen. Chou En-lai, the leading Communist representative in wartime negotiations between the Communists and Nationalists. In a stormy meeting, Chou warned Worton that the Communists would fight the Marines if they moved to Peking. Although Peking was not named in Worton's directives, he was determined that the Marines would occupy the city. He told Chou that the III Amphibious Corps was combat-experienced and that the Marines would drive through any force that tried to stop them. The gauntlet was down.

Worton's insistence on establishing a Marine presence in Peking had two purposes: to make sure the Nationalists, rather than the Communists, gained control of the ancient city that was a potent symbol of national power and to use Peking's two first-class military airfields to bring in the Nationalist troops who would relieve the Marines—especially since Worton had found Tientsin's airfield inadequate. The meeting between Worton and Chou pointed to the coming clashes between the Marines and Chinese Communists.

Although the 1st Division expected to occupy its assigned places in North China peacefully, Maj. Gen. DeWitt Peck brought it in from Okinawa ready for trouble. The 7th Marines, designated the division's assault troops, landed at Tangku on September 30. While the 2d Battalion stayed in the port, the 3rd Battalion went by train directly to Tientsin, where it was met by a noisy, cheering throng of thousands and was billeted in the buildings of the race track west of the city. On the first day, 5,400 Marines were ashore.

That evening, Lt. Col. John J. Gormley took his 1st Battalion, 7th Marines to Chinwangtao, an ice-free port 150 miles north of Tangku. The British had developed Chinwangtao as the port for their Kailin coal mines. The situation was tense; troops of the Communist Eighth Route Army were in the area and small-arms fire was frequently heard. Gormley disarmed the Japanese troops at Chinwangtao and Peitaiho, and the Communist leaders in the area sent word that they would cooperate with the Marines—an attitude that did not last long.

The 1st Marines were posted at Tientsin, where, on October 6, 50,000 Japanese troops surrendered to Rockey, acting in the name of Chiang Kai-shek. They were allowed to keep one rifle and five rounds of ammunition for every ten men to protect themselves and their supplies. The Marines found the teeming city exciting. "Although the billets were 'musty, damp and dirty (the Japanese had ripped out plumbing, sabotaged heating and water supplies), wine, women and steaks were cheap.'" The Marines hired "roomboys" to do onerous housekeeping chores and quickly discovered the British concession where "bad vodka, poor wine and poisonous Chinese whiskies and Russian women were the main attractions" and the French concession where there was "a large five-story bazaar and a larger house of ill-repute."[126] As in pre-war days, the younger officers were especially attracted to the White Russian girls. The Marines soon whipped up an inflation that slowed down the most extravagant living.

On October 6, the Marines had their first fire fight with the Chinese Communists, pretty much as Chou En-lai had promised. In preparation for the movement of the 2d and 3rd Battalions of the 5th Marines to Peking, Engineers guarded by a rifle platoon of the 1st Marines tried to remove a series of roadblocks 22 miles northwest of Tientsin and were fired on by

40 to 50 Communist soldiers. Three Marines were wounded. The detachment returned to Tientsin. On the seventh, a 1st Marines rifle company and a platoon of tanks, covered by carrier planes, removed the roadblocks; and the 5th Marines went into Peking. Later on, a Communist general in civilian clothes appeared at III Corps headquarters in Tientsin and apologized for the attack on the road.

The Communists beat Maj. Gen. Lemuel C. Shepherd, Jr.,'s 6th Marine Division to Chefoo, on the north coast of the Shantung Peninsula. The Marines' landing was cancelled; and the 29th Marines, who had been assigned to Chefoo, were switched to the port of Tsingtao on the south side of the Shantung Peninsula. Tsingtao, 475 miles southeast of Peking, was an important industrial city with the best harbor and airfield north of Shanghai.

The 6th Marine Division landed on October 11 under a show-of-force umbrella of carrier air power. Soon enough, Maj. Gen. Shepherd received a message from the area's Communist commander warning that the arrival of Nationalist troops at Tsingtao would bring civil war. Shepherd replied that he had no control over the movement of Nationalist troops to Tsingtao and pointedly added that in case disorders broke out "my Division of well-trained combat veterans will be entirely capable of coping with the situation."[127]

By now, the Communists were attacking Marine units guarding communications routes in the 1st Division's zone. On October 18, six Communist soldiers were killed while firing on a Marine-guarded train between Peking and Langfang. Jeep patrols were also fired on, and three Marines were wounded in October. In the 6th Division's area, the Communists harassed low-flying Marine reconnaissance planes with small-arms fire. The Marine pilots were ordered not to reply, and MAG-32 arrived on October 21 and began flying patrols over the Shantung Peninsula.

Life was not all tension for the Marines in Tsingtao. There were many pleasures. For 25 cents a Marine could have a hot bath, manicure, pedicure and brisk massage. Chinese sold everything from watches to freshly made "Scotch." Inflation soon took hold; Japanese beer increased six times in price, and speculators had a heyday trading for American dollars. On

Thanksgiving Day, the 22d Marines' football team beat the 29th Marines, 25-14, in the Rice Bowl in Tsingtao Stadium.

Meanwhile, Maj. Gen. Claude A. "Sheriff" Larkin, who had commanded MAG-21 at Ewa on Pearl Harbor Day, brought the 1st Marine Aircraft Wing to Tientsin. At the end of October, Maj. Gen. Louis E. Woods relieved him. MAG-12 and MAG-24 were based at Peking and MAG-25 and MAG-32 at Tsingtao.

In both Tientsin and Tsingtao, Chinese mobs attacked and robbed Japanese and German civilians. At Tientsin, the 1st Marines waded into the fighting and stopped the rioting; and in Tsingtao, squad-sized street patrols of the 22d and 29th Marines kept the peace. Meanwhile, the repatriation of 326,375 Japanese military personnel and 312,774 civilians began on October 22. It was a huge job.

Japanese troops continued to guard outlying bridges and stretches of railroad track between Peking and Chinwangtao because Maj. Gen. Peck did not want to expose small units of Marines to Communist attacks. Two Nationalist armies totaling 56,000 men were airlifted to Peking and Tientsin and garrisoned the cities. But their commanders were in no hurry to replace the Japanese on the roads and rail lines.

The Marines were caught in a fluid and dangerous situation. Pressure grew to start withdrawing them and avoid involvement in a civil war once Nationalist troops were present in North China.

Chiang Kai-shek was eager to recover the industrial complex and rich agricultural resources of Soviet-occupied Manchuria. But the Soviet commanders refused to let Nationalist troops land there and turned over some ports to the Communists under Gen. Lin Piao. This meant Chiang Kai-shek would have to enter Manchuria overland through the Chinwangtao region and increased the danger that the Marines would become involved.

On November 14, Chiang's American-trained divisions attacked north into Manchuria. Lt. Gen. Wedemeyer reported, "He visualizes utilizing the Marines as a base of maneuver."[128] The Marines were in an impossible position. Wedemeyer and senior Marine officers felt that the directives under which they operated were "ill-considered and ambiguous."[129] Back home in November, seven joint resolutions were introduced in the Congress calling for the withdrawal of the Marines from China.

When Ambassador Patrick J. Hurley resigned suddenly on November 27, President Truman instantly appointed General of the Army George C. Marshall to be his special representative to China. Truman called for a ceasefire in China, a unified government and army and an end of the civil war "particularly in North China."[130] Marshall suspended the movement of Nationalist troops to North China. That meant the Marines would stay.

They were ordered to protect the ports and the rail traffic bringing out the coal urgently needed in Shanghai, Peking and Tientsin. The 7th Marines provided most of the rail and bridge guard detachments between Chinwangtao and Tangku. It was lonely dangerous duty in the cold of the Chinese winter.

On the morning of November 14, the Communists, firing from a village, stopped a train carrying Maj. Gen. Peck to Chinwangtao. The next day, Peck started out again and found several hundred yards of tracks torn up. A Chinese track gang made repairs while the Marines answered sniper fire. A mine exploded killing several of the work gang, and Peck finally had to fly to Chinwangtao.

On December 4, two members of the 1st Battalion, 29th Marines were shot by two Chinese. One Marine was killed; the other survived by pretending to be dead and watched the Chinese disappear into a nearby village. The battalion executive officer set up a 60mm mortar and gave the village head man a half hour to surrender the two killers or he would shell the village. When the deadline expired, 24 rounds of white phosphorus were fired outside the village walls. Nobody was hurt, but word got back to the United States that the Marines had fired into an unarmed village, and criticisms appeared in the press.

Increasingly, the Marines aided the Nationalist armies that were fighting Communists. The Marines provided the Nationalists with arms, ammunition and replacement parts. When the Eighth Chinese Nationalist Army fought the Communists near Tsangkou, Maj. Gen. Shepherd turned over to the Nationalists one unit of fire for the infantry weapons of a Marine division.

A disaster occurred on December 8 when planes from MAG-32 flew back to Tsingtao after a Pearl Harbor anniversary air show-of-strength at Tientsin. VMSB-343's scout-bombers tried to fly through a snow storm, and six pilots crashed into the mountains of the Shantung Peninsula. Communist villagers rescued the only two survivors. The Communists treated the Marine fliers well and later released them and several other fliers who had also crashlanded.

Clashes between the Marines and the Communists subsided once General Marshall arrived in Chungking and organized a cessation of hostilities. The fighting practically stopped; there was hope for peace in China.

On January 11, 1946, 45,981 Marines (of the Corps' declining strength of 301,700) were in North China. General Marshall's January order for a 20 percent reduction of all Marine units in China was welcomed by Marine Corps Headquarters; available manpower was being stretched thin. By now, the Marines in China were chiefly repatriating Japanese and Koreans and making certain that the coal essential to the cities was brought safely from the mines. Marshall also directed the Marines to supply men for the new truce teams until Army replacements arrived. In mid-March, the Marines created six six-man liaison teams, including a Nationalist and Communist officer and headed by a colonel or lieutenant colonel. Two teams were assigned to the railroad lines and the others to troubled areas. The situation of those teams in the depths of China was frequently tense; sometimes, their members were shot at.

Marshall regarded the Marines' presence in North China as an embarrassment to his peace negotiations. He and Wedemeyer became convinced that the Nationalists would provide adequate security forces only when they were persuaded that the Marines were leaving. Instead, the Nationalists increased their activities in Manchuria and occupied Mukden. By mid-April, Nationalists and Communists were battling in Manchuria. Chiang was now less willing than ever to divert troops to relieve the Marines from rail and mine security details.

Economies and demobilization forced the reduction of the 6th Marine Division to the 3rd Marine Brigade, built chiefly around the 4th Marines, and required the 1st Division to disband the third infantry battalion of each regiment and one battery of each battalion of the 11th Marines. By the end of April, III Corps strength was down to 30,379.

In succeeding months, despite a substantial reduction of Marine forces in China and a complicated shifting of commands, the Marines continued to support the truce teams, protect coal production, keep open communications between Tientsin and Chinwangtao and maintain garrisons at Peking, Tientsin, Tangku, Peitaiho, Chinwangtao and Tsingtao. During those early months of 1946, the situation quieted in North China. Only one Marine was killed in combat there in the first half of the year. But by the end of June, political negotiations between the Nationalists and Communists broke down completely. General Marshall's mission for unification and peace had failed.

In July, the Communists began their "Third Revolutionary Civil War." They reorganized their forces, greatly expanded now, as the People's Liberation Army and demanded that all American military forces be withdrawn from China immediately. The Communists began to make their objections perfectly clear.

The Marines promptly were caught in two serious incidents. In the heat of Saturday, July 13, eight Marines from the Bridge 109 Detachment at Lin-Shou-Ying, 15 miles from Peitaiho, went into a nearby village to get ice for their beer cooler. This violated a directive that the men stay within their barbed wire defensives. As they left the icehouse, 80 blue-uniformed Communists surprised and surrounded the Marines. One man escaped in the gathering dusk. In response to a radio call, all available men of the 1st Battalion, 7th Marines boarded a special train to Lin-Shou-Ying and pursued the Communists and their captives through a rainy night and into the next day. On the sixteenth, a 200-man combat patrol from the 2d Battalion continued the chase. The patrol returned on the eighteenth without having found the missing Marines.

Once the Marines obeyed a Communist demand that all Marine units return to their positions of July 13, the men were finally returned on July 24, after each had written a letter attesting to his good treatment. Throughout the long negotiations, the Communists hammered at the point that the Marines were supporting the Chinese Nationalist Army.

Five days later occurred an even more violent encounter. A Marine supply convoy left Tientsin at 9:15 that morning for Peking. The escort, commanded by 2d Lt. Douglas A. Cowin of Ann Arbor, Michigan, consisted of 31 men from the 1st Battalion, 11th Marines and a 10-man 60mm mortar section of the 1st Marines. The escort rode at both ends of the 15-vehicle convoy.

Two of its Jeeps had TCS radios; but when the convoy was ambushed, the radios were out of range of the Marines at either Tientsin or Peking. The Communists had planned their attack well.

Shortly after 11 A.M., 44 miles from Tientsin, the point of the convoy had to thread its way through rocks spread across the road. Ahead was a roadblock of oxcarts. The Marines dismounted cautiously. Immediately, a dozen grenades were thrown from a clump of trees 15 yards to the left of the road. As he jumped from his Jeep, 2d Lt. Cowin was killed; and most of the men with him were killed or wounded. The survivors took cover and returned the Communist fire. The main body of the convoy was hit by steady rifle fire from trees 100 yards to the right of the road. Few men in the trucks or passenger vehicles were armed; they took cover in a ditch. The rear guard was attacked by fire from both sides. Platoon Sgt. Cecil J. Flanagan took command of the escort and went up and down the long line of vehicles directing fire. The machine gun and mortar in the rear guard prevented the Chinese from rushing the convoy. At 1:15, when there was a lull in the firing, three Marines turned a Jeep around and dashed for help.

At 3:30, the Communists, estimated at 300, started withdrawing to the sound of bugles. Gathering up the wounded and covered by a rear guard of Flanagan's men, the convoy headed for Peking, leaving behind three damaged trucks. The Marines had three killed, one man who died of his wounds and 10 others wounded.

Meanwhile, the Jeep racing back to Tientsin overturned on the outskirts of the city, injuring two of the three Marines. They commandeered a passing vehicle and brought word of the ambush to Col. Wilburt S. Brown, commanding the 11th Marines. A heavily armed combat patrol of 400 Marines rushed out; but when it arrived at the scene at 8:45, the enemy dead and wounded had been removed. All the Marines could do was tow in the shot-up trucks.

General Marshall recognized that the incident represented a toughening of the Communists' attitude. As a result, patrols were strengthened, more powerful field radios were used and many Marine bridge and rail detachments were withdrawn. But there were no more attacks.

By the summer of 1946, the combat efficiency of the

Marines in China had dropped drastically because of the turnover of experienced personnel. MAG-24 was operating with only 20 percent of its aircraft available because of a shortage of qualified mechanics. And 1st Division units were rated at 25 and 35 percent of combat efficiency.

The Marines at Tsingtao were reduced to the reinforced 3rd Battalion, 4th Marines under Col. Samuel B. Griffith, II, the former Raider and Chinese-language student. On September 3, the rest of the 4th Marines sailed for Camp Lejeune. The regiment was finally home after nearly 20 years overseas. In September 1948, the 4th Marines joined the Sixth Fleet in the Mediterranean; and after the American Consul General was killed by a sniper during the Arab-Israeli war, 62 Marines from the regiment were at Haifa and 41 were in Jerusalem to guard the American consulate. Two Marines were wounded on duty in Jerusalem.

In August 1946, 4,700 Marines of the 1st Marine Division were stationed from Tangku to Chinwangtao. Within 15 miles on both sides of the railroad were 25,000 Communist soldiers. On August 4, a coal train heading for Tientsin was derailed. Four Marines in the caboose and Chinese railroad police fought off the ambushers until a relief train rescued them. Frequently, snipers shot at bridge and station outposts. This harassment worked. By September 30, Marine rail guards were replaced by Nationalist troops at all the most exposed outposts. The Marines ended their responsibility for guarding the delivery of coal to Chinwangtao.

On September 18, Maj. Gen. Samuel L. Howard, who had commanded the 4th Marines in Shanghai in 1941, replaced Rockey as commander of the 1st Division. Maj. Gen. Howard addressed a statement to the people of North China that said in part: "The U.S. Marines have no part in the establishment of our nation's policy. We are an organization whose traditional duty is to support and uphold that policy and to protect American lives and property in any part of the globe. We are in China to carry out the directives of our State Department or those of General Marshall. This we propose to do."[131]

The division's ammunition supply point at Hsin Ho, six miles northwest of Tangku, was an oval two miles across and one wide, ringed with barbed wire fence and spotted with eight sentry towers. On October 3, at about 10 P.M., the sentry at Post 3 was fired on by a large group of Chinese. They cut the wire fence and began carrying off ammunition boxes. The remainder of the guard—52 Marines in all—dashed up and took firing positions. At 11 P.M., when 100 men from the 1st Battalion, 5th Marines at Tangku arrived, the Chinese had disappeared, leaving behind one dead and one wounded Communist soldier. Thirty-two cases of ammunition were missing in the well-executed raid by the 53rd Communist Regiment.

On January 7, 1947, General Marshall left China, his peace mission washed out; and Truman nominated him as Secretary of State. At the end of January, mediation officially ended.

Plans were already underway to bring the rest of the Marines home from China. The 7th Marines embarked for the United States; and the 11th Marines headed for Guam. The air units started leaving. The 1st Marines stayed in Tientsin, with one battalion ready to fly to Shanghai on six hours' notice; and the 5th Marines remained in Peking and Tangku. Their prime responsibility now was to evacuate Americans and support the U.S. Army detachment in Peking.

While the 1st Division was pulling out of China, "the Communists made their most punishing attack against the Marines."[132] The target again was the ammunition at Hsin Ho, which the Communists wanted to seize before it was turned over to the Nationalists. The enclosure was now triangular with two long sides about two miles in length and the short side a mile long. At 1:15 A.M. on April 5, 1947, a bugle sounded, followed by rifle and machine-gun fire. The two sentries at the most distant northern post returned the fire for about 10 minutes until they were killed. The Communists killed three Marines in a patrol Jeep and drove back the main guard. Eight Marines were wounded. The raiders took all the ammunition they could carry.

C Company, 5th Marines came out from Tangku; but the Communists were ready for them. When the self-propelled 105mm howitzer in front of the column reached a narrow place in the road near Hsin Ho, it struck a land mine and blocked the road. Marines were hit by intense fire from an irrigation ditch 40 yards east of the road. They took cover behind their trucks and fired back. Two waves of Communist soldiers, 35 or 40 men, rushed forward throwing grenades and then continued the fire fight for 15 minutes before they were driven off. Eight more Marines were wounded in the ambush.

By the end of the month, the Hsin Ho ammunition dump was handed over to the Nationalist army. At Hsin Ho and Tsingtao, the Marines turned over to the Nationalists 6,500 tons of ammunition.

In May, Lin Piao's People's Liberation Army command, equipped with Japanese weapons, attacked in Manchuria and defeated the Nationalist armies. The Communists had the initiative, and they never again lost it.

By the end of August, the 1st Marine Division had pulled out of China. All that remained was the Fleet Marine Force, Western Pacific at Tsingtao under Brig. Gen. Omar T. Pfeiffer. He had 4,026 men, including the 3rd Battalion, 4th Marines and the 2d Battalion, 1st Marines, and VMF-211 and VMR-153. Their job was to guard American naval installations and by airlift to provide emergency protection for the 7,500 Americans still in China.

By this summer of 1947, the Communists—supplied with Japanese and captured American arms—were clearly winning the civil war. Lt. Gen. Wedemeyer visited China as the head of a special commission and warned that the Communists, by furthering the aims of the Soviet Union, were a danger to America's strategic security. He recommended, as the only alternative, giving military assistance to the Nationalists, whom he described as "the presently corrupt, reactionary and inefficient Chinese National Government."[133]

That fall, the 2d Battalion, 1st Marines was designated the 1st Marines; and the 3rd Battalion, 4th Marines became the 3rd Marines. Cordoned behind Nationalist defenses at Tsingtao, they had little contact with the Communists. But on Christmas Day, 1947, Communists killed one Marine and seized four more in a hunting party and did not release them until April 1, 1948. Four days later, the four-man crew of a Marine plane that crashlanded near Tsingtao was captured by the Communists and not returned until July 1.

In the summer of 1948, while the Russians began their blockade of West Berlin, the Chinese Communists advanced into northern and central China. In Manchuria by November 1948, the Nationalists lost 400,000 troops "and mountains of

American military supplies."[134] The senior American Army general in Nanking blamed the disaster on "the world's worst leadership."[135]

The Marines, now under Brig. Gen. Gerald C. Thomas, were given the job of evacuating Americans from North China and Manchuria, while the Army brought them out through Nanking and Shanghai. The 9th Marines from Guam arrived at Tsingtao.

In January 1949, the Communists won the massive 65-day battle of the Hwai-Hai and swept through Peking and Tientsin. The complete defeat of the Nationalists was now inevitable. The 9th Marines moved to the Whangpoo River at Shanghai to protect American lives. Tsingtao was doomed; and by February 3, all the Marines there were on board ships except for C Company, 3rd Marines, which served as a shore patrol. In March, the bulk of the 3rd Marines relieved the 9th Marines at Shanghai. On April 20, the Communists shelled and machine-gunned British warships in the Yangtze, killing 40 men and wounding 73. Corpsmen and stretcher bearers from the 3rd Marines took the wounded aboard the American hospital ship *Repose.*

With the last 119 American civilians evacuated, the 3rd Marines sailed from Shanghai on April 29 for the United States. It left behind only its C Company at Tsingtao, the remnant of the task force that had once numbered more than 50,000. C Company stayed aboard a cruiser and sent patrols ashore. In mid-May, it was relieved by C Company, 7th Marines, which had come out from Camp Pendleton. By May 26, when Shanghai had fallen to the Communists and Tsingtao was about to be taken, the last Marines left China. They had had 10 killed and 33 wounded there since the end of World War II. It was the close of the long and colorful era of the China Marines.

By using the Japanese and helping the Nationalists to oppose the Communists' takeover of China, the Marines "ensured the enduring enmity of the Communists."[136] In essence, the Marines had provided a base for the Nationalists to recover North China and Manchuria, much as the Marines had been used earlier to support governments favored by American policy in the Caribbean. The Marines had begun to confront the Communists in Asia—a confrontation that in the years ahead would be played out in Korea and Vietnam.

16
Summing Up the War

The Marine Corps had grown to maturity in World War II. It had done its job, proved itself.

By V-J Day, the Corps had ballooned to an all-time peak of 485,833 men and women, of whom 242,043 were overseas. Of the overall total, 116,628 were in Marine aviation. The Corps' readiness and the amphibious nature of the Pacific war had stimulated this vast expansion.

Approximately 450,000 new Marines had been trained at the Recruit Depots at Parris Island and San Diego. Not all those who joined the Marines in World War II were volunteers; 70,729 were draftees and 5,241 were Selective Service volunteers inducted into the Marine Corps Reserve. In legalistic terms, the Corps could not accept volunteers ages 18 to 36 after December 5, 1942; so 224,875 World War II Marines came in through the Selective Service System—though most of them volunteered to become Marines.

The war saw the first black Americans in the Corps since 1798. This was the result of President Franklin D. Roosevelt's Executive Order 8802 in 1941. A Marine Corps study states, "There is no question but that the order was unpopular at Headquarters Marine Corps."[137] The month after Pearl Harbor, Commandant Holcomb said, ". . . the Negro race has every opportunity now to satisfy its aspirations for combat, in the Army—a very much larger organization than the Navy or Marine Corps—and their desire to enter the naval service is largely, I think, to break into a club that doesn't want them."[138] Many Marines felt theirs was a small "elite" service, and there was a strong Southern tradition among the commissioned officers. But

Secretary of the Navy Frank Knox insisted that the Marine Corps start recruiting a thousand blacks per month.

The first black Marines to enlist on June 1, 1942, were Alfred Masters and George O. Thompson. One of the earliest recruits was Edgar R. Huff of Gadsden, Alabama, who was to become the senior sergeant major in the Corps. Huff, who served 30 years, said, "I wanted to be a Marine because I had always heard that the Marine Corps was the toughest outfit going and I felt that I was the toughest going."[139]

The first black unit, the 51st Composite Defense Battalion, was activated in August 1942 at the new camp built near Camp Lejeune at Montford Point, North Carolina. The battalion was to consist of 1,085 Marines commanded by white officers headed by Col. Samuel A. Woods, Jr., a native of South Carolina and a Marine for 25 years. Among the recruits were college graduates and veterans. Charles W. Simmons, who became sergeant major of the 51st, had a masters degree from the University of Illinois. George A. Jackson had been an Army lieutenant and Gilbert H. "Hashmark" Johnson had served in both the Army and the Navy. By May 1943, the last white Drill Instructor had left Montford Point; and from then on, all recruit training was done by black DIs led by Sgt. Major "Hashmark" Johnson.

During World War II, 19,168 blacks enlisted in the Corps. They served in two defense battalions, the 51st and 52d; 51 depot companies, and 12 ammunition companies. Segregated units with 12,738 blacks served overseas in all major campaigns from Saipan on.

After they participated in their first amphibious assault at Saipan, Commandant Vandegrift said, "The Negro Marines are no longer on trial. They are Marines, period."[140] Pvt. Kenneth J. Tibbs of Columbus, Ohio, and Pfc. Leroy Seals of Brooklyn, New York, were fatally wounded on Saipan on D-Day—the first black Marines to die in combat. Pfc. Luther Woodward, a former Memphis truck driver, tracked and killed Japanese on Guam and received the Silver Star, the highest decoration won by a black Marine in World War II.

Nine black Marines were killed in action or died of wounds in World War II and 78 others were wounded in action. They were almost all in "labor troop" units. The 3rd Ammunition

Company received the Presidential Unit Citation for its role with the 4th Marine Division on D-Day at Saipan; and the 6th Ammunition Company and the 33rd, 34th and 36th Depot Companies were awarded the Navy Unit Commendation in the Iwo Jima campaign.

In March 1945, three black Marines were sent to Platoon Commanders class at Quantico. None of the three was commissioned although they became a lawyer, a doctor and a college professor after returning to civilian life. The next three black officer candidates also washed out. At last, on the Corps' 170th birthday, Frederick C. Branch of Hamlet, North Carolina, who had served in the 51st Defense Battalion, became the Marines' first black officer. Lieutenant Branch returned to active service in the Korean war. In 1946, three black Marines were commissioned from the V-12 program; one of them, Lt. Herbert E. Brewer of San Antonio, served in the Korean war and by 1973 was a colonel, the highest-ranking black in the Marine Corps Reserve. By June 1949, blacks were integrated into the Corps and segregated basic training ceased at Montford Point.

Because of Commandant Holcomb's initial resistance, the Marines were the last of the services to form a Women's Reserve. Holcomb liked to tell the story that, when he finally approved the idea, Archibald Henderson's picture fell off the wall of the Commandant's House in Washington. The program was announced on February 13, 1943; and Mrs. Ruth Cheney Streeter of Morristown, New Jersey, was chosen to lead the women. Major Streeter, who had been the president of her class at Bryn Mawr College, was the mother of three grown children and held a pilot's license.

"Free a Marine to Fight" was the slogan designed to attract women recruits, and Commandant Vandegrift told them that they were responsible for putting the 6th Marine Division into the field. By the end of the war, 18,460 women were on duty from Washington to Pearl Harbor, filling jobs from clerks to control tower operators. Eighty-five percent of the personnel at Marine Corps Headquarters were women. Mrs. Streeter was a full colonel when she was succeeded after the war by Col. Katherine A. Towle. It was decided to keep a nucleus of trained women in the postwar Corps. In 1948, women Marines were legally integrated into the Regular Corps, as were women in all the services.

The rapid demobilization of all the armed services deflated the Corps by July 1946 to 156,000 and by the following July to the low point of 92,000. After that, the Corps rebuilt to its assigned postwar level of 108,200. This was only one-fifth of its wartime high, but still four times what its strength had been in 1939 when World War II began. The Fleet Marine Force was down from six to two divisions, one at Camp Lejeune and one at Camp Pendleton, and a reinforced brigade on Guam.

The Marines' wartime performance had been monumental. They had suffered 91,718 casualties, of whom 19,733 were killed in action, died of wounds or missing, presumed dead. In addition, 67,207 Marines were wounded and 4,778 were "non-battle" casualties in combat zones. Eighty Marines received the Medal of Honor, 48 of them posthumously; and Marines earned 957 Navy Crosses for heroism. Seven Navy corpsmen serving with the Marines were awarded the Medal of Honor, and corpsmen and other naval medical personnel received 69 Navy Crosses.

Of course, the Marine Corps' role in the Pacific war was part of a larger whole involving all the services. The purpose of amphibious assault was not to capture Japanese islands for themselves but to make possible an attack on the enemy's homeland. Wartime leaders argued over the best routes to approach Japan and which islands should be assaulted and which neutralized or bypassed. But the United States did not have the long-range power to reach Japan directly. There was no shortcut. It could be done only by men seizing advanced naval and air bases from which land-based and carrier-based aircraft could bomb Japan intensively and from which the final invasion could be mounted. The Marine Corps had prepared itself to do precisely that job.

Along the way, the complexities of amphibious assault had to be conquered. Command of the sea and air around the target had to be mastered. The Marine landing force commander had to win from the Navy the responsibility for the conduct of operations ashore. Logistics, combat loading and beach control had to be perfected. All kinds of technical advances had to be created and absorbed: communications, air support control, radar, landing craft, underwater demolition teams, escort carriers, flamethrowers, demolitions and the essential amphibian tractor. The Navy had to learn to deliver ships' gunfire effectively against an entrenched enemy. Ashore, infantry fire teams increased small-unit flexibility and infantry-tank teams provided riflemen with artillery. Rifle companies grew from 183 men to 242, chiefly by the addition of a machine-gun platoon. Some problems were not solved satisfactorily, especially the actual use of close air support and the feeding of replacements into battle.

The most significant fact was that the Marines were ready for the mission the war thrust upon them. Years before, their best minds had seen the future and the Marines' role in it. They had developed the doctrine of offensive amphibious warfare and started to build the means to fight it. They stumbled often; they did things wrong as well as right; but through trial and error, they learned from their successes and their mistakes. They won some of the toughest fighting in all man's history of killing other men.

That spirit that Ernie Pyle wrote about on Okinawa was crucial to the Marines' triumph. They had a belief in themselves, the conviction every winner needs that he is the best. Certainly, there were a few "supermen": Basilone, Boyington, Edson, Hawkins, Shoup and others, both celebrated and unnoted; they were precious models. But more important still was the ingrained faith that a Marine does not let another Marine down, in a bar or on a beachhead. It was the spirit that Carlson dramatized with the phrase "Gung Ho"; it was the spirit that drove Marines forward in the face of danger and almost certain death.

Now, the Marines' biggest war was over. The early defeats and the later victories were memories. Unforgettable names had been added to the Marine Corps' story: Wake, Corregidor, Guadalcanal, Tarawa, Iwo Jima, Okinawa.

In the beginning, the United States had been thrown out of the Western Pacific; but it had fought back and returned in even greater strength. Americans were willing to die because they believed they had a right to be there; and they would not permit another power to deny them that right. They defeated Japan neither to preserve Western colonialism in Asia nor to free

Asians from Japanese domination. They fought from the defense of Pearl Harbor to the surrender in Tokyo Bay for their own national purpose. It had not been easy; it had been a long and bloody war in which more than 400,000 Americans had died around the world. It had taught Americans the extent of their strength. They had still to learn its limits.

In his 1946 Commandant's report, General Vandegrift summarized the Marines Corps' postwar mission: "To provide a balanced Fleet Marine Force, including its air support component, for service with the Fleet in the seizure or defense of advanced Naval Bases or for the conduct of such limited land operations as are essential to the prosecution of a Naval campaign."[141] And the Marines would continue to develop amphibious operations, serve on armed naval vessels and protect naval property.

An analysis of the Marines' performance in World War II concluded, "It is imperative that the United States have a branch of the service which devotes full time to devising ways of projecting land power overseas against targets held by hostile forces."[142]

All too soon, the need for this capability would be brutally evident. The Marines' experience in North China was a clear signal of this. World War II had made the United States a Pacific power—the only Pacific power. The western frontier of that power now stood on the far side of the Pacific—5,000 miles west of San Francisco. There, it would come up against new forces; and the nation would call on the Marine Corps once again.

*Marines of the 1st Division return from a sniper patrol
in the Punchbowl area of eastern Korea in December
1951. Front to back, they are Sgt. Albert L. Ireland, Pfc.
Linden L. Brown, and Pfc. Robert D. Glover, Jr.
Master Sgt. R. Olund, USMC Photo*

SEMPER FIDELIS

VI
THE
KOREAN
WAR
1946-1953

1
Changes between the Wars

Following its great triumphs of World War II, the Marine Corps should have been riding high. But during the brief interlude—less than five years—between the surrender in Tokyo Bay and the North Korean attack across the 38th Parallel, the Corps wrestled with four critical problems at home: the pressure to demobilize, the effect of the atomic bomb on the battlefield, the integration of blacks into the armed forces and the unification of the military services. The solutions to these problems changed the Corps significantly.

It was a time when the United States and the Soviet Union were becoming locked in an ideological and power struggle. In Europe, the "Iron Curtain" dropped between the communist and western armies—except for the aberration of West Berlin 100 miles east of the Curtain. The Truman Doctrine and the Marshall Plan held that line in 1947. The Soviet bloc swallowed Czechoslovakia in 1948, but the Soviet attempt to dislodge the Western Powers from West Berlin in 1948–49 was defeated. The Soviet Union was not prepared to start World War III for West Berlin.

On the other side of the globe, the United States refused to allow the Soviet Union to participate in the occupation of Japan, but otherwise no sharp "line" was drawn. As a result, the Soviet-supported North Koreans tried to reunite the Korean peninsula by force in 1950 and started a major war. When United States soldiers and Marines counterattacked and approached the border of the year-old People's Republic of China, the Chinese shoved them back to the 38th Parallel. Some Americans would have "unleashed" Chiang Kai-shek's forces on Taiwan and extended the war into China. But the United States refused to pay the price to conquer North Korea, and both sides settled for a divided Korea.

In Southeast Asia, American power first supported and then supplanted French colonialism. In less than a generation, nationalist movements, heavily supported by Communist China and the Soviet Union, threw the United States out of South Vietnam, Cambodia and Laos. American leaders were forced to learn something about the limitations of American power.

For the first half of this short period, Marine Corps problems had to be solved by Commandant Alexander A. Vandegrift, the hero of Guadalcanal who in April 1945 had become the first four-star general on active duty in the history of the Corps.

Demobilization was the immediate headache. Pressure to get the men home after V-J Day was, in Vandegrift's word, "torrential."[1] In all the services, demonstrations erupted among civilians-in-uniform demanding to go home. On January 10, 1946, a delegation of Marine noncoms delivered a petition to Lt. Gen. Roy S. Geiger in Hawaii; he broke all of them to privates and had his sergeant major rip off their chevrons. Vandegrift wrote Geiger that a demonstration "to an old-line Marine . . . still borders on near mutiny."[2]

By early 1946, the 3rd, 4th and 5th Marine Divisions had been disbanded and the 6th Division reduced to the 3rd Marine Brigade. By the end of that year, the Corps was out of Japan and its forces in China had been cut severely. One year after World War II ended, the Marine Corps has shrunk from a wartime peak of 485,000 men and women to 156,000—and by February 1948, it was down to an actual strength of 92,000.

The Corps' postwar leaders had not only to absorb the lessons of World War II but to prepare for atomic war. Official Marine Corps historians later wrote: "the atomic bomb of Hiroshima rendered obsolescent in 10 seconds a system of amphibious assault tactics that had been 10 years in the making. Obviously, the concentrations of transports, warships, and aircraft carriers that had made possible the Saipan and Iwo Jima landings would be sitting ducks for an enemy armed with atomic weapons."[3]

Lt. Gen. Geiger, as commanding general of Fleet Marine

Force, Pacific, observed the test atomic explosions at Bikini Atoll in July 1946 and urged a complete review of amphibious concepts. A special board of Maj. Gen. Lemuel C. Shepherd, Jr., Maj. Gen. Field Harris and Brig. Gen. Oliver P. Smith studied the mysteries conjured up by atomic weapons. The crucial question: How can Marines achieve the surprise, speed and dispersion needed to survive on a potentially atomic battlefield?

The answer: "vertical envelopment." Instead of assaulting a beachhead frontally in concentrated, slow-moving waves of landing craft, Marines would leapfrog it with carrier-based helicopters.

In 1948, Marine Helicopter Experimental Squadron I (HMX-1) commanded by Col. Edward C. Dyer began training at Quantico with a few small helicopters. Colonels Merrill B. Twining and Victor H. Krulak led the creation of the first manual of helicopter amphibious doctrine, known as *Phib-31*. At the time, Sikorsky helicopters could lift only two combat-equipped Marines. The choppers brought ashore their first Marines from the escort carrier *Palau* in an amphibious exercise on May 23, 1948, at New River, North Carolina. In August, the squadron received its first Piasecki HRP-1 helicopter. Six combat-ready Marines could be lifted in this to-be-famous "Flying Banana."

As soon as Marines landed in Korea, in August 1950, their commander, Brig. Gen. Edward A. Craig, started using a Sikorsky HO2S-1 helicopter for reconnaissance and to reach his forward units. A year later, transport helicopter squadron HMR-161 arrived in Korea with larger Sikorsky HRS-1s and began troop- and supply-carrying operations. In theory at least, Marine assaults were freed from both landing beaches and airfields.

During the next two years in Korea, the HRS-1s of HMR-161 and the smaller HO2S-1s of VMO-6 airlifted more than 60,000 men and 7.5 million pounds of cargo and evacuated 9,815 wounded. The HRS-1s carried companies and battalions into combat. By the war's end, the helicopter was firmly established as the vehicle of vertical envelopment.

None of these revolutionary developments signaled the end of waterborne amphibious assault. The landing at Inchon, Korea, proved that. The Corps continued to perfect its skill at conventional warfare and amphibious operations. The combining of Marine ground and air elements under a single command became the keystone of the Marine Corps' image of itself as a balanced ground-air amphibious force-in-readiness.

On July 26, 1948, President Truman signed Executive Order No. 9981 ending segregation in the armed services. Commandant Clifton B. Cates protested that segregation was not a problem to be solved by the armed forces but by American society.

Although there were only 2,200 blacks among a total of 93,000 Marines in mid-1947, the change wrought by integration was fundamental. The process began slowly. Athletic teams were integrated. And at Parris Island, by the spring of 1949, Maj. Gen. Alfred H. Noble, Navy Cross winner at Belleau Wood, integrated recruit platoons and NCO clubs. The deactivization of the camp at Montford Point in September 1949 marked the end of the seven-year segregated era for blacks in the Marine Corps. Black women had not been enlisted when the Corps was segregated; the first two, Annie E. Graham of Detroit and Ann E. Lamb of New York, became Marines in September 1949. Finally, on November 18, 1949, the Corps issued instructions that all individual black Marines be assigned to vacancies in any unit where they could be used effectively.

The Korean war buildup hastened integration. When the war began, the Corps' overall strength of 74,279 included 1,502 black Marines on active duty; of those, 427 were stewards. Three years later, the Corps' strength was at 249,219 and included 14,731 blacks on active duty (of whom 538 were stewards). The percentage of blacks in the Corps had risen from two to six. After the war, Maj. Gen. Oliver P. Smith said that he had had a thousand black Marines in Korea and that two had won the Navy Cross and many, the Silver Star and Bronze Star. He added, "They did everything, and they did a good job because they were integrated, and they were with good people."[4] The day of black labor and stevedore units was over.

After each war the Marine Corps has had to scramble for its life. One would think that its unchallengeable record in World War II would have finally made the Corps invulnerable. Not so.

World War II was not yet won before the pressure was intensified to unify the armed services. This was an old idea given new strength by the enormous wartime growth of the military, by the development of air power and by the abject failure of coordination at Pearl Harbor. For the most part, the Army leadership wanted unification; the Navy did not. An acrimonious debate began in Congress as early as 1943; and once the war was over, President Truman pressed to modernize "the antiquated defense setup."[5]

The Marine Corps opposed unification, and Commandant Vandegrift was the spokesman of that opposition. Marines feared that under a single Department of Defense they would be devoured by the Army and at the very least they would lose their air arm to the Air Force. Vandegrift wrote former Commandant Holcomb, "The Army is back on the job in full force trying to absorb the Navy and with it the Marine Corps."[6]

In May 1946 at hearings before the Senate Naval Affairs Committee, Vandegrift charged that the Army was trying to limit the Corps to ceremonial functions and small ineffective units on landing beaches. Declaring that he placed the Corps' fate in the hands of the Congress and ultimately the American people, he made an emotional statement:

> We have pride in ourselves and in our past but we do not rest our case on any presumed ground of gratitude owing us from the nation. The bended knee is not a tradition of our Corps. If the Marine as a fighting man has not made a case for himself after 170 years of service, he must go. But I think you will agree with me that he has earned the right to depart with dignity and honor, not by subjugation to the status of uselessness and servility planned for him by the War Department.[7]

Vandegrift testified that in the years since 1829 the Congress had five times rejected proposals to destroy or severely damage the Corps. He felt that he was fighting for the Corps' survival and that if the Army had its way it would take "the first step in the total abolition of the Corps."[8] Marines saw themselves as members of an organizational David among Goliaths.

When HR 2319 was introduced in February 1947, it did not

mention the Marine Corps. Vandegrift wanted its roles and missions defined by law; he feared that otherwise the Corps would be exposed to any future president's wish to reduce or eliminate it. He pointed out forcefully that Andrew Jackson and Theodore Roosevelt had attempted to curtail the Corps and that President Truman "unfortunately held no particular love for the Marines."[9]

To plan the Corps' defense through this struggle, Vandegrift created a team headed by Brig. Gen. Gerald C. Thomas and Brig. Gen. Merritt A. Edson. Vandegrift and Navy Secretary James V. Forrestal went to see Truman personally and argued for a Congressional charter for the Corps. Gen. Dwight D. Eisenhower, now the Army's Chief of Staff, opposed having "two land armies"[10] and recommended that the Marines be limited to units of regimental size. He told Vandegrift that the Army dreaded the Corps' expansiveness ever since the publicity over Belleau Wood. Vandegrift assured him that the Marine Corps had no ambition to become a second army; it wanted to remain the amphibious partner of the Navy and not to build up for protracted campaigns on large land masses.

On July 26, 1947, while flying to his mother's deathbed in Missouri, President Truman signed the National Security Act organizing the military under a single Secretary of Defense and establishing the Air Force as a separate arm.

The Marines won their basic point: The act formalized in law for the first time the Corps' special amphibious function. The Corps was assigned the mission of seizing and defending advanced bases and engaging in land operations related to a naval campaign; it retained the Fleet Marine Force and was given responsibility for amphibious doctrines and representation on the Joint Staff.

Because the new law created a host of problems, Forrestal, as the first Secretary of Defense, called a conference at Key West in March 1948 (the Commandant was not invited) and began to hammer out the services' roles and missions. The Corps did, in fact, remain virtually a "second army" with a manpower ceiling of 400,000. In 1949, despite the opposition of the second Secretary of Defense, Louis A. Johnson, the Commandant sought a place on the Joint Chiefs of Staff for discussion of matters affecting the Marine Corps.

Finally, during the Korean war, the Corps won its long and intense political struggle. Public Law 416 of the 82nd Congress, enacted on June 28, 1952, guaranteed that the Corps would consist of at least three combat divisions and three air wings and that the Commandant would have co-equal status with members of the Joint Chiefs in matters of direct concern to the Marine Corps. The new law, said Commandant Shepherd, affirmed "that the Marine Corps shall be maintained as a ready fighting force prepared to move promptly in time of peace or war to areas of trouble."[11]

The Congressional hearings on the bill, sponsored by former Marines Senator Paul Douglas and Congressman Mike Mansfield, showed that all the members of the Joint Chiefs opposed the concept that the Marine Corps should come directly under the Secretary of the Navy rather than the Chief of Naval Operations. That battle was not won until 1954, when Secretary of the Navy Robert B. Anderson issued orders putting the Commandant on a level with the Chief of Naval Operations rather than subordinate to him. The Corps saw itself as a partner—not a part—of the Navy.

Vandegrift was not around for these later battles. Some Marines were convinced that he was not re-appointed because of the bitter unification fight. He was succeeded at the end of 1947 by Maj. Gen. Clifton B. Cates, the decorated veteran of World War I who had led a regiment on Guadalcanal and a division at Tinian and Iwo Jima.

The interservice in-fighting more clearly cost the Corps "Red Mike" Edson, holder of the Medal of Honor and two Navy Crosses. The great Raider leader, who had served longer overseas in World War II than any other Marine officer and was a leading candidate to become Commandant, opposed unification with vigor. Some ardent Marines credit him with saving the Corps. When he was ordered not to oppose unification in public, Edson retired to rouse support for the Marine position. In an article entitled "Power-Hungry Men in Uniform," he wrote that he disliked "an American replica of the Prussian general staff system."[12] Immediately after he retired, he said:

> I am a military man and proud of it. But when we reach the point where the military are directing, rather than

435

supporting, our country's policies, we are far along the road to losing what this country has always stood for. It was because of this trend of events that I finally reached the very difficult decision to resign from the Marines and return to Vermont.[13]

Edson was recalled to active duty briefly in the Korean war and on August 14, 1955, at the age of fifty-eight, was found dead in his garage of carbon monoxide poisoning.

1st Lt. Baldomero Lopez leads the men of the 3rd
Platoon, A Company, 5th Marines over the stone seawall
at Red Beach, Inchon, Korea, on September 15, 1950.
Within minutes, Lopez was shot while throwing a
grenade. He smothered the explosion with his body and
earned the Medal of Honor posthumously.
Sgt. W. W. Frank, USMC Photo

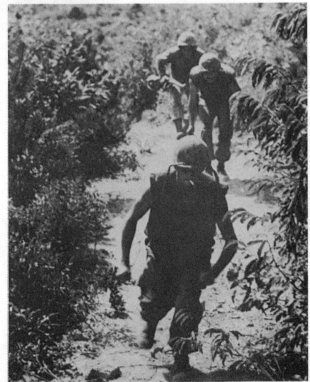

Under fire, Cpl. Reule Fake leads a
Navy corpsman and another Marine
up Siberia Hill, Korea, to rescue a
wounded Marine.
USMC Photo from United Press
International

*Marine sniper Lt. Fred J. Fees fires
at enemy troops across the Han River
near the Seoul railroad bridge.
U.S. Army Photo*

*Supported by tanks, Marines fight
their way into the center of Seoul.
Wide World Photos*

*Hunched in their parkas against the
shrieking wind, the column of
Marines moves torturously back from
the Chosin Reservoir after being hard
hit by the Chinese Communists at the
end of November 1950.
David Douglas Duncan; courtesy,
Museums Branch, USMC*

Cold, exhausted Marines take a brief break on the march south from Yudam-ni. The Chinese repeatedly severed the escape route of the 5th and 7th Marines as they fought to link up with other Marine units at Hagaru.
USMC Photo

The long line of Marines moves again down the winding road among the frozen North Korean hills.
David Douglas Duncan; courtesy, Museums Branch, USMC

Only the dead and wounded ride. The rest walk out.
David Douglas Duncan; courtesy, Museums Branch,
USMC

Bone-weary, hungry, unceasingly
cold, they endured.
David Douglas Duncan; courtesy,
Museums Branch, USMC

The breakout from the Chosin
Reservoir was one of the great
fighting retreats of military history.
David Douglas Duncan; courtesy
Museums Branch, USMC

The Marines trudge southward from Koto-ri through the snow-covered, wind-swept Korean hills. Sgt. F. C. Kerr, USMC Photo

Marines rush a wounded comrade on a stretcher down a Korean hillside to a waiting HRS-1 helicopter for a life-saving flight to a hospital. Staff Sgt. M. McMahon, USMC Photo

Marine F4U supplies accurate close air support for Marines fighting on the ground in Korea. Staff Sgt. Ed Barnum, USMC Photo

Panther jet of the 1st Marine Aircraft Wing makes a napalm run against an enemy troop area in Korea as part of a ninety-two-plane attack, June 10, 1953. USMC Photo

After the tragic 1956 Ribbon Creek "death march," Marine Corps drill instructors came in for public attention. Tech. Sgt. John H. Groves, one of the best DIs at Parris Island, bawls out a recruit for not knowing the name of a pack buckle.
Bob Lerner, Look Collection, the Library of Congress. Copyright © Cowles Communications, Inc., 1957

Groves drills his recruit platoon in the manual of arms.
Bob Lerner, Look Collection, the Library of Congress.
Copyright © Cowles Communications, Inc., 1957

2
The Pusan Perimeter

When the Korean war exploded in June 1950, the first combat troops to ship out from the United States mainland were Marines. General of the Army Douglas MacArthur was threatened with a Dunkirk-like disaster; but he was even then concocting a daring amphibious assault behind the invading North Korean army. And he wanted Marines to make his gamble work.

The war they went to fight resulted from mammoth postwar changes in Asia. With Japan's defeat, United States power, ideology and self-interest clashed with Soviet (and then Chinese) power, ideology and self-interest along the ill-defined border on the Pacific edge of Asia.

During World War II, the United States had proposed the 38th Parallel as the temporary line for dividing the bleak, mountainous Korean peninsula into sectors in which the Russian and American armies would accept the surrender of Japanese forces. That seemed a practical arrangement in 1945. The Russians were already in Korea, and a line even that far north stretched American capabilities to their utmost. It also kept 21 million of the 30 million Koreans—and the capital city of Seoul and its port of Inchon—under American control. But after the Soviet Union refused to let a United Nations commission hold elections in its half of Korea in 1948, the 38th Parallel hardened into a rigid frontier. The United States and the Soviet Union each created a satellite state in its own zone.

The United States grew ambivalent about Korea and the "harsh and fumbling" American occupation.[14] After the Joint Chiefs of Staff decided they had little strategic interest in keeping 45,000 American military personnel in South Korea, the United States withdrew the last of its forces in June 1949. It left

[For the location of places in the Korean war see map No. 9 in the map section.—*Au.*]

500 military advisors to the government of President Syngman Rhee, the autocratic nationalist leader who had returned from long exile to head the Republic of Korea. President Truman was wary of the men "of extreme right-wing attitudes" surrounding Rhee; Truman said, "I did not care for the methods used by Rhee's police to break up political meetings and control political enemies."[15] Because Rhee threatened to attempt to reunite the Korean peninsula by force, the United States gave the South Koreans no tanks, fighter planes or heavy weapons.

On January 12, 1950, Secretary of State Dean Acheson, speaking before the National Press Club in Washington, defined the United States' strategic frontier in Asia. He said, "The defensive perimeter runs along the Aleutians to Japan and then goes to the Ryukyus . . . to the Philippine Islands."[16] He excluded Korea and Formosa. The Communists took him at his word.

On Saturday evening, June 24, 1950, Secretary Acheson on his Maryland farm telephoned President Truman at home in Independence, Missouri. He told the President that some eight hours earlier—before dawn on June 25 Korean time—eight North Korean divisions led by Russian-made T-34 tanks had invaded South Korea.

The United States government was totally surprised—even though this was a period of Communist pressure around the globe: Berlin, Czechoslovakia, China, Indochina.

The United Nations' Security Council convened in New York on Sunday afternoon. That evening, Truman decided to send the Republic of Korea ammunition and military supplies and to evacuate American citizens; and on Monday, he authorized MacArthur to use his air and naval forces south of the 38th Parallel. Although the Republic of Korea (ROK) army was disintegrating, Truman did not commit U.S. ground forces because he feared other Communist strikes elsewhere. But he enlarged the arena of concern by ordering the U.S. Seventh Fleet into the Formosa Strait to protect the Nationalist Chinese from attack and prevent Chiang Kai-shek from attacking mainland China. (This intervention between the Chinese political foes would have enormous political effects later on.)

With the Soviet Union absent and unable to use its veto power (it had been boycotting the Security Council for six months over the presence of Nationalist China), the United Nations on Tuesday night called on its members to help repel the armed attack on South Korea and to restore peace. The UN and U.S. decisions to intervene caught the American commanders in Tokyo off guard. Vice Adm. C. Turner Joy, MacArthur's naval commander, said later, "As a consequence, we had no plans for this type of war."[17]

Events moved swiftly. On Wednesday in Washington, Commandant Cates proposed to the Chief of Naval Operations that the Fleet Marine Force be used in Korea. On Wednesday in Korea, American fighter planes, covering the evacuation of Americans and other foreign nationals, shot down seven North Korean aircraft. That same day, Seoul fell; most of the ROK army was trapped north of the Han River. On Thursday, the U.S. Navy began bombarding the Korean coast and made its first kill: a South Korean minecraft.

MacArthur visited the Korean front on Friday and found that of the 98,000-man ROK army only 25,000 troops could be accounted for. He urged President Truman to use United States combat troops. Truman immediately approved sending an Army regimental combat team from MacArthur's four understrength divisions on occupation duty in Japan. By Friday night (Washington time), the United States was fully committed to the defense of the Republic of Korea.

Unlike both World Wars I and II, this was America's war from the beginning. But, as in both those earlier wars, the United States military was not ready. On July 1, Lt. Col. Charles B. Smith and 406 soldiers from the 1st Battalion, 21st Infantry flew to Korea. In the rain on July 5, Task Force Smith, now 540 strong, went into battle above Osan near the west coast and was overwhelmed by two North Korean regiments with 33 tanks. The next day, the enemy scattered two battalions of the U.S. 34th Infantry, which had moved in behind Smith's original positions. The United States had to throw in its forces piecemeal, and they were getting beaten.

During the night of July 11–12, a demolition party including a Marine officer and four enlisted Marines from the cruiser *Juneau* were the first Americans to land in North Korea. In a whale boat from the destroyer *Mansfield*, they went ashore south of Songjin on the east coast and rigged two 60-pound charges in a railroad tunnel. Later, broadcasts by the North Korean radio indicated that the next train had detonated the charges.

The rapid American buildup was chaotic and expensive. On July 8, Truman named General MacArthur head of the United Nations Command in Korea. On July 13, Lt. Gen. Walton H. Walker took charge of the U.S. Eighth Army's 18,000 soldiers then in Korea. On July 20, Maj. Gen. William F. Dean's 24th Infantry Division defending Taejon was shattered and lost nearly 30 percent of its 12,200 men. Dean, after wandering in the mountains for 36 days, was captured and held prisoner for more than three years. By the third week of July, the decimated 24th and the understrength 25th Infantry Division and 1st Cavalry Division from Japan with 39,000 men—many of them neither physically nor psychologically ready for combat—were being squeezed into the southeastern corner of Korea around the port of Pusan, a pocket 100 miles north to south and 50 miles wide.

It was now a race between the North Korean advance and the arrival of reinforcements from the United States. American pilots and soldiers helped slow down the North Koreans. Some ROK divisions fought valiantly. On July 29, Lt. Gen. Walker called a halt to the Eighth Army's retreat and ordered his forces to stand or die. He said, "A Marine unit and two regiments are expected in the next few days to reinforce us. . . . There is no line behind us to which we can retreat. . . . There will be no Dunkirk, there will be no Bataan. . . . We must fight until the end. . . . We are going to hold this line. We are going to win."[18]

By the end of July, the U.S. Army had taken 6,003 casualties and the ROK army about 70,000; but the North Koreans were losing the race for Pusan. Their enveloping drive from the west was held at the Naktong River and outside the town of Masan. By August 5, 47,000 U.S. ground combat troops were in Korea, and U.S. and ROK forces had numerical superiority. Some 500 American planes were destroying bridges and railroads vital to the North Koreans' long supply lines. Then, the United Nations Command took its first offensive action. Maj. Gen. William B. Kean led the 35th Infantry, the 5th Regimental Combat Team from Hawaii and the 1st Provisional Marine Brigade to meet the North Korean 6th Division southwest of Masan.

MacArthur had requested a Marine regimental combat team

on July 2, and the Marines landed at Pusan's docks on the night of August 2. They were the first troops to leave the continental United States. (The 9th Infantry—which had fought with the Marines before—left Tacoma, Washington, three days later and, because of the shorter voyage, reached Pusan two days ahead of the Marines.)

When the war began, the Marine Corps had 74,279 men and women on active duty. On July 7, it created the provisional brigade built around the 5th Marines at Camp Pendleton and Marine Aircraft Group 33 at El Toro, California. An integrated air-ground Marine team was going into combat under a single commander. This example of the Marine Corps ideal would not last long.

The Brigade was commanded by Brig. Gen. Edward A. Craig, a slim, white-haired Connecticut Yankee who had fought on Bougainville, Guam (where he won the Navy Cross) and Iwo Jima. Brig. Gen. Thomas J. Cushman led MAG-33. Their command totaled 6,534 men. Lt. Col. Raymond L. Murray commanded the major ground element, the 5th Marines. This was the regiment of Belleau Wood, Nicaragua, Guadalcanal, New Britain, Peleliu and Okinawa. Commissioned out of Texas A&M in 1935, Murray had fought at Guadalcanal (Silver Star), Tarawa (Silver Star) and Saipan (Navy Cross). The 1st Battalion, 11th Marines, commanded by Lt. Col. Ransom H. Wood, was the Brigade's artillery.

Lt. Gen. Shepherd, the new commanding general of Fleet Marine Force, Pacific, and his G-3, Col. Victor H. Krulak, flew ahead to Tokyo to confer with MacArthur. There, on July 10, they learned that MacArthur wanted to land an entire Marine division far behind the enemy lines and cut off the North Koreans from their base. It was a bold plan. Shepherd told MacArthur that the 1st Marine Division could be ready to land on September 15. On the spot, Shepherd drafted a message for MacArthur's signature requesting that the Joint Chiefs send a Marine division.[19]

It was D-Day minus 67 for the Inchon landing.

Commandant Cates saw the Brigade off from San Diego on July 14, just seven days after it had been activated and 12 days after MacArthur had requested it. Most of its officers and noncoms were combat veterans of World War II. Its equipment had been retrieved from mothball in the California desert. But its three rifle battalions had only two companies apiece.

Craig and Cushman flew to Tokyo. MacArthur told them of his plan for an amphibious landing at Inchon and agreed that the Marine air-ground team would be kept intact.

On July 19, President Truman, on the Joint Chiefs' recommendation, called up 33,000 Marines in the Organized Marine Corps Reserve to active duty. Within 12 days, reserve units began arriving at Camp Pendleton; and by September 11, all organized ground reserve units had reported for duty. On August 7, 50,000 Marines of the Volunteer Reserve were notified that they too would be called to active duty.

The Marine Brigade sailed for Japan to prepare for MacArthur's amphibious counterattack. But suddenly on July 25, plans changed. The North Koreans, on an "end run," were closing on Pusan from the west as well as from the north. The Eighth Army, too short of troops to cover the whole 120-mile front, was falling back to contract its lines. While still at sea, the Brigade's ground elements were diverted directly to Korea. Amphibious assault had to wait.

The next day, Craig flew to Taegu, Korea; reported to Walker; flew over the combat area, and scouted the southwest side of the folding Pusan Perimeter in a Jeep. When the Marines docked at Pusan on the evening of August 2, Craig still did not know where they would be sent the next morning. They would be a fire brigade. They unloaded all night under searchlights and, after a final hot meal back on their ships, boarded trains and Army trucks and headed west 40 miles to the area around Changwon. Each Marine carried only his pack, weapon, ammunition and rations.

The ROKs guarded the shorter northern face of the Pusan Perimeter. On the longer western side, the 1st Cavalry and 24th Infantry Divisions stood behind the Naktong River, with the 25th Division, reinforced by the Army's 5th Regimental Combat Team and the Marine Brigade, to the south of them. Opposing them at this southern end of the line was the veteran North Korean 6th Division reinforced by the 83rd Motorcycle Regiment with machine guns on Russian "jeeps" and motorcycle sidecars.

On August 3, in the Marine Brigade's first action, Corsairs of Lt. Col. Walter E. Lischeid's VMF-214 (the Black Sheep squadron of World War II) flew off the escort carrier *Sicily*. During the following days, the planes struck Seoul and Inchon and on August 6 were joined by Maj. Arnold A. Lund's VMF-323 off *Badoeng Strait*. The night fighters of VMF(N)-513 operated out of Japan. On August 5, Maj. Kenneth L. Reusser, now executive officer of VMF-214, won a second Navy Cross; flying at daringly low altitudes, he shot up enemy tanks, a tanker, trucks and soldiers near Inchon.

On the ground, the Marine Brigade took its first casualties on the night of August 3–4, when trigger-happy novices wounded three Marines. Brig. Gen. Craig was furious.

Task Force Kean was now ordered to launch the Americans' first counterattack of the war—from Chindong-ni to Chinji. The 35th Infantry would strike from the northeast; the 5th Regimental Combat Team would take the direct road westward through the center, and the Marines would loop to the southwest along a road 17 miles longer through Kosong and Changchon. The attack would begin on August 7, coincidentally the eighth anniversary of the Marines' landing on Guadalcanal.

On the night of August 6, the 3rd Battalion, 5th Marines dug in on Hill 255. Its commander, Lt. Col. Robert D. Taplett, a rangy thirty-one-year-old native of Tyndall, South Dakota, was ordered to rush reinforcements forward to help beleaguered F Company of the 5th Infantry hold Hill 342. Taplett sent 2d Lt. John H. Cahill with 52 men from G Company. After they had advanced three miles through artillery fire, two Marines were wounded by rifle fire from U.S. soldiers who had not gotten the word that the Marines were in the area.

The sun rose and the heat became stifling. Cahill led his platoon up the steep hill, and men fell out. Cahill and Sgt. Lee Buettner went ahead to locate the Army unit on the summit and were fired on by the enemy—the first North Korean action against the Marine Brigade on the ground. Only 37 of the 52 Marines reached the crest; by then, three Marines were dead and eight wounded.

The North Koreans surrounded the hill. An airdrop of water and ammunition fell into enemy territory. The Marines' 2d Battalion was sent forward; but D and E Companies, stopped by the 112-degree heat and some enemy fire, did not reach the perimeter until the following day.

Just before dawn on August 8, the enemy attacked in

449

hand-to-hand fighting. When D Company arrived, the Army company and Cahill's platoon pulled out. Cahill had six Marines killed and 12 wounded. D Company came under heavy fire. While trying to bring in the body of 2d Lt. Wallace J. Reid, Capt. John Finn, Jr., the company commander, was hit in the head and shoulders and crawled back to the lines. His executive officer, 1st Lt. Robert T. Hanifin, Jr., took command. The enemy attacked again. Hanifin collapsed from heat exhaustion, and veteran Master Sgt. Harold Reeves and 2d Lt. Leroy K. Wirth of the 11th Marines took over. On August 9, D Company, with eight dead and 28 wounded, turned the crest of Hill 342 over to the all-black 24th Infantry.

Other Marine elements were also receiving their baptism of fire. On August 8, the enemy seized the peak north of the Marines' Hill 255 and opened fire on the 5th Marines. From their new position, the enemy could cut the Masan–Chindong-ni supply road. H Company's commander, Capt. Joseph C. Fegan, Jr., ordered 2d Lt. John O. Williams and his 1st Platoon to attack. Grenades and machine-gun fire pinned them down 30 yards from the enemy. Fegan told Williams to fall back and ordered up the 3rd Platoon. There was no response. The men were shaken by the 1st Platoon's defeat; Fegan himself had to take over the assault. Then, Cpl. Melvin James led the assault squad into the enemy's left flank and hit them with BAR fire. James pulled six wounded Marines to safety. Tech. Sgt. Ray Morgan and Pfc. Donald Terrio attacked the enemy's right flank and destroyed two machine guns. Captain Fegan carried out Sgt. Edward F. Barnett, who had been shot in the elbow and hip. The 3d Platoon wiped out the enemy position at a cost of six Marines killed and 32 wounded. The next morning, H Company crossed a saddle and shoved the enemy from the heights.

The Marines now headed south. The 1st Battalion led by Lt. Col. George R. Newton seized Hill 308 and cleared the vital Tosan road junction. Then, the 2d Battalion, commanded by Lt. Col. Harold S. Roise of Moscow, Idaho, assumed the lead and at the narrow Taedabok Pass, nine miles short of Kosong, ran into an ambush of automatic fire from the high ground. Taplett's 3rd Battalion took an alternate route to leapfrog ahead. Maj. Morgan J. McNeely sped ahead with a patrol to scout the road. His Jeep disappeared around a bend. G Company found the bullet-riddled Jeep and McNeely and his five men lying on the ground. Three had been killed and three, severely wounded. First Lt. Jack Westerman dashed to the Jeep and brought back McNeely, mortally wounded. Westerman, wounded himself, was awarded the Navy Cross. The rest of the patrol had to be left there until the next morning.

On August 11, with Taedabok Pass cleared, the Marines pushed aggressively toward Kosong at the bottom of the Marines' road loop and started for Sachon. H Company led the way into Kosong behind two M-26 Pershing tanks. Marine air and ground worked well together. The 11th Marines and VMF-323 flushed out and destroyed an estimated hundred troop-laden vehicles of the enemy's 83rd Motorcycle Regiment. The North Koreans shot down two of the first four attacking Corsairs. Lt. Doyle Cole was pulled from the bay by Brig. Gen. Craig in his helicopter. But Capt. Vivian Moses drowned in a rice paddy after he crashlanded and was knocked unconscious. Only the day before, Moses had been shot down in enemy territory and been rescued by helicopter. His was MAG-33's first combat death in Korea.

August 12 was a fighting afternoon. At the village of Changchon, the enemy grabbed the hills on both sides of the road and tried to ambush the approaching Marine column. About 1 P.M., the Marine point—a 15-man Jeep-borne detachment of Capt. Kenneth J. Houghton's Reconnaissance Company—moving a mile ahead of B Company, sprang the trap prematurely. B Company was also taken under fire from both flanks. Pershing tanks moved up. Capt. John L. Tobin, B Company commander, sent the 1st Platoon to help the Recon Company and the 3rd Platoon to attack the hill on the right front from which the Recon Company had been fired on. The 3rd Platoon took the hill easily; but the enemy waited on the reverse slope, counterattacked and drove the Marines halfway back down. A Company attacked a hill on the right and took the crest by 5 P.M. Corsairs hit the enemy machine-gun positions and picked over a column of vehicles hightailing it back to Sachon, four miles up the road. B Company attacked on the left side of the road and seized Hill 202 by 8 P.M. The Marines had suffered three killed and 13 wounded. The men were dog-tired and without water or rations. In four days, they had driven the enemy back 22 miles.

The Marines expected to reach Sachon the next day. But that afternoon, the 3rd Battalion had been hurried all the way back to Chindong-ni to help stem an attack that had overrun two Army artillery battalions. Taplett's Marines arrived at dusk and immediately took the first ridge north of the road. By 10 A.M. the next morning, they commanded two ridgelines without a single casualty.

The Brigade was now engaged on two fronts 25 miles apart. Craig commanded both of them by helicopter. At midnight, Lt. Col. Newton received orders to return to Chindong-ni. But before the 1st and 2d Battalions could withdraw from Chang-chon, B Company had to fight off a furious night attack. At 4:45 A.M., North Korean veterans of the Chinese civil war struck the company's front and flank. The 3rd Platoon on the left flank was surprised and overrun. The enemy captured two machine guns and turned them on the Marines, until, at dawn, 3.5-inch rocket launchers destroyed the guns. Captain Tobin ordered the 3rd Platoon's survivors to hold, and artillery supported them with pinpoint shooting. The enemy kept coming. Tobin consolidated the 1st and 2d Platoons in a single perimeter. After an hour's slugging match, the enemy fell back to the lower slopes of Hill 202. Ordered to return to the road in order to move out, B Company disengaged a squad at a time. The company had 12 killed, 18 wounded and eight missing. Captain Tobin asked permission to recover the eight missing Marines on the left flank. Lt. Col. Newton denied his request because the battalion was late in obeying Brigade orders to withdraw. The 1st and 2d Battalions left for Chindong-ni with Engineers and tanks covering their rear. The men were bitter that the eight Marines— whether dead or alive—had been left behind.

The Eighth Army's first offensive had stopped the North Korean 6th Division's sweep against the southern end of the Pusan Perimeter. But further north another crisis had already erupted.

On August 15, the Brigade moved by railroad 75 miles north to Miryang. There, the Marines ate their first hot meal in 13 days, bathed in the muddy Miryang River and replaced their rotted uniforms. They came under control of the 24th Infantry Division, Brig. Gen. John H. Church commanding. They were going into the Battle of the Naktong.

The Marines were hardening now, more confident. They had marched in Korea's heat and hills. Young men had been tried in battle. A British military observer saw them pass through Miryang and reported:

> If Miryang is lost Taegu becomes untenable and we will be faced with a withdrawal from Korea. I am heartened that the Marine Brigade will move against the Naktong salient tomorrow. . . . these Marines have the swagger, confidence and hardness that must have been in Stonewall Jackson's Army of the Shenandoah. They remind me of the Coldstreams at Dunkerque. Upon this thin line of reasoning, I cling to the hope of victory.[20]

The Naktong River was the last natural barrier on the western side of the Pusan Perimeter, and its valley offered the enemy a lowland corridor to Pusan. The North Koreans had started crossing the river at a number of points on August 6. Their offensive endangered the lifeline from Taegu, the provisional capital, all the way to Pusan. They came over most threateningly at the Naktong Bulge, an area four miles by five, east of the river and west of Miryang and Yongsan. At the bulge, the river bends sharply westward around a hill mass dominated by Hill 311. Blocking the east side of this oxbow were two hills: Cloverleaf Hill north of the Yongsan–Naktong road and mile-and-a-half-long Obong-ni Ridge south of the road. By August 10, most of the North Korean 4th Division had crossed the Naktong, overrun the bulge area and begun driving eastward. On August 18, Taegu was evacuated and the South Korean government fled to Pusan.

Task Force Hill—about three Army infantry regiments under Col. John G. Hill, USA, who had brought the 9th Infantry to Korea—tried futilely to contain and counterattack the enemy. The official Army history of the war reports: "When the attack of 15 August failed, General Walker knew he must commit more strength into the bulge if he was to drive out the enemy. Impatient and angry, he came to Church's command post during the morning and said, 'I am going to give you the Marine brigade. I want this situation cleaned up, and quick.' "[21]

The all-out counterattack began at 8 A.M. on August 17. While the 19th and 34th Infantry Regiments hit from the northeast and part of the 21st Infantry blocked on the south, the Army's depleted 9th Regimental Combat Team and the Marine Brigade struck westward in the center along the Yongsan–Naktong road. On the left, south of the road, the Marines attacked Obong-ni Ridge—which was being called No Name Ridge—under cover of the 9th RCT; and then north of the road, the soldiers were to attack Cloverleaf Hill while the Marines covered them. The attack was less than expertly managed.

> Shortage of transport had delayed the arrival of the brigade and had adversely affected the artillery preparation; a misunderstanding with the Army unit on the right led to a lack of flank support; the air strike from the escort carriers was 15 minutes late, so that the 18 Corsairs had only half their intended time to work over enemy positions. The advance uphill, against a numerically superior and entrenched enemy, was carried out with great bravery but at heavy cost; of the 240 men of the 2d Battalion [5th Marines] which led the attack, 142 had become casualties by mid-day.[22]

When Roise's 2d Battalion made the Marine attack, Capt. Andrew M. Zimmer, now in command of D Company, moved up with 2d Lt. Michael J. Shinka leading the 3rd Platoon. On its right was Staff Sgt. T. Albert Crowson's 1st Platoon and on its left, the 2d Platoon of E Company. The understrength rifle platoons crossed a rice paddy in eerie silence. When they were halfway up the steep, bare slope, dozens of machine guns opened up on them, inflicting heavy casualties. With the artillery ineffectual and the Corsairs late, Crowson's platoon was stopped. Captain Zimmer sent in Tech. Sgt. Sidney S. Dickerson's 2d Platoon, which had been covering the assault. The Marines came under automatic weapons fire from both flanks.

By mid-morning, Mike Shinka had only 15 men left. When they reached the crest of Hill 109, one peak of Obong-ni Ridge, his nine remaining Marines came under intense fire. Running short of ammunition, they withdrew partway down the slope. By then, Shinka had six men able to fight. He went back up to the crest of Hill 109 looking for his wounded. He pulled Pfc. George J. Hric, who had been shot in the stomach, out of his foxhole. A bullet shattered Shinka's chin. He tossed a grenade at a North Korean who was crawling up the hill and continued to drag out the wounded man. A bullet hit Shinka's right arm and sent him spinning down the hill.

On D Company's left, 1st Lt. William E. Sweeney took E Company against Obong-ni Ridge. Second Lt. Nickolas A. Arkadis' 1st Platoon neared the crest and was hit by flanking enemy fire and short "friendly" artillery shells. At 11:30, E Company was ordered back to leave room for an air strike; but some Marines within 25 yards of the summit were caught in the strafing. Enemy machine gunners enfiladed E Company and its attack crumbled.

By noon, the 2d Battalion had 23 dead and 119 wounded—nearly 60 percent of the 240 riflemen in the attack, "2/5 took a terrible beating as platoons and squads, decimated by the heavy fighting, advanced and fell back."[23] Arkadis, Dickerson and Wirth were among the wounded. With the battalion short a third rifle company, "the ridge could not be taken."[24] The Marines had been stopped.

At 1 P.M., Brig. Gen. Craig ordered Newton's 1st Battalion to pass through the shot-up 2d Battalion and seize the ridge. Starting at 4 P.M., the 9th Infantry successfully attacked Cloverleaf Hill. When Captain Tobin was seriously wounded in the chest and arm, Capt. Francis I. "Ike" Fenton, Jr., took command of B Company. Under flanking enemy fire from the 9th RCT zone, B Company stalled. Pershing tanks and 81mm mortars blasted the enemy gunners; and by evening, the company held the crest of the two northern most hills of Obong-ni Ridge in the rain.

To the south, A Company passed through E Company at 3 P.M. and halfway up Obong-ni Ridge came under machine-gun fire. First Lt. Robert C. Sebilian, decorated as a sergeant on Bougainville and now leading the 1st Platoon, was hit, and Tech. Sgt. Orval F. McMullen pressed the attack. The 1st Platoon advanced between Hills 109 and 117 and was pinned down. On his left, 2d Lt. Thomas H. Johnston's 2d Platoon was cut in half and finally stopped. The diminutive Johnston rose and charged in a one-man assault, hurling grenades at the enemy machine gun. He reached the saddle south of Hill 117 before he was killed. Tech. Sgt. Frank J. Lawson took command of what was left of the platoon, now no more than a squad. Capt. John R. Stevens, a World War II signal officer, sent A Company's 3rd Platoon to join Lawson, and it too was stopped by machine-gun fire and grenades.

Four Pershing M-26 tanks of the 3rd Platoon, A Company Tanks had supported the Marines' attack all day and were back refueling and re-arming when word was received at 8 P.M. that four enemy T-34s were approaching the Marine lines. Second Lt. Granville G. Sweet ordered his 1st Section to load with 90mm armor-piercing shells. Corsairs destroyed the enemy's rear tank and dispersed its accompanying riflemen. The front T-34 was demolished by 75mm recoilless rifles and Tech. Sgt. Cecil R. Fullerton's lead Pershing. The second enemy tank was knocked out by 3.5-inch rockets, the recoilless rifles and the two lead Marine tanks. The Pershings' fire exploded the final enemy tank behind the two blazing T-34 hulks. In five minutes, the Marines had shattered the myth of T-34 invincibility.

By dark, the Marines held the northern end of Obong-ni Ridge. B Company was on the crest of Hills 102 and 109, and Stevens tied in his A Company on B's left to prepare for the expected enemy counterattack. On A Company's far left flank, 1st Lt. George C. Fox's 3rd Platoon dangled unprotected.

At 10 P.M., mortar shells began falling among A Company's foxholes; and white phosphorus shells wiped out the company's mortar section. Starting at 2:30 A.M. with a green flare signal, the North Koreans smashed down on A Company; and B Company was hit three times by soldiers covered by automatic fire from Hill 117. A Company's 2d Platoon fought vastly superior numbers of enemy for a half hour; Tech. Sgt. Lawson was wounded three times. The platoon was finally overrun and the Marines' line penetrated. The two companies were split. The enemy reached A Company's command post behind the 2d Platoon and pushed it back down the draw. Stevens' executive officer, 1st Lt. Fred F. Eubanks, Jr., attacked singlehandedly up the gully; he was joined by 2d Lt. Francis W. Muetzel, who had been left for dead in his foxhole when the 2d Platoon retreated.

He had regained consciousness and fought through the enemy to the Marine lines. Marine artillery helped A Company's hard-pressed riflemen; and by dawn, the enemy attack was spent. B Company still held its two hilltops.

A Company counterattacked at 7 A.M. BARman Pfc. Harold Twedt knocked out two machine guns before he was killed. Finally, the remnant of A Company, aided by a precise air strike, seized Hill 117. Major Lund ordered Capt. John P. Kelley to destroy a nest of four machine guns 50 yards in front of the Marines. Dive-bombing his Corsair with exquisite accuracy, Kelley put his 500-pound bomb right on the target. The Marines on the ground were knocked off their feet; one BARman was killed. But the strike was totally effective, and the Marine advance gained overwhelming momentum. Twenty men pushed south to take Hill 147, the next peak, and continued on to wipe the enemy from Hill 153, Obong-ni's highest crest. By mid-afternoon, the Marines held all of Obong-ni Ridge.

The next objective was Hill 207, west of Obong-ni Ridge. Taplett's 3rd Battalion climbed it from the north on the morning of August 18, with G Company on the right spur and H Company on the left. By 12:37, the two companies had taken the crest against light opposition. Now the entire Naktong Bulge was swarming with North Korean troops scurrying for the river in panicked retreat. Artillery, aircraft and mortars plastered the fleeing targets. "Victory turned into slaughter when the Brigade supporting arms concentrated on the masses of Communists plunging into the river."[25] "The enemy was killed in such numbers that the river was definitely discolored by blood."[26]

The 3rd Battalion attacked Hill 311, the final ridge in the bulge itself. When Captain Fegan was wounded and evacuated, H Company's attack bogged down. G Company circled the hill from the south, and 1st Lt. Robert D. Bohn sent Cahill's 1st Platoon around to the west. It overran the northern half of the summit until it was thrown back by the defenders facing H Company. Cahill was among the platoon's ten casualties. G and H Companies spent a quiet night and early in the morning of August 19 occupied the hilltop without opposition. The Naktong Bulge had been cleaned out at a cost to the Marines of 66 dead, one missing and 278 wounded. The North Korean 4th Division had been decisively defeated.

The Marine Brigade was shipped back to a bivouac area near Masan that became known as the Bean Patch. The men ate hot meals again, checked their weapons, received mail and beer. On August 29, Brig. Gen. Craig awarded 87 Purple Hearts at a ceremony attended by President Rhee. The 1st Battalion, 11th Marines went over to Chindong-ni to assist the 25th Division. Eight hundred replacements joined the Brigade, and volunteers were recruited out of supporting units for the rifle companies. In the ranks, there were rumors of a coming amphibious operation.

On August 29, Col. "Chesty" Puller's 1st Marines and the headquarters of the 1st Marine Division began landing at Kobe, Japan. Puller, now fifty-two, had scrambled to get this command and had reported to Camp Pendleton only 25 days before. The 1st Division was being pieced together with Murray's 5th Marines and Puller's 1st. The newly activated 7th Marines was to be the division's third rifle regiment; and the 3rd Battalion, 6th Marines, with the Sixth Fleet in the Mediterranean was shipped from Crete through the Suez Canal to complete the 7th Marines. The division's commander, Maj. Gen. Graves B. Erskine, had been sent on a secret State Department mission to Southeast Asia in July. He had been succeeded by Maj. Gen. Oliver P. Smith, a lanky native of Menard, Texas. A scholarly, meticulous and abstemious officer, Smith had been a Marine since 1917. He commanded the 5th Marines at Cape Gloucester and served on Peleliu and Okinawa. Arriving in Tokyo on August 22, he struggled to extract the 5th Marines from the Pusan Perimeter, since the 7th Marines could not arrive in time for D-Day on September 15 at Inchon. Without the 5th Marines, Smith would have only one Marine regiment for the invasion. MacArthur ordered the 5th Marines returned to the division.

But again the enemy upset the Marines' plans. On September 1, the North Koreans launched an offensive with 98,000 men and penetrated the UN lines all around the perimeter. MacArthur rescinded his order releasing the 5th Marines. Smith was offered the Army's 32d Infantry but declined because the regiment had not been trained for amphibious assault. Finally, a compromise was worked out by which the 5th Marines would join the 1st Marine Division after September 5—but first they would return to the Naktong.

On the afternoon of September 1, the well-rested Brigade was trucked back to Miryang.

> There the North Koreans threatened Miryang and with it the lifeline of the entire Eighth Army position. There, for the moment at least, was the most critical spot of the far-flung battlefield. An hour before noon General Walker ordered General Craig to prepare the marines to move at once. Just after noon the action order came and the marines made ready to depart at 1330. They were going back to the bulge area.[27]

The enemy had already reoccupied the Naktong Bulge; driven a hole eight miles deep and six miles wide into the 2d Infantry Division, which had replaced the 24th Division along the Naktong, and had briefly seized Yongsan. It was the North Koreans' final lunge to reach Pusan before the United Nations' forces could gather unbeatable strength.

Lt. Gen. Walker put the Brigade under operational control of Maj. Gen. Lawrence B. Keiser, USA, commanding the 2d Infantry Division. He was ordered to restore the river line.

The Marines were to jump off on September 3 four miles east of their earlier battleground near the Naktong. Newton's 1st Battalion was to advance south of the Yongsan-Naktong road and Roise's 2d Battalion north of it. But on the night of September 2, the enemy smashed the 9th Infantry, through which Roise was to pass.

At 7:15 A.M., D and E Companies moved forward. With tanks and artillery, the Marines' firepower stopped the North Korean 9th Division cold. At 8:55 A.M., A and B Companies attacked from below Chukchon-ni, but they were out of position and had to wade through hundreds of yards of knee-deep rice paddies under small-arms fire. At 11 A.M. they launched their attack from the edge of the paddy, making so frightful a noise that a company of North Koreans jumped from their foxholes on the forward slope of the ridge ahead and fled. Marine BAR and riflemen killed most of them. And A Company took the ridgetop.

Corsairs routed the enemy in front of the 1st Battalion and sent them fleeing north across the road to Hill 117 in front of the 2d Battalion. D Company, now commanded by 1st Lt. H. J.

Smith, raced to cut off their retreat, was isolated and took heavy casualties. Along the road, Marine tanks battled enemy antitank guns and put five North Korean tanks out of action. That night, the 2d Battalion was two miles west of Yongsan.

On the high ground south of the road, B Company, with help from A Company Engineers, continued to press the enemy into the 2d Battalion's zone. A Company enveloped Hill 91 and seized it in heavy fighting.

This had been another rough day for Roise's 2d Battalion with 18 Marines killed and 77 wounded, most of them in D Company. Therefore, on September 4, the 3rd Battalion passed through the 2d; and the 1st and 3rd pushed quickly forward past abandoned North Korean vehicles and hundreds of enemy dead. The Marines gained 4,000 yards before setting up defenses for the night.

As the Marines advanced in rain and fog on September 5, North Korean artillery and mortars greeted them from Obong-ni Ridge, their old battleground. Lt. Col. Murray planned to retake the ridge with the 1st and 3rd Battalions, while the 9th Infantry attacked toward Cloverleaf Hill. But shortly after noon, the situation changed; and Murray had to shift his attention from Obong-ni to the road. Suddenly, taking advantage of the lack of air support in the heavy weather, the enemy mounted a daytime counterattack. In a driving rain, North Korean soldiers and tanks attacked B Company, which had dug in on Hill 125. The enemy armor came up the road; and at the same curve that had been the site of the tank battle of August 17, the leading North Korean T-34 surprised and destroyed the Marines' first two M-26s. B Company's 3.5-inch rockets came to the rescue and wiped out two T-34s and an armored personnel carrier. Eight wrecked steel monsters now lay at that road bend.

Meanwhile, B Company on Hill 125 above the bend was hard pressed until the 9th Infantry threw in its artillery fire-power and Marine reinforcements from A Company were shifted over. Artillery and mortar fire finally finished off the enemy attack. For the day, the Marine Brigade had 35 killed and 91 wounded. The counteroffensive had neutralized two enemy divisions.

That night, the 2d Infantry Division took over the Marine positions; and Craig ordered the Brigade back to Pusan "for further operations against the enemy."[28] At dawn on September 6, the Marines returned to Pusan by truck through an icy rain.

That same day, another kind of battle broke out in Washington when a newspaper reported that a congressman had asked President Truman to give the Commandant a voice on the Joint Chiefs of Staff. The President had exploded and written the congressman: "For your information the Marine Corps is the Navy's police force and as long as I am President that is what it will remain. They have a propaganda machine that is almost equal to Stalin's." After the story hit the headlines, Truman gave the Marine Corps a public apology for his "unfortunate choice of language" and praised the "immediate response of the Marine Corps to a call for duty in Korea." But he did not back down from his view of the Corps.[29]

In three air-ground operations in exactly one month, the Marine Brigade had had 172 killed and 730 wounded. MAG-33 had flown 995 close-support missions, 80 percent of them directed by Tactical Air Control Parties on the ground. The Brigade's initial operation as part of Task Force Kean had been the first sustained Eighth Army counterattack of the war. "The next Brigade operation, the first battle of the Naktong, ranks with the hardest fights of Marine Corps history."[30] It drove the enemy back across the river with heavy losses. But ten days later, the Marines had to push them back again—although this time the Brigade was withdrawn before it could complete the job. The Marines had helped stop the North Korean invasion and save the Pusan Perimeter.

At Pusan for the next six days, the men slept in the open on the docks where they had landed a month before and ate their meals on the transports that would carry them around the Korean peninsula. The rifle battalions received their third rifle companies. And Marine officers gave weapons training to 3,000 men of the 1st Korean Marine Corps Regiment, which was to become the 1st Marine Division's fourth rifle regiment.

On September 13, after 67 days of existence, the 1st Provisional Marine Brigade was deactivated and its units joined the 1st Marine Division and sailed for Inchon.

3
"We Shall Land at Inchon"

General MacArthur possessed the vision and the unshakable faith that, even while his army was pinned into the southeastern corner of Korea, he could build a second assault force and strike a killing blow at the enemy's spine. He insisted that X Corps, this second force, land from the sea at the west coast port of Inchon; drive inland to the capital city of Seoul, the nexus of South Korea's communications, and sever the North Koreans' lifeline. He would reverse roles: He would invade; he would attack.

The experts—Army, Navy and Marines—tried to dissuade him. The risks were dangerous. The amphibious force would have to approach Inchon through a long, narrow channel at the one three-day period of the month when the tides were high enough (at least 29 feet) to carry the landing craft over the harbor's vast protective mud flats. His force would have to assault the urban waterfront of a large Oriental city in which determined defenders could hole up and work havoc against American ships, landing craft and Marines.

MacArthur was adamant. He rejected all the alternative landing sites proposed to him. He refused to delay the attack a month to permit time for buildup, training and rehearsals. The Army's Chief of Staff, the Chief of Naval Operations, the Commanding General of the Fleet Marine Force, Pacific, all came out to Tokyo. On August 23, the generals and admirals (but not the Marines) gathered in MacArthur's mahogany-paneled conference room in the Dai Ichi Building. They spoke of the tactical hazards: the natural obstacles, the shortage of time, the unlikelihood of surprise, the expectation of enemy mines, the advent of the typhoon season. The seventy-year-old general

462

listened to their presentations and then, calmly smoking his pipe, talked to them for 45 minutes. He stressed his belief in the overwhelming psychological advantages of the bold strategic stroke. In a dramatic near-whisper, he finished: "We shall land at Inchon, and I shall crush them!"[31]

The 1st Marine Division would deliver his amphibious blow. The 5th Marines would be shipped around from Pusan, and the newly arrived 1st Marines, from Japan. The division's third regiment, the 7th Marines, could not reach Korea until a week after the September 15 D-Day.

Fortunately, the post-World War II Marine officers and noncoms—and the Navy's leaders—were veterans of amphibious assault. And fortunately, also, the enemy—as long as the Chinese and Russians stayed out of the fight—had no aircraft, no submarines, no navy to oppose the American assault.

The landing would be conducted by the two-division X Corps, activated especially for this operation. The 7th Infantry Division would come in behind the 1st Marine Division. Overall command was given to MacArthur's chief of staff, Maj. Gen. Edward M. Almond, USA. The Marines had hoped that command of X Corps would go to Lt. Gen. Shepherd. But MacArthur decided otherwise—whether because, with Saipan in memory, the Army did not want Marines to command Army units or whether Almond wangled the job was long debated among Marines.

Time was the dragon. Inchon's extraordinary tides—among the most extreme in the world—flooded high enough for only three hours. The landing would have to be made in two parts. First, the Marines insisted, they had to capture the fortified island of Wolmi-do, which dominated the inner harbor. The 3rd Battalion, 5th Marines, would assault the island on the morning tide. The rest of the 5th Marines and the 1st Marines would land in the city itself on the evening tide. In between, the Marines on Wolmi-do would be exposed to hours of danger. And after the main landing, only two hours would remain before dark to get men and equipment ashore. "The planning was necessarily carried out in violation of all the rules and in record time."[32] It was the best that could be done.

Marine Corsairs led by Maj. Donald Bush flew photo-reconnaissance missions. And two weeks before D-Day, Navy

Lt. Eugene F. Clark, an old Asia hand, stole in with two South Koreans and scouted Inchon's mud flats and seawalls and radioed back his findings. He sent friendly Koreans to Seoul and Kimpo Airfield to check on enemy strengths. He even managed to relight the beacon of the harbor lighthouse on Palmi-do island to guide the amphibious task force.

Wolmi-do was blasted from sea and air for five days. Marine fliers of VMF-214 and -323 started napalm attacks on September 10 to burn off trees screening the North Korean guns. Navy planes followed up. On D minus two, five destroyers closed on Wolmi-do in broad daylight to entice the North Koreans into exposing their gun positions. The precarious tactic worked, the enemy batteries on the island and in the city revealed themselves—damaging three destroyers—and Wolmi-do rocked with naval and air bombardment.

Amphibious expert Rear Adm. James H. Doyle ordered the invasion force, Task Force 90, to sea a day early to avoid the 125-miles-per-hour winds of Typhoon Kezia. But still the armada had heavy going on the typhoon's edge. On September 12, the flagship *Mount McKinley* docked at Sasebo, Japan, to pick up MacArthur and his entourage. Lt. Gen. Shepherd came along as MacArthur's amphibious advisor. In addition to the 1st Division's Marines, the landing force of 25,040 men included nearly 3,000 men of the 1st Korean Marine Corps Regiment and about 2,750 specialized U.S. Army soldiers. The Secretary of the Navy required that all U.S. Marines who were not yet eighteen years old be removed from the operation, which subtracted some 500 young men from the landing force.

The column of 19 ships led by the destroyer *Mansfield* snaked through the dark passage toward Inchon, aided by the light on Palmi-do. D-Day on Friday, September 15, a warm, pleasant day, started with Marine and Navy carrier planes bombing and strafing through the early overcast. At 6:33 A.M., one platoon of Lt. Col. Taplett's G Company and three platoons of his H Company hit the northwest end of Wolmi-do. The rest of the assault companies landed two minutes later. They were greeted by only a few scattered shots.

Landing in water over his head, 1st Lt. Robert D. Bohn recovered and wheeled G Company to the right and up the northern slope of Radio Hill. Most of the North Koreans there surrendered. Capt. Patrick E. Wildman sent a detachment from H Company to hold the North Point of Wolmi-do and to block the long causeway leading to Inchon. The rest of H Company raced to the Standard Oil tanks in the industrial area of Wolmi-do facing Inchon. Ten tanks landed from A Company of the 1st Tank Battalion. At 6:55, Sgt. Alvin E. Smith, the guide of G Company's 3rd Platoon, raised the flag on the shell-torn crest of Radio Hill. On *Mount McKinley's* flag bridge, MacArthur rose from his swivel chair and said, "That's it. Let's get a cup of coffee."[33] And he sent a message to the fleet: "The Navy and Marines have never shone more brightly than this morning."[34]

It wasn't quite over. Capt. Robert A. McMullen's I Company, the battalion's new third rifle company, landed in the fourth wave and was met by a flurry of grenades from a bypassed enemy platoon at North Point. The North Koreans refused to surrender and a dozer tank sealed them in their holes. Another tank flushed out 30 North Koreans from a cave and they did surrender.

In less than an hour, the Marines held half of Wolmi-do. Engineers blocked the causeway to Inchon with mines to keep out enemy tanks. H Company moved slowly through the industrial area, and G Company cleared the rest of Radio Hill. By 8 A.M., the island and the harbor were under control. The Marines used the swimming pool at North Point, a pre-war resort, as a POW stockade. Total American casualties so far were 14 wounded. The initial phase had gone well.

At 10 A.M., Taplett ordered G Company to seize tiny Sowolmi-do, which was linked to Wolmi-do by a narrow 750-yard causeway. At the far end of the causeway waited an enemy platoon, cornered and ready to fight it out with machine guns and rifles. VMF-214 made a close support napalm attack. And a Marine mine-clearing team led over tanks followed by riflemen. At the end of the causeway, a fire fight erupted. In half an hour, it was over with 17 North Koreans dead and 19 prisoners; eight others later escaped to the mainland. On Sowolmi-do, three Marines were wounded. No Marines had yet been killed.

By 1 P.M., the tide had rolled back, leaving more than a thousand Marines stranded on their captured islands in a sea of mud. These were tense, silent hours. While Corsairs searched inland for enemy reinforcements (and found none), Lt. Col.

Taplett organized a defense against counterattack from Inchon. He proposed sending a tank-infantry force into the seemingly empty city but was denied permission.

For the main landing, Newton's 1st and Roise's 2d Battalion, 5th Marines, would land in the very heart of Inchon, on Red Beach, actually a strip of stone seawall, north of Wolmi-do. They would seize a 3,000-yard arc, with Cemetery Hill on the left and Observatory Hill in the center, and press through the city's streets and already burning buildings to the inner tidal basin on the right. Puller's 1st Marines would land three miles to the southeast on Blue Beach in a suburban industrial area at the base of the promontory on which Inchon sat. The 5th Marines would attack directly through the city; the 1st Marines would envelop it from the rear.

The final bombardment started at 2:30. Four cruisers and six destroyers and Navy Skyraiders and Marine Corsairs set the whole waterfront aflame. As the waters in front of Inchon rose again, the barrage climaxed with 6,000 rockets.

At Red Beach, two assault platoons of Capt. John R. Stevens' A Company landed on the left at 5:33 P.M., climbing their ladders up the seawall as though attacking from a trench. They met heavy fire from the northern or left flank and from bunkers directly in front. Several Marines were hit immediately; the others could advance only a few yards. With the 1st Platoon pinned down on the left, 1st Lt. Baldomero Lopez, a twenty-five-year-old Annapolis graduate from Tampa, Florida, brought in the 3rd Platoon. Casualties mounted. As Lopez tried to hurl a grenade against a machine-gun bunker, he was hit in the right shoulder and arm. Unable to throw his grenade, he swept it under him and smothered its explosion with his body.[35] Two Marines attacked the bunker with flamethrowers and were shot down.

The second wave was late; so without waiting, 2d Lt. Francis W. Muetzel took his 2d Platoon south of Cemetery Hill and up a street toward the Asahi Brewery. When the Marines reached the brewery, they were ordered back to the beach to help out. But Muetzel found the south side of Cemetery Hill a good approach and assaulted it. In ten minutes, his platoon took the summit and captured the dazed members of a North Korean mortar company. That was the key to Red Beach. At 5:55,

Captain Stevens fired an amber star cluster as a victory signal. A Company had 8 killed and 28 wounded.

On the right, Capt. Samuel Jaskilka's E Company landed at 5:31. The seawall rose four feet higher than the landing crafts' ramps; the Marines put up wooden ladders and hurled grenades over the wall. Quickly, 2d Lt. Edwin A. Deptula's 1st Platoon was on shore without casualties. It pushed inland and reached the British Consulate at 8:45. Another platoon seized the lower slopes of Observatory Hill. Together, they secured the right flank for the next 22 waves of landing craft.

From Wolmi-do, the 3rd Battalion added its firepower and removed the mines from the causeway so its tanks could move to the mainland.

C and D Companies were assigned to capture 200-foot-high Observatory Hill behind the center of Red Beach. But elements of the two companies landed on the wrong beaches, and Capt. Poul E. Pedersen, commander of C Company, was delayed when his boat took a stalled LCVP in tow. The confusion gave the enemy on Observatory Hill time to recover from the pre-assault bombardment and set up their machine guns.

Now, eight supply-laden LSTs approached the seawall against enemy mortar and machine-gun fire. LST crews fired their 40mm and 20mm cannon wildly at the beach and drove Muetzel's platoon from the crest of Cemetery Hill and down the reverse slope. Muetzel's platoon still had not had a single casualty, but the LSTs killed one 2d Battalion Marine and wounded 23. As soon as the ships came close enough, angry Marines stormed aboard and demanded that the sailors stop shooting.

As the uncontrolled firing finally stopped, 2d Lt. Byron L. Magness led the 2d Platoon of C Company against Observatory Hill. Second Lt. Max A. Merritt's 60mm mortar section followed the riflemen, and Tech. Sgt. Max Stein was wounded knocking out a machine gun with grenades. Magness' group seized the saddle between the two peaks of Observatory Hill as darkness took over.

Capt. Francis I. Fenton, Jr., brought B Company ashore in the 2d Battalion zone to avoid small-arms fire; and Lt. Col. Newton radioed him to assume C Company's mission and assault the northern half of Observatory Hill. In the darkness, B

467

Company fought up the hill; six Marines were wounded on the way up. Fenton gained the crest at 8 P.M. and made contact with Magness' force in the saddle on his right.

Further right, 1st Lt. H. J. Smith's D Company attacked the southern half of Observatory Hill. Smith thought Jaskilka's E Company had already taken the southern peak; and D Company, with 2d Lt. Ray Heck's 1st Platoon in the lead, marched up the street toward the top of the hill. They were greeted by machine guns on their right; and in a 15-minute fire fight, one Marine was killed and three Marines and the Navy corpsman wounded. F Company covered the extreme right flank of Red Beach.

Meanwhile, around on the southern side of the Inchon promontory, Puller's 1st Marines were assaulting Blue Beach through thick black smoke and the brown haze of wind-whipped rain. This landing—unrehearsed and conducted by a regiment which, unlike the 5th Marines, had not fought together—was chaotic.

On the left, Blue Beach One, Lt. Col. Allan Sutter's 2d Battalion started landing on schedule at 5:30. It met no opposition, but the naval bombardment had caused a landslide that blocked the only exit road. The amphibious vehicles came to a halt. F Company grounded in the mud 300 yards offshore, and the Marines had to wade in. Six hundred Marines of the two companies finally plunged ahead on foot to the high ground toward the northeast, leaving the LVT crews to dig out the road with picks and shovels.

To the right on Blue Beach Two, the 3rd Battalion ran into some scattered fire. On the left side of this area, some of I Company's aluminum ladders buckled; but the Marines had anticipated that and Engineers anchored cargo nets to the top of the 15-foot seawall. When G Company's lead LVT got stuck in the mud, it stopped the others. Capt. George C. Westover dismounted his men, and they fanned out to block the lowland corridor leading to the beach.

Lt. Col. Thomas L. Ridge found a cove and ramp on the right of the beach usable and shifted many of the LVTs there. And, having expected confusion on the beach, Puller came ashore at H-plus 30 minutes to take charge.

As G and I Companies rapidly cleared the beach, they took casualties from a machine gun in a tower 500 yards inland. The gun was silenced by fire from the LVTs. The Marines advanced through smoke-filled streets and past blazing buildings. While G Company pushed into the lowland area, I Company veered right to the tip of Hill 233 on the southern end of the beachhead. The 2d Battalion had one killed and 19 wounded.

The 1st Battalion in reserve was supposed to land behind the 2d Battalion on Blue Two, but by mistake wound up two miles to the left of the beachhead at the inner tidal basin. Lt. Col. Jack Hawkins, who had made a spectacular escape from a Japanese POW camp in World War II, rounded up most of his men and sent them in the correct direction. But the boats for one platoon of B Company had already pulled away and left the platoon at the tidal basin all night. In the morning, it hiked over to rejoin its company, rounding up prisoners on the way. Because of the heads-up work of a smart coxswain, C Company landed at the right place. And eventually most of the 1st Battalion moved forward to its assembly area half a mile inland.

Blue Beach was a dreadful example of a landing attempted without adequate time for training or rehearsal. There was a serious shortage of Navy guide boats. Groups of landing craft and entire assault waves landed in the wrong places. But despite the confusion, assault-wise Marine officers kept the attack going. Fortunately, there was no significant opposition.

By night, the 2d Battalion had secured enough of Hill 117 directly ahead to cover the Inchon–Seoul highway with fire. G and I Companies blocked the center. And H Company's 1st Platoon circled to the extreme right and attacked a North Korean company on the small cape topped by Hill 94. The enemy fled, leaving 30 casualties.

The buildup on the beaches went on all night. The 1st Shore Party Battalion, under Tarawa veteran Lt. Col. Henry P. Crowe, worked by floodlight to unload the LSTs' ammunition, rations, water, fuel, engineer supplies and combat vehicles. The ships had to be ready to pull out on the morning tide. Bulldozers moved along the seawall under some enemy fire, pushing down masonry that blocked the unloading. The Engineers managed to get a switch engine and six cars running in the Inchon railroad yards.

By 10 P.M., the 1st and 2d Battalions of the 11th Marines, delayed by the confusion in the inner harbor, were ready to deliver artillery fire. Tanks crossed the causeway, which the enemy had failed to destroy, and joined tanks landed from the LSTs at Red Beach. There were 13,000 Americans ashore. Marine casualties for D-Day had been 22 killed, 174 wounded in action and 14 non-battle casualties.

On Saturday morning, the 1st and 5th Marines attacked at dawn. Murray's 5th Marines moved through the southern part of Inchon, leaving the seaport to be cleared by the extremely zealous Korean Marines. The 5th advanced three miles and linked up with Puller's 1st Marines. That closed off Inchon. Together, the two regiments moved through the sprawling, dead seaport until they held a line about three miles long with its flanks on the water.

Five miles away, eight planes of VMF-214 intercepted six T-34 tanks heading toward Inchon in broad daylight with no infantry support. The fliers thought they knocked out all the enemy tanks, but this proved to be incorrect. Capt. William F. Simpson's Corsair was hit and failed to pull out of its dive; Simpson was killed.

At 10:45 A.M., Maj. Gen. Smith ordered Murray and Puller to advance to the Force Beachhead Line, a right-angled front pointing like an arrowhead toward Kimpo Airfield. The Inchon–Seoul highway was the boundary between the regiments with the 5th Marines north of it and the 1st Marines to the south. Where the road bent left to skirt hills and Ascom City, two of 2d Lt. Granville G. Sweet's M-26 tanks spotted three intact T-34s—survivors of the air strike—and swiftly exploded all three. The Marine tankers also found two wrecked T-34s. The last of the original six attacked by the planes must have escaped. By evening, the 5th Marines were on commanding high ground but still some 3,000 yards short of the FBHL. The division had met little opposition; casualties for the day were four killed and 21 wounded.

On this same Saturday, 180 air miles to the south at its nearest point, the Eighth Army attacked the Pusan Perimeter and engaged North Korean units that might have reinforced the defenders of Kimpo and Seoul. Raids and bombardments along both coasts sought to keep the enemy commanders off balance.

The 5th Marines now looped left to Kimpo Airfield, 16 miles

away; and the 1st Marines drove straight ahead to Yongdungpo, 20 miles up the highway.

At dawn on Sunday, 2d Lt. Lee R. Howard's 2d Platoon of the 5th Marines' D Company was dug in on a knoll west of the Inchon–Seoul highway and short of Ascom City, a large village that after World War II had ballooned into a huge United States service command base. Howard watched a column of six T-34s approach from the direction of Seoul. There were at least 200 enemy infantrymen riding on them and marching alongside. He notified 1st Lt. Smith waiting on a hill to the rear with tanks, recoilless rifles and 3.5-inch bazookas. Howard let the tanks pass, and then his platoon opened up with machine guns, rifles and BARs. Cpl. Okey J. Douglas knocked out the lead tank with his 2.36-inch bazooka and singlehandedly went on to damage the second enemy tank. The heavier weapons at Smith's position began firing. The T-34s tried to deploy into the rice paddies. First Lt. William D. Pomeroy's M-26 tanks attacked. F Company, 11th Marines on the other side of the road joined the firing. Bazookaman Pfc. Walter C. Monegan, Jr., raced down and at point-blank range wrecked two tanks in succession. All six T-34s were destroyed and almost all the enemy infantrymen were killed. One Marine was slightly wounded.

Just then, a column of Jeeps came speeding up the road from the rear. They carried Generals MacArthur, Almond, Shepherd and Smith and a host of officers and press correspondents and photographers. The officers inspected the brand-new carnage of dead bodies and blazing tanks amid a flurry of picture taking. Afterward, seven armed North Koreans were flushed out of a culvert over which MacArthur's Jeep had been parked.

The 2d Battalion, 5th Marines, advancing toward Kimpo, fought through Ascom City's sprawling maze of buildings, warehouses, streets and caves. West of the town, the 3rd Battalion and the Korean Marines skirmished with enemy detachments. By 6 P.M., Smith's D Company and a platoon of tanks swept onto the southern tip of Kimpo Airfield's main runway. The three 2d Battalion rifle companies set up independent perimeters, and Lieutenant Deptula's 1st Platoon of E Company outposted the village of Soryu-li several hundred yards northeast of E Company.

Squeezed between the advancing 5th Marines and the Han

471

River beyond the airfield, the North Koreans counterattacked at 3 A.M. Deptula's separated platoon held its fire until the enemy were in its midst. Then Sgt. Richard L. Marston leaped up, shouting "United States Marines!"[36] and firing his carbine on full automatic. Rifles and BARs joined in. A dozen North Koreans went down and the rest fled, only to rally and hit back three more times. Finally, a T-34 came up; and Deptula was forced to withdraw to E Company's main position. One Marine had been killed and one wounded.

At 5 A.M., E Company was hit by small-arms fire. Captain Jaskilka thought the shots came from D Company and stood up and shouted for it to stop. He discovered his mistake just as the enemy attacked from two sides. Cpl. Russell House rushed forward hurling grenades and was killed; he won the Navy Cross posthumously.

At F Company's perimeter, a six-man demolition team tried to blow up a bridge; Sgt. Ray D. Kearl killed four of the infiltrators. When the North Koreans launched their main attack at dawn, B Company's fire dispersed most of them before they could reach the 2d Battalion.

The 1st Battalion seized Hills 118, 80 and 85 between Kimpo and Yongdungpo. Near Ascom City, Muetzel was seriously wounded and lost his right leg. Sgt. Joseph M. Ward grabbed an enemy grenade; it exploded as he threw it back. He lived to receive the Navy Cross.

By 10 A.M. on Monday, September 18, Kimpo and its 6,000-foot-long runway were secured; and D Company occupied Hill 131 overlooking the Han River north of the airfield. The 2d Battalion had four killed and 19 wounded taking Korea's largest airfield. A helicopter with Lt. Gen. Shepherd aboard was the first American aircraft to land at Kimpo; and the next day, Maj. Gen. Field Harris deployed VMF-212, VMF-312 and VMF(N)-542 to the field. VMF-214 and VMF-323 on the carriers and VMF(N)-513 at Itazuke in Japan started flying close support for the 1st Marines.

In the south on September 18 and 19, the Eighth Army, which was finding it difficult to switch over to the offensive, finally crossed the Naktong against strong opposition. By the nineteenth, the North Korean High Command began moving its main forces northward. The Inchon strategy was working. But the slowness of the Eighth Army seemed inexcusable. It had 140,000 men in combat units—including 60,000 U.S. soldiers— against an estimated 70,000 enemy soldiers, more than half of whom were reluctant South Korean conscripts.

While the 5th Marines moved on Kimpo, the 1st Marines advanced up the Inchon–Seoul highway, punched its way through the village of Mahang-ri and ran into an enemy strong-point in a defile halfway to Sosa. There, the enemy hit 2d Lt. Bryan J. Cummings' lead tank and threw back the accompany-ing riflemen. Although his engine went dead, Cummings opened his hatch and dragged in the lone Marine still clinging to his tank, as the enemy scrambled down the hill. Inside, the rescued Marine went berserk and had to be knocked out. Chok-ing from his gun's fumes, Cummings opened a port; a grenade flew in and exploded, wounding Cummings and two Marines. At that moment, Sgt. Marion C. Altaire brought up his M-26 and swept the back of Cummings' tank with machine-gun fire, killing the swarming North Koreans. Corsairs poured bombs and rockets on the ridges, G Company fought for the hills above the pass and more tanks added their fire. Finally, the 2d Battalion drove the enemy from the high ground on the left of the road and sent the survivors fleeing toward Sosa. Behind, they left 250 dead and wounded and 70 prisoners. It had been the Marines' stiffest fight so far.

By noon the next day, the 3rd Battalion took Sosa against light opposition. The 1st Marines' three battalions occupied a line of hills beyond Sosa. Enemy guns and mortars hammered them there as the North Koreans prepared to hold Yongdungpo, Seoul's ugly industrial suburb on the near side of the Han River.

The capital was now the Marines' target. And the enemy was gathering to defend it. The 5th Marines was ordered to cross the Han and hit Seoul from the mountainous northwest, and the 1st Marines was to fight straight up the highway and through Yongdungpo. The Korean Marines would protect the division's left flank and the 32d Infantry, its right.

The 5th Marines faced the difficult task of crossing the 400-yard-wide river without bridging materials. Why such mate-rials were not at hand is unclear. The LVTs of the Marines' 1st Amphibian Tractor Battalion were collected; and Lt. Col. John H. Partridge, commander of the Marines' 1st Engineer Battalion, provided two 50-ton "rafts" to lift across tanks, vehicles and equipment. The place chosen for the crossing was a former ferry site between the village of Haengjiu and steep Hill 125, both on the far side of the river. Seoul was four ridge-broken miles away.

On the moonless night of September 19, a swimming team from the Reconnaissance Company led the way across the Han. It consisted of Capt. Kenneth J. Houghton, 2d Lt. Dana M. Cashion, ten enlisted men and two Navy officers serving as interpreter and public relations officer (with a tape recorder). At 8 P.M., the swimmers stripped to their skivvies and swam the dark river with a silent breast stroke. They towed two rubber boats loaded with arms, equipment and clothes. In 40 minutes, Houghton's team was across and had overpowered two stray Koreans. The team failed to check the crest of Hill 125 and all too quickly gave the signal that it was safe for the LVTs on the south bank to cross. Nine roaring amtracs started to bring the rest of the Recon Company led by 1st Lt. Ralph B. Crossman. Suddenly, the enemy hidden on Hill 125 opened fire; bullets and mortar shells pummeled the water and shore. The two Korean prisoners tried to escape and the Marines killed them. One of the swimmers, Pfc. Alphonse O. Ledet, Jr., was missing. Four of the LVTs grounded in the mud near the north bank. The last Recon platoon was ordered to stay on the south bank and cover them with fire. The swimming team tried to return across the river now pockmarked by Marine mortar shells. Captain Houghton was knocked out by a concussion and dragged aboard a grounded LVT. Two other swimmers were slightly wounded. Gunnery Sgt. Ernest L. DeFazio led the rest of the swimmers back to the south bank. The free LVTs also raced back to the south bank, and most of the men in the grounded vehicles swam or waded to safety. No one knew who, if anyone, had given the order for the amtracs to retreat in the face of the surprisingly strong resistance.

DeFazio with eight men went back and searched for Captain Houghton, located him in the LVT and returned with two amtracs that were finally freed from the mud.

Embarrassed by this repulse, the Marine commanders ordered Taplett's 3rd Battalion to cross the Han in strength at 6:30 A.M. The enemy was ready for them. The first assault wave of six LVTs took 200 hits, but the amtracs' armor limited casualties to four crewmen wounded. Captain McMullen's leading I Company landed under intense fire. His company, which had been the reserve force on Wolmi-do, was made up of newcomers to combat who had formed the Brigade's third rifle companies at Pusan. Their only support crossing the Han was the machine-gun fire from their own LVTs and four Corsairs of VMF-214, which clobbered Hill 125. The company landed and attacked the hill. Halfway up, the 3rd Platoon's mortar section was cut down by machine-gun fire; 1st Lt. William F. Sparks was wounded and the men fell back. Casualties were heavy. The 2d Platoon rode its amtracs a few hundred yards inland and attacked. McMullen sent the 1st Platoon through the 3rd, and all three platoons assaulted the hill. McMullen was hit but stayed in command to lead the final assault. With close support from VMF-214, the Marines took the crest. I Company had 43 dead and wounded.

By 9:40, I, G and H Companies had all taken their assigned high ground north of the river. The Marines recovered the two grounded LVTs. And Pfc. Ledet showed up after spending the night alone on the enemy side of the river and was able to report on enemy strength and movements. The 1st and 2d Battalions came across to bolster the Marine beachhead. The Marines had crossed the Han—the hard way. MacArthur pinned a Silver Star on Maj. Gen. Smith.

On September 21, Navy Lt. Thomas Coleman was shot down in North Korean territory; and Marine Lt. Arthur R. Bancroft of VMO-6 flew a helicopter to rescue him. The chopper was destroyed on the ground, and 1st Lt. Robert A. Longstaff in a second helicopter made a daring landing under fire and picked up the stranded airmen. (Bancroft was killed eight days later by antiaircraft fire while trying to rescue the crew of an OY that had been shot down. The airplane's observer, Capt. Edwin E. Rives, was killed; and the pilot, Lt. Thomas D. Odenbaugh, was captured.)

The 7th Marines and the 3rd Battalion, 11th Marines landed at Inchon on the twenty-first and began moving up to the Kimpo area. It was only 35 days since the regiment had been activated. The plan now was for the 7th Marines to swing to the division's left flank and cut off any enemy escape to the north. The 1st and 5th Marines would advance on Seoul astride the Han River. The

5th Marines would clear the north bank and open crossing sites for the 1st Marines in the Yongdungpo area. But the North Koreans' stubborn and skillful defense forced another change in plans.

South of the Han River, the 1st Marines closed on Yongdungpo from the south and southwest. The 3rd Battalion took the ridges of Lookout Hill. And the 2d Battalion fought up the highway and took Hill 72, after the Engineers cleared a minefield that had destroyed the lead M-26. A mile further at Hill 146, the North Koreans blocked the highway. A dozer tank smashed into a roadblock of trees and earth-filled rice bags and exploded in a second minefield. The Engineers led by 1st Lt. George A. Babe again went about their dangerous mine-clearing work. Sutter's 2d Battalion finally took Hill 146.

On September 19, before it crossed the river, the 1st Battalion, 5th Marines had seized the three hills between the airfield and Yungdungpo. At noon, the 32d Infantry began freeing the 1st Battalion, 1st Marines on the far right to be trucked north to relieve the 1st Battalion, 5th Marines, for its river crossing the next day. Since it was already dark when the 1st Marines arrived, Lt. Col. Hawkins did not take possession of the two forward hills (Hills 80 and 85) of the three that the 5th Marines had held. Before dawn, the enemy reoccupied them. To capture them again would take many Marine lives.

Early that same morning, September 20, a strong enemy force led by five T-34s came down the Inchon-Seoul highway. D and F Companies of the 1st Marines stood on a ridge south of the road three miles short of Yongdungpo. Further back, E Company was dug in at right angles across the highway. The Marines held their fire and let the enemy column come through until it reached E Company. Then, all three companies opened up and slaughtered the panicked enemy. An ammunition truck that had strangely been leading the column blew up with a spectacular display. In the light of the explosion, nineteen-year-old Pfc. Walter C. Monegan, Jr., of Melrose, Massachusetts, who had knocked out two tanks on September 17, charged down the hillside from F Company. The Marines shifted their fire to protect him. Monegan and Cpl. William Cheek closed within a hundred yards of the lead tank. Monegan wrecked it with one 3.5-inch projectile and then blew up a second tank. Pfc. Robert

Perkins reloaded the bazooka; and as Monegan took aim at a third tank, machine-gun fire found him and "Monegan—killer of tanks" was dead.[37] He was awarded the Medal of Honor.

The 11th Marines closed the highway behind the attacking enemy with a curtain of artillery fire. The Marines counted 300 North Korean bodies and four destroyed tanks.

Puller's regiment prepared to attack Yongdungpo. First, the city was smashed and burned with shells, rockets, incendiary shells and napalm. The 2d Battalion advanced up the highway to the first of two bridges over branches of the Kalchon River, a tributary that flowed north into the Han before Yongdungpo. The 1st Battalion attacked Hills 80 and 85, which the enemy had reoccupied. C Company recaptured Hill 80 easily, but the enemy was entrenched on Hill 85 and the battle there was vicious.

The North Koreans met Capt. Robert P. Wray's double envelopment by bending their flanks into a horseshoe and battling C Company's platoons head on. On the left, 2d Lt. John N. Guild led the attack and was badly wounded in the chest by machine-gun fire. He refused medical aid and pressed his 2d Platoon forward until he died. On the right, 2d Lt. Henry A. Commiskey raced ahead of his 3rd Platoon and charged up the steep slope under heavy fire. First onto the crest, he jumped into a machine-gun emplacement and killed four North Koreans. With his .45 empty, he grappled with a fifth enemy and killed him. Commiskey pushed forward alone and cleaned out a second position, killing two more of the enemy. Then, the North Koreans broke and ran. The twenty-three-year-old Marine from Hattiesburg, Mississippi, was awarded the Medal of Honor. John Guild was given a posthumous Navy Cross.

At dawn on September 21, B Company crossed the wreckage of the Kalchon River bridge north of Yongdungpo under cover of fire from the Marines on Hill 85. Taking heavy casualties, Capt. Richard F. Bland's company pushed ahead 2,000 yards between a dike and the Han River until it entered a fire fight with the enemy on a second dike. Artillery was slow to support B Company because it was advancing southward against the grain of the battle. Its platoon leaders were wounded, and Staff Sgt. Frank Quadros took command of the survivors of the 1st and 3rd Platoons.

Pfc. Albert H. Collins of Tulsa, Oklahoma, ducked across a fire-swept area to get a supply of belted ammunition for his machine gun. Returning, he was struck by enemy fire and crawled the last 40 yards. He found the other Marines of his machine-gun crew dead or wounded. Although he was bleeding badly, Collins loaded the gun and opened fire. As his ammunition ran out, he died. He was awarded the Navy Cross. Bland's company, with 40 wounded, held the dike and was reinforced by C Company. They could not advance into the city.

Meanwhile south of Yongdungpo, the 2d Battalion fought its way toward the burning city. By noon, D Company was slugging it out at 100 yards with the enemy entrenched behind a dike on the battalion's left front. E and F Companies assaulted a ridge on the right of the highway, took heavy casualties and had to withdraw at dusk. VMF-214 skillfully covered their withdrawal, but the enemy still controlled the high ground. The day's fighting had cost the 2d Battalion 11 dead and 74 wounded. As it had lost 28 killed and 226 wounded since D-Day, Puller put in his 3rd Battalion. After Maj. Edwin H. Simmons' Browning heavy machine guns dueled the enemy's Russian Maxims in World War I style, Ridge's 3rd Battalion waded the Kalchon against strong resistance.

The enemy had contained the 1st Marines' two main drives slanting in from the northwest and the southwest. But in the center, 200 Marines of A Company daringly penetrated the very heart of Yongdungpo. They were led by six-foot-four Capt. Robert H. Barrow, a native of St. Francisville, Louisiana, who had fought as a Marine with the Chinese guerrillas behind the Japanese lines during World War II.

After hiking through a mile of open rice paddies in grain as high as their heads, Barrow's Marines waded the Kalchon without a shot being fired and dripping with mud climbed the dike on the far side. By noon, they had advanced several hundred yards up the broad main street of the dead-seeming city. "It was an eerie kind of experience," Barrow said later.[38] Knowing he was far ahead of the other attacking columns, he radioed for instructions. Lt. Col. Hawkins told him to keep going.

As Barrow's Marines closed on the Inchon-Seoul highway coming along on their right, they ran into an enemy force.

Second Lt. John J. Swords' 3rd Platoon cut it to ribbons. Swords led his men to the top of a dike topped by a macadam road. There, on the far side of the city, their fire could cover Seoul's dirt airstrip and the approaches to Seoul itself. To the north they directed telling machine-gun fire on the enemy troops pushed back by B Company's attack. The rest of A Company quickly occupied more of the dike top and formed a "sausage-shaped" defense. They covered the junction with the highway, the location of a crucial enemy supply center in a five-story building. A Marine's grenade blew up a camouflaged mountain of ammunition, and the entire countryside shook with the explosion. The "mushroom-shaped cloud" from the exploding ammunition dump marked their position; their radio was unable to reach the battalion command post. They took plasma from the enemy supplies for their dozen wounded. They threw back small enemy attacks and hoped their ammunition would hold out. To defend the hundred-yard section of the dike reaching to the road intersection, they dug foxholes along the gently sloping incline of the 25-foot-high dike and placed machine guns and BARs on top of the dike to fire in all directions. For some unexplained reason, Lt. Col. Hawkins sent no reinforcements to support the isolated company deep behind enemy lines or to exploit its achievement.

At dusk, five T-34s rumbled down the dirt road paralleling the dike and opened fire at 30 yards with 85mm shells and machine guns. They were the first tanks that the Marines of A Company had ever fought. "They stood cool and tall and let them have it," Barrow remembered. The bazooka men let fly, and Cpl. Francis Devine exploded one tank. Like battleships, the remaining tanks cruised down the road in column, reversed course and paraded back—and then repeated the entire maneuver again, firing all the time. Bazookas damaged two more tanks. The remaining pair made a fifth pass and then rolled off. In this hour of bombardment at close range, A Company had suffered exactly one casualty, and that from concussion. Foxholes had protected the Marines against the machine guns, and the enemy's armor-piercing shells smashed deep into the dike before exploding.

At 9 P.M., a large enemy force hit the 3rd Platoon on the north end of the dike nearest the road junction. Conserving their ammunition carefully, Barrow's Marines threw the North Koreans back in a 15-minute fire fight. Half an hour later, they returned and were repelled again. By midnight, the 3rd Platoon had dispatched five such attacks. Just before the last, Cpl. Billy D. Webb from Tulsa, Oklahoma, went out into the streets among the burning buildings with his M1 and with one shot killed the enemy commander who had been exhorting his men to attack. Webb's shot finished it. Dawn found 310 dead around A Company's perimeter. At 8 A.M., the 1st and 3rd Battalions attacked and swiftly reached the isolated company. A Company's dramatic stand had won the battle for Yongdungpo.

Still ahead lay Seoul; and enemy forces, including the 78th Independent Regiment and the 25th Brigade, prepared to fight to hold it.

The 5th Marines attacked the capital in earnest from the northwest early on September 22. It was one week since D-Day and the beginning of a very bloody battle. The North Koreans, 10,000 strong and well armed, had organized a Main Line of Resistance on a formidable hill complex across the Marines' front. The 25th Brigade defended these hills; it was led by men who fought with the Communist army in China. They would not panic and run. They had to be dug out and killed.

The 5th Marines attacked with the 3rd Battalion on the left, the 1st Koreans Marines in the center and the 1st Battalion on the right. The fighting was intense, and the regiment made little progress. The 1st Battalion, in an all-day fight, did take Hill 105-S.

On the morning of September 23, the 7th Marines' headquarters and 3rd Battalion crossed the Han; and the rest of the regiment came over the following day. Its initial mission was to protect the northern flank and rear of the 5th Marines.

The Korean Marines, who had been beaten back the previous day tried unsuccessfully to straighten the line. The enemy mortars were deadly. That afternoon, the 2d Battalion, 5th Marines passed through the Korean Marines and attacked Hill 56, where enemy resistance was strongest. At the time the Marine officers did not realize this hill was a crucial part of the enemy's MLR.

F Company took heavy casualties crossing a thousand yards of paddies and hit Hill 56 directly from the east. The 1st Platoon fought furiously at close range until only seven able-bodied Marines were left. D Company attacked the adjoining ridge saddle from the north. Its 1st Platoon was caught in the open by intense fire; half its men were struck down in five minutes. The platoon leader, 2d Lt. Ray Heck, was mortally wounded, and his senior noncom, Staff Sgt. T. Albert Crowson, who had commanded the platoon at the Naktong, had his leg shattered. First Lt. Smith, the company commander, personally retrieved the battered platoon. That night, D and F Companies, isolated, clung to the slopes of Hill 56, waiting for the expected counterattack. In one of the mysteries of the war, it never came.

On September 24, the 1st Marines crossed the Han unopposed after the Engineers cleared the crossing site of mines. Puller ordered Hawkins and his 1st Battalion to pass through Sutter's 2d and drive eastward. Since Sutter was already in motion, the order was received with skepticism. But Puller was firm; he said, "You'll just have to advance a little faster."[39] The men moved out at double time.

Maj. Gen. Almond was "dissatisfied with the marines' progress,"[40] and impatiently told Maj. Gen. Smith that Seoul was to be captured by September 25. MacArthur wanted to proclaim the capital's liberation exactly three months after the North Korean invasion. It was neat public relations, but the enemy would not cooperate.

Almond changed X Corps' attack. He ordered the 32d Infantry (40 percent of its men were Koreans) and the ROK 17th Regiment to cross the Han and attack Seoul from the southeast. The 5th and 1st Marines would advance jointly from the west and southwest. The 7th Marines would still protect the left flank. Almond visited Murray's and Puller's command posts and told them what he wanted done, bypassing and infuriating the usually patient Maj. Gen. Smith.[41]

The 5th Marines went to work on the heights just west of Seoul. The 3rd Battalion attacked from the northwest. The 1st Battalion secured the north bank of the Han for Puller's crossing and then relieved the 3rd Battalion. The 2d Battalion attacked the enemy's MLR, which was now called Smith's Ridge after D Company's commander.

What was left of D Company had the job of clearing the enemy from the wooded spine of Smith's Ridge. As the company approached in the morning mist, the defenders on the ridge opened up and pinned down the Marines for two hours. Two Marine tanks were disabled. First Lt. Smith ordered every man into the line and kept two machine guns firing. First Lt. Karle Seydel made five trips under fire to bring up ammunition. The two opposing forces were now in grenade-throwing range, a competition at which the baseball-conditioned Marines excelled. Both sides tried to flank their opponents. In one attempt, Sgt. Robert Smith's squad was wiped out, with eight men killed. Corpsman James Egresitz went to help the wounded and was killed. Only three wounded Marines ever got back.

About 10:30, the mist and smoke lifted; and artillery and VMF-323 could help out. The fliers destroyed four tanks, but five of their planes were damaged by flak.

First Lt. Smith had 40 men and four officers left when he launched the final assault. As the Marines pressed forward, Smith was killed at the head of his men. At the finish, 26 Marines remained. By then, there were more dead than living North Koreans on Smith's Ridge. The surviving enemy fled toward Seoul, and the Marines shot down as many as they could. At 1:30, their objective was secured. First Lt. Seydel was the only D Company officer unwounded. Of 206 men, the company had 36 killed, 116 wounded and evacuated and 26 who were wounded and stayed—178 casualties. Marines referred to this day's fight as "the epic of Dog Company."[42]

On the east side of Smith's Ridge, Capt. Uel D. Peters' F Company—which now had less than 90 men left, counting the wounded who refused evacuation—had two prolonged fire fights and took its objectives. Cpl. Welden D. Harris, who had killed three North Koreans in hand-to-hand combat the day before and been wounded twice, received a third and mortal wound. He was awarded the Navy Cross posthumously.

At 3 P.M., Jaskilka's E Company moved up from reserve to take Hill 105-N beyond Smith's Ridge. Two tanks were destroyed. The remaining three could advance only after Staff Sgt. Stanley B. McPherson of A Company, 1st Engineer Battalion went ahead under fire and cleared a path through the enemy minefield. By then, not enough daylight remained to take the hill. But the day's battle on Smith's Ridge had been crucial— "the western defenses of Seoul had fallen."[43] Lt. Col. Roise estimated that 1,500 North Koreans were dead on Hill 56 and

Smith's Ridge. Since landing at Pusan, the 5th Marines had had 17 of its 18 original platoon leaders and five of its six company commanders killed or wounded.

While the 5th Marines were assaulting the MLR so painfully, the 1st Marines had crossed the Han. For the first time, all three Marine regiments were in position to attack on a single front.

And at last, after overcoming fierce rearguard resistance, the Eighth Army broke out of the Pusan Perimeter on September 23. In three days, it gained 35 miles. The 31st Infantry of X Corps' 7th Infantry Division pushed south from Inchon to meet the 1st Cavalry Division, which was spearheading the Eighth Army advance.

At 7 A.M. on September 25, X Corps attacked Seoul itself. The 5th Marines smashed through the MLR ridge line, and the 1st Marines swept forward in tough street fighting. South of the city, the 32d Infantry and the 17th ROK Regiment crossed the Han and occupied South Mountain, Seoul's highest point. As programmed, Almond and MacArthur announced the city's capture. It wasn't true.

The fliers found Seoul "a flak trap." Close air support was energetic and effective, but antiaircraft fire gave Maj. Gen. Harris' 1st MAW a hellish day. Lt. Col. Walter E. Lischeid of VMF-214 was shot down in flames over the western edge of the city. In the next two hours, Lt. Col. Richard W. Wyczawski of VMF-212 and Lt. Col. Max J. Volcansek, Jr., of VMF(N)-542 were both shot down and injured. Lischeid's death started a legend. He was killed flying Corsair No. 17. On D plus two, Captain Simpson had been killed flying plane No. 17; and two days later on *Sicily*, Tech. Sgt. George C. Underwood was killed when the new No. 17 accidentally discharged its guns. On September 23, Maj. Robert Floeck was killed in this same plane, but the aircraft was saved. Now, when Lischeid was killed in No. 17, Capt. John S. Thach, USN, of *Sicily* banned that number plane from the carrier.[44]

In the northwest part of the city, the 2d Battalion, 5th Marines ran into tough fighting. E Company grabbed Hill 72 ("Nellie's Tit") and Hill 105-C. To the left, the 3rd Battalion met even stronger resistance; and H and I Companies took Hill 105-N with heavy casualties.

The 1st Marines made a 90-degree turn to the northeast and

slashed toward the heart of the city. As always, "liberation" was expensive. Watching the artillery destroy Korean homes, Puller said, "They'll remember us for a thousand years for this, and hate our guts."[45]

A small force of tanks and 50 Engineers ran into an ambush at the base of Hill 105-S, which had supposedly been secured. First Lt. Babe was shot in the arm. The detachment was in trouble until a flame tank flanked and seared the enemy emplacements with short bursts of flaming napalm. Tech. Sgt. Pasquale Paolino of the Engineers discovered a cave dug into Hill 105-S, banged on Second Lt. Cummings' tank and directed its fire into huts at the cave's mouth. A few North Koreans emerged with their arms over their heads; and when they were allowed to surrender, some 120 more followed, including two women. The women later claimed to have been stripped and mistreated by the Marines, causing a brief uproar in some newspapers back in the United States.

The tanks then took the lead in front of the 3rd Battalion, 1st Marines and fought up broad Ma-Po Boulevard through successive roadblocks and against automatic-weapons and mortar fire from the rooftops and buildings. The 1st and 3rd Battalions gained 2,000 yards by nightfall. The enemy was defending the city savagely.

The pressure continued to take Seoul fast enough to meet MacArthur's political objectives. Shortly after 8 P.M., Maj. Gen. Smith received an urgent message from X Corps saying that aviators had reported the enemy fleeing Seoul to the north. The message ordered an immediate attack. Smith was certain the fliers had spotted fleeing refugees; his Marines were still under fire. Smith and his operations officer called Corps headquarters to argue against a night assault into the city. They were told that Maj. Gen. Almond wanted the attack to begin at once. Smith obeyed orders; and the attack was directed to begin—with caution—at 1:45 A.M., following a 15-minute artillery barrage. At 1:38, Puller decided the preparation was inadequate and ordered the barrage repeated. The attack was delayed until 2 A.M. At 1:53, Puller received a flash message from Lt. Col. Ridge, commander of his 3rd Battalion, that a strong enemy force supported by tanks and self-propelled guns was moving down Ma-Po Boulevard from the center of the city toward the 1st Marines. Almond's attack was postponed.

Fortunately, these North Koreans of the 25th Brigade had run into an 11-man 3rd Battalion patrol led by Cpl. Charles E. Collins, which was out among the streets in front, seeking to make contact with a patrol from the 5th Marines. A fire fight began at 1:30. While Collins covered his men with his M-1, members of the patrol raced back to warn Maj. Edwin H. Simmons, who was coordinating the battalion's frontline defenses. Tanks attacked G Company's roadblock. Simmons called in artillery. The first enemy tank killed Pfc. Varga, his radioman. Marines destroyed that tank and forced the second to retreat. Machine gunners, riflemen and artillery blasted the enemy column out of existence with an enormous concentration of firepower. By 6:30, the last of seven tanks was destroyed, more than 475 of the enemy were killed and 83 prisoners taken. Simmons earned the Silver Star; and Corporal Collins, who had covered his patrol's retreat, "miraculously"[46] returned safely, disguised in white civilian Korean clothes.

Another enemy force hit the 32d Infantry at 5 A.M. and overran a portion of its front until a counterattack could restore the line. The Army regiment reported killing 394 of the enemy and taking 174 prisoners. X Corps' insistence that the enemy was fleeing and its announcement that the city had been captured were surely "a bit premature."[47]

Once these enemy attacks were annihilated, the two climactic days of the battle for Seoul actually began. The 7th Marines drove southeast to pinch out the 5th Marines while the 1st Marines fought northeast through the center of the city.

Col. Homer L. Litzenberg, commander of the 7th Marines, sent D Company down the Kaesong–Seoul highway at 6:30 A.M. on September 26 to meet the 5th Marines. First Lt. William F. Groggin, the company machine-gun officer, led the column through hundreds of cheering Koreans. The Marines moved through a narrow valley between Hills 296 and 838 toward Sodaemun Prison at the northwest corner of Seoul. Suddenly, machine guns opened up from a tower and the high ground. Since the welcoming throngs had prevented the use of flankers, D Company was caught on the low ground. Its counterattacks were thrown back. Groggin and Capt. Richard R. Breen, the company commander, were among the wounded. The enemy closed in behind D Company and repulsed a small tank-infantry relief force. By 4 P.M., the now-surrounded company withdrew a thousand yards to the cut between the two hills and prepared a tight perimeter for an all-night defense. Breen had 40 casualties. In the morning, a second relief column escorted D Company back to the regimental CP.

Taplett's 3rd Battalion, 5th Marines spent September 26 clearing the last resistance from the Hill 296 complex. Captain McMullen's I Company led the attack, but McMullen underestimated the enemy's strength and called off his artillery support. The North Koreans tore huge holes in the Marines' line. McMullen led the company into close-in fighting and drove the enemy to lower ground. The North Koreans counterattacked uphill; and a wild melee began. Before the enemy finally gave way, I Company was badly battered. McMullen was carried off with his seventh battle wound in two wars.

On I Company's right, G Company inched forward against stubborn resistance. When Cpl. Bert Johnson was hit while setting up his machine gun, Pfc. Eugene A. Obregon, his ammunition carrier, dashed up and, firing his pistol, dragged Johnson to the side of the road. Under fire, Obregon started to bandage Johnson's wound. A platoon of enemy charged them. Obregon grabbed Johnson's carbine, covered him with his own body and fired coolly at the enemy. The nineteen-year-old Marine from Los Angeles was killed by a machine-gun burst and was awarded the Medal of Honor. The enemy attack was repelled and Johnson was rescued.

In the 1st Marines' zone, the 1st Battalion on the right cleaned up strong resistance around Seoul's red brick main railroad station at the base of 900-foot-high South Mountain, which was in peacetime a pleasant city park. Fighting was intense among the terminal buildings and railroad cars. C Company finally cleared the station, and A Company secured the northwest tip of South Mountain. The 32d Infantry attacked from the south side of South Mountain, killing 500 North Koreans and destroying five tanks.

On the 1st Marines' left, Sutter's 2d Battalion passed through the 3rd and attacked along Ma-Po Boulevard's street car line into the center of Seoul. Every few yards, determined detachments defended rice-bag barricades eight feet high and five feet thick across the width of the avenue. Engineers, protected by riflemen, cleared mines in front of the barriers and then the M-26s smashed them. The teamwork was effective, but the Marines had to fight a battle of 360 degrees as North Koreans fired from roofs, windows and side streets. Suicide squads tried to destroy the Marine tanks and managed to blow up a flamethrower tank. It was slow, brutal street fighting.

Advancing up the broad boulevard littered with abandoned enemy gear, Capt. Goodwin C. Groff's F Company was stopped a hundred yards short of Kung Hua Noon Circle. The company was supposed to advance up the left street from the circle; and E Company, which was following, was to take the right fork. Then, the two companies were to converge again and assault the Duksoo Palace at the head of the boulevard. Lt. Col. Sutter had told them, "Move out fast and keep going."[48]

With F Company pinned down, Capt. Norman R. Stanford, the new commander of E Company, and his runner, Pfc. Edward Cavanaugh, worked up to the intersection. Stanford, an Annapolis graduate from Cohasset, Massachusetts, had won the Navy Cross on Okinawa. He and Cavanaugh kept close to the buildings. The circle was a mess of dead bodies, debris and abandoned guns; the buildings were on fire. Stanford found F Company stopped by a barricade with an antitank battery. Waving up his four tanks, he sent them against the barrier. The fighting was severe; in the last 250 yards, E Company had 20 casualties, including Stanford. Once his company destroyed the barrier, it led the way up the avenue toward the palace.

On September 27, Litzenberg's 7th Marines fought in the immense ridges just north of the city. Murray's 5th Marines battled through the streets, barricades and minefields in western Seoul; its 3rd Battalion took the Middle School and attacked toward the Capitol building.

On the right of the Marines' front, Puller's 1st Marines raised the American flag above the French Embassy at midmorning and got into a furious fight at the city's main intersection. Second Lt. Cummings' tank knocked out two 76mm self-propelled guns in the middle of the intersection, and then his tank was destroyed by mines. The North Koreans were fighting stubbornly. Sutter's 2d Battalion battled through a maze of streets and in the afternoon raised the flag over the Russian and United States Embassies.

Shortly after 3 P.M., Taplett's 3rd Battalion, 5th Marines, burst into the Government House compound; struck the North Korean flags, and raised the American. By the day's end, Tech.

487

Sgt. George W. Bolkow's 3rd Platoon of A Company captured the crest of rocky Hill 338 northwest of Government House.

As dusk fell, resistance in front of the Marines collapsed; and except for mopping up enemy pockets and snipers, the battle of Seoul was over. The next day, the 1st Marines advanced and dug in on the northeastern part of the city. The North Koreans were retreating north to Uijongbu. The 7th Marines seized the high ground north of Seoul on both sides of the main highway leading to Uijongbu.

September 29 was a day of fighting and ceremonies. The 7th Marines had a full day of battle. The 1st Marines repulsed two counterattacks before dawn. Its E Company on Hill 132 held positions 300 yards in front of the battalion. At 4 A.M., Pfc. Alfred Walsh and Pfc. Stanley R. Christianson, manning a listening post protecting the company, heard a large enemy force approaching. Christianson sent Walsh back to warn the others and opened fire. He killed seven of the enemy before their automatic weapons overwhelmed him. His one-man defense allowed his platoon to beat off the enemy attack and kill 41 North Koreans. The Marine from Mindoro, Wisconsin, was awarded the Medal of Honor posthumously.

At midmorning, General MacArthur and President Rhee arrived separately at Kimpo Airfield and drove to the Government Palace along a route guarded chiefly by the Marines. During the liberation ceremonies, Puller's Marines protected the distinguished audience. Artillery could be heard in the distance and shook glass loose from the broken skylights. At noon, MacArthur opened the proceedings restoring the capital to the Republic of Korea; his five-minute speech ended with the Lord's Prayer.

By now, the North Korean invaders had been routed throughout South Korea. On September 26, the Eighth Army had advanced a hundred miles; and the following morning, the 7th Cavalry linked up with the 31st Infantry above Osan—near where, at the war's beginning, Task Force Smith had met defeat. The North Koreans were throwing away their weapons, putting on civilian clothes and trying to escape to the north. By the last day of the month, the ROK 3rd Division was five miles below the 38th Parallel. The North Korean army had been virtually destroyed.

The three Marine regiments took blocking positions in a

semi-circle north of Seoul. There were occasional fire fights. Early on October 1, the 7th Marines drove north toward Uijong-bu, with VMF-312 flying close support. First Lt. Robert O. Crocker was shot down by small-arms fire and then killed on the ground. The enemy rear guard fought tenaciously. By the evening of October 3, the 7th Marines entered the ruins of Uijong-bu. The three-day advance had cost 13 killed and 111 wounded.

On October 5, the Marines received orders to return to Inchon where a Marine cemetery was dedicated on the 6th. The amphibious operation ended on October 7, and the Marines headed for Wonsan on the east coast—and a new war.

The entire Inchon–Seoul campaign had been executed with daring and speed. Seoul was taken in less than two weeks. The enemy lost an estimated 13,666 casualties, 4,692 prisoners and 44 tanks. Total casualties to the 1st Marine Division were 421 dead and 2,029 wounded in action, nearly half of them during the fight around and inside Seoul. Eleven 1st MAW planes were shot down. Care for the wounded was remarkable. During the entire Inchon–Seoul offensive, Navy surgical teams operated on 2,484 patients; only nine of them died after reaching an aid station. Chances that a wounded Marine would live were figured to be 199 to 1.

In his report to the United Nations' Security Council, MacArthur called the campaign "decisive." He said "the enemy is thoroughly shattered." And he added, "A successful frontal attack and envelopment has [sic] completely changed the tide of battle in South Korea. The backbone of the North Korean army has been broken and their scattered forces are being liquidated or driven north with material losses in equipment and men captured."[49] Naval historians have written: "History records no more striking example of the effectiveness of an amphibious operation."[50]

The old general's self-assurance had been responsible for this bold campaign. The desperate days of retreat and defense had been converted into victory. The North Korean aggressors had been driven from the Republic of Korea. American, South Korean and United Nations fighting men had turned back Communist expansion by force in Asia. But suddenly, somehow, this did not seem enough. Self-assurance led to arrogance and to disaster.

4
The Reservoir

The American decision to cross the 38th Parallel was a watershed of history. Not because American forces invaded a small hostile country; there was nothing unique about that. But because the decision led to a massive defeat of American arms; it brought the United States to battle with the People's Republic of China; it encouraged Asian nationalist and Communist movements to oppose the Western powers; it heated up a period of McCarthyite frustration and fear in the United States; it stimulated the concept of basing America's defenses on nuclear weapons; it convinced many Americans that they had to confront Communism and nationalism elsewhere in Asia, and it marked the first significant rollback of the long American thrust westward across the Pacific.

Secretary of State Acheson called what happened after the United States crossed the Parallel, "the greatest defeat suffered by American arms since the Battle of Manassas and an international disaster of the first water."[51]

The decision was a split one. According to Acheson, Dean Rusk and John Allison in the State Department's Far Eastern Division urged that a crossing of the Parallel "should not be precluded";[52] Paul Nitze and George Kennan opposed it. Pentagon planners favored crossing the Parallel and "uniting" Korea. The buck stopped on President Truman's desk.

On September 27, even before the liberation ceremonies in Seoul, the Joint Chiefs of Staff, with the President's approval, gave MacArthur his orders:

> Your military objective is the destruction of the North Korean Armed Forces. In attaining this objective you are

490

authorized to conduct military operations, including amphibious and airborne landings or ground operations north of the 38th Parallel in Korea, provided that at the time of such operations there has been no entry into North Korea by major Soviet or Chinese Communist Forces, no announcement of intended entry, nor a threat to counter our operations militarily in North Korea. . . . under no circumstances, however, will your forces cross the Manchurian or USSR borders of Korea and, as a matter of policy, no non-Korean Ground Forces will be used in the northeast provinces bordering the Soviet Union or in the area along the Manchurian border. Furthermore, support of your operations north or south of the 38th Parallel will not include Air or Naval action against Manchuria or against USSR territory. . . .[53]

MacArthur's staff developed a plan for the Eighth Army to drive north as far as Pyongyang, the capital of the People's Democratic Republic of Korea, and for X Corps to land at Wonsan on the east coast and cut westward to trap the North Korean forces retreating from the south. After linking up, both commands would advance north to points 50 to 100 miles below the Manchurian border. Only ROK units would proceed beyond that restraining line.

On October 1, the ROK army started crossing the 38th Parallel; President Rhee was still determined to unite Korea. Two days later, China's Prime Minister Chou En-lai warned the Indian ambassador in Peking that if American troops crossed the Parallel, China would enter the war. In Washington, some read his statement not as a realistic "announcement of intended entry" but as political blackmail. The swift momentum of the UN offensive that had begun on September 15 was not to be stopped.

On October 7, the United Nations supported the idea of a unified, democratic Korea.[54] Acheson said it encouraged "General MacArthur's adventurism."[55] Two days later, the 1st Cavalry Division attacked across the Parallel. The Eighth Army smashed the North Koreans' defenses above the Parallel. And on Sunday, October 15, President Truman met with General MacArthur on Wake Island. In reply to the President's question,

MacArthur said he saw "very little"[56] chance that the Chinese would intervene; the war would be over by Thanksgiving.

Possibly as early as October 12—three days after U.S. forces crossed the Parallel and three days before the Wake Island conference—and certainly no later than October 16, "volunteers" of the Chinese People's Liberation Army secretly entered Korea from the north. On October 26, General Lin Piao's experienced Chinese Fourth Field Army attacked ROK units at the Yalu River and 50 miles below the border. The two leading ROK regiments were destroyed. The II ROK Corps on the Eighth Army's right was driven back. On Sunday, November 1, the Chinese attacked the 1st Cavalry Division and the next day hit the 7th Marines.

Still, the initial Chinese intervention proved limited. When the Eighth Army had been forced back to the Chongchon River after 12 days of fighting, the Chinese broke off battle action on November 6. There were no further Chinese attacks for two weeks. It appeared that full-scale war with China could still be avoided.

On November 6, MacArthur asserted that the North Korean armies had been destroyed; but on November 24, the very day representatives from Peking arrived at UN headquarters at Lake Success, New York, he launched a general "end the war" offensive and sent United States troops all the way to the Yalu—despite his orders. With the North Korean army "shattered," the North Korean capital occupied and Chinese armies lurking in the distance, the reasons for MacArthur's action were at best murky.

As soon as the UN offensive began, the Chinese counterattacked again all along the front. Said one analyst, "While China crossed the Yalu on October 15th, she did not cross the Rubicon until November 26th."[57] MacArthur started blaming the political leaders in Washington for his miscalculation and failure. The world tiptoed to the brink of World War III.

Why did the Communist Chinese tackle the massed armed forces of the United States and the United Nations? In retrospect, it seemed that the Chinese wanted to preserve a buffer between themselves and American power based in Japan. Before the North Koreans invaded South Korea in June, this buffer had consisted of the two Korean states. American reoccupation of

South Korea had still left North Korea as a buffer; the October–November offensive threatened to wipe out that shield entirely. But whatever the motivation, the effect of the Chinese invasion of North Korea was that China prevented the unification of Korea by force and gained enormous prestige in Asia.

There were other factors in the Chinese decision: MacArthur, as early as August 26, had spoken out so strongly in support of the Nationalist regime on Formosa that President Truman forced him to retract his statement and considered replacing him with General Omar Bradley. The People's Republic of China started an anti-American propaganda campaign condemning the United States for preventing the "liberation" of Formosa, rearming Japan and keeping Peking out of the United Nations. The Communist Chinese invaded Tibet and helped their ideological comrades in Indochina.

And the United States made a major mistake in analyzing military intelligence, insisting, right up to the fatal November 24 offensive, that the Chinese armies were not in North Korea in strength. Said the official U.S. Army history of the war:

> . . . apparently the Central Intelligence Agency and the administration generally did not evaluate the available intelligence so as to reach a conviction on the question of whether the Chinese intended to intervene in the Korean War different from that held by General MacArthur. It must be inferred that either Washington was undecided or that its view coincided with that of the Commander in Chief, Far East, since it did not issue directives to him stating a different estimate.[58]

MacArthur refused to believe that the Chinese would intervene in full force and proclaimed that, if they did enter the war, American air power would interdict and destroy them. He and his intelligence officers were wrong. When his "end the war" offensive began, 180,000 Chinese soldiers were waiting in front of the Eighth Army and 120,000 in front of X Corps—a total of 300,000 men.

Early in November, Marine fliers of VMF(N)-542, attacking Sinuiju at the mouth of the Yalu River, had reported hordes of trucks moving from Manchuria into northwest Korea. President

Truman, after first refusing permission, finally acceded to Mac-Arthur's insistence on bombing the bridges across the Yalu, as long as dams and power plants were not hit and Manchurian territory and air space were not violated. Truman also denied MacArthur permission for "hot pursuit" across the border against MIG-15 jets, which had by now joined the war. Mac-Arthur warned that the restrictions provided enemy aircraft "a complete sanctuary."[59]

Air Force and Navy bombers attacked the 12 bridges across the Yalu and Tumen Rivers. On November 8 occurred the first all-jet air battle in history. U.S. fliers knocked out four bridges and damaged most of the others during November, but the results were disappointing and the bombings stopped on December 6 when the Yalu froze over. By then, the Chinese had already invaded North Korea.

Clearly, the interlocking invasions of North Korea by the forces of both the United Nations and Communist Chinese represented a confrontation of significance in the world's history. The armed forces of two of the world's major nations would meet in battle.

As the Eighth Army moved into North Korea in early October, the 1st Marine Division was ordered to load out of Inchon and seize Wonsan on Korea's east coast, 110 air miles above the 38th Parallel. Wonsan was Korea's petroleum refining center and one of the best natural harbors on the peninsula. But on October 10, the I ROK Corps occupied Wonsan and its deserted airfield. Five days later, the Marine transports sailed from Inchon with 30,184 troops, including 21,176 Marines. The remainder were U.S. Army and Navy personnel and members of the Korean Marine Corps.

The Navy found Wonsan harbor and beaches blocked by more than 2,000 Soviet-made mines that had been assembled and laid under Russian supervision. Attempting to clear a channel, four minesweepers were blown up by mines, and survivors rescued under fire from enemy shore batteries. Because many were magnetic mines that let 12 ships pass before they exploded, the sweeping was slow and dangerous. The crowded transports sailed endlessly back and forth for a week that the bored troops dubbed Operation Yo-Yo. Dysentery swept the men. While the Marines still fumed in their ships, Marine Air Group 12 began arriving at Wonsan; and on the evening of October 24, Bob Hope and Marilyn Maxwell put on a USO show there.

In the west, Pyongyang was captured on the twentieth; and 4,000 men of the 187th Airborne Regiment parachuted 30 miles north of the capital, trying unsuccessfully to cut the North Korean escape routes. In the center of the peninsula, ROK forces drove north. MacArthur predicted the war was almost over.

When he returned from Wake Island, MacArthur moved his restraining line north to a point 30 to 40 miles below the Manchurian border. And on October 24, he took it upon himself to eliminate the restraining line completely and instructed Lt. Gen. Walker and Maj. Gen. Almond to occupy all of North Korea with all their forces. The next day, the Joint Chiefs of Staff asked MacArthur why he had issued this "radically different" order.[60] He replied that the ROK Army was not strong enough to secure North Korea and declared that he had the authority to make this vital change. Apparently, no one had the courage to counter-mand his order.

As a result of MacArthur's new instructions, Almond on October 25 sent Maj. Gen. Smith the decisive order for the Marines to relieve I ROK Corps troops at the Chosin and Fusen Reservoirs, a hundred air miles north of Wonsan. After many chaotic changes of plans, Almond assigned the Marine division a zone of action 300 road miles north to south and 50 road miles wide, reaching all the way to the Manchurian border.

On that same day, the Marines finally began to land over Yellow and Blue Beaches at Wonsan in "as anticlimactic a landing as Marines have ever made."[61]

While the 5th and 7th Marines headed north, the 1st Marines went to work in the Wonsan area. The 1st Battalion, 1st Marines immediately entrained in gondola cars for the small lovely seaport of Kojo, 39 miles south of Wonsan, to protect a supply dump and relieve a ROK battalion. The 3rd Battalion stayed at Wonsan. Maj. Gen. Smith began to worry about the dispersion of his division; the Marines were being used like Army troops in a land campaign.

At Kojo, Lt. Col. Hawkins, the 1st Battalion commander, deployed Capt. Wesley B. Noren's B Company on three high points of ground two miles south of Kojo; Capt. Robert P. Wray's C Company on a line of hills a mile and a half to the north, and Capt. Robert H. Barrow's A Company between C Company and Kojo. Everything seemed quiet. But more than a thousand soldiers of the veteran North Korean 5th Division were based in the village of Tongchon, two miles south of B Company's outposts.

At 10 P.M. on October 27, B and C Companies were attacked. The North Koreans crept up silently, hurled grenades and surprised and overran B Company's 1st Platoon. They killed 15 Marines, seven in their sleeping bags. The 3rd Platoon repulsed an attack. C Company was hard hit; 20 Marines were cut off until morning; but Wray's Company threw back the assaults while losing six killed and 16 wounded.

B Company was struck repeatedly, and the 1st Platoon withdrew with 30 men missing. Sgt. Clayton L. Roberts covered the platoon with a machine gun until he was killed. Captain Noren organized a 360-degree defense. F Battery, 11th Marines added mortar and artillery fire. Noren brought out his wounded in ponchos through the knee-deep mud of the rice paddies. The enemy moved into Kojo and attacked 2d Lt. John J. Swords' A Company platoon. When it was already light, 200 North Koreans dashed out of Kojo for the hills; nearly half were killed. The final count of Marine casualties in the all-night battle was 23 killed, 47 wounded and four missing.

The next afternoon, in response to Hawkins' urgent calls for help, Lt. Col. Sutter's 2d Battalion and Colonel Puller's Regimental Command Group joined the 1st Battalion. Marine fliers destroyed Tongchon, and two U.S. destroyers bombarded Kojo. On the afternoon of October 31, Hawkins' battalion was relieved by Korean Marines and returned to Wonsan by LST. A week later, Hawkins was replaced. Sutter's battalion hiked back to Wonsan on November 3.

On October 28, Lt. Col. Ridge's 3rd Battalion, 1st Marines was trucked 28 miles west from Wonsan to the Taebaek mountain village of Majon-ni to relieve the 26th ROK Regiment and to control the major road net that intersected there. One road led to Pyongyang and another to Seoul. The road from Wonsan twisted through a 3,000-foot mountain pass of deep gorges and hairpin turns—soon to be known as Ambush Alley.

Ridge's Marines were to keep the enemy away fron Wonsan and block their escape route to the north. Each rifle company was assigned one of the three roads to patrol, and Major Simmons' Weapons Company set up roadblocks where the battalion perimeter crossed each road. First Lt. Leroy M. Duffy's Engineers dug out an OY strip on the edge of the mountain-ringed valley, through which ran the Imjin River. The Marines screened all Koreans who entered the perimeter. If they showed signs of having served in the North Korean army—head close-cropped, neck with a tanned line left by a uniform or feet with callouses from military shoes—they were put into the prison stockade; in 17 days, the Marines assembled 1,395 prisoners, most of them voluntary ones.

From the POW interrogations and from civilians, the Marines learned that the North Korean 15th Division was nearby, ready to use the upper Imjin as a base for guerrilla operations.

On November 2, an H Company platoon was ambushed in a deep gorge five miles south of Majon-ni. The Marines managed to get off the message, "We've been hit, send help, send help,"[62] before their radio failed. Capt. Clarence E. Corley, Jr., the company commander, rushed out with his other two rifle platoons, heavy machine guns and 81mm mortars. The mortars pounded the enemy positions on the cliffs. Pfc. Jack Golden lugged a 94-pound machine gun up to a height from which he fired down on the enemy. Maj. Edwin H. Simmons, in an observation plane, called in Corsairs, and the North Koreans vanished into the hills. The battalion medical officer, Lt. Robert J. Fleischaker, USN, and his team treated the wounded, most of whom were evacuated by helicopter the next day.

The same morning that H Company's patrol was attacked, a supply convoy escorted by a G Company rifle platoon was ambushed seven miles west of Wonsan and forced to turn back. Nine men were killed and 15 wounded. Ridge's Marines had to be supplied by an Army air drop.

Colonel Puller was determined to push a truck convoy through to Majon-ni. On the afternoon of November 4, Barrow's A Company started out with a convoy of 24 supply trucks. Barrow put his Engineer platoon in front, and they filled in four cratered roadblocks. At the fifth roadblock, the Engineers got into a fire fight with North Koreans hidden on the heights above the narrow road. Barrow had to turn back. It was now dark, and the trucks began the eight-mile trip to Wonsan with their lights out. One truck with 21 Marines missed a hairpin turn and plunged over the edge. A human chain brought the injured men 60 feet up to the road, and the convoy got back with eight men wounded, 16 injured and five vehicles destroyed.

The convoy started out again the next morning. Barrow, figuring that the enemy in Ambush Alley waited for the sound of approaching trucks, placed an infantry platoon a thousand yards ahead of the vehicles. At the scene of the previous day's ambush, the platoon surprised 70 guerrillas and killed most of them. This time, the convoy reached Majon-ni without casualties.

A Company joined the perimeter defense; and at 1:30 A.M. that night, the North Koreans attacked. After a long fire fight, the enemy overran the battalion OP when the five Marines there ran out of ammunition. The position was recaptured quickly once the early morning fog lifted. And A Company escorted 619 prisoners back to Wonsan.

On November 6, Puller sent Sutter's 2d Battalion to the hamlet of Muchon-ni near the highest pass along Ambush Alley on the road to Majon-ni. At a horseshoe bend, the convoy was stopped by a landslide roadblock and then attacked by enemy concealed on the high ground. E Company counterattacked and suffered eight killed and 38 wounded before the North Koreans were chased off.

At Majon-ni, 250 of the enemy attacked an H Company observation post on November 8; one Marine was killed and 10 wounded. On November 10, the 3rd Korean Marine Corps Battalion arrived to reinforce the perimeter. The U.S. Marines at Majon-ni celebrated the Corps' 175th birthday with a traditional cake their cooks managed to bake. On November 13, the American and Korean Marines were relieved by the 1st Battalion of the 15th Infantry, which continued the fighting there. The U.S. Marines had lost 20 dead and 45 wounded at Majon-ni and in Ambush Alley. The 1st Marines moved north.

By now, the Army's 7th Infantry Division had landed at Iwon, 60 air miles northeast of the port of Hungnam; and most of the 3rd Infantry Division had landed at Wonsan.

While the 1st Marines were busy at Kojo, Majon-ni and Muchon-ni, the 7th and 5th Marines prepared to advance to the Manchurian border. The 7th Marines, issued parkas and some other cold weather gear, moved 50 air miles north to Hamhung by road and rail during the last three days of October. North Korean forces repeatedly attacked Army and Marine convoys out of Wonsan. On one supply train, they killed six Marines and wounded eight in hand-to-hand fighting.

The 7th Marines was to relieve the 26th ROK Regiment, which already on October 29 had taken 16 Chinese prisoners north of Hamhung near Sudong. Over in northwest Korea, the 8th U.S. Cavalry Regiment and the 6th ROK Division were surprised and badly hurt by the Chinese, who had penetrated between MacArthur's two major forces.

MacArthur had divided his army. The Eighth Army and X Corps, under separate commands, were split by the Taebaek mountains, running north and south in the center of the Korean peninsula. There were no good east–west roads through the mountains north of Pyongyang and Wonsan. Most of Mac-Arthur's top commanders later said they disagreed with his strategy. MacArthur said they never told him so to his face. Courage was also needed at headquarters.

The Marines' new arena of action stretched northward from the estuary of the Songchon River, a spacious flatland containing the port of Hungnam and the industrial city of Hamhung eight miles upriver. The Marines would follow a road and narrow-gauge railroad north from Hungnam through Hamhung into the Taebaek mountains. From the port, the dirt and gravel road ran 78 miles to the little village of Yudam-ni at the western end of the Chosin Reservoir. For the first 43 of those miles, the road rose gently through fairly level terrain. But at Chinhung-ni, a one-lane road suddenly started climbing among mile-high peaks. It first rose 2,500 feet through narrow, twisting Funchilin Pass, with a cliff on one side and an abyss on the other. Two miles before the village of Koto-ri, the road entered a rugged plateau and followed the Changjin River, which flows north through the reservoir. At the larger town of Hagaru, the road divided around both sides of the reservoir's southern tip. The western branch climbed through the 4,000-foot Toktong Pass and then descended through gorges into the broad valley leading to Yudam-ni. This primitive road zigzagging through wild mountain country would become the Marines' Main Supply Route (MSR)—the focus of the attention of the world.

Although there were Chinese soldiers ahead and the Eighth

Army was some 60 air miles away across the Taebaek range from the Marines' left flank, Colonel Litzenberg's orders remained to lead the Marine division north to the Manchurian border by this route. The 7th Infantry Division, also part of X Corps, would drive northward on the Marines' right toward Hyesanjin on the Yalu River. The I ROK Corps would advance up the coastal road to the northeast.

On October 30, VMF-312 attacked 500 enemy troops at Hagaru; they were believed to be Chinese. Litzenberg gathered his officers and noncoms at the regimental command post. "We can expect to meet Chinese Communist troops," he said, "and it is important that we win the first battle. The results of that action will reverberate around the world, and we want to make sure that the outcome has an adverse effect in Moscow as well as Peiping."[63] He told his men they might soon be taking part in the first battle of World War III.

On November 2, the 7th Marines relieved the 26th ROK Regiment 37 miles north of Hungnam at Majon-dong on the MSR. As A Company moved forward carefully, it came under long-range Chinese fire and took a few casualties. The 3rd Battalion, 11th Marines fired 26 artillery missions in response.

The Marines entered a long narrow valley—Hill 698 on the left and Hill 727 on the right. D Company replaced a ROK unit on the exposed slopes of Hill 698. As the Marines climbed higher, they came under scattered fire. Hurling grenades, the two assault platoons reached the crest but took severe casualties and had to be recalled under fire. E Company passed through D Company and occupied a plateau 150 yards below the crest.

In the valley, the 7th Marines' "walking perimeter," protected on all sides, advanced under cover of close support from VMF-312 and VMF(N)-513, which blasted the ridgelines on both sides. The Chinese replied with mortar fire, and one 120mm round wounded three men in the 1st Battalion command post.

At dusk, the Marines dug in at a bridge a mile south of Sudong. Litzenberg placed the 1st Battalion's rifle companies on the high ground up front and the 2d Battalion on the slopes along the center of his position. The 3rd Battalion protected the regiment's rear. All three battalion command posts and mortars were situated in the valley along the road. The Marines did not know that the Chinese had their 371st Regiment to the north and west, the 370th Regiment to the east and the 372d Regiment hidden several miles ahead. Many of these troops had formerly been in the Chinese Nationalist Army and were armed with Japanese rifles confiscated in Manchuria and American-made machine guns and mortars captured from the Nationalists.

Two Chinese battalions began to attack at 11 P.M. in a well-coordinated double envelopment. By 1 A.M. on November 3, the Marines' 1st and 2d Battalions were under full-scale attack on both flanks. The Chinese had avoided the obvious approach down the valley from Sudong and attacked from the ridgelines. Coming swiftly and silently, they struck A and F Companies on the right and B Company on the left. They burst on the Marines with grenades and submachine guns; and where they found room between defensive positions, they flooded into the low ground.

Suddenly, a North Korean tank supporting the Chinese lumbered through A Company's roadblock and into the 1st Battalion command post, firing ineffectively. Bazookas and recoilless rifles opened up, and the tank swung around and headed north. One of its shells all but wiped out the antitank crew at the roadblock before the tank disappeared around a bend in the road.

In the hill-fighting east of the MSR, A Company's 1st and 2d Platoons and elements of B Company were forced back. Sgt. James I. Poynter of Bloomington, Illinois, was critically wounded when the Chinese surrounded his A Company squad. Poynter bayoneted several of the enemy. Then he rushed at three Chinese machine guns setting up 25 yards ahead. He grabbed grenades from fallen Marines, charged the machine-gun emplacements in succession, killed the crews of two and put the last out of action before he was mortally wounded. His swift daring disorganized the enemy and gave his squad time to defend itself.[64]

Across the road, the rest of B Company was attacked. Staff Sgt. Archie Van Winkle, a reservist from Seattle, led his platoon through withering fire. He and every man who charged with him was hit. Van Winkle's one arm hung uselessly, but the Alaska-born sergeant dashed 40 yards through enemy fire to reach his isolated left-flank squad and reunite his men. Hit in the chest by

501

a grenade burst, he refused evacuation until he was carried off unconscious.[65] Both Poynter and Van Winkle were awarded the Medal of Honor. And 1st Lt. Chew Een Lee of Sacramento, California, commander of B Company's machine-gun platoon, received the Navy Cross for exploring the slope above his position and drawing fire to expose the enemy positions to his gunners. Although Lee was seriously wounded in the right arm, he led a counterattack that drove back the enemy.

The Chinese swarmed into the valley from both sides, overran the 7th Marines' 4.2-inch Mortar Company and seized a sharp curve in the road between the 2d and 3rd Battalions. By dawn, they had cut the MSR and controlled the terrain between the Marine rifle companies on the hillsides and the 2d Battalion command post. Litzenberg had to call in supporting arms to avoid destruction. Mortars, howitzers and aircraft went to work raking the enemy. Scores of Chinese on the hillsides and along the valley floor were eradicated. Marines learned that if they could hold their positions against a Chinese night attack, once day came, Marine firepower would crush the enemy.

By midmorning, the 1st Battalion had cleared the valley. Its heavy machine guns took a fearsome toll; 662 enemy dead were later counted in the battalion's zone. The 2d Battalion fought in two directions. E Company attacked Hill 698 against a concentrated grenade barrage. The squad led by Cpl. Lee H. Phillips of Stockbridge, Georgia, had five men left when it gained the crest. The defenders counterattacked. Phillips took three men against the final rocky point. They pulled themselves over the rocks with one hand and hurled grenades with the other. He and his last two men fought off a final counterattack. And the Marines held Hill 698. (Twenty-year-old Phillips was killed in action on November 27.)[66]

D Company tried to cross the valley and attack a Chinese roadblock on a spur of Hill 727. It took until evening before the riflemen, artillery and aircraft forced the Chinese to retreat from the roadblock and freed the MSR. A hundred Marine casualties were evacuated, but accurate casualty figures were destroyed when the 7th Marines withdrew from Yudam-ni in December.

The Chinese regiments, badly hurt, pulled back three miles from Sudong to a line established by the 372d Regiment. And Marine air reported 300 enemy trucks on the move south of the Chosin Reservoir.

502

On November 4, while Maj. Gen. Smith brought the division command post north to Hungnam, Litzenberg continued his advance. The Reconnaissance Company took the lead in Jeeps and in the middle of Sudong surprised a group of Chinese soldiers. The Marines killed three and captured 20 in a half-hour fight. Then they climbed toward Chinhung-ni six miles up the road, while C Company followed the railroad tracks on the other side of the river.

The lead Recon platoon spotted Chinese soldiers at the Samgo Station just north of Chinhung-ni and killed most of them. Nearby, the Marines found a North Korean T-34 camouflaged under a pile of brush on the right side of the road. Second Lt. Donald W. Sharon, Staff Sgt. Richard B. Twohey and Cpl. Joseph E. McDermott climbed on the tank. When the periscope began to revolve, McDermott smashed its glass and Twohey dropped in a grenade. The three Marines jumped off, and the tank came after them. Twohey jumped back on it and dropped another grenade down the periscope. As it exploded, the tank stopped and began smoking. A second tank hidden in a hut emerged; a Corsair destroyed it with rockets. Almost instantly, two more tanks were discovered and, under fire, their crews surrendered. The 7th Marines settled into a perimeter around Chinhung-ni.

Up ahead, the Chinese held Funchilin Pass. Litzenberg sent the Recon Company to outpost the southern tip of Hill 891, east of the road some 2,000 yards into the pass. This spur, to be known as How Hill, commanded the road; it turned out to be part of the enemy's forward line. As they approached the main hairpin turn at 4:30 P.M., the Recon Company's two lead Jeeps were destroyed. The 3rd Platoon was pinned to the road for 45 minutes, until darkness and an air strike permitted it to retreat with two killed and five wounded.

The next morning, the 3rd Battalion took the lead. The Chinese on How Hill hit the Recon Company's 1st Platoon at the same hairpin; it withdrew with four wounded. I Company tried to advance on Hill 897 on the left and G Company toward How Hill on the right, but machine-gun fire stopped them. Capt. Thomas E. Cooney, commanding G Company, was wounded twice. An artillery duel went on the rest of the day, and further ahead Marine fliers destroyed 21 trucks. They reported the ridges between Chinhung-ni and the Chosin Reservoir were alive with enemy troops. The planes blasted all the enemy positions they could find in the 11 miles between Koto-ri at the top of the pass and Hagaru at the reservoir. But the 7th Marines were stopped at the pass.

Early on November 6, 1st Lt. Howard H. Harris led H Company around the ridgeline to envelop the strongpoint on the tip of How Hill. It took the Marines until midafternoon to cover the rugged ground and get in position for the assault. Two Corsairs bombed the mountain top. The Marines climbed the steep slope of a nose extending from the summit; they were met by machine-gun fire and grenades. As the assault platoons prepared to attack, 2d Lt. Robert D. Reem of Lancaster, Pennsylvania, collected his squad leaders for instructions. A grenade fell in their midst; Reem smothered it with his body and was killed.[67]

The Marines charged the hilltop three times and were stopped each time. On the fourth attempt, Sgt. Charlie Foster reached the top and was killed, but the Marines finally took the nose. The enemy still held How Hill's crest, and the Marines' ammunition was running low. Litzenberg ordered H Company to disengage and withdraw. The Marines fought their way back with two dead and six wounded. Artillery and mortars pounded the hill all night.

The next morning, the Chinese were gone. The 3rd Battalion occupied Hills 891 and 987 without opposition. The 7th Marines had 46 killed, 262 wounded and six missing.

Meanwhile, 1st Lt. William F. Goggin had led a fast-moving patrol of 15 Marine volunteers and Corpsman James Walsh through the mountains to the west and radioed that Koto-ri was clear of enemy. As they had in western Korea, the Chinese had pulled back in front of the Marines. On November 10, the Marine Corps' 175th birthday, the 1st Battalion occupied Koto-ri.

That day on the high plateau, winter struck. The sub-zero cold and severe wind put hundreds of Marines into shock. They were getting their first taste of the ordeal to come. The cold became a vicious enemy. To survive, men had to live with great care; the penalty was frostbite, frozen feet, hands and faces. They piled on layers of clothing. They carried their canteens inside their clothes, extra socks next to their bodies. Only the dry portions of rations could be eaten safely. Entrenching tools would not break up the frozen earth. Oil froze weapons. They had to be wiped almost dry; when possible, lubricated with light hair oil. Artillery fire was slowed and ranges shortened. The cold-weather Shoe Pac made feet sweat when marching and freeze when standing still. A new vapor-barrier boot was rushed out from the United States. Vehicle engines had to be warmed up every few hours; mechanics could not expose their hands while making repairs. Jeep ambulances were useless; the wounded would freeze to death.

The Marines did extensive patrolling as combat stopped. The 2d Battalion, 5th Marines was sent northeast up toward the Fusen Reservoir. Lt. Col. Roise's Marines set up positions blocking the Sinhung corridor and patrolled the routes to the north. They were in touch with 7th Infantry Division patrols coming down the highway but did not try to penetrate the enemy defenses near the Fusen Reservoir. After November 9, Roise was ordered back to the MSR leading to the Chosin Reservoir. The 2d Battalion came around on November 13 and 14 and relieved the 7th Marines at Koto-ri to advance toward Hagaru.

On November 11, X Corps ordered an advance to the border: I ROK Corps on the right, the 7th Infantry Division in the center and the 1st Marine Division on the left. But within the next week, these orders were changed; and the direction of the Marines' attack was shifted. Instead of heading straight north, the Marines were to go north to Yudam-ni and then west, to reduce the enormous gap between X Corps and the Eighth Army and to cut the main Chinese supply routes. Only then would the Marine division head north to the border.

X Corps' three separate columns advancing through rugged country could not support each other. "Its headlong rush to the border"[68] paid no heed to the Chinese that MacArthur knew were there. Although these were days without important contacts with Chinese forces, Maj. Gen. Smith was worried. He anticipated attacks on the MSR. His units were spread out over a single mountain road.

Smith feared his Marines were out on a limb. With the Eighth Army already thrown back in the west, his left flank was wide open. On November 15, he wrote the Commandant: "I believe a winter campaign in the mountains of North Korea is too much to ask of the American soldier or marine, and I doubt the feasibility of supplying troops in this area during the winter or providing for the evacuation of sick and wounded."[69]

Smith garrisoned the key points on the MSR and set his 1st Engineer Battalion to strengthen the Hamhung–Hagaru road for tanks and heavy vehicles. He and Maj. Gen. Harris planned an airstrip capable of taking C-47 cargo planes near the burned-out town of Hagaru, which the 7th Marines had occupied on November 15. The temperature was four degrees below zero. Three days later, enough work had been done on the road for heavy equipment to get through and begin work on the Hagaru airstrip. Maj. Gen. Smith "deliberately slowed" the Marine advance at Hagaru; his caution would "prove the division's salvation in the weeks ahead."[70]

On November 17, the 5th Marines was ordered to move up the east side of the Chosin Reservoir and seize Sinhung-ni, seven miles northeast of Hagaru. And on the twenty-first, the 1st Marines, relieved of earlier assignments around Wonsan, was free to protect the MSR behind the two forward Marine regiments. The Marines also received help from the 41st Independent Commando, Royal Marines—235 reconnaissance specialists led by Lt. Col. Douglas B. Drysdale. The unit had requested service with the American Marines and was assigned to work with the Recon Company to protect the division's endangered left flank. The two Marine forces would together fight the Chinese as they had 50 years before.

On November 21, the 17th Infantry of the 7th Infantry Division reached the Yalu without opposition at snow-covered Hyesanjin. This would be the only American unit to push through to the border (except for a small task force from the 32d Infantry, which reached the Yalu a week later).

On November 24, the day after Thanksgiving, the Eighth Army jumped off on MacArthur's "end the war" offensive. And the next day, X Corps issued new orders for the Marine division to move out from Yudam-ni on November 27, head west 55 miles, seize Mupyong-ni and then advance north to the Yalu. The 7th Division would approach the Yalu on the east side of the Chosin Reservoir. Until now, the Marines' left flank had been exposed; this plan would lay open both flanks.

The Chinese reacted swiftly to the new offensive. On November 25, they hurled back the II ROK Corps, the right wing of the Eighth Army, near Tokchon, about 70 air miles southwest of Yudam-ni.

The 7th Marines seized Yudam-ni west of the Chosin Reservoir against light resistance on November 25. On the previous day en route, the Marines were fed a belated hot turkey Thanksgiving dinner—it would be their last full meal for 17 days. The 5th Marines followed the 7th, intending to pass through it at Yudam-ni and lead the attack westward to Mupyong-ni on the twenty-seventh.

On November 26, the 7th Marines captured three soldiers of the 60th Chinese Division. They said that three divisions were now in the hills around Yudam-ni and planned to move southeast and cut the MSR below Yudam-ni after the two Marine regiments had passed.

That same day, the II ROK Corps on the Eighth Army's right flank was torn to shreds under a second day of Chinese attacks. The Eighth Army's offensive was stopped and rolled back even before the Marines could jump off. The dangerous gap between the Eighth Army and X Corps widened.

Long-range Marine patrols probed outward from Yudam-ni. One patrol of A Company, 7th Marines, with 1st Lt. Frank N. Mitchell's platoon at the point, moved southwest along a snow-covered ridgeline and when it approached the village of Hansan-ni was hit by enemy fire at pointblank range. As the Marines took many casualties immediately, Mitchell dashed forward, grabbed a BAR from a wounded Marine and fired it until his ammunition was exhausted. The enemy struck the patrol's front and left flank; and Mitchell, although wounded, led the hand-to-hand struggle that repulsed the attack. As darkness gathered, the lieutenant from Indian Gap, Texas, led a party of litter bearers through the enemy lines to search for the wounded. Alone, he covered his men's withdrawal until he was killed.[71] The company hiked back to Yudam-ni. B Company, sent out to the same area, had ten Marines wounded.

It was cold at Yudam-ni. The Manchurian wind screamed in from the north over the bare hills and down the arm of the Chosin Reservoir that approached the village from the northeast. Yudam-ni, 3,500 feet above sea level, lay in a valley surrounded by five great ridges on which waited the frozen riflemen of the 7th Marines. They were guarding the dirt roads running west and north and the vital MSR leading south to Hagaru. On the night of November 26, when Lt. Col. Roise's 2d Battalion, 5th Marines arrived, the temperature stood at zero.

The next morning, Roise's battalion and Lt. Col. William F. Harris' 3rd Battalion, 7th Marines, supported by three battalions of the 11th Marines, started west. The 5th Marines advanced along the road between the steep heights of the Northwest and Southwest Ridges and the 7th Marines along the slopes of both the ridges. The Chinese were there. Within the hour, both Marine battalions came under heavy fire. Covered by mortars, artillery and air strikes, Capt. Uel D. Peters' F Company, 5th Marines, attacked the enemy's northern flank and pushed the Chinese off a spur of Northwest Ridge. D Company, now led by Capt. Samuel S. Smith, spearheaded the main move west along the road. The Chinese were dug into the massive height of Sakkat Mountain straight ahead. They stopped D Company. Roise discontinued the attack. G Company, 7th Marines fought along the peaks of Southwest Ridge until the defenses on Sakkat Mountain drove it back. G Company's commander, Captain Cooney, was mortally wounded. B, C and I Companies of the 7th Marines came forward as reinforcements. But the Marine attack, having gained 1,500 yards, was finished. If the Chinese had permitted the Marines to move forward three more miles to their next objective, they would have been isolated and trapped. Here in front of Sakkat Mountain was the high-water mark of the Marines' advance toward the Yalu.

By 6:30 P.M. on November 27, Yudam-ni was pitch black; the temperature plunged to 20 degrees below zero. Squads took turns in the warming tents. On Northwest Ridge, the Marines were immobilized in their foxholes by the painful cold. Flesh froze; carbines and BARs froze. And silently through the night came hordes of Chinese soldiers over mountain trails leading to North and Northwest Ridges. Gen. Lin Piao was sending the 9th Army Group led by Gen. Sung Shin-lun, one of China's best field commanders, to drive X Corps into the sea and wipe out the 1st Marine Division. The 79th and 89th Divisions were to strike the knockout blow against the northwest side of the Marine perimeter, and the 59th Division would swing around to the south to hit South Ridge and Toktong Pass and cut the MSR between Yudam-ni and Hagaru. Three divisions skilled at night attacks would fall on two regiments of Marines under a full moon. If General Sung succeeded, the Marines at Yudam-ni would be completely encircled.

By 9 P.M., the Chinese were in position a few hundred yards from the Marines, who waited unknowingly on the Northwest Ridge. Suddenly, an enemy patrol jabbed at the 5th Marines' roadblock just south of the ridge and was dispersed. The Chinese probed Peters' F Company on the western end of Northwest Ridge, and Chinese mortar shells rained down on the Marine front line. Then came the first assault wave. It hit the junction of E and F Companies on the ridge. The Marines piled up dead Chinese in front of them; but the attackers kept coming, broke the link between the two companies and poured through the gap. Staff Sgt. Robert S. Kennemore of Greenville, South Carolina, a veteran of Guadalcanal, rallied his leaderless E Company platoon. A grenade landed in the midst of a machine-gun squad; Kennemore placed his foot on it to absorb the explosion and lost both legs. They gave him the Medal of Honor.

Capt. Samuel Jaskilka rushed in reinforcements to contain the penetration on E Company's side of the break. The Chinese tried to envelop F Company's rear but were cut down by the Marines' firepower. By midnight, the main enemy force here had been virtually annihilated.

At the same time just to the north, another enemy force assaulted H Company, 7th Marines on Northwest Ridge's Hill 1403. Capt. Leroy M. Cooke's right flank collapsed under the weight of the enemy's numbers. Cooke called in supporting mortar fire, stopped the onslaught and led a counterattack. Chinese grenades and machine guns smashed this assault and killed Cooke. First Lt. Howard H. Harris, returned to duty after illness, went forward to take command and found all but one of Cooke's officers wounded.

For two hours, the Chinese were silent while they brought up reserve battalions. At 3 A.M., they began a second major assault against the entire two-mile Northwest Ridge front. In the broad draw at the center, machine-gun fire from Jaskilka's E Company mowed down the first waves; the Chinese following them took cover. Pfc. R. A. Jackson destroyed an enemy machine gun with a grenade just as the gun's fire killed him. On the left, some 200 Chinese hit Peters' F Company and overran two machine-gun positions. Second Lt. Bernard W. Christofferson led a counterattack, killed 20 Chinese with his submachine gun and recaptured the machine guns. On the right, the Chinese attacked Harris' H Company for an hour and finally drove the Marines back fighting. Their surrender of Hill 1403 was dangerous, making it possible for the enemy to cut off the 2d Battalion, 5th Marines and fire down on the 2,000 Marines in the valley.

East of the MSR, another Chinese division crossed the spine of North Ridge where D and E Companies, 7th Marines were isolated on Hills 1282 and 1240. At 10 P.M., Capt. Walter D. Phillips' E Company on Hill 1282 drove off a harassing force. The Chinese struck in strength at midnight and were thrown back in savage fighting. They charged repeatedly for two hours accompanied by whistles, bugles and chants. Each wave was mowed down by machine guns, grenades and mortars. The Marines took heavy casualties but held Hill 1282.

Shortly after 10 P.M., the enemy swept down the ridge at Hill 1384, north of 1282; overran an outposted platoon of I Company, 5th Marines, and forced a platoon of South Korean police, just above Taplett's 3rd Battalion command post, to retreat. H&S Company also had to withdraw across the MSR. Taplett's command post at the bottom of North Ridge was left in a no-man's-land. The battalion commander stayed in his blacked-out tent issuing orders to his rifle companies over his field telephone. At about 3 A.M., his executive officer, Maj. John J. Canney, left the CP to retrieve the H&S Company; he was killed. With Taplett remained his S-3, Maj. Thomas A. Durham, with pistol drawn; Pfc. Louis W. Swinson was outside covering the approaches with his rifle.

Lt. Col. Murray sent two A Company platoons to support Phillips' E Company on the spurs of Hill 1282 just above the village. They arrived at the climax of the Chinese attack. E Company was dwindling to a handful of men. The enemy finally forced a wedge between the two small groups of Marines making a last-ditch stand. Captain Phillips, throwing grenades in the melee, was killed. His executive officer, 1st Lt. Raymond O. Ball, immobilized by two wounds, fired his rifle and shouted encouragement until he was hit several more times and mortally wounded. First Lt. John Yancy and Staff Sgt. Daniel M. Murphy tried desperately to hold the line. (Yancy, a former Raider, was severely wounded and won his second Navy Cross. He had earned his first on Guadalcanal eight years before, almost to the day.) E Company was reduced to a platoon, and the two A Company platoons had 40 killed and wounded. The Chinese now held the commanding ground of Hill 1282.

Meanwhile, at 1:05 A.M., the Chinese assaulted D Company, 7th Marines on Hill 1240, just southeast of 1282. By 2:30, Sgt. Othmar J. Reller's platoon had fought off three attacks and was overrun. The rest of the company came under attack, and Capt. Milton A. Hull's command post fell a half hour later. With D Company down to a few squads of effectives, Captain Hull—wounded in the forehead, his face covered with blood—led a counterattack against the crest. The Chinese retreated and then fought forward again. Hull was hit in the shoulder. By dawn, he had 16 men who could fight. The enemy had them surrounded until reinforcements cut their way through.

While the two Chinese divisions attacked Yudam-ni, the 59th Division had swept around far to the southeast. C Company, 7th Marines, less one platoon, was on Hill 1419 east of the MSR, five miles south of the village. At 2:30 A.M., the Chinese struck and inflicted heavy casualties. The seesaw battle raged until dawn. Then, artillery fire from Yudam-ni helped force the Chinese back into the hills. But they had C Company surrounded and outnumbered.

Two miles further south, the 240 Marines of the reinforced F Company, 7th Marines held an isolated hill in the middle of Toktong Pass. Capt. William E. Barber, its Kentucky-born commander, had won the Silver Star on Iwo Jima. At 2:30, the Chinese struck "Fox Hill" and began a siege of five nights and days that is one of the epic stories of the Marine Corps.

The enemy quickly overwhelmed the two forward squads of 1st Lt. Robert C. McCarthy's 3rd Platoon; of 35 Marines, 15 were killed and nine wounded. Repeated Chinese attacks seized the hill's peak and tried to drive between the 2d and 3rd Platoons. There, Pfc. Robert F. Benson, Pvt. Hector A. Cafferata, Jr., and Pfc. Gerald J. Smith and his fire team wiped out two enemy platoons and prevented a breakthrough. When the Chinese attacked, New York City-born Cafferata had jumped from his sleeping bag; he never had time to put on his boots. Every member of his fire team was hit, and the Chinese threatened to pierce the Marine line. The big Marine fought alone, a target for concentrated fire. His rifle quit, and he took another from a wounded Marine. With rifle and grenades, he killed 15, wounded many more, forced the others to withdraw. Reinforcements moved up. The Chinese attacked again. A grenade landed in a shallow entrenchment where wounded Marines lay. Cafferata, still bootless in the fierce cold, grabbed the grenade and threw it back. It exploded, severing one finger and seriously injuring his right hand. Despite the pain, he continued to fight until hit in the arm by a sniper's bullet.[72]

Another unit of Chinese, approaching along the MSR, attacked F Company's rear and was annihilated. By daybreak, F Company had 20 dead and 54 wounded; but the Chinese attack, after suffering an estimated 450 casualties, petered out.

It had been a dreadful night. From Yudam-ni south, the Marines had hundreds dead and wounded. The Chinese had cut the Marines' link with the sea repeatedly from Yudam-ni to Koto-ri. Along the MSR, the Marines held strongpoints, like covered-wagon circles—isolated and embattled.

At Yudam-ni, the Marines started counterattacking just before dawn on November 28. Two platoons of G Company, 5th Marines, led by 2d Lts. John J. Cahill and Dana B. Cashion, drove north across the MSR and reached Taplett's command post. H&S Company reoccupied its former positions. Cahill and Cashion daringly plunged ahead up Hill 1384 and nearly reached the peak before Taplett ordered them to withdraw and form a defense line overlooking Yudam-ni. Their attack had relieved some of the pressure on the Marines in the valley.

Two platoons of Capt. Jack R. Jones' C Company, 5th Marines, led by 2d Lts. Byron L. Magness and Max A. Merritt, attacked up Hill 1282 shortly after daybreak. They overran 50 Chinese in hand-to-hand combat and reached the summit in time to destroy an entire Chinese company attacking up the opposite slope. The Chinese unit lost 94 of its 116 men. Marine losses on Hill 1282 totaled 15 killed and 67 wounded in A and C Companies, 5th Marines, and an estimated 120 killed and wounded in E Company, 7th Marines. But the Marines had retaken Hill 1282.

A thousand yards to the southeast, the remnant of Hull's D Company, 7th Marines, clung to Hill 1240, surrounded by Chinese troops. The 3rd Platoon of C Company, 5th Marines fought up the hill. They could see the Chinese massing to attack but could not call in supporting fire because communications were broken. Two battalions struck the Marines at 11 A.M.; but the depleted C Company platoon and the 16 remaining D Company Marines held out under heavy mortar fire until relieved by B Company, 5th Marines, at 5 P.M. The Marines lost half of the 3rd Platoon and practically all of D Company.

West of the MSR on Northwest Ridge, the Chinese on Hill 1403's peak could enfilade the entire valley. Further west on the same ridge, E and F Companies, 5th Marines, still held out; 500 Chinese dead were piled up in front of their positions. At 5:45 A.M. on the twenty-eighth, Murray alerted Roise to the probability of withdrawing his battalion to Southwest Ridge.

At dawn, Murray and Litzenberg conferred. They canceled the Marines' scheduled westward attack; and at 11 A.M., Murray ordered Roise to pull back to Southwest Ridge. Shortly after 4 P.M., Maj. Gen. Smith ordered the Marines to head south and reopen the road to Hagaru. The drive to the Yalu was dead. Murray brought his command post to the center of Yudam-ni, where Litzenberg's was located; and the two regimental commanders together planned the defense of Yudam-ni and the breakout to Hagaru.

The first job was to rescue C and F Companies, 7th Marines, embattled on the hills down the MSR. Two futile attempts to reach F Company on Fox Hill were made from Hagaru, seven miles to the southeast. On the twenty-eighth, Litzenberg's 1st Battalion, out of Yudam-ni, tried to get through. A Company fought, marched and climbed for five hours and then was stopped a mile short of C Company on Hill 1419. Lt. Col. Raymond G. Davis sent B Company, which was following A Company, on a flanking movement west of the road. Called in by forward air controller 1st Lt. Dan C. Holland, VMF-212 flew daringly close to the ridges. The air strikes and mortar fire routed the Chinese. The two rescue companies formed a protective shield around C Company's perimeter. It was now dark. F Company was supposed to fight its way north from Toktong Pass, but its casualties and the surrounding Chinese made this impossible. Litzenberg ordered Davis to return to Yudam-ni. He reached there at 9 P.M., bringing out C Company and its 46 wounded.

At the pass, F Company had spent the day caring for its 54 wounded, collecting weapons and ammunition from Marine and Chinese dead and recovering an airdrop of ammunition and medical kits. The Navy corpsmen had a terrible time. They had to melt the morphine Syrettes in their mouths before giving injections. Because the blood plasma was frozen, Marines died. Relief columns from both Yudam-ni and Hagaru had failed to break through, but the Marines on Fox Hill felt sure they could hold.

Starting at 2:15 A.M. on November 29, the Chinese attacked F Company again. At dawn, the Marines recovered the few yards they had given up during the night. Five more Marines had been killed and 29 more wounded, including both Captain Barber, severely hit in the left leg, and 1st Lt. Robert C. McCarthy, the leader of the 3rd Platoon. Nearly half of Barber's men were now casualties. Marine planes dropped ammunition and supplies right on the target marked with the previous day's colored parachutes. And 1st Lt. Floyd J. Englehardt flew in his Sikorsky helicopter with batteries for the company radios. The helicopter was damaged by Chinese fire, but he managed to take off again.

That day, another attempt was made to rescue the Marines on Fox Hill. Maj. Warren Morris, executive officer of 3rd Battalion, 7th Marines, led a composite battalion out of Yudam-ni at 8 A.M. It was engaged by large numbers of Chinese; and at 1:15, when air observers warned Litzenberg that the battalion was about to be surrounded, he ordered Morris to return to Yudam-ni immediately.

The Marines at Yudam-ni and Fox Hill spent a third night without much sleep or a hot meal. At 2 A.M. on November 30, the Chinese hit Fox Hill again. (It was Captain Barber's thirty-first birthday.) The air drops had now brought his Marines ample mortar ammunition and grenades; in a heavy snowstorm, they destroyed three Chinese companies at a cost of one Marine wounded. Barber's men felt that the Chinese, who had been unable to take Fox Hill in three nights, now never would. And the Marines at Yudam-ni were heartened to hear that the Marines at Hagaru had successfully repulsed a large Chinese force in an all-night battle.

The Chinese had repeatedly severed X Corps' vital artery with roadblocks that isolated Yudam-ni, Fox Hill, Hagaru and Koto-ri. Then they prepared to attack the division's center at Hagaru.

Fourteen miles southeast of Yudam-ni, Hagaru sat on a frozen plain crossed by the frozen Changjin River at the bottom tip of the frozen Chosin Reservoir. Low hills rose on the west and steep ridges on the east. Here the Marines had division headquarters, supply dumps, hospital facilities and the partly finished C-47 airstrip. Lt. Col. Thomas L. Ridge, commanding the 3rd Battalion, 1st Marines, estimated that at least a regiment would be needed to defend the place adequately. He had only his battalion, two artillery batteries and service troops. His G Company and a platoon of the Weapons Company had not yet arrived. But Ridge had to hold Hagaru at all costs.

Even with the cautionary restraints of the Marine commanders, MacArthur's headlong dash for the Manchurian border had left the UN forces inexcusably exposed.

Ridge's S-2, 2d Lt. Richard F. Carey, had sent two Korean scouts to investigate the Chinese beyond the Hagaru perimeter, mingle with them, determine their concentrations and if possible their plans. In two dangerous sorties, the agents located the Chinese units south and west of Hagaru and, by talking with Chinese troops and even officers, learned that they would attack Hagaru on the night of November 28. With this information, Ridge placed H and I Companies on the southern and southwestern sides of the perimeter. They would also protect the men building the airstrip. He hoped to put G Company, scheduled to arrive late on the twenty-eighth, on East Hill just east of the MSR. Major Simmons' Weapons Company manned a roadblock where the perimeter crossed the MSR to Koto-ri and defended the southern nose of East Hill.

Ridge knew he was cut off when his attempts to reach F Company on Fox Hill to the northwest failed, and a platoon and three tanks trying to patrol south to Koto-ri were stopped within sight of the Hagaru perimeter, with one killed and five wounded. The road was cut both above and below the town.

At 11 A.M. on November 28, Maj. Gen. Smith arrived at Hagaru by helicopter and opened the division command post. A half hour later, Maj. Gen. Almond flew in, conferred with Smith and left to visit the 31st Infantry, which had been badly hurt east of the Reservoir. Then, Almond was ordered back to Tokyo, where he learned that the entire Eighth Army was in full retreat.

When G Company could not come north to Hagaru, Ridge placed detachments from the Army's 10th Engineer Battalion and X Corps' headquarters on East Hill. The 7th Marines' Antitank Company defended the area north of the hill. Other units were spread between these elements. The perimeter was very weak.

The men were ready in their foxholes, and it had begun to snow when the Chinese attacked H and I Companies at 10:30 P.M. The enemy took frightful losses smashing against the Marines, who were supported by artillery and mortars. Six-foot-two 1st Lt. Joseph R. Fisher, I Company's commander, seemed invulnerable as he dashed from foxhole to foxhole encouraging his men. Second Lt. Wayne L. Hall, commanding the 3rd Platoon, was jumped by three Chinese and killed all three with his .45. Machine-gun bullets plowed through the wooden walls of the medical clearing station behind the company, and one bullet penetrated Maj. Gen. Smith's quarters. I Company managed to hold on.

H Company was hard hit. The 3rd Platoon leader, 1d Lt. Wendell C. Endsley, was killed. By 12:30, the Chinese fought through this platoon and reached H Company's command post. But they failed to exploit the penetration. Instead, cold and hungry, they looted the provision tent and galley. First Lt. Harrison F. Betts gathered 30 Marines and counterattacked; every one of the 30 was wounded. One wounded Marine saved his life by pretending to be dead while enemy soldiers stripped off his parka. A few Chinese got close enough to fire on the men operating the bulldozers under floodlights on the airstrip. A group of Engineers counterattacked and cleared the airstrip. The men went back to work. Ridge sent a pick-up platoon of signalmen and engineers to support H Company.

On the other side of the perimeter, the Chinese overran East Hill. The service troops defending there included a large portion of newly recruited ROK troops; the Army engineer company had 77 American enlisted men and 90 ROKs. These platoons fell back; Capt. John C. Shelnutt, the Marine officer attached, was killed. His Marine radio operator, Pfc. Bruno Podolak, voluntarily remained at his post now behind enemy lines and radioed back reports. He was the only American alive up on East Hill. By 4 A.M., the defenders barely clung to the reverse slopes, and East Hill was ripe for a disastrous breakthrough. But the Chinese were satisfied to hold the high ground and did not attack the command posts and supply dumps below. Marine gunners quickly pivoted around and plugged the hole with howitzer fire.

The main Chinese assault had spent itself. A counterattack cleaned out the Chinese who had penetrated H Company and restored the southern perimeter. New snow covered the bodies of hundreds of Chinese dead.

After daylight on the twenty-ninth, 250 Marine, Army and ROK service troops led by Maj. Reginald R. Myers, the 3rd Battalion's executive officer, counterattacked East Hill against an estimated 4,000 Chinese. Myers repeatedly exposed himself to intense fire to direct the men new to combat. At 9:30, VMF-312 planes hit the hill with napalm and bombs. Myers kept his force struggling up over treacherous ground under fire, skillfully calling in mortar and artillery fire. By noon, 170 of his men had disappeared, casualties or exhausted in the subzero cold. Pfc. Podolak, wounded in the back, joined the attacking force. Some of the men led by Marine 1st Lt. Robert E. Jochums pushed onto an outlying spur, the furthest point of the advance. Stopped by enemy fire, Myers' men set up a defensive line until the Marines' A Company, 1st Engineer Battalion, came up. They could not dislodge the enemy on the hilltop. That would have to wait for G Company's arrival from Koto-ri. But the counterattack had killed an estimated 600 of the enemy and wounded 500. Ridge's defenders had more than 500 casualties. The need for reinforcements from further south was urgent.[73]

The Chinese had already struck at Koto-ri and Chinhung-ni. At the latter point, where the 1st Battalion, 1st Marines protected the division's rear, the enemy had probed the perimeter starting on the night of November 26. By November 30, Lt. Col. Donald M. Schmuck, who had replaced Hawkins, took out A Company and part of B Company and in a narrow mountain valley to the west killed 56 and with close air support routed the rest of a battalion of Chinese, many of them mounted on Mongolian ponies.

At Koto-ri, Sutter's 2d Battalion, 1st Marines first ran into fire fights with Chinese detachments on November 27. The next day, Colonel Puller ordered D Company north to clear the MSR. Less than a mile north of the perimeter, it ran into the enemy entrenched on the high ground. F Company was sent out to help. By the end of the day, both companies were forced to return to Koto-ri. They had four dead and 34 wounded.

That evening, G Company, 1st Marines; the 41st Commando, Royal Marines, and B Company, 31st Infantry arrived at Koto-ri on their way to Hagaru. Puller organized them into a task force under Lt. Col. Drysdale, the Royal Marines' commander, to fight through the 11 miles to Hagaru, where they were desperately needed. Describing the Chinese positions to Drysdale, Puller said, "They've got us surrounded. The bastards won't get away this time."[74]

Task Force Drysdale started out at 9:45 A.M. on November 29, followed by a convoy of 1st Marine Division headquarters troops under Maj. Henry J. Seeley. The British Marines seized the first hill up the road. But when Capt. Carl J. Sitter's G Company passed through them to attack Hill 1236, a mile and a half north of Koto-ri, it had to uproot entrenched Chinese. And another mile further north, at Hill 1182, G Company ran into mortar and machine-gun fire. Drysdale decided to wait there for tanks that were scheduled to join his column. When he started out again at 4 P.M., the task force was led by 17 tanks; and 12 more were coming up in the rear. In between, the column consisted of approximately 922 men in 141 vehicles. They moved slowly as the lead tanks blasted enemy pockets, climbed roadblocks and bypassed craters. VMF-212 Corsairs covered them. A Chinese mortar round wounded every man in one truck. The riflemen repeatedly had to leap from the trucks and engage in fire fights. Maj. Gen. Smith radioed for the tanks in front of the column to press on to Hagaru, even if the trucks could not get through.

In a mile-long valley nearly halfway to Hagaru, enemy fire forced Task Force Drysdale to halt just before dark. On its right rose a steep hill where the enemy had mortars and machine guns; on the left, a frozen creek wound through a flatland several hundred yards wide, with the Changjin River and wooded hills beyond. Drysdale was to call the site of this ambush Hell Fire Valley. It would be the scene of one of the ugliest defeats in Marine Corps history.

Again, the men piled out of the trucks to return the enemy fire. Pfc. William B. Baugh threw himself on a grenade that landed in his truck and was mortally wounded.[75] A mortar shell set an ammunition truck on fire, creating a roadblock that split the column. Enemy fire prevented the truck's removal. During this action, the front section of the column, including the lead tanks, G Company, three-fourths of the British Marines and a few Army infantrymen—some 400 men—fought forward, with Drysdale in command, to reach Hagaru. Remaining in Hell Fire Valley were 61 Commandos; most of B Company, 31st Infantry, and nearly all the Marine headquarters and service troops. Marine Lt. Col. Arthur A. Chidester took charge and ordered the vehicles turned around for a dash back to Koto-ri.

The Chinese would not let them escape. One attack severed the column 200 yards north of Chidester and another cut the road south of the stalled convoy. Chidester and Maj. James K. Eagan were wounded and captured. (They were never seen again.) When darkness stopped the Marine air strikes, the enemy approached. The men in the valley were now divided into four perimeters. The largest was the most northern group led by Marine Maj. John N. McLaughlin. He had about 130 men including soldiers, Marines, Commandos and Associated Press photographer Frank Noel. Three hundred yards south of McLaughlin was the remnant of two Army platoons in a drainage ditch. Thirty yards further south were about 18 headquarters troops led by Capt. Michael J. Capraro and another hundred yards south a few more Marines with Major Seeley.

The men caught in the valley hoped that the following tanks would come to their rescue. But some of the tanks were stopped by heavy resistance a mile from Major Seeley, and the rest of their convoy scurried back to Koto-ri with heavy truck losses.

Until midnight, the Chinese in Hell Fire Valley kept the little perimeters pinned down and looted trucks. Then, the enemy began probing. The headquarters and service troops, including many veterans of World War II, fought well with the combat-trained Commandos. By 2 A.M., McLaughlin's men were out of grenades. Many had exhausted their ammunition. Some Commandos slipped away to reach Koto-ri for help. Noel and two men tried to escape in a Jeep and were captured. By 4:30, the Chinese demanded that the trapped men surrender. McLaughlin and Commando Sgt. Patrick D. Murphy went out to parley, hoping to stall until air support could return at dawn. The Chinese gave him ten minutes to decide. McLaughlin talked with his 40 remaining able-bodied men. None had more than eight rounds of rifle ammunition. He agreed to surrender if the Chinese would allow the evacuation of the seriously wounded to Koto-ri. The Chinese agreed, and the battle of Hell Fire Valley was over.

McLaughlin had delayed enough so that a sizable group led by Major Seeley escaped over the mountains to Koto-ri. The Chinese did not send back the wounded but permitted the most critically wounded to be put in a Korean hut, where they were later recovered and taken to Koto-ri.

Task Force Drysdale had approximately 162 killed or missing and 159 wounded, a total of 321 casualties. Of B Company's 190 soldiers, 119 were killed, wounded or missing. Forty-four Marines were listed as missing; of these, 25 eventually escaped or were released from prison camps.

Drysdale and his half of the column fought through successive roadblocks into Hagaru, losing one tank and several vehicles. Drysdale was wounded. Sixty-one of 235 Royal Marines and 48 of 205 G Company Marines were casualties. Those who got through reported to Lt. Col. Ridge at 7:15 P.M. More than 300 men and a dozen tanks had arrived to help defend Hagaru.

The next morning, November 30, G Company repeated Myers' effort to retake Hagaru's steep, snow-covered East Hill. Captain Sitter's Marines attacked from two sides; but the difficult terrain and long-range enemy fire defeated the attempt. The Marine units along the MSR received air drops of supplies and ammunition. Among those dropped at Koto-ri was a recreation package including contraceptives. When some were taken to Chesty Puller, he said, "What the hell do they think we're doing to these Chinese?"[76]

That night at Hagaru, large numbers of Chinese poured down East Hill and wiped out half of one G Company platoon. Captain Sitter moved from foxhole to foxhole encouraging his men and deployed service troops as they came up to reinforce. The enemy repeatedly penetrated the lines and were met with hand-to-hand combat. Sitter, fighting with his men, was painfully wounded in the face, chest and arms by grenade bursts but refused to be evacuated.[77] Marine howitzers, tanks, a group of headquarters personnel under 2d Lt. Carey and the 41st Commando helped repulse the attack and restore the lines before G Company was safe.

Meanwhile, on the thirtieth, a conference was held in Hagaru with Almond, Smith and the commanders of the 7th Infantry Division. Almond wanted to fall back toward Hamhung; Smith insisted that he would evacuate his wounded and fight his way out.

Most pressing was the fate of two infantry battalions and one artillery battalion of the 7th Infantry Division east of the Chosin Reservoir. They were trying to reach Hagaru and had taken 400 casualties. They were unable to fight their way out. By the night of December 1, the first Army survivors, mostly walking wounded, reached the Marine lines at Hagaru. The three Army battalions had now suffered casualties estimated as high as 75 percent. They were fighting toward Hagaru under constant attack. Losses of officers and noncoms left units leaderless. Many of the troops were ROKs who understood no English. At dark on December 1, the column was within four and a half miles of Hagaru and safety. But Lt. Col. Don C. Faith, who had assumed command, was mortally wounded; the column disintegrated. Small demoralized bands of men, wounded and frostbitten, tried to cross the ice of the reservoir; before dawn, 670 survivors of Task Force Faith had reached Hagaru.

The next morning, Marine Lt. Col. Olin L. Beall and three enlisted men searched at the reservoir for survivors. They drove onto the ice and saved a few wounded men under Chinese fire. Beall then organized a task force of trucks, Jeeps and sleds to bring back more soldiers. The Chinese sniped at the rescuers crawling out on the ice but did not hinder the escape of the Army wounded; they actually helped in some cases. Beall rescued 319 soldiers that day, most of them wounded or frostbitten. In all, 1,050 of the original 2,500 soldiers were saved. A Marine patrol counted more than 300 dead in the abandoned trucks of Task Force Faith. The 385 able-bodied soldiers who reached Hagaru were organized into a provisional battalion.

Casualties were now an overwhelming problem. One hundred and fifty-two were flown out by VMO-6, most of them from Yudam-ni. Although the Hagaru airstrip was less than half completed, a trial landing was attempted on the afternoon of

December 1. An Air Force C-47 bounced down and took off half an hour later with 24 casualties. Three more planes made it that afternoon and carried out 60 more. In 12 days and nights, D Company, 1st Engineer Battalion had hacked out of the frozen earth enough of an airstrip to fly out the wounded, bring in supplies and reinforcements and make a breakout possible.

5
The Breakout

The Marines began to change direction late on November 29. The evening before, MacArthur had summoned his field commanders, Walker and Almond, to Tokyo and authorized them to retreat. He reported to Washington that he had gone on the defensive against "overwhelming force." He said, "We face an entirely new war."[78] He had gambled and lost. His army was divided and overextended. Washington turned down his request that Chiang Kai-shek's Nationalist army be brought into the war.

On the bitter cold Korean peninsula, weary soldiers and Marines, huddled in their parkas, fought for their lives. The 1st Marine Aircraft Wing gathered five squadrons at Yonpo Airfield below Hungnam to cover them. Navy ships, which had scattered in the euphoric expectation of the war's end, hurried back to lift them from North Korea.

On the twenty-ninth, Maj. Gen. Smith ordered the 7th Marines to turn south and open the MSR to Hagaru, where Ridge defended. Puller commanded at Koto-ri and Schmuck at Chinhung-ni at the base of the mountains. The next day, at the Hagaru conference, Maj. Gen. Almond ordered the total withdrawal of the Marines—from Yudam-ni 78 miles all the way to the sea.

Litzenberg and Murray, issuing orders jointly, established a new defensive line south of Yudam-ni, where the ground was better suited for a holding action. Maj. Maurice E. Roach took a jury-rigged battalion to hold the high ground above Yudam-ni. He had his men wear green neckerchiefs ripped from parachutes and called his unit the Damnation Battalion.

As the first tricky step, the 5th Marines pulled out of their positions north and west of Yudam-ni, freeing the 7th Marines to drop back further south. These dangerous disengagements were made in daylight when the Marines could count on air cover and artillery. Roise's 2d Battalion, 5th Marines withdrew from the west for a mile and gave up Hill 1426 to the enemy. This released Harris' 3rd Battalion, 7th Marines to take new positions astride the road 4,000 yards south of Yudam-ni.

The breakout began at 8 A.M. on December 1. While Taplett's 3rd Battalion, 5th Marines led the main force down the road, Davis' 1st Battalion, 7th Marines was to dash eight miles across the ridgetops that night to rescue Barber's beleaguered company still holding open Toktong Pass. Taplett and Davis would join up in the area of Fox Hill. Despite six inches of snow on the Yonpo runway, the Corsairs were overhead.

The one tank that had made it through to Yudam-ni before the Chinese cut the MSR took the point on the road. Because of the shortage of space, only drivers and the seriously wounded were allowed to ride the trucks. Even Litzenberg and Murray walked. Before the Marines set out, 85 officers and men were buried at Yudam-ni (their bodies were transferred to the United States after the war). There was no room for the dead.

Only the 1st and 3rd Battalions, 5th Marines remained north of Yudam-ni. "Pulling them out was to prove equivalent of letting loose of the tiger's tail."[79] G Company, the last 3rd Battalion company in place, was within grenade-throwing distance of the Chinese. To prevent them from swarming over the company as it came down off the top of Hill 1282, VMF-214 Corsairs kept down the Chinese with dummy runs. It worked. Once G Company was far enough away, planes and artillery clobbered the enemy. G Company had left behind ammunition with time charges. Hill 1282 erupted with explosives. G Company managed the difficult disengaging maneuver without a casualty and escaped across the bridge south of Yudam-ni. The Engineers blew up the bridge. The rear guard, B Company, 5th Marines, stole away from nearby Hill 1240 without supporting fire, using its own machine guns to cover its withdrawal. The Marines now held a line below Yudam-ni along a row of hills from west of the MSR eastward to the tip of the Reservoir's arm.

The Marines were now "attacking in another direction" as Smith was to call it. Below Yudam-ni, Harris' battalion attacked Hill 1542 west of the MSR and Hill 1419 (C Company's old battle site) to the east. Harris' battalion had its hands full. The Corsairs could not uproot the dug-in enemy, and G and I Companies could not hold the crest of Hill 1542. With H Company unable to take Hill 1419 by itself, Davis had to send up his A Company to help. By 7:30 P.M., it finally secured Hill 1419 and cleared the way for Davis to break off and head over the ridgetops. He quickly sent his dead and wounded to the main force on the road and replaced his casualties with H Company. Each man carried an extra bandolier of ammunition and a sleeping bag. They took only six heavy machine guns and two 81mm mortars. Mortar and machine-gun ammunition was initially carried on litters. As the ammunition was expended and casualties mounted, the litters would be put to other use.

At 9 P.M., they plunged ahead. It was 16 degrees below zero; and Davis feared that if he allowed his men to stop, their own sweat would freeze and kill them. The front men had to struggle through snow often knee-deep. Behind them, the path was pounded into ice; men slipped and fell and climbed back up the ridges on hands and knees. In the darkness, all the snow-covered peaks began to look alike. On the ridges, they guided by the stars; but in the deep valleys, the stars were blotted out. Compass orientations did not check.

On the point, 1st Lt. Chew Een Lee, his right arm still in a sling, led 1st Lt. Joseph R. Kurcaba's B Company. By mistake, they veered to the southwest and headed toward the enemy on the eastern slopes of Hill 1520. Davis tried to warn Kurcaba of the danger ahead, but the radio failed. With his radio operator, Cpl. LeRoy Pearl, and his runner, Pfc. Vincent C. Michaels, Davis struggled forward through the snow in the darkness. They overtook the point as the men were stumbling up the ridge into enemy territory. The Chinese opened fire. B and C Companies attacked and wiped out an enemy platoon.

When Davis allowed a break, the men began collapsing in the snow, despite the cold and enemy bullets. Officers and non-coms had to shake and cuff them awake. They pushed on. At 3 A.M., Davis called a halt and organized a perimeter. The men took turns sleeping in the empty silence of the bleak, icy wasteland.

At daybreak, the battalion swerved left and attacked Hill

1653, a mile and a half north of Fox Hill. Unable to communicate either with Marine planes above him or with Fox Hill, Davis worried about entering the range of friendly mortar fire. The head of the battalion met little opposition; but H Company, bringing up the rear with the wounded, had to fight off the enemy's wolflike harassment.

Fox Hill finally came through on Corporal Pearl's radio. Captain Barber, now commanding from a stretcher, wanted to send out a patrol to guide Davis in; the offer was declined. Barber covered Kurcaba's final attack on Hill 1653 with a VMF-312 strike. At 11:25 A.M. on December 2, B Company entered F Company's lines through a sea of frozen Chinese bodies.

From Fox Hill, the men of Davis' forward companies went back to help with the 22 litter cases. Supervising this, Lt. Peter A. Arioli, USN, the regimental surgeon who had volunteered to accompany the battalion, was killed by a Chinese sniper. His was Davis' only battle death, although two Marines cracked under the night's strain, had to be tied down and died before they could be evacuated.

Davis' battalion, to be known as the Ridgerunners of Toktong Pass, dug in on the high ground around Fox Hill. Barber's Marines stayed in their foxholes. Over five nights and days of fighting, they had 26 killed, three missing and 89 wounded—50 percent casualties. Six of Barber's seven officers were wounded, and most of the unwounded men suffered frostbite. Only 82 of his original 240 men could walk. Theirs was a stand that Marines compared to those of Wake Island and Edson's Ridge.[80] Both Barber and Davis were awarded the Medal of Honor.

At the same time Davis had left Yudam-ni, Taplett's battalion—with the radio call sign Darkhorse—had started leading the main body down the MSR. Taplett passed through Harris' battalion and had advanced only 1,400 yards when Chinese fire from both sides stopped it. H and I Companies fanned out but needed until 7:30 P.M. to clear the enemy. Pressing on, I Company east of the road was halted again by Chinese dug in on the western side of Hill 1520. Taplett and Davis were fighting on opposite sides of the same mile-high land mass, but they did not know it. The enemy and terrain made mutual support impossible. Taplett's Marines spent the night fighting. The Chinese attacked and cut off Capt. Harold G. Schrier's I Company. Staff Sgt. William G. Windrich of Hammond, Indiana, organized a squad and held an overwhelming enemy force at bay while the other Marines withdrew. Seven of his men were hit, and he was wounded in the head by a grenade burst. Returning to the company, Windrich gathered volunteers and rescued the wounded. Hit in the leg and unable to stand, he rallied his men to drive off another attack before he bled to death.[81]

All but 20 of Schrier's men were casualties; I Company now existed only on paper. Both G and H Companies were reduced to two-platoon strength. Taplett called for reinforcements and was sent the remnants of D and E Companies of the 7th Marines from the green-scarfed Damnation Battalion.

Tough fighting on the ground and daring flying among the ridges were needed before Taplett could resume the advance. The Engineers built a bypass around a bridge the Chinese had blown. G and H Companies attacked along either side of the MSR, and the composite D-E Company moved down the road behind the Engineers and Staff Sgt. Russell A. Munsell's lone tank.

While the spearhead battalions moved south, the three battalions holding the rear line below Yudam-ni were under tremendous pressure. Five VMF(N)-542 planes helped Roise's rearguard battalion during the early hours of December 2. F Company was forced off the left flank of Hill 1276, and Roise ordered it retaken. Two attempts in the darkness were repulsed by enemy machine guns. After dawn, planes strafed and rocketed the Chinese. F Company took the crest; the machine guns on the reverse slope drove them off again. Corsairs blasted the Chinese at midmorning; but by then, it was time for Roise to pull out; and the futile, costly counterattack was dropped.

Simultaneous Chinese night attacks all along the rear line were driven off, except on the extreme left where the Chinese shoved Lt. Col. Harris' G and I Companies off Hill 1542. Although reinforced by about a hundred artillerymen and headquarters troops thrown together as J Company, Harris had to give ground under persistent attack until he had less than 200 men left. When J Company was routed, artillery Sgt. James E. Johnson of Pocatello, Idaho, took charge of his leaderless platoon and covered its withdrawal. He was last seen, wounded, struggling hand-to-hand with the enemy.[82] Harris' Marines were finally able to hold enough of Hill 1542's slopes to keep Chinese small-arms fire off the MSR.

As the vehicle train started creeping south on the morning of December 2, there were not enough riflemen to protect the high ground. Air cover kept major Chinese elements away, but infiltrators were able to knock off a number of Marine drivers.

Leading the breakout, Taplett's Darkhorse battalion had to fight for nearly every foot of the road. What was left of his G Company took Hill 1520 on the left by noon. H Company on the right fought through a Chinese strongpoint. D-E Company was stopped 300 yards further on, where a bridge over a rock ravine had been blown out. Twelve Corsairs drove the enemy out of the ravine; but by 2 A.M. on December 3, D-E Company was exhausted and ineffective with heavy losses, particularly among its noncoms. The battalion had to halt 1,000 yards short of Fox Hill.

At dawn on December 3, the ground was covered with six inches of new snow. Tech. Sgt. Edwin L. Knox's Engineer platoon held the point behind the tank. G Company came down to the road to take over from D-E Company, the remnant of which was now commanded by 2d Lt. John J. Cahill, the same officer who had led the first Marines into action four months before—when the temperature had been more than 100 degrees higher.

During the night of December 2, Davis' men around Fox Hill counterattacked to clear Toktong Pass and dislodge the battalion of Chinese barring the way to Hagaru. The Marines drove the enemy right into the path of Taplett's H Company. Pvt. James T. Beard, firing his BAR from the hip, crushed a series of enemy positions. He killed a machine-gun crew with a grenade, turned the gun on the retreating enemy and killed 17 before he ran out of ammunition. Helicopter pilot 1st Lt. Robert A. Longstaff was shot down and killed while trying to rescue a badly wounded Marine. By 10:30 A.M., the enemy battalion had been slaughtered by mortars, machine guns, rockets and napalm. At 1 P.M., Munsell's tank came into the pass and Davis' and Taplett's battalions met.

Davis', Taplett's and Barber's wounded were put aboard

trucks. Taplett's rifle companies had been reduced in three days from 437 men to 194. To make room, the walking wounded had to get off and struggle painfully toward Hagaru on foot. Litzenberg walked alongside his Jeep filled with wounded.

Munsell's tank led off again, followed by Davis' Ridgerunners and Lt. Col. Stevens' 1st Battalion, 5th Marines. Marine Corsairs blasted the enemy in front and on the flanks. Planes from six Marine squadrons flew 145 sorties, mostly in close support. Taplett's Marines provided security for the artillery, followed by Roise and finally Harris as the rear guard. And up from Hagaru moved the Royal Marine Commandos with a platoon of tanks to clear the road. As the point from Yudam-ni came within a few hundred yards of Hagaru that evening, the men in the front closed ranks—the wounded who were able climbed down off the trucks—and they marched silently into the perimeter.

As the rest of the column moved toward Hagaru, at 2 A.M. on December 4, the prime movers for eight 155mm howitzers ran dry of diesel fuel. Unaware of this break in the line behind them, the troops in front pushed ahead. But Chinese hit the cannoneers and drivers of the 4th Battalion, 11th Marines. Two drivers were killed, and a few others panicked and tried to bypass a blown-out bridge by crossing the ice of a small stream. Chief Warrant Officer Allen Carlson of the 11th Marines dashed after one of the fleeing trucks, cursing loudly, and brought back a howitzer. He rounded up a crew and started firing point-blank at the enemy. E Company, 5th Marines circled around; by 8:30, the enemy strongpoint had been eliminated. The stalled howitzers were abandoned; and at 2 P.M., the last elements of Harris' rear guard entered the Hagaru perimeter.

The head of the column had needed 59 hours to cover the 14 miles to Hagaru, the rear units, 79 hours. Some 1,500 casualties had been brought out, a third of them suffering from frostbitten feet, hands and faces.

While the Marines rested, regrouped and prepared to fight their way to the sea, the Chinese were strangely absent. Two B-26s mistakenly bombed and strafed the perimeter on the evening of December 5. The evacuation of the wounded was the most urgent problem. The division surgeon, Capt. Eugene R.

Hering, USN, set the standard: To be approved for evacuation, a man had to be in worse condition than Lt. Cmdr. Chester M. Lessenden, USN, the 5th Marines' surgeon, who had both feet painfully frozen and refused to be flown out. By nightfall of the fifth, 4,312 men—3,150 Marines, 1,137 soldiers and 25 Royal Marines—had been flown out of Hagaru by Marine and Air Force aircraft.

Five hundred and thirty-seven replacements were flown into Hagaru. Many of them were Marines wounded in the Inchon-Seoul campaign. The Air Force offered to evacuate the troops at Hagaru, but Maj. Gen. Smith refused. He wanted all able-bodied men to come out with all possible equipment.

The press met with Smith at Hagaru, and a British correspondent asked if this were a "retreat" or "retirement." Smith replied quietly that since the Marines were surrounded, there was no rear and therefore there could be no "retreat." So much for rhetoric.

To prepare the next stage of the breakout, more than 370 tons of supplies were flown into or air-dropped on Hagaru: ammunition, hand grenades, gasoline and diesel oil, rations and communication wire. The air-drop damage rate was especially high among the artillery and mortar ammunition, but Smith said that the amount received gave the division a vital margin.

Even though delay would allow the Chinese time to get in position in the hills down along the MSR, the need for recuperation was so compelling at Hagaru that the move to Koto-ri was postponed until December 6. The plan was for the 7th Marines to lead the way while the 5th Marines and Ridge's 3rd Battalion, 1st Marines protected the rear. After Koto-ri, the remaining elements of the 1st Marines would take over the rear guard. Everyone except drivers, relief drivers, radio operators and casualties would walk out.

MAW-1 would cover the column with 24 planes, while Marine, Navy and Air Force search and attack planes scouted ahead and among the ridges on the flanks. Four hundred and ninety soldiers including 385 survivors of Task Force Faith were organized into a provisional battalion ("the 31/7") and attached to the 7th Marines. Maj. Gen. Smith flew ahead to Koto-ri by helicopter to organize the next step southward. By air, the trip took only ten minutes.

Although the Chinese had not attacked at Hagaru, Intelligence reported masses of enemy troops were assembling both at Hagaru and above the road to Koto-ri. Seven Chinese divisions were identified in the area.

On the morning of December 6, Murray sent Roise's 2d Battalion against East Hill where the Chinese still threatened Hagaru itself and dominated the road south to Koto-ri. Capt. Samuel S. Smith's D Company led the assault. After two hours of fighting, Chinese resistance collapsed; and the hill was taken with one Marine killed and three wounded.

D Company was unable to secure the next ridge of the same land mass until 2:30 P.M. F Company occupied the first hill, and both companies hit the Chinese assembling at the saddle between the two hills. First Lt. George C. McNaughton led a patrol onto the saddle and captured 220 Chinese. The saddle was then turned over to a small force from the Antitank Company and the Army's 4th Signal Battalion.

This became the fiercest battle of the entire breakout. From dusk until 2 A.M., the Chinese attacked there again and again, taking frightful losses. Mortars and machine guns on both sides took their toll. D Company, which had been virtually wiped out on Smith Hill northwest of Seoul, was hard hit again. First Lt. Seydel, the company's only officer not wounded in the earlier battle, killed seven Chinese and was himself killed. D Company had 13 dead and 50 wounded and was forced to fall back and tie in with F Company. Next, the Chinese attacked A, C and E Companies of the 5th Marines on the perimeter to the northwest of East Hill. The Marines' firepower was devastating. Estimates of Chinese dead in the 22-hour battle ran as high as 800. The enemy had made a major effort to destroy the Marines and been crushed.

The 7th Marines were already following the route of Task Force Drysdale—in the opposite direction. Three hundred artillerymen filled the regiment's ranks, giving Litzenberg about 2,200 men. The 1st Battalion moved out on the east of the road; the 2d Battalion supported by tanks, along the MSR; the Provisional Battalion ("31/7"), in the valley along the west side of the road, and the 3rd Battalion behind the regimental train.

They started leaving the perimeter at 6:30 A.M. on December 6 in a silvery fog. The survivors of F Company of Fox Hill had the point. Barber had been flown out, and 1st Lt. Welton R. Abell commanded the reinforced company. Almost immediately, the lead dozer tank was hit by three rounds from a 3.5-inch bazooka; and then after allowing F Company to pass, the Chinese opened up on the column. Not until two companies and tanks attacked the hill could the advance start again at noon. F Company's last remaining officer of the Fox Hill battle, 1st Lt. John M. Dunne, was killed. Four thousand yards out of Hagaru, another strongpoint stopped the column until 3 P.M. The flank battalions ran into continual opposition. Along the ridgeline to the east, long columns of Chinese reinforcements were sighted moving toward the MSR. Air attacks could not stop them.

The Marines fought past a succession of strongpoints, roadblocks and blown bridges. In Hell Fire Valley, a Chinese machine gun held up the 2d Battalion; it was midnight before Army tank fire destroyed the gun. Another 1,200 yards and everything stopped while the Engineers repaired one blown-out bridge, and soon afterwards, a second. Fearing the arrival of the Chinese reinforcements, the column kept going all night long.

The 2d Battalion covered the last few miles into Koto-ri without trouble. But at 2 A.M., the regimental train was hit by enemy fire; three officers in the regiment's command group were killed and wounded. When Chaplain Cornelius J. Griffin entered an ambulance to console a dying Marine, machine-gun bullets shattered his jaw and killed Sgt. Matthew Caruso by his side. Lt. Col. Harris and Major Roach directed H Company in beating off the attack. At 5:30, Harris disappeared and was never seen again; presumably the son of Maj. Gen. Field Harris had been killed. The 2d and 3rd Battalions were sent back up the MSR again from Koto-ri to keep the road open for the other units. The 2d Battalion also helped rescue 22 British Marines who had been stranded ever since Drysdale's fight a week earlier. They had survived for five days on food and medical supplies air-dropped after an OY pilot had spotted the letters HELP stamped in the snow.

With the 7th Marines safe at Koto-ri, the Chinese moved in and attacked the flanks of the Division Train No. 1, which had been delayed starting out from Hagaru. After dark on December 6, the 3rd Battalion, 11th Marines had to repulse an enemy attack. Further on, Chinese mortar shells set several trucks on fire and blocked the convoy again. And at dawn, the enemy attacked in force. They almost overran the artillerymen before they were stopped; several hundred of the enemy were killed.

The Chinese also attacked the Division Headquarters Company and burned several trucks. Bandsmen set up two machine guns and kept the Chinese at a distance. Six-foot-four, 240-pound 1st Lt. Charles H. Sullivan emptied his carbine, then hurled it like a javelin and drove the bayonet through a Chinese chest at 15 yards. By daylight, a company-strength group of the enemy closed to within 30 yards before strafing runs by VMF(N)-513 helped stop them. Four planes of VMF-312 dropped four tons of explosives and napalm, and the Chinese broke and ran.

During this ambush, the Military Police Company was guarding 160 Chinese prisoners, lying in the middle of the road. When the Chinese fired on them, the prisoners tried to break. Both Chinese and Marines fired into them and killed 137.

Division Train No. 2; Steven's 1st Battalion, 5th Marines; Ridge's 3rd Battalion, 1st Marines, and the 41st Commando moved out of Hagaru. Drysdale held an inspection of his Royal Marines before setting out.

By 10 A.M. on December 7 only Roise's battalion; 1st Lt. Vaughan R. Stuart's tank platoon, and Capt. William R. Gould's A Company, 1st Engineer Battalion were left in Hagaru. Five demolition teams prepared piles of equipment and clothing for burning, placed charges in the ammunition dumps and bull-dozed the mountain of surplus rations and saturated them with fuel oil. While Roise's Marines were still pulling off the southern tip of East Hill, explosions shook the earth. Roise was furious; rockets, shell fragments and all kinds of debris rained down but fortunately did not injure any of the Marines. And finally, the Engineers blew the bridge, leaving Hagaru to small groups of Chinese who dared the flames and explosions to pick over the ruins of the Marines' former forward base. The name of Hagaru had joined Belleau Wood, Guadalcanal and Iwo Jima in Marine Corps history.

As the final units moved on Koto-ri, the Engineers blew all the bridges along the route. Pathetic hordes of Korean refugees scurried after the troops in blind panic. Many were killed in the fighting. By midnight, the last of the 1st Marine Division reached Koto-ri. In the two frantic days of December 6 and 7, the division had suffered 103 killed, 7 missing and 506 wounded— 616 casualties. But it had brought to Koto-ri 10,000 troops and a thousand vehicles. The perimeter was bursting to its seams. The "advance" southward would continue as soon as it became light.

In the Koto-ri perimeter were approximately 2,300 U.S. Army soldiers, 40 ROK police, 150 Royal Marines and more than 11,600 United States Marines. With OYs spotting from the Koto-ri strip, tanks, mortars, artillery and planes kept the Chinese at bay. Colonel Puller had the strip lengthened so that larger aircraft could evacuate casualties.

The mountainous ten miles from Koto-ri to Chinhung-ni were expected to be especially dangerous. It was decided to have Schmuck's 1st Battalion, 1st Marines strike northward from Chinhung-ni. Task Force Dog from the 3rd Infantry Division was rushed up from Hamhung to relieve Schmuck. On December 2, Schmuck himself had led a squad-sized patrol north and located a large body of Chinese. He called in artillery fire from Koto-ri and slaughtered them.

Before the force at Koto-ri could get out, a critical problem had to be solved. The Chinese had blown a bridge three and a half miles south of Koto-ri. There, water from the Chosin Reservoir flowed out of a tunnel and into four large steel pipes to run the turbines of a power plant in the valley below. Where the pipes crossed under the road, they had been covered by the destroyed one-way bridge. On the uphill side was a concrete gatehouse and on the other, a sheer drop. There was no possibility to construct a bypass. The gap of 16 feet (24 feet with the abutments) had to be spanned if the division would bring out its vehicles, guns, tanks and the wounded.

Lt. Col. Partridge studied the break from the air and figured it required four 2,500-pound sections of an M-2 steel Treadway bridge. He ordered eight sections air dropped in case any were damaged. A hundred-man detail worked all night at Hungnam's Yonpo Airfield, and eight Air Force C-119s parachuted the sections inside the Koto-ri perimeter on December 7. One section was damaged and one fell into Chinese hands. Plywood panels were also dropped. Tanks could cross on the metal spans alone, but the narrower vehicles had to keep one wheel on the metal span and the other on the plywood center. Two Army Brockway trucks would carry the bridge sections to the site.

On December 8, in a heavy snowstorm, and with the temperature at 14 degrees below zero, the 7th Marines moved out from Koto-ri. Puller held the perimeter there and formed the rear guard. Visibility was 50 feet; air cover was absent. Schmuck's battalion hiked up from Chinhung-ni. Its mission was to seize Hill 1081, which controlled the narrow, tortuous Funchilin Pass three miles above Chinhung-ni—and the vital bridge site. Schmuck's Marines took only a radio Jeep and two ambulances. Captain Wray's C Company seized the southwestern nose of the hill. Captain Noren's B Company attacked its western slope, while Captain Barrow's A Company assaulted the steep ridge leading to the summit. The snowstorm hid them from the Chinese 6th Division, which was dug in to meet an attack from the north. Said Robert Barrow much later, "They were clearly in a position to control, dominate and absolutely stop the 1st Marine Division from moving south. They had to be dislodged."[83]

Two machine guns stopped Noren's company until a patrol worked around and routed the gunners. Struggling through the deep snow, the company took an enemy bunker complex by surprise in a brief savage fight. Barrow led his three platoons up the ice-covered "almost sheer cliff" in the wind-lashed blizzard. As the storm lifted momentarily, they deployed slightly, attacked the razor-backed ridge and enveloped the Chinese strongpoint on one crest of Hill 1081. So complete was the surprise that only one enemy machine gun offered effective resistance; and it was knocked out by Cpl. Joseph R. Leeds and his fire team, who had crawled up to it on hands and knees. Leeds went in first and killed nine Chinese in the bunker; he was mortally wounded. Marine losses were 13 killed and 17 wounded who had to be taken down. About midnight, when it was 25 below zero, the Chinese counterattacked along the ridgeline; and Barrow's men drove them off.

For the troops trying to come down from Koto-ri, December 8 was a frustrating, snow-blinded day. After 117 Marines, soldiers and Royal Marines were buried in a common grave at Koto-ri, the 3rd Battalion, 7th Marines moved out and met fire from automatic weapons west of the road. Litzenberg urged

Major Morris, who had replaced Lt. Col. Harris, to commit his reserve company. Morris replied, "All three companies are up there—50 men from George, 50 men from How, 30 men from Item. That's it!"[84] Lt. Col. Randolph S. D. Lockwood's 2d Battalion moved from the road to get behind the enemy position. By then it was dark, and the attack had to be postponed.

Litzenberg's Army Provisional Battalion found less opposition east of the road. The Ridgerunner battalion, commanded by Maj. Webb D. Sawyer since Davis had become regimental executive officer, pushed down the road itself and ran into heavy Chinese fire. First Lt. Kurcaba was killed and Lieutenants Chew Een Lee and Joseph R. Owen were wounded. Stevens' 1st Battalion, 5th Marines moved east of the road and took Hill 1457. Because the advance had fallen short, the trucks following the 7th Marines had to back up and the Brockway trucks returned closer to Koto-ri. All told, casualties were light on December 8; weather and terrain had prevented the division from securing its objectives.

When December 9 broke cold and clear, American planes went to work; and Schmuck's Marines discovered that they had not occupied the final slopes of Hill 1081. In hard fighting, A Company took the crest. The entrenched Chinese doggedly defended the last 200 yards. Staff Sgt. Ernest J. Umbaugh led a grenade attack and was killed in the final assault. By 3 P.M., with help from mortars and four Corsairs, the Marines seized Hill 1081 just as the point of the 7th Marines' column appeared on the snaking road far below. Barrow had only 111 able-bodied men left of the 223 he had brought to battle. He, Umbaugh and Leeds were awarded the Navy Cross. The Marines counted 530 enemy dead for the crucial, desperately defended ridge. No Chinese surrendered; none escaped. It was the last Chinese large-scale effort to stop the Marines.

The clear weather made air and artillery support possible, and the 7th Marines could advance more easily. C Company came upon 50 Chinese so badly frozen in their foxholes that the Marines simply lifted them up and sat them on the road under guard. Frequently now, Chinese who were freezing to death, whose fingers had to be broken from their rifles, were surrendering to the Marines.

About noon, the bridge sections arrived at the pass, and

even Chinese prisoners were put to work constructing the abutments and laying the Treadways and plywood panels. By 3:30, the job was done; and by 6 P.M., the first vehicles began to inch across.

Suddenly, an accident crushed every hope. A tractor towing an earth-moving pan broke through the plywood center panel. The bridge became impassable for wheeled vehicles. An expert tractor driver, Tech. Sgt. Wilfred H. Prosser, carefully backed the tractor off the wrecked bridge. Lt. Col. Partridge calculated that if the Treadways were placed as far apart as possible, M-26 tanks could pass with two inches to spare and Jeeps with barely half an inch on the 45-inch interval between the inboard edges of the Treadways. Bulldozers skillfully positioned the Treadways while Sawyer's battalion kept the Chinese away from the bridge site. When the repairs were made, the vehicles started across. Engineers guided them over with flashlights. The column crossed the bridge all night long. Marines, Korean refugees and even cattle crunched southward on the crisp snow.

At 2:45 A.M. on December 10, the first elements of Sawyer's battalion began arriving at Chinhung-ni. (It was Robert Taplett's thirty-second birthday.) For the rest of the column, it was a march of stops and starts. The Chinese were sighted east of the road and kept moving south despite artillery and air attacks that cut up their ranks. There were occasional fire fights along the twisted mountain road to Chinhung-ni. By mid-afternoon, the last elements left Koto-ri; the tanks brought up the rear. Chesty Puller stayed until they started. His Jeep carried out several wounded and three dead Marines. Puller walked to the pass.

The forward units were already aboard trucks heading for Hungnam. But there was a severe shortage of vehicles, and most of the men had to continue to walk out. Shortly after midnight, the Chinese struck at Sudong, south of Chinhung-ni. Armed with grenades and burp guns, they killed several drivers and set their vehicles on fire. The whole column came to a halt. A confused fight erupted until Lt. Col. John U. D. Page, USA, and Marine Pfc. Marvin L. Wasson teamed up and routed 20 Chinese at the head of the vehicle column. A grenade killed Page and wounded Wasson. After getting first aid, the Marine went back into the fight with Lt. Col. Waldron C. Winston, USA, who directed a counterattack by Marine and Army service troops. UPI correspondent Harry Smith also fought in the ambush. Wasson, calling for machine guns to cover him, fired three white phosphorus rounds from a 75mm recoilless rifle and destroyed a house serving as a Chinese strongpoint. Then, he helped push trucks of exploding ammunition off the road. It was daybreak before the road was cleared. Eight men had been killed and 21 wounded; and nine trucks and an armored personnel carrier, lost. Wasson received the Navy Cross.

At the rear of the division came 40 tanks, guarded only by the Recon Company. The Recon Marines also had to keep back the thousands of refugees, infiltrated by Chinese soldiers, who followed the Marine column. Because of a mix-up in orders, Schmuck had not received Maj. Gen. Smith's instructions that the 1st Marines were to protect the tanks.

The brakes of the ninth tank from the rear froze. The tanks in front moved ahead, but the tail of the column stalled 2,000 yards from the Treadway bridge. Five Chinese soldiers emerged from among the refugees, and one called in English that they wanted to surrender. First Lt. Ernest C. Hargett, leader of the Recon platoon guarding the last tanks, went out cautiously to meet them. Cpl. George A. J. Amyotte covered him with a BAR. Suddenly, the leading Chinese stepped aside and the others opened up with burp guns and grenades. Hargett's carbine failed to fire in the sub-zero cold. The former Marine football star hurled himself at the Chinese, swinging his carbine. He crushed one skull. A grenade explosion wounded him. Amyotte shot down the other four Chinese one by one. As Chinese attacked from the high ground on the flanks, Hargett's platoon fell back fighting. The enemy overran the last tank and killed its crew. Half of Hargett's men were wounded. Amyotte, wearing fiberglass body armor and firing from prone, covered the platoon. A grenade exploded squarely on his back, but he coolly continued to pick off the enemy.

A Chinese explosive charge blew Pfc. Robert D. DeMott over the cliff. He was thought dead. But he landed unconscious on a ledge and later managed to climb up to the road and walk among the Korean refugees to Chinhung-ni. He was the last Marine out from the Reservoir.

Hargett and his remaining 24 men fought their way through. His platoon had two killed and 12 wounded. Tank crewmen finally freed the frozen brake. Cpl. C. P. Lett, who had never driven a tank before, took over a second tank, which had been deserted by its crew, and maneuvered it to safety.

After the freed tank and Letts' tank crossed the Treadway bridge with Hargett's men, Chief Warrant Officer Willie S. Harrison of the Engineers blew up the bridge. By midnight on December 11, the division's last elements arrived at the staging area at Hungnam. From Koto-ri south, the division had suffered 75 more dead, 16 missing and 256 wounded. But the breakout was complete.

The 1st Marine Division had beaten off at least seven Chinese divisions and left the 9th Army Group impotent to prevent the Hungnam evacuation or to march westward and reinforce the attack on the Eighth Army.

The issue had, in fact, been decided by the failure of the enemy's initial attacks at Yudam-ni. Marine firepower had inflicted heavy casualties on the Chinese and enabled the Marines to consolidate at Hagaru and avoid destruction in detail. The Chinese had also suffered from the Korean cold and from shortages of transport, supplies, food and communications. They could not save their wounded. Their problems became progressively more difficult the longer the Marines were able to hold out.

No one knew better than the Marines on the ground that the breakout could hardly have been successful without the air support of Marine, Navy and Air Force pilots. Crash landings threatened death in the frozen hills, and a pilot could not survive 20 minutes in the frigid waters off the coast. To make air support possible, runways had to be cleared of snow and carrier decks scraped free of ice inches thick. One time, VMF-214 had to cancel all flights because of 68-knot winds and the coating of ice on *Sicily's* flight deck.

Despite all the hazards, Marine aviators flew hundreds of close-support and search-and-attack missions for Marine, Army and ROK ground units. The Marine Corps system of a forward air controller on the ground talking directly to the pilot overhead proved itself invaluable. And from November 1 until Christmas, the transports of VMR-152 lifted five million pounds of supplies to the troops and evacuated more than 4,000 casualties. VMO-6's OYs and helicopters performed unending rescue and evacuation missions and were often the only physical contact between ground units separated by the enemy.

On December 10, VMF-311, the first Marine jet squadron to fly in combat, arrived at Yonpo. Its fliers covered both X Corps and, with Fifth Air Force jets, the Eighth Army.

As Maj. Gen. Smith wrote Maj. Gen. Harris, "During the long reaches of the night and in the snow storms many a Marine prayed for the coming of day or clearing weather when he knew he would again hear the welcome roar of your planes as they dealt out destruction to the enemy."[85]

Even before the last elements of the 1st Marine Division arrived at Hungnam, the first were loading out. X Corps organized a defensive line around the port. Lt. Gen. Shepherd was on the scene to help with the evacuation of the Marines. The job was enormous. More than 105,000 troops, 91,000 Korean refugees, 17,500 vehicles and mountains of supplies had to be sea-lifted out.

Col. Edward H. Forney, deputy chief of staff of X Corps, was the Corps evacuation officer. By December 14, 22,215 Marines were on board ships; they headed for Pusan the next day. On the eighteenth, MAG-12's command post flew to Itami, Japan. The disastrous Chosin Reservoir campaign was over.

A Marine Shore Party Company, an Air and Naval Gunfire Liaison Company and part of the 1st Amphibian Tractor Battalion helped finish the cleanup at Hungnam. Among the last troops off the beaches on Sunday afternoon, the day before Christmas, were A and B Companies of the Marine Amtrac Battalion, covering the flanks of the final withdrawal. Then, the remaining ammunition and supplies were blown up in one volcanic eruption that seemed to destroy the entire Hungnam waterfront.

Time magazine summed up the feat that had been accomplished:

> The running fight of the Marines and two battalions of the Army's 7th Infantry Division from Hagaru to Hamhung—40 miles by air but 60 miles over the icy, twisting mountainous road—was a battle unparalleled in U.S. military history. It had some aspects of Bataan, some of Anzio, some of Dunkirk, some of Valley Forge, some

of the "Retreat of the 10,000" (401–400 B.C.) as described in Xenophon's *Anabasis*.[86]

Newsweek called the overall debacle "America's worst military licking since Pearl Harbor,"[87] and *Time*, "the worst defeat the United States ever suffered."[88] MacArthur later decried these assessments as "the emotional reaction of irresponsible writers."[89]

But no one could point to a worse American defeat. Blunt-spoken Chesty Puller, who was to receive his fifth Navy Cross—the only Marine ever awarded five—for "superb courage" commanding the division's rear guard out of Koto-ri, wrote his wife: "The leadership, especially that of the higher command during this operation, has not been of top grade, especially in determining an estimate of the situation and the capabilities of the enemy."[90]

The only saving grace was the truly heroic effort of disciplined, determined American Marines and soldiers against an able enemy and sub-zero cold. Puller wrote his wife, "We were ordered to retreat and did so."[91] They saved themselves and restored some share of the nation's pride despite the arrogant hubris of the politicians and the generals.

General MacArthur painted the picture rose: "This was undoubtedly one of the most successful strategic retreats in history, comparable with and markedly similar to Wellington's great Peninsula withdrawal. Had the initiative action not been taken and an inert position of adequate defense assumed, I have no slightest doubt that the Eighth Army and the X Corps would have been annihilated." He called the action "the most successful and satisfying I have ever commanded."[92].

The 1st Marine Division alone from November 30 until December 11 had 2,103 battle casualties—342 dead, 78 missing and 1,683 wounded. And the United Nations forces had been ignominiously thrown out of North Korea.

6
Fighting Back

After its trial in the north, the 1st Marine Division recuperated in the 5th Marines' old Bean Patch at Masan. Strengthened by nearly 3,000 replacements, as well as new weapons and equipment, the Marines ate fresh food and played touch football and got ready again for battle.

On December 23, the Eighth Army's doughty commander, Lt. Gen. Walton H. Walker, was killed when a ROK truck crashed into his Jeep head on. Lt. Gen. Matthew B. Ridgway, the paratroop leader, came out and took command the day after Christmas. He found his army nervous, apprehensive, uncertain. He set out to rebuild its self-confidence. The Marines liked his style.

On New Year's Eve, the Chinese attacked. They drove the United Nations' front back from approximately the 38th Parallel and reconquered Seoul, Inchon and Wonju. The U.S. 2d and the ROK 8th Divisions were badly mauled.

Four Marine air squadrons supported the retreating UN ground forces, but the 1st Marine Division was out of action this time. On January 9, 1951, Ridgway assigned the division a blocking and anti-guerrilla mission, still far behind the front, in the Pohang area on the east coast. Another 1,800 Marine replacements were rushed out. The next month was devoted to sending out "rice paddy patrols" and hunting elusive North Korean guerrillas, who were more eager to escape than fight. At least the exercise served to restore morale and combat-readiness and introduce the division's replacements to the Korean winter. The month's work cost the division 26 dead, 10 missing and 148 wounded in action.

On February 10, the 27th Infantry Division recaptured

Inchon and Kimpo Airfield. The Chinese reacted immediately; they attacked at midnight of the eleventh. Although Maj. Gen. Smith wanted his division kept on the UN flank near the sea, the Marines were shifted to Chungju in the middle of the peninsula. There, they served under Maj. Gen. Bryant E. Moore, commanding general of IX Corps, who had fought with the Marines for Henderson Field. And the 1st Marine Aircraft Wing came over from Japan to Airfield K-3 near Pohang.

As the Chinese offensive died out, Ridgway started Operation Killer, a limited counter-offensive along the entire Eighth Army front. He wanted the pressure kept on. At 8 A.M. on February 21, the Marine division advanced north from Wonju, with the 5th Marines on the right and the 1st Marines on the left. They moved against negligible resistance through an area of rocky heights and narrow valleys; mud and poor roads snarled traffic. They reached their first objective, a ridgeline about three and a half miles south of the high ground dominating Hoengsong, by dusk on February 24.

For the most part, Fifth Air Force planes supported the Marines while Marine aircraft flew for U.S. Army units. The Marine air wing was no longer directly under division control, and the Marine commanders protested the breakup of their ground-air team and the frequent delays in receiving close air support through the Joint Operations Center. But their complaints went unanswered.

On February 24, Maj. Gen. Moore's helicopter crashed into the Han River; and he died of a heart attack a half hour later. Maj. Gen. Smith commanded IX Corps for nine days. As the commander of a major U.S. Army unit, he followed in the footsteps of Lejeune, who had led the 2d Infantry Division in World War I, and Geiger, who had commanded the Tenth Army on Okinawa after Buckner was killed. Chesty Puller, who had been promoted to brigadier general and replaced Maj. Gen. Craig as assistant division commander, took over the division while Smith had the corps.

Puller moved the 1st Marines straight ahead toward Hoengsong with the 7th Marines on its left. The 3rd Battalion, 1st Marines, now commanded by Lt. Col. Virgil W. Banning in place of Ridge, had to cross the 200-foot-wide, chest-deep Som River. The Engineer Company was unable to help; and Major

543

Simmons, commanding the Weapons Company, proposed a field-manual designed "Swiss bent bridge" of A-shaped trusses of timbers tied together with telephone wire. This solution enabled the battalion to cross on March 1.

The Marines found the second half of Operation Killer tougher; but by the end of March 4, they occupied the line of hills north of Hoengsong. In eight days, the division had 48 killed, 2 missing and 345 wounded. Since the Chinese still proved more willing to retreat than to fight, Ridgway had been unable to achieve his objective of killing many enemy troops.

Dissatisfied, he continued the northward pressure under the name of Operation Ripper. The Marine division moved out on the morning of March 7. This time, MAG-33 was able to send 11 flights of four planes each to support the Marine regiments. For the next week, individual platoons fought rearguard defenders screening the Chinese withdrawal. On March 15, the 1st ROK Division found Seoul deserted by the enemy. The capital, in changing hands four times in nine months, had been pounded into rubble.

At this time, the 1st Marine Division had 25,642 men and the 1st MAW 4,645. All told, there were 277,119 Americans serving in Korea, 21,184 men from 10 other nations and 249,815 members of the ROK army. That made a total of 493,503. The enemy was estimated to have 504,000 Chinese and North Korean soldiers in Korea.

The second phase of Operation Ripper began on March 14. Mud, flooded streams and inadequate roads continued to hamper progress more than the enemy. The next afternoon, Major Sawyer's 1st Battalion, 7th Marines, on the extreme left of the Marines' zone, took the town of Hongchon without a fight. But the units toward the right began to meet more determined opposition in the hills east and north of Hongchon. The 1st Marines' 2d and 3rd Battalions ran into a fire fight around Hills 246 and 428 in the middle of the division's sector and suffered seven killed and 87 wounded without taking the hills. In the morning, the enemy had vanished. Sawyer's battalion captured Hill 399, just east of Hongchon, by attacking its bunkers with grenades. On March 20, the Marines easily reached Phase Line Buffalo.

The 1st Korean Marine Corps Regiment rejoined the division on the twentieth and advanced through a trackless wilderness between the 5th Marines on its left and the 1st Marines on the right. In a tough three-day fight, the Korean Marines seized Hill 975. Once that strongpoint fell, the objectives of Operation Ripper had been reached. The Eighth Army had returned nearly to the 38th Parallel.

Ridgway, wanting to maintain the momentum, set a new objective: Phase Line Kansas, partially north of the 38th. The 7th Marines was chipped off from the Marine division and attached to the 1st Cavalry Division. The 1st Marines was sent to division reserve, and the 5th Marines and 1st KMC Regiment continued to drive northward. On April 2, the 5th Marines had to ford the deep Soyang River. After Lt. Col. Joseph L. Stewart, the regimental executive officer, planned the crossing, he found a Jeep waiting to start him on his journey home. He was the last man to leave Korea from the 1st Provisional Marine Brigade, which had landed at Pusan exactly eight months before.

The 5th Marines and the KMC Regiment were pulled out of the line. On April 4, the 7th Marines was among the first Eighth Army units to recross the 38th Parallel. Ridgway's purpose now was to break up the spring offensive that the Chinese were known to be mounting in the Iron Triangle area in the center of Korea. On April 8, the 1st Marine Division was ordered to relieve the 1st Cavalry Division and prepare to press the attack.

Then, on April 11, President Truman announced that he had fired General MacArthur. Trouble between the general and the President had been long simmering. At the heart of the dispute was a difference of views over the Constitutional arrangement that the civilian leadership determines foreign policy and the military carries it out. Back in August, the President had forced MacArthur to withdraw a public statement to the Veterans of Foreign Wars recommending that Chiang Kai-shek be brought into the war. MacArthur believed that opening a second front in China would compel the Communist Chinese to reduce their effort in Korea. Truman believed it would bring in the Soviet Union and start World War III.

On March 24, while Washington was working toward a Korean ceasefire, MacArthur issued a statement demanding that the Chinese surrender and announcing that he was ready to meet the enemy commander in the field. "By this act MacArthur left me no choice—I could no longer tolerate his insubordination," Truman said afterwards, "General MacArthur had openly defied the policy of his Commander in Chief, the President of the United States."[93] When a letter from MacArthur, again advocating the use of Chinese Nationalist troops, was read in the House of Representatives on April 5, the die was cast. Four days later, the President relieved him on the recommendation of the Joint Chiefs of Staff. Truman explained, "General MacArthur was ready to risk general war. I was not."[94]

MacArthur had miscalculated. Based on his conviction that Communist China would not enter the war, he had sent American troops to the Yalu, despite his orders, and advanced his army into North Korea on widely separated fronts. It had been beaten. The Administration in Washington, for failing to control his activities, had to share the blame for the resulting "shattering defeat."[95]

MacArthur asserted that the war's goal was an open-ended "victory." Both the Joint Chiefs and America's allies feared a widening of the war. MacArthur's civilian superiors tried to make him understand that this was not World War II but a war of limited aims. The general was still fighting the last war. His dismissal insured that this war would be confined to the Korean peninsula.

During these events, the fighting paused. Ridgway, replacing MacArthur, took over the United Nations command; and on April 14, Lt. Gen. James A. Van Fleet assumed command of the Eighth Army.

In the first three weeks of April, enemy antiaircraft fire shot down 16 Marine planes; nine pilots were killed, one captured. Capt. Valdemar Schmidt and Cpl. Robert Sarvia flew their helicopter 20 miles behind enemy lines to rescue an Air Force pilot. The chopper was shot down, crashlanded and rolled over. While Marine fighter pilots covered him, Capt. Frank E. Wilson in another helicopter picked up the two Marines and the Air Force flier and brought back his chopper to a field lit by headlights and flares.

The Eighth Army was moving forward again toward the vital Iron Triangle when, on the night of April 22, the Chinese opened their massive Fifth Phase Offensive. They hit the 6th ROK Division on the Marines' left. The entire ROK division collapsed before midnight and opened a vast gap, ten miles deep and ten miles wide, on the Marines' flank. The 1st Marines rushed up from reserve by truck through thousands of retreating ROKs. About midnight, the KMC on the right and the 5th Marines in the division's center came under attack. The KMC struck back and drove the Chinese from Hill 509. Capt. James T. Cronin, commander of the 5th Marines' B Company, sent 2d Lt. Harvey W. Nolan's platoon racing the enemy for possession of Hill 313 just north of Hwachon. Nolan's Marines climbed the last 200 yards on hands and knees. Machine-gun fire stopped them, killing seven and wounding 17. In the morning, the enemy had abandoned the hill.

The heaviest fighting came on the extreme left where Major Sawyer's 1st Battalion, 7th Marines stood off nearly 2,000 Chinese. During three hours of furious fighting, the Marine line bent but did not break. Lt. Col. Robley E. West's 1st Battalion, 1st Marines came up and extended Sawyer's left to prevent the enemy from widening the penetration.

With dawn's light, VMF-232 and VMF-214 went into action supporting the Marine regiments. Marine aircraft flew 205 sorties that embattled day. The division was ordered to fall back to Line Pendleton centered on the town of Hwachon. The 1st and 3rd Battalions, 1st Marines faced west to contain the breakthrough and permit Sawyer's battalion to disengage and fall back. Banning's 3rd Battalion, 1st Marines seized Hill 902, a 3,000-foot mass dominating the area. By the day's end, the division formed a front that bent around like a fishhook on its exposed left end.

At 8 P.M., the Chinese attacked Captain Wray's C Company, 1st Marines on Horseshoe Ridge. The assault continued for four hours; if it succeeded, the entire battalion would be endangered. Ammunition ran short until Cpl. Leo Marquez started lugging ammunition and grenades to the men in the firing line. He escaped unwounded although bullets holed his helmet, cartridge belt and shoe. C Company held.

At midnight, Capt. Horace J. Johnson's G Company, on the center of Hill 902, was almost overrun. Tech. Sgt. Harold E. Wilson of Birmingham, Alabama, was repeatedly wounded leading his platoon to hold off the attackers. Unable to fire his weapon, he resupplied his men with rifles and ammunition taken from the wounded. He brought up and placed reinforcements. A mortar round blew him off his feet. Although dazed by the concussion, he refused medical aid and moved from foxhole to foxhole directing fire. At dawn, with help from the 11th Marines, the Army's 987th Armored Field Artillery Battalion and Marine aircraft, the final attack was repulsed. Wilson accounted for every man in his platoon and finally walked a half mile to the aid station. In addition to the concussion, he had been wounded in the head, shoulder, right arm and left leg. He received the Medal of Honor.

On the division's center and right, the 5th Marines and the KMC Regiment continued to withdraw. The division's line contracted enough so that the 7th Marines could drop into reserve.

On the afternoon of April 25, a mortar round scored a direct hit on the 3rd Battalion, 1st Marines' command post and wounded Col. Francis M. McAlister, the regimental commander; Lt. Col. Banning, the battalion commander; Maj. Reginald R. Myers, the executive officer, and Maj. Joseph D. Trompeter, the battalion S-3. Banning and Myers had to be evacuated; Trompeter took over the battalion and Major Simmons replaced Myers. In 48 hours, the 1st Marines had had nearly 300 casualties.

With the crisis under control, Maj. Gen. Smith, who had led the division at Inchon, Seoul and the Chosin Reservoir, was relieved by Maj. Gen. Gerald C. Thomas. A native of Missouri and graduate of Illinois Wesleyan University, Thomas had enlisted in May 1917; won the Silver Star at Belleau Wood and Soissons, and been wounded in the Meuse-Argonne. He had served in Haiti and China and during World War II had served on Guadalcanal and Bougainville. He had been a longtime associate of General Vandegrift.

The Marines pulled back east of the Pukhan River and then continued to withdraw south of the Soyang River and past Chunchon to form a new line northeast of Hongchon. There the retreat stopped.

Van Fleet shuffled units, and the Marine division again came under Almond's X Corps. Action diminished to patrolling and artillery firing, until the Chinese attacked en masse again on May 16. This time, they struck the eastern side of the front, broke through the 5th and 7th ROK Divisions and made a 30-mile penetration.

Although the Marines were not in the path of this attack, an enemy force in regimental strength slashed in behind the 7th Marines and tried to cut the MSR. Two Marine tanks were disabled, but Capt. Victor Stoyanow's I Company held and the company commander led a counterattack. Tanks and riflemen sealed off the Chinese escape route and slaughtered most of the attacking force.

Air Force, Navy and MAW planes, controlled chiefly by VMO-6, hurled air strikes at the enemy's main offensive. On May 18, the Marines extended their lines eastward to ease the pressure on the 2d Infantry Division, enabling that division to face east against the hole in the Eighth Army line. All four Marine regiments (including the KMC) were in action. The Chinese swiftly ran out of steam and supplies and paid for their aggressiveness with enormous losses. They began to retreat, often out of control. Remnants of units surrendered. The fleeing enemy left behind a screen of North Korean troops as their rear guard. The North Koreans were told that if they did not stand and die they would be executed.

The United Nations army pursued through mountainous terrain that gave every advantage to its defenders. The Marine division jumped off on May 23 and at first made progress easily. But resistance soon stiffened. Marine aircraft shot up the Chinese escaping westward along the southern side of the Hwachon Reservoir. By the last day of May, the 7th Marines broke through the pass leading into Yanggu at the eastern end of the reservoir; and the 5th Marines advanced to a ridgeline 6,000 yards northeast of the burnt-out town. The division's losses for May totaled 83 killed and 731 wounded.

Marine officers, having lost control of the air wing, were increasingly displeased with their close air support. During the Inchon–Seoul campaign, the average delay in receiving requested air support had been 15 minutes. In May–June 1951, with air support under Air Force control, the delay was 80 minutes—35 minutes of which was taken up clearing the request through the Joint Operations Center. And only 65 to 70 percent of the sorties called for were ever received. Maj. Gen. Thomas complained to

Maj. Gen. Almond that on May 29, when the 5th and 7th Marines were under heavy enemy fire, they had requested 92 sorties and received 55—of which 20 were Marine Corps planes. And practically all of those delivered were two to four hours late.

Starting on June 1, the 5th and 7th Marines pushed up from Yanggu and as far east as the Soyang River valley. The enemy stood in a maze of nameless ridges and well-placed positions. The Marines fought over ridge after endless ridge. The ground in the middle was dominated by a large land mass that rose toward the peak of Hill 1316 on the southern rim of a valley to be called the Punchbowl.

On the morning of June 2, the 3rd Battalion, 1st Marines' command group was again the victim of an enemy mortar barrage. It killed one officer and wounded 40 Marines, including four company commanders, and prevented the battalion from attacking.

By June 4, three Marine regiments were in line—the 1st on the left, the KMC in the center and the 5th on the right. The Korean Marines fought a furious five-day battle over the rugged terrain leading up to Hill 1316. At 8 P.M. on June 10, the 1st Marines, briefly led by Col. Wilburt S. "Bigfoot" Brown, a colorful veteran of both World Wars, Nicaragua and China, ran into expertly defended enemy bunkers that had to be wiped out with grenade and bayonet attacks. Despite strong support from the 11th Marines, Maj. Clarence J. Mabry's 2d Battalion engaged in what Colonel Brown called "the hardest fighting I have ever seen"[96] and suffered 14 killed and 114 wounded. On Mabry's left, Lt. Col. West's 1st Battalion had nine killed and 97 wounded against determined North Korean resistance. Nineteen-year-old Cpl. Charles G. Abrell of Terre Haute, Indiana, three times wounded, attacked a bunker; he clutched an armed grenade that killed the enemy gun crew and himself.[97]

Because of the heavy casualties, Maj. Gen. Thomas brought the 7th Marines, now commanded by Col. Herman Nickerson, Jr., onto the line to advance up the So-chon valley. In the next week, 10 Marine tanks were lost to mines.

During the last days of June, two months of hard fighting came to an end. The Marine division started digging in on the heights above the Punchbowl. And the Eighth Army occupied the lower half of the strategic Iron Triangle, which had been the enemy's main assembly and supply area.

The war was one year old on June 25. An estimated 1,250,000 men had been killed, wounded or captured in battle. Two million civilians were dead and three million homeless. The border between the Communist and free worlds was virtually back at the 38th Parallel where the war had started.

At last, the United States was prepared to accept the *status quo ante*, make peace along the 38th Parallel and leave the unification of Korea to be achieved by peaceful means. On June 23, following informal meetings with George Kennan, the Soviet delegate to the United Nations, Jacob Malik, suggested truce talks. And on June 25, this idea was supported by the rulers in Peking. The talks began at Kaesong on July 10. Action on the battlefront slowed down; and in mid-July, the 2d Infantry Division relieved the Marines.

On August 22, the Communist delegates walked out of the truce talks. The war heated up again, and the Marine division went back into action. What followed was the division's final month-long explosion of mobile warfare in the Korean war. The objectives were two complex, strongly defended ridges just north of the Punchbowl depression: Yoke Ridge immediately to the north and Kanmubong Ridge further north across a narrow valley. Here, the North Korean defenders fought with tenacity and strong artillery support.

On August 27, when the division was ordered back into action, it had few veterans left from the Chosin Reservoir campaign. The 7th Marines and the KMC Regiment moved up through a quagmire created by torrential rains. On August 31, the 7th Marines attacked the section of Yoke Ridge east of Hill 924 and the KMC attacked on its left against Hills 924 and 1026. By the end of September 1, the KMC's 3rd Battalion had taken Hill 924 despite enemy mines, mortars and automatic-weapons fire. The Korean Marines were driven from Hill 924's crest by a surprise midnight counterattack and retook it the following morning. The 3rd Battalion, 7th Marines needed until the afternoon of September 2 to take its objective, Hill 602. The following day, the KMC Regiment broke up a North Korean counterattack in a three-and-a-half-hour battle and finally seized Hill 1026. By that evening, the Marine division held the northern rim of the Punchbowl.

The cost of the four-day battle had been 109 dead and 494 wounded, including the losses in the KMC Regiment. Despite the Air Force's interdiction campaign, the North Koreans' strength in artillery, mortars and machine guns was estimated to have equaled that of the Marines and their attached Army units.

The effort to take Yoke Ridge forced a six-day halt to bring up a new reserve of artillery and mortar ammunition over the almost impassable supply routes. And as the Marines moved deeper into the rugged highlands, the logistic problem became ever more difficult.

On September 11, the 7th Marines resumed the offensive to seize Hills 673 and 749, the first objectives on Kanmubong Ridge. Mortar and machine-gun fire stopped H and I Companies halfway up the steep southeast spur of Hill 680, an intermediate objective. The battered companies were twice driven back. Although most of his men were hit, 2d Lt. George H. Ramer of Meyersdale, Pennsylvania, led I Company's 3rd Platoon to the top and wiped out a bunker. He was wounded twice. The enemy counterattacked and forced the Marines off the peak. Twenty-four-year-old Ramer covered their retreat until the enemy killed him.[98]

Across a valley to the east, the 1st Battalion could make no more progress against Hill 673. Sgt. Frederick W. Mausert III of Cambridge, New York, rescued two wounded Marines under fire. He was wounded in the head but led his men in a bayonet charge against a bunker and silenced its machine gun. As his unit approached the ridgeline, twenty-one-year-old Mausert made a target of himself to draw enemy fire and allow his men to attack. Wounded again, he stormed the topmost bunkers and destroyed another machine gun before he was killed.[99]

In the darkness, Colonel Nickerson sent the 2d Battalion into the valley between the assault battalions in order to trap the North Koreans on Hill 673. At dawn, the 2d Battalion swept upward, surprised the defenders, grabbed the crest of 673 and moved on against Hill 749. Across the valley, G Company attacked; and all three 3rd Battalion companies met on the summit of Hill 680. The two-day fight cost the Marines 22 killed and 245 wounded.

Part of the reason for the heavy casualties was the scarcity of close air support. The Fifth Air Force was giving first priority to interdicting the enemy's buildup. The entire Eighth Army was assigned only 96 close support sorties a day. To cripple the enemy's concentration of artillery dug into rock emplacements much more was needed. "As a consequence, General Thomas reported, many of the 1,621 casualties suffered by the 1st Marine Division during the hard fighting in September were due to inadequate close air support."[100] The men on the ground paid with their lives.

One air development, on the other hand, was saving lives: the helicopter. On September 13, the Marine Transport Helicopter Squadron 161, which had arrived in Korea on the last day of August with 15 HRS-1 Sikorsky helicopters, lifted a day's supplies to the 2d Battalion, 1st Marines. The choppers brought in 18,848 pounds of cargo and evacuated 74 casualties. Lt. Col. George W. Herring's squadron performed a similar feat on the 19th and two days later brought the first combat troops into action by helicopter. "A new era of military transport had dawned."[101]

On the thirteenth, Col. Thomas A. Wornham's 1st Marines relieved the 7th Marines attacking Hill 749. Lt. Col. Franklin B. Nihart's 2d Battalion drove to the summit at 3 P.M., after a battle of small arms, automatic weapons and hand grenades. The 3rd Battalion finally took Hill 751 on the left by the end of September 14. The next day was comparatively quiet, but after midnight a North Korean regiment counterattacked to drive the 2d Battalion off Hill 749. The depleted Marine companies stopped wave after wave of enemy attackers. As casualties mounted, Cpl. Joseph Vittori of F Company led a three-man counterattack. On the extreme flank, he leaped from foxhole to foxhole to fire on the enemy and manned a machine gun when its gunner was struck down. The young BARman from Beverly, Massachusetts, made repeated trips through heavy shell fire to bring up ammunition before he was mortally wounded.[102] The next day, the 1st Battalion passed through the 2d and finished the job of occupying Hill 749. During the four-day battle for

Hill 749, the division had 90 killed, one missing and 714 wounded.

The 5th Marines then attacked Hill 812, a bare hill mass 1,000 yards ahead, and, after two days of hard fighting, seized the hill on the eighteenth. The enemy counterattacked twice; and by day's end, Lt. Col. Houston Stiff's 2d Battalion had 16 killed and 98 wounded. The enemy still occupied Hills 980 and 1052 looming above the battalion.

On the nineteenth, the 2d Battalion battled the enemy for control of The Rock, a huge granite knob on the ridgeline 700 yards west of Hill 812. The Marines held the top and eastern side of The Rock, the North Koreans the western side. At 3:15 A.M. on the twentieth, the enemy tried to retake Hill 812. They pushed back E Company's left platoon, but the company counterattacked and the 2d Platoon struck the enemy flank and sent them scurrying to their own side of The Rock, leaving 60 dead.

On September 20, 1951, Lt. Gen. Van Fleet called off the X Corps offensive because of the high casualty rate and because "it was unprofitable to continue the bitter operation."[103] As it turned out, that was the end of the war of movement in Korea.

7
The Long Outpost War

The war settled down into a static conflict with sudden bursts of vicious local battle for the next 22 months. Changes in the ground held by both sides were minute, but the piling up of casualties was horrendous. The Marines suffered about 40 percent of their total dead and wounded in Korea during those long, disheartening months.

With the end of the war of movement, the Marine division held a 13-mile section of the 125-mile front. It stretched from the Punchbowl eastward to the I ROK Corps, which guarded the coastal end of the line.

To relieve a ROK regiment on remote Hill 884 near the eastern end of the Marine sector, Maj. Gen. Thomas tried an experiment. He ordered HMR-161 to airlift the Division Reconnaissance Company to the hill by helicopter. Such a sizable troop lift had never before been attempted. On September 21, each helicopter brought five fully equipped Marines, who descended from the hovering craft by knotted 30-foot ropes. A total of 224 men, including a heavy machine-gun platoon, was landed in four hours. On foot, it would have taken the Marines 15 hours just to climb the hill.

Another helicopter experiment was less successful. E Company, 1st Marines was moved from reserve at night to meet a threat against the front line. Although 223 Marines were lifted on the evening of September 27, the operation was not attempted again; and it was decided that night lifts should be confined to movements within friendly territory.

On October 11, the entire 3rd Battalion, 7th Marines was flown close to the front by 12 helicopters in 156 flights. The lift carried 958 combat-equipped Marines in five hours and 50 minutes. Four days later, six HMR-161 helicopters brought 19,000 rounds of ammunition to help a surrounded ROK unit and evacuated 24 wounded. On the Marine Corps Birthday, the 5th Marines relieved the 1st Marines in the line. Nearly 2,000 combat-equipped men were transported by helicopter—the largest helicopter lift so far—952 men were carried in and the same number taken out, all in 10 hours.

During this period, the ground troops confined their activities to extensive patrolling in order to take prisoners, plant mines and fight guerrillas behind the lines. One Marine, Sgt. Albert Ireland, earned his ninth Purple Heart, five in World War II and four in Korea. Both sides spent a lot of time and energy building complicated and formidable defenses in depth.

On October 25, the truce talks were resumed at Panmunjom, just south of the 38th Parallel. And by November 27, a cease-fire was agreed upon based on a line of demarcation. A lull set in all along the front. On December 18, lists of prisoners of war were exchanged. The Communist list named 3,198 American POWs of whom 61 were Marines, including two naval corpsmen. By the end of the year, there were 24,535 Marines in Korea; none of them had arrived prior to January 1, 1951.

On January 1, 1952, Lt. Gen. Franklin H. Hart relieved Lt. Gen. Shepherd as commander of FMFPac, and Shepherd became the Commandant of the Corps.

Maj. Gen. John T. Selden replaced Maj. Gen. Thomas as commander of the 1st Marine Division on the eleventh. Selden had served two years in Haiti before being commissioned during World War I. He had commanded the 5th Marines at New Britain and served as chief of staff of the 1st Marine Division on Peleliu. Brig. Gen. William J. Whaling continued as assistant division commander.

By this time, the division was occupied by the routine of trench warfare, sniping by day and patrols and raids at night. Action was so light that Camp Tripoli was set up near Wontong-ni for training in small unit leadership and offensive tactics. The arrival of new thermal boots and lightweight armored vests helped keep down casualties from frostbite and shell fragments. And Col. Keith B. McCutcheon, the innovative helicopter pioneer who had taken over HMR-161, continued to experiment with troop and supply lifts that made movement easier in the Korean hills.

Starting on March 17, the Marine division was shifted to the extreme western side of Korea as part of a realignment of divisions along the entire front. The Marines replaced the 1st ROK Division just above the Imjin River to strengthen the protection of the ancient invasion route to Seoul. Here, the division took responsibility for 32 miles of the Jamestown Line, and here it would remain for the rest of the war.

This was an area of coastal lowlands, climbing into steep hills and narrow valleys toward the northeast. The Marine sector started on the Kimpo Peninsula in the west, crossed the Han River and ran along the southern side of the Imjin. Crossing that river, it continued northeast along the key terrain until it crossed the 38th Parallel and, two and a half miles further on, met the 1st Commonwealth Division at the Samichon River. Instead of North Koreans, the Marines now faced the 65th and 63rd Chinese armies.

By the end of April, MAG-12 also moved to the west side of Korea. VMO-6 and HMR-161, of course, had come up behind the Marine division even more promptly. The 1st Marine Aircraft Wing headquarters and MAG-33 remained in the Pohang area. The wing, continuing to operate under the Fifth Air Force, was commanded by Maj. Gen. Christian F. Schilt, who had won the Medal of Honor at Quilali in 1928. On April 11, he was relieved by Brig. Gen. Clayton C. Jerome, a veteran of five campaigns in World War II and most recently Assistant Commandant for Air.

Through the spring of 1952, the Marine division and the enemy opposite pounded each other with artillery barrages and probed with patrolling jabs. At first, the Marines established an outpost line in front of the Main Line of Resistance. Occasionally, patrols suffered casualties in hand-to-hand fighting. On the night of April 15, the Chinese twice attacked a platoon of E Company, 5th Marines positioned on a 400-foot hill known as Outpost 3. Machine gunner Cpl. Duane E. Dewey of Grand Rapids, Michigan, smothered a grenade that landed in his position while he and his assistant gunner were having their wounds treated by a corpsman. Miraculously, Dewey survived and a year later received the Medal of Honor at the White House from the new President, Dwight D. Eisenhower.[104] In the struggle at Outpost 3, the Marines had 6 killed, 5 missing and 25 wounded.

Late in April, the Marine front was extended another 6,800 yards to the west; and the outpost lines were withdrawn and replaced with forward outposts and listening posts. The 5th Marines created an infantry-tank Everready Rescue Force to dash in and rescue the United Nations Truce Team at Panmunjom in case that became necessary.

On May 12, Gen. Mark W. Clark relieved Ridgway as United Nations commander in Korea. To increase the pressure on the enemy, Clark assigned UN aircraft to knock out major industrial targets, including hydroelectric plants, in North Korea. Prime target was the Suiho plant at the Yalu, which supplied a quarter of northeast China's electrical power. Strikes flown between June 23 and 27 by Marine, Navy and Air Force planes virtually blacked out North Korea for two weeks. Col. Robert E. Galer led MAG-12's planes and Col. John P. Condon led MAG-33 in these strikes. All 150 Marine aircraft returned safely.

On August 5, Galer, a Medal of Honor winner in World War II, was leading a flight of 31 aircraft when his engine was hit. He had trouble breaking loose from his cockpit; and as he dropped spreadeagled before his parachute opened, his plane nicked his shoulder. He recovered in time to pull the ripcord and landed safely deep in enemy territory. After eluding enemy soldiers, he guided a rescue helicopter to him with a small survivor radio and was hoisted aboard. On the return flight, the helicopter was hit by enemy aircraft fire but landed safely on a rescue ship at Wonsan.

The Marines sent out repeated patrols between the two dug-in armies. On May 8, the 1st Battalion, 5th Marines launched a raid to dislodge the Chinese from former Outpost 3. While C Company feinted against a nearby hill, 1st Lt. Ernest S. Lee's A Company assaulted the 450-foot hill on which Outpost 3 marked the forward point. The Marines ousted a reinforced enemy platoon but came under artillery and mortar fire. As they approached the peak, the 1st Platoon threw back a counterattack but had to withdraw when it received a barrage of more than 400 rounds in five minutes. A Company was unable to reach its final objective and suffered 7 killed and 66 wounded.

After the 7th Marines replaced the 5th Marines in the line, the 1st Battalion went out early on May 28 to seize Hill 104 and Tumae-ri Ridge. C Company made a feint to the left and got into hand-to-hand fighting. Second Lt. John J. Donahue and his platoon of Capt. Earl W. Thompson's A Company took Hill 104 with bayonets fixed. But the company was unable to take Tumae-ri Ridge and returned to the MLR with 9 killed and 107 wounded.

Two Marines were awarded posthumous Medals of Honor in this costly miscarriage. Nineteen-year-old Cpl. David B. Champagne of Wakefield, Rhode Island, saved three members of his A Company fire team when he threw back an enemy grenade, which exploded and blew off his hand. Pfc. John D. Kelly of Homestead, Pennsylvania, a radio operator with C Company, turned his radio over to another man and joined the assault. Kelly personally wiped out one position, killing two of the enemy, and then singlehandedly attacked a machine-gun bunker. He was painfully wounded but destroyed the bunker and killed three Chinese. As he tried to reach a third bunker, he was mortally wounded.[105]

The Chinese celebrated the end of the war's second year by attacking the 2d Battalion, 5th Marines late on June 24. They overran Outpost Yoke, killing nine and wounding 23 of its 34 Marines. Artillery fire finally drove off the attackers.

The Marines celebrated the Fourth of July by having all their front-line battalions attack the enemy's forward positions. One 2d Battalion, 5th Marines patrol got into an hour-long fire fight, losing one Marine killed and 11 wounded. On the night of July 2, G Company, 7th Marines met a battalion-sized Chinese force on Outpost Yoke. Many Marines were hit immediately. Staff Sgt. William E. Shuck, Jr., led his machine-gun squad and a rifle squad up the hill and was wounded. Ordered to pull back, he made sure all the dead and wounded were evacuated. He was killed by a sniper's bullet.[106] Four Marines were killed and 40 wounded in this action. In further celebration, the division fired 3,202 artillery rounds at the enemy on the Fourth. And on July 6–7, the 1st Battalion, 7th Marines climaxed the festivities by an abortive two-company raid in the Outpost Yoke area. C Company took Yoke but Chinese artillery drove it off again with heavy casualties. The official history of the war concluded baldly: "Marine casualties from the operation were out of proportion to the results achieved—12 dead, 85 wounded, and 5 missing. It had been a high price to pay for a venture of this type, particularly when the primary objectives went unaccomplished. During the entire 4–7 July period, 22 Marines had lost their lives in combat operations. Division reported that 268 Marines had been wounded during the long Fourth of July."[107] Maj. Gen. Selden had objected to the attack order, but "Corps turned a deaf ear."[108]

The next battle was big and long. At 1 A.M. on August 9, the Battle of Bunker Hill (Hill 122) opened when a Chinese raiding party forced a squad of Marines from E Company, 1st Marines to evacuate Hill 58A, which was a quarter mile in front of the MLR and halfway to the Chinese outpost line. It had been held by the Marines since June.

To recapture the lost hill, a reinforced E Company platoon set out at 4 A.M.; but enemy fire sent it back to the MLR. After daybreak, Marine and Air Force jets poured bombs and napalm onto Hill 58A. Artillery pounded it. At midmorning, an A Company platoon reoccupied the hill, and an E Company platoon quickly reinforced it. But a few minutes later, the Chinese drove the Marines down the southern slope. By midafternoon, the Marines had taken 75 casualties and given up Hill 58A again.

That night, the embattled hill changed hands twice more. C Company forced the Chinese off the crest, but they stormed back and retook it. Concentrated shelling caused most of the 1st Marines' 17 killed and 243 wounded.

At this point, Col. Walter F. Layer, who had recently taken command of the 1st Marines from Col. Walter N. Flournoy, changed the objective from Hill 58A to Hill 122—Bunker Hill. This hill had a 350-yard-long crest about 700 yards in front of the MLR and across a long draw southeast of Hill 58A. Hill 122 ran south to Hill 124; Hill 122-124 was known as Bunker Ridge. Much of the enemy fire on the Marines had been directed from an observation post on Hill 122. By moving the attack to Hill 122, Colonel Layer hoped to surprise the enemy and neutralize the capture of Hill 58A.

A diversionary attack was launched against Hill 58A on the night of August 11 by a reinforced rifle platoon and eight gun and flame tanks. The flame tanks climbed the hill firing their machine guns and then reversed course and ran over the hill again before retiring. The gun tanks remained east of the hill to support the 3rd Platoon of D Company, which assaulted and took the hill. The Chinese counterattacked, and then both infantry elements withdrew.

Meanwhile, B Company, led by Capt. Sereno S. Scranton, Jr., made the main assault on Bunker Hill. As the Marines swept forward, the Chinese answered with small-arms fire and hand grenades and then gave ground in close-in fighting. By 3 A.M. on August 12, the Marines had a precarious foothold on Bunker Hill and quickly began digging in.

At 3 P.M., the Chinese opened an intense artillery and mortar barrage. The resulting casualties forced a decision for B Company to pull back from the ridgetop and take positions on the reverse or eastern slope. An hour later, 350 Chinese attacked from the west. B Company, now reinforced by Capt. Howard J. Connolly's I Company, fought them off; and the Chinese withdrew to the northern slope of Bunker Ridge. At the same time, the 3rd Battalion's reconnaissance platoon occupied Hill 124. Marine mortars and artillery supported the defenders, and gun and flame tanks covered the steep draw on Bunker Hill's right flank. B and I Companies dug into Bunker Hill's reverse slope.

The Chinese tried some diversionary tactics of their own. They attacked Hill 48A, Stromboli, a Marine outpost far to the east of Hill 122, and hit the 1st Marines' main line shortly after midnight on August 13. Although they did not penetrate the 2d Battalion, they turned back a reinforcing squad sent out to Hill 48A and repeatedly struck at the isolated defenders there. When a second reinforcing unit finally crashed through, the Chinese broke off the action.

At 1 A.M., the Chinese stepped up their fire at the Marines on Hill 122. The 11th Marines boxed the area with defensive fire. Half an hour later, the Chinese attacked; and a four-hour battle raged on Hill 122 until they were repulsed by the Marines' artillery, tanks, rockets and mortars.

Capt. William M. Vanzuyen's G Company, 7th Marines came out from reserve to reinforce Captain Connolly's positions on Bunker Hill just before dawn. And at mid-day, Capt. John G. Demas' H Company, 7th Marines relieved the other Marines on the hill. During August 12 and 13 at Bunker Hill, the 1st

Marines reported 24 killed and 214 wounded. An additional 40 Marines had been casualties in the Stromboli area.

At 9 P.M., an enemy battalion hit Bunker Hill again. The few Chinese who penetrated Captain Demas' positions were killed. Enemy mortar and artillery fire had killed seven H Company Marines and wounded 21. One of the dead was Corpsman John E. Kilmer of Highland Park, Illinois, who was wounded while aiding the casualties. As enemy mortar fire increased, Kilmer shielded a wounded Marine with his body and was mortally wounded.[109]

Bunker Hill was reinforced by a platoon of A Company, 1st Marines late on August 14; and that night, the whole Bunker Ridge complex erupted in a fire fight. Marine artillery protectively boxed in the hill and held the attackers in check. By 4 A.M. the battle was over. Captain Demas' Marines suffered 7 killed and 28 wounded before being relieved by B Company, 1st Marines. The enemy attacked the hill again on the sixteenth in their persistent effort to destroy the Marines; and the next morning, C Company relieved B Company. The Chinese continued sporadically to attack the hills—on the night of August 25 alone, F Company had 65 casualties there—and on September 4, E Company had 12 killed and 40 wounded. But the issue was no longer in doubt.

Throughout the August struggle for Bunker Hill, the Marines on the ground had received full close air support. And in a 24-hour period starting 6 P.M. on August 12, Marine artillery fired a record 10,652 rounds in support.

The Bunker Hill battle became a subject of debate. Since the Marines proved unable to neutralize Hill 58A from Bunker Hill, the value of the entire bloody operation was questioned. And the decisions to feed in companies piecemeal and to fight a reverse-slope defense were severely criticized.

Marine casualties had been 48 killed and 313 listed as seriously wounded and "several hundred additional wounded were treated at 1st Marines medical facilities and returned to duty shortly thereafter."[110] Rear area units had to be culled for 200 replacements, and Commandant Shepherd authorized an airlift of 500 enlisted Marines to the division. He also increased the next two monthly replacement drafts by 500 men, and emergency replacements came out from Camp Pendleton. The first major Marine action in west Korea's war of position and attrition had been costly.

By now the Marine division was being used as one more infantry division holding the transpeninsula front. In this positional war, there was no rationale for having a Marine division in the line rather than an Army division. This assignment did not diminish the Corps' eagerness to do its share, but it increased the Corps' need to justify its existence as a specialized elite organization. And, incidentally, it weakened the Corps' argument that it required its own aviation element for close support.

In the two months following the dubious Battle of Bunker Hill, the Marines did not especially distinguish themselves. During August, three daylight-manned outposts in front of the 5th Marines, at the right of the division's line, were lost to the enemy. The last of the three was Outpost Irene. When the 2d Battalion outpost detail went out to man it at dawn on August 17, the Marines found it already occupied. The Chinese forced the Marines and two reinforcement parties to withdraw. During this clash, Pfc. Robert E. Simanek of Detroit, Michigan, threw himself on a grenade and was gravely wounded but survived to receive the Medal of Honor from President Eisenhower.[111]

Early on September 5, the enemy made a coordinated attack against Bunker Hill, Stromboli and four outposts in front of the 5th Marines on the east end of the Marine sector. A reinforced company attacked Outpost Bruce, on Hill 148, a mile in front of the line, and caused 32 Marine casualties. Two Marines and a Navy Corpsman won the Medal of Honor in this fight. Pfc. Fernando L. Garcia of San Juan, Puerto Rico, threw himself on a grenade to save his platoon sergeant's life and was killed. Corpsman Edward C. Benfold moved forward to check on two Marines in a large crater. Two enemy grenades dropped into the crater. Benfold picked them up in both hands, leaped from the hole and hurled himself at two charging Chinese. He pushed the grenades against their chests, killing them, and was himself mortally wounded. Pfc. Alford L. McLaughlin, a machine gunner from Leeds, Alabama, was painfully wounded but fired two machine guns alternately from the hip until his hands were blistered. Then, standing up in full view, he defended his position with a carbine and grenades and killed an estimated 150 Chinese and wounded 50 more. He was the only one of the three who survived that night's battle.

The Chinese continued to assault Outpost Bruce the next two nights. Although every defender was either killed or wounded, the Marines held the hill. In the 51-hour siege there, 19 Marines were killed and 38 wounded. At the other outposts, five more were killed and 32 wounded.

Starting on September 5, the enemy also began attacking three outposts in front of the Korean Marine Corps Regiment at the western end of the division line on the mainland. Maj. Gen. Edwin A. Pollock, who had relieved Maj. Gen. Selden as the division's commander on August 29, emphasized the need for holding ten of the key outposts along the division front. (Pollock had earned the Navy Cross on Guadalcanal and fought at Iwo Jima.) On September 19 and 20, the Chinese twice gained control of Outpost 36 in fierce fighting. With air support from three Marine attack squadrons, the Korean Marines regained the hill and held it. Early in October, Outpost 37, nearby, changed hands four times before the Korean Marines were forced to give it up on the afternoon of October 5. In the same battle, Outpost 36 was lost again. And Outpost 86, at the southwestern end of the Korean Marine front, changed hands four times before it was given up.

On the eastern end of the division line, the 7th Marines, which had replaced the 5th Marines, tried to defend nine permanent outposts. Beginning on the night of October 2, the Chinese assaulted Outposts Seattle and Warsaw and overran them in less than an hour. At Warsaw, Pvt. Jack W. Kelso picked up a grenade that landed in his bunker, rushed outside and hurled it back at the enemy. He was wounded as it left his hand. Then the eighteen-year-old from Madera, California, covered four Marines escaping from the bunker and was mortally wounded.[112] A platoon from his I Company counterattacked and recaptured Outpost Warsaw. But three counterattacks to recover Outpost Seattle failed. At the two outposts, 13 Marines were killed and 88 wounded. A fourth attempt to retake Outpost Seattle on October 6 failed after five hours of heavy fighting with 12 Marines dead and 44 wounded. That night, the Chinese made determined attacks against five outposts and two MLR positions. A company overran the two squads holding Outpost Detroit;

only two wounded Marines escaped. To the east, a company also attacked Outpost Frisco and overwhelmed its defenders. A platoon from I Company came out from the MLR and restored control. Staff Sgt. Lewis G. Watkins of Seneca, South Carolina, a guide of this platoon, led the assault up the hill. He was hit but took an automatic rifle from another wounded Marine and stopped the fire of a machine gun holding up the attack. A grenade came near him and several Marines; he picked it up and was about to throw it away when it exploded, killing him.[113] Later in the day, the decision was made to abandon Outpost Frisco. In the outpost fighting of October 6–7, 10 Marines were killed, 22 missing and 128 wounded. By the end of the first week of October, the Marine division had surrendered to the Chinese six outposts on commanding ground in front of its sector.

During the attacks on the Marine outposts in September and October, air strikes received by the Marine division increased. Marine fliers also participated in two massive air raids against Pyongyang, the North Korean capital, on July 11 and August 29. And 1st Lt. John W. Andre of VMF(N)-513 shot down a Yak fighter, which added to his four kills in World War II, made him the first Marine nightfighter ace in Korea. Late in September, Maj. Alexander J. Gillis of VMF-311, flying with an Air Force squadron, became the first naval aviator to destroy three enemy aircraft in Korea. All three of his kills were MIG-15s. The third plane disabled Gillis' F-86, and he spent four hours in the Yellow Sea before a helicopter picked him up. On September 10, 22 jet fighters from VMF-115 attacked troop concentrations 35 miles south of Pyongyang. On the return flight, six of the pilots flew in formation into a 3,000-foot mountain, failing to clear the peak by 600 feet.

The enemy's next significant move was to mount a major attack at the most vulnerable point on the Marine division's Main Line of Resistance. This was the Hook, a deep salient pointing north near the western end of the division's sector. It was protected by two outposts: Warsaw, 600 yards to the northeast, and Ronson, 275 yards west of the Hook, replacing the enemy-seized Seattle. The Hook was important because it overlooked the Samichon valley, a major corridor to Seoul, and dominated the Imjin River behind the MLR.

Col. Thomas C. Moore's 7th Marines defended this western

end of the Marines' sector. All three battalions were on line to protect an overextended six-mile front. Only one company was in reserve. Col. Moore had 3,844 Marines, 144 medical officers and corpsmen, 3 Army communicators and 774 Korean service troops and interpreters. Opposite them were two Chinese regiments and 120 artillery pieces. The Chinese had closed in on the MLR for months by digging intricate trench systems.

The attack on the Hook was preceded by 48 hours of intense enemy artillery fire, directed mostly against the Hook, Ronson and Warsaw. About 2,850 artillery and mortar rounds devastated bunkers, trenches and communications lines in the 1st Battalion's area. The destruction exceeded the Marines' ability to repair the damage. The coming attack was well advertised.

The MLR sector that included the Hook was defended by Capt. Paul B. Byrum's C Company. One squad was outposted on Ronson and a reinforced platoon on Warsaw. On the right flank was Capt. Dexter E. Evans' B Company. The enemy advanced its 3rd Battalion, 357th Regiment for the attack.

At 6:10 P.M. on October 26, Outpost Ronson was hit and in half an hour was overrun. No one escaped. By 7 P.M., Warsaw's defenders were locked in hand-to-hand fighting and trying to keep their attackers from their bunkers. Artillery and mortar fire smothered the Hook. Lt. Col. Leo J. Dulacki, the 1st Battalion commander, ordered Capt. Frederick C. McLaughlin's A Company forward to support C Company on the MLR.

The enemy struck in battalion strength and by 7:38 had reached the main trenches 400 yards southwest of the Hook. A few minutes later, the Chinese hit both east of the salient and directly against the nose of the Hook. The enemy, under artillery support, overran the trenches and advanced along the crest and on both sides of the ridge. The Marines pulled back covered by a small rear guard. To the southwest, the attack penetrated C Company's line; the 1st Platoon formed a perimeter defense. At 11:30 P.M., Colonel Moore reported Warsaw in enemy hands.

Colonel Moore sent up his reserve, H Company from Lt. Col. Charles D. Barrett, Jr.'s, 3rd Battalion. And Maj. Gen. Pollock ordered Lt. Col. Sidney J. Altman's 3rd Battalion, 1st Marines out of reserve to support the hard pressed 7th Marines. The 2d Battalion, 11th Marines pounded Warsaw and the enemy formations.

At 12:30 A.M., the Chinese launched a diversionary attack against Outpost Reno, two miles west of the Hook. An ambush patrol hidden behind Reno surprised and dispersed the first enemy attack. At 4 A.M., another Chinese company hit Reno for 40 minutes before withdrawing. Nine Marines were killed and 49 wounded there.

At the Hook, Captain McLaughlin's A Company passed through C Company and counterattacked until heavy fire stopped its advance. Then, Capt. Bernard B. Belant's H Company moved up to continue the counterattack. By this time, the Chinese controlled more than a mile of the MLR. At 8 A.M., Captain Belant started his attack and was met by a barrage of enemy fire. Immediately, 2d Lt. George H. O'Brien, Jr., leaped from his trench and, shouting for his platoon to follow, zigzagged across an exposed saddle and up the enemy-held hill through a hail of fire. He was shot through the arm and thrown to the ground; getting up, he urged his men onward, stopped to assist a wounded Marine and raced for the trenchline. He killed at least three Chinese with his carbine and grenades. He was knocked down three more times by grenade concussions but continued to lead his men for four more hours. As enemy fire stopped the Marine advance. O'Brien organized his remaining men's defense; and when they were relieved, he covered their withdrawal. The Marine from Fort Worth, Texas, received the Medal of Honor.

A second Marine, 2d Lt. Sherrod E. Skinner, Jr. (whose twin brother was also a Marine officer), won the Medal of Honor posthumously that night. Skinner was an artillery forward observer; and when the enemy hit the MLR, he organized the surviving Marines at the observation post, fought off the attackers and called in artillery fire. He twice left his bunker to direct machine-gun fire and bring up ammunition. He was wounded both times. When the position was overrun, he directed his men to feign death. They were searched several times by enemy groups. When an enemy soldier tossed a grenade into the bunker, Skinner rolled on top of it to shield two other Marines and was killed.[114]

H Company had driven a wedge into the enemy position and regained the initiative. Planes from three Marine squadrons dumped bombs and napalm on the enemy. That day, 72 planes,

567

including 67 Marine aircraft, flew close support missions. The 11th Marines and A Company, 1st Tank Battalion also supported the frontline troops.

Capt. Murray V. Harlan, Jr.'s, I Company moved up to recapture the Hook. The 1st Platoon crept forward under fire at 1:50 P.M., taking severe casualties. By 5 P.M., a few Marines reached the trenches; but a heavier barrage sent them back to the reverse slope. By midnight, B Company, 1st Marines joined the attack on I Company's left. The Chinese met them with small-arms fire and grenades, and for an hour and a half the battle was a stand-off. B Company pulled back to leave space for an artillery and mortar barrage. At 3:40 A.M., on October 28, B Company made the final charge; and by 6 A.M., the Marines again held the Hook. In the next two hours, the 7th Marines also reoccupied Ronson and Warsaw. The battle for the Hook was finished. Marine losses were 70 killed, 386 wounded and 39 missing of whom 27 turned up as prisoners. It was calculated that Chinese supporting fire had laid at least 15,500 artillery and mortar rounds on the Marines. They had withstood a heavy blow and come back to win.

The fall's upsurge of fighting ended with a Chinese attack against four Korean Marine outposts just before midnight on the last day of October. After some sharp fighting that cost the Korean Marines 154 casualties, the attacks were thrown back.

Winter crept in. Van Fleet strengthened his line by inserting another ROK division; and by year's end on line were 11 Korean divisions, three U.S. Army, 1 Marine and 1 British Commonwealth. In reserve were one Korean division and three U.S. Army divisions.

In its third winter, the war was a dragged-out conflict that was unpopular both at home and in the battle theater. In the 1952 Presidential campaign, Dwight D. Eisenhower had promised he would go to Korea if elected; and he began a four-day visit to the battlefront on December 2. Maj. Gen. Pollock briefed the President-elect at his command post. But the peace negotiations were stalled on the issue of the exchange of war prisoners. The Communists demanded the repatriation of all North Korean and Chinese prisoners; the United Nations refused to force the return of 60,000 men who did not want to return to their homelands. On October 8, the senior UN delegate had recessed the talks hoping to force the Communists' hand. In December, the United Nations voted an Indian compromise based on the concept of voluntary repatriation run by a repatriation commission. The change of Administrations in Washington in January 1953 and the death on March 5 of the Soviet premier, Joseph Stalin, which changed the Communist world, apparently made negotiations on the prisoner issue possible. By the war's end, 7,190 Americans had been captured and an estimated 2,730 had died in enemy hands. Of the survivors, 21 U.S. Army soldiers (plus one British Marine) chose to go to China rather than return home.[115]

The winter was relatively quiet. Both sides eased their offensive activity if not their vigilance. Lt. Gen. Maxwell D. Taylor replaced Van Fleet as Eighth Army commander. Every Marine regiment and air group changed commanders. Maj. Gen. Jerome turned over the 1st MAW to Maj. Gen. Vernon E. Megee, who had enlisted in the Corps in 1919, earned his wings in 1932 and served at Iwo Jima and Okinawa.

The Marine aviators in Korea ran into a maelstrom of controversy when a broadcaster in the United States charged that Marine planes were the most careless about bombing and strafing friendly troops. The Marine Corps replied that of the 63 incidents between January and October 1952 in which UN casualties resulted from Fifth Air Force flights, 1st MAW pilots were responsible for 28.5 percent. Although Marine aircraft accounted for only 14.5 percent of the FEAF planes, Marine fliers were performing 30 to 40 percent of the close support missions and virtually all of the very close support.*

In February 1953, the fighting on the ground started to pick up again with small-unit efforts against enemy strongpoints in no-man's-land. On the division's right, the 5th Marines was particularly aggressive. The regiment was now commanded by Col. Lewis W. Walt, who had won two Navy Crosses in World War II. Early on February 3, Colonel Walt sent A Company against Hills 31 and 31A and a tank-artillery feint against three hills west of the target area. With A Company, young 2d Lt.

---

*On February 16, 1953, Capt. Ted Williams, the baseball star, crashlanded his burning Panther jet at a forward base while returning from his first mission, a large-scale raid in North Korea. Williams, who had also flown in World War II, flew 37 combat missions in Korea.

Raymond G. Murphy of Pueblo, Colorado, although wounded himself, made several trips up and down the fire-swept hill carrying wounded Marines to safety. Then, he covered the Marines' retreat and killed two of the enemy. At the base of the hill, he organized a party and led it back up to search for missing men.[116] The main purpose of the raid was not achieved: no prisoners were taken. But enemy casualties were estimated at 390. The Marines had 14 killed and 91 wounded.

On February 25, Walt sent a two-platoon assault against Hill 15, the site of former Outpost Detroit two miles east of Hills 31 and 31A. This time, bad weather wiped out almost all the planned air strikes, and the raid was unsuccessful. B Company made another attack against Hill 31A on March 19 but withdrew with heavy casualties.

One week later, the 5th Marines became involved in the bloodiest fighting yet in western Korea. This four-day battle for Outposts Carson, Reno and Vegas (previously called Allen, Bruce and Clarence) would cost the Marines 1,015 casualties.

The fight was part of a Chinese attack against Eighth Army outposts across the front. On March 23, the enemy had overrun the Army position called Old Baldy, 25 miles northeast of the "Nevada Cities" outposts. The Chinese hoped to shortcircuit an unexpected UN spring offensive and seize dominant ground that could remain in their hands when a truce went into effect.

The three Nevada Cities outposts stood on high ground in front of the 5th Marines' 1st Battalion and about 10 miles northeast of Panmunjom. Reno, the middle outpost, was the nearest to the Chinese line and 1,600 yards from the Marine line. Vegas to the east was the highest and 1,310 yards from the MLR. Carson was furthest west and 820 yards from the MLR. Each was manned by about 40 Marines (a rifle platoon) two corpsmen and weapons company personnel. A reinforced squad held a blocking position called Reno Block on a small hill between and slightly to the rear of Reno and Vegas.

At 7 P.M. on March 26, 1953, the Chinese on the hills facing the Nevada Cities outposts opened up with a barrage. In 20 minutes, 1,200 mortar rounds hit Carson. Coordinated fire struck outposts and the MLR all along the Marine division front. Small-unit attacks felt out several outposts.

At 7:10, 3,500 Chinese converged on the Nevada Cities outposts from three directions. Another company made diversionary probes at Outposts Berlin and East Berlin in the 3rd Battalion's sector and were driven off. Marine artillery replied in force. But the sheer weight of numbers, 20 to 1, proved decisive. In an hour, the 54 Marines on Carson were fighting with bayonets, knives, rifles and bare fists. They stopped the Chinese. But the 40 Marines at Reno were pushed back into their cave defense, and the Chinese were sealing the entrances. Within two hours, only seven of the Marines on Reno were still able to fight. On Vegas, the Chinese in overwhelming numbers swarmed over the Marines.

Reinforcements were rushed out from the MLR. An advance platoon from F Company was ambushed but fought its way to Reno Block. Two squads from C Company came under fire all the way out; 10 Marines were wounded. Both those units were trying to reach the defenders on Reno. A D Company platoon heading for Vegas had to fight hand-to-hand near the Block. Two F Company platoons then struggled to the Block through a storm of shells; one platoon took 70 percent casualties in minutes. But slowly the Marines were building up strength at the Reno Block.

A final message from Reno received at 11 P.M. could not be understood. Three minutes before midnight contact with Vegas was lost. A platoon from E Company was on its way to Vegas, but both outposts had fallen. The Marines at the Block, now at company strength, fought off three Chinese attacks. At 1:44 A.M. on the twenty-seventh, Capt. Ralph L. Walz, the commander of F Company, reported that he had one platoon left at the Block. His remaining Marines stood off three more attacks in the next hour. By 3 A.M., the relief forces from F and C Company were ordered to return to the MLR. They had 35 percent casualties. When they withdrew, Corpsman Francis C. Hammond of Alexandria, Virginia, remained behind with C Company's wounded and was killed by a mortar shell.[117]

Trying to reinforce Vegas, two platoons from D and C Company got within 400 yards of the outpost; and F Company, 7th Marines joined them. By 3 A.M., they were within 200 yards of Vegas, but the position was in Chinese hands and the relief elements were ordered to return. It was later learned that 1st Lt.

571

Kenneth E. Taft, Jr., in charge at Vegas, had been killed and some of his H Company Marines captured. At Reno, 2d Lt. Rufus A. Seymour, the officer in charge, was captured with several of his men. All of the original Marines on Reno except five had been killed. The 1st Battalion had 5 killed, 51 wounded and 39 missing (at Reno) for a total of 95 casualties; the 3rd Battalion had one killed, eight wounded and 40 missing (at Vegas) for a total of 49. The 1st Marines had 4 killed and 16 wounded.

During the morning of the twenty-seventh, planes from three Marine squadrons, Air Force jets and artillery pounded the enemy-held area. The Marine commanders made a decision to try and recapture Vegas but let Reno, further away, go. At 11:20 A.M., D Company, 5th Marines set out for Vegas but took such a beating from Chinese artillery and mortars that in 50 minutes only nine men in the 1st Platoon were still able to carry on. D Company crawled up the muddy slope to within 200 yards of Vegas. The 2d Battalion's Provisional Company joined the counterattack. E Company, 5th Marines and F Company, 7th Marines were thrown into the fight and replaced D Company in the van on Vegas' slopes. Three platoons of Marines seized part of the hill in a 90-minute hand-to-hand fight. Two F Company platoons made it to within 50 yards of the peak before being repulsed by machine-gun and mortar fire. Corpsmen William R. Charette of Ludington, Michigan, with F Company moved about helping the wounded under intense fire. When a grenade landed near a Marine he was aiding, he threw himself over the wounded man. The blast wounded Charette in the face and tore off his helmet and medical kit. He ripped part of his uniform to make emergency bandages. Finding a Marine whose armored vest had been blown off by an exploding shell, he put his own battle vest on the wounded man. He saved many lives that night and was the only corpsman in the Korean war to receive the Medal of Honor and live to wear it.[118]

Before midnight, Capt. Ralph F. Estey's F Company, 7th Marines withstood three enemy attacks and set up a perimeter defense at the base of Vegas. In the early morning hours of the twenty-eighth, it made three assaults on the summit but was repulsed every time, despite repeated Marine air strikes. F Company reached to within 15 yards of the trenchline on the left side of Vegas and battled the Chinese in a 22-minute fire fight. Squad leader Sgt. Daniel P. Matthews of Van Nuys, California, saw a corpsman trying to remove a wounded Marine exposed to fire from a machine gun on the peak. He worked his way to the gun emplacement and leaped onto the rock fortification surrounding the gun. Although severely wounded, Matthews shot two Chinese, routed a third and silenced the machine gun before he was killed. The wounded man was carried to safety.[119]

By noon, Estey's F Company had 43 effectives left after six assaults on Vegas and was relieved by Capt. Herbert M. Lorence's E Company, 5th Marines. MAG-12 flew seven four-plane strikes against the outpost and nearby enemy-held hills. E Company attacked the crest at 1 P.M., digging the Chinese out of their holes. The final assault was made by the 1st Platoon led by Staff Sgt. John J. Williams, who had taken charge after 2d Lt. Edgar R. Franz had been wounded and evacuated. In six minutes, the Marines held Vegas again.

Fifteen minutes later, the Chinese counterattacked. Enemy artillery and mortar shells hit the Marines on the crest at the rate of one round every second. Marine tanks and artillery placed a protective curtain of fire around the outpost. And gradually the Chinese opposition began to slacken. By 2 P.M., the enemy held only the topographical crest at the northernmost point of the ridge. Maj. Benjamin G. Lee, operations officer of the 2d Battalion, 5th Marines who had won the Silver Star as an enlisted man on Guadalcanal, directed the buildup of the Vegas defense. After 10 hours of fighting, there were only 58 Marines from E and F Company on the hill. During the afternoon, 150 men from F Company, 5th Marines strengthened the rear trenches. Panther jets of MAG-33 joined the MAG-12 planes in bombing enemy postitions.

That night, the Chinese attacked both Carson and Vegas and were beaten off. In a second assault, they managed to drive the Marines from the high ground; but it was swiftly retaken. Just before midnight, at least 200 of the enemy made a third attempt to recapture Vegas. The 11th Marines' fire and the defenders, bolstered by E company, 7th Marines, threw them back and seized the critical northern segment of the outpost. Virtually at the end of the battle, Major Lee and Captain Walz were killed instantly by a 120mm enemy mortar round. Maj.

Joseph S. Buntin, executive officer of the 3rd Battalion, 5th Marines, took charge as outpost commander.

After a day of furious digging-in in the rain, the Marines on Vegas met another attack at 6:50 P.M. on the twenty-ninth. Three companies approached both flanks. Marine artillery fired 6,404 rounds and sent the Chinese battalion reeling. The enemy came back twice more before midnight and still again in battalion strength in the early hours of the thirtieth. By 2:15 A.M., they gave up their persistent efforts to take Vegas.

Marine casualties in the battle totaled 1,015: 116 killed, 801 wounded and 98 missing, of whom 19 were taken prisoner. The Marines figured they had caused 2,221 enemy casualties and destroyed the Chinese 358th Regiment as a fighting unit.

The 1st Marine Aircraft Wing had flown 218 close support missions against the Nevada Cities hills. The enemy fired 45,000 rounds of artillery and mortar fire at the Marines, and Marine and Army artillery units replied in kind. In addition to the Medal of Honors cited, 10 Marines won the Navy Cross in the battle.

In view of the loss of Reno, a new Outpost Elko was established on Hill 47, southeast of Carson and 765 yards in front of the MLR; and Vegas was strengthened with a detachment of 135 men. The 7th Marines replaced the 5th Marines after 68 days on the line. Some Marine dubbed Vegas "the highest damn beachhead in Korea."[120]

On March 28, in the midst of the Vegas battle and three weeks after Stalin's death, the Communists notified the United Nations that they were prepared to discuss the return of sick and wounded prisoners. After six months of stalemate, the two sides sat down again at Panmunjom on April 6. A provisional command was established at Munsan-ni to process the prisoners of both sides. Marine Col. Wallace M. Nelson commanded the United Nations Personnel and Medical Processing Unit. Marines swiftly built the Freedom Village POW recovery station. Operation Little Switch began on Monday, April 20; and in the next week, 6,670 North Korean and Chinese prisoners were returned and 684 were received from the enemy. Among the 684 were 149 Americans, including 15 Marines and three Navy corpsmen who had been attached to the 1st Marine Division. All the Marines had been wounded before they were captured. The first Marine freed was Pvt. Alberto Pizzaro-Baez of Puerto Rico and H Company, 7th Marines, who had been captured in October 1952.

On April 26, the plenary truce talks resumed at Panmunjom; and by June 4, the final agreement on the repatriation of prisoners had been hammered out. But President Rhee denounced the armistice plan and boycotted the Panmunjom meetings. The South Korean National Assembly unanimously rejected the truce terms. On June 17, the details of the truce line were settled; but the next day, ROK guards released 27,000 North Korean POWs who did not want to be repatriated. They quickly disappeared into the South Korean populace. At the end of the month, General Clark was authorized by Washington to sign the armistice without the South Koreans if necessary.

Meanwhile, back at the front, the Chinese attacked Outposts Carson and Elko on April 9. In the resulting fire fights, 14 Marines were killed, 4 missing and 66 wounded. A few smaller skirmishes followed before the Marines were relieved on May 5, after 13 months in line, by the 25th U.S. Infantry Division and its attached Turkish Brigade. News reports said the Marine commanders protested, wanting the division to remain on the line. The 11th Marines artillery units and the 1st Tank Battalion did remain up front.

In reserve, the division served as a counterattack force and pursued a training program that included two regimental amphibious exercises. A third was cancelled because of the impending POW repatriation. On June 1, Maj. Gen. Pollock gave over command of the division to Maj. Gen. Randolph McC. Pate, a veteran of the Dominican Republic, China and World War II and an experienced staff officer who had most recently commanded the 2d Marine Division at Camp Lejeune.

During the last days of May, the Chinese conquered Outposts Carson, Vegas and Elko and in the middle of June drove ROK units back more than 4,000 yards in the center of the UN front. In the former action, the 25th Division was supported by Marine artillery, tanks and planes.

While the division was in reserve, the 1st Marine Aircraft Wing continued to fly as part of the Fifth Air Force. Pilots had to fly a hundred combat missions before being rotated. In April, the wing flew 3,850 combat sorties, including 1,319 in close support. On April 17, VMF-115 set a record with 262 sorties in a single day. In one series of three interdiction strikes that day, Lt. Col. Joe L. Warren; Maj. Samuel J. Mantel, Jr., and Maj. John F. Bolt, Jr., led 23 Panther jets in firing 4,630 rounds of 20mm ammunition and dropping 22 tons of bombs on an enemy supply concentration point on the east coast. In May and June, flying was restricted by seasonal bad weather; but the wing still flew 3,359 and 3,276 sorties. By July 11, Major Bolt, who had shot down six planes in World War II, became the first Marine jet ace, with six MIG-15s downed. Between February 27, 1951, and June 11, 1953, Marine fliers had executed more than 80,000 combat sorties for the UN divisions.

The 1st Marine Division went back into the line on July 7 and 8 and immediately entered heavy fighting. Since Outposts Carson, Vegas and Elko had all been lost in the meantime, the eastern sector of the division front was now considerably weakened; and Outposts Berlin and East Berlin were more vulnerable to enemy attack. On the night of July 7, the Chinese attacked those two outposts, only 325 yards from the MLR. Berlin, manned by both 7th Marines and Turkish troops, repulsed the onslaught; but East Berlin, 500 yards to the east, fell in close-in fighting. Two relief platoons were forced to return to the MLR. At dawn, only 18 men were still holding out at Berlin. A two-platoon unit tried to retake East Berlin at mid-morning. Chinese shells reduced the first platoon to 20 men; the second platoon fought at the outpost's main trenchline and by 12:33 P.M. recaptured East Berlin. There were only 20 able-bodied Marines left after an hour of hand-to-hand fighting in which Marines literally threw Chinese down the reverse slope. That night, the Chinese attacked both outposts again; and the reinforced Marines pushed them back. In the two-night battle, the 7th Marines had 19 killed, 2 captured and 140 wounded.

It was a period of monsoon rains and for the next ten days there was little action. Patrols occasionally ran into ambushes and fire fights.

On July 19, the truce negotiators at Panmunjom reached final agreement on all the remaining points in dispute. But that night, a Chinese battalion again struck at the Berlin complex. Thirty-seven Marines were then on East Berlin and 44 on Berlin. In a fierce two-hour battle, both outposts were overrun. A decision was made not to try to recapture them; and finally, a defense-in-depth replaced the outpost system. Artillery, tanks and air blasted the now-enemy-held position. Fifty Marines had been killed, 12 captured and 118 wounded.

The 1st Marines replaced the 7th Marines in the line on July 26; but during the transfer period, the Chinese attacked late on the twenty-fourth. This time their targets were Hills 111 and 119 on the MLR itself. Hill 119, called Boulder City, was directly behind the former Berlin outposts, and Hill 111, to the far right at the eastern end of the division's line. The attack on Hill 111 was a diversion but it temporarily penetrated the Marine lines. The main enemy force hit Boulder City, and hand-to-hand combat developed along 700 yards of frontline trenches. G Company, 1st Marines was cut to half strength. I Company came up in relief, but the Chinese intercepted a coded message and their artillery created 35 more casualties as G Company moved to the rear.

In the 5th Marines' sector, the Chinese struck at Outposts Esther and Dagmar. They seized part of the forward trenches at Esther. The H Company defenders led by 2d Lt. William H. Bates hung on to the rear trenches. Flamethrowers and hand-to-hand fighting finally broke up the attack by 6:40 A.M. of July 25. Twelve Marines were killed and 98 wounded there.

The fighting at Hill 119 continued into the early morning hours. The enemy held most of the forward trenches and briefly occupied the rocky crest itself. Capt. Louis J. Sartor of I Company, 1st Marines led a counterattack at 1:30 A.M. Two hours later, the MLR had been restored; and by 5:30, additional Marines had secured Hill 119. The fighting there went on through the morning of the twenty-fifth before the last of the enemy were driven off the forward slope of Boulder City. That night, the Chinese attacked again and reached the trenchline. They killed 19 Marines and wounded 125 before being driven off. Since July 24, Marine casualties totaled 43 killed and 316 wounded. One of the dead was Staff Sgt. Ambrosio Guillen of El Paso, Texas, the last Marine to earn the Medal of Honor in Korea. Though critically wounded in hand-to-hand fighting, he rallied his men, refused medical attention and saw that the wounded were evacuated before he succumbed.

On the night of July 26, with the armistice approaching, the

Chinese made two final lunges at the 1st Marines on Hill 119. This was to be the last ground action for the 1st Marine Division in Korea. Had the Chinese succeeded in winning Boulder City, they would have forced the Eighth Army to withdraw, under the terms of the armistice, so that it no longer controlled all of the Imjin River. But the Marines held.

It had been a costly finale for both sides. Eighth Army officers estimated that the Chinese suffered 72,000 casualties in July. The Marines alone had 1,611. During those last weeks, the enemy had made substantial local gains at key points along the UN front.

On Monday morning, July 27, 1953, the armistice agreement was signed at Panmunjom. Marine Col. James C. Murray, who had been involved in the truce talks for two years, was in charge of the UN Command staff group that worked out the final line of demarcation.

The war was finished after three years, one month and two days of battle. The Marines had 4,262 killed in battle and 20,038 wounded. Forty-two Marines had been awarded the Medal of Honor for valor—26 of them posthumously. When the armistice became effective at 10 P.M., thousands of white star cluster shells illuminated the sky all along the 155-mile front.

8
The Marine POWs

Two hundred and twenty-one U.S. Marines had been captured by the enemy. Forty-nine were officers and 172 enlisted men; 190 were ground troopers and 31 aviators. All but one of the aviators were officers. By one estimate, one in every 570 of the Marines who served in Korea was taken prisoner in contrast with the U.S. Army's one in 150.[121]

Of the 221 Marines captured, 194 (43 officers and 151 enlisted men) returned. The Marine POW survival rate was 87 percent. The survival rate of all U.S. POWs was only 62 percent.

Of the 194 Marines who made it back, 172 returned in the two prisoner exchanges, 18 escaped in May 1951; two enlisted men escaped within a week after being taken, and two others were released by the enemy after a brief captivity.

Fifteen wounded Marines had been returned in April's Operation Little Switch, and 157 were repatriated after the armistice in Operation Big Switch. Six corpsmen who had served with the 1st Marine Division were also returned then.

During Operation Big Switch, Marine Col. Albert F. Metze, who had been a POW himself in World War II, was the Processing Unit Commander. On August 5, the first day of the exchange, Marine Pfc. Alfred P. Graham, Jr., was the fifth man to be processed. Sgt. Robert J. Coffee and Pfc. Pedron E. Aviles were the only other Marines returned the first day.

It took a month before all 3,597 U.S. servicemen were returned during Big Switch. The Marine who had been a POW longest was Capt. Jesse V. Booker, who had been shot down on August 7, 1950. Col. Frank H. Schwable, the senior Marine captured, and Maj. Walter R. Harris were released on September 6, 1953, the last day of the switch.

Two of the most renowned Marine POWs were Lt. Col. William G. Thrash, a VMA-121 pilot, and Maj. John N. McLaughlin, who had been taken prisoner in the November 1950 ambush of Task Force Drysdale. Both had defied their captors throughout their long imprisonment and provided strong leadership for their fellow captives.

Of the 190 ground Marines captured, 42 were taken prisoner in the Task Force Drysdale debacle, 40 in the outpost fighting in October 1952 and 39 in the final outpost battles in March and July 1953. Those groups totaled 121 and left only 69 ground Marines captured during the rest of the war.

Three Marines captured with Task Force Drysdale had been POWs in World War II: Staff Sgt. Charles L. Harrison, who had been captured on Wake Island; Warrant Officer Felix J. McCool, captured on Corregidor; and Master Sgt. Frederick J. Stumpges, a survivor of the Bataan Death March.

In general, the Marine POWs who returned felt that they had been given much harsher physical treatment by the North Koreans than by the Chinese. The Chinese used mental pressure rather than physical brutality and made great efforts to indoctrinate them politically. The Chinese attempted to separate "progressive" or cooperative prisoners from "reactionary" or resistant ones. Major McLaughlin in particular was subjected to intimidation and maltreatment because he was a leader among the officer-prisoners and persistently non-cooperative toward his captors.

Among the worst punishment, in addition to beatings and near-starvation, was solitary confinement in a vermin-infested "hole" in a crouched position for 56 hours or more. Second Lt. Roland L. McDaniel was confined to the hole for ten days and emerged with pneumonia and tuberculosis. Second Lt. Richard L. Still was sentenced to the hole for three months for trying to escape. First Lt. Felix F. Ferranto spent more than two years of his 33 months as a prisoner in solitary confinement or isolated with small units of "non-cooperative" POWs. And two aviators, Capt. Gerald Fink and Capt. Arthur Wagner, received especially severe treatment for their resistance.

In January 1952, six ranking officers, including Major McLaughlin, were sentenced to solitary confinement for periods of three to six months. After that, tension among the prisoners in

Camp 2 was highly charged with suspicion of informers and opportunists until Lt. Col. Thrash arrived in June and restored discipline. As a result, in September, Thrash was confined to solitary for eight months. On one occasion, he was beaten and thrown outside half naked in sub-zero weather and nearly died.

On November 10, 1952, Marines at Camp 2 managed defiantly to observe the traditional Marine Corps Birthday by making a cake with stolen eggs, sugar and flour and celebrating with stolen rice wine.

During the last months of the war, with the approach of the truce agreement, the treatment of prisoners improved. They received warmer clothing and better medical care. Clearly, the Communists wanted to repatriate the prisoners in as good condition as possible for propaganda purposes.

In the summer of 1952, the Chinese gained a propaganda weapon that had a world-wide effect. They extracted false confessions from two U.S. Air Force fliers that the United States had used germ warfare by dropping bacteriological bombs on North Korean towns. After that, all captured fliers were subjected to severe stress, beatings and torture to confess to such war crimes. Marine Master Sgt. John T. Cain, an enlisted pilot with VMO-6, refused to make such a confession even though he was confined to the hole and actually taken before a firing squad. Capt. John P. Flynn of VMF(N)-513, who had been shot down over Japan in World War II, also withstood brutal interrogation and refused to "confess."

Thirty-nine Air Force men and one Marine did succumb to intense pressure and torture and made confessions. The Marine was Colonel Schwable, the 1st MAW Chief of Staff, who had been shot down on a reconnaissance flight on July 8, 1952. Schwable was held in solitary confinement until December, interrogated incessantly, kept near starvation and refused medical attention. He finally signed a false statement. The forty-five-year old Annapolis graduate and veteran of 20 years' service had been a pioneer night-fighter pilot who had shot down four planes as commander of VMF(N)-531 in World War II. A Court of Inquiry in 1954 decided that he had resisted "to the limit of his ability before giving in." The Court recommended that Schwable should not be disciplined but judged that his usefulness as a Marine officer had been "seriously impaired."[122]

One enlisted Marine POW was disciplined for cooperating with the enemy by writing a pro-Communist magazine article. Fourteen Marines admitted signing peace appeals or petitions but were judged not to have acted dishonorably.[123]

Despite published reports that no American POWs attempted to escape from captivity in this war, Marine Corps records show that 18 Marines and a U.S. Army interpreter attached to the 1st Marine Division escaped in May 1951 after several months as prisoners. The Marines were 1st Lt. Frank E. Cold and 17 enlisted men (including Staff Sgt. Harrison, the Wake Island survivor). They had been brought south to perform work details behind the enemy lines. When an artillery barrage dispersed their guards, they fled in the opposite direction. They made their position known to an Army observation pilot with panels of wallpaper stripped from a Korean house and were rescued by three Army tanks.

In addition, two enlisted Marines escaped after a few weeks' captivity and two were released after four days in enemy hands. Although no Americans escaped from a permanent enemy prison camp and reached friendly lines, the Corps credits Marines with seven unsuccessful escape attempts, for which they were severely punished by their captors. First Lt. Robert J. Gillette managed to evade his captors for several weeks and Capt. Paul L. Martelli, for 10 days.

Five Marines later received awards for their conduct while prisoners of war: Lt. Col. Thrash, Major McLaughlin, Major Harris, Captain Flynn and Master Sgt. Cain.

But the nation was distressed by the behavior of many American POWs in Korea. Said one investigator, "Almost one of every three American prisoners in Korea was guilty of some sort of collaboration with the enemy. . . . some of them had behaved brutally to their fellow-prisoners."[124] As a result, in 1955, Secretary of Defense Charles E. Wilson appointed an Advisory Committee on Prisoners of War, headed by Assistant Secretary of Defense Carter L. Burgess and including among its ten members retired Marine Maj. Gen. Merritt A. Edson. The committee recommended and President Eisenhower put into effect a new Code of Conduct, which said clearly that a prisoner of war should give only his name, rank, service number and date of birth. It said he will not surrender willingly. If captured, he will resist and try to escape. He will do nothing that might be harmful to his fellow prisoners or disloyal to his country and its allies. After the record of the Korean war, such a Code of Conduct appeared necessary.

The Marine POW record had been clearly superior. When the United States Congress investigated the issue of prisoner-of-war conduct in Korea, the Senate report summarized: "The United States Marine Corps, the Turkish troops, and the Colombians as groups, did not succumb to the pressures exerted upon them by the Communists and did not co-operate or collaborate with the enemy. For this they deserve greatest admiration and credit."[125]

9
The Korean Experience

The 1st Marine Division remained in Korea for more than a year and a half after the armistice was signed. One regiment, initially the 5th Marines, defended the division's sector north of the Imjin River, while the other two stood guard behind the river. The forward regiment was also responsible for security in the UN's half of the division's 28-mile-long slice of the 4,000-yard-wide demilitarized zone.

In August 1954, the 3rd Marine Division under Maj. Gen. Robert H. Pepper, and MAG-11 and MAG-16 came out and took up stations in Japan to provide an amphibious capability there. The 1st Marine Division was relieved in March 1955 by the U.S. 24th Infantry Division and returned to Camp Pendleton after an absence of nearly five years. In mid-1956, the 1st Marine Aircraft Wing transferred from Korea to the Naval Air Station at Iwakuni, Japan.

This had been a major war in the number of men involved, the duration of the fighting, the number of casualties and the significance of the conflict to the world. It ended pretty much where it began—at the 38th Parallel. North Korea gained 850 square miles and South Korea gained 2,350 square miles north of the 1950 boundary. But the results could not be measured on the ground. Whether the war had been a defeat for the United States and its allies, a stalemate or a defeat for the Communist powers depended entirely on the perception of the viewer. Both sides had tried to reunite Korea by force and failed. But the Communist world had been shown that its armies could not overrun a non-communist neighbor, and the United States had been shown that even its enormous power had limits.

The price paid for these lessons was tremendous. Communist military casualties were estimated at 1.4 million. The United Nations had 996,937 killed, wounded and missing. Of this total, the Republic of Korea's casualties were 850,000. United States casualties were 136,937: 33,629 were battle deaths and 103,308 wounded in action. The U.S. Marine Corps had 30,544 casualties; 4,262 killed, 244 non-battle deaths and 26,038 wounded. For the Corps, these were more casualties than in any conflict until that date except World War II.

There had been 74,279 men and women on active duty in the Corps when the war began. An estimated 424,000 Marines served during the hostilities; the peak was September 30,1953, when 261,343 were in uniform. The greatest strength in Korea was in April 1953, when 35,306 ground and air Marines were there.

The war created several fundamental problems for the Corps. Perhaps the most important was the use of the 1st Marine Division, after Inchon, as one more infantry division engaged in a major land war. Although the division (with the Korean Marines attached) was the largest in the Eighth Army and was respected as a crack outfit, Marine analysts recognized that its role during most of the war "could be considered an inefficient, though not ineffective use of Marines."[126] As a military organization specialized in amphibious warfare, the Corps was being misused. Essentially, this occurred because of the Marines' own desire to be a fighting force-in-readiness. They were ready and able and were used as needed.

Utilization of the Marine division as part of a large land army also led to the loss of integration with its own air arm. The 1st Marine Aircraft Wing flew 127,496 combat sorties in Korea, far more than the 80,000 sorties flown by all Marine aviation in World War II. But less than a third of the Korean sorties, about 39,500, were flown in the Corps' aviation specialty: close support of ground troops. And after October 1950, when the 1st MAW was put under operational control of the Fifth Air Force for the rest of the war, it primarily flew interdiction and bombing raids deep into enemy territory. The 1st MAW's commanding general had "virtually no tactical control over his own units."[127]

The issue was doubly frustrating because the interdiction program failed to prevent the enemy from building up its troop and artillery strength. The Commander of the Seventh Fleet said after the war, "The interdiction program was a failure."[128] And General Ridgway wrote years later, "In Korea, where we had air mastery over practically the whole peninsula, MacArthur himself acknowledged our inability to isolate the battle area by air bombardment or to choke off the flow of reinforcements and supply."[129]

Not only did the Air Force give close support a low priority, but differences in close support doctrines and tactics were never resolved. Where Marine procedures filled close support requests in five to 15 minutes, Air Force procedures, Marines said, resulted in delays from 30 minutes to nearly four hours. Toward the war's end, some of the conflicts were eased by informal understandings, increased cooperation and greater decentralization of control among Air Force, Army and Marine commanders.

Marine pilots saw a lot of action. They downed 35 enemy planes. In addition to Major Bolt's six kills, Maj. Alexander J. Gillis and Maj. John H. Glenn, Jr., destroyed three MIGs each and Maj. Roy L. Reed, two. By late 1952, the F9F Panther jet had pretty much replaced the venerable Corsair. Marine aviators suffered 258 killed and 174 wounded in action. A total of 436 planes were lost in combat or operational accidents.

At the same time, the war enabled the Corps to make enormous progress in the use of the helicopter and the evolution of vertical envelopment. In September 1951, the Marines had executed "the first helicopter lift of a combat unit in history."[130] The helicopter also cut to minutes the time needed to carry wounded to hospitals; it saved lives. And it swiftly laid miles of communications wire that would have taken weeks by men on the ground. HMR-161 lifted 60,046 men and 7.5 million pounds of cargo during the war. It evacuated 2,748 wounded, and VMO-6 flew out 7,067 wounded.

Another major change in the Corps during this war was the integration of black Americans into Marine units. At the war's beginning, there were 1,502 black enlisted men on active duty; by 1953, there were 19 officers and 14,468 men. The first black officer to lead Marines in combat was Lt. William K. Jenkins of Elizabeth, New Jersey, who served with B Company, 7th Marines. The Marines in Korea had only one black pilot, 2d Lt. Frank E. Petersen, Jr., of Topeka, Kansas, who flew 64 combat missions with VMF-212 and earned the Distinguished Flying Cross. Petersen was the fourth black to become a naval aviator. The first, Navy Ensign Jesse L. Brown, was killed on December 4, 1950, flying close support for the Marines breaking out of the Chosin Reservoir.

One black enlisted man who made an outstanding record in combat was Pfc. A. C. Clark of Minden, Louisiana. An automatic rifleman with H Company, 5th Marines, Clark earned the Bronze Star in August 1952 for rescuing his platoon leader, who had been wounded on a combat patrol. He earned the Silver Star the following December 13 when, although wounded, he covered the evacuation of two wounded Marines, killed three of the enemy and silenced a machine gun.

In tactical terms, the static warfare that dominated most of the war reduced the 1st Marine Division's combat and amphibious efficiency. Amphibious assault was an offensive capability that received no call in Korea after 1950. Individual unit amphibious readiness was rated in mid-1953 at between 25 and 60 percent.

In western Korea, the division tried to solve the problem of being spread over so wide a front by setting up a long, thin MLR with outposts. These vulnerable outposts were manned by too few Marines to stand off determined enemy attacks. The outpost system of defense was expensive in lives. Ultimately, as vital outposts were lost to the enemy, the division switched to the defense-in-depth posture used by its neighbor, the British 1st Commonwealth Division, and by the Chinese, who built entrenched defenses to a depth of four to 14 miles behind their own MLR.

During the long period of static warfare, Marine leaders felt that some UN policies hampered combat aggressiveness and counter-defense measures. One example cited was the restriction late in 1952 on previously encouraged large-scale raids to capture prisoners. Plans for raids of company size or larger thereafter required the approval of higher headquarters. The purpose was to minimize casualties in forays initiated by lower-echelon commanders. But regimental and battalion commanders felt such limitations prevented them from capitalizing on local targets of opportunity. In a war that had settled into an essentially political and propaganda confrontation, the cost of such "aggressive" operations was often unjustifiable. The offensive-minded tradition and training of Marine professionals made this dispute particularly acute, while higher headquarters worried about overall casualty rates and the fragility of the truce negotiations.

The Chinese, on the other hand, appeared more willing to take large numbers of casualties to achieve local gains. They became expert in limited-objective warfare. They developed adroit "creeping tactics," digging trenches toward UN positions, and built up artillery strength to hammer UN troops. They would invariably smother an advanced outpost with artillery fire, make an initial frontal attack that was actually a feint and envelop the outpost from the rear. At the same time, they would set up an ambush behind the outpost to prevent its defenders from escaping and reinforcements from reaching them.

The prolonged outpost warfare was predominantly night fighting, and the Chinese "had a marked superiority in night operations."[131] They were also skilled in the construction and camouflage of bunkers, trenches and tunnels and artillery and mortar emplacements. Their well-prepared reverse slope fortifications were often impervious to anything less than 1,000-pound bombs.

The Marines gained a high respect for Chinese combat effectiveness, the leadership of their officers and the patience and tenacity of their soldiers. The Chinese soldier traveled light and, armed with a submachine "burp" gun, achieved great mobility over the traditionally more heavily burdened American fighting man.

This mobility gave the enemy the advantage of tactical surprise in the darkness. Often, American soldiers and Marines were unaware of the enemy's presence until he was suddenly within grenade-throwing range. The military historian S. L. A. Marshall wrote of the Chinese that by 1953, "They had become as tenacious and earth-seeking as ants, and in that lay a great part of their success. Two and one half years of war in Korea were a bonanza for Communist China. On that training ground her armies became as skilled as any in the world in the techniques of hitting, evading and surviving."[132] The Chinese were tough and able opponents, prepared to resist the extension of American power onto the Asian mainland.

In this war, the United States had proved that it would help defend a nation that was prepared to defend itself against aggression. But as the Vietnam war was to demonstrate, some in the United States had not yet recognized the fact that it could not effectively project its power into Asia at will.

As for the Marine Corps, in the Korean war's first months, it had fulfilled its modern roles as a force-in-readiness and as experts in amphibious assault; and throughout the long conflict, it had proved itself again an elite fighting Corps that would do the job assigned with professionalism and courage.

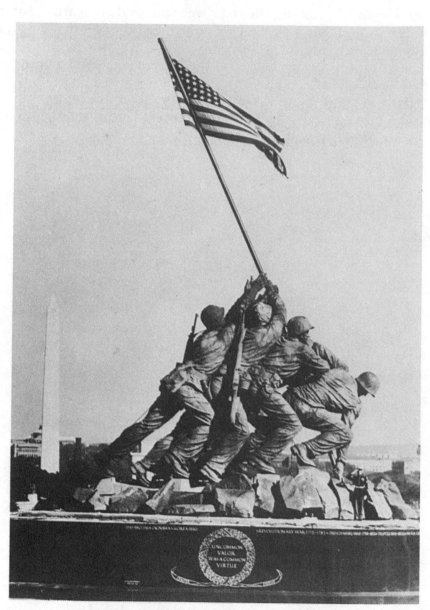

A Marine sergeant is dwarfed beside the thirty-two-foot
high figures of the Marine Corps War Memorial. The
statue, modeled on Joe Rosenthal's photograph
of the Iwo Jima flag-raising, was sculpted by Felix de
Weldon and dedicated at the Arlington National
Cemetery on November 10, 1954.
Wide World Photos

SEMPER FIDELIS

VII
TUMULTUOUS
TIMES
1953-1965

1
Around the World

Between the Korean armistice in July 1953 and the Marines' landing at Da Nang, South Vietnam, on March 8, 1965, Marines met a variety of crises abroad, as Marines have throughout the nation's history. The two most crucial overseas ventures during this period were the landing in Lebanon in 1958 and the intervention in the Dominican Republic in 1965. The other major events can be summarized in a brief sampling that suggests the range of the Corps' modern responsibilities.

1953: In April, a 2d Marine Provisional Brigade, totaling 2,200 Marines under Brig. Gen. Wilburt S. Brown and 40 Marine helicopters, maneuvered at Yucca Flat, Nevada, when a large atomic device was exploded over the desert, simulating an atomic battlefield. In August, the 2d Battalion, 6th Marines rescued victims of an earthquake in Greece's Ionian Islands.

1954: During the United States-supported coup against the government of Col. Jacobo Arbenz Guzman of Guatemala, the 2d Battalion, 8th Marines stood by to protect American citizens and property. On the Marine Corps Birthday, the Marine Corps memorial statue of the Iwo Jima flag-raising was officially dedicated at Arlington National Cemetery.

1955: In January, a battalion of Marines helped evacuate 26,000 Chinese to Taiwan from the Tachen Islands off the Chinese mainland. In October, Marine pilots brought emergency supplies to flood-inundated Tampico, Mexico.

1956: Gen. Randolph McC. Pate succeeded General Shepherd as Commandant of the Corps. On January 7, Master Sgt. Bertrum E. Strickling and Cpl. Thomas E. Rhodes of the Marine Security Guard used small arms and tear gas to fight off a stone-throwing mob trying to break into the American Consulate in

East Jerusalem. The mob was dispersed by the Arab Legion, which killed four of the attackers and wounded many. But as a result of the incident, Jordan, which occupied East Jerusalem, banned the Marines. E Company, 2d Marines reinforced the U.S. Naval Air Station at Port Lyautey, Morocco, during fighting between the French and Moroccans. In November, during the Suez crisis, the 3rd Battalion, 2d Marines evacuated U.S. nationals from Alexandria, Egypt, and a UN truce team from Haifa, Israel.

1957: In February, the 3rd Marines stood by during an Indonesian revolt. Marine helicopters assisted flood victims in Ceylon and Spain. The Commandant restored the post of Sergeant Major of the Marine Corps, the first occupant being Sgt. Major William Bestwick.

1958: On May 13, when Vice President Richard M. Nixon's car was stoned by a mob in Caracas, Venezuela, the 1st Battalion, 6th Marines was flown to U.S. Caribbean bases. In June, sailors and Marines from the Guantanamo Naval Base in Cuba were kidnapped and later released by forces of Fidel Castro; and in July, Marines entered Cuban territory to protect the base's water supply during fighting between the Cuban army and Castro's forces. In mid-year, MAG-11 arrived in Taiwan to strengthen Nationalist Chinese air defenses after the People's Republic of China began bombarding the Kinmen Islands of Quemoy and Little Quemoy.

1960: Bypassing nine senior officers, Maj. Gen. David M. Shoup, Medal of Honor winner at Tarawa, succeeded Gen. Randolph McC. Pate as Commandant of the Corps. In March, Marines helped rescue earthquake victims at Agadir, Morocco. In June, when White House Press Secretary James C. Hagerty and Ambassador Douglas MacArthur II were besieged by a mob in Tokyo, a Marine helicopter rescued them from their car.

1961: In May, Marines from the 3rd Battalion, 6th Marines and HMR-262 helped with relief work after an earthquake in Turkey. In November, eight helicopters from HMR-264 aided hurricane victims in British Honduras.

1962: The M-14 rifle replaced the M-1 and the M-60 machine gun, the venerable Browning. On February 20, Marine Lt. Col. John H. Glenn, Jr., of New Concord, Ohio, orbited the

594

earth three times in the first manned American space capsule.*
In May, the 3rd Marine Expeditionary Brigade, commanded by
Brig. Gen. Ormond R. Simpson, landed in Thailand. Before the
last Marines left Thailand early in August, 5,000 Marines had
been sent there. In October, the entire 189,000-man Marine
Corps participated in the worldwide alert of U.S. military forces
during the Cuban missile crisis. The 5th Marine Expeditionary
Brigade of more than 11,000 men sailed from Camp Pendleton
for the Caribbean, and the 2d Marine Division was deployed to
Key West, Florida, and Caribbean waters.

1963: In January, Marines from the Eighth and Eye Barracks
in Washington helped keep watch over the painting of the Mona
Lisa while it was on display in the National Gallery of Art.

1964: Gen. Wallace M. Greene, Jr., an Annapolis graduate
from Waterbury, Vermont, succeeded General Shoup as Commandant of the Corps.

Throughout the period, Marines engaged in amphibious exercises around the world as well as cold-weather and desert training in California and jungle training in Panama.

*In the next 20 years, a dozen more Marines and former Marines became
astronauts. Among them, Lt. Col. R. Walter Cunningham flew in Apollo 7, the first
manned Apollo mission. Fred Haise was on the aborted Apollo 13 mission. Col. Jack
Lousma flew in the second Skylab mission in 1973 and commanded the third flight
of the space shuttle *Columbia* in 1982. Lt. Col. Gerald P. Carr commanded Skylab
3, the record-setting 84-day earth-orbiting mission in 1973–74. Vance D. Brand flew
with the Russians in the joint Apollo-Soyuz space mission in 1975. In 1983, former
Marine Story Musgrave, M.D., after 15 years as an astronaut, flew in the space
shuttle *Challenger* on its first orbit of the earth.

2
Tragedy at Ribbon Creek—1956

The Corps' most traumatic experience during this period occurred at home. At Parris Island, South Carolina, on Sunday night, April 8, 1956, an angry drill instructor, Staff Sgt. Matthew C. McKeon, marched 74 Marine recruits into a tidal swamp called Ribbon Creek. Six young men were drowned.

The tragedy shocked the nation and tarnished public support of the Marine Corps. Calls were widespread to reform the Corps' recruit-training practices, which gave non-commissioned drill instructors (DIs) virtually absolute control over their "boot" charges. The newly installed Commandant, General Pate, relieved the general commanding the Recruit Depot and created a recruit training command to effect reforms. He explained, "In a very real sense the Marine Corps is on trial for the tragedy of Ribbon Creek just as surely as is Sergeant McKeon."[1]

After a 15-day-long public trial, Staff Sgt. McKeon was found guilty of negligent homicide and drinking on duty. He was acquitted of oppressing recruits and of manslaughter. He was sentenced to be confined at hard labor and forfeit some pay for nine months, to be reduced to the rank of private and to be given a bad conduct discharge. The Secretary of the Navy reduced the sentence to three months' confinement at hard labor and demotion to private. Following the trial, McKeon spent only 12 more nights in the Parris Island brig.

The high point of the trial was the appearance, at the request of the defense lawyers, of retired Lt. Gen. "Chesty" Puller. Puller defended the Corps. He said, "The definition of military training is success in battle. . . . I'll quote Napoleon. He stated that the most important thing in military training is discipline. Without discipline an army becomes a mob. . . . In my opinion

596

the reason American troops made out so poorly in the Korean war was mostly due to lack of night training. . . . I would say that this night march was and is a deplorable accident."[2]

In the year after the Parris Island "death march," 197 drill instructors were relieved for a variety of causes; and an emotional battle raged between Marine generals and many veteran officers and noncoms. Under public and Congressional pressure, the Corps ordered an end to "hazing and maltreatment" of recruits. But some young combat leaders argued that a civilian teenager had to be kicked around if he was to be hardened enough to obey a sergeant's order to crawl forward into enemy fire, even to his death. The DIs were warned that they could no longer order recruits to dry-shave while double-timing, "to march in swamps, marshes or streams," to scream obscene phrases about themselves. DIs were forbidden to bury recruits in dirt, lock them in wall lockers or scrub them with sand.

But the conversion of a civilian youngster into a battle-ready Marine continued to be a tough and toughening process. Brig. Gen. Wallace M. Greene, Jr., who was assigned to reform training at Parris Island, said, "A DI's real reward is being able to shape men into Marines." And Tech. Sgt. John H. Groves, a Korean veteran and one of the best of Parris Island's DIs at the time, added, "We have to train men so we can tell them to go forward and draw enemy fire—and we're not going to reward them with a 72-hour pass."[3]

3
Landing in Lebanon—1958

Bikini-clad sunbathers and soft drink vendors greeted F Company, 2d Marines when it "stormed" ashore on Red Beach four miles south of Beirut, Lebanon, on the afternoon of July 15, 1958. Four companies of Marines drove 700 yards inland and secured the Beirut International Airport. There was no opposition at all.

The Marines landed because Lebanon's President Camille Chamoun had asked for help to restore peace in his unstable, riot-torn little country on the eastern end of the Mediterranean. Lt. Col. Harry A. Hadd's 2d Battalion, 2d Marines was the United States Sixth Fleet landing force nearest Lebanon when President Eisenhower made the decision to intervene. Thirteen hours later, Hadd's Marines were ashore.

The landing followed in the long tradition of U.S. Marine interventions. The Middle East was torn by another outburst of the disruption that bubbled up repeatedly after the British and French presence had been diminished by World War II. The entire strategic, oil-rich area had become a hotbed of nationalism and a pressure point in the Cold War.

In 1954, Gamal Abdul Nasser had risen to power in Egypt and excited a militant pan-Arabism. After he made an arms deal with the Communists, the Arab world split, Jordan and Iraq siding with the Western powers and Egypt and Syria, with the Soviet Union. In July 1956, Nasser nationalized the Suez Canal. In response, the Israelis, British and French attacked Egypt until the United Nations and the United States forced them to stop.

Throughout this turmoil, Lebanon, smaller than Connecticut, tried to walk a tightrope. It chose that pose because of both its commercial interests and its conglomerate population—half

[For the location of places in the Mediterranean see map No. 3 in the map section.—Au.]

its people belonging to several Christian communities and most of the rest Moslem, with some Jews and Druze. After nearly 80 years of French hegemony, by 1943 the Lebanese had worked out a domestic political formula with a Christian president and a Moslem premier. The situation was highly explosive.

International events hammered at Lebanon's delicate internal compromises. When President Chamoun refused to break with Great Britain and France over the 1956 Suez crisis, his Moslem premier resigned. The following spring, Chamoun was the only Middle Eastern leader to accept the Eisenhower Doctrine, which promised military and economic assistance to any Middle Eastern nation threatened by Communist aggression. Then, in February 1958, Chamoun's antagonists, Egypt and Syria, merged into the United Arab Republic.

Tension inside Lebanon mounted that summer as Chamoun's six-year term approached its end. The constitution prohibited a president from succeeding himself; but Chamoun controlled a large majority in the parliament, where presidents were elected. Tension turned to violence on May 8; the anti-Chamoun editor of the Beirut newspaper *Telegraph* was murdered. Riots broke out in Tripoli, an oil port and Moslem center in northern Lebanon. Led by Rashid Karami, rebels burned the United States Information Agency building there. On May 12, leaders of the Basta, the Moslem quarter of Beirut, began a general strike led by Saeb Salam, a former premier. Rebel groups in various parts of the country rose to arms. Conditions in Lebanon became chaotic.

Gen. Fuad Chehab, the Christian commander of the Lebanese army, feared the army's disintegration into Moslem and Christian factions. He tried to stay neutral and contain the anti-government forces in their strongholds in Tripoli, the Basta and the central countryside.

President Chamoun asked the United States, Britain and France to intervene if the situation got out of hand. On June 6, Lebanon filed a complaint against the United Arab Republic with the United Nations' Security Council, which then sent observers to Lebanon.

Chamoun's internal troubles came to be seen as part of an international crisis on July 14, when military officers in Iraq deposed the pro-Western government and murdered the king and premier. King Hussein of Jordan feared he would be overthrown next. The Western position in the Middle East seemed threatened. Chamoun formally appealed for help, and President Eisenhower immediately ordered Gen. Nathan F. Twining, Chairman of the Joint Chiefs of Staff, to land the amphibious units of the U.S. Sixth Fleet.

The crisis caught the Sixth Fleet off balance. Its landing force had been built up to the 2d Provisional Marine Force led by Brig. Gen. Sidney S. Wade, who had commanded the 1st Marines in the latter days of the Korean war. But on July 14, Wade's force was divided: The 1st Battalion, 8th Marines was north of Malta on its way home. The 3rd Battalion, 6th Marines, which was relieving the homebound battalion, was enroute from Crete to Athens. Only Hadd's 2d Battalion, 2d Marines, off the southern coast of Cyprus, was in position to land in Lebanon on 24-hour notice. And even the Landing Ship, Dock carrying its artillery battery, shore party detachment, underwater demolition team, heavy equipment and two of its M-48 tanks, was steaming to Malta for repairs. Fortunately, the LSD *Fort Snelling* supporting the 3rd Battalion, 6th Marines, was near Rhodes and some 400 miles from Lebanon.

Earlier, Marine Maj. Victor Stoyanow, a Korean veteran, had traveled to Beirut incognito and inspected the possible landing beaches. The Marines' contingency plan called for one Battalion Landing Team to go ashore northeast of Beirut and a second one to land south of the city and seize the airport. When this second BLT was relieved, it would move into the city. The military objective was to guard the Lebanese government against an invasion by neighboring Syria's army of 40,000 men and 200 Russian T-34 tanks.

At 12:30 A.M. July 15 (Beirut time), Adm. Arleigh A. Burke, Chief of Naval Operations, notified Adm. James L. Holloway, Jr., in London and Vice Adm. Charles R. Brown, commanding the Sixth Fleet, of Eisenhower's decision to intervene. The Marines were ordered to land south of Beirut at 3 P.M. and grab the airport.

The chance that the Marines would face opposition was remote. It was possible that rebel groups would try to repulse the invasion, that factions of the Lebanese army might resist or that the Syrian army would counterattack. But none of these was a serious threat, and none happened.

600

President Chamoun welcomed the promptness of the intervention. But when U.S. Ambassador Robert McClintock informed General Chehab an hour and a half before the landing, he was "visibly upset."[4] He had not approved the invasion and feared that it would split his army and incite the rebels. The general asked the ambassador to have the Marines stay aboard their ships and come around to Beirut's harbor and unload only a few tanks. McClintock agreed and tried to radio the Sixth Fleet, but it was too late to stop the Marines. Their amphibian tractors reached Red Beach at 3:04 and rumbled onto the airfield. E Company cleared the civilians from the beach, G Company secured the airport terminal and F and H Companies set up defensive positions around the airfield. No shots were fired.

At 3:30, Ambassador McClintock's naval attache arrived at the beach and told Hadd that the ambassador and General Chehab wanted the Marine battalion to return to its ships and land only its tanks on the Beirut docks. Hadd and then Capt. Victor B. McCrea, USN, the amphibious force commander, both refused. Vice Adm. Brown approved McCrea's decision.

President Chamoun, who had by now received reports that he was to be assassinated, asked McClintock over secret voice radio to send a Marine company with tanks to guard the Presidential Palace in Beirut. McClintock rushed a military attache to Hadd, who, believing his battalion was "extended to the maximum," again refused the ambassador's request.[5] Shortly thereafter, Captain McCrea directed Hadd to supply a 100-man detail. But by then, General Chehab, under McClintock's pressure, had promised that the army would guarantee Chamoun's safety. Hadd said later that if the order had not been rescinded, he would have told McCrea that the Marines could not comply. They already held a long perimeter; they lacked shore party support, and the Palace was next to the rebel-held Basta. McClintock was critical of what he regarded as the Marines' lack of flexibility. The hurry-up invasion was not prepared for all contingencies.

In cooperation with the Lebanese army, the Marines kept the airport open for commercial air traffic. McClintock asked Hadd and McCrea to meet with him in the American Embassy. But none of the three Americans was willing to leave his post. When McClintock insisted, Hadd and McCrea finally called on the ambassador separately and tried to resolve the "bizarre disagreements"[6] between the American diplomatic and military leaders. McClintock later described the meeting with McCrea: "The captain did arrive, puffing, accepted a large bourbon and soda, and said, 'Ambassador, by our landing today we have prevented an economic depression in the United States!' "[7]

The combination of tension and farce continued as the amphibious force tried to unload its ships. On shore, wheeled vehicles could not negotiate the soft sand; and off shore, an overlooked sandbar prevented the LSTs from beaching. The Marines had to improvise until *Fort Snelling* showed up that evening. Even then, the landing craft carrying the shore party was caught on the sandbar and did not reach the beach until 2:30 A.M. And the tanks arrived ashore short of ammunition. As Lt. Col. Hadd commented later, "the delay in the beaching of the causeway and the unloading of the LSTs would have been disastrous if the landing had been opposed."[8]

Early the next morning, the 3rd Battalion, 6th Marines, commanded by Lt. Col. Robert M. Jenkins, landed over Red Beach. Brig. Gen. Wade ordered Hadd's battalion to prepare to advance into the capital. Wade drove ahead into the city and met with McClintock at the embassy. When Wade arrived, the ambassador was talking on the telephone with General Chehab, who was asking McClintock to halt the Marines' move into the city. Both McClintock and Chehab were concerned that Lebanese army units might try to stop the Marines.

McClintock asked Wade to hold up the Marines. The general said he had no authority to cancel the order but he would delay the move an hour. McClintock and Wade rushed to see President Chamoun, who agreed that the Marines should enter Beirut. Chehab asked for another 30-minute postponement, to which Wade agreed. He ordered Hadd to start out at 10:30.

By now, a detachment of Lebanese army tanks had set up a roadblock on the main road between the airport and the capital. Wade returned to the airport past the Lebanese tanks. Receiving another request from Chehab for a delay, Wade again postponed the Marine advance until 11 A.M.

At that hour, the Marines boarded their tanks, trucks and LVTPs and moved out. They halted in front of the Lebanese tanks, one mile from the airport. The Lebanese had their guns pointed at the Marines' lead vehicles. McClintock, Chehab, Admiral Holloway and Wade all met at the roadblock and retired to an army schoolhouse a short distance from the road to confer about the awkward situation: A United States Marine force invited ashore by the government of Lebanon was threatened by the guns of that government's army.

At the schoolhouse, General Chehab asked the Marines to take a different route into the city. Holloway and Wade refused. McClintock found a compromise: He, Chehab and Holloway would ride together at the head of the Marines into Beirut; and they would bypass the Basta. At 12:30, the column started with the ambassador's car leading the way into Beirut. The Marines took control of the port area, patrolled the bridges over the Beirut River on the road leading north to Tripoli and furnished guards for the embassy and the ambassador's residence.

During the night, a few rebels sniped at Marine positions south of the airfield; the Marines replied with rifle fire. There were no casualties on either side. The next day, two Marines in a Jeep made a wrong turn and entered the Basta. They were disarmed and taken to a rebel command post. After receiving a long lecture about American imperialism, they were released; their Jeep and weapons were later returned.

In the following days, cooperation increased between the Lebanese army and the Marines. And on the morning of July 18, the 1st Battalion, 8th Marines under Lt. Col. John H. Brickley landed at Yellow Beach four miles north of Beirut and formed a perimeter to guard the beachhead and the northern approaches to the city. They were met only by spectators, ice cream and watermelon vendors and children swimming in the Mediterranean.

Not knowing what reaction the Lebanese intervention would arouse, the 2d Marine Division at Camp Lejeune and the 2d Marine Aircraft Wing at Cherry Point, North Carolina, were prepared to move to the Mediterranean; and the 3rd Battalion, 3rd Marines on Okinawa was ordered to sail for the Persian Gulf, to land in Iran or Saudi Arabia if needed. None of these units was brought to Lebanon.

On July 17, British paratroopers landed in Jordan at the request of King Hussein. On the eighteenth, the 2d Battalion, 8th Marines under Lt. Col. Alfred A. Tillman arrived at Beirut from Camp Lejeune by an airlift via Port Lyautey, Morocco. It took 34 hours in the air and 54 hours overall for 26 transport planes to bring the approximately 800 men.

The next day, the U.S. Army's 24th Airborne Brigade from Germany began arriving at the Beirut airport. This created the usual interservice problem over command of American forces ashore. Admiral Holloway asked the Joint Chiefs of Staff to name an officer to coordinate the units of the two services. The Marines wanted Lt. Gen. Edwin A. Pollock, now commanding general, Fleet Marine Force, Atlantic, to get the assignment. But the Joint Chiefs selected Maj. Gen. Paul D. Adams, USA, who took command from Brig. Gen. Wade on the twenty-sixth.

Meanwhile, the military scene was peaceful except for some harassment of the Marines' outlying positions. On July 19, a patrol from the 6th Marines went out to disperse rebels who were sniping at American planes as they landed at the airfield. The Marines got involved in a confused three-cornered fire fight with the rebels and Lebanese police in civilian clothes. A Lebanese army unit moved into the area to halt the rebel aggressiveness.

General Chehab placed Lebanese troops between the Americans and rebel positions in the Basta area. And the 1st Battalion, 8th Marines began sending out motorized platoon-strength patrols with helicopter cover. They reconnoitered as far as 20 miles east of the battalion's position north of the city. On the twenty-ninth, the Army relieved the Marines at the airport. All three Marine battalions took up positions in and northeast of the city. By the end of July, the Army and Marines had encircled Beirut with an armed perimeter. Some sniper activity continued, but the only two Marine deaths resulted from accidental shootings by other Marines. One Army sergeant was killed and another wounded by rebels.

Plans to end the intervention began as soon as it started. President Eisenhower called on the United Nations to safeguard Lebanese independence, but a Japanese resolution in the Security Council to have the UN protect Lebanon was vetoed by the Soviet Union.

Robert D. Murphy, Under Secretary of State for Political Affairs, arrived in Beirut as President Eisenhower's personal representative to speed a political solution for the internal

Lebanese problems that had instigated the intervention. Murphy and Admiral Holloway agreed that the causes of Lebanon's internal conflict were domestic and bore little relationship to international issues. Murphy worked toward getting the Lebanese to hold a presidential election.

Col. William A. Eddy, a Lebanon-born, Arabic-speaking retired Marine officer employed by the American Arabian Oil Company, arranged a meeting between Murphy and two of Saeb Salam's colleagues on July 24. Murphy assured the rebel leaders that the Americans had not landed to keep President Chamoun in office. After that, the rebel harassment of American troops lessened. In long discussions, Murphy also convinced the left-wing Druze chieftain Kamal Jumblat and the Tripoli Moslem leader Rashid Karami of the United States' intentions. These understandings led to an election on July 31. The parliament chose General Chehab as president.

The Americans began to withdraw their nearly 15,000 soldiers and Marines. On August 14, the 2d Battalion, 2d Marines re-embarked; and on September 15, the two 8th Marines' battalions sailed for the United States. The Army assumed responsibility for the Beirut dock area; and the 3rd Battalion, 6th Marines guarded the northeastern approaches to the city.

When Chehab took over the presidency on September 23, he named Rashid Karami as his prime minister with a cabinet composed chiefly of anti-Chamoun leaders. In reaction to this and to the torture and murder of a journalist of the militant Christian Phalange Party, Chamoun's supporters called a general strike of Christians. American forces stayed out of the conflict, but the Lebanese army had to break up a clash between the irregular forces of the two factions. Beirut continued to resemble an armed camp.

On September 29, the 3rd Battalion, 6th Marines left Lebanon; and the regiment's newly arrived 2d Battalion assumed the job of serving as a ready reserve for the Army troops ashore. On October 23, the Lebanese formed a more balanced government with representatives from each of the major parties. Two days later, the last U.S. Army troops left the country.

Although the intervention could not solve the bloody musical chairs of Lebanon's chronic political chaos, it helped maintain peace and demonstrated that the United States would support a small country that feared for its independence. Violence was minimized by well-disciplined American soldiers and Marines who did not permit harassment to escalate. The United States did not use its military power to sustain one partisan faction against the other, but its presence made a temporary political solution possible. And the landing force was pulled out again voluntarily as soon as possible.

4
Dominican Power Play—1965

The overthrow of two dictators—Cuba's Fulgencio Batista and the Dominican Republic's Rafael Trujillo—combined to bring the Marines back to battle in the Caribbean in 1965.

The drama began in Cuba on New Year's Day 1959 when Fidel Castro destroyed Batista's American-supported regime.* This led to the disastrous effort on April 17, 1961, to oust Castro with the Bay of Pigs invasion, planned by the Central Intelligence Agency and executed by Cuban refugees.** In October 1962 came the attempt by the Soviet Union to install nuclear weapons 90 miles off the United States coast and the nerve-wracking Cuban missile crisis. These events aroused fears in the United States over Communist exploitation of unrest elsewhere in Latin America.

Six weeks after the Bay of Pigs fiasco, Generalissimo Trujillo was shot to death. The CIA-assisted assassination generated exactly the kind of dangerous disquiet that Washington feared would lead to a Castro-oriented takeover.

In the prolonged disorder created by Trujillo's successors and rivals, the Marines landed in the Dominican Republic on April 28, 1965. "Armed and authorized to return fire, they were the first combat-ready U.S. forces to enter a Latin American country in almost forty years"[9]—ever since Franklin D. Roosevelt had apparently ended the era of unilateral military interven-

*A few weeks later, a Marine team led by Col. Robert D. Heinl, Jr., arrived in Haiti to strengthen the army of François "Papa Doc" Duvalier. The mission was withdrawn in 1963 after Duvalier declared Heinl *persona non grata*. In 1972, the State Department reported that former Marine noncoms were training Haitian militiamen through a private American corporation.

**Marine Col. Jack Hawkins played a significant role in the preparation of the Bay of Pigs invasion. Commandant General Shoup complained to President Kennedy that he had not been informed in advance of the invasion.

[For the location of places in the Caribbean see map No. 5 in the map section.—*Au.*]

tion. With Castro declaring his intention to spread his revolution, President Lyndon B. Johnson was determined to prevent a "second Cuba."

After the Marine occupation of the Dominican Republic from 1916 to 1924, Trujillo's 30-year-long tyranny had "presented the United States with no real difficulties";[10] he insured political and economic stability. And the dictator, who had been trained as a soldier by the Marines, continued his close ties to the Corps through Col. Richard M. Cutts. After Trujillo's death and with his "front man for many years" Joaquín Balaguer[11] still in the presidency, a U.S. Navy squadron with Marines aboard stayed off the Dominican coast for several months to discourage a pro-Castro revolution.

In November 1961, two of Trujillo's brothers returned to the country; and Secretary of State Dean Rusk warned them against seizing power. U.S. warships with 1,800 Marines again steamed off Santo Domingo (Ciudad Trujillo), the capital. The brothers left. In January, Balaguer was forced out of office.

The United States played an active hand in the fluid Dominican political scene and helped, through the Organization of American States, to encourage the elections that brought the popular Juan Bosch to the presidency in February 1963. The U.S. Military Assistance and Advisory Group at the time was headed by Marine Col. David C. Wolfe, who had commanded VMF(N)-513 in Korea. After Bosch was in office seven months, a military coup, supported by conservative business interests, sent him into exile in Puerto Rico. In December 1963, President Johnson finally recognized the military-imposed government on the understanding that elections would be held in 1965.

Bosch's overthrow was followed by a period of low sugar prices, unemployment, demonstrations, riots and finally civil war. The government, dominated now by Donald J. Reid Cabral, grew increasingly weak and unpopular. On Saturday, April 24, 1965, a faction in the Dominican army, seeking the return of Bosch and the 1963 constitution without elections, revolted against Reid Cabral's government. Overnight, pro-Bosch soldiers took up positions in Santo Domingo. Crowds rioted in the streets and demanded Bosch's return. The rebellious troops handed out thousands of guns to the crowd. Reid Cabral asked

Marine Lt. Col. Ralph Heywood, the U.S. naval attache, if the United States would intervene.

Sunday, the pro-Bosch rebels captured the National Palace and arrested Reid Cabral. He resigned and was allowed to go into hiding. At noon, the U.S. Navy's six-ship Caribbean Ready Group began moving from Puerto Rico toward the Dominican Republic, in case it became necessary to evacuate U.S. citizens. Aboard were the 3rd Battalion, 6th Marines and Marine Medium Helicopter Squadron 264—1,702 Marines in the 6th Marine Expeditionary Unit.

The government in Washington worried about a Communist takeover if Bosch and his supporters regained power. It hoped the anti-Bosch elements of the Dominican armed forces would form a junta and restore order. As Bosch seemed on the verge of returning to the island Sunday afternoon, the Dominican Air Force strafed the rebellious Army camps near Santo Domingo and with the Navy attacked the National Palace. The Navy fired a few shells into the city. Fighting in the capital spread swiftly.

On Monday morning, the U.S. Navy Ready Group stood 30 miles off the Dominican coast, out of sight. Gen. Elías Wessin y Wessin, leader of the anti-Bosch military, asked for United States troops to intervene. That would have been awkward. It would have put the United States in the posture of intervening to support an unpopular regime that had overthrown the constitutionally elected President Bosch. Washington instructed the embassy to stay neutral, obtain a ceasefire and begin evacuating U.S. citizens.

When efforts to negotiate a ceasefire failed on Tuesday, Wessin y Wessin led anti-Bosch military units into the capital. The Dominican Air Force rocketed and strafed the city. U.S. Ambassador W. Tapley Bennett, Jr., who had just returned to the island, refused to mediate and urged the pro-Bosch forces to surrender. He asked the U.S. Navy to make a show of force off Santo Domingo. A confused battle raged in the streets. Hundreds were killed and wounded in "the bloodiest single battle in Dominican history."[12]

Evacuation operations began Tuesday morning. American civilians and foreign nationals gathered at the large resort Hotel

El Embajador in the western suburbs near the sea and were moved by buses and trucks to Port Haina, six miles west of Santo Domingo. (In 1921, the Marines had established a camp at Haina to train officers for the Policia Nacional Dominicana. A graduate of its first class was Rafael Trujillo.)

Unarmed Marines were carried to Port Haina by helicopter to manage the evacuation when the high speed transport *Ruchamkin* and the tank landing ship *Wood County* reached the pier. The helicopter carrier *Boxer* and the amphibious transport dock ship *Raleigh* steamed off downtown Santo Domingo. Rapidly, 1,178 U.S. nationals were taken aboard the Navy ships.

By Tuesday night, it seemed that the crisis was over; and the anti-Bosch forces had won. But they failed to follow up their advantage against stubborn rebel resistance, and the tide turned. The pro-Bosch forces pushed back Wessin y Wessin's troops and tanks and consolidated their hold on most of downtown Santo Domingo. By Wednesday afternoon, the anti-Bosch forces clearly could not put down the revolt. Dominican Air Force Col. Pedro Benoit, who headed a new anti-Bosch junta, asked that U.S. Marines be landed.

Now, there was no concern about awkwardness. Asserting that the rebels were Communist-dominated, Ambassador Bennett supported Benoit's call and recommended that Marines be landed near the Hotel El Embajador, where more civilians had gathered. The Dominican police said they could not guarantee the evacuees' safety. Bennett asked the Navy to take them from the hotel by helicopter and to reinforce the Marine Guard of one noncom and six men at the embassy.

A Marine platoon promptly landed by helicopter on the embassy grounds and started shooting at pro-Bosch snipers. Unarmed Marine pathfinders, an unarmed rifle platoon and helicopter support teams landed on the polo field next to the Hotel El Embajador, followed by an armed platoon wearing body armor.

At 6 P.M., President Johnson authorized the landing of 500 Marines from *Boxer* to protect American lives. The Marines were not to fire unless fired upon. Although no Americans had been hurt, Johnson said, "Where American citizens go that flag goes with them to protect them."[13]

As soon as the order arrived from Washington at 6:53, Col.

George W. E. Daughtry, commanding the 6th Marine Expeditionary Unit, put ashore two rifle companies and his battalion headquarters by vertical envelopment. HMM-264 helicopters took in 536 fully armed Marines from *Boxer* and brought out 684 civilians from the hotel. By 11:30 P.M., the operation was completed without a casualty. *Raleigh,* which had rushed 200 evacuees to San Juan, Puerto Rico, was ordered back to Santo Domingo at best speed. She was prepared to land the remaining rifle company and supporting arms over the beach at Port Haina so that they could move down the main highway to join the Marines at the hotel.

On Thursday afternoon, Colonel Daughtry, who had commanded the 1st Battalion, 7th Marines in the fighting in west Korea, visited the embassy with Commodore James A. Dare, commander of the Ready Group. Sniper fire pinned them down in the building, and Marines returned the fire.

By now, President Johnson and his advisors were resolved to forestall the establishment of what they perceived as a pro-communist Bosch government. The Joint Chiefs of Staff ordered the rest of the Marines to land at Haina at 5:30 P.M. The LVTs, tanks and anti-tank Ontos joined the rest of the battalion an hour later. Fifteen hundred Marines were now ashore.

The 3rd Brigade of the U.S. Army's 82d Airborne Infantry Division began landing in C-130s at San Isidro Airfield, eight miles east of Santo Domingo, at 2:30 A.M. on Friday. Because the Dominicans did not man the control tower after dark, a naval aviator and two Marine officers rushed there by helicopter to turn on the lights and talk down the planes. The commanding general of the airborne division took charge of all U.S. ground forces ashore.

Lt. Col. Poul F. Pedersen, another Korean veteran, took the 3rd Battalion, 6th Marines eastward from the polo grounds into the city with its flank at an intersection designated Checkpoint Charlie. At 4 P.M. Friday, the left flank platoon advanced north along Avenida Presidente Rios to occupy Checkpoint Delta at the junction with Avenida San Martin. Several hundred yards up the street, the Marines were hit by small-arms and machine-gun fire from rebels holed up in a housing project west of Avenida Presidente Rios. In minutes, one Marine was killed and eight were wounded. Because the housing project was full of civilian families, the Marines could not use their recoilless rifle; but the riflemen swept through the area. Since darkness was approaching and the Marines were new to combat, the platoon was ordered to consolidate its position at Checkpoint Charlie and try to reach Checkpoint Delta at dawn.

Meanwhile, the paratroopers had advanced from the airfield on the eastern side of the city and fought the pro-Bosch rebels near the Duarte Bridge over the Ozama River. Four soldiers were wounded. The paratroopers established a bridgehead west of the river and occupied the electric power plant nearby, relieving the junta's soldiers there to move into the area between the two American forces according to plan. But the Dominican soldiers promptly left for the military base at the airfield, taking with them their tanks, half-tracks and artillery. "They made an impressive sight as they came into San Isidro. The only trouble was that they were headed in the wrong direction."[14] There were now no friendly troops between the Marines and U.S. Army soldiers. Both commanders called for more forces.

Fearing the spread of fighting between Americans and Dominicans, President Johnson ordered that a ceasefire be obtained through the OAS and the Papal Nuncio, even though the anti-junta forces still controlled downtown Santo Domingo. The Papal Nuncio arrived at the U.S. Embassy Friday afternoon when the building was under fire. He had to confer with Ambassador Bennett in the ambassador's bathroom. After a meeting at the junta's headquarters at San Isidro late that afternoon, a ceasefire was finally signed.

Early Saturday morning, May 1, the Marines tried to advance again from Checkpoint Charlie to link up with the Army. One Marine was killed and three were wounded by the rebels in the housing project. The Marines moved north up Avenida Presidente Rios and then east along Avenida San Martin. And a 200-man armored paratrooper force came westward, suffering two killed and two wounded. The two U.S. forces met at 12:45 on Avenida San Martin.

Ambassador Bennett, stressing that "Castro-like" elements had taken over the anti-junta movement,[15] urged that the American forces on both sides of the city be allowed to link up. But former Ambassador John Bartlow Martin, who had returned to the Dominican Republic as President Johnson's personal representative, met with the anti-junta forces and agreed that the U.S. Marines and soldiers would stay out of the city, except for an enlarged zone around the U.S. Embassy. Therefore, the anti-junta leaders protested against the meeting of the two forces on the Avenida San Martin; and at 3:45 P.M., they were ordered to return to their original positions.

The rebels also agreed to an International Safety Zone running west from Checkpoint Charlie around the polo grounds and to the sea. This arrangement left a gap between the U.S. Marines and soldiers.

Meanwhile, early Saturday morning, Lt. Gen. Bruce Palmer, Jr., USA, arrived from Washington to command the American forces. He had the stated mission to protect American lives and the unannounced mission to prevent a Communist takeover. He brought with him the 82d Airborne's 2d Brigade. That same day, the 1st Battalion, 6th Marines landed at the airport; and Brig. Gen. John G. Bouker arrived with the 4th Marine Expeditionary Brigade staff. There were now two Marine battalions and four Army battalions on hand.

On his arrival, Lt. Gen. Palmer told his military commanders that he did not recognize the ceasefire; and he warned Washington that, if American forces were not permitted to link up, there was a risk that the country would be taken over by the opposition. He wanted to establish an armed cordon through the center of the city to confine the pro-Bosch rebels and give the U.S. forces control of the city's key installations. Former Ambassador Martin strongly opposed moving American troops downtown, fearing that the killing of Dominicans by Americans would aid the Communists.

The link-up problem was solved on Sunday with the Washington decision to open a corridor connecting the American forces from the International Security Zone to the airport but detouring around the anti-junta stronghold in the center of Santo Domingo. A newly arrived OAS Special Committee approved the plan. It was executed right after midnight on Monday, May 3; and by 1:30 A.M., the link-up had been accomplished and the rebel forces were sealed off in the central city. Shortly afterwards, the Marine detachment from *Newport News* landed at Haina and occupied the University of Santo Domingo, where arms were reportedly hidden. The following day, the 1st

Battalions of both the 2d and 8th Marines and HMM-263 arrived. The buildup continued until 22,200 armed Americans were ashore and another 10,000 stood by off the coast. In good part, these unnecessary numbers resulted from overenthusiastic Army and Marine Corps rivalry. While the Dominicans continued to fight sporadically, the intervention settled into armed vigilance and political maneuvering. Sniping and brief skirmishes caused American casualties. Four Marines were killed and one was wounded in downtown Santo Domingo on May 6. Several Marines were hit at the embassy, but the two main objectives had been achieved: to "prevent a Communist takeover" and to avoid major fighting between Americans and Dominicans.

An Inter-American Peace Force was created with units from five Latin American countries; and on May 25, the first contingent of Brazilian troops arrived. President Johnson immediately ordered the withdrawal of 600 Marines; and by June 6, all the Marines had left. Among the approximately 6,000 who had served ashore, nine had been killed and 30 wounded.

On June 1, 1966, the Dominicans elected Balaguer president over Bosch. Johnson offered Balaguer his full support; and by the end of the summer, the international peace-keeping force, which consisted mainly of United States troops, was removed. Balaguer was re-elected four years later and again in 1974.

Fearing a "second Cuba," the United States had used its ready power to support a military faction opposed to the democratically elected Juan Bosch. But the time had passed when the United States could march into Latin America; the Marine-led intervention was widely condemned. Even America's friends called President Johnson's action imperialistic. What hope the United States had stirred in Latin America with the start in 1961 of the Alliance for Progress and what prestige it had gained in its handling of the 1962 Cuban missile crisis were converted, said a Council of Foreign Relations analyst, into "violent hostility. . . . The impetuosity of the original U.S. intervention had alienated practically the entire hemisphere but the studied moderation of subsequent U.S. policy had at least partially redeemed the initial adverse effects."[16] The most recent retired Marine Commandant, Gen. David Shoup, was highly critical of the size of the American reaction. He wrote, "Only a fraction of the force deployed was needed or justified. A small

1935-model Marine landing force could probably have handled the situation."[17]

But the fundamental objection was to the renewal of the American policy of intervention in a small nation's internal politics. Former Ambassador Martin called the intervention necessary but "illegal."[18] And Senator J. William Fulbright, chairman of the Senate Foreign Relations Committee, criticized it as "a unilateral military intervention in violation of inter-American law, the 'good neighbor' policy of thirty years' standing, and the spirit of the Charter of Punta del Este . . ."[19]

*Marines of E Company, 3rd Marines, hurl grenades as
they attack up a ridge near Vietnam's
demilitarized zone in 1968.
Staff Sgt. Shearer, USMC Photo*

SEMPER FIDELIS

VIII
THE
VIETNAM
WAR
1954-1975

1

The 11 Years to Da Nang

When the first men of the 3rd Battalion, 9th Marines hit the beach north of Da Nang on the morning of March 8, 1965, they were greeted with festivity. Giggling Vietnamese girls draped the Marines, including Brig. Gen. Frederick J. Karch, with garlands of red and yellow flowers.

But the welcome was deceptive. Before this was over, 14,691 Marines would die and 88,633 would be wounded in Indochina. This American attempt to gain a military foothold on the mainland of Asia would be the highwater mark of America's thrust across the Pacific.

The 9th Marines' Vietnam landing capped off a very long prologue. It had begun during World War II, when the U.S. Office of Special Services had helped Ho Chi Minh's guerrillas fight the Japanese; and Ho's Viet Minh had helped rescue downed American pilots and supply intelligence about Japanese military movements.

Ho Chi Minh's Indochinese Communist Party had formed the Viet Minh in 1941 as a national-front organization to fight both the Japanese and the French. The French had been the colonial power in Vietnam for most of a century, and Ho had joined the Communist Party in France in 1920 after failing to convince the post-World War I Versailles Conference to support self-determination for the peoples of Indochina.

During World War II, the Japanese let the pro-Vichy French manage rice-rich Vietnam for them. But by 1945, the French there had become increasingly pro-de Gaulle. The Japanese interned French civil servants and troops and governed Vietnam through Prince Bao Dai, who had been the front man for the French in central Vietnam before the war. After Japan surren-

[For the location of places in Indochina see map No. 10 in the map section.—*Au*.]

619

dered to the Allies, Bao Dai abdicated and Ho Chi Minh proclaimed Vietnam's independence as the Democratic Republic of Vietnam.

With the end of World War II, the British occupied southern Vietnam and Chiang Kai-shek's forces moved into the north. The British used Japanese soldiers to keep Saigon out of Viet Minh hands—as the Americans were doing against the Communists in North China—and rearmed 5,000 French troops. The French took over the Saigon government; and by the end of 1945, the British pulled out. In the north, the Chinese allowed Ho Chi Minh's government to remain in Hanoi; but early in 1946, Chiang Kai-shek agreed to withdraw in favor of the French. Ho made a deal with the French under which French troops would enter northern Vietnam and Paris would recognize Ho's regime as a free state within the French Union.

Ho had two goals: national liberation and the "modernization" of Vietnam. Tensions rose between the French and the Viet Minh. On November 23, 1946, a war began that climaxed with the defeat of the French at Dien Bien Phu in 1954.

United States interest in Vietnam started slowly and grew during the Cold War. The United States had repeatedly urged the French to move toward granting Vietnam its independence. But after the Communist victory in China in 1949 and Ho's recognition by Peking and Moscow, the United States recognized the regime of Bao Dai, whom the French had installed once again. With the outbreak of the Korean war in 1950, President Truman increased arms shipments to the French in Indochina. The containment of communism in Asia was American policy, and the French fight in Indochina was seen as a way to effect that policy. Vietnam became part of the Cold War. "Anticommunism preempted anticolonialism or pronationalism in importance."[1] By 1954, American aid was paying for 80 percent of the French war against the Viet Minh and running at more than $1 billion per year. In April, Lt. Col. Julius W. Ireland landed VMA-324 at Da Nang and turned over 25 dive bombers to the French.

That spring, the French lost most of the country to the Viet Minh and their Chinese instructors who had come south in greater numbers after the Korean armistice in 1953. Because the French did not send draftees overseas, they were short of soldiers. Less than half of those who defended Dien Bien Phu were French. The French asked for American intervention; one suggestion was that President Eisenhower send a division of Marines. After a major debate in Washington over how far the United States should go to prevent a French defeat in Indochina, the Eisenhower Administration finally decided not to send American troops or air or naval manpower to battle in Vietnam. The French position deteriorated.

Partly as a result of these events, the major powers held the Geneva Conference from April 26 to July 21, 1954. On May 7, after an eight-week battle, Dien Bien Phu near the Laotian border fell, despite the infusion of $10 million worth of U.S. equipment. The French weakness in Indochina was obvious. (At least one non-active-duty Marine, John Verdi, flew "Boxcar" missions over Dien Bien Phu.)

At Geneva, the Viet Minh agreed to evacuate the forces it had south of the 17th Parallel in return for nationwide elections in July 1956. Civilians could cross the 17th Parallel for 300 days after the armistice went into effect. An International Control Commission with representatives from Canada, India and Poland would oversee the agreements. Dismayed by the results of the conference, the United States refused to sign the agreements and wanted to insure that the southern, French-occupied portion of Vietnam would not also be lost to Ho Chi Minh's Communists. Secretary of State John Foster Dulles led in the formation of the Southeast Asia Treaty Organization (SEATO) to prevent the further spread of communism and try to fill the power vacuum in Southeast Asia.

At the time of the Geneva Agreements, the U.S. Military Assistance Advisory Group, commanded by Lt. Gen. John W. O'Daniel, USA, and based in Saigon, already had 342 men. In June 1954, an anti-insurgency team headed by Col. Edward G. Lansdale, USAF, a Central Intelligence Agency specialist, also arrived; at least one Marine officer, Capt. Richard Smith, became a member of this team. The United States also started to help train and build up the Vietnamese armed forces. In August, Lt. Col. Victor J. Croizat became the first U.S. Marine assigned to the MAAG. He helped create refugee centers and later became the senior U.S. advisor to the small Vietnamese Marine Corps, which had been formally organized in October 1954 to serve with the budding Vietnamese Navy's river and coastal forces. In working with the Vietnamese Marine Corps, Croizat was joined by Capt. James T. Breckinridge. He and Tech. Sgt. Jackson E. Tracy worked at Nha Trang as small-unit tactics instructors. By the end of the year, the Vietnamese Marine Corps, now at two-battalion strength, was better disciplined than most Vietnamese units. Croizat left Vietnam in 1956 and was succeeded by Lt. Col. William N. Wilkes, Jr.

Prime Minister Ngo Dinh Diem, a nationalist and Roman Catholic protégé of New York's Francis Cardinal Spellman, sought the departure of the French Expeditionary Corps from South Vietnam. And by 1955, Lt. Gen. O'Daniel had taken over the French responsibility for training and organizing the Vietnamese armed forces.

In October 1955, Diem held a referendum in the south, defeated Bao Dai and proclaimed the establishment of the Republic of Vietnam with himself as president. Diem refused to start the process toward the nationwide elections decreed by the Geneva Agreements. His power base was strengthened by large American military aid and the movement from the North of more than 800,000 Vietnamese, the great majority of them Catholics. Diem consolidated his rule by political arrests and "re-education," and South Vietnam became a repressive and corrupt police state.

Resistance mounted against Diem's rule and the American presence; and in late 1960, Hanoi's Communist government began to support the guerrillas in the south. At the year's end, the National Liberation Front of South Vietnam (loosely called the Viet Cong) was created to overthrow the Saigon government and get rid of the Americans. During the following year, the Viet Cong insurgency spread rapidly. The Viet Cong launched a campaign of terrorism, assassinating and kidnapping thousands of civilian leaders. President John F. Kennedy quietly sent 400 Special Forces soldiers and 100 more military advisors to South Vietnam.

The United States in 1962 built up the level of military aid and advisors and appointed Gen. Paul D. Harkins, USA, commander of the new U.S. Military Assistance Command, Vietnam (MACV). His chief of staff was Marine Maj. Gen. Richard G. Weede, who had commanded the 5th Marines in Korea. President Kennedy authorized U.S. advisors to return Viet Cong fire. Three U.S. Army transport helicopter companies arrived to give the Vietnamese army greater tactical mobility against the Viet Cong. The first Marines in the Vietnam buildup were 42 men of the 1st Radio Company, FMF, at Pleiku. In less than a year, U.S. helicopter crews were firing at insurgents and flying strafing missions. Vietnam was to be a helicopter war.

Among the early arrivals was a Marine helicopter squadron, which on Palm Sunday, April 15, 1962, set up near Soc Trang, an abandoned Japanese fighter airstrip in the Mekong Delta, 85 miles southwest of Saigon. This was Marine Medium Helicopter Squadron 362 (HMM-362) commanded by Lt. Col. Archie J. Clapp; it flew from *Princeton* into an area dominated by the Viet Cong. Vietnamese troops provided perimeter security. The Marine task unit, called "Shufly," consisted of about 450 Marines commanded by Col. John F. Carey. Its Sikorsky UH-34D helicopters carried supplies and troops to isolated or threatened Vietnamese villages and troop concentrations. Before being relieved by HMM-163 on August 1, HMM-362 flew 50 combat troop lifts involving 130 landings against Viet Cong opposition. On some missions as many as 24 helicopters participated. Seventeen of its choppers were damaged. On one such mission on May 9, eight of the 22 helicopters carrying Vietnamese soldiers were hit at least once. On July 18, the largest helicopter lift in Vietnam thus far took Vietnamese troops north of Saigon in 18 Marine helicopters, followed by 12 of the U.S. Army and 11 of the Vietnamese Air Force. Although HMM-362 suffered no Marine casualties during its tour, 109 Americans were killed or wounded in combat in Vietnam during 1962.

In September, HMM-163 moved to the air base at Da Nang, 380 miles north of Saigon. This was the Marines' operating area in contingency plans. On October 6, during a Vietnamese troop lift, five Marines and two Navy men from Marine Task Unit 79.5 were killed in a crash caused by mechanical failure. In April 1963, a 3rd Marine Division platoon was flown in from Okinawa to strengthen security at the Da Nang base. An air-ground team was formed. The addition of American helicopters to the guerrilla war substantially supported Diem and discouraged the Viet Cong—for the moment.

Meanwhile, the Soviet Union began aiding the Pathet Lao

army in Laos. In response, on May 17, 1962, the 3rd Marine Expeditionary Brigade began landing 3,000 men as part of Joint Task Force 116 at Bangkok, Thailand. They were flown 350 miles north to Udorn, which was 35 miles from Vientiane, Laos' political capital. The brigade was commanded by Brig. Gen. Ormond R. Simpson, assistant commander of the 3rd Marine Division, and included the 3rd Battalion, 9th Marines; HMR-261, and VMA-332. The Marines show-of-force was out of Thailand by August 7.

In Vietnam during the spring and summer of 1963, militant Buddhists rebelled against Diem's government. There were armed clashes, and seven Buddhist bonzes set themselves on fire to protest the regime's immorality. Mao Tse-tung announced his support of the Buddhists. As students rallied to the Buddhists' leadership, Diem's forces raided the pagodas and killed and jailed their bonzes; Diem closed the universities in Saigon and Hue and arrested thousands of students. The United States deplored Diem's actions and his failure to win popular support. On November 1, Vietnamese army officers, with American encouragement, executed a coup. They murdered Diem and his brutally powerful brother and set up a military junta headed by Gen. Duong Van Minh. Three weeks later, President Kennedy himself was assassinated (by a former Marine).

At this crucial juncture, the United States pledged support to General Minh and opposed efforts to neutralize South Vietnam. By now, the Viet Cong controlled much of the South Vietnamese countryside. The non-communist political forces in South Vietnam had been seriously weakened and fragmented by both the NLF and the Diem regime. When Minh was overthrown in a coup in January 1964, Gen. Nguyen Khanh, the commanding general of I Corps, took over the government in Saigon by force. The Vietnamese army held the capital but could make little progress against the Viet Cong. Saigon itself was political chaos. "Over the next months Saigon took on the pace and style of a Marx Brothers movie."[2]

In June, Lt. Gen. William C. Westmoreland replaced Harkins at MACV and Henry Cabot Lodge succeeded Gen. Maxwell Taylor as ambassador. And the United States announced it was sending 5,000 more men to South Vietnam.

On another level, during the first half of 1964, extensive

clandestine operations were carried out against North Vietnam. Marine Maj. Gen. Victor H. Krulak, the Pentagon's chief specialist on counterinsurgency warfare, played a leading role in planning these attacks. Air operations were also staged against North Vietnamese and Pathet Lao troops in Laos. And destroyer patrols were sent into the Gulf of Tonkin to collect intelligence information and exert pressure on North Vietnam.

The Republican Presidential nominee, Senator Barry Goldwater, and the Pentagon recommended greater U.S. involvement and carrying the war to North Vietnam. The Secretary General of the United Nations, French President Charles de Gaulle and the Soviet government all pressed for reconvening the Geneva Conference to find a neutralist non-military solution. In July, the United States announced that its military aid mission would be increased from 16,000 to 21,000 men. But President Lyndon B. Johnson promised American boys would not be sent to fight in Vietnam.

The issue was soon settled. North Vietnamese torpedo boats attacked the destroyer *Maddox* in the Gulf of Tonkin on the night of August 2, 1964. Two nights later, a second attack was reported against *Maddox* and *C. Turner Joy*. Hanoi denied the second attack had taken place. President Johnson ordered carrier air attacks against North Vietnamese torpedo boat bases, naval craft and a major oil storage depot. And at his instigation, the Congress passed overwhelmingly the Gulf of Tonkin Resolution authorizing the President to "take all necessary measures to repel any armed attack against the forces of the United States and to prevent further aggression." It allowed the President to use force to assist any SEATO country that asked for help.

The United States went into this war in force to stop Communism and to save the Vietnamese people. That was the rationale. As had Wilson, Roosevelt, Eisenhower and Kennedy before him, Lyndon Johnson "believed in the essential goodness of the United States and its almost infinite capacity for righting the wrongs of mankind."[3]

While American military intervention was vigorously debated in Washington, the political situation in Saigon grew more and more chaotic. Then, on February 7, 1965, the Viet Cong attacked the American compound at Pleiku, killing eight Americans and wounding at least 80. The United States retaliated by bombing North Vietnam—while Soviet Premier Alexei Kosygin was in Hanoi. And the Marines' 1st Light Anti-Aircraft Missile Battalion, equipped with Hawk surface-to-air missiles, began arriving by air at Da Nang.

Prolonged political infighting in Saigon resulted by mid-1965 in the coming to power of a group of younger officers led by Maj. Gen. Nguyen Van Thieu and Air Vice Marshal Nguyen Cao Ky (age thirty-four). But the NLF was steadily blanketing the countryside, and the South Vietnam Army (ARVN) was increasingly demoralized. On March 2, American bombers attacked North Vietnam "in the first nonretaliatory raid"[4] and began flying against North Vietnamese targets on a sustained basis. On March 8, the Marines landed to defend the American air base at Da Nang. The war on the Asian mainland was now openly American. Vietnam would become the Marines' longest war, and during it more Americans would serve in the Marine Corps than did during World War II. During World War II, approximately 600,000 men and women served in the Corps; and between 1965 and 1973, some 800,000 were Marines, of whom about 448,000 actually served in Vietnam.

2
"The Dirty War"—1965–1967

The Marines were the first Americans to be committed to the Vietnam war overtly as combat troops. They landed at Red Beach just north of Da Nang an hour late because the sea was rough; but by 9:18 A.M., Lt. Col. Charles E. McPartlin, Jr., had his battalion ashore. Lt. Col. Herbert J. Bain's 1st Battalion, 3rd Marines started to come in by air from Okinawa in Marine KC-130s; and by the end of March 12, all the Marines, including two batteries of the 12th Marines,* were on hand. The planes were attacked by Viet Cong small-arms fire.

Two Marine helicopter squadrons, HMM-162 and -163, were already operating out of Da Nang; and two Hawk batteries were also on the base. The newly arrived ground forces of Brig. Gen. Karch's 9th Marine Expeditionary Brigade were to provide close-in security for the airfield and defend the ridgeline west of the field. I Company, 9th Marines took over Hill 327, the dominant terrain feature, and K Company, Hill 268 to the north. The 3rd Marines stayed on the air base to protect against infiltrators and mortar attacks. Across the Cau Do River, a mile south of the field, the area was all Viet Cong territory, except for the thin ribbon along Highway One.

The Marines found themselves in the center of the I Corps Tactical Zone, the northernmost military region of South Vietnam. The I Corps Zone stretched from the North Vietnam border at the 17th Parallel, down a narrow strip of coast to a spur of the Annamite Mountains at Sa Huynh—north to south about 265 miles. The zone was only 30 to 70 miles wide. In it lived some 2.6 million people. Government troops held the sizable towns and the cities; but the Viet Cong controlled the countryside. To cope with them, the Zone contained

*The first artillery battery to land, Battery F, was commanded by Capt. Robert C. McFarlane, who from 1983 through 1985 served as National Security Advisor to President Ronald Reagan.

some 25,000 regular ARVN soldiers plus regional and militia forces.

The 5,000 Marines in the Da Nang area were strengthened on April 10 by Lt. Col. David A. Clement's 2d Battalion, 3rd Marines. One of its reinforced companies was sent by chopper 42 miles north to Phu Bai, eight miles below Hue, which was South Vietnam's ancient capital and third largest city. The company was relieved four days later by Lt. Col. Donald R. Jones' 3rd Battalion, 4th Marines from Hawaii.

The first Marine fixed-wing tactical aircraft, the F4B Phantom II jets of VMFA-531, arrived at Da Nang on April 10. Maj. Gen. William R. Collins, commanding general of the 3rd Marine Division, arrived in Da Nang in May. Maj. Gen. Paul J. Fontana established the 1st Marine Aircraft Wing's advanced headquarters at Da Nang. The Marines were redesignated the III Marine Amphibious Force.

As the Marine buildup sped rapidly ahead, Brig. Gen. Marion E. Carl, a leading Marine World War II ace, brought in a 6,000-man brigade with the 4th Marines. On May 7, it started landing at Chu Lai, a difficult stretch of beach 57 miles south of Da Nang. Lt. Gen. Krulak, now commander of the Fleet Marine Force, Pacific, had long recommended building a second jet air base there. The field was a radically new expeditionary Short Airfield for Tactical Support (SATS) with aluminum runway matting, arresting gear and later a catapult. On June 1, Seabees and Marine Engineers had the airstrip ready for MAG-12's Douglas A-4 Skyhawks.

By early June, Maj. Gen. Lewis W. Walt, the junior major general in the Corps, had taken over III MAF and the 3rd Marine Division, while Brig. Gen. Keith B. McCutcheon replaced Fontana as commanding general of the 1st MAW.

The Viet Cong ambushed an ARVN battalion near Ba Gia on May 30; only three American advisors and 65 of 400 Vietnamese soldiers broke through. Marine helicopters and VMFA-531 went to their aid, but requests for support from a Marine battalion were not acted on in time.

The Viet Cong was displaying new strength; and by the first week in June, the Marines had suffered 208 casualties, with 29 killed in action. Clearly, the Marines—and the Army's 173rd Airborne Brigade at Bien Hoa near Saigon—were in the war to fight. The policy of simply "advising" the South Vietnamese army and securing coastal bases had failed. Commandant Wallace M. Greene, Jr., had visited Da Nang and told the press that the Marines were in Vietnam to "kill Viet Cong."[5]

There were now 51,000 U.S. servicemen in Vietnam, including 16,500 Marines. The Americans' job had been to secure the major bases and free the South Vietnamese to carry the fight to the enemy. But even with this help, the war was going badly. On June 26, General Westmoreland received authority to commit his American forces to battle when he decided they were needed.

At 1:30 A.M. on July 1, an 85-man enemy demolition force infiltrated the Da Nang airfield and destroyed three planes and damaged three more. The raiders killed one Air Force airman and wounded three Marines. As a result, the Marines extended their area of responsibility to the heavily populated areas south and east of the field; and the 2d Battalion, 9th Marines arrived to guard the area to the south.

On July 12, 1st Lt. Frank S. Reasoner of Kellogg, Idaho, and A Company of the 3rd Reconnaissance Battalion became the first Marine whose courage earned the Medal of Honor in Vietnam. His reconnaissance patrol was ambushed deep in Viet Cong territory. Enemy machine-gun and automatic weapons fire struck Reasoner and five men on the point and isolated them from the rest of the patrol. One of his men was hit; Reasoner killed two Viet Cong and silenced an automatic weapons position in an effort to evacuate the wounded Marine. He organized a base of fire. Casualties mounted. Reasoner's radio operator was hit and tried to reach a protected spot; he was hit again. Reasoner raced through machine-gun fire to help him and was mortally wounded.

The Marines established a fourth but temporary coastal enclave to the south in the II Corps Tactical Zone when a battalion of the 7th Marines went ashore at Qhi Nhon, 175 miles below Da Nang, to secure the beach for the 1st Cavalry Division and support the Pleiku–Kontum area inland to the northwest.

By the end of July, the decision was made in Washington to send the 1st Cavalry Division to Vietnam and to increase the U.S. military presence there from 75,000 to 125,000 men. The authorized strength of the Marine Corps was increased in August from 193,000 to 223,000 men. And a decision was made not to call up the American armed forces' reserves. Instead, voluntary enlistments were stepped up and the draft was doubled from 17,000 to 35,000 a month. That crucial decision would intensify opposition to the war in the United States during the years ahead.

By mid-August, the Marines had four regiments and four air groups in Vietnam.* The 3rd and 9th Marines were in the Da Nang area. The 3rd Battalion, 4th Marines was at Phu Bai. The rest of the 4th Marines; the 3rd Battalion, 3rd Marines, and 1st Battalion, 7th Marines were at Chu Lai. The 2d Battalion, 7th Marines was at Qui Nhon under Army control. Among Marine air units, MAG-16 and MAG-11 were at Da Nang, with one helicopter squadron at Phu Bai. MAG-12 was at Chu Lai and MAG-36 would arrive there on September 1. One MAG-36 helicopter squadron went to Qui Nhon.

On August 18, the Marines launched Operation Starlite, their first offensive operation. Col. Oscar F. Peatross led three battalions out of Chu Lai against the 1st Viet Cong Regiment on the Van Tuong Peninsula, 15 miles south of the Chu Lai airstrip. One company in LVTs crossed a river from the north; a battalion landed by helicopter on the west, and a battalion in amphibian tractors attacked the southeastern beach.

That day, two Marines earned the Medal of Honor. New York City-born Cpl. Robert E. O'Malley of I Company, 3rd Marines led his squad against the strongly entrenched enemy. He raced across a rice paddy, jumped into a trench and with his rifle and grenades killed eight Viet Cong. Then he led his squad to help a neighboring unit that was taking heavy casualties. Though wounded three times, he covered the evacuation of his squad's wounded by helicopter. Lance Cpl. Joe C. Paul, a native of Williamsburg, Kentucky, fought with H Company, 4th Marines near Nam Yen. When five of his platoon were wounded, Paul rushed forward, placed himself between them and the enemy and fired his automatic weapon to divert the enemy attack and allow the casualties to be evacuated. He was mortally wounded but continued firing until he collapsed.

*The Marines were involved in their first charges of atrocities in Vietnam on August 3 when men of the 1st Battalion, 9th Marines destroyed most of the houses in the village of Cam Ne, six miles southwest of Da Nang. CBS television pictures of a Marine burning one house with a cigarette lighter and Morley Safer's report horrified Americans back home. Keyes Beech of the *Chicago Daily News* reported that Marines "have killed or wounded Vietnamese civilians and burned dozens of homes in the dirtiest war Americans ever had to fight."

*Marine patrol struggles through rice paddy near Gio
Linh on March 25, 1967.*
UPI Photo

*In Hue, Marines battle North Vietnamese during the
1968 Tet offensive.
Kyoichi Sawada, UPI Photo*

*Marine carries wounded buddy to
evacuation helicopter near Khe Sanh.
Kyoichi Sawada, UPI Photo*

Exhausted Marines find momentary refuge in church at An Hoa during enemy mortar attack in 1967.
Frank Johnston, UPI Photo

Under intense enemy fire, Marines advance to recapture the Citadel in Hue after the North Vietnamese 1968 Tet offensive.
Kyoichi Sawada, UPI Photo

Tank brings out bodies of dead Marines killed in hand-to-hand combat with North Vietnamese north of Con Thien in July 1967.
Dana Stone, UPI Photo

Marines hurry refugees aboard helicopter on American Embassy parking lot just before the 1975 fall of Saigon. Nik Wheeler, Sipa-Liaison

On April 12, 1975, helicopters of HMH-463 come in to extract Marines and last U.S. civilians from soccer field near Phnom Penh's U.S. Embassy. Gunnery Sgt. Donnie Shearer, USMC Photo

Marines board the deserted container ship Mayaguez from the destroyer escort Harold E. Holt in futile attempt to rescue Americans captured by Cambodians on May 12, 1975. Official U.S. Navy Photo

Navy surgeons at Marine First Medical Battalion field
hospital near Da Nang start working to save the life of
Cpl. Andre A. Williams, who was shot in the chest by a
Viet Cong while on night patrol. The doctors' swift,
expert skill kept Corporal Williams off the list of 14,691
Marines killed in Indochina and among the 88,633
wounded Marines who survived.
James Hansen, Look Collection, the Library of
Congress. Copyright © Cowles Communications, Inc.,
1967. With permission of Andre A. Williams

*Body bags with fallen Marines are lifted aboard
a helicopter during the battle for Khe Sanh. Over 200
years, 41,411 Marines have been killed at action
in their nation's wars.
David Douglas Duncan; courtesy Museums Branch,
USMC*

The Viet Cong had entrenched themselves with their backs to the sea and fought tenaciously in close combat. But the Marines' firepower was too strong. Despite the enemy's rocket launchers, mortars and automatic weapons, they were cornered; few surrendered. By August 24, 45 Marines and 614 Viet Cong were reported killed. The enemy fled inland from the coastal peninsula, and the Marines' initial effort was less than a total success.

This operation was followed on September 7 by Operation Piranha on the Batangan Peninsula, eight miles south. This time, results by the 7th Marines "were not so spectacular."[6]

Meanwhile, on August 5, the Viet Cong attacked the Esso storage terminal on the Hai Van Peninsula across the bay from Da Nang. The peninsula was defended only by two under-strength Vietnamese Regional Force companies. The raiders destroyed nearly two million gallons of fuel.

Marines, Navy and Seabees built up China Beach on the South China Sea east of Da Nang. This eight-mile oceanfront was bounded by 2,000-foot-high Monkey Mountain to the north and Marble Mountain to the south. On October 27, 47 Viet Cong raiders attacked China Beach by boat. A handful got through and destroyed 19 helicopters and damaged 35 more and wrecked the nearly completed naval hospital across the road. Three Americans were killed and 91 wounded. At that same time, 20 Viet Cong attacked the airstrip at Chu Lai and destroyed two and damaged six of MAG-12's A-4s with satchel charges.*

On November 10, United States and Vietnamese Marine units for the first time participated in a combined amphibious operation. They landed at Tam Ky, between Chu Lai and Da Nang, and swept the area but met no opposition. Six days later, the 3rd Battalion, 3rd Marines, loaded out from Chu Lai and landed south of Hoi An, the capital of Quang Nam province. This area was controlled by Viet Cong, and the three-day operation killed 25 and captured 15. That same rain-swept night, the 1st Viet Cong Regiment, supposedly destroyed in Operation Starlite, overran the district capital of Hiep Duc, in the narrow Que Son valley 25 miles west of Tam Ky. MAG-16 and -36, airlifting in 788 ARVN troops, encountered heavy antiaircraft machine-gun fire; 21 of the 30 helicopters were hit. With air cover support by MAG-11 and -12, Hiep Duc was retaken; but because of the

*On November 4 near Chu Lai, correspondent Dickey Chapelle was killed by a booby trap while accompanying a Marine patrol.

637

frustrating shortage of ARVN troops was later abandoned. This was now the period of the northeast monsoon with rains averaging an inch per day; the Viet Cong attacked isolated garrisons and outposts and ambushed units coming to the rescue. It was classic guerrilla warfare, striking weak spots and keeping regular forces on the move. The Viet Cong would not risk a stand-up battle.

The enemy ran into trouble when they attacked Thach Tru on Highway One on November 22. They met a Vietnamese Ranger battalion supported by gunfire from two U.S. destroyers and by Marine aircraft. The 3rd Battalion, 7th Marines was brought in by helicopter and the next day attacked to the west. It was later determined that the enemy force was not Viet Cong but the 18th Regiment of the North Vietnamese army, the PAVN.

The 3rd Marines had already begun a "pacification" program intended to liberate hamlets and villages from Viet Cong domination, provide them with security and encourage the acceptance of government control. The first such Marine effort was at the hamlet of Le My, eight miles northwest of the Da Nang air base; it became a Marine civic action showplace. The program worked well enough in thinly populated areas but was less successful in the 9th Marines' densely populated zone south of the air base, where the Viet Cong were stronger.

The Marines also undertook small-unit patrolling and night ambushes to protect the rice harvest from the Viet Cong and tried to extend the pacification program to the south. Its success depended on the Popular Forces militia to provide the villages with security, but these troops proved inadequate to the job. As a result, the Marines called on their Caribbean experience and a bit of the British model in Malaya. Combined Action Companies were created with a Marine squad and a Navy corpsman assigned to work with each Popular Forces platoon. The first of these units was established at Phu Bai by the 3rd Battalion, 4th Marines—partly as an expedient way to stretch the thinly spread battalion there. The Marines assigned received some training in counterinsurgency techniques as well as the Vietnamese language and history. By January 1966, a second Combined Action Company was formed at Da Nang under Lt. Col. William W. Taylor, who had organized the original company at Phu Bai under 1st Lt. Paul R. Ek. The concept offered the possibility of effective civic action and eventually grew to a regiment-sized force.

Operation Harvest Moon, which began on December 8, was supposed to attack Viet Cong units that had moved into the Que Son valley and harassed garrisons north of Hiep Duc. The enemy destroyed two ARVN battalions that came into the valley from Highway One. Two Marine battalions were "helilifted" in; and on December 10, a third battalion, flown in against heavy opposition, landed between the two Marine battalions. This Task Force Delta was first commanded by Brig. Gen. Melvin D. Henderson until he was relieved by Brig. Gen. Jonas M. Platt. B-52s made their first four strikes in support of Marine ground forces. By December 16, the Viet Cong had faded away. But Lt. Col. Leon N. Utter's 2d Battalion, 7th Marines was ambushed at Ky Phu and accounted for 105 enemy dead before it reached Highway One. Capt. Harvey C. Barnum, Jr., of Waterbury, Connecticut, won the Medal of Honor when, making a hazardous reconnaissance, he found the commander of H Company, 9th Marines mortally wounded and his radio operator dead. Barnum strapped on the radio, took charge of the decimated company under heavy fire and led it against the enemy. The Marines had 45 killed and 218 wounded. Harvest Moon was a failure. Since the Da Nang landing, U.S. Marine casualties totaled 454 dead and 2,093 wounded at year's end.

At the beginning of 1966, 180,000 American troops were in South Vietnam, including 38,000 Marines. There were brief periods of truce over Christmas and during the Vietnamese holiday of Tet in mid-January. President Johnson halted the bombing of North Vietnam from December 24 to January 31, 1966, and tried to begin peace talks. Early in February, he met in Honolulu with Thieu and Ky to restate their common war aims.

The rest of the 1st Marine Division was ordered to Vietnam to occupy the two southern provinces of I Corps. This actually meant that the remainder of the 1st Marines and all of the 5th Marines would join Maj. Gen. Walt's forces by the end of June.

Once the Tet holiday was over, a major offensive was planned against the 325A PAVN Division in the area between I Corps and II Corps at the southern end of the Marines' zone. The 3rd Battalion, 1st Marines and 2d Battalion, 4th Marines landed near Thach Tru on January 28 in the largest amphibious operation of the war until that time. And the next day, the 2d Battalion, 3rd Marines was flown in by helicopter five miles west of the landing beaches. On D plus 4, the 2d Battalion, 9th

Marines was brought into the mountains northwest of the beaches. But most of the North Vietnamese had moved south into Binh Dinh province, where they were attacked by the 1st Air Cavalry Division and II Corps troops. The operation went on until March 1 but resulted in little action for the Marines.

In an effort to make the civic action program work, Col. Edwin H. Simmons' 9th Marines tried out a new technique called County Fair south of Da Nang. Combined units of Vietnamese and Marines sealed off a hamlet, searched it and checked identity cards to try to spot the Viet Cong guerrilla cell left in the community. It was hoped that if the Viet Cong infrastructure were eliminated, pacification would succeed. The process was made more palatable by giving the villagers medical help, setting up a community kitchen and providing entertainment while the hamlet was searched. Arms caches, propaganda materials and Viet Cong themselves were uncovered.

February and March saw the Marines engaged in some hard fighting. On the night of February 27, the 2d Battalion, 1st Marines went to the rescue of an ARVN regiment northeast of Phu Bai in the north and attacked well-prepared Viet Cong positions. On March 4, Marine helicopters lifted an ARVN battalion to a battle near Quang Ngai city; and the 2d Battalion, 7th Marines followed it into the fight. Three more Marine battalions were thrown into the action by the next day. The Marines and ARVN reportedly destroyed a third of the 36th PAVN Regiment. On March 9, the Special Forces camp at A Shau near the Laotian border was wiped out in a vicious two-day fight. Marine and Air Force pilots flew close support, resupply and medical evacuation missions. The Marines lost three helicopters and one A-4C. "There was no saving the camp. On 11 March evacuation began. There was panic among the irregulars. Some tried to rush the helicopters, had to be cut down by U.S. Green Berets and Marine crewmen."[7] Twelve of the 17 Green Berets and 172 of the 400-man Vietnamese garrison were finally lifted out. On March 20, the 3rd Battalion, 7th Marines and 2d Battalion, 4th Marines were flown in to help an ARVN battalion under attack at An Hoa; and in four days of heavy fighting, 405 Viet Cong were killed. Before March was over, the 1st Battalion, 7th Marines had to help out an ARVN battalion northwest of Quang Ngai city. The war had heated up for the Marines.

By now the 1st Marine Division under Maj. Gen. Lewis J. Fields was based in Chu Lai. Walt, now a lieutenant general, retained command of III MAF and turned over the 3rd Marine Division at Da Nang to Maj. Gen. Wood B. Kyle.

Emboldened by President Johnson's support at Honolulu, Prime Minister Ky on March 10, 1966, fired his I Corps commander, Gen. Nguyen Chanh Thi, an able rival for power, and triggered a major crisis throughout South Vietnam. Buddhists, students and workers demonstrated against the Saigon junta. They called for national elections in the South and an end to the war. Da Nang, Hue and Hoi An were all rocked by riots and disruption. The port of Da Nang was closed down entirely. Thousands of Vietnamese vented their stifled anger against the military, the Americans and the suffering they were forced to endure. In Saigon, mobs burned American vehicles. In Hue, the Buddhist-student "struggle movement" seized the radio station and closed the university. The 1st ARVN Division demonstrated against the government. In Da Nang, a general strike was staged; and the mayor joined the opposition to the Saigon regime. Americans feared the downfall of South Vietnam's military government.

Ky declared Da Nang an enemy-held city; and to liberate it, on April 5, he brought 1,500 Vietnamese marines and two companies of National Police in American-piloted transport planes. The American commander closed the air base's gates to prevent bloodshed, and Ky flew back to Saigon weaker than ever. American noncombatants were evacuated from Da Nang and Hue by Marine helicopters. F Company, 9th Marines blocked an anti-Ky military force marching on Da Nang. The Buddhists controlled central Vietnam, and President Thieu agreed to hold elections for a constitutional assembly and to transfer power to the civilians. The American policy of supporting the stability of the military regime was for the moment totally undermined.

On May 15, Ky struck back. He airlifted a thousand Vietnamese marines into Da Nang and seized the city's key installations in a week of confused fighting. In Saigon, 50,000 workers struck in protest. Vietnamese troops fired shells at the Da Nang air base where Ky's marines were stationed.[8]

Lt. Gen. Walt himself had to go to the Tourane River bridge, east of Da Nang, where Vietnamese Army engineers had armed the bridge and an ammunition dump with high explosives. When Walt arrived with his G-3, Col. John R. Chaisson, a Marine platoon was facing the Vietnamese. While a very angry Walt met the Vietnamese warrant officer in the middle of the bridge, the U.S. Army advisor to the Vietnamese troops and a couple of Marines sneaked under the bridge to try to cut the wires between the detonator and the explosives. The Vietnamese officer refused to pull back his men and threatened to blow the bridge if the Marines advanced. When the Army advisor gave Walt a thumbs-up signal, the general warned the Vietnamese he had five minutes to remove his men and disconnect the detonator. He refused. Time ran out. Walt told the Marines—now built up to a company—to cross the bridge. The Vietnamese ordered the detonator's plunger pushed down. But nothing happened. Walt walked off the bridge and the Marines took over.[9]

Ky's troops invaded the Buddhist pagodas and created hundreds of casualties. Vietnamese aircraft rose to bomb Da Nang, and Walt sent up Marine jets to shoot them down if they attacked the city. The Vietnamese pilots backed down. Ky's forces than lay siege to Hue, where, on May 26, workers and students destroyed the USIS library. Nine Buddhist bonzes and nuns burned themselves to death across the country. On May 31, the United States consulate at Hue was sacked and burned. The Americans deserted Hue. By mid-June, Hue surrendered to Ky's army. The Buddhist "struggle movement" was crushed. The Ky junta remained in power, as the Americans desired and made possible.

During this same period, the 3rd Marine Division pressed southward from Da Nang in a series of "search and clear" operations, cordoning off areas and attempting to eradicate the guerrillas. Five Marine battalions fought the Viet Cong's skillful Doc Lap Battalion. After three months, the Marines had opened Highway One as far south as An Hoa.

Deep in enemy territory, 25 miles west of Chu Lai, Staff Sgt. Jimmie E. Howard, a former Marine football player and coach at San Diego, commanded the 18-man 1st Platoon of C Company, 1st Reconnaissance Battalion. The tall, big sergeant from Burlington, Iowa, had earned the Silver Star and three Purple Hearts in Korea. His job now was to hold an observation post atop grass-covered Hill 488 and spot enemy troops trying to descend out of the hills to the coast.

At 10 P.M. on June 15, the platoon's third night on Hill 488, it was attacked by a North Vietnamese battalion. Lance Cpl. Ricardo Binns' four-man observation team out front was hit first. Binns shot the nearest enemy soldier; each Marine flung a grenade, and they scrambled to the crest. Lance Cpl. John T. Adams of Portland, Oregon, emptied his rifle at the enemy and using it as a club killed two more before he was shot to death. Cpl. Jerrald R. Thompson of Palmer, California, was wounded by a grenade; he killed two North Vietnamese with his knife before he died.

The 16 remaining Marines formed a tight perimeter and threw back assault after assault. Howard directed their defense. A grenade wounded him severely; he could no longer move his legs. He distributed his ammunition to the other men, maintained radio communication and called in artillery fire and air strikes. The enemy taunted them: "Marines, you die!" Flares lighting the bare mountainside revealed hordes of the enemy. The planes worked them over, bombing and strafing. The Marines used up their grenades. They squeezed off single shots and threw back rocks.

By dawn, five of Howard's men were dead and all the rest but one were wounded. Corpsman Billie D. Holmes, badly hurt himself, cared for the wounded. The Marines held.

When evacuation helicopters approached, Howard coolly waved them off and called for more air strikes to secure the landing zone.

Maj. William J. Goodsell brought his helicopter in 10 feet off the ground. It was hit, and Goodsell died of gunshot wounds. A second chopper was hit; its crew chief was killed. Helicopters finally brought in 1st Lt. Marshall Darling's C Company, 5th Marines onto the southern slope. The Marines climbed rapidly, wiping out enemy positions as they went. When they reached Howard's position, his men had eight rounds of ammunition left. The battle went on. Four more Marines were killed, including 2d Lt. Ronald Meyer, just a year out of Annapolis. Darling and Lance Cpl. James Brown crawled out and carried in Meyer's body under fire. By noon it was over. Binns and Holmes were recommended for the Navy Cross. Howard received the Medal of Honor for saving his platoon from annihilation.[10]

In June up north, North Vietnamese units crossed the Demilitarized Zone (DMZ) to support the Viet Cong. The

Marines responded by building up to five-battalion strength. Task Force Delta, commanded by Brig. Gen. Lowell E. English and including some 8,000 Marines and 3,000 South Vietnamese, did battle with the 324B North Vietnamese Division (while other enemy units attacked Pleiku and Saigon). Operation Hastings opened on July 15 in the vicinity of Cam Lo on the east-west Route 9 below the DMZ and at a 700-foot hill called the "Rock Pile." Three battalions attacked north of the enemy and the others hit them from the south.

On July 18, two Marines with K Company, 4th Marines earned the Medal of Honor. The company had been put down to block an enemy jungle trail network on July 15 and was immediately attacked. Capt. Robert J. Modrzejewski of Milwaukee led his men to capture an enemy strongpoint and then fought off a series of counterattacks over the next three days. The surrounded company was assaulted by a regiment-size enemy force on the eighteenth. Although wounded, Modrzejewski led the defense and brought in air and artillery strikes at close range. When the 3rd Battalion was ready to withdraw, rear security was assigned to a platoon of 32 Marines led by Staff Sgt. John J. McGinty III of Boston. They held off the enemy for four hours. When two squads were isolated, McGinty charged through heavy fire and found 20 men wounded and the corpsman killed. He reloaded weapons and magazines for the wounded and directed their fire. He was wounded but led his men in driving off their attackers. The enemy tried to flank the Marines, and McGinty killed five with his pistol and brought in supporting fire within 50 yards of his position, finally routing the enemy.

In another scrap on a narrow jungle trail near the DMZ on July 24, I Company, 5th Marines was ambushed and its lead platoon hard hit. Lance Cpl. Richard A. Pittman of San Joaquin, California, with the second platoon in line, heard the lead unit's cries for help, dropped his rifle, took a machine gun and several belts of ammunition and rushed forward. Coming under fire, Pittman silenced it with his gun. Two automatic weapons opened on him, and he destroyed them both. He kept going 50 yards further up the trail until he reached the spot where the leading Marines had fallen wounded. Attacked by 30 or 40 of the enemy, Pittman braced himself in the middle of the trail and raked them with machine-gun fire. When his gun jammed, he picked up an enemy submachine gun and then another Marine's pistol and forced the enemy to flee. Out of ammunition, he hurled a final grenade at them and rejoined his platoon. He was awarded the Medal of Honor.

When the enemy started pulling out and Operation Hastings ended on August 3, the Marines had killed 824 of the enemy. But the North Vietnamese had succeeded in pulling substantial numbers of Marines and ARVN soldiers to the north and away from protecting the population centers.

Four miles below the DMZ near Cam Lo on August 8, a reconnaissance patrol flushed a large enemy unit. A platoon of E Company, 4th Marines was flown in to go after it. But the search was futile. The enemy remained hidden until the helicopters returned just before dark to recover the platoon. When most of the Marines had been lifted out, the enemy opened fire. They damaged two choppers, stranding 21 Marines. Back at Dong Ha, E Company's commander, New York City-born Capt. Howard V. Lee heard the radio messages from his trapped men. He took seven Marines and all the ammunition they could manage in two light choppers and raced out to the encircled perimeter. Lee took command. The enemy attacked in full force. A grenade wounded Captain Lee in the body and eye, but he continued in command throughout the embattled night. Another chopper flew in with more ammunition. It was hit and its crew picked up rifles and joined the fight. The 20 remaining Marines fought on through the night against repeated attacks until they were rescued the next morning.[11]

Soon, the North Vietnamese 324B Division struck again in the same area between Route 9 and the DMZ. Three Marine battalions met them. Maj. Gen. Kyle moved his advance 3rd Division command post to Dong Ha, where Route 9 and Highway One intersect. Operation Prairie I continued until the end of January 1967 and involved seven Marine battalions and three ARVN battalions. The Marines had 225 killed and 1,159 wounded.

Down in Quang Tin province six miles west of Tam Ky, two days after Captain Lee's fight, the 1st Battalion, 5th Marines fought a tough battle against well-entrenched North Vietnamese. Lt. Col. Hal L. Coffman's battalion was sweeping the area as part of Operation Colorado. At about 3 P.M., it was ambushed by a large enemy force in the hamlet of Cam Khe. Capt. James Furleigh's A Company was met by heavy fire from a tree line and had to pull back through the fire-swept paddies. Five Marines were immediately killed. The enemy had fire superiority. Heavy rain made it impossible to call in supporting arms. Lance Cpl. R. P. Donathan tried to knock out the machine gun that had stopped the company, and was killed. Corpsman T. C. Long, who went to his rescue, was hit in the right knee and trapped under Donathan's body. The other Marines could not get to them. Coffman sent in 1st Lt. Darling's C Company on Furleigh's right flank. The enemy tried slipping around the Marines' left, and Furleigh had Staff Sgt. Albert J. Ellis bring up the 3rd Platoon there. The skill of the Marine riflemen was pitted against the enemy superiority in numbers and firepower. Pfc. George Fudge, a deadly sharpshooter, picked off at least ten North Vietnamese and knocked out a machine gun with a grenade. Lance Cpl. Robert Goodner destroyed two automatic weapons with his 66mm rocket launcher (LAAW). But Ellis' platoon needed help to prevent the enemy from turning the flank.

Coffman sent B Company there. It came under fire from the enemy holding a trench to its front. A 60mm mortar zeroed in on the company command post until Sgt. Peter Rowell's mortar silenced the enemy weapon. The rain continued, but the ceiling had risen enough to let four medical evacuation helicopters come in. Two of the H-34s were shot down. In the third, 1st Lt. Ellis Laitala made ten trips bringing in ammunition and medical supplies and taking out the wounded. Capt. Robert J. Sheehan flew the fourth chopper spectacularly; he made nine trips and his chopper was hit three times, while flying out 20 casualties. As the weather cleared, Marine A4D jets roared in with 2,000-pound bombs.

On the far right, Darling's C Company had the toughest part of the fight. It had to dig the enemy out of a long, deep trench near the road. Darling put his 2d and 3rd Platoons on a firing line and sent the 37 men of Lt. Arthur Blades' 1st Platoon to assault the enemy. In the 3rd Squad on the platoon's right nearest the trench line, all six of its men were hit, three of them killed. Responding to Blades' call for help, Darling sent forward a group of Marines and a machine-gun crew. His executive officer, 1st Lt. Ron Benigo, was hit in the back of the head while carrying a wounded Marine from the paddy but brought out two more men before he was forcibly evacuated.

Blades placed his reinforcements on his left flank and freed his remaining two squads to attack the trench line with automatic-weapons fire and grenades. Four of the six Marines in the 2d Squad were hit and a corpsman rushing up to help them was killed. Blades led his last squad forward. Its leader, Cpl. Christopher Cushman, stood up to spot a sniper. Lance Cpl. Walter McDonald, a combat photographer, shot the sniper and dropped a grenade on another enemy soldier in the trench.

The enemy now began to fall back before the Marines' onslaught. Three engineers with the platoon worked their way up the trench itself to press the enemy from the rear while Blades' Marines attacked their front. Blades kept his men moving forward, firing and hurling grenades. Finally, the enemy broke and ran; Cushman shot one and McDonald two more. The rest died in a blaze of grenades and automatic rifle fire. K Company, 5th Marines was flown in, but the main battle was over.

The next morning, Commandant Greene and Lt. Gen. Walt arrived in a chopper and walked the trench line. Greene asked 1st Lt. Darling what had happened. "Well, General, we got into a fight with the enemy," Darling said. The Commandant asked what he did. "General," he said, "we killed them."[12]

That night, enemy 82mm mortars bombarded the battalion command center; and the enemy assaulted the battalion perimeter. B Company threw them back with a wall of fire.

In fiscal 1966, the Marine Corps took in 80,000 volunteers and nearly 19,000 draftees. It was authorized to reach a strength of 278,184 by July 1, 1967; its peak during the Korean war had been 261,343. As a result of these increases, elements of the 5th Marine Division, which included the 26th, 27th and 28th Marines with the 13th Marines as artillery, began arriving in Vietnam. Its first commander was Maj. Gen. Robert E. Cushman, Jr. A native of St. Paul, Minnesota, and an Annapolis graduate, Cushman had won the Navy Cross on Guam and spent four years on the staff of Vice President Richard M. Nixon.

The South Vietnamese election for a constituent assembly to draft a new constitution was held on September 11, 1966. All communists and neutralists were barred from running; the Buddhists boycotted the elections. The following month in Australia, President Johnson declared, "I believe there is a light at the end of what has been a long and lonely tunnel."[13] He was using the same figure of speech as had French Lt. Gen. Henri Navarre before the battle of Dien Bien Phu.[14]

By now, there were 60,000 Marines in South Vietnam. They claimed 7,300 enemy killed. The Marines had suffered 1,700 dead and more than 9,000 wounded. The Marines' area of responsibility covered 1,800 square miles and nearly a million people. In contrast to the U.S. Army's primary policy of "search and destroy," the Marines were believers in "clear and hold" tactics that would pacify the hamlets and eradicate Viet Cong control. Said Lt. Gen. Walt, "It is slow because you are changing minds. That takes time."[15]

The war effort required enormous resources. There were now nearly 400,000 Americans in Vietnam, and the war was costing the American taxpayer $2 billion a month. American forces tackled the enemy's main forces and killed many of their troops, but the countryside seemed impenetrable. Most ARVN soldiers lacked the will or discipline to risk their lives either to defend the American shored-up government in Saigon or to oppose the Communists. The Saigon politicians went through the American-prodded motions of writing a constitution and holding national elections. When the presidential election was finally held in September 1967, the military ticket of Thieu and Ky predictably won. But it was surprisingly close. The runner-up was an unknown politician who declared he wanted to recognize the NLF and start peace negotiations. The election was "a fiasco of noble proportions."[16] President Thieu promptly put a number of the defeated candidates in jail, including the runner-up.

The war itself seemed to run on a treadmill. Soon there would be half a million American troops in Vietnam. Counting Vietnamese, Koreans and others, Thieu's side had 1.3 million men in uniform. They attacked enemy bases in the south and fought a series of battles with North Vietnamese troops in the Central Highlands and near the DMZ. Hundreds of Americans and thousands of Vietnamese died. It all seemed to make no progress, no difference—except that the fighting created uncounted hundreds of thousands of homeless refugees, whose villages had been destroyed and their crops killed with herbicides. The cities, bulging with American goods and dollars, were wracked by horrendous inflation and flagrant corruption—and hatred of the foreign invaders.

In mid-October 1966, Secretary of Defense Robert S. McNamara returned from Vietnam and gave President Johnson a highly pessimistic report. He said in part: "There is no sign of an impending break in enemy morale and it appears that he can more than replace his losses. . . . Pacification is a bad disappointment. . . . full security exists nowhere (not even behind the U.S. Marines' lines and in Saigon); in the countryside, the enemy almost completely controls the night."[17]

Lt. Gen. Walt began 1967 with 67,729 Marines and 2,649 Navy personnel in the III Marine Amphibious Force. The South Vietnamese had 75,000 troops in I Corps, counting all levels of soldiers and militia. The Marines had Maj. Gen. Kyle's 3rd Division in the two northern provinces. Maj. Gen. Herman Nickerson, Jr.'s, 1st Division covered Quang Nam province and had Task Force X-Ray, commanded by Brig. Gen. William A. Stiles, with two battalions in each of the two southern provinces. The Korean Marines' 2d Brigade was in Quang Ngai province. Maj. Gen. Louis B. Robertshaw commanded the 1st Marine Aircraft Wing.

Vietnam was unlike World War II or Korea. It reminded Marines like Walt and Krulak of the occupations of Nicaragua and Haiti. But Vietnam was on a vast and more deadly scale, and half of the country was in the hands of a hostile and dedicated government and army.

There were those who believed that the Marines were in the wrong place—that they should have been posted in the Mekong Delta, where they could have utilized their 30-year-old amphibious capability. The criticism made sense, but the Marines were not about to move under Army control. In the north, they were again in the ambiguous situation of serving quite like an army force. They were in Vietnam—and stayed in Vietnam—not because they were specialists but because they existed. They were needed and they wanted a piece of the action. But it was increasingly hard to justify "a second army" in Vietnam, even in

"Marineland," as I Corps was called back in Saigon. Once again, a separate Marine command with its own air force would, in time, become a source of trouble.

In early 1967, Lt. Gen. Walt was deeply concerned about the guerrilla war. As he expressed it, "This is first a political war, second a psychological war and third a military war." He said, "Fighting the guerrilla is not the easy part of the war. In 1966, half my casualties were from guerrillas, and these are the nasty kind of casualties—the dirty war." Walt wanted to reorient the ARVN from fighting the enemy's main force to fighting the guerrillas and from living off the villages to helping them. As he saw it, "The more troops I get in here, the larger my area of control. We're taking over hamlets every day. We're protecting more people every day." But he was not sanguine about the prospects: "Some of these areas have been VC-controlled for 20 years. The kids are hard-core communists today. Some people say it will start snowballing, but I don't see any sign so far."[18]

In the first weeks of 1967, the Marines performed assorted "clear-and-secure" operations to block infiltration routes leading down out of the hills toward Hue and to open sections of Highway One. Two battalions of the 26th Marines fought Operation Chinook; four Marines were killed and 73 wounded. The 1st Division had 17 killed and 52 wounded south of Da Nang. And further south, Task Force X-Ray had 10 killed and 50 wounded.

Down in the inhospitable Mekong Delta, the Marines had one chance to perform amphibiously. On January 5, the 1st Battalion, 9th Marines, as the Seventh Fleet's Special Landing Force, with HMM-362 landed 62 miles south of Saigon and worked with two Vietnamese marine battalions. This operation, called Deckhouse V, introduced U.S. combat troops to the Delta. "Intelligence proved bad and results were unimpressive: 21 enemy killed, 7 Marines were killed, and 35 Marines were wounded."[19] During the rest of 1967, Special Landing Force Marines made 22 more landings—but all of them were up north in the I Corps area.

The minute the 1967 Tet holiday truce ended at 7 A.M. on February 12, the 1st Marines began Operation Stone in the familiar area south of Da Nang. Typically, the Marines had to go back over previously "cleared" territory. In ten days, the Marines claimed 291 enemy dead and took 65 prisoners, while suffering nine killed and 77 wounded.

On February 25, the Marines were given permission to fire artillery into the DMZ and into North Vietnam itself. The reaction was quick. Early on February 27, the enemy hurled some 50 140mm Soviet rockets into and near the Da Nang airfield. Later, patrols found 134 firing points within five miles of the base. The attack damaged 17 aircraft and destroyed five communication vans. It killed 32 civilians and wounded 40, and killed 11 American servicemen (including one Marine) and wounded 26.

The Special Landing Force, now the 1st Battalion, 4th Marines and HMM-363, landed at the southern end of I Corps on February 16 and in 10 days accounted for 204 enemy dead; five Marines were killed and 55 wounded. Then, the Landing Force landed again near Thach Tru to support the 7th Marines and three ARVN battalions—fighting over an area that had been the battleground more than a year earlier. In the same period, a battalion of the 5th Marines supported an attack by ARVN and ROK Marines southwest of Chu Lai. Up north in Quang Tri province, five Marine battalions fought Prairie II near the DMZ, losing 93 killed and 483 wounded. As soon as that operation was over, Maj. Gen. Kyle returned to Camp Pendleton to take over the 5th Marine Division; and Maj. Gen. Bruno A. Hochmuth assumed command of the 3rd Division.

On March 20, the same Special Landing Force went ashore four miles south of the DMZ near Gio Linh to help with Prairie III and was greeted by a thousand rounds of mortar, rocket and artillery fire. An ammunition convoy was ambushed and badly cut up the next day. Sgt. Walter K. Singleton of Memphis and A Company, 9th Marines was killed on the twenty-fourth when he took a machine gun and singlehandedly entered the enemy strongpoint, killed eight of its defenders and scattered the rest to save his wounded.[20] Before the Landing Force re-embarked on April 1, it had had 29 killed and 230 wounded. By the time Prairie III was called off on April 19, the Marines had lost 55 killed and 529 wounded. Prairie IV started the next day in the same place. It would be the toughest yet.

In this period, the first Marine A-4 was shot down by a SAM missile from a site inside the DMZ. Electronic warfare-capable

651

EF-10B and EA-6A aircraft were used against the missiles. And the Marines' new A-6A Intruder aircraft were already hitting targets in North Vietnam.

In Quang Nam province in the center of I Corps, the 2d Battalion, 5th Marines had 5 killed and 55 wounded in three days of battle; and the Da Nang air base was hit by another rocket attack on March 15. At the southern end of the Marines' zone, Operation Desoto ended on April 7 with 76 Marines killed and 573 wounded. After that, two Army brigades came into the Chu Lai area under III MAF and allowed the 7th Marines to shift north to Da Nang. The war's leaders thought a greater concentration of troops up north might help. On April 12, Commandant Greene asked Congress for 40,000 more Marines for Vietnam. And shortly afterwards, General Westmoreland told the press: "We'll just go on bleeding them until Hanoi wakes up to the fact that they have bled the country to the point of national disaster for generations. Then they will have to reassess their position."[21]

Between Chu Lai and Da Nang, the Marines now focused their efforts in the Que Son valley. Again, this inland battleground had been fought over repeatedly; but the Viet Cong still dominated it. In an initial skirmish, eighteen-year-old Pfc. Gary W. Martini of Lexington, Virginia, won the Medal of Honor in death. He tried to save two Marines wounded when the enemy killed 14 and wounded 18 Marines in his platoon of F Company, 1st Marines. Two more Marine battalions were airlifted into the valley and coordinated their attack with ARVN Rangers in Operation Union. Before it was over in mid-May, more units had joined the fight and 110 Marines had been killed and 473 wounded. Enemy dead were figured at 865 dead and another 777 "probable."

In the north began the first bloody battle for the U.S.-built airstrip on the Khe Sanh plateau in the mountainous jungle of the northwest corner of South Vietnam. This had been Green Beret country since 1962—guarding the east-west invasion path along Route 9. On March 16, E Company, 9th Marines was ambushed and had seven killed and nine wounded near Hill 861, five miles northwest of the Khe Sanh Combat Base. On April 24, B Company, 9th Marines, working north of Hill 861, was attacked furiously and lost 14 killed and 17 wounded. The next day, the 3rd Battalion of Col. John P. Lanigan's 3rd Marines flew into Khe Sanh and fought the enemy entrenched on Hill 861. The 2d Battalion was also airlifted in and by the end of April 28, the two battalions had taken the hill.

Then, the 2d Battalion went further west after Hill 881 North and the 3rd Battalion after Hill 881 South. Marine casualties were heavy before the latter objective could be taken with the help of massive artillery support and more than 150 sorties by the 1st MAW. The 2d Battalion found itself up against a North Vietnamese regiment and finally captured Hill 881 North in heavy fighting. On May 9, the battalion again was engaged in a major fire fight and had 24 Marines and 19 wounded. That night, a seven-man reconnaissance team was ambushed and four were killed and the rest wounded; three CH-46 helicopters trying to rescue the team were hit. The 325C North Vietnamese Division pulled back, and the 26th Marines came in to relieve the 3rd Marines and protect the Khe Sanh airstrip. In that first battle, the Marines had had 155 killed and 425 wounded. It was only the beginning at Khe Sanh.

While the fighting was going on around Khe Sanh, to the east the enemy was attacking Marine bases and cutting Route 9 to prevent the reinforcement of the Khe Sanh area. At Con Thien on May 8, the 1st Battalion, 4th Marines was assaulted by two enemy battalions and had 44 killed and 100 wounded.

On May 18, the 9th Marines moved up into the southern half of the DMZ itself for the first time, with strong Marine-Air Force air support. The Seventh Fleet now had two special landing forces: Alpha and Bravo. Alpha made an amphibious assault with helicopters, landing craft and naval gunfire support in the northernmost corner of the DMZ. It ran into heavy resistance along the sandy bank of the Ben Hai River. Bravo joined the operation, and Vietnamese police removed 13,000 civilian refugees from the buffer zone. By landing behind the enemy battalions south of the DMZ, the Marines forced them to pull back into the hills. At the end of May, seven Marine battalions finished up Prairie IV with 489 of the enemy killed. Marine losses were 164 killed and 999 wounded. The whole series of Prairie operations to that date had cost the Marines 525 killed and 3,167 wounded.

On June 1, Lt. Gen. Walt, who had commanded III MAF for

two years, was relieved by Lt. Gen. Cushman, who had been his deputy. Maj. Gen. Nickerson replaced Cushman; and Maj. Gen. Donn J. Robertson, who had earned the Navy Cross on Iwo Jima, took over the 1st Marine Division. At the 1st Marine Aircraft Wing, Maj. Gen. Robertshaw was relieved by Maj. Gen. Norman J. Anderson.

In the south in Quang Tin province, Union II developed into a fierce 11-day battle in the Que Son valley with the 5th Marines fighting two North Vietnamese regiments. The enemy was strong and well dug in. After much artillery and air pounding, the fighting became bunker-to-bunker. Capt. James A. Graham of Wilkinsburg, Pennsylvania, earned the Medal of Honor posthumously on June 2. He led his F Company across a wide rice paddy in the face of mortar and small-arms fire. When his 2d Platoon was pinned down by two machine guns, Graham charged with his company headquarters men through the 2d Platoon and forced the enemy to abandon one machine gun. Graham himself killed 15 of the enemy. As his men and the 2d Platoon withdrew, Graham stayed with one Marine too seriously wounded to be moved. His last radio message reported that he was being attacked by 25 of the enemy.

Together, Union I and II took a toll of 1,566 enemy dead. The Marines lost 220 killed and 714 wounded. Ten days later, the fighting was resumed with a new name: Operation Adair, and continued through the end of June.

At the northern end of the zone, June and July saw a series of hard-fought operations. The enemy continued to build up around Khe Sanh and sporadic fighting went on through June. Between May 13 and July 16, the Marines there had 52 killed and 555 wounded. Operations Crockett, Ardmore, Cimarron, Buffalo and Hickory II cost hundreds of Marine casualties. The 11th Engineer Battalion cut a "firebreak" 600 meters wide and nine miles long between Con Thien and Gio Linh, stripped it of vegetation and filled it with barbed wire, minefields, sensors, watchtowers and strongpoints. On July 2, B and C Companies, 9th Marines were heavily attacked and took severe casualties. The 3rd Battalion helicoptered in to join the rest of the 1st Battalion and hit the enemy's left flank. That first day, 84 Marines were killed and 190 wounded. Two battalions of the 3rd Marines were flown into the battle area, and the fighting continued until July 14 with 159 Marines dead and 45 wounded. The enemy reportedly lost 1,301 dead—and two prisoners.

The Da Nang air base was hit by 122mm rockets shortly after midnight on July 15 from launchers in a village six miles southwest of the city. The results of the attack were serious. Eight airmen were killed and 138 wounded and 37 Marines were wounded. Ten planes were totally wrecked and a number severely damaged.

On August 19, Capt. Stephen W. Pless of Atlanta, Georgia, was piloting a small helicopter gunship near Quang Ngai when he heard on his radio that a U.S. Army helicopter was down on a remote beach and under attack. On the beach, Pless saw four Americans being bayoneted and beaten by more than 30 Viet Cong. Diving low, he scared off the enemy. As they raced to the trees, Pless fired his machine guns and rockets at them. One of the Americans on the ground waved, and Pless landed under fire to rescue the downed men. The wounded man stumbled toward the helicopter. Gunnery Sgt. Leroy N. Poulson ran out and found two others still alive. The copilot, Capt. Rupert E. Fairfield, jumped out to help. Lance Cpl. John G. Phelps fired his machine gun at the Viet Cong, who rushed Pless' craft repeatedly. With the three wounded men aboard, Pless took off. A U.S. Army gunship arrived and attacked the enemy. Pless' overloaded helicopter struck the water four times before it was able to rise and carry out the three wounded soldiers.[22]

The enemy stepped up their artillery and rocket attack on major Marine bases during late August and early September. The attacks killed men and destroyed aircraft and ammunition dumps at Dong Ha, Marble Mountain, Phu Bai and Da Nang.

Since the bombing of North Vietnam had failed to suppress North Vietnam's support of the Viet Cong, a barrier of barbed wire and "highly sophisticated devices," mines and sensors was begun across the northern border of South Vietnam. The plan met serious doubts in the Pentagon. Commandant Greene candidly opposed the project, and Marines on the scene felt the enemy would simply circumvent the barrier and continue to walk in through Laos. It was predicted that "McNamara's Wall" would be no more effective than the Maginot Line.

Navy Chaplain Vincent R. Capodanno of Staten Island, New York, earned the Medal of Honor in death on September 4 when he went into a large-scale battle with the 2d Platoon, M Company, 5th Marines south in Quang Tin province. Disregarding intense enemy fire, Lieutenant Capodanno moved unarmed around the battlefield giving medical aid to the wounded and administering last rites to the dying. A mortar round tore off part of his right hand and wounded him in the arms and legs. He refused medical attention. He raced over to help a wounded corpsman under fire from a machine gun 15 yards away and was killed by a burst from the enemy gun.

In this action, Sgt. Lawrence D. Peters of Johnson City, New York, was killed leading his squad in the same 2d Platoon. Although seriously wounded four times, Peters stood in full view of the enemy to force them to expose their positions, until he died. He too was awarded the Medal of Honor posthumously.

As more Army troops of the Americal Division moved into the southern part of I Corps, the 5th Marines shifted north to Da Nang and the 1st Marines were sent still further north to join the 3rd Marine Division. That division focused its attention on the defense of Con Thien, a red clay hill 500 feet high just south of the DMZ and west of Highway One. It was held by one battalion; and in early September, the enemy tried to attack the Marine strongpoint. Heavy fighting went on repeatedly into early October against various elements of the 4th, 9th and 26th Marines. When the pressure against Con Thien lessened, MACV in Saigon declared the battle a substantial victory.

Two pieces of Marine equipment came under debate during this period. The Colt-manufactured high-velocity M-16 rifle, which had replaced the M-14, was accused of jamming and causing American deaths.* This new 5.56mm rifle had been chosen as the successor to the controversial M-14 and filled the need for a lightweight weapon with a high rate of fire. Admittedly, the new weapon still had "bugs" in it and failed under combat conditions. Modifications reduced its rate of fire, improved extraction and brought down the malfunction rate. During the same period, the CH-46 helicopter was found to have structural faults that caused a number of accidents.

In October, the 1st Marines, newly moved north, went to work in the Hai Lang National Forest, an enemy base area. Spe-

---

*The M-16 rifle was designed by Eugene M. Stoner, a World War II enlisted Marine.

cial Landing Force Alpha (1st Battalion, 3rd Marines) and two ARVN battalions joined them. By the end of the month, the 3rd Division's Operation Kingfisher was closed down. Since July 16, it had cost 340 Marines killed and 3,086 wounded; III MAF claimed 1,117 enemy dead and five captured. In the Hue area, the 3rd Division screened the western approaches to the populated coastal area, killed 123 enemy and suffered 17 dead and 260 wounded.

On November 1, Vice President Hubert H. Humphrey visited the Marines and at Da Nang presented the 3rd Division with the Presidential Unit Citation for more than two years of fighting in the five northern provinces. Clearly, this had become a long and costly war. The list of American casualties seemed endless. And, although "body counts" of enemy dead were notoriously unreliable, the North Vietnamese and Viet Cong were also paying a heavy price for trying to wage war in South Vietnam.

Twice, early in November, the Viet Cong hit district headquarters and refugee settlements 15 miles southwest of Da Nang; they killed civilians and destroyed 559 houses. Two Marine battalions retaliated and by the month's end had killed 125 of the enemy, losing 21 Marines dead and 137 wounded. On November 14, Maj. Gen. Hochmuth was killed when his UH-1E helicopter exploded and crashed near Hue. Maj. Gen. Rathvon McC. Tompkins, winner of the Navy Cross on Saipan, took over the 3rd Division.

During the last weeks of 1967, Marine operations, although expensive in casualties, harvested fewer results in hurting the enemy. And as more Army units moved into the southern area of I Corps, the Korean Marine Brigade moved north to Da Nang.

On December 20, the 1st Platoon of D Company, 7th Marines fought an all-night battle near Da Nang with a North Vietnamese infantry battalion. Second Lt. Michael I. Neil led the platoon into hand-to-hand combat. All his squad leaders were killed or wounded before a relief column reached the unit at dawn. One squad leader, Cpl. Larry E. Smedley, received the Medal of Honor posthumously, and Lieutenant Neil received the Navy Cross. This was the only Marine rifle platoon in the war to receive a Meritorious Unit Commendation.

"The year ended almost exactly as it had begun."[23] The Marines had been in the midst of some of the heaviest fighting and so far had been able to keep some semblance of control over the northern boundary of South Vietnam. At year's end, 77,679 Marines were in III MAF. There were 21 Marine battalions, 31 ARVN battalions, 15 U.S. Army battalions and 4 Korean Marine battalions in I Corps. The Marines were now concentrated in the three northern provinces with four of their seven infantry regiments along Route 9 south of the DMZ. Commandant Leonard F. Chapman, Jr., of Key West, Florida, who succeeded Greene on January 1, 1968, reported that the Marines had killed 17,876 enemy soldiers during the past year. The toll had been high: 3,452 Marines killed and 25,994 wounded. Marine casualties since 1962 now totaled 5,479 dead and 37,784 wounded. Only in World War II had the Corps suffered more.

The Marines took particular pride in their pacification efforts, but admittedly these had been a mixture of success and failure. The heavy influx of North Vietnamese troops had succeeded in drawing American forces from the populated coastal areas and reduced the effectiveness of the pacification program. The ARVN proved incapable of "pacifying" areas cleared by the United States Army and Marines, and Ky's 1966 offensive against the civilian supporters of Gen. Nguyen Chanh Thi and the Buddhists had destroyed much of the non-communist infrastructure in I Corps. In addition, the year of heavy fighting and the spread of "free-fire zones," from which civilian population was banned, had doubled the number of refugees. There were now an acknowledged 530,000 refugees in I Corps. Although the American commanders were highly optimistic, the light at the end of the lonely tunnel still seemed a long way off.

3
Tet and Khe Sanh—1968

The Americans later insisted that they had known the Tet Offensive was coming; they said that the North Vietnamese buildup had been no secret. But at the time, few believed Intelligence reports that the enemy intended to attack South Vietnam's cities and towns. General Westmoreland, expecting battle at Khe Sanh, started shifting forces northward. Afterwards, some would say that he did exactly what North Vietnam's Gen. Vo Nguyen Giap wanted him to do—pull American strength away from the cities.

Along the six-mile-deep DMZ stood the North Vietnamese 324B and 325C Divisions. In mid-January 1968, the 304th Division came in from Laos and joined the 325C near Khe Sanh. Soon, elements of three more North Vietnamese divisions were identified south of the DMZ.

The 3rd Marine Division was strung out along the northern face of South Vietnam. Units of the 1st Marine Division were moved north, and Westmoreland sent the 1st Air Cavalry Division and the 2d Brigade of the 101st Airborne Division into the two northern provinces. As 1968 began, there were a quarter of a million allied soldiers in I Corps.

By now, the Marine Corps had 21 of its 36 ground battalions, 14 of its 33 fixed-wing squadrons and 13 of its 24 helicopter squadrons in Vietnam. Of the Corps' total strength—298,498 Marines—81,249 were in Vietnam.

Westmoreland keyed his northern defense on holding the Khe Sanh Combat Base on the plateau in the coffee-growing hills near Route 9. He saw Khe Sanh as the plug at the western end of the DMZ and believed that, if the base fell, the North Vietnamese would flank the Marine defenses along the DMZ.

He strengthened Khe Sanh; he did not want it to become an American Dien Bien Phu.

The decision to defend Khe Sanh was certainly controversial. President Johnson involved himself intimately. The Joint Chiefs of Staff supported the decision in writing. Their former chairman—and former ambassador in Saigon—General Taylor disagreed. Critics said the enemy was luring American strength into the remote hills. As one official Marine historian has written, "In the last analysis, Khe Sanh was defended because it was the only logical thing to do. We were there, in a prepared position and in considerable strength. A well-fought battle would do the enemy a lot more damage than he could hope to inflict on us."[24] And an Air Force historian added, "The base had become a symbol of U.S. determination to see the war through."[25]

Khe Sanh itself was the responsibility of Col. David E. Lownds' 26th Marines. When four enemy regiments were reported within 20 kilometers of its airstrip, Lownds' 2d and 3rd Battalions were moved over from the coast to help the 1st Battalion defend the base.

After some small-scale contact, the second battle of Khe Sanh opened on January 20. Two 3rd Battalion companies attacked a North Vietnamese battalion entrenched between Hills 881 North and 881 South. The next day, the enemy bombarded the Khe Sanh base, destroying 1,500 tons of ammunition, and captured the village of Khe Sanh on the highway. The Marines had to replenish the ammunition by air.

Lt. Col. John F. Mitchell's 1st Battalion, 9th Marines was rushed into the area; and more than a thousand civilians were airlifted out. The 37th ARVN Ranger Battalion of 318 men and two additional Marine 105mm howitzer batteries joined the garrison. More guns could have been added, but the limiting factor was the number of artillery shells that could be flown in. The monsoon rains—and the enemy—had closed Route 9.

Despite the American planning and buildup, when the Tet Offensive began the enemy simply bypassed Khe Sanh and attacked the population centers. General Giap's strategy worked.

In an enormous, surprise, coordinated offensive, more than 60,000 of the enemy—starting early on Tuesday, January 30—attacked every important American base and most of the cities and provincial and district capitals throughout South Vietnam. A great portion of the ARVN troops charged with defending the cities was absent for the Tet holiday.

At 2:47 A.M. Wednesday, a team of Viet Cong commandos armed with antitank rockets and explosive charges blasted their way into the walled compound of the United States Embassy in Saigon. They killed four U.S. Army MPs and wounded Cpl. George B. Zahuranic; he, Sgt. Ronald W. Harper and Sgt. Rudy A. Soto, Jr., were the only Marines on guard in the building. The commandos drove off a helicopter-borne paratrooper assault force. Marine Cpl. James C. Marshall was killed on a compound rooftop. The invaders held the embassy compound for six and a half hours before 12 were killed and two wounded men were captured. Pictures of the bloody raid against the center of the American presence in Vietnam shocked Americans back home.

Viet Cong battalions penetrated Saigon; a commando unit attacked the Presidential Palace, and two battalions blew up aircraft and fought American troops at Tan Son Nhut airfield. The enemy hit the Bien Hoa Air Base and the Long Binh military headquarters. They holed up in Cholon, Saigon's Chinese section, for two weeks and kept the city in chaos. Destruction was widespread; tanks and helicopter gunships demolished buildings, and fire swept through entire areas of huts.

In the north, the enemy overran all five provincial capitals. They opened the jails and released thousands of prisoners. Their troops had infiltrated in advance, hidden among the holiday traffic and an apathetic—or sympathetic—people. They attacked Tam Ky and Quang Ngai city and in heavy fighting were thrown back. They attacked Quang Tri city, where the 1st ARVN Division and the 1st Air Cavalry Division stopped them.

Further northwest at Cam Lo, the North Vietnamese smashed the defenses of the District Headquarters. There, young Cpl. Larry L. Maxam of Glendale, California, a fire team leader with D Company, 4th Marines spotted the enemy massing to assault the remaining defensive wire. Repeatedly wounded by grenade fragments, Maxam grabbed an abandoned machine gun and fired on the advancing enemy. A grenade struck him in the face; he was hit by rifle fire. But continuing to fire his machine gun, he forced the enemy to retreat. Despite further wounds, he defended half the perimeter singlehandedly for an hour and a half, until he was finally overwhelmed by the enemy fire.[26]

One objective of the enemy's Tet Offensive was to crush the Americans' air mobility and close support capability. On January 29 and 30, rockets and mortars hammered MAG-11 at Da Nang and MAG-16 at Marble Mountain; and rockets crashed into MAG-12 and -13 at Chu Lai.

At Da Nang, mortar shells and rockets hit U.S. and ARVN positions in the early hours of January 30. The enemy attacked I Corps headquarters; the duty section and a Combined Action Platoon stopped the first assault. Marine and Vietnamese MPs and Vietnamese Rangers rushed up; and in a formless battle, the attackers were killed or expelled. The North Vietnamese 2d Division approached the city from the south and west and was intercepted by reconnaissance elements of the 1st Marine Division. Overhead in his command helicopter, Lt. Gen. Cushman spotted 200 of the enemy across the river south of the air base. He radioed Maj. Gen. Robertson, who sent the 3rd Battalion, 5th Marines, followed by the 2d Battalion, 3rd Marines, to stop them.

Further south at Hoi An, the enemy invaded the city until ARVN troops counterattacked. On February 5, the enemy again fought into Hoi An and again were thrown back.

At the ancient imperial capital of Hue, enemy battalions infiltrated the city. Some of their soldiers waited in the tea rooms and bars until the pre-arranged time to change into uniform. They swiftly and easily took the center of the city on January 31. South of the Perfume River, they captured the provincial headquarters and the university and to the north, most of the imperial Citadel, except for the corner occupied by the 1st ARVN Division headquarters. They seized all the key installations but the high-walled MACV compound and some isolated pockets of resistance. They murdered hundreds of selected Vietnamese and foreigners.

The North Vietnamese forced the Americans and ARVN to fight in the cities. In most places, Americans and ARVN troops dislodged the enemy in a few days; but in Hue, the battle would go on for a month.

Early on the morning of January 31, A Company, 1st Marines rushed to Hue by truck to reinforce the MACV compound. A Company was followed by the command group, 1st Battalion, 1st Marines; G Company, 5th Marines, and a tank platoon. They fought through to the compound by mid-afternoon, and then two Marine platoons crossed the Perfume River bridge with heavy casualties. But they could not breach the Citadel wall and at dusk withdrew across the river.

F and H Companies, 5th Marines joined the Marines at Hue. At first, there was reluctance to use American firepower to retake the revered city. But when the ARVN counterattack slowed down and its commander asked for Marine help south of the river, the Marines went to work under the command of Col. Stanley S. Hughes of the 1st Marines. Fighting was house-to-house, reminiscent of the battle for Seoul. The Marines used recoilless rifles, tank guns, rockets and tear gas.

In this battle, Sgt. Alfredo Gonzalez of Edinberg, Texas, commanded the 3rd Platoon of A Company, 1st Marines. On the way into Hue, he led his platoon to clear out snipers. One Marine on top of a tank was hit and fell exposed to enemy fire; and Gonzalez, although wounded himself, carried him to safety. Then, he and his men destroyed the enemy strongpoint. When his company was pinned down on February 4, Gonzalez moved from position to position firing antitank weapons at the enemy's fortified emplacements until he was mortally wounded. He was awarded the Medal of Honor posthumously.

Not until February 6 did five companies of Marines recapture Hue's hospital, jail and provincial headquarters. Resistance south of the river was wiped out by February 9, with an estimated 1,053 enemy dead. Then, the Marines crossed the river and joined the ARVN in the final assault on the old city.

On February 12, Lt. Col. Robert H. Thompson's 1st Battalion, 5th Marines moved into the city from the north by helicopter and landing craft. The monsoon rains washed out most tactical air support. The Marines advanced on the left flank, with the 3rd ARVN Regiment in the center and the Vietnamese marines on the right. It took until February 22 for them to seize the southeast wall of the Citadel and drive the North Vietnamese from the city. The U.S. Marines stayed out of the struggle for the Imperial Palace; and on the twenty-fourth, the South Vietnamese flag finally flew over the Citadel. On March 2, the battle was declared finished. After more than a month of fighting, in which

142 Marines died and 857 were seriously wounded, the ancient city on the Perfume River lay in ruins.

The Marines' 27th Regimental Landing Team, commanded by Col. Adolph G. Schwenk, and the 3rd Brigade of the 82d Airborne Division were rushed to Vietnam. Schwenk's 27th Marines began arriving in Da Nang by air from Camp Pendleton by February 17 and took over the troublesome area between Marble Mountain and Hoi An. Schwenk's third battalion, which had been based in Hawaii, arrived directly from an amphibious exercise at sea. By the end of February, there were 24 Marine and 28 U.S. Army battalions operating in I Corps. Lt. Gen. Cushman headed the largest combat command ever held by a Marine, excepting Lt. Gen. Roy S. Geiger's brief command of the Tenth Army on Okinawa.

But command changes began to recognize the new Army–Marine mix in I Corps and also suggested wider concern over the way the war was going. Westmoreland established a MACV forward command post at Phu Bai on February 9 under Gen. Creighton W. Abrams, Jr., USA, the former Vice Chief of Staff of the Army. And Westmoreland asked for 206,000 more men, in addition to the 535,000 already in Vietnam.

On March 10, Westmoreland made two moves that seriously affected the Marines. First, he organized the Provisional Corps under Lt. Gen. William D. Rosson, USA, with Marine Maj. Gen. Raymond G. Davis, who had earned the Medal of Honor at the Chosin Reservoir, as his deputy. Prov Corps took operational control of the 3rd Marine Division, the 1st Air Cavalry Division and the 101st Airborne Division. And, secondly, the 1st MAW's fixed-wing aircraft were finally, after much debate and compromise, turned over to the "mission direction" of the Commanding General, Seventh Air Force. This change had been fiercely opposed by the Marine leaders; to a significant degree, it broke up the Marine air-ground team again.

The creation of Abrams' and Rosson's commands and the "single manager" for tactical air resulted from the Army, and Westmoreland especially, being dissatisfied with the Marines' leadership in Vietnam. "Disclaimers by both Army and Marine Corps spokesmen did not completely still the clamor."[27] The old interservice wounds from Bellau Wood, Saipan, Okinawa and Korea ached once more.

The most important question was: What had the enemy accomplished with his Tet Offensive? American military leaders insisted that the enemy had gained no new territory, rallied no general popular support and been badly hurt as a fighting force. That was all true. U.S. estimates were that the enemy had lost more than 15,000 soldiers. The enemy had caused tremendous destruction and chaos and killed an estimated 165,000 civilians. But if their goal had been to occupy most of the two northern provinces, as Westmoreland said, they had failed. U.S. military spokesmen called Tet a victory—as they had once heralded the raising of the Berlin Wall as a triumph for the West.

The true effect of Tet was much more devastating. The enemy had demonstrated that, despite the enormous American military buildup and the best available American military brains, they were able to mount a powerful invasion of South Vietnam. The massive bombing of North Vietnam had weakened neither their will nor their capability. The government in Saigon was rocked; the sense of hopelessness spread among the people of South Vietnam. And above all, the North Vietnamese dramatically undermined support for the war back in the United States. All the optimistic statements of progress and victory were no longer—and never again—credible.

On March 1, Clark Clifford replaced McNamara, who had become disillusioned with the war, as Secretary of Defense. On March 22, President Johnson suddenly recalled General Westmoreland, who had commanded MACV since 1964, and announced that General Abrams would succeed him. And on March 31, Johnson halted the bombing of North Vietnam except near the DMZ, urged the start of peace talks and took himself out of the 1968 election campaign. Preliminary talks started in Paris on May 13, but the war went on—for a very long time.*

First, the four Marine battalions and the ARVN Rangers at the remote Khe Sanh Combat Base fortified the perimeter around the airstrip and the chain of hills to the north and west. During the last weeks of January, the North Vietnamese had probed and bombarded the Marine positions. Early on February 5, while the Tet Offensive was still alive, electronic sensor

---

*March 16, 1968, was the date of the massacre of several hundred South Vietnam civilians by U.S. Army troops in the village of My Lai in Quang Ngai, the southernmost province under III MAF command.

devices warned the two companies of the 3rd Battalion, 26th Marines on crucial Hill 881 South that the enemy were approaching through the 20-foot-high elephant grass. Artillery and air hit them hard. A battalion attacked the north slope of Hill 861A; and Capt. Earle G. Breeding, Jr.'s, E Company, 26th Marines stopped them in a hand-to-hand brawl, leaving 109 enemy bodies hanging on the barbed wire. The Marines had seven dead and 35 wounded.

During the night of February 6, the 66th North Vietnamese Regiment accompanied by nine Russian-made tanks captured the relocated Special Forces camp near Lang Vei on Route 9 six miles southwest of the airstrip. The Marines at Khe Sanh could not send a rescue force, but Marine helicopters pulled out 14 of the 24 Green Berets and most of the Montagnards. Air and artillery pounded the abandoned base and destroyed three enemy tanks. The next day, the enemy attacked the Marine defenses around Khe Sanh and penetrated Capt. Henry J. M. Radcliffe's A Company, 9th Marines until a counterattack drove them out. Twenty-one Marines were killed and 26 wounded. The enemy kept up their bombardment; and on February 23 alone, 1,307 mortar and artillery rounds smashed into the Khe Sanh base. On the twenty-fifth, a patrol from B Company, 26th Marines was ambushed south of the base. A platoon sent out to help the trapped patrol was also hit by the enemy. In all, 26 Marines were killed and 21 wounded.

The North Vietnamese lay siege to Khe Sanh, digging their trenches ever closer. Round-the-clock bombing, including B-52 strikes, and heavy artillery fire tried to halt them. The base was supplied and 852 wounded were removed by air, despite fire from concentrations of enemy antiaircraft weapons. On February 29 and March 1, the enemy made their last major effort to breach the perimeter and were repulsed by the ARVN Rangers. The shelling and bombing continued, but the worst of the battle was over. Between November 1967 and the end of March, the Marines at Khe Sanh had had 205 killed and 1,668 wounded. The Marines figured that two North Vietnamese divisions had been destroyed.

As the monsoon season ended, Lt. Gen. Cushman planned a triple spring offensive: the relief of Khe Sanh, a raid into the A Shau valley in Thua Thien province and an attack into the DMZ.

To relieve Khe Sanh, the 1st Air Cavalry Division with an ARVN battalion approached Khe Sanh from the east and south, while the 1st Marines and three ARVN battalions moved westward to open Route 9. The cavalrymen established a base and airstrip at Ca Lu, five miles east of Khe Sanh; by April 6, they linked up with the 9th Marines south of the airstrip. By the twelfth, Route 9 was open to traffic again. The Lang Vei camp was reoccupied. When the 3rd Battalion, 26th Marines took Hill 881 North on Easter Sunday, April 14, the 77-day battle for Khe Sanh was declared over. It had been a tremendous effort of artillery fire, air supply and bombing. The Americans had poured on the enemy 100,000 tons of bombs and 150,000 artillery rounds. There had been 679 air drops; and while 455 aircraft had actually landed at Khe Sanh, the enemy had destroyed only four fixed-wing aircraft and 17 helicopters.

But the Marines' troubles there were not over. Two nights later, two platoons engaged the enemy in a fight that grew to involve three companies of the 1st Battalion, 9th Marines. The Marines finally pulled back, leaving 13 dead and two wounded. In the end, one wounded Marine, Cpl. Hubert H. Hunnicutt, was recovered. The battalion commander was relieved of his command.

On May 23 at the White House, President Johnson presented the Presidential Unit Citation to the 26th Marines. Colonel Lownds, who had shaved off his handlebar mustache for the occasion, and Sgt. Major Agrippa W. Smith, the senior enlisted man at Khe Sanh, received the award for the regiment.

The A Shau valley operation was carried out by elements of the 1st Air Cavalry and 101st Airborne Divisions and a number of ARVN battalions. Between April 19 and May 16, they had many small unit actions, counted 735 enemy dead and captured large quantities of enemy weapons and trucks.

But the III MAF's attack into the DMZ was frustrated when the enemy in force attacked Dong Ha, at the intersection of Highway One and Route 9, in an effort to reach the 3rd Marine Division command post. On April 29, the 2d ARVN Regiment tackled a North Vietnamese regiment four miles north of the base; and then the 2d Battalion, 4th Marines engaged the enemy's main body in a tough three-day battle a mile and a half northeast of Dong Ha. On May 1, three companies attacked the fortified village of Dai Do. G Company led by Capt. M. Sando

Vargas, Jr., of Winslow, Arizona, was pinned down by enemy fire and isolated from the rest of the battalion. Although wounded, Vargas set up a defense perimeter at the edge of the village, and G Company fought off counterattacks throughout the night. The next morning, Capt. James E. Livingston of Telfair, Georgia, led his E Company through several hundred yards of intense fire to reinforce Vargas' men. They destroyed more than 100 bunkers and drove out the enemy. Although he was twice wounded, Livingston consolidated his remaining men and Vargas' company and tried to attack the next village. They were stopped by a counterattacking enemy battalion. Wounded a third time and now unable to walk, Livingston stayed on the field, deploying his men and getting the wounded evacuated. Vargas was also hit a third time; but when he saw the battalion commander, Lt. Col. William Weise, seriously wounded, Vargas crossed the fire-swept field and carried Weise to a protected position. Then, he helped organize the battalion's defense. Both Vargas and Livingston received the Medal of Honor.

The 3rd Battalion, 9th Marines plus U.S. Army and ARVN elements tried to trap the enemy; and heavy fighting continued until May 16. The North Vietnamese 320th Division attacked again at the end of the month and was battered by units of the 4th, 9th and 3rd Marines.

The enemy's aggressiveness had been weakened but not rubbed out by the losses of the Tet Offensive. On May 5—in what was called Mini Tet—they launched 119 rocket and mortar attacks throughout South Vietnam. In I Corps, they hit III MAF headquarters at Da Nang, the MACV compound at Hue and the 101st Airborne Division headquarters, as well as airfields at Da Nang, Marble Mountain, Quang Tri and Chu Lai. More such attacks took place on May 11 and 13; and on the nineteenth, rockets blew up an ammunition dump, destroying 80,000 gallons of fuel and several helicopters.

The rocket and mortar attacks called for a change in tactics, and the 1st Marine Division started more mobile operations to push the North Vietnamese further away from Da Nang. As a result, the 2d Battalion, 7th Marines on May 9 got into a fight with a large enemy force near the ruined railroad bridge over the Ky Lam River; and four days later, the 3rd Battalion met the well dug-in enemy two miles further west. The enemy was in the area in strength. The 27th Marines took over the fight and pressed the battle toward the west, while the 7th Marines screened the corridors leading from the mountains toward Da Nang. The Marines' "Sting Ray" technique of sending six-man recon teams to spot the enemy for air and artillery fire was used effectively.

Further south in Quang Tin province's western reaches, the North Vietnamese on May 10 hit the Special Forces camp at Kham Duc, which was supported by a section of Marine 105mm howitzers. Lt. Gen. Cushman sent in U.S. Army reinforcements; but when the enemy attacked in regimental strength, the camp was abandoned.

In May, action also heightened around Khe Sanh where six Marine and two Army battalions had been posted the previous month. The enemy's 304th Division ambushed convoys and engaged the 3rd Battalion, 4th Marines in a two-day battle west of Khe Sanh. Other fights broke out east and south of the base. When the fresh 308th North Vietnamese Division replaced the battered 304th, Task Force Hotel, led by Brig. Gen. Carl W. Hoffman, staged a counteraction from two large fire support bases, Loon and Robin, which were blasted out of the rain forest five miles south of Route 9 near the Laotian border. By early June, Marine companies there were heavily engaged; and on June 16 and 18, the enemy attacked the 3rd Battalion, 4th Marines and were repulsed. The fighting cost the enemy 725 killed and captured and forced the 308th to withdraw after two weeks of battle.

Westmoreland left Saigon on June 11, and Lt. Gen. Cushman's proposal that Khe Sanh be abandoned was finally acted on. Everything possible was removed and the rest burned, blown up or buried. Working east along Route 9, the 1st Marines and the 11th Engineer Battalion dismantled six tactical bridges behind them. By July 5, the base at Khe Sanh had been razed and was replaced by Landing Zone Stud at Ca Lu further east. The North Vietnamese proclaimed the "fall" of Khe Sanh a victory; in Washington, the White House spokesman insisted it was a military decision. In Paris, the North Vietnamese spokesman called the American explanation that the base was no longer essential "sour grapes." MACV said that the new mobile tactics in Quang Tri province made the base unnecessary. Maj. Gen.

Davis, now commanding the 3rd Marine Division, announced that combat bases and strongpoints would either be closed down or made defendable by a single reinforced company. The new emphasis would be on mobility. Clearly, if the defense of Khe Sanh had served any purpose, it had been outlived.

Throughout June, enemy artillery damaged 3rd Marine Division bases. At Dong Ha on June 20, an ammunition dump exploded, destroying a quarter of a million artillery and mortar rounds. But by the end of the month, enemy offensive activity decreased noticeably in conjunction with North Vietnamese professions in Paris of a desire to negotiate a settlement.

For seven days beginning on July 1, the American Operation Thor blasted an area 10 miles by 16 miles, north from the southern edge of the DMZ. It was bombarded by Marine, Navy and Air Force planes, Strategic Air Command B-52s, two cruisers and six destroyers and 118 pieces of artillery. After that paroxysm of fire, the 3rd and 9th Marines and the 2d ARVN Regiment swept the area from Route 9 to the DMZ.

In Quang Nam province, the 27th and 5th Marines tried to keep the enemy off balance. But on August 18, the enemy hit a number of targets and especially Da Nang again with rockets and mortars. And on August 22, they shelled Saigon for the first time in two months. ARVN Rangers intercepted the 38th North Vietnamese Regiment south of Da Nang; but before dawn on August 23, the Viet Cong routed a Popular Force detachment south of the air base and seized the southern end of the Cam Le Bridge that carried Highway One northward into Da Nang. The Marines' C Company, 1st Military Police Battalion stopped the Viet Cong at the northern end of the bridge; and at dawn, A Company, 27th Marines struck the Viet Cong rear and broke their hold on the bridge. ARVN Rangers came to the rescue of the Popular Force men under attack. The enemy continued the pressure south of Da Nang and by the end of August had lost some 1,072 dead there.

Highway One and the railroad had been opened again from Da Nang north to Hue. And the 27th Marines on September 10 began to leave Vietnam for California and Hawaii. Its place south of Da Nang was taken by the 1st Marines, which was relieved up north by U.S. Army troops. Further south and west, elements of the 7th and 5th Marines fought occasional sharp actions. The 9th and 3rd Marines operating near the DMZ, thwarted an attack across the line by the rejuvenated North Vietnamese 320th Division. On September 30, the 16-inch rifles of *New Jersey* added gunfire support ranging 24 miles inland. If not spectacularly effective, it was a dramatic gesture.

In the fall, with the DMZ seemingly more secure, the 1st Cavalry Division (Air Mobile) was pulled back from I Corps, leaving the northern front to the 3rd Marine Division and the 101st Airborne Division (Air Mobile). As the monsoon rains returned, the enemy made an attack on the Thuong Duc Special Forces camp in central Quang Nam province between Da Nang and Laos; it was broken up by Marine artillery and bombing. The 2d Battalion, 5th Marines counterattacked up Route 4, while the 7th Marines and other units of the 5th attempted to land behind the enemy. The fighting went on in the area around Hill 163 until October 19.

Just before the American elections, President Johnson announced the cessation of all air, naval and artillery bombardment of North Vietnam starting on November 1. Two days later, North Vietnamese in Paris announced they were ready to participate in peace talks and began withdrawing most of their regiments out of South Vietnam. But on November 5, they charged that the United States was continuing reconnaissance flights over North Vietnam. The United States replied that those flights revealed increased North Vietnamese efforts to resupply their forces in the south through Laos.

November 1 marked the beginning of two programs. The first was Le Loi, a stepped-up pacification campaign to return control of the rural population to pre-Tet levels and restore the damage done by the enemy's 1968 offensives. The second was the Phoenix program aimed at eradicating the Viet Cong infrastructure in the villages and hamlets.

In an area 10 miles south of Da Nang called "Dodge City," the 1st Marine Division staged an intensive "cordon and search" operation. Six Marine battalions were used to cordon off the area five miles wide and three miles deep. Three-man fire teams were positioned every 50 feet around the perimeter. As the cordon tightened in the first week of December, the fighting grew heavier until, by December 9, 1,210 of the enemy had been killed and 182 captured. Throughout the Marine Corps zone of responsibility, aggressive operations killed hundreds more of the enemy as the year wound down.

More than 62,000 enemy were claimed killed in the Marine zone during the year, while Marine casualties totaled 4,618 killed and 29,320 wounded.* Marine Corps strength peaked in September with 85,520 Marines in Vietnam. After the tremendous exertions at Tet and in the fighting at Hue and around Da Nang and Khe Sanh, the quality of enemy forces was judged to have declined. North Vietnamese increasingly filled in for the worn-thin Viet Cong units. But 1968 had by no means been a vintage year for the American war in Vietnam.

*Just before Christmas, two Marines, Staff Sgt. Robert J. Hammond and Sgt. Robert J. Chicca, were among the members of the crew of *Pueblo* who were released by North Korea after 11 months of captivity.

4
Getting Out — 1969-1973

As 1969 began, Richard M. Nixon entered the White House. During the election campaign he had suggested to the American people that he had a plan for getting the United States out of Vietnam. He had said, "Vietnam has been a profoundly sobering lesson in the limits of U.S. power. . . . What we must do is to work . . . toward ensuring that we have no more Vietnams."[28] Staying there had suddenly become no longer "vital" to America's national interest.

After months of resistance and haggling, the Saigon government agreed to join in four-party negotiations that included the National Liberation Front. On January 24, all four delegations sat down in Paris at one round table.

In Vietnam, American forces kept up the military pressure. The enemy launched a late February burst of rapid jabs and rocket attacks against American military installations. President Thieu pressed a repressive heel down harder on critics of his regime. By May, the NLF began calling for new elections in the South to establish a coalition government.

The Nixon Administration spoke of a "Vietnamization" of the war—strengthening the ARVN to take over more of the fighting and release American forces from actual combat. This would "change the color of the dead," said the critics. On May 14, the President proposed a "mutual withdrawal" of American and North Vietnamese forces and leaving a final political solution to all factions in South Vietnam that renounced the use of force. On June 8 at Midway, Nixon announced that the first 25,000 of the 540,000 United States troops in Vietnam would be pulled out by the end of August. Troop withdrawals quieted the American "doves" while Vietnamization reassured the "hawks."

Despite these hopes and expectations—and the angry peace movement in the United States—the fighting went on. During the next three years, 15,000 more Americans and hundreds of thousands of Vietnamese were killed; the ARVN suffered more casualties than it had in the previous three years, and the ground war spread beyond Vietnam into Laos and Cambodia.

The enemy was now less active, apparently hurt by the fighting of the previous year. General Abrams reduced the big-unit, search-and-destroy operations and concentrated on attacking their base areas and interdicting their supply lines. Pacification, which had once meant "winning hearts and minds," continued to mean bombing villages, defoliating crops and jungle and removing peasants from the land to clean out Viet Cong-dominated areas.

In April 1970, after the overthrow of Prince Norodom Sihanouk, 74,000 American and ARVN troops invaded Cambodia. There were demonstrations of protest in Saigon. In the United States, the reaction was vigorous and led, most dramatically and tragically, to the killing of four students at Kent State University by Ohio National Guard troops. The Cambodian invasion itself destroyed North Vietnamese equipment, and the Cambodian army stopped the Viet Cong from receiving military supplies through the port of Sihanoukville. When American forces pulled back from Cambodia at the end of June, the North Vietnamese occupied the country's northern provinces and organized new supply routes through the Mekong valley.

In February 1971, 21,000 ARVN troops, supported by American air power, crossed into Laos to cut the Ho Chi Minh trail. Planning by both the ARVN and the Americans was weak. And not even American advisors were supposed to accompany the ARVN into Laos. The North Vietnamese counterattacked in strength. American aircraft reportedly killed thousands of North Vietnamese. Marine planes and helicopters participated in this action. Eighty-nine American helicopters were destroyed. Although some ARVN units fought well, the South Vietnamese were no match for the enemy; after 45 days, their units had suffered nearly 50 percent casualties. Marine helicopters helped get the ARVN out again. The traffic continued down the Ho Chi Minh trail. This late in the day, it was a pretty poor show.

During this entire period, the air war against both halves of

Vietnam, Laos and Cambodia was stepped up. "After two years and a few months of his [Nixon's] administration the United States had dropped more bombs on Indochina than it had in both the European and the Pacific theatres during World War II."[29] Anger and resentment rose against the American strategy.

This was the environment in which the Marine Corps fought the final years of the Vietnam war. As 1969 began, the 3rd Marine Division, commanded by Maj. Gen. Raymond G. Davis, was screening the DMZ. The division was under the operational control of the U.S. Army's XXIV Corps, which also contained the 1st Brigade of the 5th Mechanized Infantry Division and the 101st Airborne Division. The 1st Marine Division under Maj. Gen. Ormond R. Simpson guarded the approaches to Da Nang. Maj. Gen. Charles J. Quilter commanded the 1st Marine Aircraft Wing.

On January 13, in the largest Special Landing Force operation of the war, the 2d and 3rd Battalions of the 26th Marines landed at Batangan Peninsula, south of Chu Lai. This had been the battlefield of the first regiment-sized combat action of the war back in August 1965. Resistance now was minimal; and by February 9, both battalions were back on board the ships of the Seventh Fleet. The Marines were keeping alive their amphibious expertise and image.

Col. Robert H. Barrow's 9th Marines went aggressively into the mountains in the southwestern corner of Quang Tri province on January 22 in Operation Dewey Canyon. The enemy had built up a well-stocked jungle base area with a number of artillery pieces near the Laotian border. Despite the unpredictable monsoon weather, Barrow's regiment had to be supported entirely by helicopters. The Marine air groups flew 1,617 sorties in support. For one ten-day period no resupply at all was possible. By February 18, fighting was heavy; the 1st Battalion in the center of the line found strong resistance. In one action on Washington's Birthday, 1st Lt. Wesley L. Fox of Herndon, Virginia, was serving as commander of A Company when it was ambushed in the northern A Shau valley. The enemy charged, and Fox and all but one of his command group were wounded. Advancing into heavy fire, Fox knocked out one enemy position and led his men to drive the enemy into retreat. He was

675

wounded again but stayed in command, set a defense and evacuated his casualties. H Company successfully ambushed Route 922, part of the Ho Chi Minh Trail network across the border inside Laos. Three days later, Cpl. William D. Morgan of Pittsburgh, a squad leader with H Company, charged an enemy bunker to draw its fire. Morgan was killed, but he enabled his men to save two wounded Marines and overrun the North Vietnamese position. Lance Cpl. Thomas F. Noonan, Jr., of Brooklyn, New York, a fire team leader in G Company, also lost his life trying to save a wounded Marine under fire.[30] In Dewey Canyon, 130 Americans were killed and 932 were wounded.

During Tet 1969, which began on February 16, the enemy again infiltrated into Da Nang and the surrounding countryside. They followed their earlier patterns of attack, hitting particularly through the Viet Cong-dominated hamlets south of the Cau Do River. They were quickly routed. Both the 1st and 7th Marines participated in the counteractions. Lance Cpl. Lester W. Weber of Aurora, Illinois, a machine-gun squad leader with M Company, 7th Marines was sent with his 2d Platoon to help a squad under heavy attack near Bo Ban. When his platoon was attacked, Weber plunged into the tall grass of the rice paddy, killed one enemy soldier and forced 11 others to retreat. He fought a second North Vietnamese hand-to-hand and killed him. Seeing two enemy soldiers firing from behind a dike, Weber dived into their position and wrestled their weapons from their hands and killed them. As he dashed forward to attack a fifth enemy soldier, he was mortally wounded. He was awarded the Medal of Honor posthumously.

On March 19, when an enemy battalion penetrated the perimeter of D Battery, 11th Marines near An Hoa, Corpsman David R. Ray of Nashville, Tennessee, went to the aid of the wounded. He was hit, killed one enemy soldier and wounded a second who attacked him. Ray continued to treat the wounded until he was fatally wounded. As his last act, he threw himself over a wounded Marine when an enemy grenade exploded nearby.[31]

On March 26, Lt. Gen. Nickerson succeeded Lt. Gen. Cushman as commanding general of III Marine Amphibious Force. Nickerson had commanded the 1st Marine Division and subsequently been deputy commander of III MAF. Lt. Gen. Cushman returned to Washington to become deputy director of the Central Intelligence Agency; at the beginning of 1972, he would succeed General Chapman as the Commandant of the Marine Corps.

Marine fighting during the first half of 1969 was less intense than it had been in 1968. When the first 25,000 American troops left Vietnam by the end of August, among them went 8,388 Marines, including the 9th Marines and part of the 1st MAW.

In Quang Nam province, Pipestone Canyon was the most significant 1st Division operation of the year. Four Marine battalions and ARVN units went after the 36th North Vietnamese Regiment south of Da Nang. It was a "clearing" operation typical of many in the later years of the war. Behind the Marines came a U.S. Army engineer company with giant Rome plows that dug up the land at the rate of 200 acres a day. When the operation was finished in early November, 54 Marines had been killed and 540 wounded. In August, the 7th Marines moved into the Que Son valley and joined the U.S. Army in battling the 2d North Vietnamese Division outside Hiep Duc. On the twenty-eighth, Mexican-born Lance Cpl. Jose F. Jimenez, a fire team leader with K Company, led a charge against well-camouflaged North Vietnamese. He killed several and destroyed two enemy positions in the face of concentrated automatic weapons fire before he was mortally wounded.[32] By the end of the month, more than a thousand of the enemy had been killed.

Through the fall, the 3rd Marines fought a number of engagements along the DMZ. The 3rd and 4th Marines and MAG-36 left Vietnam by mid-December, as 45,000 more Americans were withdrawn, including 18,483 Marines. The 3rd Marine Division finished its Vietnam service after 40 months of combat and moved to Okinawa. More and more, the U.S. Army was taking over the Marines' responsibilities in the northern provinces. The enemy had reduced their activity mostly to guerrilla and terrorist activity.

The seventy-second and last Special Landing Force operation of the war began on September 7 when the 1st Battalion, 26th Marines landed south of Hoi An. While a Korean Marine battalion held a blocking position, the Marines attacked by helicopter and landing craft. A second Korean Marine battalion landed to the north and swept south against the combined U.S.-Korean block.

The first serious action of 1970 was a North Vietnamese

attack on Fire Support Base Ross in the Que Son valley. On the dark, rainy night of January 6, three enemy sapper teams penetrated the perimeter behind an enemy barrage. Although 38 of the sappers were killed and three captured, the Marines lost 13 killed and 40 wounded.

The Marines faced their own mini My Lai on February 19, 1970, when B Company, 7th Marines was fighting in a heavily populated area of southern Quang Nam province. The company had had 14 men killed and 85 wounded since November. That night, a five-man "killer team" patrol led by Lance Cpl. Randell D. Herrod, who had recently transferred into the company, entered the hamlet of Son Thang. Corporal Herrod had been recommended for a Silver Star by his previous platoon commander, 1st Lt. Oliver L. North. Herrod's patrol killed five unarmed Vietnamese women and 12 small children. Four members of the patrol were charged with unpremeditated murder. First Lt. North testified for Herrod. After a six-day trial, two Marines were found guilty; Herrod was found not guilty and received his Silver Star.

The war seemed to be slowing down for the Marines, but men were still being killed and wounded and performing exceptional feats of courage. Early on May 8, Lance Cpl. Miguel Keith, an eighteen-year-old from San Antonio, Texas, was serving as a machine gunner with Combined Action Platoon 1-3-2 in Quang Ngai province when his platoon was attacked by a larger enemy force. Keith was seriously wounded but moved across a fire-swept field, firing his gun at the enemy. He attacked five enemy soldiers, firing as he advanced, killing three and dispersing the others. A grenade knocked him to the ground. Bleeding severely, he charged 25 enemy soldiers massing to attack, killed four and drove off the rest before he was mortally wounded. He was the last Marine in Vietnam to be awarded the Medal of Honor.

By April 15, another 12,900 Marines left the country, including the 26th Marines, MAG-12 and the 1st Antitank Battalion and most of the 1st Tank Battalion, the 3rd Amphibian Tractor Battalion and the 1st Shore Party Battalion. Four tactical air squadrons departed.

During the Vietnam war, 730,000 men and women served in the Marine Corps compared to some 600,000 in World War II. At its peak in 1968, the 85,755-man Marine force in Vietnam included two divisions, two regimental landing teams and the aircraft wing. (The first woman Marine to be ordered to a combat zone was Master Sgt. Barbara J. Dulinsky, who arrived at MACV in Saigon in March 1967.)

By 1970, Marine redeployment had left the Army outnumbering the Marines in I Corps. As a result on March 9, XXIV Corps became the senior U.S. command in the zone. Lt. Gen. Keith B. McCutcheon became the new commanding general of III MAF, which was now a division-wing team under operational control of Army headquarters. III MAF's area of responsibility was limited to Quang Nam province and small pieces of the neighboring provinces. It was headquartered at Da Nang's Red Beach, near where the 9th Marines had first landed five years earlier. The 1st Marine Division consisted primarily of the 1st, 5th and 7th Marines and the artillery regiment, the 11th Marines. It totaled about 21,000 Marines and 1,200 Navy men. Their main job was to keep the enemy away from Da Nang.

On April 18, Maj. Gen. Edwin B. Wheeler, the 1st Marine Division commander, broke his leg in a helicopter crash and was succeeded by Maj. Gen. Charles F. Widdecke, Navy Cross winner on Guam.

In July and August, the 7th Marines supported ARVN troops attacking enemy bases and on August 31 made one last sortie into the Que Son area. Called Operation Imperial Lake, this proved to be the final major Marine offensive effort of the war. It also involved the 5th and 1st Marines, the Korean Marines and U.S. Army units.

Then, the 7th Marines left Vietnam and the 5th Marines took its place. Lt. Gen. McCutcheon went home terminally ill in December, and Lt. Gen. Donn Robertson took over command of III MAF. In all of 1970, the Marines had 403 killed and 3,625 wounded, compared to 1,051 killed and 9,286 wounded in 1969.

The 5th Marines started for home in February 1971, leaving only the 1st Marines outside Da Nang. Of the air groups, only the fixed-wing MAG-11 and the helicopters of MAG-16 were left. On April 14, III MAF removed to Okinawa; the 1st Marine Division to Camp Pendleton, and the 1st MAW headquarters left for Japan. The Marines were organized now as the 3rd Marine Amphibious Brigade with 13,600 men under Maj. Gen. Alan J. Armstrong. And as the Combined Action Program phased out, terrorist activity in Quang Nam province increased.

Marine ground and air operations in Vietnam stopped on May 7, the day VMA-311 flew its last air strike into Laos. On the air side, the Marines had lost 252 helicopters and 173 fixed-wing aircraft in combat and 172 helicopters and 81 aircraft operationally during the war. The last ground troops sailed on June 25.

As Commandant Cushman said in April 1972, "We are pulling our heads out of the jungle and getting back into the amphibious business."[33]

When the North Vietnamese opened a major Easter offensive on March 30, 1972, only about 500 Marines were in the country. MAG-12 and -15 moved into Vietnam with their Skyhawks and Phantoms. An air task force and MAG-15 set up at Nam Phong, Thailand. Intensive bombing of North Vietnam was resumed; and on May 8, President Nixon ordered Haiphong harbor mined.

Although there were still 70,000 U.S. soldiers in South Vietnam, the ground battle was left to the Vietnamese. Marine Capt. John W. Ripley, advisor to the 3rd Vietnamese Marine Battalion, won the Navy Cross for personally blowing up the bridge at Dong Ha. Marine helicopters from *Okinawa* carried South Vietnamese marines into battle; but by May 4, all Quang Tri province had been lost.

The last U.S. combat troops left Vietnam on August 11. In September, the ARVN stopped the enemy's drive north of Hue and recaptured Quang Tri province.

On December 18, after the Paris peace talks broke down again, President Nixon ordered the heaviest bombing of the war against North Vietnam. For the first time, B-52s bombed Hanoi; more than a dozen were shot down by North Vietnamese missiles.

At last, agreement was reached in Paris; and a ceasefire began in Vietnam on January 28, 1973. MAG-12's Skyhawks flew the final sorties of the American war over the Mekong Delta. By the end of March, the last American soldiers were out of the country. It had been the longest war in U.S. history.

Twenty-six Marine prisoners of war were repatriated; 12 others had returned earlier. The Marine Corps listed eight Marines as dead while captured; two were still counted as captured and 47 as missing in action. In 1985, there were returned from Vietnam the remains of Sgt. Robert C. Sherman of Danville, Illinois, who had died after having been taken prisoner of war on June 24, 1967. As late as 1991, the remains of Staff Sgt. Robert L. Greer and Staff Sgt. Fred T. Shreckengost were returned and interred in Arlington National Cemetery.

On August 14, 1973, the American bombing of Cambodia finally stopped. It was more than four years since the decision had been made to get out of the war.

5
Black Americans—Green Marines

By the time of the Vietnam war, the Marine Corps was totally integrated. Marines leaders liked to say there were no white or black Marines—all were "green Marines" wearing combat green.

Of the 448,000 Marines who served in Vietnam from 1965 on, 41,000 were black. The stories of a few of them demonstrate their contribution to the Corps' share in this war.

Five black Marines earned the Medal of Honor in Vietnam. All five were killed shielding fellow Marines from exploding enemy grenades. For his heroism on February 28, 1967, Pfc. James Anderson, Jr., of Compton, California, was the first black Marine to earn the Medal. The others were Pfc. Oscar P. Austin of Phoenix, Arizona; Sgt. Rodney M. Davis of Macon, Georgia; Pfc. Robert H. Jenkins, Jr., of Interlachen, Florida, and Pfc. Ralph H. Johnson of Charleston, South Carolina.

The senior black officer in Vietnam was Lt. Col. Frank E. Petersen, Jr., of Topeka, Kansas. He had received the Distinguished Flying Cross in Korea and in May 1968 was named commanding officer of Fighter Attack Squadron 314, a Phantom jet unit at Chu Lai. He flew 280 combat missions, was shot down and rescued and awarded the Legion of Merit.

The first black to command a Marine infantry battalion was Lt. Col. Hurdle L. Maxwell who commanded the 1st Battalion, 6th Marines in 1969 and retired in 1971 with 20 years of service.

Sgt. Major Edgar R. Huff became the first black battalion sergeant major in an infantry battalion and senior sergeant major in point of service in the Corps. He served two tours in Vietnam and was severely wounded in January 1968 while rescuing a radioman trapped in an open field by enemy fire. Huff received

681

the Bronze Star and two Purple Hearts and later became sergeant major of the III MAF. When he retired in 1972, he was the first black Marine with 30 years' service.

Sgt. Major Agrippa W. Smith of the 1st Battalion, 9th Marines was the senior enlisted man in the battle for Khe Sanh. He had enlisted at Montford Point back in 1943 and eventually became sergeant major of the 26th Marines.

James E. Johnson, who had joined the segregated Corps in 1944 as a "steward duty only" private, rose to be a chief warrant officer. He retired in 1965 and later became Assistant Secretary of the Navy for Manpower and Reserve Affairs.

In 1968, Maj. Edward L. Green, a Vietnam veteran, became the first black officer on the faculty at the Naval Academy. In the Annapolis Class of 1972, eight of the 12 black midshipman joined the Marine Corps. In 1972, Green succeeded Lt. Col. Petersen as Special Assistant to the Commandant for Minority Affairs.

In 1964, the Marine Corps had only 48 black commissioned officers; by 1973, it had 282. But only 24 were majors or higher among a total of 5,300 Marine officers in those ranks. In 1964, the Corps had only 184 blacks in the top three enlisted ranks; by 1973, it had 1,394. Still, only two percent of Marine officers were black, and the 28,839 black enlisted men were disproportionately in the lower ranks.

Even this record was not achieved painlessly. There were ugly incidents and violent clashes during the 1960s in the United States; at Kaneohe, Hawaii; on Okinawa, and in Vietnam. Both the nation and the Corps were adjusting to the new battle for desegregation and racial equality that followed the Supreme Court's 1954 decision. Camp Lejeune reportedly had 160 incidents of assaults, muggings and robberies with racial overtones in 1969.[34] On the night of July 20, just before the 1st Battalion, 6th Marines, was to ship out for the Mediterranean, a big party was held and some white Marines were assaulted by groups of blacks. One white Marine, Cpl. Edward Blankston, died of head injuries and two other white Marines were stabbed. Forty-four men were charged and 13 convicted of riot, disobedience or assault. One black Marine was sentenced to nine years at hard labor for manslaughter. A special inquiry criticized leadership at Lejeune and young militant blacks. But the tension was widespread.

There were clashes and "fraggings" between the races on Okinawa and in the rear areas in Vietnam. In December 1969, Commandant Chapman said, "We've got a problem."[35] In 1970, 1,060 violent racial incidents occurred throughout the Corps; 79 Marines were seriously injured and two killed.[36]

Time, concern and effort were needed to try to solve the problem. Major Green has written, "Although it is doubtful that the influence of racial prejudice will ever be completely eradicated . . . the military has made commendable progress in moving toward this objective. . . . When a commander makes his subordinates aware that discriminatory behavior will not be tolerated within his command, it will not exist."[37]

By late 1984, 20 percent of the Corps' enlisted personnel and 4.4 percent of its officers were black. Among the black officers were one general (Brig. Gen. Frank E. Petersen, Jr.), four colonels and 17 lieutenant colonels. The highest-ranking black enlisted men included 202 sergeant majors or master gunnery sergeants, 535 first sergeants or master sergeants and 1,680 gunnery sergeants. By the 1980s, integration had become a fact.

By 1991, 35,261 enlisted Marines (20.2 percent of the total) and 1,009 officers (5.1 percent of the total) were black. The officers included one general, eight colonels and 41 lieutenant colonels. The highest-ranking black enlisted men were 274 sergeant majors or master gunnery sergeants (including four women), 760 first sergeants or master sergeants (including 26 women) and 1,966 gunnery sergeants (including 78 women). Progress seemed slow but steady.

6
Defeat and Bravado

The end came one week shy of 21 years after the fall of Dien Bien Phu and nearly three years after the last combat Marine had been withdrawn from Vietnam. When the last GIs had marched to their ships in 1973, they had left behind $5 billion worth of military equipment, including hundreds of tanks, 500 fighter-bombers, 625 helicopters and enough arms to equip a 700,000-man South Vietnamese army. But it was not enough; nothing could have been.

In March 1975, the North Vietnamese army, well trained and well armed with Soviet weapons, drove down from the north and sliced into the central highlands from the west, chopped up South Vietnam and surrounded Saigon. Da Nang, the Marines' old base, fell on March 29 without a struggle. The ARVN dropped back and was squeezed into an ever-tightening circle around the capital. As the South Vietnam retreat turned into confusion and panic, ships of the U.S. Seventh Fleet began gathering in the South China Sea to support an evacuation from Saigon.

Meanwhile, Cambodia fell to communist-led Khmer Rouge troops. Marine Col. Sydney H. Batchelder, Jr., flew into Phnom Penh on April 3 to manage the evacuation of the Cambodian capital. On Saturday morning, April 12, 360 Marines and corpsmen of the 2d Battalion, 4th Marines took off in CH-53 helicopters of HMH-462 from the amphibious assault ship *Okinawa* in the Gulf of Siam and landed in Phnom Penh. Lt. Col. George P. Slade's Marines swiftly formed a perimeter around a soccer field 1,000 yards from the United States Embassy while the last Americans and 159 Cambodians were evacuated. Then, under rocket and mortar fire, the Marines were flown out by HMH-463;

and their command group was lifted out by two Air Force helicopters. The entire operation took two hours and 23 minutes.

Off the coast of South Vietnam, the Seventh Fleet flotilla carried the 6,800-man 9th Marine Amphibious Brigade commanded by Brig. Gen. Richard E. Carey. The Marines and their 68 transport helicopters were embarked in 16 Navy amphibious ships and eight American merchant ships of the Military Sealift Command. There were also 10 U.S. Air Force helicopters in the carrier *Midway.* All stood in readiness to pluck out the last Americans from Saigon.

The evacuation was delayed because Ambassador Graham A. Martin did not want to alarm the already desperate South Vietnamese. Finally, U.S. Air Force jet transports began frantically carrying out the last thousand Americans and tens of thousands of Vietnamese from Saigon's Tan Son Nhut airfield. Many pro-American Vietnamese were unable to escape, and some Americans were forced to pay Vietnamese officials large bribes to obtain exit visas for their Vietnamese wives and children. Ambassador Martin's aloofness and stubbornness were blamed by many, and the ambassador's management of the evacuation was widely and bitterly criticized.[38]

Once the process did begin, Marines in Jeeps escorted buses filled with refugees to the U.S. Defense Attaché Office compound next to Tan Son Nhut. There, 18 Marines of the Embassy Security Guard under Gunnery Sgt. Vasco D. Martin, Jr., held a perimeter with M-16s and machine guns. On April 25, 40 men of 1st Lt. Bruce P. Thompson-Bowers' 3rd Platoon of C Company, 9th Marines were quietly flown in from *Hancock* to help them. President Thieu fled to Taiwan, blaming the Americans for not coming to his aid. Former Vice President Ky was taken to Camp Pendleton.

Communist bombs, shells and rockets rained down on Tan Son Nhut on Monday evening, April 28, and early Tuesday, killing two Marine security guards. The airfield could no longer be used. At Ambassador Martin's urgent telephone call, President Gerald R. Ford set in motion Operation Frequent Wind, the final evacuation of Saigon by helicopter.

On Tuesday afternoon and evening, HMH-462 and -463 flew in elements of Col. Alfred M. Gray's Regimental Combat Team-4, principally units of the 2d Battalion, 4th Marines, to the

DAO compound at Tan Son Nhut and brought out, under fire, 395 Americans and 4,475 Vietnamese and others. By midnight, the Marines set fire to the buildings and were flown out. Tens of thousands of South Vietnamese tried to reach the American fleet in barges, fishing boats, sampans and rafts. Fourteen 54-man detachments from the 3rd Marine Division under Maj. David A. Quinlan helped evacuate 67,437 Vietnamese on American ships.

Unexpectedly, the Marines were called on to evacuate more than 2,000 people from the American Embassy itself, instead of 100 as originally planned. There was room for only one CH-46 at a time on the embassy roof and one heavier CH-53 at a time on the parking lot. Starting at 5 P.M. Tuesday, two strings of helicopters put down at the embassy.

Late Tuesday, 130 Marines were flown over from Tan Son Nhut to beef up the 41-man embassy security guard led by Master Sgt. Juan J. Valdez. The Marines manned the gates with bayonets, and some used rifle butts to knock off Vietnamese trying to climb the barbed-wire-topped wall.

The last night was pandemonium. After dark, the rooftop landing zone was marked only with a barrel of burning oil and rubbish; from 2:15 A.M. on, a chopper was sent into each landing zone every ten minutes. Ambassador Martin went home to get his poodle and boarded a HMM-165 helicopter piloted by Capt. Gerald Berry on the roof at 5 A.M. In all, 978 Americans and 1,120 Vietnamese and others were lifted out of the embassy.

Eleven Marines with M-16s crouched on the roof. Maj. James Kean and Master Sgt. Valdez had pulled their men into the main building and barricaded the doors. Then, they moved up through the building until they held only the top floor and the roof. Vietnamese raced through the building's six floors and tried to reach the roof through the tear-gas smoke. The Marines, now under small-arms fire on the roof, marked their position with a red-smoke grenade. The last CH-46 landed; and just before 8 A.M., the Marines piled on board. The last man brought out the embassy's flag in a brown paper bag.

A total of 1,373 Americans and 5,595 Vietnamese and others had been evacuated from Saigon by helicopter. It required 530 evacuation sorties to get them out.

Four Marines were killed in those final days. Lance Cpl. Darwin J. Judge, a nineteen-year-old Eagle Scout from Marshalltown, Iowa, and Cpl. Charles McMahon, Jr., twenty-two, of Woburn, Massachusetts, both members of the Embassy Security Guard, were killed early Tuesday in a rocket attack on Tan Son Nhut. Capt. William C. Nystul of Coronado, California, and 1st Lt. Michael J. Shea of El Paso, Texas, were also killed Tuesday when their CH-46 helicopter crashed into the South China Sea near the carrier *Hancock*.

Left behind in the confusion at the embassy was the plaque commemorating the five Americans who had been killed defending the embassy during the Tet attack in 1968. Also left behind were the bodies of Corporal McMahon and Lance Cpl. Judge. The Provisional Revolutionary Government that took over Saigon returned them later; and they were buried on March 4, 1976, in their hometowns.

In Southeast Asia, Marines were involved in one more convulsion of violence. On Monday, May 12, 1975, two weeks after the evacuation of Saigon, a Cambodian gunboat stopped and seized the old, unarmed American container ship *Mayaguez* steaming from Hong Kong to Sattahip, Thailand. In Washington, America's leaders decided to use the ship's capture to prove to the world that, despite the loss of the Indochina war, the United States had not become a "paper tiger."

President Ford put on alert a 1,100-man battalion landing team of the 3rd Marine Division on Okinawa and rushed ships and planes to the scene. By Tuesday noon, the Cambodians had taken *Mayaguez* to three-mile-long Koh Tang (Tang Island), 34 miles from the mainland. On Wednesday, Capt. Charles T. Miller and his 39-man crew were transferred by fishing boat to an island—ironically named Koh Rong—at the harbor of Kompong Som, formerly Sihanoukville. (The ship's third mate, David C. English of Seattle, was a former Marine who had fought in Vietnam.) U.S. Air Force jets sank three Cambodian gunboats. Trying to turn back the fishing boat, the planes strafed it, reportedly hitting several of the Americans, and dropped tear gas that left everyone retching.

The alerted 2d Battalion, 9th Marines, commanded by Lt. Col. Randall W. Austin, sped from Okinawa to U Tapao Air Force Base in Thailand despite the usual official Thai protests. Early Thursday, 227 Marines flew 195 miles from U Tapao in 11 Air

Force helicopters to recapture the ship and attack Koh Tang.

Forty-eight Marines of D Company, 4th Marines, and 12 sailors, commanded by Maj. Raymond E. Porter, climbed down by rope from three Air Force HH-53s to the deck of the destroyer escort *Harold E. Holt*, which then went alongside *Mayaguez*. At 7:25 A.M., led by Cpl. Carl R. Coker, the Marines boarded the ship—eighteenth-century-style. *Mayaguez* was empty.

Under fighter cover, 179 Marines from Capt. James H. Davis' G Company assaulted Koh Tang an hour before the Marines boarded *Mayaguez*. One platoon was to land on the western side of the island's narrow neck leading to its northern end. The remainder of the company and the battalion command group headed for a larger landing zone on the eastern side of the neck. A second wave of E Company under Capt. Mykle E. Stahl was prepared to follow G Company in.

The attack on Koh Tang was a mistaken effort to rescue *Mayaguez'* crew. They were not there. And Cambodian armed strength on the island was seriously underestimated.

The Cambodians shot down the first two helicopters approaching the island's eastern landing zone at 6:15 A.M. One crashed in flames; seven Marines, two Navy corpsmen and the Air Force co-pilot died in the chopper; three Marines were killed in the surf. The remaining 13 men swam out to sea. After more than three hours in the ocean, they were rescued by the guided-missile destroyer *Henry B. Wilson*. While in the water, 1st Lt. Terry Tonkin, using a survival radio, managed to direct Air Force planes in firing runs against enemy positions on the island. The other helicopter landed on the beach with its tail shot off, and the 3rd Platoon Marines and the helicopter crewmen formed a defensive perimeter in the trees at the water's edge. No more helicopters dared land on the eastern side. There, the 20 isolated Marines and four airmen, led by Marine 2d Lt. Michael A. Cicere, held out all day under intermittent enemy fire. One Marine and one airman were wounded.

On the western side of Koh Tang, one of the first two helicopters—with Captain Davis aboard—was shot up and limped back to Thailand. The second helicopter disembarked the 1st Platoon under 2d Lt. James McDaniel. When the chopper took off again, it crashed, killing one of its four crewmen.

The remaining four helicopters were diverted to the western landing zone, and three were able to land there. The fourth, with Lt. Col. Austin's command group and an 81mm mortar section, landed 1,300 yards to the south to avoid enemy fire.

First Lt. James D. Keith, G Company's executive officer, took charge of the men on the western landing zone beach and set up a perimeter. The command group moved northward against resistance. Of the 179 Marines in the landing force, 131 made it ashore; and of those, 20 were isolated on the eastern shore and 29 were with the separated command group.

The main force of 82 men had landed at the western tip of a man-made cut across the heavily jungled island. On both sides of the cut, visibility was limited to 5 to 15 feet. The Marines were pinned down by fire from a wooded area 75 yards from the beach. The Cambodians fought hard.

Second Lt. McDaniel led a reinforced squad south against an enemy strongpoint. The patrol—all new to combat—was hit by fire on its flank. Lance Cpl. Ashton N. Loney of Albany, New York, was killed and five Marines, including McDaniel, were wounded. The fighting was sharp and at close range. Staff Sgt. Seferino Bernal, Jr., and Pfc. Jerome N. Wemitt rescued wounded men under fire. Keith, fearing the patrol would be encircled, ordered it back to the landing zone. The Cambodians followed the Marines, attacked the perimeter and were driven off. Keith called in Air Force strikes at the enemy's strongpoints. The fire fight and grenade duel continued all morning.

Meanwhile, the *Mayaguez'* crew had already been released two hours before the Marine attacks. But that was not known at the time. Planes from the carrier *Coral Sea* bombed Ream Airfield in Cambodia and an hour later bombed the Ream Naval Base and an inactive oil refinery near Kompong Som. At 10 A.M., the fishing boat bringing the *Mayaguez'* crew back to their ship approached the destroyer *Wilson*. The men were safe.

Since all but one of the eight helicopters bringing the first wave of Marines to Koh Tang had been destroyed or damaged, only five helicopters could be rounded up to fly in the second wave of 127 Marines. Before they reached Koh Tang, the crew of *Mayaguez* was aboard *Wilson*; and the assault was briefly called off. The five helicopters headed back toward U Tapao but, at Lt. Col. Austin's insistence, reversed course again for Koh Tang.

After Air Force strikes and a mortar barrage, 2d Lt. Richard H. Zales led a platoon against the Cambodians between Keith's perimeter and the approaching battalion command group and scattered the enemy into the jungle. At 12:45 P.M., the two Marine elements linked up.

Four of the five helicopters carrying the second wave managed to land and discharge 100 Marines—19 of G Company and 81 of E Company—and pick up six wounded Marines. The fifth chopper, trying to land in the isolated eastern zone, was damaged by enemy fire and made an emergency landing in Thailand. There were now 225 Americans on Koh Tang.

The only remaining job was to get them out. After an attempt to rescue 2d Lt. Cicere and his men at 2:15 P.M. failed with damage to one helicopter, the men on the eastern side were finally evacuated by one helicopter at 6:10 P.M. under heavy fire from Cambodian automatic weapons. On the western side, a C-130 dropped a 15,000-pound bomb; and by 8:10, a helicopter hovering at the water's edge lifted out the last 29 men under automatic weapons fire in total darkness. The destroyer *Wilson* had an armed boat close to the shore covering the final departure. Three missing Marines were left on the western side of Koh Tang; nobody knew whether they were dead or alive. It had been a tough vertical assault.

All told, connected with the *Mayaguez* operation, 41 Americans had been killed (including 23 Air Force men killed in a Thailand helicopter crash) and 50 wounded. That made 56,869 Americans in uniform who had died and 303,704 who had been wounded in connection with the Vietnam war. The totals included 14,691 Marines killed and 88,633 wounded.[39] Although Marines made up only one-tenth of all U.S. forces that served in Vietnam, one in every four names carved in the Vietnam Memorial in Washington, D.C., is that of a United States Marine.[40]

In Washington, the political leaders felt the *Mayaguez* affair had made their point. It was, somehow, an appropriate finish to the United States Marines' longest and most disastrous overseas war.

On July 2, 1976, North and South Vietnam were officially declared reunited as the Socialist Republic of Vietnam with Hanoi as its capital.

7
"Men Stalking Each Other"

The Vietnam war divided the American people as had no other overseas war. Many condemned it as immoral; others believed it vital to America's national interest. These views were irreconcilable. They tore the nation apart.

The United States had tried to move into the post-World War II power vacuum in Southeast Asia. This intervention repeated a long tradition of sending American force to impose the American will across the seas. Over and over again, American power had thrust outward, and the Marines had repeatedly served as the spearhead: Tripoli, Mexico, Canton, the Philippines, Peking, the Caribbean, two World Wars, Korea and Vietnam. The process would continue in Lebanon, Grenada and Kuwait.

In Vietnam again, the Marines, as a force-in-readiness, had been among the first to fight. The Marine Corps had not been responsible for the decisions that shipped hundreds of thousands of Americans into Vietnam, but its leaders were certainly eager to go. As former Commandant Shoup saw it, "In early 1965, there was a shooting war going on and the Marines were being left out of it, contrary to all their traditions."[41] As in all the nation's wars, the Corps outspokenly sought a fighting role.

Not only ordinary Americans were divided over Vietnam. Leaders in Washington also differed over whether it was essential to the United States that Southeast Asia not go communist. Shoup, who could never be faulted for either his courage or his candor, said:

> From the beginning of our growing involvement in the affairs of Vietnam, I had opposed the idea that such a

691

small country in that remote part of the world constituted either an economic interest or a strategic threat to the welfare of the United States. In the past I have frequently expressed concern about military policies or plans which would commit American troops to a land war against the oriental peoples of Southeast Asia.[42]

When Lyndon Johnson sent a largely drafted and draft-driven civilian army to fight an undeclared, ideological war on the mainland of Asia, many young Americans were not prepared to die to prevent Indochina from going communist. But some were, and more than 56,000—willing or not—had been killed in the effort. In 1967, a Navy chaplain with the Marines in Vietnam said, "Most of these kids know why they are here. Today I talked with a kid with his third Purple Heart in three months here. I asked him if he wanted to go home. He said he wanted to go home and see his wife and new baby, but he'd be back."[43]

It was certainly the ugliest war in which the Marine Corps ever fought. It was a war against civilians as well as armies—a war of booby traps and assassinations, murder and terror. In February 1967, Lance Cpl. Ralph D. Mase of Little Rock, Arkansas, a fire team leader with I Company, 1st Marines, went on a patrol looking for Viet Cong only a mile south of Marble Mountain. He was the second man in the column. His foot touched a wire and tripped a booby trap. It was simply a grenade in a C ration can. Kicking the wire, Mase pulled the grenade out of the can. The grenade exploded, sending fragments into his right arm. It was that kind of war.

Late that same night, Cpl. Andre A. Williams of Springfield, Massachusetts, and his sentry dog, Rocky, served as the point of a patrol from Combined Action Company E-2 out of the village of Nam-O. Half an hour later, Rocky smelled danger. Instantly, a Viet Cong stepped from a doorway and shot Williams through the chest. His patrol leader killed the Viet Cong; and a Medevac helicopter rushed Williams to the Marine First Medical Battalion field hospital, where a swift operation saved his life. It was that kind of war.[44]

After the Marines had been fighting for four years, I visited Vietnam again in July 1969 and at Hoi An wrote in my notebook: "Here in the countryside, there is firing every night, assassinations every month. The refugee camps are filled with wives and children of men still hiding out in the 10-foot-high grass with the Viet Cong. Twelve-year-old girls carry rifles and wear black pajamas. Marines must go armed and wear steel vests to walk in the road." It was still that kind of war.

Lt. Gen. Walt called it "the chevron war"—small unit actions and patrols in the hamlets and rice paddies led by noncoms in their teens and twenties. He compared it to fighting the Indians in the American West—"men stalking each other in the thick green gloom of deep forest."[45]

But in Vietnam, the guerrillas—"bandits," the Marines had called them in the Caribbean—had a real army of their own. The Marines had to fight two wars: the nasty guerrilla war in the populated areas—the villages and paddies, and the big-unit, artillery-supported conventional war against the North Vietnamese army up north in the jungle. American strength and technology fought a native nationalism dressed in communist ideology and supported by major powers. Each side had the capability of using and experimenting with modern weapons. Vietnam was both the most impersonal and the most personal of wars.

At its core, it was a matter of heart and spirit. The Americans, so far from home, were the foreigners; in a long Vietnamese tradition, they were the hated. Even those Vietnamese who huddled under the protection of American guns in fear of Viet Cong terror knew that they could buy only some small piece of time. In the end, the war was lost because the military dictatorship in Saigon failed to win the loyalty of its people and the American leaders failed to wage a guerrilla war successfully. As the Americans had taught the British 200 years before, it is difficult for soldiers and guns to suppress a revolution across the sea.

This war ripped at men's souls. In Vietnam, men bombed and were killed; men booby-trapped and were maimed. Marines did kill civilians and torture prisoners. They burned homes and they built schools and hospitals. They brought the Vietnamese guns and napalm, food and medicines. They created orphans and constructed orphanages. They both killed and cared for. It was an impossible assignment—a most terrible war.

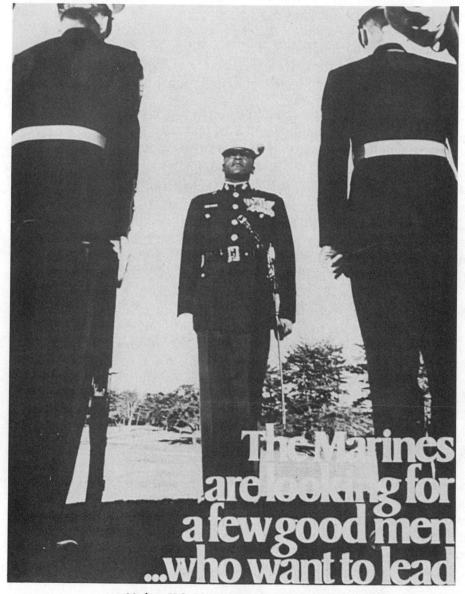

The Marines
are looking for
a few good men
...who want to lead

Modern U.S. Marine Corps recruiting poster.
The Marines first advertised for "a few good men"
in the Providence Gazette in 1779. USMC Photo

SEMPER FIDELIS

IX
STARTING
THE THIRD
CENTURY
1975–1989

1
November 10, 1975

In a cold, drizzling rain on the morning of November 10, 1975, several hundred green-raincoated Marines gathered silently before the Marine Corps War Memorial at Arlington National Cemetery. Standing in the sanctuary of America's heritage, they could see the Washington Monument and the Jefferson and Lincoln Memorials through the gray mist. It was the Corps' official two-hundredth birthday, and the Marines were assembled at the giant green-bronze statue of the Iwo Jima flag-raising to remember the three million Americans who have been United States Marines.

Two Marines who had raised that flag on Mount Suribachi 30 years before lay in nearby graves. The last former Marine alive of the six men portrayed in the famous statue, Rene A. Gagnon, attended the ceremonies. (He died in 1979, at the age of fifty-five.) Former Navy corpsman John H. Bradley was the only other survivor. Leading the Marines at the memorial service was the new Commandant of the Corps, tall, lean Gen. Louis H. Wilson, who had won the Medal of Honor as a twenty-four-year-old captain on Guam in World War II.

The Marine Band played. Prayers were said. And the President of the United States spoke. Quoting the golden inscription on the gleaming black marble base of the statue—"Uncommon valor was a common virtue"—President Ford called the Marine Corps Birthday "the bicentennial of its uncommon valor." The President said, "The Corps has become a living monument to devotion and self-sacrifice. . . ."

At the ceremony's end, a rifle salute cracked out, echoing among the hills. A Marine bugler sounded Taps.

That evening, some two thousand Marine officers and their

ladies attended a Birthday Ball in Washington, one of many held around the world. They watched a pageant review the Corps' "200 years proud." Their greatest applause resounded for the tableaux of a Navy corpsman and a Marine rifle squad. The pageant swept over the American saga and brought back to mind Marines who had helped shape that story:

John Basilone, the kid who drove a laundry truck in New Jersey and wiped out a Japanese regiment on Guadalcanal. William Deane Hawkins, "The Hawk," the first man ashore at Tarawa. "Chesty" Puller and his five Navy Crosses. William Barber and Fox Company holding Toktong Pass. "Hiking Hiram" Bearss, with his shirttails flapping. Dan Daly, the New York City newsboy who fought around the globe. John Quick, under fire, signaling at Guantanamo and carrying ammunition through to Bouresches. James Swett, the youngster who shot down seven Japanese planes in his first 15 minutes of combat. The Raiders: Merritt Edson and Evans Carlson. John T. Myers and bantam Smedley Butler in China. Herman Hanneken and Christian Schilt. Littleton Waller Tazewell Waller. Earl Ellis. George Terrett. Archibald Gillespie. John Marshall Gamble. Archibald Henderson and John Lejeune. David Shoup and Lewis Walt. The long line from John Trevett to John Glenn.

As anyone who has gone to war knows, only a few heroes are remembered. Many Marines performed acts of courage and gave their lives, unwitnessed and unsung. They deserve commemoration as much as those whose moment of valor was recognized with the Medal of Honor or Navy Cross.

When the pageant had run its course and the Marine Corps story had been told again, the Commandant cut the traditional birthday cake with the sword that the state of Virginia had given Presley O'Bannon in 1807 on his return from "the shores of Tripoli." The first slice of cake, as custom dictated, was handed to the oldest Marine present, Gen. Gerald C. Thomas, the eighty-one-year-old retired veteran who had fought as a sergeant at Belleau Wood.

It had been a day for looking back over 200 years. The Commandant's birthday message also looked forward. It closed: "Marching shoulder to shoulder we shall gain in strength and readiness as we move ahead, in step and smartly."

The bicentennial came at a time when the Marines were

once again under attack. The Vietnam war had disrupted the nation and the Corps, left them uncertain of both their responsibilities and their power.

The Corps was by then almost unique among the world's major nations. Its nearest competitor was the 17,000-man Soviet Naval Infantry. The British Royal Marines were down to 6,000 men. Of course, there were marine corps—usually created with the help of the U.S. Marine Corps—throughout East Asia and Latin America. But the question was raised: Were the American Marines a vestige of a bygone imperial age?

The Senate Armed Services Committee told the Corps to re-evaluate its mission and clean house of substandard manpower. General Wilson took office as Commandant in July 1975, when General Cushman retired early.* Wilson immediately appointed the so-called Haynes Board, chaired by Maj. Gen. Fred E. Haynes, Jr., a veteran of three wars, to find anwers to the questions being asked both inside and outside the military establishment:

Was there need for a 196,000-strong Marine Corps when the nation after the Vietnam war seemed no longer willing to intervene abroad?

As the Marines had not made a major amphibious assault since Okinawa (1945) and Inchon (1950), should the Corps' main mission still be to attack enemy shores from the sea?

What should be the Marines' role in the future?

Was the Marine Corps prepared to fight an enemy armed with sophisticated modern weapons?

Should the Marine Corps continue to possess its own air wings?

Why did this "elite" force have higher rates of desertion, absence-without-leave and drug abuse than the other services?

The Marine Corps has been challenged throughout its history—after the War of 1812, the Civil War, the Spanish-American War and both World Wars—after every major war the nation has fought. There was nothing new about that. These repeated attacks were not the work of some perennial cabal out to destroy the Corps. They resulted from the nature of the Marine Corps itself.

*Gen. Earl E. Anderson, the Assistant Commandant, also retired early, in part because of an internal controversy over succession procedures.

After Vietnam, nobody proposed mothballing the Corps. Not only would that have meant getting rid of some of the nation's best; but, said the authors of one critical study, "doing away with the Corps would be politically infeasible in any event."[1] That was true. In a political brawl, the Corps always managed to take care of itself.

The most serious post-Vietnam challenge questioned the Corps' future purpose. Its mission had evolved over the years; as Lt. Gen. Krulak put it, "The Marines don't have a role except to be malleable enough to do what comes on the horizon."[2]

The single thread running through the entire Marine Corps story was that the Corps is the armed force that can best project American power onto hostile shores. The early Marines, starting out as soldiers on American men-of-war, put armed force ashore with the Navy at Nassau, the Penobscot, Tripoli, the Falkland Islands, Sumatra, Africa, California, Mexico and China.

With the coming of steam propulsion, steel ships and long-range naval guns in the mid-nineteenth century, naval warfare changed. And there was a greater urge to extend American power overseas. In 1898, half the Corps was on shipboard duty; but 20 years later, only two percent was afloat.[3] Down to World War I, the Corps fought small or decrepit nations (Mexico, China, Spain, the Philippines, Nicaragua, Haiti). It was "more closely associated than the other services with American intervention abroad,"[4] as America expanded overseas.

The turning point, if there was any single moment, came in 1908 when President Theodore Roosevelt's Executive Order 969 removed Marines from warships and enlarged their duties to "furnish the first line of mobile defense of naval bases and naval stations beyond the continental limits of the United States."[5] The Marine Corps kicked like a mule, and sea duty was retained. But Roosevelt had pointed to the future.

The Corps went on from defending to seizing advanced naval bases and, in World War II, to capturing island air bases for the strategic bombing of Japan. Until the atomic bombs were dropped, the Marines were ready to join in the climactic assault on the enemy's homeland itself.

With the end of World War II, the unification of the armed services and the opening of the Cold War, the Marine Corps emphasized that it was a force-in-readiness—in Commandant Cates' words "a ready striking force."[6] The idea and the slogan

"First to Fight" had been there since World War I, and the Corps came to see its mission as stepping in swiftly to deter or contain aggression until the Army could mount the major land effort. "Our first and paramount characteristic is readiness," Commandant Wilson told the Senate Armed Services Committee in February 1976. "This mission is meant to provide the fleets with a ready capability to project combined arms combat power ashore. . . . we have extensive overseas interests that are vulnerable."[7]

The experiences in Korea and Southeast Asia demonstrated limits of America's power and for the moment cooled American ardor for costly interventions overseas. It became clear to all that the United States was not an Asian power but a Pacific power. Massive American military muscle had ruled the Pacific Ocean—43 percent of the earth's surface—since the Japanese surrender in 1945. No nation was able to challenge the United States there. The long westward thrust of American power had been stopped only when it tried to climb onto the mainland of Asia— threatening the Yalu River border in the north and injecting a half million men into Vietnam in the south. But it still dominated the high seas and the island chain skirting Asia's Pacific coast.

The United States had been pushing its power across the Pacific for a century and a half. It based an East India naval squadron at Hong Kong as early as 1835; and between then and 1900, American Marines fought at Quallah Battoo, Canton, Formosa, the Han River, Manila Bay and Tientsin. Americans have been fighting and dying on the rim of Asia for a very long time. Even after the defeat in Vietnam, American power still stood 5,000 miles west of San Francisco. The Far East was still the American Far West.[8]

But the frontiers of American power had been shoved back. In the Pacific, the line of the Philippines, Taiwan, Okinawa, South Korea and Japan was not secure. In Europe, Mediterranean bases were under threat. General Shoup wrote, "It is a grim revelation that there are limits of U.S. power and our capabilities to police the world."[9] These limits and the uncertain future of bases overseas promised a reduction of prepositioned American forces abroad and increased the need for a mobile readiness force.

At the same time, Americans were determined to avoid "another Vietnam." Some analysts interpreted this as a lasting opposition to any military interventions. A Brookings Institution study of the Marine Corps said, "There is growing public disenchantment with military ventures overseas, particularly those involving the use of ground troops."[10]

This post-Vietnam view implied that a neo-isolationist United States, pulling back into a "fortress America" stance, no longer needed the Marines' offensive capability. But to limit military capabilities to temporary political moods was always precarious.

As the story of the Marine Corps demonstrates, military interventions abroad have been a constant feature of American life. They have had a variety of purposes: show of force, evacuation of U.S. nationals, protection of U.S. interests, control of "choke points" to guard free transit of the seas and intervention on a lasting basis. Except for the brief preoccupation with the Civil War, there never was a period when American military and naval forces have not been engaged in "ventures overseas." The Marines' ventures ranged from New Providence (1776), Santo Domingo (1800) and Tripoli (1803) to Lebanon (1958), the Dominican Republic (1965), Vietnam (1965–1973), Koh Tang (1975), Lebanon (1982), Grenada (1983), Panama (1989) and Kuwait (1991). The Marines calculate that they made 180 landings in the 134 years starting in 1800. The American people have never been disenchanted with military ventures overseas for long.

The widespread "disenchantment" over Vietnam was not with the original intervention. It was with the escalation of the immoral and frightful cost of that involvement to both Americans and Vietnamese and the refusal of the responsible American leaders to find and take an "exit." The Vietnam war, fought in good part by unwilling and draft-compelled young Americans, became unpopular as it was intensified and protracted.

In the future, the United States' political leaders will need to make rational, hardheaded assessments of the relationship between the national interest and the cost in blood and money: to get in when a vital national interest warrants the cost and to get out if the cost exceeds the stake. There will be a continuing need for professional military forces capable of reacting swiftly and successfully when the American people's elected leaders deem intervention essential to the nation.

Commandant Wilson talked about the Marine Corps' future role this way:

> Everyone knows we need an Army, we need a Navy and we need an Air Force. It is very difficult to explain why we

need a Marine Corps. [With] a country such as ours that has an $180 billion investment overseas and roughly overseas trade of some $74 or $80 billion a year, we need a force that can project power overseas. . . . I think it is inconceivable that we should not have this capability to project power ashore overseas. . . . [The Marine Corps] is not a defensive force but a means of projecting power ashore where we may be required. Of course, that's our mission. . . . I am not concerned about the future of the Marine Corps so long as we have ready forces such as we have today, because I am convinced that when the call comes, they have my telephone number—and I expect a call.[11]

The United States has always sought—and will presumably continue to seek—to project its power overseas when it feels its vital interests or the rights of its citizens are endangered. As a member of the Haynes Board wrote: "History has demonstrated again and again the cyclic nature of political affairs. It is dangerous to reduce the only viable forcible entry capacity the nation has as long as the U.S. continues to have overseas interests that are both vital and vulnerable."[12]

After the American pullback from Indochina and Thailand in the mid-1970s, military planners began to direct renewed attention to the United States' military interests in Europe. Some planners believed the Corps should strengthen its firepower and help defend Europe. They said that a prepositioned conventional deterrent remains credible only if it can be reinforced and that the Marine Corps' ready force serves this purpose. Others saw the Corps' future value not in supplementing U.S. Army forces in Europe but in intervening against non-major powers, where American interests and citizens are endangered or where the major powers' interests clash. After Vietnam, the entire concept of what battle the Marines should prepare to fight came under challenge.

The crux of the post-Vietnam attack on the Marine Corps was the charge that the Corps, in classic military habit, was preparing to fight World War II over again. Specifically, the Corps was criticized for continuing to emphasize amphibious assault—"this peculiar type of combat."[13] Critics warned that the multi-division World War II Marine Corps trained for amphibious assault would never be needed again.

703

No one advocated that the United States eliminate all amphibious-trained Marines. Even the Brookings Institution study acknowledged the value of one and a third divisions of amphibious Marines. The question became: What should the greater part of the Corps be prepared to do? If most of its amphibious mission were obsolete or if it were to supply just more "army," there could be no military justification for keeping a three-division Marine Corps.

The Brookings study proposed four options: that the rest of the Corps be eliminated; that it replace the Army garrisoning the Pacific islands; that it beef up the Army defending Europe; or that it take over the airborne readiness assignment from the 82d Airborne Division, the Army's own elite competitor as a "quick insertion" force.

Among these options, the deactivization of the bulk of the Corps would be militarily foolish and politically impossible. The Pacific garrisoning option offered a rationale for maintaining a three-division Corps, but it would be a geographically limiting mission and obliterate the concept of a worldwide readiness force. To have the Corps serve as supplementary Army manpower could erase any Marine Corps uniqueness and open the way for eventual Army absorption.

The Corps already had a responsibility in the Joint Strategic Objectives Plan to provide two Marine Amphibious Forces— 80,000 men and 1,000 planes—"ready to go" as a strategic reserve for NATO. Marine planners desperately wanted an assignment on Europe's flanks—not in the center. Said Lt. Gen. Leslie E. Brown, then Chief of Staff of Headquarters, Marine Corps, "We are not desirous to have the central European commitment. We prefer to stay light and maneuverable."[14] Commandant Wilson pointed out that there are 8,000 miles of coastline between Europe's North Cape and Greece, and added, "We are the only ones who can project this power ashore."

But the prospect of simply reinforcing the Army was disconcerting to many Marines. In Vietnam, the Marines had to serve pretty much like Army troops in the Corps' longest war. Commandant Wilson said candidly that the Marines could have been used better if they had exercised their amphibious expertise down in the Mekong Delta.

Finally, replacing the Army airborne division would stir interservice conflicts; but it would eliminate the duplication of readiness strike forces, whether air-delivered or sea-delivered. Rivalry between the Army Airborne and the Marines went back at least to the post-Korean war Strategic Army Corps and Strike Command. The 1965 Dominican Republic intervention ballooned beyond all need with the 82d Airborne Division and the Marine Corps competing to prove their ability to get there fast. And shortly after the first Marine battalions landed at Da Nang, the 173d Airborne Brigade reached Saigon. As General Shoup commented, "With these initial deployments the Army-Marine race to build forces in Vietnam began in earnest and did not slow down again until both became overextended, overcommitted, and depleted at home."[15]

To some serious degree, the Corps on its two-hundredth birthday was once again a service in search of a mission that justified its size. The Corps' mission always determined how it would be structured, trained and equipped. It was said that amphibious warfare had "shaped the Corps into a distinctively tailored light infantry force" and left its ground units "short on firepower and cross-country mobility." Although others believed the Corps was already too heavily equipped, the question remained: Could the Marines, as armed and equipped, survive in a European war or a conflict like the 1973 Middle East war, which would feature armor and precision-guided weapons and an enemy with the will and skills to use them?

2

The Post-Vietnam Corps

When the post-Vietnam debate erupted, the Corps had an authorized strength of 196,300 men and women. Of these, 113,000 were in its combat forces: 51,000 in three divisions, 37,000 in three air wings, and 24,900 in "force troops"—tanks, amphibian tractors, support troops, etc. Elements of its three division-air wing Marine Amphibious Forces were deployed at sea in the Mediterranean and Western Pacific and intermittently in the Caribbean. Additionally, the Corps was authorized to have an Organized Reserve of 35,000 Marines, essentially a fourth division and air wing.

The Corps constructed its combat forces on "a building block principle" that gave it flexibility. Tank battalions and LVT battalions could be added to an expeditionary force as the situation required. Thus, a Marine Amphibious Force (a combined division and air wing) could be mounted out with the kind of mobility, firepower and air cover best suited to the fighting ahead.

By its own estimate, the Corps was short of everything from people to amphibious shipping and naval gunfire support. (There was virtually not a gun larger than 5 inches left in the entire U.S. Navy until, in the early 1980s, out of mothballs came four *Iowa*-class battleships with their 16-inch guns and a new array of missiles to strengthen the Navy's gunfire support of Marine amphibious assaults.)

The Marines' worst bottleneck was their difficulty in getting to where they would fight. In 1968, during the Vietnam war, the Navy had the amphibious lift capability to deploy two complete Marine Amphibious Forces (MAFs), but by 1982 this was down to less than one MAF of 50,000 men. The Navy's goal was to deploy

706

one MAF in one theater and one Marine Amphibious Brigade (16,500 men) in another.

In 1976, the first super-sized *Tarawa*-class amphibious ship was commissioned; and in 1981, the keel was laid in Seattle for the amphibious ship *Whidbey Island* (LSD-41), the first of a new class of Landing Ship Dock. It was the first amphibious ship built by the nation in more than five years.

Since 1971, the Corps was operating the VSTOL vertical-short-takeoff-landing AV-8A Harrier aircraft. The British-made Harrier's ability to use short runways, roads and decks and its agility made it valuable for close support. Its performance for the British in the Falkland Islands war in 1982 bolstered the Corps' desire to acquire a new model AV-8B with twice the range or payload. The first production model was flown in 1982.

And the Corps acquired the heavy-lift helicopter, the CH-53E Super Stallion, which can carry 16 tons 50 miles. It can lift virtually anything in a Marine division's inventory except the tanks.

The Corps had precision-guided bombs, improved Hawk and Stinger antiaircraft missiles and one-man Dragon medium anti-tank guided missiles. The Sidewinder missile and laser-guided Hellfire missile provided helicopters with added tank-killing punch.

The M-48 tanks with their 90mm guns were replaced by the M-60 with a 105mm gun. A Light Armored Vehicle (LAV), armor-protected and helicopter-transportable, was introduced for assault support, to fight armor, for command purposes and air defense.

The Marines were trying to intensify firepower in the 192,000-person active-duty Corps and the 37,000 "selected reserves." The goal was to make a Marine infantry battalion 10 percent smaller while increasing its firepower by 25 percent. The basic squad was briefly changed from three four-man fire teams to two five-man fire teams—the first change in the structure of the squad in the memory of anyone on active duty.

The M-16 rifle was given a heavier barrel and a more durable stock. Fifty-caliber machine guns were added to battalions. The SMAW "bunker buster," an 83mm bazooka-like weapon, was used by weapons platoons. Each Marine division would have a total of 44 TOW platoons, and each battalion would have 32 Dragons. Mortars, machine guns and even pistols were modernized. The Corps especially strengthened its antitank power with precision-guided weapons.

A 155mm howitzer that could be carried in the CH-53E helicopter replaced the 105mm howitzer. The MULE, a portable laser-directed rangefinder for forward observers, pinpointed targets for laser-guided munitions. The Seafire targeting system directed five-inch laser-guided projectiles. And new concepts for landing craft strung out into the next decade. Revolutionary high-speed "surface-effect" air cushion ships (hovercraft, etc.) carried at 50 knots a 60-ton payload—VSTOL aircraft and forces armed with electronic and laser-beam-aimed weapons—in dispersed formations inland across hostile beaches.

In 1976, the Haynes Board recommended to the Senate Armed Services Committee that the Corps remain a global strategic force-in-readiness. It opposed organizing the Corps specifically for combat in one theater; Maj. Gen. Haynes said, "the Marine Corps has basically a global role. It has to be prepared to go anywhere. . . . If maintained as a combined arms air-ground team, we can go anywhere and fight and make a good account of ourselves."[16]

Focusing on "mid and high intensity wars," the Board urged that the Marines retain their three division-air wing strength and improve their firepower by adding antitank and antiaircraft missile and artillery punch. It proposed that ground reconnaissance units be strengthened so that they could search and fight, rather than search and run. In the air, the Board supported the VSTOL force and keeping the A-6 all-weather attack plane for close support. Said Haynes, "We reject out of hand any reduction in the close support attack role."[17]

The Corps' integrated air arm had long been its most controversial element. Over half a century, the Marines increased their firepower and mobility with aircraft and helicopters. At first, the Corps, because it was lightly armed with artillery and tanks, built up its own air force to reach beyond the range of naval gunfire for close support. Its aviation capability grew to include fighter and attack aircraft that could dogfight enemy planes and bomb deep inside enemy territory. The Corps accumulated 13 types and 22 models of combat aircraft and helicopters. The question was widely asked whether the Corps was justified in maintaining fighter-attack squadrons primarily for air-to-air combat and interdiction, when the Air Force and Navy were equipped to perform these jobs.

The questioning also attacked the Corps' need for its own

close air support if Marines were to be used in land campaigns with the Army rather than in amphibious assault. And the development of sophisticated surface-to-air missiles complicated the job of close air support. Marines argued persuasively that they had created highly effective air-ground close support coordination surpassing anything that the Air Force could provide. Marine close air support for Marines on the ground has been superlative.

In reaction to the Vietnam experience, some analysts opposed loading down Marines with more armor, artillery and mechanized vehicles. They feared increasing a Marine task force's weight and slowing its strategic mobility and reaction time. They called such thinking the "Fort Benning mentality" and blamed it for losing the Vietnam war against a lightweight, flexible enemy.

They believed the Vietnam war and the enormous tank losses of the 1973 Middle East war showed that the day of Guderian's tank-fighter-bomber team was over. The battlefield of the future, in this view, would be dominated not by tanks and manned aircraft but by precision-guided antitank and antiaircraft missiles carried by small units skilled in camouflage and night operations.

The new military technology of electronics and lasers promised to revolutionize warfare. Vietnam and the 1973 Middle East war (and the 1991 Gulf war) were laboratories for a historic evolution of warfare, pushing armies apart again as did the arrival of the rifle and the machine gun a century ago. The "one-shot one-kill" weapons made tanks, planes and helicopters exceedingly vulnerable.

The "smart weapons" revolution required basic changes in Marine Corps thinking. To fight and survive and win on a battlefield now, Marines had to be adequately armed and armored, possess the means for dispersal and rapid mobility and carry modern weapons that could destroy attacking tanks, aircraft and the enemy's new weapons at greater distances. To coordinate these new requirements with the mission of "projection of power" by sea or air was the Corps' real post-Vietnam challenge.

While the Marine Corps was rethinking its mission and structure, its quality as an "elite force" also came under attack. Could the Corps sustain its right to be regarded as an elite force at its three-MAF size? The Vietnam war draft had driven resentful young men to "volunteer," and later the pressure to compete for recruits in a peacetime all-volunteer armed force saddled the

Corps with serious problems of recruiting and discipline. The Marine Corps was ill-prepared for the all-volunteer era because it erroneously thought that virtually all its Vietnam recruits were "true volunteers." It found itself with the highest per capita rates of desertion, absence-without-leave and drug abuse in the armed forces.[18]

Several explanations were offered for this disturbing record of "troop quality": the large number of high school dropouts among recruits, the Corps' changed racial makeup and its insistence on severe standards of discipline. While the other services were selling the attractions of career-training and beer-in-the-barracks, the Corps was advertising its need for "a few good men" and warning young men it was not promising them a rose garden.

At the end of 1975, Commandant Wilson presented the Senate Armed Services Committee a report from the Haynes Board admitting that the Corps "has had a manpower quality problem" and stating that it had begun to take corrective measures. It got rid of 4,000 "unsuitable" Marines and raised to 75 percent the desired proportion of high school graduates among recruits. (Only 46 percent were high school graduates in 1973). The increased requirement for high school graduates reduced the percentage of blacks being enlisted in the Corps from 19 to 15 percent.

Commandant Wilson also sought to raise the quality of leadership, improve living and working conditions, curtail excessive reassignment of individuals and units and revamp training techniques. Above all, he put the emphasis on the quality rather than the quantity of recruits.

The key problem remained to attract and keep intelligent and motivated young people. Because only 27 percent of recommended first-term enlistees—and 12 percent of all first-termers against an optimum of 25 percent—re-enlisted, the Marines had to recruit 50,000 young men and women a year.

Recruit training abuses further undermined the Corps' reputation as an elite force. In 1974 and 1975, 178 Parris Island drill instructors and 182 San Diego DIs were punished for abusing recruits. After the senseless and fatal beating of Pvt. Lynn E. McClure of Lufkin, Texas, at the San Diego training center and the grotesque shooting of a recruit by a Parris Island DI, subcommittees of the House and Senate Armed Services Committees ordered investigations into Marine Corps recruiting and training practices. And a *New York Times* editorial referred to the Corps as "once the elite of the United States armed forces." The *Times* commented that "not all Marines have yet learned to draw the line between toughness and sadism."[19]

In the most shocking case, Private McClure, a "problem recruit" who had reportedly been emotionally disturbed and rejected by both the Army and Air Force, was beaten into unconsciousness with pugil sticks on December 6, 1975, by other recruits in training at San Diego and died three months later after surgeons removed part of his skull. Training abuses reminded the public of the indefensible practices exposed after the Ribbon Creek "death march" 20 years earlier.

Many Marines denied that training abuses were widespread. Commandant Wilson called them "infinitesimal" among all the recruits who go through boot camp. He said, "Sadism has no part in Marine training. Punishment to where a man drops has no part in Marine training. But stress does have, to a certain point. . . . The ultimate is not to have abuses at the recruit depot. The ultimate is to train a man to be able to take care of himself and to live in the stressful situation of battle."

One Marine with an intimate grasp of the recruit training problem was Gen. Robert H. Barrow, who had been the Deputy Chief of Staff for Manpower before becoming Commandant in 1979. A DI himself long ago, Barrow was a combat commander in Korea and Vietnam and served as commanding general of the Parris Island recruit depot for nearly three years. When he was Deputy Chief of Staff for Manpower, he said:

> We had more abuse at Parris Island and San Diego than the Marine Corps is willing to admit or the public ever understood. . . . The odd thing about this [was] almost without exception the individual who experienced it believed it was good for him. . . . That is why it never comes out. . . . The Marine Corps has been unwilling to recognize that it is a problem because people believe it was good for them. . . . A lot of DIs don't raise their voice, they don't raise their hand, they don't engage in any form of hazing, and they get the same good results. But they are powerful people of strong character, who have great confidence in themselves and don't need to engage in this kind of nonsense. . . .
> [Recruit training] is the guts of the Marine Corps. . . . "readiness" comes from the boot camp experience because

711

that's where discipline is taught. One of the training objectives at Parris Island is "to develop in the individual a sense of discipline and insure a respect for authority and an instant and willing obedience to orders." When you've said that, you've said everything.[20]

Pointing out that 55 percent of the Marine Corps was twenty years of age and under, Barrow explained that young men become Marines mainly for two reasons:

> First, many, if not most, want desperately to believe in something. Most of us want one or more strong personal commitments—religion, home, community, or some other institution which would extract from us involvement and strong beliefs. In today's world, the opportunity for such positive commitment has waned significantly and many young people look around them in vain for such opportunities. For many, the search ends with the Marine Corps. . . . Second, there is an inherent need in all males of the animal world to prove their masculinity or manliness. . . . In the past, it has accounted for such decisions as opening the new frontier, "going to sea" and other forms of adventure. . . . The opportunity for legitimate proving of one's manliness is shrinking. A notable exception is the Marine Corps. The Marine Corps' reputation, richly deserved, for physical toughness, courage and demands on mind and body, attracts those who want to prove their manliness. Here too their search ends.
>
> Perhaps unwittingly, the Marine Corps exploits and builds on these two basic desires, to believe in something and to prove one's manliness; and in the process, the Marine Corps gains from it two of its most important virtues—spirit and discipline—virtues which are the mark of excellence in any military organization and which are absolutely essential to success in combat.[21]

Congressman Paul N. McCloskey, Jr., a Korean war Marine officer, put it clearly when he said that he objected to physical abuse of recruits but that Marine Corps training should be "as tough as combat itself."

The Marine Corps had long experience with young men who

ended up in the brig while on garrison duty but proved valiant fighters in battle. No responsible Marine commander condoned abusing such men to make them cooperate or to turn them into effective Marines. The system broke down, as it repeatedly did, when noncoms and officers charged with training these men were inadequate to deal with them intelligently.

It is difficult to train and lead young men so that they will remain thinking human beings and still react instantly and unquestioningly to a sergeant's order that they advance into deadly enemy fire. The requirements of an "elite" killing force like the Marine Corps run opposite to all meaning of the term "elite" in a democratic society where the ideal is individuality, self-determination and the questioning of authority. But the preservation of a free society can depend on young men willing, trained and disciplined to fight and die on order.

3
Ready in the 1980s

In the 1980s, a series of violent events on the world scene—the Iranian revolution; the seizure of, and the attempt to rescue, the American hostages in Teheran; the Soviet invasion of Afghanistan; the continuing tensions in the Middle East, including the Iran-Iraq war and the Israeli invasion of Lebanon; revolutions in Central America; the war in the Falkland Islands (where in 1832 a party of 18 U.S. Marines and sailors from the sloop *Lexington* had landed and freed three American schooners and 38 civilians)—made Americans aware that armed interventions might again be a neccessity for the United States.

The Marines began to get squared away in the eras of General Wilson and his successor, Gen. Robert H. Barrow, who took charge of the Corps on July 1, 1979. General Barrow had fought behind the Japanese lines in China in World War II, daringly helped take Seoul in the Korean war, received the Navy Cross in the breakout from the Chosin Reservoir and commanded a regiment in Vietnam. After serving as Deputy Chief of Staff for Manpower in 1975–76, he became Commanding General, Fleet Marine Force, Atlantic, and then Assistant Commandant.

As Commandants, Wilson and Barrow found the beginnings of a post-Vietnam mission. They pushed arming the Corps with modern weapons and vehicles. And they upgraded the quality of Marine Corps personnel. General Barrow said, "We have global usefulness. We are a deterrent force. We are a force that can forcibly enter some other country. We are the precursor force to open the door."

The Administration of President Jimmy Carter went so far as to set up on March 1, 1980—after the capture of the hostages in Iran and the Soviet invasion of Afghanistan—the structure of an interservice Rapid Deployment Joint Task Force (RDF). Its command was given to fifty-one-year-old Marine Lt. Gen. Paul X. "P. X." Kelley, a feisty, Boston-born, red-headed graduate of Villanova University who had been commissioned in 1950. He had commanded the newly activated 2d Force Reconnaissance Company, Force Troops, Fleet Marine Force, Atlantic. In 1960 and 1961, he served with the British Royal Marines Commandos in England and with the 45th Commando in Aden. He was Commander "C" Troop, 42d Commando in Singapore, Malaya and Borneo. In 1965, he was assigned to Vietnam and commanded the 2d Battalion, 4th Marines. In Vietnam his decorations included the Silver Star. He commanded the 1st Marines, the last Marine ground combat unit to leave Vietnam.

The RDF was initially intended to tailor forces to operate primarily in the Persian Gulf and Arabian Sea area, where the U.S. military presence was inadequate. Many Marines and some political leaders felt the Corps itself was already the "rapid deployment force" and, when the RDF bogged down in interservice rivalry, urged that it be turned over to the Corps entirely. But the solution went another way. In July 1981, Lt. Gen. Kelley was replaced by an Army lieutenant general, although one Marine Amphibious Force was still available to the RDF and the Marines remained part of the RDF concept. Promoted to general, Kelley was appointed Assistant Commandant of the Marine Corps and in 1983 was named Commandant.

Also in 1983, the RDF was converted into a unified command, the U.S. Central Command, led by an Army general, for the rapid deployment for U.S. forces in an area covering 19 countries of Southwest Asia from Pakistan through the Middle East to Africa as far as Kenya, plus the Persian Gulf and Red Sea, but not including Syria, Lebanon and Israel. In 1985, Gen. George B. Crist, who had been chief of staff at Headquarters, Marine Corps, was given command of the U.S. Central Command. This was the first time a Marine had headed a unified command and the first time the Corps had three four-star generals on active duty simultaneously.

Meanwhile, as the Marine Corps regained its sense of mission, it planned and trained to intervene in various strengths and formulations anywhere on the globe from Thailand to Norway. Marines exercised on the European front in Norway, Denmark, Germany and Turkey and prepositioned equipment in Norway in case a Marine brigade had to prop up NATO's northern flank. And with overseas advanced bases growing ever scarcer, 30 days' worth of equipment and supplies for the 7th Marine Amphibious Brigade of 12,000 men, based at Twentynine Palms, California, were stored aboard prepositioned cargo ships at Diego Garcia in the Indian Ocean. The one ammunition ship at Diego Garcia contained the equivalent of the payload of 500 sorties of C-141Bs from the United States.

These supplies could be linked up rapidly with the men who would be flown out to fight with them, as long as there was a "benign" port in which they could meet. This prepositioning system provided "rapid response" but had no "forcible entry" capability. The Marine Corps developed three sets of four or five prepositioned ships, each set with equipment for a 16,500-man brigade. The prepositioned ships could be moved into areas of expected trouble. Some Marines disliked the limitations of the system, the lack of forcible-entry capability and the possible vulnerability to precision-guided weapons. But the Corps' leaders believed it would reduce the time and replace the sealift needed to get a significant force of Marines to battle.

In 1982, the U.S. Navy was down to 67 amphibious ships, scattered on both coasts and abroad. Assembled, they could carry only the assault elements of one MAF to battle. Commandant Barrow expressed to Congress his concern about Marine Corps mobility, both the nation's "inadequate amphibious capability" and "our limited means of strategic mobility."

During these same years, the place of the Marine Corps in the structure of the Defense Establishment became more sharply defined. The Corps gained increased recognition of its claim to be one of two naval services within the Department of the Navy. This meant that both the Commandant and the Chief of Naval Operations were directly responsible to the Secretary of the Navy.

And through a progression of small steps begun by Commandant Wallace M. Greene, Jr. (1964–67), the Commandant became a full-fledged member of the Joint Chiefs of Staff. This followed an occasion on May 4, 1978, when all the members of the Joint Chiefs were unavailable for a meeting except the Commandant. Instead of having the Commandant serve as acting chairman, that role was assigned to the Vice Chief of Staff of the Army. Commandant Wilson raised the issue and before the year's end Congress granted and the President approved the Commandant's full membership on the JCS.

Another post-Vietnam problem that needed solving was the quality of personnel. The Corps energetically worked at raising standards and exceeded its goal of having 75 percent of its recruits be high school graduates. Twenty-nine percent of those recruited in 1980 would have been ineligible in 1982. Retention rates increased. Serious racial incidents declined significantly, although the percentage of black enlisted Marines grew to 22 percent. More married Marines were allowed to bring dependents to Japan and Okinawa. And starting in 1980, a major campaign to eliminate drug and alcohol abuse in the Corps made gains. AWOL and desertion declined, and cases of the abuse of recruits in boot camp diminished on orders from Headquarters.

All the 7,500 women Marines were high school graduates, and the Corps had more qualified women applicants than it could absorb. By the end of 1985, the number of women Marines had increased to 9,695, and their training was broadened to include drill under arms and marksmanship qualification. In that year, Brig. Gen. Gail M. Reals became the first woman Marine to be selected on a competitive basis as a brigadier general.

Two Marines were awarded the Medal of Honor for past bravery. In 1979, the widow of Col. Donald G. Cook was presented the Medal of Honor for her husband who had died 12 years earlier in a Viet Cong prison camp. Brooklyn-born Cook, then a Marine captain and a military advisor to the South Vietnamese, was ambushed and captured in Phuoc Tuy Province on December 31, 1964. The thirty-year-old Marine courageously provided leadership to other POWs and refused to cooperate with his captors until his death from mistreatment, malnutrition and malaria on December 8, 1967. President Carter praised his "unselfish and exemplary conduct."

Anthony Casamento of West Islip, Long Island, New York, received the Medal of Honor from President Carter on September 12, 1980, after a long campaign to recognize his bravery on Guadalcanal on November 1, 1942. The then twenty-one-year-old corporal commanded two machine-gun crews in D Company of the 1st Battalion of Edson's 5th Marines. All but two of his 29 men were killed when the Japanese attacked and cut off his company which had just crossed the Matanikau River. Although wounded 14 times, Corporal Casamento took over a machine gun and held

717

the ridge singlehandedly. When reinforcements arrived, dead Japanese soldiers were piled up in front of his gun. For years, Casamento thought all his men had been killed. But eventually the two survivors who had been wounded surfaced and verified his heroism. He was fifty-nine when he received the Medal of Honor in the White House Rose Garden, sitting in the wheelchair he needed because of the wounds received nearly 38 years before.

In contrast to the behavior of Colonel Cook as a POW was the highly publicized case of Pfc. Robert R. Garwood of Adams, Indiana, a nineteen-year-old Jeep driver who was captured near Da Nang on September 28, 1965, and 14 years later revealed himself to a Finnish economist in a Hanoi hotel and returned to the U.S. After a long, flamboyant trial, he was found not guilty of desertion but convicted of collaborating with the enemy and striking another prisoner. He was dishonorably discharged.

4
The Fighting Security Guards

The United States does not have to be at war for Marines to be called on to risk their lives. In the post-Vietnam period, anti-government forces in the smaller nations repeatedly turned to guerrilla warfare, terrorism and violent demonstrations. On this scattered battlefield around the world, the Marine Security Guard Battalion was thrown into the front line.

The modern Marine Security Guard program began following the murder in May 1948 of U.S. Consul General T. C. Wasson by a sniper in war-torn Jerusalem. On June 28, Wasson's successor requested that a detachment of Marines be sent to Jerusalem; and on July 18, 12 Marines were assigned to the consulate. They were supplemented in October by 30 additional Marines. During the next weeks, two of the guards were wounded in the line of duty.

Since 1949, Marines have served as security guards at U.S. Foreign Service posts under agreements between the Corps and the Department of State. This responsibility had grown by 1967 to require the formation of the Marine Security Guard Battalion. By 1991, 1,281 Marines—small units of 6 to 35 men—were serving in 138 embassies, consulates and missions in 119 countries, as well as with American delegations to international conferences. The Marine Security Guard Battalion had overseas company headquarters in Frankfurt, West Germany; Casablanca, Morocco; Manila; Panama City, and Nairobi, Kenya. The Marines protected classified materials, office personnel and government property. External security was the responsibility of the host countries—although they were not always eager to aid the Americans.

These small Marine Security Guard detachments of selected enlisted men (and at times a few women Marines) were lightly armed with pistols, shotguns and tear gas and under the imme-

719

diate control of the State Department leadership on the scene. Their effectiveness was often determined by a civilian's estimate of a violent situation and the ability of the Marine noncommissioned officer in charge to respond.

Lance Cpl. Darwin J. Judge and Cpl. Charles McMahon, Jr., who were killed at Tan Son Nhut Airfield in 1975 during the final fighting in Saigon—and James C. Marshall, who was killed at the U.S. Embassy in Saigon during the 1968 Tet attack—were members of this Marine Security Guard Battalion. And Staff Sgt. Charles W. Turberville of the battalion died during a September 26, 1971, terrorist attack on the U.S. Embassy in Phnom Penh, Cambodia.

In March 1973, the Marine Security Guard detachment secured the U.S. Embassy at Khartoum, Sudan, after armed Palestinian terrorists abducted and murdered the U.S. ambassador and chargé d'affaires who were at a reception at the Saudi Arabian Embassy. And when a United States Liaison Office was opened in Peking in May 1973, nine Marines served there in civilian clothes for a year before the Chinese government insisted that they be replaced by civilian guards. By the mid-1980s, the United States had an embassy in Peking (now Beijing), with a Marine Security Guard detachment the members of which wore their uniforms while on duty.

When Greeks overthrew the government on Cyprus and Turkish forces armed with American weapons invaded the island in the summer of 1974, Marines of the 16-man Security Guard detachment under Gunnery Sgt. Robert L. Boyd defended the U.S. Embassy in downtown Nicosia. They were armed with .38 caliber pistols. Just after noon on August 19, only five Marines of the detachment were in the embassy when hundreds of well-organized, rock-throwing Greek Cypriotes attacked. They entered the grounds, broke windows and burned automobiles and an effigy of Secretary of State Henry A. Kissinger. Two Marine sergeants were sent to the embassy roof and tried to disperse the mob with tear-gas grenades. Armor-piercing bullets from an AK-47 killed a woman secretary and mortally wounded Ambassador Rodger P. Davies, who was standing in a hallway near his office behind shuttered windows. The ambassador died on the way to the hospital. The next January, a crowd broke into the embassy building and was routed by Marine tear gas.

Four actions that took place within one month demonstrate

the kind of problems with which the Marine Security Guards have to contend.

One unit that performed exceptionally well, although denied the use of "deadly force," was the seven-man detachment in Islamabad, Pakistan, on November 21, 1979. Master Sgt. Loyd G. Miller and his men held off with tear gas canisters a mob that surrounded and burned the U.S. Embassy until 137 employees and other civilians could find refuge in a third-floor steel-walled vault room. The Marines had permission to use deadly force if the Pakistanis finally entered the vault. After four hours, the heat of the flames forced the Americans out. Miller tried to lead them and met a wall of flames. He then led the way to the roof and safety. Early in the attack, Marine Cpl. Steven J. Crowley, twenty, of Selden, New York, was shot through the head and fatally wounded while manning his rooftop post. He was the fifth Marine Security Guard to be killed in the line of duty. Miller, who later received the Legion of Merit, carried Crowley's body out of the burning building.

When thousands of Pakistanis stormed the American Consulate in Karachi on that same day, two women Marines, Cpl. Vicki Lee Gaglia and Cpl. Betty Jo Rankin, stood ready in helmets and flak jackets and with weapons to defend the building alongside the male detachment members. After the all-day stand-off, Corporal Gaglia lowered the American flag while two male Marines covered her with their shotguns.

In Latin America, Marine Security Guard detachments saw frequent action, especially at La Paz, Bolivia; Bogotá, Colombia; Managua, Nicaragua; and San Salvador, El Salvador. The fourteen-man detachment at San Salvador had to deal with repeated trouble during the civil war in that country. At midday on October 30, 1979, more than 200 armed leftists attacked the embassy. When the mob entered the compound, the Marines, led by Gunnery Sgt. Stephen J. Csabon, fired over their heads. Csabon and Cpl. Robert A. Fowler were wounded but the crowd was driven off with tear gas. An hour later, government security forces arrived and surrounded the embassy. The following May 12, the Marines had to use tear gas again to rescue Ambassador Robert E. White from his official residence and bring him to the tightly guarded embassy.

The most widely known action took place in Teheran, Iran, on Sunday morning, November 4, 1979. The U.S. Embassy in

Teheran had already been attacked the previous February 14, and demonstrators protesting U.S. hospitality to the deposed Shah had captured several Marines. One, Sgt. Kenneth L. Kraus, was taken from his hospital bed and held hostage for a week before Iranian revolutionary authorities intervened.

Then, on November 4, two weeks after the Shah was allowed into the United States for cancer treatment, the embassy in Teheran was overrun and 13 Marines were among 65 Americans taken hostage. Five unarmed off-duty Marines were captured in their apartment house. The seven Marines in the chancellery building fought back with tear gas until the embassy official in charge, who had been taken prisoner by the demonstrators, ordered the Marines to stop resisting. Staff Sgt. Michael E. Moeller of Loup City, Nebraska, the noncom in charge and a former Vietnam rifleman, directed the shredding of classified material. Sgt. James M. Lopez, twenty-one years old, of Globe, Arizona, the lone Marine on duty in the consulate building, held off the mob for three hours with tear gas and sent civilians out into the streets in small groups. Most were captured, but five managed to reach the Canadian Embassy, where they were helped to get out of Iran. Sergeant Lopez destroyed the visa plates, put on a civilian shirt, tore the red stripe off his trousers and tried to escape. But he was caught a few blocks away. He survived and remained in the Corps.

Two weeks after the embassy was seized, four black Marines and nine other Americans were released. The remaining nine Marines were among the 50 American men and two women who endured mistreatment during 444 days in captivity.

Except for Corporal Crowley in Islamabad, the first Marines killed in action subsequent to the *Mayaguez* affair in 1975 were three Marine members of the combined-forces team that tried to rescue the Teheran hostages on the night of April 24, 1980. Most of the force flew to a desolate landing site in the Iranian desert 200 miles from Teheran and known to the team as Desert One. There, the mission was aborted because it was left with less than six RH-53D helicopters regarded as minimal for success. Marine Col. Charles H. Pitman, the commander of the helicopters and a decorated flier who had been shot down seven times during 1,200 helicopter combat missions in Vietnam, was a passenger aboard a helicopter that turned back to the aircraft carrier *Nimitz* before reaching Desert One.

Helicopters were manned by men from Marine Aircraft Group 26. The Marines' function on the failed mission was to fly their aged and heavily loaded Navy helicopters to Desert One; pick up the 90-plus men of the Army Special Forces so-called "Delta" anti-terrorist team, flying in on C-130s from an Egyptian air base, and take the choppers to Teheran to pick up the hostages and the raiding party in the final stage of the rescue.

When the attempt was called off and the last five of the original eight helicopters were refueling at Desert One to return to the carrier *Nimitz*, one helicopter collided with a C-130 on the ground and both craft burned, killing Marine Staff Sgt. Dewey L. Johnson of Dublin, Georgia; Sgt. John D. Harvey of Roanoke, Virginia; Cpl. George N. Holmes, Jr., of Pine Bluff, Arkansas; and five Air Force personnel. Marine Majors Leslie B. Petty and James H. Schaefer, Jr., were among the five wounded.

The fatal accident at Desert One was a tragic end of the brave but controversial rescue attempt.[22] The hard-charging Army colonel who planned and ran this "impossible dream" blamed the Marine pilots for his failure and even called them "cowards." The Marine Corps did not permit its helicopter pilots to defend themselves. The Pentagon issued a formal statement that said the Secretary of Defense considered the performance of the helicopter pilots "far above the call of duty."

Nine months later, the nine Marine hostages were finally released on January 20, 1981, upon the inauguration of Ronald Reagan as President of the United States.

Marine Security Guards have performed a variety of duties. In Moscow in August 1977, the Marine detachment (which had first "landed" there in 1934 after the U.S. recognized the U.S.S.R.) evacuated the chancellery and guarded classified materials and equipment while Soviet firemen fought a fire that raged for 18 hours in the top floors of the American Embassy. Another fire occurred in the embassy on March 28, 1991.

The six-man consulate detachment in Asmara, Ethiopia, in 1977 evacuated 48 Americans and destroyed classified documents and communications equipment when the military regime protested American plans to cut off military aid to Ethiopia. The Ethiopian army tried to take over the consulate prematurely, and the Marines met them with drawn weapons.

Seven Marines led by Staff Sgt. Mark A. Hughes defended

the U.S. Embassy in Taipei, Taiwan, after President Carter announced the normalization of relations with the People's Republic of China. Before midnight on December 16, 1978, a mob of thousands bombarded the embassy with rocks and bricks, and some forced their way into the compound. The Marines drove them out with tear gas and nightsticks.

Members of the Marine guard at Managua, Nicaragua, helped evacuate 1,423 civilians during fighting in the city in June and July 1979, which ended with the departure of President Anastasio Somoza Debayle. Spanish-speaking Master Sgt. Peter I. Delandero, the noncom in charge and nephew of the President of Mexico, helped organize the evacuation.

In December 1979, anti-American violence stirred up by the crisis in Iran resulted in the bombing of the U.S. Embassy in Thailand and an attack on the embassy in Libya. And angry Moslems were beaten back from the embassies in Kuwait and the Philippines.

In May 1980, six Marines, who served in civilian clothes, were protecting the American Interest Section in Havana, Cuba, when more than a million Cubans marched by in an anti-American demonstration. Three Marines in San José, Costa Rica, were wounded on March 17, 1981, when the vehicle carrying them to guard duty at the embassy was hit by a command-detonated mine. The vehicle was destroyed, and Sgt. Steven Garcia of New York City suffered two broken legs.

While a Marine Amphibious Unit was serving as a part of the Multinational Force in Lebanon, terrorists blew up the U.S. Embassy in Beirut on April 18, 1983. Among the 63 dead was a member of the embassy's Marine Security Guard detachment, Cpl. Robert McMaugh of Manassas, Virginia, who was on post at the time.

San Salvador again became the scene of serious trouble at 8:45 P.M. on the evening of June 19, 1985, when terrorists killed six Americans sitting at a sidewalk café. Four off-duty Marines and two U.S. businessmen were among 13 people slain when nearly a dozen men in camouflage uniforms opened fire and then fled. The dead Marines were Sgt. Thomas T. Handwork, twenty-four, of Boardman, Ohio; Sgt. Bobby J. Dickson, twenty-seven, of Tuscaloosa, Alabama; Cpl. Gregory H. Weber, twenty-two, of Cincinnati, Ohio; and Cpl. Patrick R. Kwiatkowski, twenty, of Wausau, Wisconsin.

A left-wing faction claimed responsibility, and Washington spokesmen said the four Marines, unarmed and in civilian clothes, were apparently the prime targets of the attack. They were the first fired on. The Marines were among 18 assigned to the Security Guard detachment at the U.S. Embassy.

During this period, the Marine detachments in Beirut, Lebanon, and Kabul, Afghanistan, were functioning in situations of extreme unrest, danger and terrorism. In place after place, a few enlisted Marines were called on to defend their nation's interests; in case after case, they performed superbly.

However, at the very end of 1986, the reputation of the Marine Security Guard Battalion was severely tarnished when a Marine sergeant told U.S. officials that, while serving in the Marine Security Guard detachment at the U.S. Embassy in Moscow in 1985 and 1986, he had been involved in "espionage-related" activities with Soviet citizens. As a result, the Corps placed him and several other Marine Security Guards in custody and in early 1987 charged them with espionage and other illegal activities, such as allowing Soviet citizens into classified areas of the embassy in Moscow and of the consulate in Leningrad as far back as 1982. At least seven Marines were suspected of unlawful conduct with Soviet citizens while on duty in the Soviet Union. Usually, this conduct involved sexual relations with Soviet women. The press called the affair a "sex-for-secrets scandal." Some of the original charges were dropped for lack of evidence.

Marine Sgt. Clayton J. Lonetree of Chicago became the focus of public interest in the case. He was the first U.S. Marine ever to be tried for spying. Lonetree confessed to having an affair with a Soviet woman who worked at the U.S. Embassy in Moscow and introduced him to a KGB agent. He was also accused of continuing to spy after he was transferred to the U.S. Embassy in Vienna until he turned himself in to a CIA officer.

In August 1987, Sergeant Lonetree was convicted by a general court-martial of espionage, identifying covert agents of the United States and other charges. He was sentenced to 30 years' confinement, which was later reduced to 25 years. The Court of Military Review affirmed the sentence in 1990. He continued to appeal.

The Marine Corps was widely shaken by the case. One Marine general said, "The Security Guard detachments are supposed to be the elite of this elite corps." The entire detachments were recalled from both Moscow and Leningrad. The Marines reviewed their Security Guard selection process and in April 1987 began by shortening Security Guards' tours of duty, primarily in Eastern Bloc countries. And several investigations studied the issue of embassy security.

The Corps sought to see the problem in the context of the fact that 15,000 enlisted Marines had served in the Marine Security Guard Battalion over the previous twenty years and that Marine Security Guard detachments around the world continued to meet their responsibilities with honor.

5
Disaster at Beirut

A yellow Mercedes-Benz five-ton open-bed truck came down the road just west of the headquarters compound of the 24th Marine Amphibious Unit at Beirut International Airport at 6:22 A.M. on Sunday, October 23, 1983. The driver entered the parking lot south of and in front of the headquarters of the 1st Battalion, 8th Marines. In the four-story building slept more than 300 men, most of them Marines. The truck's driver accelerated, circled the lot once, ran over a concertina wire barricade and sped between Sentry Posts 6 and 7.

Lance Cpl. Eddie A. DiFranco, wearing helmet and body armor, was on duty at Post 6. At Post 7, Lance Cpl. Henry P. Linkkila inserted a magazine into his M-16 rifle, put a round in the chamber and shouldered his weapon. Before he could fire, the truck plunged into the building and the equivalent of more than 12,000 pounds of TNT exploded.

Sergeant of the Guard Stephen E. Russell had spotted the truck heading straight toward his sandbagged post at the main entrance of the building. He instantly recognized the threat. He ran from his plywood guard shack and across the lobby, shouting, "Hit the deck!" The explosion hurled him, severely injured and unconscious, out of the building and into the road. One sentry said later that the truck's driver was smiling.

The building was reduced to rubble in seconds. Almost everyone inside was killed. When the last body was retrieved, the American dead totaled 241; 220 of them were Marines, the remainder, 18 Navy medical corpsmen and three soldiers. More Marines died that Sunday morning than on any single day since D-Day on Iwo Jima.

This disaster was the climax of a Marine Corps involvement in

Lebanon that had begun 25 years before with the landing of elements of three Marine regiments at Beirut in July 1958. At that time, all the Marines, except the Security Guard at the embassy, left Lebanon by mid-October. Their intervention in Lebanon was brief, and they suffered no casualties.

But in the 1980s, the story was different. In 1971, several thousand fighters of the Palestine Liberation Organization (PLO) had been pushed out of Jordan into Lebanon. As a result, they confronted the Israelis along the Lebanon-Israel border; and on June 6, 1982, the Israeli army invaded Lebanon. At 5 A.M. on August 25, 1982, 800 men of the 32d Marine Amphibious Unit (MAU) of 1,800 men, commanded by Col. James M. Mead, a decorated F-4 squadron commander in Vietnam, came ashore at the port of Beirut from the U.S. Sixth Fleet. They were part of a 2,000-man Multinational Force (MNF) of French, Italian and American troops whose job was to see that the PLO forces and other Palestinians were removed from Beirut peacefully. The Marines evacuated 6,436 armed Palestinians and Syrians.

The most important Palestinian, PLO leader Yasir Arafat, left Beirut on August 30, led through the Marine lines by a French escort. By September 3, life in Beirut seemed to return to near normal. The Marines had not fired a round; they reboarded their ships on September 10.

An unstable mix of Christians, Moslems and Druze made Lebanon vulnerable to internal violence and big-power pressures. On September 14, 1982, four days after the Marines left, Lebanon's Israeli-backed, Christian Phalangist President-elect Bashir Gemayel was assassinated. The next day, the Israeli army rolled into Moslem West Beirut. And two days later, Lebanese Christian Phalangists massacred hundreds of civilians in the Palestinian refugee camps of Sabra and Shatila south of Beirut. After the massacre, the new Lebanese President, Amin Gemayel, brother of Bashir, requested an MNF to protect the Moslems of West Beirut and gain the withdrawal of Israeli and Syrian forces.

Although the U.S. Joint Chiefs of Staff opposed the decision to send in the Marines, they were rushed back to Beirut. The mission of the 32d Marine Amphibious Unit now was defined as providing "a presence in Beirut, that would in turn help establish the stability necessary for the Lebanese government to regain control of their capital."[23] The Joint Chiefs of Staff Alert Order of September 23 in part defined the mission as: "To establish an environment which will permit the Lebanese Armed Forces to carry out their responsibilities in the Beirut area."[24] The confusion was there from the beginning: Were the Marines in Lebanon as a neutral presence or to help the government of Lebanon maintain order against dissident factions? "Peacekeeping" was not explicit in the mission statement.

President Reagan told Congress that "the American force will not engage in combat."[25] A military analyst later wrote, "Their presence was based on the absurd political premise that they could pacify Lebanon."[26]

Eventually, the Marines, and the United States, came to see that they were stuck in a bitter civil and religious war in which Lebanese were killing Lebanese, and Soviet-backed Syria was arming one side while the United States backed another. When the Marines themselves were attacked by Syrian and Lebanese Moslem artillery, rockets and small arms, they would finally fight back and wonder why precisely they were in Lebanon.

In this deployment of the MNF, the French were stationed in the city itself, the Italians to the south near the densely occupied refugee camps, and 1,200 U.S. Marines still further south at the Beirut International Airport. They totaled about 3,000 men. (A small British contingent of 155 men joined the MNF in February 1983.)

When the Israeli forces reluctantly moved out from the airport on September 29, three Marine rifle companies occupied the area, bordered on the west by the sea and on the east by the Old Sidon Road. Colonel Mead also wanted to occupy the heights beyond the road; but since the Israelis used the road, the Marines were not permitted to appear to be protecting Israeli military resupply routes.

The next day, the Marines suffered their first casualties while they were clearing the airfield. An abandoned American-made bomb exploded and killed Cpl. David L. Reagan of Chesapeake, Virginia, and wounded three others.

At first, the Marines were relaxed. The local Shiite Moslems were friendly. They perceived the Marines as protecting them from the Israelis and Christian Phalangists. Later, the Shiites would be shooting at the Marines.

The airport was busy; in the two weeks prior to the bombing on October 23, 1983, for example, it served an average of 35 flights and 2,400 passengers per day. MAU headquarters was set up in a two-story concrete building that had been the Airport Fire Fighting School. Just southwest of the MAU headquarters, the Marine battalion occupied the bombed-out four-story reinforced-concrete building that had once housed the Lebanese government's Aviation Administration Bureau.

On October 30, 1982, the 32d MAU was relieved by the 24th MAU, commanded by Col. Thomas M. Stokes, Jr., another Vietnam veteran, and consisting of 1,806 Marines and 81 Navy personnel. The newly arrived Marines were greeted with the explosion of a car bomb at the entrance to the beach. To emphasize their being a "presence," the Marines started conducting daily daylight motorized and foot patrols. They also began training a rapid reaction force of the rebuilt Lebanese Armed Forces (LAF). Although the Marines saw themselves as peacekeepers, training the LAF made them seem pro-government partisans.

Strangely, the Marines' first confrontations came not with the Lebanese dissident "militias" but with the Israel Defense Forces (IDF)—two tough-minded fighting outfits on virtually the same turf. In January 1983, Israeli supply columns on the Old Sidon Road were ambushed, and the Israelis thought they were attacked out of Marine territory. On the morning of February 2, the commander of the Marines' L Company, Capt. Charles B. Johnson, saw three Israeli Centurion tanks coming toward his perimeter. As the tanks approached the fence, Captain Johnson stood in the road. The lead tank stopped just in front of him. The Israeli lieutenant colonel in the tank dismounted, told Johnson he was going through and climbed back into his tank. Johnson later said he replied: "You'll have to come through me." He drew his pistol, chambered a round and pointed the weapon skyward. The tank commander pulled over; the two other tanks revved up their engines and headed for the fence. Johnson climbed onto the lead tank and yelled at the Israeli officer to order his tanks to stop. He did.

Arab radio stations told and retold the story of the American who had stopped three Israeli tanks, and the Israeli press accused Johnson (a teetotaler) of being drunk. Back home, he was a momentary hero.

On February 14, the 22d MAU relieved the 24th MAU. The 22d MAU was the redesignated 32d MAU, and this was Colonel Mead's third tour in Beirut. Marine amtracs and two helicopters of Marine Medium Helicopter Squadron 264, with Syrian permission, made repeated precarious attempts to try to rescue Lebanese civilians caught by snowstorms in the mountains and by flooding in the Bekaa Valley.

Trouble with the Israel Defense Forces continued. On March 12, two Marine patrols were stopped at Israeli checkpoints. U.S. Ambassador Philip C. Habib warned the Israeli Defense Minister that the MAU commander himself would lead the next patrol through an Israeli checkpoint. Commandant Barrow wrote the Secretary of Defense asking "firm and strong action." Finally, the Marine commander and Israeli Brig. Gen. Amnon Lifkin established a direct radio link between their headquarters, and the incidents ceased.

But Lebanon was heating up. Moslem attacks now began against the Multinational Force, which was increasingly seen as an ally of the Christian-dominated government. The first assault occurred on March 15, when an Italian patrol was ambushed; one soldier was killed and nine were wounded. The next day, a grenade thrown from an apartment building at a Marine patrol north of the airport wounded five Marines. Their flak jackets saved them from death. The Lebanese blamed a pro-Iranian organization and sentenced a Lebanese civilian to death. This was the Marines' first major encounter. They suspended foot patrols, increased mobile patrols north of the airport and began conducting all patrols with loaded weapons.

On April 17, for the first time, a Marine who was shot at returned fire. The next afternoon, a man drove a pickup truck loaded with explosives past a sleepy Lebanese guard and into the lobby of the American Embassy on the Beirut waterfront. The explosion killed 63 people. One of the 17 American dead was Cpl. Robert McMaugh of Manassas, Virginia, a member of the embassy's Marine Security Guard, who was on post. The MAU, four miles away, rushed a company of the 2d Battalion, 6th Marines to secure the area, and the nearby French marines of the MNF came to help. The British offered the United States use of their embassy on the Corniche, the boulevard along the Mediterranean; and a Marine platoon commanded by Lt. William G. Leftwich III helped secure the building—perhaps the first time U.S. Marines had guarded a British Embassy.

In reaction to the attacks, the MAU's mission expanded to include security, and rules of engagement were changed to permit a Marine to fire if he "perceived hostile intent." Guards were doubled on all posts, and amtracs were used to block entry routes.

731

On May 5, Colonel Mead's helicopter was hit by three 7.62mm rounds. In Beirut the fighting spread. Lebanese anti-government Moslems were furious that the United States sponsored the May 17 Israel-Lebanon withdrawal agreement. They welcomed the support of Syria, which opposed the agreement and, since its defeat by Israel, had been rearmed by the Soviet Union. The environment was growing more dangerous.

At the end of May, the 22d MAU was replaced by the 24th MAU, commanded by Col. Timothy J. Geraghty. The 22d MAU returned to Camp Lejeune, where Colonel Mead was succeeded on June 27 by veteran flier Col. James P. Faulkner. Colonel Geraghty's 24th MAU included the 1st Battalion, 8th Marines and HMM-162. During the next five months, the Marines filled 500,000 sandbags and placed 10,000 feet of concertina barbed wire. The area around the airport became more and more hostile, and in June Colonel Geraghty arranged for Lebanese Army fire teams to accompany Marine patrols.

On July 22, a dozen Soviet-built Katyusha rockets and mortar shells, fired by a Syrian-backed, Druze-led faction, struck the airport. One civilian was killed; among the 13 wounded were two Marines. This shelling, aimed at the Marines, was later called the "point in time when the Marine situation began to deteriorate markedly."[27] In addition to those killed in the bombing of October 23, 1983, almost exactly three months later, all 18 MAU Marines killed in Lebanon by hostile fire were killed after this date.

The fighting built up in Beirut and in the hills nearby. Lebanese fought Lebanese, and anti-American feelings rose as the Marines continued to train units of the government army. Now the Marines were targets. When Druze artillery and rockets hit the airport on August 8 and 10, the Marines used their two newly arrived counterartillery radars. On the tenth, Marine mortars sent up flares, which quieted the Lebanese fire. One Marine was wounded, and the busy airport was closed from August 10 to 16. On the sixteenth, the new Commandant, Gen. Paul X. Kelley, visited the MAU.

When the Israelis started to leave the Beirut area on August 28, the fighting in the Marines' area intensified. The Marines began returning fire. The next morning, Druze 82mm mortar fire hit an A Company position, killing 2d Lt. Donald George Losey of Winston-Salem, North Carolina, and his platoon sergeant, Staff

Sgt. Alexander M. Ortega of Rochester, New York, and wounding three. Four more Marines were wounded that day. For the first time, the Marines fired their new 155mm howitzers, silencing the Druze position. And the 5-inch guns of the guided missile cruiser *Belknap* fired illumination rounds to support the Marines.

An armored personnel carrier machine-gunned a Marine-LAF checkpoint, and two Cobra helicopters destroyed the machine guns with a 5-inch Zuni air-to-ground rocket. But one Cobra took three machine-gun hits and had to make an emergency landing on the helicopter carrier *Iwo Jima*.

On August 31, as the fighting continued, the Joint Chiefs of Staff ordered the MAU to deliver 500,000 rounds of 5.56mm small-arms ammunition from its contingency supply to the LAF. (Additional artillery ammunition was ordered delivered on September 5 and 14.) Also on the thirty-first, the 155mm howitzers again fired on aggressive Druze artillery positions in the hills east of the airport. On the same day, however, because of the rising tension and threat to the Marines, patrols into Beirut were suspended, plans were made to reinforce the MAU and the nuclear carrier *Eisenhower* and a French aircraft carrier moved closer to Lebanon.

Starting before dawn on September 4, Israeli forces withdrew to the Awwali River in southern Lebanon; and although the move was no surprise, the Lebanese Army was unprepared to fill the resulting vacuum. Syria refused to withdraw its forces. Paradoxically, the United States government, which had condemned the original Israeli invasion of Lebanon, was now privately pleading with the Israelis to stay and enforce order around Beirut. When the Israelis refused, the Marines were caught in a rapidly mushrooming civil war: the Christian-led Lebanese Army and the Phalangists versus the Syrian-backed Druze and Shiite Amal militia. The LAF moved south of the airport near the C Company position, bringing it under heavier fire. A 106mm recoilless rifle fired on Marine bunkers, and mortars peppered the airport. The Marines' situation had changed.

Before dawn on September 6, 21 rockets hit the Marines. Lance Cpl. Randy Clark of Minong, Wisconsin, and Cpl. Pedro J. Valle of San Juan, Puerto Rico, were killed, and two were wounded. Cobras could not find the launching sites. Lebanese troops were pushed eastward, leaving the Druze in command of the high ground overlooking Beirut and the airport. By the end of

September 7, more than 130 rounds exploded at the airport and two more Marines were wounded.

The next day, rockets landed near two VIP visitors, Lt. Gen. John H. Miller, commander of Fleet Marine Force, Atlantic, and Maj. Gen. Alfred M. Gray, commanding general of the 2d Marine Division. The response was a 155mm volley and a 5-inch salvo from the frigate *Bowen;* for the first time, naval gunfire supported the Marines ashore.

Colonel Geraghty wrote on September 11, "Our contribution to peace in Lebanon since 22 July stands at 4 killed and 28 wounded. . . . 24th MAU will hang tough."[28] President Reagan telephoned, relaying the nation's support. But the Marines felt they could neither attack nor withdraw; the problem was political, not military.

On September 12, the 31st MAU, commanded by Col. James H. R. Curd, arrived off Beirut, coming through the Suez Canal to serve as the afloat reinforcement for the beleaguered 24th MAU. (The 31st MAU stayed exactly one month before sailing off.) On the night of the sixteenth, the frigate *Bowen* and the destroyer *John Rodgers* fired 72 rounds and silenced artillery that had been shelling the American ambassador's residence.

Three days later, for the first time, two U.S. naval ships fired 360 5-inch shells to help the LAF hold its ridgetop position at Suk al Gharb, nine miles southeast of the center of Beirut, against a Syrian-backed Druze and Palestinian assault. This was a crucial escalation for the American forces. The order to support Lebanese government troops with U.S. naval gunfire was given to Colonel Geraghty by Special Presidential Envoy Robert C. McFarlane, who was at the ambassador's residence in Beirut. McFarlane was responding to a request from the Lebanese Ministry of Defense. McFarlane, a former Marine, had replaced Philip C. Habib in July as the President's chief Middle East negotiator and had been arguing to send the Marines into the mountains to back up the LAF.[29] Colonel Geraghty "strenuously opposed the order [to call in naval gunfire to support the LAF] . . . but he was overruled."[30] He saw that such support of the LAF would endanger his exposed Marines on the airport's low ground.

This massive combat support of the LAF erased for the Shiite Amal Moslems and the Druze any argument that the Marines were a neutral presence. In their view, the MNF had become supporters of Lebanon's ruling Maronite Christian faction. Now naval gunfire was used repeatedly; it became the weapon of choice. On September 25, the battleship *New Jersey*, armed with 16-inch guns, added its naval gunfire support.

The entire MNF came under heavy attack; the Marines replied with mortar and howitzer fire. On September 20, for the first time, two Navy carrier-based aircraft were attacked by a Russian SA-7 surface-to-air (SAM) missile. On September 24, the MAU pulled back from two vulnerable outlying checkpoints. Then a fragile and much violated ceasefire started on September 26, and the airport was closed for six days. During this period, the LAF received American armored personnel carriers, tanks and howitzers; and PLO members attempted to fight their way back into the Sabra and Shatila refugee camps. Iranian members of the so-called Islamic Amal built bunkers opposite the Marine positions. In Washington, the U.S. Congress voted, and on October 12 President Reagan signed, an extension of Public Law 98-119 giving the President authorization to keep the Marines in Lebanon another 18 months.

The Marines engaged in a sniper war. Virtually all members of HMM-162 were sent back to the helicopter carrier *Iwo Jima*. On October 14, Sgt. Allen H. Soifert of Nashua, New Hampshire, was mortally wounded in the chest by sniper fire. The Marines closed the airport perimeter road, and a sniper team eliminated targets pinpointed by sniper scopes.

A Company came under heavy fire starting on Sunday, October 16; and at a rooftop observation post, forward air controller Capt. Michael J. Ohler, a Naval Academy graduate from Huntington, New York, was killed and three were wounded. The Marines answered with rifles, machine guns and Dragon anti-armor missiles. The fire fights were now almost continuous. On the nineteenth, four Marines were wounded when a remote-controlled bomb hidden in a blue Mercedes was detonated next to their supply convoy.

By now, six Marines had been killed by hostile fire, and more than 40 wounded; the Marines felt they were getting picked off almost one by one. The so-called peacekeepers had become full-fledged fighters in a nasty, undeclared war. The Marines were fighting professional Syrian soldiers and Iranian Revolutionary Guardsmen right outside the MAU perimeter. But this was barely realized by Americans back home. Under orders from Washington, the almost daily combat was minimized; it was said that shells landing in Marine areas had not been aimed there.

735

Briefly, Beirut seemed to quiet down; and on Saturday, October 22, the Marines and a sprinkling of soldiers and sailors watched a USO country-and-western show in front of the MAU's battalion building and enjoyed a pizza party. Early Sunday morning, the yellow Mercedes truck sped through the party site and exploded in the building's lobby.

"The Iranian behind the wheel of the big yellow Mercedes truck—and most of the truck itself—was [sic] vaporized. On a hill about four kilometers from the center of the blast, an Iranian cameraman waited patiently until he heard the detonation. He released the shutter of his camera—which had been set up and focused at dawn—thirteen seconds after the driver of the big yellow Mercedes immolated himself."[31]

Hearing the explosion, Colonel Geraghty ran from his office/sleeping quarters on the second floor of the MAU headquarters building. Outside, he saw that the concrete battalion headquarters building had collapsed. Survivors began desperately to rescue the injured. The colonel called the Sixth Fleet commander and sent a flash message to the National Military Command Center in Washington. He asked that the battalion headquarters be replaced by the 2d Marine Division's air alert force and that he be sent an extra rifle company. Within 24 hours, Lt. Col. Edwin C. Kelley arrived with 2d Battalion, 6th Marines headquarters, which was redesignated 1st Battalion, 8th Marines. And his E Company arrived on October 30.

The explosion badly wounded the battalion commander, Lt. Col. Howard L. Gerlach. Colonel Geraghty's executive officer, Lt. Col. Harold W. Slacum, informed the MNF by radio of what had happened and requested medical assistance. He asked *New Jersey* to send ashore her Marine detachment to provide security. MAU headquarters had to establish direct radio contact with the line companies and restore the fire support coordination net. On board *Iwo Jima*, Capt. Morgan M. France, USN, the commodore of Amphibious Squadron 8, flew in medical teams and working parties, alerted the Royal Air Force Hospital on Cyprus and requested medevac aircraft from Stuttgart, Germany. The first doctor from *Iwo Jima* reached the site within the hour.

Marines dug by hand through the ruins to save the living. They were soon joined by Italian and Lebanese soldiers. The French were occupied with their own disaster. Almost simultaneously, another suicide driver had driven a small red truck loaded with explosives into their barracks two miles away; the barracks had been destroyed and 58 paratroopers killed. Nevertheless, they and the British sent contingents to help. An offer of Israeli medical assistance was rejected by Commodore France. The Lebanese construction firm of Oger Liban arrived with heavy equipment to lift large blocks of steel-reinforced concrete. Although no one was brought out of the rubble alive after about 1 P.M. on Sunday, the Marines worked through the following nights under the glow of spotlights. Some Lebanese civilians came to help, others to loot, and snipers fired on the rescue scene.

The leader of the Iran-backed Shiite Islamic Amal, the prime suspect, denied any role in the bombing but called it a "good deed." In the United States, officials, including Secretary of Defense Caspar Weinberger, blamed the bombing on Iranians backed by the Syrian government, and President Reagan said the Soviet Union "assisted and encouraged the violence. . . ."

The first aircraft to evacuate the severely wounded was an Air Force C-9 "Florence Nightingale" from Germany, which at 10:30 brought in a surgical team. Then a Royal Air Force C-130 took 20 wounded to Cyprus. A stream of aircraft poured in. Those treated for wounds numbered 112. And the grisly job of digging out the dead continued.

On Monday, President François Mitterrand of France visited the bombed French compound and came and paid tribute to the dead Marines. Commandant Kelley landed at Frankfurt as a plane arrived with the remains of Marines who had been killed in the bombing. Early the next morning, while Marines were assaulting Grenada, Kelley visited the wounded in the intensive care ward of a U.S. military hospital in Wiesbaden. Lance Cpl. Jeffrey L. Nashton of Rome, New York, who was badly wounded, felt the stars on Kelley's collar and tried to write something on the bed sheet. Given a pad of paper, he spelled out "Semper Fi."

The Commandant reached Beirut that afternoon, and Vice President George Bush arrived in the evening. The next Monday, the Commandant testified before the Senate and House Armed Services Committees that Marine security at Beirut "was adequate to meet what any reasonable and prudent commander should have expected. . . ." But, he added, "Our security measures were not adequate to stop a large heavily laden truck, loaded with . . . high explosive, traveling at a high speed and driven by a suicide driver, which executed the attack in seconds from start to finish. . . ."[32]

The Federal Bureau of Investigation determined that the explosion had been caused by explosive material wrapped around tubes filled with propane or another highly volatile gas and detonated with the force of more than 12,000 pounds of TNT. It collapsed the four-story building and made a crater eight feet deep and 39 by 29 feet under the seven-inch-thick concrete floor.

A commission appointed by Secretary of Defense Weinberger and headed by Admiral Robert L. J. Long, USN, recently retired as Commander in Chief Pacific, investigated and issued the so-called Long Commission Report. Among the commission's six members was Lt. Gen. Lawrence F. Snowden, USMC (Ret.). The commission found that the MAU's "rules of engagement" did not cover the attacks on the embassy and the battalion building. And it blamed higher headquarters for not supervising the MAU's security.

The commission found that Colonel Geraghty had not received intelligence information that would have led him to defend against this kind of attack. It faulted the battalion commander for concentrating one-quarter of the battalion in a single building as protection against hostile fire. And it criticized the decision that sentries on Posts 4, 5, 6 and 7 carry unloaded weapons. The commission said Syria and Iran were at least indirectly involved in the bombing.

A House armed services subcommittee found that security was "inadequate" and that Colonel Geraghty "made serious errors of judgment in failing to provide better protection for his troops. . . ."[33] It blamed Commodore France and higher commands for not reviewing the MAU's security as conditions changed in the weeks before the bombing, and it criticized the policy-makers for putting the Marines in a situation where security was "inevitably inadequate."

During the last week of October, three more Marines were wounded by incoming mortar fire. The MAU buttoned up, protecting its perimeter with concrete barriers, ditches and machine guns. It came under fire repeatedly, and Colonel Geraghty pulled back A Company from its isolated position, dispersed his men and started transferring administrative and support elements to the ships offshore. The Marines blocked the two entrances to their camp with six-foot-high mounds of dirt, tar-filled steel drums, concertina wire and mazes to slow down speeding vehicles until a .50-caliber machine gun could stop them.

On November 19, the 24th MAU was relieved by the 22d MAU, which on the way over had landed on Grenada. Col. James P. Faulkner, who had commanded the MAU in that landing, was now its chief of staff under Brig. Gen. Jim R. Joy, assistant commander of the 2d Marine Division, who had taken command of the MAU two days earlier. It included the 2d Battalion, 8th Marines and HMM-261. (On February 20, 1984, Colonel Faulkner would again command the MAU, and Brig. Gen. Joy became Commanding General, Joint Task Force, Lebanon.)

This was the 22d MAU's third trip to Lebanon. Some of its Marines had been with the MAU when it landed in September 1982. Under new security rules, most headquarters personnel and other Marine elements were sent aboard ship, and the rifle company at the north end of the airport was replaced by LAF troops. All helicopters were returned to *Guam* at night. MAU headquarters was moved to the airport maintenance building. The Marines dispersed their units; and 40 Seabees flew in from Rota, Spain, to help build more than 190 underground bunkers and command posts, a barrier protection system for the rifle companies and platoon-size strongpoints. Command posts and "barracks" were made of more than 130 sea-land shipping containers, reinforced and buried in the ground. The MAU was under siege.

Early on December 4, 28 Navy jet bombers attacked Syrian targets east of Beirut. Two U.S. planes were shot down, and one pilot was killed, and one, captured. That night, with the Marines under heavy fire, a 122mm rocket landed directly on a combat outpost manned by Capt. Robert K. Dobson, Jr.'s G Company atop a small building, killing eight enlisted Marines and wounding two. Six were off-duty Marines who, when the fire on the checkpoint increased, had rushed out of their bunker to reinforce the four there. Two nights later, G Company, tanks and Dragon rounds destroyed the Amal occupants of two fortified bunkers. And on December 8, after taking more fire, the Marines destroyed all of the Amal's bunkers opposite G Company in Burj al Barajinah, known to the Marines as "Hooterville." Still again on December 15, G and E Companies came under heavy fire. The Marines' battle went on.

Following the example of the recent press blackout of Grenada, higher headquarters now severely restricted reporters' access to the Marines. Some people in power found the national spotlight on the barracks explosion too much to handle. But it could not be switched off.

Everything from SA-7 missiles to small arms fired on Marine helicopters; and on January 8, 1984, Marine Cpl. Edward D. Gargano of Norfolk, Massachusetts, was killed while helping unload a helicopter at the embassy in Beirut.

Between November and February, the entire MAU perimeter at the airport was surrounded by a nine-foot-high dike, a tank ditch, concertina barbed wire and 800 dragon-teeth obstacles. The MAU even prepared for "kamikaze air attacks" and brought in 10 Stinger Missile Teams. Before it was over, the Marines had filled more than a million sandbags. The "presence" mission was now secondary; security came first.

Still, on January 30, the Amal militia killed G Company Marine Lance Cpl. George Dramis of Cape May, New Jersey, mortally wounded Lance Cpl. Rodolfo Hernandez of El Paso, Texas, and wounded two more.

In February, the fighting exploded between Lebanese government forces and the various Moslem militias, now strongly backed by Syria and its Soviet mentors. The Lebanese Army could not control the situation. The Amal called on all Moslems to leave the LAF. On the night of February 5, the Amal and Druze forces went on the offensive. The LAF Army collapsed. Moslem militiamen took control of Christian West Beirut. An Amal leader told the Marines his men did not want to fight them. LAF units along the airport road from Beirut to the airport terminal laid down their arms and left. And at dawn, the LAF captain commanding opposite G Company told Captain Dobson that all his Moslem soldiers, three-quarters of his force, had deserted and he wanted to withdraw through the Marine lines. E Company filled the former LAF positions, and the Amal pulled back to avoid fighting the Marines. LAF forces around the airport disintegrated and sought haven in U.S. lines. It was over.

Brig. Gen. Joy learned from the commander of the British MNF contingent, and from the BBC, that President Reagan had told the other three governments that the United States would withdraw the Marines from Lebanon. The British pulled out on February 7, and the Italians began to pack up.

Lebanese President Amin Gemayel did Syrian bidding on February 17 and revoked his peace arrangement with Israel. The

Syrians, Iranians and Soviets had won. The U.S. Joint Chiefs of Staff on February 18 ordered the withdrawal of the U.S. elements in the MNF.

On Sunday, February 26, 1984, the Marines' E and F Companies were helilifted out to the ships. The next day, G Company left by armored amphibian vehicles and landing craft. At the Beirut International Airport, Druze militia finally occupied the Marines' positions.

The MAU remained aboard ship until April 10, when it was relieved by the 24th MAU, commanded by Col. Myron C. Harrington, Jr. The new amphibious task force took position just over the horizon, out of sight of the Beirut shoreline. The 80 Marines of the 24th MAU guarding the embassy were removed on July 31. Only the Security Guard detachment was left inside the new embassy building in East Beirut.

During the 18 months the MAUs were in Lebanon, 238 Marines were killed in combat and 151 were wounded. (Of all the services, 266 were killed.) "Lebanon" was inscribed on the Marine Corps Memorial as the Corps' forty-second battle honor. But on this assignment, the Marines had been stripped of their mobility and their freedom of action. The Marines had spent 533 days in Beirut and felt they had accomplished virtually nothing.[34]

A terrorist spokesman bragged later that two "martyrs" had forced the U.S. Marine Corps out of Lebanon: one who died to blow up the embassy and the other who drove the truck that destroyed the barracks.

On September 20, 1984—only weeks after the MAU Marines outside the embassy had been replaced by Lebanese guards—23 people were killed and four Marines were wounded when the annex of the new U.S. Embassy was hit by another suicide driver in a van loaded with explosives. What everyone called "terrorism" had proved to be an effective form of warfare.

Nearly four years later, on February 17, 1988, Marine Lt. Col. William R. Higgins, a former aide to Defense Secretary Weinberger, disappeared while serving in Lebanon as the senior U.S. military observer for the United Nations Truce Supervision Organization (Palestine). A pro-Iranian Shiite Moslem terrorist group claimed it had kidnapped him and in July 1989 announced that it had hanged him.

6
Urgent Fury—Grenada

Marine Capt. Timothy B. Howard, thirty, and Capt. John Patrick Giguere, thirty-three, of Marine Medium Helicopter Squadron 261, lifted their two AH-1 Cobra gunships from the amphibious carrier *Guam* and flew without lights toward the Caribbean island of Grenada through the predawn darkness. They led CH-46 helicopters loaded with men of E Company, 2d Battalion, 8th Marines toward Pearls Airfield on Grenada's northeast coast. The Cobras circled for five minutes, drawing inaccurate fire from the hill north of the airport. Then they brought in the Marines just south of the airfield.

Firing 20mm cannon and 2.75-inch rockets, the Cobras knocked out two 23mm antiaircraft guns on the hill and during the morning returned to *Guam* three times to refuel and rearm. About noon, they were summoned to support U.S. Army units on the other side of the island near the capital city of St. George's. With the radio frequencies they had been given, Howard and Giguere could not reach the controlling Air Force AC-130 gunship or any Army unit. They returned to *Guam* to refuel.

Their replacements, Capt. Douglas J. Diehl and Capt. Gary W. Watson, were able to radio a forward air controller but discovered the Army was using different maps from theirs. With a mirror, the Army controller spotted their target—a house concealing a 90mm recoilless rifle. Diehl fired his 20mm cannon, and then Watson destroyed the house with a TOW missile. Three men ran out of the house to a truck, which Watson blew up with a second TOW. Diehl and Watson returned to *Guam* and gave the radio frequency to Howard and Giguere, already airborne again.

They were ordered to attack Fort Frederick on high ground east of St. George's. Antiaircraft defenses had not been suppressed. On Howard's fifth run at about 3 P.M., three missiles hit his helicopter. One missile shattered his right forearm and broke his right leg in 14 places. Capt. Jeb F. Seagle, thirty, his copilot, of Lincolnton, Nebraska, was knocked unconscious.

Howard, using his left hand, slammed down the damaged gunship on a grassy field. The hard landing blew out all the windows and revived Seagle. Howard dropped from the smoking plane to the ground, and Seagle dragged him by the collar some 40 yards from the helicopter and tied a tourniquet of radio wire about the remains of his arm. From the area near Fort Frederick, Spanish-speaking Cubans with AK-47 automatic weapons taunted them and fired at them. Overheated ammunition aboard the Cobra started exploding wildly, and the helicopter blew up. Howard ordered Seagle to take his .38-caliber pistol and find help. Seagle ran off, and the Cubans followed him. His body, riddled with bullets, was found on the beach.

Above Howard in the second Cobra, Captain Giguere, a native of Fort Lee, Virginia, attacked an antiaircraft gun position with a TOW missile, called in a medevac helicopter and swept down and fired his 2.75-inch rockets to keep away the returning Cubans. Lying on his back, Howard felt he was finished, but Marine Maj. Melvin W. De Mars, Jr., swooped in with his CH-46 Sea Knight rescue helicopter and landed 60 feet from him. Giguere courageously attacked a building containing an antiaircraft position to make it possible for De Mars to land. Gunnery Sgt. Kelly M. Neidigh, with an M-16 in one hand, dashed out of the Sea Knight under small-arms fire, put his arm around Howard and dragged him aboard. Cpl. Simon Douglas Gore, Jr., covered them from the chopper. Not knowing Seagle was already dead, De Mars tried to wait for him, but they finally left to save Howard.

After De Mars was gone, Giguere was shot down into the bay; and both he and his copilot, 1st Lt. Jeffrey R. Scharver, twenty-five, of Canton, Ohio, were killed. They had saved Tim Howard, tried to save Jeb Seagle and covered De Mars' rescue. On *Guam*, the Navy doctors kept Howard alive. Although the native of Fort Jackson, South Carolina, lost his right forearm, he won permission to stay in the Corps.

As soon as De Mars delivered Howard to *Guam*, he refueled and went back to look for Giguere. There were no survivors. Navy divers later recovered their bodies. The three Cobra fliers,

Giguere, Scharver and Seagle, were the only Marines killed on Grenada. Seagle was the only Marine to be awarded the Navy Cross.

The United States' armed assault on Grenada, melodramatically misnamed Urgent Fury, began on Tuesday morning, October 25, 1983, on a tiny Caribbean island noted primarily for white tourism and black unrest. Urgent Fury's urgency was dubious, and the only fury was the haste with which the operation was planned. It was called the "largest U.S. combat action since the Vietnam War,"[35] but the Pentagon and higher political authorities censored the true story of the one-sided little battle. Official documents and studies stayed classified through the Presidential election of 1984 and beyond.

Urgent Fury was publicized as a picture-book operation in which elite elements from all the armed services joined together to seize control of the island swiftly and smoothly. The truth was quite different. And even official embargoes could not conceal it. Reminiscent of the attempted rescue of the Iranian hostages and of the Dominican Republic intervention in 1965, the Joint Chiefs of Staff system and interservice rivalry ended up with every service participating, confusions of command, overkill in the thousands of troops involved, mistakes blamed on faulty communications and Americans shooting Americans.

Players in the Grenada spectacle included 1,200 men on the battalion landing team formed around the 2d Battalion, 8th Marines, which in turn were part of the 22d Marine Amphibious Unit (MAU) embarked in Amphibious Squadron Four to form Amphibious Ready Group I-84; a Navy battle group of 11 ships led by the carrier *Independence*, with 90 planes and support ships with 5-inch guns, and the guided missile cruiser *Richmond K. Turner;* two battalions of the Army's 75th Rangers with 600 men each; 6,140 members of the 82d Airborne Division; at least two SEAL Navy Underwater Demolition Teams; and the hush-hush Delta Force, which had tried unsuccessfully to rescue the U.S. hostages in Iran.

All this power and talent had very little enemy to fight—chiefly some 750 often middle-aged Cuban construction workers who were supplying labor for a British contractor to build a 10,000-foot airfield runway. About 100 Cuban soldiers were on the island. Marines felt that if there had to be an intervention, a small Marine landing force could have handled it with ease.

744

The original design called for Marines and Army units to land together; the Marine Corps refused. With the lack of preparation and the high-speed planning, the amphibious landing-wise Marines knew that Americans from different services who had not trained together would be killing each other by mistake. As a result, Army Rangers and elements of the 82d Airborne Division landed at the southwest corner of the island, where the Cubans were concentrated, and the Marines were relegated to capturing the island's functioning airfield on the remote northeast coast, where there was no one much to fight.

Grenada, a former British colony, had been a member of the British Commonwealth since 1974. On the island, only about twice the size of the District of Columbia, lived some 110,000 people. The British Prime Minister opposed the American intervention, tried to talk President Reagan out of it and was reportedly "humiliated" by it. The invasion was also opposed by the French, West Germans, Italians, Canadians and most of the members of the Organization of American States.

The reasons given for the attack varied. There were 600 American medical students at the St. George's University Medical School on the island, and some officials in Washington feared another Teheran-like hostage situation. A second declared purpose was to stop Cuban involvement on the island, but information about the Cubans and their arms proved badly flawed. When it was over, President Reagan said, "Grenada, we were told, was a friendly island paradise for tourism. Well, it wasn't. It was a Soviet-Cuban colony being readied as a major military bastion to export terror and undermine democracy. We got there just in time."[36]

The intervention was triggered when Grenada's leftist Prime Minister Maurice Bishop was murdered on October 19, probably because he had been seeking cooperation with the United States. Deputy Prime Minister Bernard Coard and the People's Revolutionary Army (PRA) seized power and wanted a Marxist regime on this southernmost Windward Island. With Bishop's murder, the Revolutionary Military Council, led by the Army commander, Gen. Hudson Austin, imposed a curfew and closed the airport.

Some official American strategists said Marxists in power on Grenada would endanger the oil routes between Venezuela and the United States. They feared Cuba was planning to export its brand of communism to Grenada and create a military air base for Soviet use.

The Grenada crisis erupted the very same week that the Marine barracks was blown up at Beirut. The assault on Grenada was not a response to that disaster; the Caribbean attack had been decided on days before. The 22d Marine Amphibious Unit (MAU) had sailed for Lebanon on October 18 and was at sea on its way to relieve the 24th MAU in Beirut. The 22d MAU consisted of the 2d Battalion, 8th Marines; Marine Medium Helicopter Squadron 261, and a command and logistical group. The Marine battalion had 43 officers and 779 enlisted men, 10 percent less personnel than before. Rifle platoons had been reduced from 45 men to 36, organized with three 11-man squads. But the battalion's firepower had been increased with additional grenade launchers, Dragon antitank weapons and .50 caliber machine guns. Forty percent of the men had been with the 2d Battalion, 8th Marines for two years or more, and many men of the 22d MAU had already served in Lebanon. They were commanded by Col. James P. "Pat" Faulkner, forty-seven, of Charlotte, North Carolina, who had won four Distinguished Flying Crosses in Vietnam combat.

The 22d MAU was diverted to the Caribbean about midnight on October 20–21, two-plus days before the Sunday-morning explosion in Beirut. But President Reagan did not sign the order to invade Grenada until after the Beirut tragedy. Although the squadron's original diversion to the Caribbean was supposed to be secret, a U.S. news telecast reported it on Friday, October 21.

On the afternoon of October 22, the amphibious-ready group was ordered to head for Grenada and was informed that the U.S. Army would conduct an airborne assault there. At first, Colonel Faulkner assumed his MAU would serve as a reserve. Not until Sunday, October 23, did the Organization of Eastern Caribbean States, made up of six small Caribbean nations, formally request the United States' help.

By that Sunday, the Grenada operation had grown to be a joint combat operation; and that evening, President Reagan signed the order for an assault landing by dawn on Tuesday. U.S. Army units would seize the Point Salines airfield at the southwestern corner of the island, while the Marines would secure Pearls Airfield and the town of Grenville on the northeast coast. The carrier battle group built around *Independence* would provide air cover and support. Every service was in the act.

Preparation was so skimpy that "no maps of any type were available on the ships."[37] A naval commander aboard who had vacationed in Grenadian waters six years earlier was able to supply some information. Operating without guidance, the Marine commanders at sea began planning to evacuate civilians from the island. Later, Marine Commandant Gen. Paul X. Kelley wrote that the operation "in the apparent absence of a detailed, integrated planning process was a significant challenge. As one example among many, on very short notice USMC helicopters were used by U.S. Army forces in a vertical assault."[38]

Serious planning could begin only on Sunday afternoon, about 30 hours before H-hour, when Navy officers flew to *Guam* from Antigua with draft operations orders. The Marine assault plan was to land E Company, commanded by Capt. Henry J. Donigan III, by helicopter on the Pearls Airfield runway and send in G Company, commanded by Capt. Robert K. Dobson, Jr., across the beach. The battalion's third company, F, commanded by Capt. Michael E. Dick, would remain in reserve to provide support via helicopter if needed. Later, the initial helicopter landing site was moved 80 meters southeast in case the airstrip was defended. SEALs sent ahead into the beach reported six-foot-high surf and coral obstacles, and the surface amphibious assault was canceled. Instead, early Tuesday, in total darkness with intermittent rainsqualls, two companies went in by helicopter. E Company headed for the airstrip, and F Company, toward Grenville. G Company stayed aboard ship in reserve.

Helicopter Landing Zone Buzzard just south of Pearls was marked as an unused racetrack, but the helicopters encountered tall palm trees and high scrub brush. The leading pilots, equipped with night-vision goggles, discovered that the northwest corner of the zone was open. They were greeted by antiaircraft fire from the lone hill north of the runway. The Marine battalion commander, Lt. Col. Ray L. Smith, reported the two Cobra attack helicopters quickly silenced the fire, and the Grenadian gun crew fled. E Company attacked the airfield at dawn, cut through the chain-link fence, and, despite a brief burst from Grenadian automatic weapons, seized the airfield. A platoon was sent to take Hill 275, from which the antiaircraft fire had come. The defenders, dressed in T-shirts and shorts, ran down the rear slope; the Marines did not fire but pursued them—a futile chase for Marines encumbered with packs, flak jackets and weapons. The enemy disappeared. Pearls Airfield was declared secure at 7:25 A.M., and E Company pushed on toward the west.

At the same time the Marines were landing at Pearls, 700 men of the 1st Battalion of the Army's 75th Ranger Regiment began parachuting onto the runway of the Point Salines airfield. An hour before, the Delta Force was supposed to have cleared the runway for airborne troops; but of the Delta Force unit of 35 men, six were killed, and 16 wounded, trying to get to the runway. The Rangers were forced to jump dangerously at 500 feet without reserve chutes to duck under fire from antiaircraft guns locked in at 800 feet.

The Rangers' job was to secure the airfield and the True Blue Campus of the St. George's University School of Medicine, 100 yards east of the end of the runway. They encountered fire from AK-47 automatic rifles, mortars and three armored personnel carriers, but no paratroopers were hit in the jump. They quickly cleared the runway. Most of the resistance came from Cuban construction workers; Air Force gunships attacked their concentrations. A Ranger company went after them on the high ground above the airfield. The Rangers lost five men killed and five wounded in the fighting. By 10:28 A.M., the Rangers secured the airfield, the medical school campus and the high ground around the airfield. Meanwhile, at 10 A.M., two battalions of the 2d Brigade, 82d Airborne Division, began landing at Point Salines airport in Air Force C-141s. All the services were there.

In the northeast at 6:30 A.M., the Marines' F Company was helilifted into the Grenville area. The chosen Landing Zone Oriole proved unusable, and the helicopter squadron commander, Lt. Col. Granville "Granny" R. Amos, selected a walled soccer field in the center of town. F Company landed, three choppers at a time, and quickly secured the town and port. No opposition was encountered, and Grenville was declared secure by 7:28 A.M.

Because of the failure of radio equipment, Lt. Col. Smith had trouble bringing in more men. With the help of local residents, the Marines ashore rounded up enemy soldiers, located caches of weapons and equipment and expanded their area westward. By 8 A.M., Lt. Col. Smith had 800 Marines on land. The local people welcomed them.

By noon, Vice Adm. Joseph Metcalf III, commander, Second Fleet, and commander, Joint Task Force 120, called on the Marines to relieve the pressure on the lightly armed Ranger units and to rescue the governor-general, Sir Paul Scoon.[39] F Company was ordered to move by helicopter to Grand Mal Bay on the west coast. G Company, reinforced with five M-60 tanks, 13 amphibious vehicles, TOWs and heavy machine guns, was sent in two amphibious ships around the island to Grand Mal Bay. The site was selected by the naval officer who had vacationed at Grenada. The Marines' battalion commander, Lt. Col. Smith, was not briefed until after 3 P.M. because of communications failures, and then he managed to have H-hour postponed from 4:30 A.M. to 6:30 P.M.

The situation at the governor-general's mansion on a hill above St. George's seemed the most precarious. Early on Monday, a day before the invasion, a special mission force was sent in to assure the governor's safety. The governor's party and the rescue force were surrounded by men of the Grenadian People's Revolutionary Army. Vice Adm. Metcalf diverted the four Marine Cobra gunships to help the Army, and the two Cobras were shot down by hidden Soviet-built antiaircraft batteries.

G Company circled the north end of Grenada by ship and was finally put ashore at 7 P.M. in complete darkness near Grand Mal Bay at Landing Zone Fuel, which had not even been reconnoitered. Captain Dobson still did not know his mission and had several hundred Marines crowded onto the tiny beachhead with limited exit routes and large fuel tanks nearby. At 11 P.M., Maj. William J. Sublette arrived by helicopter with more information and an hour later brought back Lt. Col. Smith, who had spent six frustrating hours trying to catch up to his troops.

F Company was helilifted to Landing Zone Fuel near Grand Mal Bay at 4 A.M. on D plus one. In the dark, the Battalion Landing Team commander established his headquarters and collected tanks and amtracs at the Queen's Park racecourse, south of Grand Mal Bay and north of St. George's, to support the attack southeast on the governor-general's residence. By 7:10 A.M., 12 hours after arriving on the island's west coast, G Company (minus) easily rescued the governor-general, his wife, nine other civilians and 22 men of the special mission team, who were all barricaded in the residence. That afternoon at 4:30, Captain Dobson's* G Company attacked Fort Frederick, the ancient masonry fortress that served as the headquarters of the Grenadian PRA. As the Marines approached, they saw Grenadians discard their uniforms

---

*Captain Dobson won the Leftwich Trophy in 1984 for his service on Grenada and subsequently in Lebanon. The trophy is awarded annually to the best ground combat element captain in the Fleet Marine Force. It is named for Lt. Col. William G. Leftwich, Jr., who received the Navy Cross and was later killed in Vietnam.

and disappear over the fort's walls. Dobson and his men took the fort unopposed and captured stocks of weapons and ammunition. A Navy jet on Tuesday had bombed the nearby civilian mental hospital by mistake. The capture of Fort Frederick finished organized resistance on the island.

Not until late on Tuesday afternoon did the American commanders discover that the St. George's University Medical School had a second campus at Grand Anse Beach, four miles from Point Salines near St. George's. Plans were made to "rescue" those medical students the following day.

Vice Adm. Metcalf ordered the Marines' HMM-261 helicopters to help the Army's 2d Ranger Battalion extract the U.S. medical students from the Grand Anse campus. At 4:15 P.M. on Wednesday, nine CH-46 helicopters carried in a company of Rangers. The rotor blade of one CH-46 brushed a palm tree on the narrow beach, and the damaged helicopter finally was flown back to the Point Salines airfield. In minutes, four CH-53s arrived to evacuate the 224 medical students, and then the eight CH-46s returned to extract the Rangers. Another CH-46 struck a palm tree and was lost; the Marine crew and Rangers all were rescued. The students were evacuated in less than an hour without any friendly casualties and were taken to the Point Salines airfield and flown to the United States in C-141s. In all, 599 Americans and 88 other nationals were evacuated from the island.

By D plus two, the invasion was actually over. Says one official Marine Corps analysis, "The Cuban defenses were hastily organized, incomplete and in some places made poor tactical use of the terrain." The analysis referred to "the low state of training on the part of the Cuban troops (actually only construction workers)."[40]

The Marines still had a roster of minor-league missions. G Company seized the Richmond Hill Prison by 8 A.M. and found four prisoners. Then it set out to attack Fort Adolphus, which was flying a flag of "unknown type." Lt. Col. Smith and Captain Dobson considered softening the target with preparatory fire but fortunately changed their minds. Fort Adolphus turned out to be the Venezuelan Embassy.

Captain Dick's F Company cleared the city of St. George's, and the boundary line between the Army's 82d Airborne Division and Marine units was shifted south so that all of the city was in the Marines' area of operations. But communications between the Marines and the Army was haphazard at first. With the help of civilians, the Marines collected members of the PRA. Protected by close air support from *Independence*, F Company took Fort Rupert without trouble and found a sizable cache of Cuban weapons.

As the Marines' territory was enlarged, the patrol of St. George's was joined by the Marines of Battery H, 3rd Battalion, 10th Marines as a provisional rifle company. Capt. Bradley M. Gates commanded the artillerymen. Staff Sgt. Clyde M. Trout led his artillery squad down a hill three miles northeast of St. George's and in a nearby house captured Deputy Prime Minister Bernard Coard. By October 31, Gen. Hudson Austin himself was aboard *Guam*.

The Army-Marine boundary was shifted still further south to permit the Marines to occupy the Ross Point Hotel on Martin's Bay just south of St. George's, and by evening St. George's and its dominant terrain were secured. Reports were that 400 foreigners were at the hotel eager to be evacuated; but the Marines found fewer than two dozen foreign nationals, mostly Canadians, and almost none wished to be evacuated.

In the north, Captain Donigan's E Company patrolled inland and on D plus two captured the Mount Horne Agriculture Experimental Station without encountering resistance. But on a nearby hilltop, a fire team found three men who, when ordered to halt, fled. The Marines shot two, one of whom later died; they were identified as Cubans.

At the Ross Point Hotel, the Marines and elements of the 82d Airborne finally linked up at 8 A.M. on D plus three, October 28. The Army commanders were surprised to find the Marines on the scene; they had considered the area of the hotel a free-fire zone. The word about the change in boundaries had not gotten down the chain of command.

On the morning of October 30, the Marines of E Company occupied the town of Sauteurs on Grenada's north coast, and G Company moved north to occupy Gouyave and Victoria on the west coast. Neither force met opposition. And that day, the Marines turned over their area of responsibility to the 82d Airborne. The next day, the 82d replaced the Marines at Pearls Airport. In all, 6,140 members of the 82d Airborne Division were put ashore on Grenada. By that evening, all ground combat units of the 22d MAU were back aboard ship.

At dawn on November 1, 300 Marines made an amphibious landing on the island of Carriacou, 20 miles north of Grenada, in a fruitless search for Grenadian or Cuban resistance. F Company landed by helicopter, and G Company by amphibious assault. They met no resistance, found no enemy and fired no shots but seized stores of arms and ammunition. As on Grenada, the equipment was old and contained no surprises. The island was declared secure by 8:20 A.M. G Company went back to the ships, and F Company stayed ashore overnight. The 82d Airborne took over, and the Marines concluded their role in the invasion of Grenada at 9 A.M. on November 2.

The cost in American lives was given as 19 military dead and 115 wounded, of which the Marine Corps had 3 dead and 15 wounded, the Army 12 dead and 71 wounded and the Navy 4 dead and 3 wounded. Not all American casualties were from hostile fire. In one reported case, a Navy plane strafed and killed one U.S. soldier and wounded 15 more.

The United States took 691 prisoners, including 30 Soviet advisors. Reportedly, the Cubans lost 24 dead and 59 wounded, and the Grenadians had 45 military and civilians killed and 337 wounded, including 21 casualties (15 killed) in the mistaken bombing of the civilian mental hospital on Tuesday.[41] The bombing of the mental hospital was concealed by the military authorities until it was revealed by a reporter, once the press was allowed on Grenada.

The Grenada operation will be remembered because, perhaps for the first time in American history, U.S. military commanders prevented the press from covering an invasion. The only source of public information about what happened on Grenada— when it happened—came from the military. Responsible sources later said that General Austin on Grenada and Cuban authorities knew in advance that the assault was to take place. Before it did, Radio Free Grenada was calling the island's militia to active duty. Only the American people were kept in the dark.

On Thursday, October 27, 15 journalists—none from daily newspapers—were finally permitted to go to Grenada for the afternoon. The fighting was over by then. Howard Simons, managing editor of the *Washington Post*, summed up the press' view: "I think a secret war, like secret government, is antithetical to an open society. It's absolutely outrageous."[42] On October 30, the ban was eased, and 168 reporters were flown in from Barbados.

The press speculated that the military censored its war because of the intense coverage that the press had given the Vietnam war and because of the limits the British had put on press coverage of the Falkland Islands invasion. James Reston commented in the *New York Times* on November 2, "Reporters and TV cameras were kept out in the reasonable belief that if the American people knew and saw what gunships did in such an invasion, they might not approve."

The military's public rationale was that it could not guarantee the safety of American reporters and cameramen. It ignored the history of Stephen Crane at Guantanamo, Floyd Gibbons at Belleau Wood, John Hersey on Guadalcanal, Robert Sherrod at Tarawa, David Douglas Duncan at The Reservoir, Sean Flynn and Dana Stone in Vietnam. Objections were so widespread that Gen. John W. Vessey, Jr., Chairman of the Joint Chiefs of Staff, created a commission to investigate the issue.

A final hassle resulted when it was revealed that the Army had given out 8,612 medals for the operations, although it had barely more than 7,000 men on the island. Some awards went to people in the rear echelons, all the way back to the Pentagon. The Marines gave out 205 awards, including 50 combat awards and 10 Purple Hearts. Their one Navy Cross and five Silver Stars were all received by helicopter personnel. Only six noncommissioned Marines received combat awards.

The enemy, poorly armed and trained, never seemed to have much will to fight. Cubans frequently tried to surrender. In one case, 160 armed Cubans surrendered to two American Rangers with M-16s.

The Department of Defense estimated that the Grenada mission cost $134.4 million, not including the military payroll. That figured out at $224,000 for each U.S. medical student evacuated or $1 million for each square mile of Grenada.[43] The United Nations General Assembly voted overwhelmingly to deplore the United States' armed intervention.

Before long, the members of the Revolutionary Military Council that had overthrown and murdered Maurice Bishop were in the Richmond Hill Prison. "We blew them away," Vice Adm. Metcalf said proudly.[44] The medical students returned to their studies. The Cubans were removed from the island. The United States spent $20 million to complete the construction of the airfield at Point Salines. And as it did in Haiti and Cuba in the old days, the United States kept a token presence on the island to train a Grenadian law-and-order paramilitary force.

7
"A Golden Decade"

By the mid-1980s, the Corps had turned around—worked its way out of its post-Vietnam problems. After every major conflict, a fighting organization seems to require a period in which it can switch from a wartime to a postwar stance and, instead of looking back at its recent stress, swivel around and concentrate on future tasks and challenges. The Corps made this transition and entered a forward-looking period in terms of mission, manpower, movement and weapons. Although political demands dumped on the Corps two unusual experiences, in Lebanon and Grenada, its main thrust was to prepare for the future.

The turnaround from the post-Vietnam period was dramatic. Commandant Gen. Paul X. Kelley explained: "Two things started it. The Reagan Administration has done an awful lot, but what changed our whole outlook came in 1979 when Harold Brown [Secretary of Defense under President Jimmy Carter] gave us the maritime prepositioning ship concept. That poured money into our coffers that gave us a whole new base line. It included money for ships and an awful lot of money for equipment. Then, when Ronald Reagan came in, we took off."[45]

The total budget appropriated for the support of the Marine Corps in 1978 was $4.6 billion. By 1986, the total had ballooned to $14.8 billion in current dollars. And by 1991, it had leveled off at $9.6 billion. But the sizable increase changed the Marines' manpower and equipment—and outlook. General Kelley said, "This is a golden decade for the Marine Corps."

By the mid-1980s, the Corps had reduced the priority of a NATO Western European role. The Marine Corps was too small and too "light" to be a significant battle force in central Europe, and its training exercises on skis in Norway on NATO's northern flank seemed to prove mostly that the Corps had the "right stuff." In a major European confrontation, it could hardly make a difference. Strategic planners had become freshly alert to other needs and possible uses for the Marines.

Despite the prolonged land assignments in Vietnam and Lebanon, General Kelley could say in 1985: "We are not a second land army, nor should we be. The Army should have the capabilities for those long land campaigns. That's their bag, and we shouldn't be competing with them at all in that.

"The Marine Corps is what you want it to be. Amphibious operations are our primary mission, and we have to be ready to cope with every level of conflict. We can make it light; we can make it heavy, because the whole concept is based on a 'task' organization."

The Corps returned to thinking about a worldwide role and the relationship of that role to possible future threats. This meant planning for swift insertion, battlefield mobility, concentrated firepower, over-the-horizon amphibious capabilities—better rifles and grenade launchers, swifter vehicles, tactical dispersion, large helicopters, VSTOL (verticle-short-takeoff-landing) aircraft, prepositioned supplies. And the Reagan Administration's bounty made it all possible.*

Readiness and swiftness were again the bywords. Relatively small units were the formulations of the day—from embassy Security Guard detachments to MAUs and MABs and even coordination with non-Marine antiterrorists forces that might want to strike from the sea. In a strange and rational way—and without abrogating the possibility of massing power in the future—the Corps was going back to a reborn version of what it had been before the massive actions of World War II.

In line with this thinking, by 1986 Commandant Kelley had replaced the temporary formation of amphibious ground-air units of various strengths to meet specific crises with a permanent Marine Air-Ground Task Force (MAGTF) concept. The Corps established 14 permanently manned headquarters to command three

---

*James H. Webb, Jr., who became Secretary of the Navy on April 10, 1987, assured the Marine Corps of another sympathetic ear near the top of the Reagan Administration's military-political hierarchy. Webb, an Annapolis graduate, was a former Marine who received the Navy Cross, the Silver Star, two Bronze Stars and two Purple Hearts as a platoon commander with the 5th Marines in Vietnam in 1969. And he wrote a highly successful novel, *Fields of Fire*, about the Vietnam war.

amphibious forces, six amphibious brigades and five amphibious units.

Tactical mobility on the battlefield received new emphasis. Ground mobility was increased with a variety of new trucks, most notably the eight-wheeled Light Armored Vehicle (LAV-25) and the High-Mobility Multipurpose Wheeled Vehicle (HMMWV), nicknamed the Hummer and planned to replace the classic Jeep.

Said Commandant Kelley, "And we still have 'FEETs.' That's still a very valid way for an infantryman moving around the battlefield. Sometimes we forget that, but it's still on the list." The 13-man rifle squad with three four-man fire teams, which served in World War II, Korea and Vietnam, was brought back to replace the brief 1983 experiment with an 11-man squad of two five-man fire teams.

In the air, modernization was just as intense. Marine Attack Squadron 331 at Cherry Point became the first squadron to fly the AV-8B Harrier II, the second-generation VSTOL aircraft. And the Corps by 1986, after a long controversy, had four active squadrons (and planned 12 squadrons), each with 12 F/A-18 Hornets, replacements for the aging A-4 Skyhawks and F-4 Phantoms. The Corps saw the F/A-18 supplying both an air-to-air combat and a close support capability. In April 1986, two Marine F/A-18 squadrons, flying off *Coral Sea*, operated in Navy Carrier Air Groups in the Gulf of Sidra against Libya.

Cobra attack helicopter gunships were upgraded with the AH-W SuperCobras handling TOWs and the AH-1J Cobras with Hellfire missiles. And the MV-22A Osprey, a fixed-wing tilt-rotor aircraft, was being developed to replace the Vietnam-vintage medium CH-46E helicopter. The Osprey could carry 24 combat-equipped troops, take off vertically and fly 250 miles per hour. Kelley said his aviators called it "probably the most revolutionary advance in aircraft since the jet engine."

The new infantry weapons in place included the vastly improved M-16A2 5.56mm rifle, the brand-new M249 5.56mm Belgian-made squad automatic weapon (SAW), the 83mm antitank rocket launcher (SMAW), the M60E3 7.62 light machine guns and the Mark 19 40mm machine gun, and the updated M224 60mm mortar. To strengthen fire support from the sea, all four *Iowa*-class battleships were to be recommissioned. And the M1A1 Abrams main battle tank was approved to replace the M60A1. At the same time, the TOW-2 was said to be able to defeat any known armor. And with the Corps following the Army's lead, the venerable M-1911 Colt .45 was replaced with the 15-round 9mm Beretta pistol.

In the name of strategic mobility, the Corps adopted "prepositioning." The prepositioning idea was to place up front near a potential combat zone the matériel needed to sustain a Marine Amphibious Brigade for 30 days, because both shipping and forward bases were in short supply. There were two kinds—sea-based and a land-based version entrenched in Norway for a 12,000-man Marine Amphibious Brigade. Construction of the "in rock" storage site at Figaard, Norway, began in 1986.

Three brigades were earmarked for use with maritime prepositioning shipping. The original transitional Near-Term Prepositioning Force (NTPF), which concentrated heavy equipment and 30 days of supplies for a 16,500-man Marine Amphibious Brigade in the Indian Ocean and the Western Pacific, was replaced by one of three permanent Maritime Prepositioning Squadrons (MPS). By 1986, the MPS program had in place 13 ships, with one squadron in the eastern Atlantic, a second at Diego Garcia in the Indian Ocean and a third at Guam and Tinian in the Western Pacific. Kelley said, "The troops merely have to fly in."

The MPS program was a substitute that would reduce the pressure and the need for a larger, even more expensive amphibious assault fleet. Whether it was more or less vulnerable than integrating that equipment in an amphibious task force was debatable. In the Persian Gulf war of 1990–91, it would get well-supplied Marines to the battlefield faster.

The MPS program could not replace amphibious assault shipping. MPS ships have no assault capability and require a nonhostile shore to unload. This "benign environment" could exist on a peaceful shore or in an area from which a Marine assault force had removed the hostility.

In 1982, even if the U.S. Navy's 67 remaining and scattered amphibious ships could have been assembled, they could have carried the assault elements of only one MAF to battle. But by 1985, the amphibious ship *Whidbey Island* (LSD-41), the first of eight of a new class of Landing Ship Dock, was completed. It supplied an assault capability and was the first ship designed to carry a Marine landing force and the new air-cushion landing craft (LCAC). The Marines acquired the first of 200 LCACs, which promised to give the Corps its first capability for "over-the-horizon" surface amphibious assault. The LCACs have a 200-mile range, 50-knot speed and carry a payload of 60 tons. They crack the old 8- to 10-knot limit on ship-to-shore movement.

Amphibious lift was also boosted when the helicopter carrier *Wasp* was begun in 1985. Designed to put ashore 2,000 Marines from over the horizon, *Wasp* was commissioned on July 29, 1989. It was the first of the new class of amphibious assault ships to replace *Iwo Jima* and update the 1976-vintage *Tarawa*-class ship.

But weapons and equipment were only part of the story. Marines always believe that the key is Marines. But by 1987, 75 percent of the officers and 83 percent of the enlisted men had never seen combat.

Marine manpower improved from the period when the Corps could not enlist or retain enough recruits of high quality and when it was shaken with personnel problems. Manpower strengths leveled off at just under 200,000 men and women on active duty. The quality of recruits climbed from 46 percent high school graduates in 1973 to 97 percent in 1986. (Room was left for exceptionally able youngsters who did not finish high school.) The average 1986 recruit was twenty years of age; males averaged 5 feet 9.4 inches and 161.5 pounds; females, 5 feet 4.5 inches and 127.9 pounds.

And because more young Marines wanted to stay in the service—actually more than the Corps could reenlist and still stay "young"—the number of new recruits needed annually dropped from 50,000 to 37,000 in 1986. Commandant Kelley said at the time, "Number one, you need quality people, and we now have the highest quality in the history of the Corps. I cannot keep all the kids who want to stay."

With a surplus of quality personnel and a forthcoming new generation of weapons and equipment, the Marine Corps came to the end of Commandant Kelley's four-year term feeling optimistic about the future.

In one of the most competitive successions in decades, General Kelley turned over the Corps on July 1, 1987, to a new Commandant, Alfred M. Gray, Jr., who most recently had been the Commanding General, Fleet Marine Force, Atlantic. Official announcement of Gray's nomination was not made until virtually the last moment; the selection seemed hard for the participants in the selection process to agree on.

When he became Commandant, Gray, a native of Point

Pleasant Beach, New Jersey, was fifty-nine. He had enlisted in 1950 and made sergeant before being commissioned in 1952 and serving as an infantry officer in the Korean war. He was one of the first Marines into Vietnam, and one of the last out. In 1964, he commanded the first Marine ground unit to conduct independent operations in Vietnam, collecting intelligence at Khe Sanh near the Laotian border; and he commanded the Ground Security Force in the evacuation of Saigon in 1975. He commanded the 2d Marines and the 4th Marines, and as a major general led the 2d Marine Division when the barracks were blown up in Beirut in 1983. His long career as a field commander was regarded at the time both as an asset and as leaving him less experienced with the ways things are accomplished in Washington. In the end, he would leave his own personalized imprint on the Corps.

Essentially, General Gray was chosen to be Commandant because he was regarded as an experienced and respected "warrior." At the change of command ceremony at the historic Marine Corps Barracks in Washington, D.C., General Gray set the tone for his tour as Commandant when he said: "The nation's Corps of Marines, and the sailors who serve with us, are warriors. We are warriors and people who support warriors and we must always keep that focus. Some people don't like to hear about war—people who fight don't like to have to do it—but that's what we are about. The nation expects her Marines to be the finest fighting force on earth, prepared to go tonight, tomorrow or whenever. This our Corps can do tonight. . . . The nation demands that [Marines] . . . be a little bit special. The nation demands that we be the best led, the best trained, the best disciplined, particularly self-disciplined, force on earth. The nation demands that we teach nothing but winning—in battle and in life."

With the changing of command at Marine Corps Headquarters, the Corps' leaders, like any astute managers, worried how long their decade would remain "golden." They were sensitive to Congressional and public attitudes that questioned increases in military spending against cutbacks in domestic programs and that attacked military "waste." They wondered about the effect of a change in Presidential administrations.* They worried whether the recruiting pool would dry up, as some predicted. And they feared that the huge expenditure for strategic nuclear forces and the Strategic Defense Initiative ("Star Wars") would reduce the spending for conventional forces. The Corps' history proved that there would always be lean and fat years.

The Corps' insertions in Lebanon and Grenada and its prepositioning installations demonstrated its worldwide availability. To retain the Corps franchise as "the epitome of the global operation of maneuver warfare,"[46] elements of the Marine Corps participated in some 90 exercises overseas per year with as many as 34 allies. They conducted exercises from Thailand all the way round to northern Norway. They performed as many as 60 amphibious operations a year. They trained for desert, jungle, and cold-weather warfare. They trained globally. The Corps felt itself ready to go and to fight anywhere it was needed.

Commandant Kelley put the emphasis on well-trained fighting people: "In the final analysis, that's the tiebreaker: the quality of people on the battlefield. Battles are won by remnants that are left on the battlefield."

---

*A dramatic event occurred during the Reagan Administration when, in 1986 and 1987, Marine Corps Lt. Col. Oliver L. North received worldwide headlines for his role, while assigned to the White House's National Security Council staff, in supplying arms to Iran and diverting funds from a Swiss bank account to the antigovernment rebels in Nicaragua. Dismissed from the White House, he was assigned to duty at Headquarters, Marine Corps, and subsequently retired.

8
Just Cause—Panama

In the darkness, Marine Staff Sgt. Samuel French drove the lead Light Armored Vehicle (LAV) through the barbed wire gate. Sgt. Thomas P. Bernius and Cpl. Garreth C. Isaak leaped out and with grenade launchers shattered the glass door of Panama's National Department of Traffic and Transportation Station #2. Marine scouts poured from the two LAVs and stormed into the building.

It was 1 A.M. on Wednesday, December 20, 1989—H-Hour for Operation Just Cause to capture the Republic of Panama's dictator, General Manuel Antonio Noriega. The Marines were scouts of D Company, 2d Light Armored Infantry (LAI) Battalion, and members of the 1st Platoon, Fleet Anti-terrorist Security Team (FAST).

Firing their AK-47s at the Marines, Panama Defense Forces (PDF) soldiers inside the building fell back room by room. Corporal Isaak took the point and entered the large room at the end of the hall. The last PDF officer in the building fired at him. Isaak fell with a bullet in his neck.

Cpl. Thomas C. Camp moved up and pumped buckshot and lobbed a grenade into the room. One PDF soldier was killed, and three were captured. Then, suddenly, the fire fight was over. In 10 minutes, the Marines had cleared the building on the Pan-American Highway near the U.S. Navy's Arraijan Tank Farm. This naval storage facility, two miles from the vital Howard Air Force Base, supplied fuel to all the U.S. forces.

Corporal Isaak, a twenty-two-year-old Marine from Greenville, South Carolina, died that evening; he was the only Marine killed in action in Operation Just Cause. Three Marines were wounded in action.

The D Company and FAST Marines were part of the 22,500-man American force attempting to remove General Noriega. Less than a battalion of Marines were in Panama for this quick little conflict.

The Marines were ordered to seize two military compounds in the vicinity of the tank farm. As they drove from the tank farm three miles to the town of Arraijan, they found two gasoline tanker trucks and a platoon of some 20 PDF troops blocking the highway. The Marines' fire hit one of the tankers, and the PDF troops at the roadblock fled.

In Arraijan, a 17-man FAST urban warfare team and D Company Marines forced open and swiftly seized a local political headquarters of the Panamanian dictator. A vehicle attempted to attack the Marine position. Sgt. Gregory A. Johnson, twenty-four, of Anchorage, Alaska, was shot in the jaw and hit by the vehicle. The Marines occupied the Arraijan Town Hall and searched nearby houses.

Marines had handled troubles in Panama over the previous 130 years, and Marine landing parties had gone ashore in 1856, 1873, 1885 and 1895. In the largest of these interventions, the first brigade of Marines ever organized served in Panama in April and May 1885. Their main job was to guard the American-owned railroad and keep open traffic across the 47-mile-wide Isthmus of Panama.

After the Spanish-American War, Marines landed on the isthmus repeatedly to preserve the U.S. interest in Panama's independence and ensure the building of the Panama Canal. A Marine battalion protected American lives and property there in 1902. The Panamanians revolted from Colombia in 1903, and when Colombia threatened the new, U.S.-sponsored Republic of Panama, a Marine brigade again was on the scene. A Marine battalion stayed near Panama City on the Pacific Ocean until 1914, when the Canal finally opened.

In 1989's Operation Just Cause, the U.S. Army's airborne forces led the way. American soldiers were flown in from as far away as Fort Lewis, Washington. Marine Forces Panama was assigned to isolate Panama City from the west and to protect Howard Air Force Base. The Marines' three major areas of responsibility were all on the west bank of the Panama Canal Zone: the Arraijan Tank Farm; Howard Air Force Base and the high ground to the west; and the Bridge of the Americas, which controls traffic into Panama City from the west.

General Noriega came to power in August 1983. He was a favorite of the U.S. intelligence community, but a grand jury in the States indicted him for drug trafficking in January 1988. A coup against him the following month failed.

In the face of violence and attacks on the Arraijan Tank Farm, a Marine Corps Security Force (MCSF) Company and Marines of the 6th Marine Expeditionary Brigade were sent to Panama to protect U.S. military facilities. Repeatedly, Marines of the MCSF company and later I Company, 3rd Battalion, 4th Marines clashed at night with Noriega partisans on the tank farm's wooded grounds. On the night of April 11, members of a divided patrol fired on each other, and a Marine was killed.

The Marines had their largest and most controversial fire fight on the following night. It lasted two hours until the commander of Joint Task Force (JTF) Panama ordered a ceasefire. The Panamanians accused the Marines of being drunk and firing at palm trees. Furious, the Marines charged that JTF headquarters was accepting and spreading the Panamanian lies. By mid-September, they had 14 encounters on the west side of the Canal. The JTF Panama commander thought the Marines too aggressive; he restricted their patrolling. In early 1989, the U.S. Southern Command tried to have the Marines redeployed but was overruled in Washington.

Despite a violent political campaign, Noriega was beaten at the polls in the elections of May 7, 1989. He annulled the results and attacked the winners. A company of the 2d LAI Battalion with LAVs reinforced the Marines, and two U.S. Army infantry battalions arrived by the end of May. The Marines conducted a series of exercises named "Sand Fleas" to demonstrate their freedom of movement and to rehearse contingency plans. Whenever the LAI Company extended its exercises outside the Canal Zone, the PDF harassed it.

PDF officers attempted a coup, this one supported by the United States, against General Noriega on October 3, 1989. The rebels captured Noriega, but he reached a telephone and called in friendly forces. The rebel leaders were killed. During the coup attempt, the Marines blocked traffic on the Pan-American Highway leading into the city from the west and reinforced the U.S. Embassy and security checkpoints.

Operation Just Cause was finally triggered by the death on Saturday night, December 16, 1989, of Marine 1st Lt. Robert Paz of the MCSF Company. He was killed by Panamanian Defense Forces soldiers while riding in a cream-colored Chevrolet, unarmed and in civilian clothes.

Paz and three other unarmed, off-duty American officers were looking for a restaurant in Panama City at 9 P.M. At a PDF checkpoint near the Commandancia, the PDF headquarters in Panama City, Panamanians, including six uniformed PDF soldiers carrying AK-47s, stopped them. The Panamanians tried to pull one of the Americans from the car. The driver stepped on the accelerator. The PDF soldiers fired, and Paz, sitting in the backseat, was mortally wounded. The twenty-five-year-old Marine from Dallas died that night in Gorgas Army Hospital. The PDF grabbed an unarmed U.S. Navy lieutenant and his wife, who had witnessed the shooting; they were taken into custody, handcuffed and beaten.

The next day President George Bush ordered U.S. troops to Panama to capture General Noriega and destroy his forces. He was accused of drug running and laundering the profits. U.S. Ambassador Deane R. Hinton later called Operation Just Cause "the best drug bust in history."[47]

Noriega had neither an air force nor tanks. His PDF contained 13,000 men of whom only a quarter were judged combat capable. On December 19, the first day of Operation Just Cause, 7,000 American troops were airlifted into Panama to join the 12,700 already stationed there. The U.S. Army's 82d Airborne Division dropped 4,500 paratroopers in the largest airborne assault since World War II. Four Navy SEALs were killed disabling the dictator's private plane.

Not a single reporter was permitted to cover Operation Just Cause. A Pentagon pool of eight press people arrived four hours after combat started and could not file till midmorning.

At the start of Operation Just Cause, 650 Marines were in Panama under the command of Col. Charles E. Richardson. Marine Forces Panama included Company K, 6th Marines; Company D, 2d LAI Battalion; Marine Corps Security Force Company, Panama; the 1st FAST Platoon; and Detachment G, Brigade Service Support Group 6. They were assigned to the west side of the Panama Canal Zone. I Company, 6th Marines arrived from Camp Lejeune on December 28.

At H-Hour, 1 A.M. on Wednesday, December 20, the LAI company seized the PDF traffic police stations on the Pan-

American Highway and in Arraijan. K Company, 6th Marines established a roadblock south of Howard Air Force Base. Fifty Marines of Brigade Service Support Group 6, supported by Army MPs, sealed off both ends of the Bridge of the Americas.

Within a half hour after the U.S. attack started, the PDF fired six rocket-propelled grenades into the embassy compound where eight Security Guard Marines were on duty. No one was injured. By 4:20 A.M., Army reinforcements came up to secure the perimeter.

Two lightly armed Army Ranger battalions jumped into action, expecting an 82d Airborne brigade to reinforce them; but an ice storm kept half the brigade in North Carolina. Rangers and paratroopers closed in on PDF units and the international airport outside Panama City. Four Marine LAVs helped battle snipers and at midday supported the Army's attack on the Commandancia.

In the afternoon, D Company, 2d LAI Battalion and the FAST team attacked the 10th Military Zone Headquarters at La Chorrera, 15 miles west of Panama City. Their attack was supported by two Air Force A-7 attack jets. Marines fired 25mm Bushmaster guns on the turrets of their LAVs at the concrete buildings and quickly cleared the PDF barracks. They exchanged fire with a roadblock of six buses. By 6 P.M., all the scouts crowded into two LAVs and the FAST team into two Chevrolet Suburban vans, and they returned to Arraijan.[48]

K Company, 6th Marines secured the ramshackle seaside town of Vera Cruz south of Howard Air Force Base and occupied steep jungle hills west of the base. The PDF had abandoned the towns, and K Company did not have to fire a shot.

On Thursday, the FAST team continued to search houses in Arraijan, while D Company Marines accepted surrendering PDF personnel. That afternoon they searched and secured a ranch where they saw fleeing soldiers they suspected were Cubans. The Marines found drugs at the ranch.

As the Marines extended their area of operations farther west, Marine Forces Panama was given operational control over the Army's 2d Battalion, 27th Light Infantry Regiment, which on Friday night was brought into La Chorrera by helicopter. On December 28, I Company, 6th Marines arrived to help maintain security in the countryside.

More than 200 Panamanians were killed. Noriega eluded his

pursuers and finally sought sanctuary in the Vatican consulate four days later. He ended up in a U.S. prison awaiting trial for months.

With the PDF eliminated, the Marines stood watch in the countryside until the new Panamanian government could organize its own force. Marines captured hundreds of Noriega officials and patrolled to control crime and looting. The new government decided to use former PDF personnel in its new Panama Public Force (PPF), and the Marines found themselves working with people they had only recently pursued.

The American forces suffered 347 casualties in Operation Just Cause. Sixty percent of them were reportedly from "friendly fire," as were nine of the 23 killed.

Two years after Operation Just Cause, drug smuggling was restored in Panama; cocaine still made its way from neighboring Colombia to the U.S. market. Nothing much had changed.

SEMPER FIDELIS

X
THE NINETIES
1990–

1
The Gulf War—Desert Shield

The United States-led war against Iraq involved more U.S. Marines than any single operation in Marine Corps history. There were 92,990 Marines in the theater, organized in 24 combat battalions and 40 squadrons. The five-month war climaxed in January–February 1991 with a 38-day air campaign and a four-day ground battle. When it was over, 24 Marines had been killed and 92 wounded in action; eight fixed-wing aircraft and three helicopters were lost. A reporter who accompanied the 1st Battalion, 5th Marines (which had fought at Belleau Wood, Peleliu and the Reservoir) called it "the most lopsided victory in Marine Corps history."[1]

At 2 A.M. on August 2, 1990, President Saddam Hussein of the Republic of Iraq ordered 80,000 soldiers of three elite Republican Guard divisions to charge down a six-lane highway and invade neighboring Kuwait. He had only recently finished an eight-year war with another neighbor, the Islamic Republic of Iran.

By noon of August 3, the Iraqi troops reached the Kuwait border with the Kingdom of Saudi Arabia. The virtually unopposed invasion totally surprised the White House and intelligence chiefs in Washington and diplomats at United Nations headquarters in New York.

Saddam Hussein's nationalist-socialist Baath Party had been in power for 22 years. He was a client of both the Soviet Union and the United States. He bought an estimated $40 billion of weapons: Hawk missile systems from the United States, tanks and SS-1 (Scud) missiles from the Soviet Union, $16 billion in Exocet missiles and Mirage F-1 aircraft from France, tanks from China, munitions from Germany, long-range artillery from Brazil, cluster

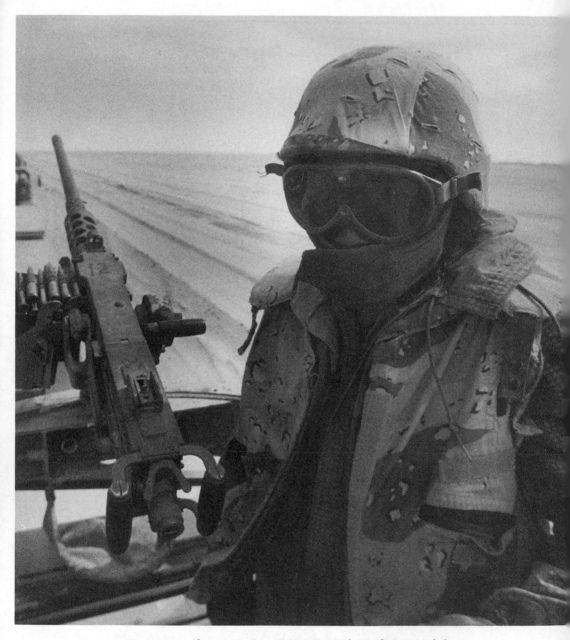

*Penetrating deep into Kuwait, Lance Cpl. Earl Cross of the
1st Marine Division and Lake Charles, Louisiana, is armed
and dressed for instant desert warfare.*
© David Leeson 1991/Dallas Morning News/JB Pictures

bombs from Chile and plastic mines from Italy. The Marines would have to face all of these.

The Iraqi dictator claimed he wanted to take from the rich Kuwaitis and give to the poor Arab masses. He demanded that Kuwait, which had given him billions of dollars in aid during his long war with Iran, now limit its oil production to allow oil prices to rise and enable Iraq to pay its war debts. He insisted that Kuwait cede territory to Iraq.

When he attacked, Kuwait's rulers, frightened of his million-man army, fled by helicopter and touring car; and the rulers of Saudi Arabia, fearful that Saddam Hussein would roll on into their country, asked the United States for help.

No one had warned Saddam Hussein not to invade Kuwait. He miscalculated; the U.S. Government would not permit his invasion to stand. The United States had not sent troops when Turkey invaded Cyprus or China invaded Tibet or the Soviet Union invaded Afghanistan, but President George Bush was determined to upset the conquest of oil-rich Kuwait. And Prime Minister Margaret Thatcher of Great Britain supported his resolve. The U.S. Government convinced Saudi Arabia's cautious leaders to allow massive numbers of American troops into their country and persuaded the Soviet Union to stop sending arms to Iraq.

As soon as Iraq invaded Kuwait, the United Nations Security Council passed Resolution 660 demanding its immediate withdrawal. Four days later, UN Resolution 661 imposed economic sanctions on Iraq.

The United States rushed 50 warships, including two aircraft carriers, to enforce the UN embargo. Many European countries and Arab rulers were unenthusiastic about an American-led armed intervention; but on August 7, President Bush ordered 125,000 U.S. troops to the Persian Gulf.

The announced objectives were to protect Saudi Arabia and to pressure Iraq to get out of Kuwait. This policy sustained the U.S. desire to preserve the status quo in the oil-rich Persian Gulf area, but it reversed U.S. strategy, which had preferred to let others fight their own Middle East battles.

Seventeen nations formed a Multinational Interception Force (MIF) of 80 ships to intercept vessels carrying embargoed goods to or from Iraq. Marine special operations teams worked with the MIF; each team was made up of 10 Marines trained to board an uncooperative vessel from a helicopter.[2]

And the U.S. Joint Chiefs of Staff began Operation Desert Shield. At first, they worked with "a hopelessly outdated plan of battle" that the U.S. Central Command had organized on the now irrelevant assumption that the United States was going to fight the Soviet Union.[3] But over time they hammered out new plans.

Three Marine Expeditionary Brigades (MEBs)—the 7th in California, the 1st in Hawaii and the 4th on the East Coast—were alerted. The 7th and 1st prepared to fly out to the Persian Gulf and meet up with 30 days' worth of supply and combat equipment already stored and waiting under the Maritime Prepositioning Force program. The next day, August 8, four ships of Maritime Prepositioning Shipping Squadron 2 (MPS-2) sailed from Diego Garcia in the Indian Ocean, 2,500 miles away, and MPS-3 sailed from Guam. The Prepositioning Force program allowed a quick-reaction force to move in fast.

Responsible for any U.S. military action in the Middle East was Army Gen. H. Norman Schwarzkopf, the Commander in Chief, U.S. Central Command. On Friday, August 10, he ordered the airlift of the 1st and 7th MEBs and the sealift of the 4th MEB to the Persian Gulf area. The Army's 82d Airborne Division sent 2,300 paratroopers from its ready brigade; then came larger units from the Army's 101st Airborne Air Assault Division and the 24th Mechanized Infantry Division (with 216 M1A1 tanks). At first, their mission was to defend Saudi Arabia, not to free Kuwait.

General Schwarzkopf had been an Army operations advisor in the "problem-plagued" invasion of Grenada in 1983[4] and succeeded Marine Gen. George B. Crist at U.S. Central Command in November 1988. Although Schwarzkopf's chief of staff was Marine Maj. Gen. Robert B. Johnston, Schwarzkopf saw the Persian Gulf mobilization as an Army show. The Marine Corps had to fight steadily for what Gen. Alfred W. Gray, Jr., then Commandant of the Corps, called "the right size and balance of forces."[5]

On September 10, *Newsweek* reported, "Schwarzkopf has been forced to give them [the Marines] the primary role in a buildup he wanted to make a showcase for the Army. Taking command, he knows, means going with the folks who get the job done."[6] Two things—the prepositioning program and the 7th MEB's prompt response as a force-in-readiness—made the Marines literally the first ready to fight.

Commandant Gray said, "The Marine deployment was next

to perfect. They came with combined arms capability and they were able to sustain themselves."

In California on Tuesday, August 7, the 1st Battalion, 7th Marines canceled its 45-mile training graduation march and within seven hours was flown in Marine C-130s from the Marine Corps Mountain Warfare Training Center at Bridgeport to Twentynine Palms.

Five days later, 17,000 Marines of the 7th MEB and Marine Aircraft Group 70 moved out of Twentynine Palms. The 7th MEB had long trained in the California desert and was earmarked for possible use in the Middle East. Moving the brigade—four battalions and an LAV-mobile light armored battalion—by air required 259 trips by C-141s or their equivalent.

The brigade's first elements reached the Saudi port city of Al Jubayl, 110 miles south of Kuwait, on Tuesday, August 14; its commander, Maj. Gen. John I. Hopkins, arrived the next day. So did MPS-2 from Diego Garcia. The 1st Battalion began landing at Dhahran, Saudi Arabia, by commercial airline that evening.

The brigade was stitched together at Al Jubayl; despite the 120-degree heat, it was combat-ready in four days. On August 25, Maj. Gen. Hopkins told General Schwarzkopf that he was ready to defend the approaches to Al Jubayl. Hopkins set up a defensive position at the so-called "cement ridge," 40 miles north of Al Jubayl. He had 15,248 Marines with 123 tanks, 425 heavy weapons and 124 aircraft. But the Marines saw themselves as only a "speed bump" to slow down an Iraqi attack against Saudi Arabia.

Meanwhile, 8,000 Marines of the 4th MEB sailed from Morehead City, North Carolina, on August 17. On August 25, the 1st MEB started to arrive by air from Hawaii with two battalions of the 3rd Marines. The next day, MPS-3 arrived from Guam and started to equip the 1st MEB. If the Iraqis had attacked then, "it would have been one hell of a battle."[7]

Lt. Gen. Walter E. Boomer took control of all Marine Corps forces in the Central Command on September 2 as the commander of the I Marine Expeditionary Force (MEF). This would become the largest armor and mechanized expeditionary force in Marine Corps history. North Carolina–born Lt. Gen. Boomer, fifty-two, a graduate of Duke University, had been a Marine for 30 years; he had received two Silver Stars in Vietnam.

By the week's end, the 1st Marine Division from Camp Pendleton was in place with Brig. Gen. James M. Myatt in command. He assumed control of all ground combat units in I MEF and quickly received a second star. Maj. Gen. Royal N. Moore, Jr., commanded the 3rd Marine Aircraft Wing (3rd MAW); and Brig. Gen. James A. Brabham, Jr., commanded the 1st Force Service Support Group (FSSG).

The 4th MEB and the 13th Marine Expeditionary Unit, Special Operations Capable [13th MEU (SOC)] arrived during September. Both were commanded by Maj. Gen. Harry W. Jenkins, Jr., another Vietnam combat veteran, and were kept aboard ship in the Gulf of Oman just outside the Persian Gulf. The shipboard Marines began holding amphibious exercises; the first was Exercise Sea Soldier in which the 13th MEU (SOC) led the 4th MEB across the beaches of the Sultanate of Oman in a simulated night amphibious raid. The prime surface vehicle for the landing was the AAV7A1 assault amphibious vehicle; an improvement on the LVT, it is capable of carrying 25 Marines at a road speed of 45 mph.

I MEF was given operational control over the 14,000 soldiers of the British 7th Armoured Brigade, the "Desert Rats" who fought with the British Eighth Army in the North African desert in World War II. They brought with them British Challenger tanks to supplement the Marines' main battle tank, the 58-ton M60A1. Later, the Desert Rats, at London's demand that they be used in "the main attack," rejoined the British 1st Armoured Division and were replaced by 4,200 soldiers of the 1st Brigade, 2d U.S. Armored Division, the "Tiger Brigade," with 118 M1A1 Abrams tanks.

Recon Marines with Col. John E. Rhodes' 13th MEU (SOC) saw action on October 28, when the frigate *Reasoner* ordered the Iraqi oil tanker *Amuriyah*, sailing in the North Arabian Sea toward Iraq, to slow down. The Iraqi captain refused even when *Reasoner* and the Australian frigate *Darwin* fired warning shots across his bow. While one helicopter gunship hovered over *Amuriyah*, a second helicopter from *Ogden* set 24 Marines aboard the tanker by ropes. Despite a hostile 38-man Iraqi crew, the Marines secured the bridge and took control of the ship. A multinational boarding party joined them, found no contraband and permitted the tanker to go on. Before the war was over, the allies performed nearly 7,000 such interceptions and boarded nearly 1,000 vessels.

By the beginning of November, 42,000 Marines were on

hand. This was close to one-fourth of the Corps' active-duty strength and one-fifth of the total U.S. force present for Operation Desert Shield. Marine leaders took pride in the fact that this had been achieved without calling up the Marine Corps Reserve, except for a few specialists.

On October 30, President Bush approved a timetable for military action against Iraq: an air attack to begin in mid-January and a ground offensive, in February. On November 8, two days after the U.S. Congressional elections, he announced that he would send another 220,000 troops to the Persian Gulf.

On November 29, the United Nations Security Council passed Resolution 678 authorizing the use of force against Iraq if Saddam Hussein did not remove his troops from Kuwait by January 15. During the Cold War, U.S.-Soviet hostility would have made such a vote impossible.

Imminent Thunder, a large-scale international and multiservice amphibious exercise, was held on November 18 on the Saudi Arabian coast to sharpen the allies' amphibious assault operations. A Marine battalion afloat linked up with I MEF forces ashore in a helicopter assault starting from over the horizon. But the surface landing was canceled because of high winds and shallow water. The Marines said that if this had been an actual operation, the landing could have been made. The exercise seemed to notify the Iraqis of the amphibious threat that the Marines posed.

The Marines got a lift when President and Mrs. Bush had Thanksgiving dinner on November 22 with a gathering of Marines from many units at the 1st Division command post. Mrs. Bush ate her dinner seated on a pile of sandbags.

A thousand Marines a day (nearly 30,000 in all) from the II Marine Expeditionary Force were flown into the area. II MEF itself stayed in the States, but the 2d Marine Division and most of the Marines with the 2d Force Service Support Group from Camp Lejeune and the 2d Marine Aircraft Wing from Cherry Point, North Carolina, went to Saudi Arabia. The 2d Division, which had not been in combat since World War II, was commanded by Maj. Gen. William M. Keys, who has a Navy Cross and a Silver Star from Vietnam. The 2d MAW was absorbed into the 3rd MAW. The 3rd MAW grew to 16,000 Marines and 467 aircraft; it flew 18,000 sorties.

The 5th MEB sailed from San Diego on December 1, scheduled to train in the Philippines and reach the Gulf in mid-January.

Like the 4th MEB, the 5th would serve afloat in the Gulf. And the call-up of Marine Corps Reserve units began.

In Saudi Arabia, the Marines had several concerns. Most urgent was the need to defend themselves against nuclear, biological and chemical warfare; the Iraqis were known to have all these capabilities. The Marines built in the Saudi desert vast replicas of the barriers and minefields that the Iraqis had created in Kuwait, and trained against them. Another concern was the shortage of water for large numbers of troops and equipment in the desert; this problem was handled with huge reverse osmosis water purification units (ROWPUs).

The allies' buildup was awesome. The U.S. Army had two corps in the Saudi desert; the Marines had two divisions and an oversized air wing ashore, plus two MEBs and an MEU at sea. Thirty-nine nations mobilized some 900,000 troops and an air armada of 1,300 planes. Before it was over, 540,000 "American fighting men and women," all volunteers, would be in the theater. Britain, Saudi Arabia, France, Italy, Canada and the United Arab Emirates all had forces ready to participate in the air war against Iraq.

In nearby waters were 120 U.S. naval ships and 50 allied ships. The U.S. Navy had six carrier battle groups, two battleships and an amphibious task force. Its guided-missile frigates immediately began seizing Persian Gulf oil platforms from which the Iraqis launched missiles.

The buildup was in part the result of the concept of overpowering force: overwhelm the enemy; don't give him an opportunity to stand and fight. It was also the result of the usual interservice insistence on a share of the action. The Air Force believed it could win the war alone; when its Chief of Staff said that publicly, he was fired.

As Lt. Gen. Lewis W. Walt called Vietnam "the chevron war," some started calling the Gulf war "the stars war" or the generals' war. The Central Command staff accumulated 485 officers, including 83 Marines. The Marine Corps had 26 general officers in the field. One officer said, "Officers were stacked two and three deep in some jobs."[8] The Gulf war would feature logistics and planning even more than fighting.

Against the massive allied force, the Iraqis were estimated to have in Kuwait alone 300,000 soldiers, 2,272 tanks and 1,296 artillery pieces.

Although the United Nations Security Council had set January 15 as the deadline for Iraq to get out of Kuwait, Middle East politics did not often permit a nation to back down when presented with an ultimatum. Sanctions and the naval blockade had cut off 90 percent of Iraq's imports and exports, but Iraq was able to absorb a lot of punishment. And it was evident that Saddam Hussein was not under enough pressure to allow him to back down and still save face.

2
The Gulf War—Desert Storm

At 2:30 A.M. on Thursday, January 17, under a new moon, Operation Desert Shield exploded into Desert Storm. A one-sided air war began. Tomahawk cruise missiles and F-117A Stealth fighter-bombers blasted Iraqi targets. Marines flew in the first waves over Iraq and Kuwait, and Marine artillery exchanged fire with Iraqi gunners at Al Khafji on the Gulf coast.

The Iraqis replied with Soviet-made SS-1s, Scud missiles. The first evening, the first Scud missiles crashed into Tel Aviv. The 91 inaccurate but terrifying Scud missiles aimed at Saudi Arabia (48), Israel (40) and Bahrain (3) were a form of international terrorism. Patriot missiles intercepted some of them in midair, but one Scud hit a barracks at Dhahran, Saudi Arabia, and killed 28 U.S. Army soldiers.

The allies initially aimed at knocking out Iraq's command-and-control net and communications and transport systems. The pilots also hunted for nuclear and chemical war facilities and for Scud bases and launchers.

In the first 14 hours, the allies flew 1,000 sorties and dropped more than 2,200 tons of ordnance. The bulk of the bombing was done by B-52 bombers and F-16 fighter-bombers, cruise missiles and Tomahawks. Four aircraft were lost. Within two weeks, air superiority would become air supremacy. In all, the allies would fly more than 100,000 air sorties. Air Force generals controlled the entire air campaign.

The 3rd MAW had 467 planes, including one-fourth of the fixed-wing aircraft in the theater. Six Marine Harriers, two OV-10 Broncos and three helicopters were downed in the war. Two Marines from Marine Observation Squadron 2 were shot down by a ground missile over Kuwait on January 18 while on forward air control duty for Marine Attack Squadron 542 (VMA-542). Lt. Col. Clifford M. Acree, the pilot of a Bronco, and his aerial observer, Chief Warrant Officer Guy L. Hunter, Jr., were taken prisoner by Iraqis with AK-47s. They were among the captured airmen shown on television from Baghdad on January 21. They were held in dark solitary confinement for most of seven weeks, beaten and abused.

As time for the start of the ground campaign approached, air targeting shifted from the Republican Guard divisions in southern Iraq to the armored divisions already in Kuwait. And allied and Iraqi ground forces began probing each other. Much of the action took place at night. At 3:14 A.M. on January 21, 1st Marine Division artillery fired 155mm howitzers across the border into Kuwait.

Just before midnight the next night, 20 Marines of the 6th Platoon, 1st Force Reconnaissance Company, patrolling in the small, deserted Saudi town of Hamaltyat on the southwest border of Kuwait, were attacked by 115 soldiers of Iraq's 36th Division. The Marines, who were watching for activity across the high sand berm that marked the international boundary, returned fire. They killed five Iraqis and suffered one man slightly wounded.[9]

The 1st Force Reconnaissance Company experimented with dune buggies fitted with a .50 caliber machine gun and an M-60. These Light Strike Vehicles (LSVs) ran silent and fast for patrolling at night. Navy SEALs trained two teams of six Marines each for fighting the quiet, stealthy LSVs.

The Marines also experimented with Remotely Piloted Vehicles (RPVs). These pilotless single-propeller Pioneer planes carried a tiny video camera and sent back reconnaissance pictures and a target's exact location. The Israeli-developed aircraft were operated from mobile command centers as far as 100 miles from the target. The RPVs flew more than a thousand sorties. On February 25, one unit of Iraqi soldiers on the ground tried to surrender to a Marine RPV.

Elements of the 4th and 5th MEBs participated in Exercise Sea Soldier IV on the coast of Oman on January 24. This was called "the largest amphibious operation since Inchon."[10] The Marines had landed at Inchon, Korea, 40 years before, but, of course, against enemy opposition.

At midnight on Monday, January 28, two 2d Marine Division artillery batteries, six miles from the border, fired salvos of cluster bombs from 8-inch howitzers at Iraqi positions inside Kuwait. It was the 2d Division's first offensive action since World War II. The next night, Marine AV-8B Harriers shot up 24 Iraqi tanks. And on January 29, Marines in LAVs fired on an Iraqi mechanized battalion moving into Kuwait.

At noon on January 29, 50 Marines of C Company, 1st Battalion, 4th Marines from Colonel Rhodes' 13th MEU (SOC) landed on the Kuwaiti island of Umm al Maradim, a sand spit 12 miles off the coast. Led by Lt. Col. George W. Flinn, they flew from the amphibious assault ship *Okinawa* in four CH-46E helicopters of Marine Medium Helicopter Squadron 164 (HMM-164).

They found the island deserted and blew up antiaircraft weapons, artillery pieces and a cache of Iraqi ammunition. They sprayed "Free Kuwait" on the largest building and left a Kuwaiti flag flying.[11]

Late on that cold, moonlit night, three brigades of the Iraqi 5th Mechanized Infantry Division—3,000 infantrymen and 80 armored vehicles—advanced in three columns from Kuwait into Saudi Arabia. The most eastern column roared down the hard-surface coast road and seized the nearly deserted town of Al Khafji, eight miles into Saudi Arabia. They met resistance.

The Iraqis tripped the allied picket line, and this became the first sustained ground action of the war. The Marines' two Light Armored Infantry (LAI) Battalions turned back the two western probes. In the east, Saudi and Qatari ground forces, supported by 1st Marine Division artillery, Harriers, helicopters and armored vehicles, moved into the outskirts of Al Khafji. Iraqi tanks approached the Saudis with their turrets pointed to the rear, the signal that they wanted to surrender. But as they neared the Saudi positions, the Iraqis spun their guns around and began firing. The Saudis retreated rapidly. Marine artillery opened up; Saudi tanks moved forward; air strikes were unleashed.

Two 3rd Marines reconnaissance teams from the 1st Surveillance, Reconnaissance and Intelligence Group (SRIG) were in Al Khafji. On Monday night, the two six-man teams were on guard atop a building. Seeing the enemy advance in their armored personnel carriers, the Marines slipped over to a four-story building, barricaded themselves in the top floor and called in artillery fire and air support. They burned their codes and classified materials. They set Claymore mines on the stairwell leading up to their hideout and watched the Iraqis in the street below looting a grocery store.

Twice, Iraqi patrols searched their building and departed. Iraqi armor massed just north of them, and the Marines radioed for supporting fire. Cpl. Jeffrey Brown of Cincinnati was wounded by shrapnel from an artillery burst he had called in.

Two trucks from the Iraqis' 5th Mechanized Infantry Division drove into the fighting by mistake. One crashed into a wall. A motorized patrol, led by Maj. Craig S. Huddleston, executive officer of the 3rd Battalion, 3rd Marines, drove into Al Khafji with antitank missiles and machine guns and escorted by AH-1W Sea Cobra helicopter gunships. They arrived while Saudis and Iraqis were locked in combat. The Marines formed a perimeter around the crashed truck but found no soldiers. The Cobras covered their withdrawal.

The Marine reconnaissance teams sat tight for 36 hours until Saudi and Qatari forces, with Marines in support, counterattacked and retook the town. Then, one recon team dashed a half mile to meet a rescue unit from the 3rd Marines, and the second team drove out of Al Khafji in vehicles with punctured tires.

When the fighting was over, the allies had destroyed 22 tanks and taken 600 prisoners. And the Marines learned something; as Lt. Gen. Boomer put it, "We learned they couldn't shoot straight."[12]

That same night, 30 miles to the west, near the Al Wafrah oil field, Marines of the 1st LAI Battalion called in air strikes and artillery to repulse another Iraqi probe. In the intense, close-range night battle, two Marine Light Armored Vehicles (LAVs) were hit and 11 Marines were killed, the first Americans to die in ground action.[13] Four of them were killed when an American TOW antitank missile struck their LAV; an hour later, the other seven were killed when an Air Force A-10 mistakenly fired a Maverick missile at their LAV-25. A member of the 10th Marines was killed early on February 2 when his position was strafed by an American aircraft.[14]

Death by "friendly fire" became a public concern in this war. One quick attempt at a remedy was to paint an inverted V—Λ—on vehicles for identification. After the war, the military would seek more high-tech solutions.

The time for ground combat grew closer. By February 20, Brig. Gen. Charles C. Krulak, commanding general, Direct Support Command (DSC), set up a huge base in the middle of the desert in sight of the Iraq border. He named it Al Khanjar (the dagger). It included a command post, a C-130 landing strip, a helicopter landing strip called Lonesome Dove and a support base with ten days' worth of ammunition, fuel and water. The two Marine divisions sidled westward, leaving behind so-called Task Force Troy to deceive the enemy.

While bringing *Wisconsin* into position to fire on Iraqi shore positions on February 18, *Tripoli* (LPH-10) and *Princeton* (CG-59) struck enemy mines at the northern end of the Persian Gulf. The amphibious assault ship *Tripoli,* carrying 2,000 Marines, had a 20-foot hole blown in her bow but stayed on station. An hour later and 10 miles away, the Aegis-guided missile cruiser *Princeton* detonated a proximity mine, which damaged a propeller; the cruiser had to return to port.

Extensive minefields, which the Iraqis planted off Kuwait over five months and which repeatedly gave the allied navies trouble, clearly made a Marine amphibious landing dangerous. The mines played a significant part in the final decision to limit the Marine Corps' amphibious force in the Gulf to a deterrent role when the ground war began.

In the end, General Schwarzkopf actually ordered two decoys: the Army's First Cavalry Division to advance up the Wadi al-Batin corridor along the western border of Kuwait, the obvious invasion route; and the Marines' 4th MEB at sea to stage a fake amphibious invasion. Marine Lt. Gen. Boomer protested to Schwarzkopf about the Marines' non-combat assignment, and Commandant Gray objected to Gen. Colin L. Powell, Chairman of the Joint Chiefs of Staff. The Marines were turned down. The final decision was that an assault through mined waters against enemy-held beaches backed by difficult marshes would result in unnecessarily heavy losses. And the shortage of engineering equipment also argued against an amphibious assault. The Marines would have to wait for another war to show their amphibious capability.[15]

Before G-Day (for Ground action), Marine units in front of both Marine divisions penetrated deep into enemy territory. Among them were elements of Lt. Col. Timothy J. Hannigan's 3rd Battalion, 7th Marines, and three platoons of C Company, 2d Light Armored Infantry Battalion. An infiltration force from the 3rd Marines crossed the border into Kuwait on foot during the night of February 22 and took blocking positions on the 1st Marine Division's right flank. They remained hidden during the daylight hours and the following night crawled on hands and knees through the first obstacle belt and cleared three vehicle lanes for the main assault. Similarly, elements of the 4th Marines infiltrated into Kuwait on foot on the 1st Division's left flank.

At 10:35 on Thursday morning, February 21, 65 hours before H-Hour, 144 Marines from C Company of the 2d LAI Battalion crashed through the barriers on the Saudi Arabian border and began a probe into Kuwait. Their job, and the job of other similar units inside Kuwait, was to uncover gaps in the barriers, draw enemy fire and deceive the Iraqi army about the location of the main coalition attack.

In LAVs, which at 50 mph could outrun a tank on hard-packed sand, the C Company Marines headed for a ridgeline more than a mile into Kuwait; there, the Iraqis had observers to spot their artillery and tank fire. As the Marines neared the ridge, they attracted artillery and rocket fire. Although they moved every five or six minutes, the fire grew heavier. Capt. Kenneth W. Amidon, C Company's commander, led his LAVs back across the border to coordinate air and artillery support, and in two hours they were back inside Kuwait.

The Marines called in artillery fire from the 5th Battalion, 10th Marines to destroy Iraqi T-62 tanks dug into the desert south of Kuwait City. They flanked the ridge and on it rounded up 73 Iraqi observers. And they explored a large but well-marked minefield.

A mortar round made a direct hit on the Jeep-like "Hummer" (HMMWV) vehicle carrying the unit's Stinger surface-to-air missile team. The men miraculously were able to walk away. When darkness closed in, the 1st Platoon's 25mm Bushmaster guns blew up two trucks loaded with ammunition and fuel. The trucks exploded in huge fireballs. LAV "Fat Chick" of 2d Platoon destroyed another ammunition truck.

Iraqi tanks counterattacked, and Captain Amidon called in air support. Planes bombed within 200 yards of the 2d Platoon. The LAVs kept maneuvering to avoid enemy fire; but shortly after 3 A.M., two missiles hit LAV "Banger" and the 3rd Platoon.

After dawn on Friday, T-62s spotted them, and the LAVs crisscrossed the flat desert to avoid the enemy tanks' fire. The Marines' 25mm guns could not penetrate the heavy tanks, but TOW missiles were effective. Master Sgt. Richard Harrison's LAV

"Croaker" kept one tank buttoned up, and a TOW ripped it apart. Maneuvering to outflank the tanks, the 1st Platoon destroyed four. Harriers dropped napalm, engulfed the ridge in fire and destroyed three more tanks.

Before this mission and the main ground attack were over, Lance Cpl. Frank Steiner IV, a twenty-year-old TOW gunner from Ontonagon, Michigan, destroyed four tanks, three trucks and a bunker complex. On Friday, he quickly knocked out two tanks and two trucks while under artillery fire. Saturday, he destroyed a bunker complex and a tank behind it, and Monday night, advancing through huge orange jets of flame and the black smoke of tremendous oil field fires, he got his fourth tank.[16]

Early on Friday, A Company, 2d LAI Battalion approached the distant end of the ridge to seize an Iraqi police outpost. The Iraqis blasted both companies with mortar, antitank fire and 122mm rockets. Cpl. Stephen Scott, gunner on LAV "Known Distance," was hit by shrapnel from an air burst and medevaced. Two more missiles hit the 3rd Platoon, but no one was wounded.

All through the second night, the C Company Marines targeted enemy tanks, artillery and soldiers; called in artillery fire from the 10th and 12th Marines; and destroyed the Iraqis. At night, the Marines had the advantage. The enemy had trouble finding them, while the Marines' thermal night scopes located the heat of enemy tanks and guns miles away.

C Company made enough disruption to convince the enemy that the ground war had started at that spot. Intelligence picked up Iraqi commanders calling for reinforcements. The Marines advanced to another ridge and ran into an Iraqi brigade with tanks. C Company attacked formations of Iraqi troops with Bushmasters, automatic weapons and M-16A2 rifles. Supporting air and artillery crippled nearly a dozen enemy tanks and bunkers.

"Tanks, armored personnel carriers, trucks, everything, was being blasted all around. It was like being in hell," said Captain Amidon. "They must have hit a couple of ammo or fuel dumps two kilometers north of us because huge mushroom clouds shot up out of the desert—it was unreal!"

The Marines kept moving forward. At 2 P.M. on Saturday, 20 Iraqi tanks closed on them from the north. Despite heavy anti-aircraft fire, Marine Cobras came in low and destroyed the tanks. At 4:17 P.M., C Company pulled back from the ridge, its job well done.

An artillery unit of Tiger Brigade, the 1st Brigade of the Army's 2d Armored Division, radioed to ask if it could help, and at 7 P.M. fired massive barrages that silenced the Iraqi infantry and armor. Into the night, the Tiger Brigade fired in support of the Marines. Baghdad Radio announced that the ground war had started.

C Company's Marines were called back at midnight to join the 6th Marines for the official start of the ground war. They had already had two days of combat.[17]

Three days before G-Day, the Soviet Union announced that it had finally persuaded Saddam Hussein to leave Kuwait within three weeks. Col. Carlton W. Fulford, Jr., commander of the 7th Marines, was asked whether the Russians could upset the battle plans. He replied, "It's too late. The toilet's already been flushed."[18]

On Friday, President Bush, eager and ready to fight, demanded that the Iraqis withdraw by Saturday. When they did not move, the allies did.

3
The Gulf War—G-Day

Desert Storm's G-Day—the start of the ground war—finally came on Sunday morning, February 24. The allies had more than five months to mobilize overwhelming force and hammer out tactical plans. Now they selected the time to attack. Their incessant bombing had battered the Iraqi army; it was time to see how well they had done the job. Whether the enemy would fight effectively and whether he would react with chemical, or even biological or nuclear, weapons were unknowns.

On G-Day, General Schwarzkopf commanded a front 300 miles wide with combat troops from four European and 14 Islamic nations, plus 537,000 American troops and 3,500 tanks. The assembled Marine Corps power included 24 infantry battalions, 19 fixed-wing squadrons and 21 helicopter squadrons, all organized in an MEF ashore, plus two MEBs and one MEU afloat. The I MEF had 66,000 Marines (including 2,276 women Marines) and 357 tanks (181 M60A1s and 176 M1A1s, most of the latter belonging to the attached Army Tiger Brigade).

The Marine Force Afloat totaled another 17,800 Marines— the 4th MEB had 8,000; the 5th MEB, 7,500; and the 13th MEU, 2,300. When together, these shipboard forces made up the largest amphibious force since World War II. As it turned out, the Marine amphibious forces would not land in this war but held in place an estimated three Iraqi divisions facing the Gulf[19] and served as the allies' strategic reserve.

Plans for the ground war and for using the Marines evolved over the months of Desert Shield. At first, the generals wanted to bull straight across into Kuwait and overwhelm the enemy. But as concern about casualties grew and after the air war had "blinded" the Iraqis, General Schwarzkopf shifted a major part of his force

786

to the west. The allied nations participating in the ground war would now combine a direct assault into Kuwait with a huge, risky "Hail Mary" end sweep to the west that would envelop and cut off the best of the Iraqi army.

The American commanders found putting together the efforts and the egos of all the coalition generals "an absolute nightmare," as one senior American general put it.

In mid-December, the commanders adopted a plan called Southern Option (Mod). The Marines remained in front of Kuwait, where Saddam Hussein expected to be attacked.[20] They would drive into Kuwait between the Persian Gulf coast and the Al Wafrah oil field. They would move north, seize the Al Jaber Airfield and link up near Ash Shuaybah on the Kuwaiti coast with amphibious forces landing from the Gulf. The 1st Marine Division would go in first, followed by the 2d.

The Marines' job was to destroy the Iraqi forces in front of them, prevent them from reinforcing their divisions to the west and block the survivors' retreat from Kuwait. The U.S. Army would cross into Iraq west of Kuwait and encircle the enemy.

The Marines faced a 15-foot-high sand berm that the Saudis had built on the border and Iraqi-constructed obstacle belts of trenches, minefields, bunkers and concertina wire. To conquer them, the Marines modified 26 bulldozers with armor and 15 M-60 tanks with mine rollers and mine plows. They provided shipping for the Army's Armored Combat Excavators (ACEs) and kept 30 for themselves. They hurriedly sent an officer to Israel and obtained 12 "towed assault bridges" and mine plows.

With ingenuity, the Marines fitted 30 assault amphibious vehicles (AAVs) with inverted A-frames to carry bundles of plastic pipe up to the Iraqi antitank ditches and release them with explosive charges. Tanks with blades would push the pipe into the ditches to allow tanks to cross.

The arrival of the badly needed breaching equipment made it possible to modify plans again on February 14, just 10 days before G-Day. In the second week of February, Secretary of Defense Richard B. Cheney and General Powell visited General Schwarzkopf and discussed offensive plans. Maj. Gen. William M. Keys suggested that his 2d Marine Division also was capable of breaching the Iraqi defenses. It was decided that the 1st Division would shift westward, screened by the 1st LAI Battalion out front. The 2d Division would sidle another 80 miles to the northwest. With this sixth change of plans, the two Marine divisions could assault the border barriers simultaneously; the 2d Division would attack alongside and on the left of the 1st.

Lt. Gen. Boomer preferred the "dual breach" because it widened the front and enabled the Marines to move faster. But this change delayed the G-Day attack from February 21 to 24 and started the ground war during four days of terrible weather.

Marine units aboard ship in the Gulf would simultaneously stage well-publicized amphibious rehearsals. Many Marines hoped to stage a classic amphibious assault on the beaches of Kuwait. But the idea was rejected because of a concern over casualties, because such an assault would destroy much of Kuwait City where the best beaches were located and because mine clearance would then control the timetable and slow down the entire campaign.

General Schwarzkopf asked Lt. Gen. Boomer if he could accomplish his objectives without an amphibious assault. Boomer thought for 30 seconds and told Schwarzkopf that he could if amphibious deceptions were used to tie down the three enemy divisions on the coast so that they would not turn on the Marines attacking overland.

On the right of the two Marine divisions, between the main road going north and the Gulf, stood Joint Forces Command East, comprising five Saudi, Kuwaiti, Omani and United Arab Emirate mechanized brigades. On the Marines' left was a pan-Arab force, Joint Forces Command North.

Farther west was the heavily armored U.S. VII Corps, which had arrived from Germany in November. Finally, still farther west stood the U.S. XVIII Corps, with the French 6th Light Armored Division, including French Foreign Legion units, up front screening its exposed far-left flank. They had moved across some 250 miles of desert over the so-called Tapline Road in 10 days without the Iraqis discovering them in time to react.

Toward dusk on Saturday, February 23, small elements of the 3rd and 4th Marines began to cross the border and pierce the sand berm. They crawled and walked into Kuwait before the main assault, cutting through barbed wire and passing thousands of mines just lying in the sand. They met no defenders.

The 3rd Tank Battalion, supported by A Company, 1st Battalion, 7th Marines, rolled into Kuwait just after midnight and took positions south of the first obstacle belt. They were followed by the 1st Battalion, 5th Marines and the rest of the 1st Battalion, 7th Marines.

At 1 A.M., the 16-inch guns of the battleships *Wisconsin* and *Missouri*, far offshore in the Gulf, started hurling shells at the Kuwaiti coast. Three hours later, the ground offensive began officially. With two giant arms, 120 miles apart, the allies advanced to embrace the enemy.

The Marines attacked into the enemy's strength, precisely where Saddam Hussein had concentrated his forces. They moved forward easily. At Quantico, the Corps had been analyzing responses to the Iraqi defenses and minefields since August; the Marines were ready.

At 4 A.M. in the darkness of that cold, wet Sunday, Maj. Gen. James "Mike" Myatt's 1st Marine Division ground into Kuwait. The men advanced under a half-moon through rain squalls and a biting wind. The fog was so thick that they could not see 100 yards, and it threatened to eliminate their close air support. But the wind shifted; now coming out of the southeast, it blew the smoke from the burning oil fields at the enemy.

The 1st Division attacked between the Al Wafrah and Umm Gudair oil fields, aiming to take Al Jaber Airfield. Then, the division would go on to capture Kuwait International Airport and to isolate Kuwait City. The 2d Division was pointed at Al Jahra and Mutla Ridge to block the Iraqis from fleeing west or north.

The 1st Division was organized in five task forces: Ripper (Col. Carlton W. Fulford, Jr.), based on the 7th Marines; Papa Bear (Commandant Gray's code name) (Col. Richard W. Hodory), built on the 1st Marines; Grizzly (Col. James A. Fulks), built on the 4th Marines; Taro (Col. John H. Admire), built on the 3rd Marines from Hawaii; and Shepherd (Lt. Col. Clifford Myers), built on the 1st and 3rd LAI Battalions. Plus the artillery of the 11th Marines.

The first four task forces each contained two infantry battalions. Ripper and Papa Bear led the attack because they were totally mechanized and had an assault amphibious company attached to each battalion. Moving more slowly, Colonel Admire's Task Force Taro secured the division's right flank, and Colonel Fulks' Task Force Grizzly guarded the left. Then they would drop behind the mechanized charge.

Task Force Ripper, seven miles southwest of the heel of the

Kuwait border, led the way into two obstacle belts of field fortifications, sand berms, barbed wire and minefields. The barriers appeared formidable, and the Marines, dressed in their heavy chemical-warfare suits and boots and stuffed into thin-skinned amtracs, expected the worst—at least heavily armed defenders protecting wickedly intricate minefields.

The Marines hit the first obstacle belt at 6:15 A.M. Tanks and bulldozers punched through the berms and opened the way for other tanks. Engineers shot live charges across minefields and exploded them. Amtracs sought to drop their ingenious fascines of plastic pipe, but there proved to be no antitank trenches in this area. Every seven minutes, 3rd MAW planes roared over in support. Amtracs loaded with Marines stormed through the cleared lanes.

The first line of Iraqi defenders fled. The Marines met dummy tanks and abandoned bunkers. Oil fires enveloped them in thick, black smoke and the stench of burning oil, but the Marines moved steadily onward, with no one to fight.

Miles inside Kuwait, they found the enemy. At a second obstacle belt some seven miles north of the first, the Iraqis resisted both Marine divisions. This was as the Marine commanders had anticipated. By 11:25 A.M., Lt. Col. A. B. "Buster" Diggs, Jr., and his 3rd Tank Battalion penetrated the second obstacle belt and met Iraqi tanks dug in behind it. When TOWs and tanks fired, Iraqis began popping up out of the desert floor, arms raised in surrender.

Two young Marines, Cpl. Michael S. Kilpatrick and Cpl. Bryan K. Zickefoose, were fighting the Badger recon vehicle of the 3rd Battalion, 9th Marines with Task Force Papa Bear. Corporal Kilpatrick was the driver, and Corporal Zickefoose, a sniper. Out in front of their unit seeking enemy positions, they came under intense mortar and artillery fire. Shrapnel peppered their vehicle. Kilpatrick maneuvered the Badger through exploding rounds; Zickefoose remained exposed on top directing air attacks against the enemy. Air strikes destroyed the enemy position. The next morning, when Task Force Papa Bear's command post was attacked by enemy tanks and infantry, the two corporals moved forward into the thick fog and destroyed an enemy tank with a perfectly aimed AT-4 shot.

Task Forces Papa Bear and Shepherd drove up the right flank, and Task Force Ripper isolated Al Jaber Airfield by Sunday at 5 P.M. Hordes of Iraqis came to them and surrendered. The 1st Marine Division destroyed 21 enemy tanks and took 4,000 prisoners at the cost of one Marine killed in action and nine wounded.

Meanwhile, at 5:30 A.M. Sunday, the 2d Division attacked west of the 1st between the Umm Gudair and Al Manaqish oil fields and moved ahead just as easily. The division had 20,500 Marines with 257 tanks. Before the assault began, 2d Combat Engineer Battalion bulldozers cut through the sand berm along the border. The engineers exploded narrow lanes through the minefields and marked the paths with red, blue and green trash cans. The 6th Marines went first, followed by the Tiger Brigade and the 8th Marines.

Lance Cpl. James D. Burrell, a nineteen-year-old Reservist from La Follette, Tennessee, rode into Kuwait in a tank as a member of a mine-clearing team. At 10 A.M. in his second minefield, a charge failed to detonate, and Burrell went forward and exploded it manually with a C-4 charge. Then he detonated a second mine lodged in his tank's plow blade.[21]

The 2d Division's 6th Marines and 2d LAI Battalion advanced rapidly through the two obstacle belts that here were relatively close together. The LAI battalion was screening the division flanks. The 6th Marines leading the way through the minefields came under machine-gun and mortar fire and some 300 rounds of indirect fire from enemy artillery.

On the division's right flank, 1st Battalion, 8th Marines, commanded by Lt. Col. Bruce A. Gombar, ran into well-placed non-metallic Italian mines that were hard to detect. As a result, the division took longer than it expected to move through the obstacle belts and create a breach head.

Five battalions of the 10th Marines supplied artillery support; and, in six hours, six narrow lanes were cleared through the minefields. The Marines advanced through two minefields and Iraqi artillery fire before engaging the first major enemy positions.

Repeatedly, a Marine-loaded amtrac hit a mine and its radio crackled "Gas! Gas! Gas!" The hatch slammed shut, and the men quickly put on their gas masks. Every time, the alarm was false.

By Sunday afternoon, the U.S. Army's Tiger Brigade, commanded by Col. John B. Sylvester, USA, was with the 2d Division. Moving north through the minefields, the brigade came under artillery and mortar fire. The brigade had been part of George Patton's Second Armored Division in World War II and was now an M1A1 tank unit. Its heavy tanks destroyed dug-in T-55 tanks from two miles away.

At the end of that first day, the 2d Marine Division consolidated north of the Umm Gudair oil field in central Kuwait. The 6th Marines, the Tiger Brigade and four battalions of artillery had moved through the breach. They had taken 5,000 Iraqi prisoners.

The Iraqis, as they had threatened, torched more than 700 Kuwaiti oil wells. The sky filled with roaring yellow flames and huge plumes of black smoke. To some it looked like Hell.

In the first 24 hours of the ground war, the 18 squadrons of the enlarged 3rd MAW, the largest Marine air command and control system in Marine Corps history, flew 671 sorties in support of the I MEF. The 3rd MAW's mission was to provide the Marines with close air support and to destroy Iraqi tanks and strategic reserves. For the first time, fixed-wing aircraft flew close support from an LHA assault ship when AV-8Bs flew off *Nassau*. On G-Day, the Wing destroyed 97 tanks and 57 armored personnel carriers. During the war, Marine air dropped more than 29 million tons of ordnance.

Conflicts arose over tactical air control, as they have repeatedly in the Corps' history. The Marines complained that they were outranked and overruled in the Joint Forces Air Component Command (JFACC), the single authority that managed all tactical air. Lt. Gen. Boomer later said, "With a more formidable enemy than the Iraqi turned out to be, the lack of battlefield preparation by JFACC could have had disastrous consequences."[22]

Near the coast, two Saudi task forces penetrated the Iraqi defenses. The Iraqis' Third Corps counterattacked and was driven back. The Saudis met little opposition but moved up the coastal road slowly, delaying the retaking of Kuwait City.[23]

Offshore on Sunday, 18,000 Marines of the 4th MEB tied down the Iraqi divisions defending the coast. The 13th MEU (SOC) performed early-morning deceptions, and in the afternoon, the 5th MEB began to be helicoptered ashore to serve as the I MEF reserve. Lt. Gen. Boomer had to bring them ashore because, with both his divisions committed, he had no other reserve.

Far to the west, the U.S. Army's XVIII and VII Corps, more than 200,000 troops and thousands of tanks, advanced to cut off the enemy. British armored troops accompanied VII Corps, and French troops went in with XVIII Airborne Corps.

The giant and daring envelopment had begun before H-Hour. The U.S. Army's 101st Airborne Air Assault Division quickly advanced 60 miles into Iraq and established a forward fuel-and-ammunition base with huge bladders of fuel far ahead of the advancing allied troops. The roads leading to Kuwait were cut. Then the 101st and the 24th Mechanized Infantry Division, Schwarzkopf's old command, moved into the ancient valley of the Tigris and Euphrates rivers. The French 6th Light Armored Division and a U.S. 82d Airborne Division brigade took the western airfield at Al-Salman.

Twenty-one Iraqi divisions were destroyed or cut off, and hundreds of Iraqi tanks were destroyed from the rear. The Army and Marines moved so rapidly that General Schwarzkopf moved up his timetable by hours and canceled an 82d Airborne Division airdrop.

At 4 A.M. on Monday, the 4th MEB demonstrated off the Kuwaiti coast in the vicinity of Ash Shuaybah, supported by gunfire from *Missouri*. The MEB's job was to hold in place Iraqi divisions along the Gulf coast.

The Marines fought their largest battle of the war on Monday. At 4:30 A.M., a mechanized column from the Iraqis' 83rd Brigade swept down along the power line on the left side of the 1st Division's front in Task Force Ripper's sector. The 1st LAI Battalion and Lt. Col. Diggs' 3rd Tank Battalion stopped them.

Then, at 8:05 A.M., on the right side of the division's front, tanks and armored personnel carriers of the Iraqis' 22d Brigade, 5th Mechanized Infantry Division and 501st Brigade, 8th Infantry Division rolled out of the heavy fog and smoke of the vast, burning Al Burgan oil field. An Iraqi regimental commander of the 22d Brigade in the lead T-55 tank surrendered near Task Force Papa Bear's command post. But a massive tank force still hidden in the fog behind him fired on the command post and Lt. Col. Michael M. Kephart's 1st Tank Battalion.

The jumbled, close-quarters armored battles continued through the morning, the confusion heightened by the fog and smoke from the burning oil wells. The main guns of the 1st Tank Battalion; antitank weapons of I Company, 9th Marines; Task Force headquarters personnel; and the artillery of the 11th Marines all went into action. Lt. Col. John B. Sollis, commanding officer of the 1st Battalion, 11th Marines, directed Cobras with TOWs and Hellfire missiles to destroy enemy multiple rocket launchers preparing to fire. The combined effort beat off the Iraqi attack.

Toward 11 A.M., the 501st Brigade made still another stab at the Task Force Papa Bear command post. The 1st Tank Battalion's TOWs and Cobra gunships routed the brigade's last-gasp attack. About 50 tanks and 25 armored personnel carriers were destroyed; the Marines suffered no casualties in the fight.

Meanwhile, at 7:30 A.M., the 1st Battalion, 1st Marines, commanded by Lt. Col. Michael Fallon, advanced into the huge oil field. An hour later, these Marines hit the southern side of the Iraqis' 15th Brigade, 3rd Armored Division, which was moving from east to west across the division front.

The northern flank of this enemy force wheeled, thundered directly south and moved to a fight. At 9:30 A.M., the Iraqis struck hard at the 1st Division's forward command post, located near a wooded area known as The Emir's Farm. A confused, smoke-shrouded fire fight began.

C Company, 1st Marines; B Company, 1st LAI Battalion; and division headquarters personnel fought through the fog and dense black smoke rising from the hundreds of oil well fires and threw back the counterattack. Cobra gunships destroyed several tanks. Battery H, 14th Marines, a Reserve unit from Richmond, Virginia, knocked out an Iraqi multiple rocket launcher. And Task Force Taro executed the war's only helicopter-borne assault near the flaming oil fields to screen the division's right flank. The Iraqis fought for an hour before being driven off.

After another 15 minutes, the Marines took fire from a second Iraqi force coming toward the division command post. The Marines pushed it back. The Iraqis attacked a final time at 11 A.M. and then, clobbered by artillery and air, surrendered. Although Iraqis were flushed from strong points and hidden bunkers for hours, the battle was over.[24]

In the 2d Division sector on the left, the 6th Marines and the Tiger Brigade began Monday south of Al Abdaliyah. The 8th Marines moved through the breach. At 3:30 A.M., enemy tanks and mortars fired on the 6th Marines. And at 6:55, the so-called "reveille counterattack" hit the 1st Battalion, 8th Marines on the division's right flank. A battalion-size column of armor and mechanized infantry came down a hard-surface road. Marine tanks and air support repulsed the Iraqis and destroyed 39 tanks and armored personnel carriers.

Tiger Brigade advanced on the division's left. Its big guns covered the Marines' flank, beyond which were the Arab units. Tiger Brigade's gunners destroyed 50 tanks in the first two hours of Monday.

In the division's center, the 6th Marines, commanded by Col. Lawrence H. Livingston, pushed forward into a built-up area called the "ice tray." The 8th Marines, led by Col. Larry S. Schmidt, took the smaller "ice cube." These landmarks were squared-off inhabited areas built by the Kuwaiti government.

AV-8B Harrier jets from VMA-542 flew support for the 2d Marine Division and attacked Iraqi tanks advancing in a column through clouds and black smoke. Capt. John S. Walsh's Harrier was hit by a shoulder-fired Iraqi SAM missile. He tried to land at Al Jaber Airfield, which he thought the Marines had just captured, but the Iraqis still controlled the field. Aflame and flying upside down at 900 feet, he ejected over friendly lines, landed in sand and was rescued by a patrol from Task Force Shepherd. Two nights before, Capt. Trey Wilbourn of Huntsville, Alabama, had crashed and was killed while leading a VMA-542 night mission, his thirty-eighth flight over Kuwait.[25]

On Tuesday the 26th, the 1st Marine Division raced ahead, led by the 7th Marines and the 1st LAI Battalion. As Task Force Ripper approached its objective—the Kuwait International Airport, south of Kuwait City—T-72 tanks of the Iraqi 3rd Armored Division counterattacked. Visibility was terrible; Colonel Fulford read his maps with a flashlight at noon.

Reacting with air, artillery and armor, the division began its final attack on the airport at 4 P.M., led by Task Forces Shepherd and Taro, and destroyed more than 300 tanks in the assault. Heavy black smoke filled the sky as the division pushed forward, collecting prisoners. By nightfall, Task Force Ripper held a blocking position west of the airport.

In the darkness at 2:30 Tuesday morning, a two-pronged Iraqi assault of armored personnel carriers and dismounted infantry came at the 2d Division from the northeast and northwest. The Iraqis attacked a road intersection held by B Company, 8th Marines and the 4th Tank Battalion. During the hour-and-a-half fight, the enemy reached within 100 yards of the Marines. The Iraqis were finally beaten back with the help of the 10th Marines' artillery. Two hours later, the 10th Marines opened fire again on the retreating Iraqis attempting to regroup.

Early that morning, planes from MAG-11 and MAG-33 found more than a thousand Iraqi vehicles jamming the six-lane expressway leading north from Al Jahra. They attacked for six hours and destroyed everything they could see. Lt. Gen. Boomer called it "absolute carnage." Young Marine fighter pilots shot up the highway, returned for fuel and ammunition and went back to the shoot on what became known as "Death Valley" and the "Highway to Hell."

The 2d Division, urged on by Lt. Gen. Boomer, who was at its forward command post, moved to cut off the Iraqis' escape. Tiger Brigade advanced northward along the top of Mutla Ridge, passed the Ali Al Salem Airfield on its left and reached the intersection with the highway coming out of Kuwait City.

That afternoon, Tiger Brigade seized the city of Al Jahra and to the northeast secured the high ground of Mutla Ridge. It found an enormous traffic jam of tanks, trucks and cars pouring out of Kuwait City into the area shot up by the Marine pilots in the morning. The Brigade swung east; its guns destroyed 166 tanks, cut the highways leading north and west from Kuwait City and blocked the Iraqis' escape toward Basra. The 6th and 8th Marines joined in the destruction of the vehicular column trying to flee north on the jammed-up highway.

Afloat, the 4th MEB conducted predawn helicopter demonstrations at Bubiyan and Faylaka islands, which dominate the seaward approaches north of Kuwait City. Marines of the 5th MEB, now ashore, helped control the unexpected mass of prisoners.

On Tuesday evening, 10 miles to the north, 12 Marines from the 1st Platoon, 2d Force Reconnaissance Company, 2d Surveillance, Reconnaissance and Intelligence Group, followed by Army Special Forces soldiers, entered the compound of the U.S. Embassy in Kuwait City.

The recon Marines had been in the field for more than three weeks; they were dirty and unshaven, hardly prepared for embassy duty. They left their base near the Saudi-Kuwait border at 4 P.M. in three "Hummer" vehicles and five hours later were guided to the embassy by three carloads of Kuwaiti resistance fighters wearing red armbands on their left sleeves.

In the darkness, the Marines found Kuwait City gutted, the buildings without electricity and water. The embassy gates were locked, and the Marines were surprised that everything appeared untouched since the American ambassador had left on December

13. The embassy vehicles still had full fuel tanks. The embassy's flag was still flying.

The Kuwaitis set up a perimeter. Forty-one Iraqi soldiers, walking by and headed north, surrendered. The next day, the Americans raised on a 40-foot fireman's ladder a flag that had flown in Vietnam.

Early on Wednesday, February 27, the 1st LAI Battalion attacked Kuwait International Airport and secured it at 9 A.M. By noon, Task Force Ripper had finished its job. Now the 1st Division stepped aside and let the Arab Joint Forces Command have the honor of being the first unit to enter Kuwait City officially. The 2d Division stayed near Al Jahra, and the Tiger Brigade blocked off retreating Iraqi forces while the Arab units crossed its front on the way to the celebrations in Kuwait City.

During the ground war, the 2d Division captured 16,376 prisoners, almost one per Marine. The Tiger Brigade alone destroyed 172 tanks and 126 armored personnel carriers since G-Day.

By now, the Army's 24th Mechanized Infantry Division stood on the Euphrates River, trapping Iraq's armor. B-52s were bombing Iraqis trying to flee. Republican Guard divisions were being attacked, although they were never destroyed. The allies began calling off the flow of reinforcements and resupply. By afternoon, the 3rd MAW reported it was hard to find targets between Kuwait City and Basra. Iraqis everywhere were waving white cloths. The enemy disintegrated.

The entire Iraqi army of 300,000 men in Kuwait was encircled; an estimated 4,000 tanks were destroyed, 42 divisions were rendered ineffective, and the allies held 50,000 prisoners of war. The Marines alone captured 22,000 prisoners. General Schwarzkopf said, "If we thought it would have been such an easy fight, we definitely would not have stocked 60 days worth of supplies. . . . We certainly did not expect it to go this way."[26]

Lt. Gen. Boomer and 34 Marines of his I MEF command group drove in a 10-vehicle convoy through the streets of Kuwait City under an oil-fire blackened sky at midafternoon Wednesday to observe the devastation the Iraqis had left behind. They were greeted by thousands of cheering, flag-waving Kuwaitis.

Early on Thursday, February 28, President Bush called off the mayhem and declared a ceasefire. The ground offensive stopped officially at 8 A.M., precisely 100 hours after the start of this orchestrated ground war. There was not much left to destroy—except maybe Saddam Hussein himself. The allied coalition had suffered 88 Americans; 41 Egyptians, Saudis and Kuwaitis; 16 British; and 2 French killed in action. Since H-Hour, Marine losses were eight killed in action and 48 wounded. In all, the Marines had 24 killed in action (14 of them from friendly fire) and 92 wounded in action. Iraqi losses, military and civilian, were estimated conservatively at 100,000.

On February 27 in Riyadh, Saudi Arabia, General Schwarzkopf held a press briefing and spoke about the Marines:

> I can't say enough about the two Marine divisions. If I use words like "brilliant," it would be an under-description of the absolute superb job that they did in breaching the so-called impenetrable barrier. It was a classic, absolutely classic military breaching of a very, very tough minefield, barbed wire, fire trenches–type barrier. They went through the first barrier like it was water. They went across into the second barrier line, even though they were under artillery fire at the same time. They continued to open up the breach. And then they brought both divisions steaming through that breach. Absolutely superb operation, a textbook, and I think it'll be studied for many, many years to come as the way to do it.[27]

Back at Camp Pendleton on April 24, a huge ceremony welcomed home the Marines from Desert Storm. The colors of all the units that had served with I MEF were paraded: 1st Marine Division; 2d Marine Division; 4th Marine Division; 2d MAW; 1st FSSG; 2d FSSG; 1st SRIG; Tiger Brigade of the Army's 2d Armored Division; 3rd Naval Construction Regiment; and the King's Own Scottish Borderers of the 1st United Kingdom Armored Division.

Lt. Gen. Boomer awarded the Silver Star to the first five Persian Gulf Marines to be so honored:

Staff Sgt. Daniel A. Kur of Michigan on Sunday night led his team of the 1st Platoon, B Company, 8th Engineer Support Battalion to remove enemy mines. While under mortar fire, he dug out mines by hand and carried them out of the minefield. He guided through the minefield an armored bulldozer; antitank fire hit and disabled the dozer and knocked Staff Sgt. Kur to the ground. He brushed himself off and continued clearing mines.

Sgt. Gordon T. Gregory of Ohio was a reconnaissance platoon

sergeant in Task Force Grizzly. On the first day of the ground fighting, while his platoon searched for a breaching point, he led the men through a minefield under intense enemy fire. He halted friendly fire on his unit and rescued two Marines from the minefield.

Cpl. Bryan K. Zickefoose of Nebraska, a sniper in a Badger reconnaissance and fire support vehicle for the 3rd Battalion, 9th Marines, was forward during breaching operations on Sunday. His vehicle came under intense fire, and he guided in two air strikes that destroyed the enemy in front of his battalion. The next morning, when the enemy counterattacked, he grabbed an AT-4 and, advancing through fog and automatic weapons fire, destroyed an enemy tank single-handedly.

Cpl. Michael S. Kilpatrick of Pennsylvania was the driver of a 3rd Battalion, 9th Marines' Badger reconnaissance vehicle. Sunday night, sprayed by shrapnel from intense mortar and artillery fire, he maneuvered his vehicle coolly and called in air strikes that destroyed the enemy's weapons. The next morning, the enemy counterattacked the Task Force Papa Bear command post with tanks. Corporal Kilpatrick grabbed a light antiarmor weapon and moved forward through fog and enemy fire. He disabled one tank and helped turn back the counterattack.

Cpl. Bryan R. Freeman of Washington was a scout for the 1st Division's 1st Tank Battalion, which on Monday was counterattacked by an Iraqi mechanized brigade. He targeted four enemy tanks, which were then destroyed by Hellfire missiles. And under small-arms fire, he guided Marine Cobra helicopters to destroy Iraqi antiaircraft artillery.

Purple Hearts were awarded to 92 Marines.

Five Marine aviators were prisoners of war: Harrier pilots Capt. Michael C. Berryman and Capt. Russell A. C. Sanborn and OV-10 aviators Lt. Col. Clifford M. Acree, Maj. Joseph J. Small III, and Chief Warrant Officer Guy L. Hunter, Jr. They were abused, but they were all returned on March 5 after the ceasefire.

What had the spectacular logistical effort and the massive presence of half a million Americans in Saudi Arabia accomplished? Saddam Hussein was still in power; the Middle East was still a bubbling, dangerous political caldron. The industrial powers were still selling arms of all kinds to the Middle Eastern nations.

This telegenic war restored a sense of military victory and pride to the United States, which—after the prolonged tragedy of

Vietnam and as a superpower in the last decade of the 20th century—was not satisfied by minor-league sorties into Grenada and Panama.

The war and its predictable and surprisingly easy victory restored Kuwait and its oil supplies to the Emir, Sheikh Jaber al-Ahmad al-Jaber al-Sabah. Saddam Hussein's publicized promise to make this "the mother of all battles" was totally deflated. Although the war carefully left him and the Sunni Moslem minority in power, it crushed his ability to threaten his neighbors with conventional warmaking power, and it punched irreparable holes in the overblown reputation of Iraq's large army. It strengthened traditional, western-supported governments in the area. It restored the haphazard balance of power that had been upset when Iraq defeated Iran in their long war. It precipitated U.S. Secretary of State James Baker's first official visit to Israel after two years in office. It reminded Americans once again to think about becoming less dependent on Middle East oil. And it injected an American military presence in a highly volatile part of the world where nothing had really been resolved.

The American military leaders managed to control the battlefield not only from the enemy but also from the American press. When reporters tried to cover Desert Storm outside of public-affairs-controlled "pools," they were arrested. A television network reporter who latched onto Saudi and Egyptian forces found he could report the war more effectively.

Powerful U.S. military leaders reverted to the stance taken by their predecessors of the 1930s, who did not worry much about public support to acquire manpower or money. From World War II through Vietnam, the American military encouraged and fostered press coverage of their battles. This won them public support for the draft and billion-dollar military budgets. The Vietnam war was painfully called off when the military lost public support back home.

That public support was vital to the military's ability to defend the United States was the real military-media lesson of Vietnam. But at Grenada, Panama and the Persian Gulf, the commanders misread this lesson and did what they could to stifle press coverage.

And what about the Marine Corps? The Gulf war certainly burnished the Corps' reputation for getting to the fight first. If it did nothing to demonstrate the Corps' amphibious assault value, the war confirmed its ability to win on the battlefield.

"The strategic impact of keeping some amphibious forces at sea in the Gulf was just tremendous. We had to fight to develop that strategy," said Gen. Alfred M. Gray, Jr., Commandant at the time. "They were going to take the Marines off the ships, put them in foxholes, I guess. We got that straightened out. Sometimes, the supporting effort becomes the main effort. That is why the Marines took most of Kuwait.

"We were up against 22 enemy divisions—60, 70 percent of the enemy force—and all the obstacles. There was no way we were going to have an attrition-type environment out there. We had to fight smart, and we did."

Lt. Gen. Boomer, who commanded 80,000 Marines in the Gulf war, was more restrained. He said later, "Because it happened so quickly, we didn't have much of a fight."[28] Both were true: the Marines reconquered Kuwait, and they didn't have much of a fight doing it. Boomer estimated that no more than 25 percent of the enemy was prepared to fight. The rest just wanted to quit.

The allied armies' main attack was not supposed to jump off until Monday; but by Sunday noon, General Schwarzkopf found that the Marines were moving ahead so fast that he ordered the army to attack. The Marines' assault had been originally labeled a "supporting attack." It became the heart of the ground war. The Marines believed that they saw more combat than anyone else, division for division. For them, their supporting attack had become the main attack.

Some observers claimed that the Gulf war displayed a new invention: maneuver warfare. It is supposed to emphasize surprise, deception, multiple thrusts and bypassing strong points.[29] But Marines had never preached fighting a static battle.

Desert Storm was an enormous exercise that tested the Marines' newest technologies, prepositioning logistics and warmaking esprit (which used to be called fighting spirit). The Corps had no opportunity to prove it was different; but with overwhelming mobility and firepower, it proved once more in battle that it is as good as they come.

From the Americans' viewpoint, this "Nintendo" war was rightly cheered as "antiseptic." But some thoughtful observers expressed fears that the young fighting generation of Americans, which did not remember dirtier, bloodier wars, would march into the future believing that war was always this easy and that only the bad guys got blown away.

4

The Gulf War—The Kurds

As soon as Desert Storm was over, two groups of Marines served on humanitarian assignments in Asia.

On April 30, 1991, a cyclone, with a wall of water 20 feet high, killed 100,000 people and left a million homeless along the southern coast of Bangladesh on the Bay of Bengal. A Joint Task Force, commanded by Marine Maj. Gen. Henry C. Stackpole III, mobilized planes, helicopters and landing craft from all the services. The Joint Task Force was part of a multinational effort; in the Task Force were Marines of the 5th Marine Expeditionary Brigade, commanded by Brig. Gen. Peter J. Rowe. The 5th MEB was on its way home through the Indian Ocean from duty afloat in the Persian Gulf and ashore during Desert Storm. The U.S. joint operation also included Special Forces teams, Army Blackhawk helicopters and Air Force transport aircraft, as well as Navy SEALs and ships. The operation demonstrated the U.S. military's post–Gulf war emphasis on joint responses to wartime and peacetime contingencies.

The 3rd Battalion, 5th Marines set up a logistics center at Cox's Bazar, a resort city on Bangladesh's southern coast. Most of the joint force stayed offshore while contributing helicopters, medical teams and engineers. Tasks ranged from clearing cattle off the Cox's Bazar runway before a plane landed to mediating Moslem officials' objections to bringing medical care to a Hindu village.

Over two weeks, starting on May 15, the Joint Task Force brought in massive amounts of relief supplies, trucks and 34 water purification units for the devastated population.

In Iraq in April, Marines of the 24th MEU (SOC), which had been practicing amphibious assault landings on Sardinia, joined

802

an even larger effort to help hundreds of thousands of Kurds, who were being killed by starvation, disease and Saddam Hussein. [The 24th MEU (SOC), then called the 24th MAU, had been the unit in the barracks at Beirut, Lebanon, on October 23, 1983, when 241 U.S. servicemen were killed by a terrorist's bomb.]

Despite his defeat, Saddam Hussein had salvaged enough power to smash two rebellious groups: the Shiite Moslems in the south and the Kurds in the mountainous north. He sent tanks, artillery and helicopter gunships against lightly armed guerrillas and unarmed women and children. A million desperate Kurds, fiercely independent Sunni Moslems who lived under the rule of several nations in the area, fled into the nearby mountains and across the border into Turkey. There, disease and starvation were killing 1,000 Kurds a day.

On April 14, the 24th MEU (SOC), commanded by Col. James L. Jones, Jr., was ordered to the Iraq-Turkey border. The MEU included the 2d Battalion, 8th Marines; HMM-264; and MSSG-24. After a forward element established a support base at Silopi, Turkey, G Company, 8th Marines came into Iraq on April 20 to secure sites for a tent city for 20,000 Kurds near the town of Zakko on the Iraqi side of the Turkish border. The Marines also established defensive positions toward the southeast near Dohuk.

The 3,000 Marines who helped support the multinational relief effort, called Operation Provide Comfort, came under the command of Lt. Gen. John M. Shalikashvili, USA. He led 21,000 troops, chiefly from the United States with contingents from Britain, France, Italy, the Netherlands and Spain. Marine Brig. Gen. Anthony C. Zinni was his chief of staff. Colonel Jones' command was also international and included the 45th Commando, Royal Marines and 1st Air Combat Group, Royal Netherlands Marines, as well as French, Italian and American paratroopers. Their missions were to establish a security zone for the Kurds free from Iraqi attacks and to prepare temporary camps to house them.

Iraqi aircraft were ordered not to fly north of the 36th parallel, and Iraqi ground troops were supposed to pull back 30 kilometers south of Zakko. But when the Marines landed, Iraqi soldiers armed with AK-47 assault rifles were still there. U.S. and Dutch Marines cordoned off the city of Zakko, and the Royal Marines, just arrived from Northern Ireland, patrolled the deserted streets.

The terrified Kurds had to be persuaded to come down out of

the mountains and return to Iraq. MEU engineers cleared the border-crossing of mines by April 21, and Marines occupied landing zones, ridges and road intersections. Blue tents were pitched about a mile from Zakko, but it took six days to convince the suspicious Kurdish leaders to be flown by helicopter out of the Zagros Mountains to inspect the site. When the tent city was finally occupied, the Marines moved 72 miles east and built another refugee tent city. Thousands of Kurds began moving toward Dohuk.

CH-46 Sea Knight helicopters of HMM-264 flying out of Turkey brought meals-ready-to-eat (MRE) and bottled water to starving and dehydrated Kurdish refugees in the cold, windswept mountains on the Iraqi side of the border. The helicopters came in at a rate of 150 per day. A mass of hungry human beings charged the helicopters as soon as they touched down, attacking the pallets for a bit of food or sip of water.

In May, Marine Contingency MAGTF 1-91, commanded by Lt. Col. Robert A. Bailey, arrived from Okinawa and was based at Silopi. Its main job was to shepherd the Kurds back to their homes in Iraq. Seven support teams and two air traffic control teams were dispersed across northern Iraq and western Turkey. Tens of thousands of Kurds returned. On June 7, the relief effort was turned over to the United Nations High Commission on Refugees. Colonel Jones and Lt. Col. Tony L. Corwin, commanding officer of the 2d Battalion, 8th Marines, were two of the last Marines to leave northern Iraq on July 15. The Marines had helped provide supplies and protection to an estimated 760,000 displaced people.[30]

5
Special Operations—Liberia and Somalia

Throughout its history, the Marine Corps has performed a variety of what it now calls "special operations." Marines execute amphibious raids, board hostile ships, rescue civilians from civil violence and natural disasters, reinforce embassies and battle terrorists. Marine leaders figure that in the decade before the Persian Gulf war, they handled 35 such emergencies.

Commandant Alfred M. Gray, Jr., started giving Marine Expeditionary Units (MEUs), which were trained for such special operations, the label "SOC" as evidence that they were "special operations capable." The function is old; the title, new. Commandant Gray also switched the name of Marine "amphibious" units back to "expeditionary," the name they had before the Vietnam war. This traditional and broader description had been discarded in May 1965 because the South Vietnamese were said to hate the name of the French Expeditionary Corps.

Even during Operations Desert Shield and Desert Storm, SOC-trained MEUs were performing special operations. When Saddam Hussein invaded Kuwait, the 13th MEU (SOC), commanded by Col. John E. Rhodes, was at Subic Bay in the Philippines. Its job was to save people from the natural disasters connected with the volcanic eruption of Mt. Pinatubo and to help a force of 2,000 Marines from Okinawa, chiefly the 3rd Battalion, 7th Marines, deter anti-American outbreaks. The 13th reached the Gulf of Oman on September 7, 1990.

During Operation Desert Shield, Marine SOC units also conducted two dramatic evacuations of civilians endangered by civil strife in Africa. And afterwards, there were assignments with the Kurds in Iraq and with the people of Bangladesh. These small-unit actions demonstrated again the relevance of the Marine

Corps' two-century-old mission to land and get things in hand.

The action called Operation Sharp Edge took place at the very start of the Gulf war but on the Atlantic Ocean side of Africa.

During the 1980s, tribal violence tore at the Republic of Liberia, a poor West African nation founded by freed American slaves in 1847. U.S. interests there were endangered; Liberia was the site of a Firestone rubber plantation, the largest in the world, and of important U.S. telecommunications facilities.

In 1980, an insurgency of Liberian army enlisted men overthrew the government of descendants of the American slaves. The rebels were led by Samuel K. Doe, a young sergeant who had been trained by U.S. Special Forces. He became president in 1985 and was opposed in turn by the National Patriotic Front of Liberia (NPFL), led by Charles Taylor. In June and July 1990, Taylor's NPFL forces and a splinter group headed by Prince Johnson closed in on Liberia's capital of Monrovia.

On May 27, 1990, the 22d Marine Expeditionary Unit (SOC), which was the Landing Force Sixth Fleet in the Mediterranean, sailed from Toulon, France, for the waters off Monrovia. Flagship of the joint task force was *Saipan;* its landing team was the 2d Battalion, 4th Marines. The 22d MEU (SOC) was led by Col. Granville R. Amos, who had commanded Medium Helicopter Squadron 261 (HMM-261) at Grenada seven years earlier. On June 3, the 22d MEU (SOC) arrived off Monrovia and sat aboard ship 20 miles offshore for the next 62 days.

The fighting at Monrovia approached the U.S. Embassy at the end of July; and on Saturday, August 4, Prince Johnson threatened to take American hostages. U.S. Ambassador James K. Bishop requested the evacuation of civilians and the reinforcement of the embassy.

On Sunday at 9 A.M., three Marine elements of 22d MEU (SOC) were landed by HMM-261 helicopters in heavy thunderstorms. Five CH-46s brought 45 Marines of the 3rd Platoon, E Company into Landing Zone Dove north of the capital and in 13 minutes carried out 18 Americans to *Saipan.* A few minutes later, E Company's 2d Platoon was put down from three helicopters at Landing Zone Condor south of Monrovia and quickly flew three civilians out to *Saipan.* Both landing zones were the sites of communications facilities.

At the same time, five CH-46E and eight CH-53D helicopters set down one by one and placed at the embassy 237 Marines from H Company, commanded by Capt. Daniel S. Rogers. The Liberian government insisted that they stay on American soil inside the embassy compound; they patrolled the perimeter and flew 40 civilians out to *Saipan*.

Fighting near the embassy compound was intense. Each day, 22d MEU (SOC) helicopters evacuated civilians to the ships and then north to Freetown, Sierra Leone; 96 evacuees were taken out through the Liberian port city of Buchanan. On August 21, 26th MEU (SOC) relieved the 22d and continued the evacuation.

In September, Prince Johnson's insurgents killed President Doe. Four thousand soldiers from 16 African countries arrived to restore the peace. When the last U.S. naval ship left the coast of Liberia on January 9, 1991, the Marines had evacuated 2,415 civilians from 21 countries, including 230 Americans.[31]

Marines from the 4th Marine Expeditionary Brigade (SOC) stationed in the Gulf of Oman just outside the Persian Gulf rescued 281 Americans and other foreign nationals from Mogadishu, the capital of Somalia on the Horn of Africa.

At the end of 1990, three armies of Somali rebels were fighting the troops of the authoritarian President Mohammed Siad Barre, who had long been bolstered by U.S. military aid. Government troops using mortars, heavy machine guns and MIGs killed hundreds of people. The fighting cut off escape through the Mogadishu International Airport. On January 3, 1991, U.S. Ambassador Bishop, now at Mogadishu, cabled the Department of State that looters armed with AK-47s had entered the embassy compound in Mogadishu. As he had at Monrovia, Bishop once again requested swift military assistance and evacuation. The nearest U.S. naval vessels were the amphibious assault ship *Guam* and the amphibious transport dock *Trenton*, 460 miles away. Aboard were elements of the 4th MEB (SOC) with CH-53E Super Stallion helicopters. The Marines were commanded by Col. James J. Doyle, Jr.

The embassy at Mogadishu was the world's largest diplomatic facility—160 acres, including a nine-hole golf course. It stretched out in the northeastern section of the capital, three miles from the airport. As the ships raced toward Somalia, embassy personnel and Somali militiamen exchanged fire with free-ranging looters.

The U.S. Embassy people could not hold out until the ships

neared Mogadishu. At 2:45 A.M. on Friday, January 4, two Super Stallions from Marine Heavy Helicopter Squadron 461 took off from *Trenton* with a reinforced rifle platoon from 1st Battalion, 2d Marines and a team of SEALs. At the same time, two KC-30 tankers, flown by Marine Corps Reservists from Fort Stewart, New York, took off from Bahrain to refuel the helicopters over the Indian Ocean.

The Super Stallions refueled twice in the air and set down on the embassy grounds at 6 A.M. The 60-man Marine relief force took places on the perimeter and tore down ladders on which looters were trying to enter the embassy compound. A team of Marines and SEALs escorted in Americans and the Kenyan ambassador, who were trapped at the military mission compound a quarter of a mile away. Then 62 evacuees piled into the two choppers and were flown out to *Trenton*.

By that night, the naval ships steamed nearer, and five CH-46 helicopters from Marine Medium Helicopter Squadrons 263 and 365 lifted off from *Guam*. In four waves, they took out the rest of the civilians: 144 men, 72 women and 47 children from 30 countries, including 11 ambassadors. For a fee, President Barre's troops escorted the Soviet ambassador and 37 members of his staff and dependents in a convoy for more than a mile through the corpse-littered city streets to the U.S. Embassy. As armed looters scaled the embassy compound's walls, the civilians were flown to Oman and the relief force returned to *Trenton*.

The job took 24 hours; not a shot was fired by or at the Marines. No one was injured, and 281 people were evacuated.[32]

The post–Gulf war world promised many more occasions on which Marines would be called out for such missions. They did not have to wait long. On September 29, 1991, a military junta violently overthrew the Reverend Jean-Bertrand Aristide, the Roman Catholic priest who was Haiti's first democratically elected president.

The poorest country in the Western Hemisphere, Haiti was familiar ground to the Corps. Marines were posted in Haiti from 1915 to 1934, the Corps' longest Caribbean intervention. Maj. Smedley D. Butler and Gunnery Sgt. Daniel J. Daly won the Medal of Honor fighting there. In 1958, a Marine Corps mission helped François "Papa Doc" Duvalier build his army.

Exiled President Aristide appealed to the United Nations

Security Council to restore democracy to Haiti, and the Organization of American States imposed sanctions to isolate the junta. On October 1, 1991, a joint task force was formed, commanded by Marine Brig. Gen. Russell H. Sutton; and 300 Marines of the 2d Marine Division and elements of the 2d Marine Aircraft Wing were sent to U.S. Naval Base, Guantanamo Bay, Cuba. Again, U.S. Marines were ready to move in to rescue endangered Americans.

Gen. Carl E. Mundy, Jr., who became Commandant on July 1, 1991, said that Marines

> are not kept around just waiting for an amphibious assault, or waiting for World War III or the start of the next regional war. They are out there every day. Twenty-three percent of the Marine Corps is forward-deployed, away from their families for periods of six months, every day of the year. They were last month; they are this month; they will be six months hence. . . . If those forward-positioned forces do their job, they either prevent or handle the crises. This has been the historic use of Marine forces. . . . As an historical average, we have called upon Marine forces to go somewhere and do something about three or four times a year. That is not going to go away just because the Cold War is over.[33]

6
Women Marines

Women first served as United States Marines during World War I, when 305 "Reservists (Female)" became clerks in uniform to "Free a Marine to fight." In July 1919, with the war over, Commandant George Barnett ordered all women out of the Reserve.[34]

The Corps became again a bastion of maleness until World War II. On November 7, 1942, Commandant Thomas Holcomb reluctantly approved the formation of the Marine Corps Women's Reserve under legislation sponsored by Congressman Melvin J. Maas of Minnesota, who was a major general in the Marine Corps Reserve. Secretary of the Navy Frank Knox announced the Women's Reserve program on February 13, 1943, and that date became the birthday of women Marines.

The Marine Corps was the last of the services to admit women. Major, later Colonel, Ruth Cheney Streeter led the wartime Women's Reserve. When World War II ended, the Corps had 820 officers and 17,640 enlisted women in the Women's Reserve.

Half a century later, the Corps was still a bastion of maleness; but 2,276 women Marines served overseas in the Gulf war, and afterward, 9,300 women were in uniform as Regular Marines. Women were unlikely ever again to disappear from the Corps.

At the end of World War II, the Corps had no intention of keeping Women Reserves. But they proved useful, and in 1946, Commandant Alexander A. Vandegrift approved retaining first 100 Women Reserves and then 300. No more than 100 Women Reserves were on active duty at any time. They were organized as Company E, 1st Headquarters Battalion; Maj. Julia E. Hamblet, a graduate of Vassar College, was the first postwar Director of the Women's Reserve.

810

On June 12, 1948, after a long and hard fight in the Congress, President Truman signed the Women's Armed Services Integration Act, Public Law 625, which allowed women to serve in the Regular military services. Under the law, women could make up 2 percent of Regular strength and have unlimited admission to the Reserves. But women were prohibited from serving in aircraft on combat missions or on Navy ships, except for transports and hospital ships. Col. Katherine A. Towle was recalled to active duty, accepted a Regular commission and became the first Director of Women Marines, reporting directly to the Commandant.

The first eight enlisted women Marines were sworn in on November 10, 1948, and the first recruit platoon of new enlistees started training at Parris Island on February 23, 1949. In June, the first Women Officers' Training Class began at Quantico with 67 candidates from 35 colleges. At its conclusion, 34 of the women were recommended for commissions, including seven Regular commissions. Women now held a firm place in the Regular Marine Corps in peacetime.

Before the outbreak of the Korean war, 13 Women's Reserve platoons were organized across the country, with places for 25 officers and 594 enlisted women.

The summer of 1949 saw the enlistment of the first black women Marines. New York Congressman Adam Clayton Powell had protested that no black women had served in the Marine Corps Women's Reserve during World War II. Now, at a time when male Marines were still segregated by race, women's Platoon 7 of the 3rd Recruit Training Battalion at Parris Island became one of the first integrated units in the Corps. Annie L. Grimes, the third black woman to join Platoon 7, became the first black woman officer to retire from the Corps with 20 years' service.

In the Korean war, women were, for the first time in American history, drafted for military service; but women Reserve Marine officers were not mobilized. When the war started in 1950, the 3rd Recruit Training Battalion was closed down for the summer; recruitment had been disappointing, and the Corps was not pressing too hard. But during the war, women joined the Corps in growing numbers, and the jobs they could fill in uniform began to spread beyond clerical work. Two photographers were the first women to be assigned jobs in an occupational field other than administration. The total number of women Marines on active duty rose from 580 to 2,787.

A 1951 study found that the Corps could actually use 6,500 women if they were employed properly. With manpower in short supply during the Korean war, the limiting factor became not male monopoly but the availability of trained women. The 1951 study found that 95 percent of women Marines worked in six specialties, although 27 were theoretically open to them. By the end of the Korean war, a few women were in some new occupational fields, such as weapons repair and truck driving. Women Marines served from Pearl Harbor to Stuttgart, Germany. One woman Marine who worked as a dispatcher at Pearl Harbor was Sgt. Barbara Jean Dulinsky; in 1967, as a master sergeant, she would be the first woman Marine to report for duty in Vietnam.

In 1953, Colonel Hamblet again succeeded Colonel Towle, whom she had followed as Director of the Women's Reserve in 1946. This time, she became the Director of Women Marines, and she led the Regular Women Marines until 1959.

Between the Korean and Vietnam wars, the number of women Marines dropped by 50 percent, from 2,787 in 1953 to 1,448 in 1964. Although the law permitted women to be 2 percent of the Corps' authorized strength, the Corps set its goal at 1 percent and never reached even that level during that decade. The Corps insisted that the 1 percent policy was not arbitrary but took into consideration the Corps' heavy combat component. Fifty percent of women Marines continued to work in administration.

When Gen. Wallace M. Greene, Jr., became Commandant on January 1, 1964, he ordered a re-examination of the selection, training and utilization of women Marines. A board headed by Lt. Gen. Robert H. Pepper made 83 recommendations; and, despite considerable debate, General Greene approved 75 of them. The Pepper Board opened to women a broader range of occupational fields and more duty stations, and improved their training.

During the Vietnam era, the number of women Marines on active duty returned to a peak of 2,780 in 1969. The main reasons were the larger size of the Corps and the improvement in the retention rate of women by eliminating marriage as a condition for discharge.[35] More enlisted women now went on to advanced schools. In 1968, the Marine Corps Command and Staff College opened to women; and, in 1970, so did the Armed Forces Staff College at Norfolk, Virginia. But the Commandant still had to step in and press some local commanders to assign women Marines to a greater range of jobs.

Women Marines who volunteered were sent to the western Pacific starting in 1966. Okinawa and Vietnam opened up to women rather easily. The local commander objected to sending women Marines to the Marine Corps Air Station at Iwakuni, Japan, but by the following March, the first women Marines reported there for duty.[36] Eight women officers and 28 enlisted women Marines served in Vietnam between 1967 and 1973.

During the Vietnam war, women served briefly in the Marine Security Guard Battalion on embassy or consulate security duty. A woman officer served in each of Manila, Panama and Beirut in 1967 and 1968. But relatively few women Marines served outside the continental United States in any capacity.

The Security Guard program was opened to women again in 1979–82, when 19 women Marines entered the program, and in 1988–89, when 11 women Marines served in 10 posts. Of the 123 countries where Marine Security Guards served, 25 were first approved for the assignment of women Marines; later, posts were opened in 57 countries.

In 1991, a new policy allowed women Marines to be assigned to any Security Guard Battalion post at which the commanding officer of the battalion thought they could contribute.[37] By midyear, 13 women Marines were serving in Security Guard detachments at 11 posts.

The Marine Corps was not ready for the women's liberation movement in the 1970s. But pressure from the Department of Defense resulted in the creation, in 1972, of an ad hoc committee chaired by Col. Albert W. Snell to ensure women Marines equal opportunities for assignment, training and advancement. Commandant Robert E. Cushman, Jr., surprised even women Marines by approving all of the Snell Committee's recommendations for increasing the occupational fields open to women; they would now include logistics, military police and aircraft maintenance.

In 1973, amid great furor and many headlines, Col. Mary E. Bane was named the first woman to command a predominantly male Marine battalion, the Headquarters and Service Battalion at Camp Pendleton. Eleven months later, a new base commander reassigned her—to a major's billet.[38]

The Paris Peace Accords officially ended the Vietnam war in 1973, and a national All-Volunteer Force policy replaced the draft. All the armed services were stimulated to increase the value they placed on recruiting and retaining personnel, male and female. In 1975, Commandant Louis H. Wilson opened all occupational fields to women except four related to combat: infantry, artillery, armor and flight crews.

In the same period, the number of women Marines increased significantly. The Department of Defense, in 1975, stopped the involuntary separation of servicewomen because of pregnancy; women were given the choice of staying or resigning. By June 1977, 407 officers and 3,423 enlisted women were in uniform.

The Organized Reserve program for women Marines was re-established after the Korean war and by 1955 included 35 officers and 664 enlisted women. The program was dropped again in 1958, despite the objections of Colonel Hamblet, the Director of Women Marines; but 227 women Marines were allowed to serve with male Reserve units. In 1971, a new special enlistment program began with a quota of 88 women; they drilled and trained with platoons of Regular women Marines. By 1973, women were allowed to command Organized Reserve units. In 1975, women were authorized to be a maximum of 5 percent of the Organized Reserve.

Training at The Basic School at Quantico was integrated for both sexes in 1977, and the rules that prevented women officers from firing the rifle and pistol for qualification were waived, although Commandant Wilson firmly stated that this was only for non-combat roles. The 22 female lieutenants of 2d Platoon, Company C, BC3-77 were divided into groups of five or six and joined field exercises with the company's 243 male lieutenants. The 2d Platoon became known as "Charlie's Angels" after a television show of that name.

Women enlisted recruits still trained separately from male recruits.

Women Marines have received a variety of awards for heroism and achievement. Col. Hazel E. Benn in 1975 was the first woman Marine, except for the Directors of Women Marines, to receive the Legion of Merit. She had worked for 24 years developing educational programs for Marines. In 1953, Staff Sgt. Barbara O. Barnwell was the first woman Marine to win the Navy and Marine Corps Medal; she saved the life of a Marine drowning in the Atlantic Ocean off Camp Lejeune. Three women Marine officers were awarded the Bronze Star with combat "V" for service in Vietnam: Lt. Col. Ruth J. O'Holleran, Lt. Col. Ruth F. Reinholz and Capt. Shirley E. Leaverton. The first woman Marine to serve under hostile fire was Staff Sgt. Josephine S. Gebers, in the Dominican Republic in 1965.

In 1974, for the last time, Commandant Cushman recognized February 13 as the anniversary of women Marines. Thereafter, all Marines would share one Birthday: November 10. The next step in this process of integration was the elimination in 1977 of the position of Director of Women Marines. Six women had served in the position since 1943: Col. Katherine A. Towle, Col. Julia E. Hamblet, Col. Margaret M. Henderson, Col. Barbara J. Bishop, Col. Jeanette I. Sustad and Col. Margaret A. Brewer. Colonel Brewer became in 1978 the Corps' first woman brigadier general.

In ceremonies on June 30, 1977, marking the end of the position of Director of Women Marines, Commandant Wilson remembered the story of Archibald Henderson's portrait falling to the floor when the decision was made that women could be Marines. General Wilson said that if there ever should no longer be women Marines, he hoped that his portrait would fall to the floor.

And in January 1980, Commandant Robert H. Barrow sent all Marine commanders this message: "Women Marines and male Marines serve side by side in our ranks. They are equal in every sense. They are Marines. They deserve nothing less than outstanding leadership, equal treatment, and equal opportunity for professional development."[39] Still, women Marines continued to be excluded by law from combat-related jobs.

Commandant Gray liked to say that there were no women Marines, just Marines. But no one believed that women were fully accepted by all Marines. After all, the story of Archibald Henderson's portrait falling to the floor is less than 50 years old.

When Brig. Gen. Gail M. Reals, the first woman Marine to be selected in competition with male Marines for the rank of brigadier general, retired in 1990, she said of her fellow women Marines: "Many times we're more loyal to the organization than the organization is loyal to us." She added, "There is still a very basic issue of acceptance. We talk about sexual harassment, we talk about all these things, but to me they're all symptoms. To me the illness is basic acceptance."[40]

Over the years, the debates about women in the Corps have narrowed. Once women were admitted, the debate focused on which occupational specialties would be opened to them. Then the Gulf war hammered the debate down to the issue of combat.

Nearly 35,000 women served overseas in all the U.S. services in that conflict, including 2,276 women Marines. After the war, Lt. Gen. Boomer, commanding general of I MEF, wrote Commandant Gray that "our women have performed superbly."[41]

Four women Marines, communicators with the 11th Marines, passed through the breach on G-Day of Desert Storm and entered Kuwait the next day. They came under enemy artillery fire, and all four earned the Combat Action Ribbon.

Maj. Gen. Keys, commanding general of the 2d Marine Division, which had 12 women Marine officers, 90 enlisted women Marines and 5 women Navy Corpsmen overseas during the Gulf war, praised their work as "nothing short of outstanding." Lt. Col. Mary K. Lowery served as division assistant chief of staff G-1. First Lt. Nancy E. McCarthy located enemy tactical intelligence material and command bunkers inside Kuwait.

The 1st Force Service Support Group included 320 women Marines; some of its truck drivers delivered supplies inside Kuwait and brought back enemy prisoners of war. Capt. Kate Tate of the 1st Radio Battalion provided crucial intelligence during the battle for Khafji.

Lt. Col. Ruthann Poole served as G-1 of the 2d FSSG, while her husband, Lt. Col. John Poole, served with I MEF. They left their four-year-old daughter with her grandparents. Capt. Kim E. Foss left her five-month-old son with her husband, a Marine captain at Camp Pendleton. A I MEF report summed up: "Gender was never an obstacle. Both male and female made equal sacrifices."[42]

Brig. Gen. Charles C. Krulak, commanding general of the 2d FSSG, said of the women under his command in the Gulf war:

> They were magnificent. The first Marine out of the 2d FSSG to be recommended for a Bronze Star was a woman. My G-1 was a female lieutenant colonel; my G-2 was a female major. The noncommissioned officer in charge of our communications center was a woman; 50 percent of the communications watch sections were women. We had female platoon commanders. After dark on the first day of the ground attack, ten of my female truck drivers went through the breach to bring back enemy prisoners, so they actually cleared the breach ahead of some of our hard-charging infantry units. . . . I am not saying that they should be infantrymen, but there is a role for them in

combat—certainly in the combat service support area. They did a great job.[43]

The Gulf war precipitated Congressional debate over women in combat, and the House of Representatives voted to repeal the restrictions against women flying aircraft in combat.

By the end of the Gulf war, women Marines were accepted in 19 occupational categories—from personnel to military police, from music to air traffic control. Although policymakers agreed that being a Marine is "inherently a dangerous business," no woman could have a combat assignment. A woman Marine could, for example, be a truck driver, but not a truck driver in an infantry unit. Commandant Alfred M. Gray, Jr., said, "They don't want to be grunts. Why would they want to be grunts?"

He added, "They don't have the physical makeup, thank God. They don't come into the Marine Corps to be infantry. The average woman can't throw a hand grenade outside the safety fan."[44]

General Gray insisted that women should not serve as pilots because Marine pilots must be ready to fight as infantrymen and forward air controllers and because the Corps did not have non-combat aircraft.

General Gray's successor, Gen. Carl E. Mundy, Jr., agreed. Immediately after becoming Commandant, General Mundy told the Women Officers Professional Association that infantry troops "in some cases wrestle an opponent to the ground and kill him in the most violent and debasing human forms. It's a very dirty, distasteful and physical business. I am not prepared to tell you that is something I would want to see American women involved in." He found that some women officers disagreed.[45]

The Corps' leaders said proudly that a woman could go to the top of any career ladder to which she was admitted; the Corps had no "glass ceilings" for women Marines. But some women officers felt strongly that if combat jobs were closed to them, they could not climb the most important military career ladders.

After the Gulf war, some 8,670 enlisted women and 670 officers were on active duty in the Corps. This meant that 4.9 percent of the enlisted personnel and 3.4 percent of the officers in the Corps were female. This was considerably below the 18,400 women Marine Reservists during World War II, but it was the largest number of women who have ever been active-duty Regular Marines.

7
Bright Future

Two events at the beginning of the nineties changed the future for the Marine Corps: the crumbling of the Soviet Union and the war in the Persian Gulf.

The disarray of the Communist monolith squelched the threat from Eastern Europe and shrank the importance of the Corps' role on NATO's flanks. As a symbol of the change, 70 musicians of the Marine Band, led by Col. John R. Bourgeois, toured the Soviet Union in February 1990; in five cities, Soviet citizens heard not military threats, but "The Stars and Stripes Forever." The Cold War seemed over.

The massive military involvement of the United States in the Middle East's violence showed off the Marines' ability to get there fast, ready to stay and fight.

By 1990, the Corps faced not only a brand-new decade but a radically different era. The Commandant who led it into this era chewed tobacco, talked about "warriors" and felt more at home in fatigues than dress blues. Gen. Alfred M. Gray, Jr., believed there is no such thing as "a low-intensity war."

At the end of his tour as Commandant, General Gray looked ahead and saw a time of contraction. The full wallet of the Reagan Administration would be zip-closed, and the military services would no longer get all the funds they asked for. General Gray said, "We are a very lean outfit, and we are committed throughout the globe."[46] Lean times fit a lean Marine Corps, but it already had little fat and a broad assignment.

The Marine Corps insisted it was a military bargain. Marines estimated that the Corps cost 4.8 percent of the defense budget but supplied 12 percent of the nation's active, general purpose divisions and 11 percent of the tactical fixed-wing aircraft.

The breakup of the Soviet Union and the breaking away of its Eastern European satellites created pressure to reduce the Marine Corps. When Iraq invaded Kuwait, both Congress and the Pentagon were planning to cut all U.S. troop strengths. The Pentagon proposed to reduce forces by 25 percent over five years and reorganize the military into four Forces: Atlantic, Pacific, Contingency and Strategic.

And during Desert Shield, Congress ordered the Corps' strength cut 9.9 percent by 1995, to 177,000 men and women. The Pentagon wanted the Corps sliced even thinner, to 159,000. General Gray objected, saying, "The Marine Corps should not go below 180,000."

The competition for fewer dollars promised an inevitable struggle among the military services for roles and missions. The Gulf war, Panama and Grenada all warned that the Marine Corps had to fight repeatedly for a place in the decision-making process and in the fighting. This competition has always been part of the modern Marine Corps story.

Traditionally, the Corps has been a contingency force that can move in wherever national interests are challenged or endangered. Marines feel they must have enough strength to get to the scene and enough staying power to do the job. General Gray said, "What matters is not how quickly you can deploy but how quickly you can employ. If you want to come and stay long enough to get a political and military decision in your favor, you've got to include coming from the sea."

The major point of conflict was whether the Army or the Marine Corps was better able to fight "small wars." General Gray was not worried about the Army's airborne elements supplanting the Corps. He said, "If the 101st and the 82d were to take over the Marine Corps' jobs, you are going to have to make them Marines. They can't support themselves and you will have to buy a lot of sealift. It doesn't make any sense. The 82d Airborne is at their best when they are around people like us who can support them when they come from the sea. That was demonstrated in Desert Shield."

His successor as Commandant, Gen. Carl E. Mundy, Jr., agreed: "The thing we don't need is two Marine Corps or two Armies. People get enthusiastic and they tend to get carried away that you can do everything with light forces, that you can fly everywhere that you need to go. But the fact is that you can't."[47]

Desert Shield proved his point. More than 90 percent of the

equipment and supplies for the coalition forces in the Persian Gulf war went by sea. Because the Corps' prepositioning program was in place, the 7th Marine Expeditionary Brigade (MEB) from California and the 1st MEB from Hawaii were able to fly swiftly and dramatically into Saudi Arabia and marry up with sea-delivered supplies stored in Diego Garcia and Guam.

General Gray looked around the post-Soviet world and saw a widespread "potential for instability." He said, "If containment was the one-word description of the strategy of the last 40-some years, stability is the key word for the strategy of the future in the less developed parts of the world." They contain the resources vital to the free world, and the free nations will have to ensure their access to those resources.

Instability makes for war. Therefore, General Gray said, "The future in terms of usefulness is very bright for the Marines."

The nineties opened with an especially useful year for the Corps. Its 216th year, 1990–91, saw most of the Corps involved in Saudi Arabia and Kuwait. At the same time, Marine units were evacuating civilians from Liberia, lifting people out of Somalia, protecting the Kurds, providing disaster relief in the Philippines and Bangladesh and going on alert for possible trouble in Haiti. Seldom has the Corps been more valuable worldwide.

Since today's Marines have to be ready for such a variety of assignments, throughout his four years as Commandant, General Gray stressed that Marines are "warriors." Some Marines resented the idea that he felt there was any word more warrior-like than "Marine." But Gray insisted that "warrior" expresses what Marines are all about. As he put it, "Only the Marines are a profession. These other outfits are occupations." He said, "You don't spend much of your career in warfighting, but when you do, you better be ready to do it."

The key for the Corps, Gray believed, is a trained and disciplined force prepared to perform a wide spectrum of missions. He required that Marine Expeditionary Units (MEUs) be "special operations capable" (SOC), and ready to do everything from urban fighting to rescuing people to lightning-like raids. He had Marines train in 39 cities and on oil rigs in the Gulf of Mexico so they could seize oil rigs in the Persian Gulf.

General Gray emphasized learning in the Corps. He gave birth to the Marine Corps University and the Marine Corps Research Center at Quantico. Ground was broken for the $14.2

million Research Center in June 1990. During the summer of 1990, he opened two schools at the Command and Staff College in Quantico: the School of the Art of War Studies and the School of Advanced Warfighting. And he created the Commandant's Reading List, which identified books of value to Marines.

General Gray was succeeded as Commandant on July 1, 1991, by newly promoted Gen. Carl E. Mundy, Jr., fifty-five, the Commanding General, Fleet Marine Force, Atlantic. Mundy was born in Atlanta, graduated from Auburn University and had been a Marine for 34 years. He landed in Lebanon with a rifle company as a new lieutenant in 1958 and served in Vietnam in 1966–67.

On August 9, 1991, Marine Gen. Joseph P. Hoar was appointed Commanding General of the U.S. Central Command, succeeding Army Gen. H. Norman Schwarzkopf. General Schwarzkopf had taken over Central Command from Marine Gen. George B. Crist. During the Gulf war, General Hoar served in Washington as the Corps' Deputy Chief of Staff for Plans, Policies and Operations, responsible primarily for Joint Chiefs of Staff matters.

One of Commandant Mundy's first significant acts was to revive the tradition of holding a symposium of the Corps' general officers. He summoned 60 Marine generals to several days of classified meetings in October 1991. They discussed the implications of Desert Shield and Desert Storm; the Goldwater-Nichols Act, which made the Chairman of the Joint Chiefs of Staff the President's chief military advisor; and the expected reduction of the military budget. They thought hardest about the future of the world and the Marine Corps. They also, in the new Commandant's style, did some dancing to country music.

The main point to come out of the discussions was that since 1945 the U.S. military had aimed primarily at countering the threat from the Soviet Union. Now the Corps had to get ready for the unpredictable.

More than ever, the Marine Corps had to be a force-in-readiness able to respond worldwide. It faced tough decisions because of tighter budgets. Commandant Mundy said that he favored eliminating entire units rather than sprinkling the belt-tightening cuts around and weakening many units. And he recognized that he had to deal with competition from the other services that wanted a piece of the Marine Corps' role as the nation's rapid-response contingency force.

Although the Gulf war failed to give the Corps a chance to demonstrate its classic amphibious skills in a modern high-tech environment, Marines continued to think "amphibious." Coming in from the sea was still their reason for being. They sought constantly to improve their ability to attack from the sea, whether by ship or aircraft, in an age when enemy missiles could find them before they ever reached the beach.

General Mundy, like the two Commandants before him, wanted the MV-22A tilt-rotor Osprey airplane, which had been at the top of the Corps' procurement wish list until Secretary of Defense Cheney deleted it. The Corps hoped the Osprey would replace its aging fleet of CH-46 helicopters. Mundy said many still saw the Osprey as the Marines' "aircraft of the future."

The Osprey could provide the over-the-horizon amphibious assault capability that Marines felt was vital in an era of missiles like the Exocet. The Osprey could carry 24 Marines at speeds up to 300 mph and fly more than 1,000 miles without refueling. By 1990, four test aircraft had been constructed. But the Corps' original plan to have 552 Ospreys by 1991 was obviously dead; the Marines had to sit by and watch the Japanese develop the aircraft.

The Corps tightened up on aircraft generally, planning to cut back from 15 types of aircraft in 1989 to about nine by the turn of the century.

Although the Marines' air-cushion landing craft, the LCAC, did not work well in the high seas and 35-mph winds of Exercise Imminent Thunder, General Mundy retains full faith in it. The Corps also developed an "advanced assault amphibious vehicle," the AAAV, the next generation of the AAV7A1, to provide both ship-to-shore assault capability and battlefield mobility ashore. It will be available at the end of the century. And the Corps has modernized its armor by switching over to the M1A1 Abrams tank that proved so effective in Kuwait.

The Corps also continued to look forward to a new amphibious assault ship that would deliver a Marine landing force including troops, helicopters and landing craft. The first of 27 ships in the new amphibious assault class is to be delivered by the end of the decade. In the meantime, the number of available amphibious ships was down to 63 and shrinking; and work continued on more amphibious assault ships of the *Wasp* LHD class, as well as the *Whidbey Island* LSD class.

Experience in the Gulf war, General Mundy said, clearly

verified the importance of the Marines' prepositioning concept. After the war, the Corps also organized "crisis-action modules" to supply an expeditionary force smaller than a 16,000-man brigade from only one or two ships.[48] The war's experience also brought to the surface the need to prepare for night fighting and for the Navy to improve its shallow-water mine clearing. General Mundy candidly told the Senate Armed Services Committee that in Desert Storm "the risk from mines was a factor in deciding not to conduct a landing."[49] After the war, the Corps and the Navy began exploring laser technology for mine detection.

General Mundy told the committee that the Marines must continue to provide a "robust forcible-entry capability." Although he was enthusiastic about the potentials of lasers, super-high-frequency communications and other modern technologies, he believed the Marine Corps was still, at its core, about "close and personal combat."

The Corps continued to probe for its role in a changing world. When General Gray changed back the designation of all Marine combat units from "amphibious" to "expeditionary" in 1988, this was much more than gung-ho semantics. He said expeditionary would "more accurately reflect Marine Corps missions and capabilities. The Marine air-ground task forces which we forward deploy around the world are not limited to amphibious operations alone. Rather they are capable of projecting sustained, combined arms combat power ashore in order to conduct a wide range of missions essential to the protection of our national security interests."[50] Neither Vietnam nor the Gulf war gave the Corps a chance to be amphibious; but it certainly continued to be expeditionary.

The tugging among the services for roles and dollars was quieted by the Goldwater-Nichols Act, which reduced the power of the service chiefs, and by post–Gulf war Department of Defense policies that sought to replace service competition with joint efforts. The Corps had long emphasized its own "joint-ness" with its Marine Corps air-ground task forces. More and more, the Corps had to figure out how to maintain its uniqueness and still fit into interservice efforts.

Looking ahead, General Gray said, "The reason that the American people support the Marine Corps is credibility. Marines have done what they say they're going to do. And they did it in spades in the Gulf war. The future of the Corps rests in young Marines' hands."

The world's tough realities continue to ensure a place for the Marines of the future. The modern Marine Corps is not a defensive but an attack force. The world will certainly again need mobile strike forces that are ready to go anywhere "in step and smartly" and are prepared to stay and fight. To do this, whether sealifted or airlifted into battle, is the legitimate role of the Marines in modern three-dimensional warfare.

Even if the superpowers' nuclear confrontation has seemed to subside, the world, with its proliferation of nuclear weapons, still lives with the threat that wars will escalate to use them. The fear that gripped the world before the start of Operation Desert Storm was proof of that.

During the long, tense showdown between the United States and the Soviet Union, many felt confident that mankind would never again see the kind of slugging match between the massed armies of the great powers that dominated warfare during the century and a half between Napoleon and Hiroshima. But the confrontation had hardly eased before one of the superpowers again sent half a million men and women overseas to fight a war—an old-fashioned war with new technology and weapons.

Certainly, human beings have not outgrown the vicious insanity of war. The United States Marine Corps will continue to serve as an elite corps of expert, volunteer killers trained and inspirited to give their lives to take their objective—members, to repeat Stephen Crane's words, of "a mysterious fraternity born of smoke and the danger of death." And a great nation's fate and freedom will continue to rest in the hands of such a band of brothers.

We few, we happy few, we band of brothers;

For he today that sheds his blood with me

Shall be my brother.[51]

Commandants of the
U.S. Marine Corps

COMMANDANT	YEARS	BIRTHPLACE
Samuel Nicholas	1775–1781	Philadelphia
William Ward Burrows	1798–1804	Charleston, South Carolina
Franklin Wharton	1804–1818	Philadelphia
Anthony Gale	1819–1820	Dublin, Ireland
Archibald Henderson	1820–1859	Colchester, Virginia
John Harris	1859–1864	East Whiteland, Pennsylvania
Jacob Zeilin	1864–1876	Philadelphia
Charles G. McCawley	1876–1891	Philadelphia
Charles Heywood	1891–1903	Waterville, Maine
George F. Elliott	1903–1910	Utah, Green County, Alabama
William P. Biddle	1911–1914	Philadelphia
George Barnett	1914–1920	Lancaster, Wisconsin
John A. Lejeune	1920–1929	Pointe Coupee, Louisiana
Wendell C. Neville	1929–1930	Portsmouth, Virginia
Ben H. Fuller	1930–1934	Big Rapids, Michigan
John H. Russell	1934–1936	Mare Island, California
Thomas Holcomb	1936–1943	New Castle, Delaware
Alexander A. Vandegrift	1944–1947	Charlottesville, Virginia
Clifton B. Cates	1948–1951	Tiptonville, Tennessee
Lemuel C. Shepherd, Jr.	1952–1955	Norfolk, Virginia
Randolph McC. Pate	1956–1959	Port Royal, South Carolina
David M. Shoup	1960–1963	Battle Ground, Indiana
Wallace M. Greene, Jr.	1964–1967	Waterbury, Vermont
Leonard F. Chapman, Jr.	1968–1971	Key West, Florida
Robert E. Cushman, Jr.	1972–1975	St. Paul, Minnesota
Louis H. Wilson	1975–1979	Brandon, Mississippi
Robert H. Barrow	1979–1983	Baton Rouge, Louisiana
Paul X. Kelley	1983–1987	Boston, Massachusetts
Alfred M. Gray, Jr.	1987–1991	Point Pleasant Beach, New Jersey
Carl E. Mundy, Jr.	1991–	Atlanta, Georgia

(The term Commandant was not used until 1800. Nicholas was the senior officer of the Continental Marines.)

U.S. Marines Who Have Received the Medal of Honor

The Medal of Honor is the United States' highest award for military valor. Since its first presentation in 1863, 293 Marines have received 300 Medals of Honor. A number of Navy corpsmen, chaplains and other personnel serving with Marine Corps units in combat have also earned the Medal.

Only two Marines have earned the Medal of Honor for two separate courageous acts: Daniel J. Daly in 1900 and 1915 and Smedley D. Butler in 1914 and 1915. Five Marines received both the Navy and Army Medals of Honor for the same act during World War I, when separate medals existed.

Of the 293 Marines, 70 were officers and 223 enlisted men. Of the total 120 were killed as a direct result of the action for which they were cited. The posthumous awards are indicated in this listing by an asterisk following the Marine's name.

NAME	PLACE	DATE	UNIT
	The Civil War 1861–1865		
Sgt. Richard Binder	Fort Fisher	1864–65	USS *Ticonderoga*
Sgt. J. Henry Denig	Mobile Bay	1864	USS *Brooklyn*
Orderly Sgt. Isaac N. Fry	Fort Fisher	1865	USS *Ticonderoga*
Sgt. Michael Hudson	Mobile Bay	1864	USS *Brooklyn*
Cpl. John F. Mackie	Drewry's Bluff	1862	USS *Galena*
Sgt. James Martin	Mobile Bay	1864	USS *Richmond*
Sgt. Andrew Miller	Mobile Bay	1864	USS *Richmond*
Orderly Sgt. Christopher Nugent	Florida	1863	USS *Fort Henry*
Cpl. Miles M. Ovaitt	Mobile Bay	1864	USS *Brooklyn*
Cpl. John Rannahan	Fort Fisher	1865	USS *Minnesota*
Sgt. James S. Roantree	Mobile Bay	1864	USS *Oneida*
Pvt. John Shivers	Fort Fisher	1865	USS *Minnesota*
Cpl. Willard M. Smith	Mobile Bay	1864	USS *Brooklyn*
Orderly Sgt. David Sprowle	Mobile Bay	1864	USS *Richmond*
Pvt. Henry A. Thompson	Fort Fisher	1865	USS *Minnesota*
Cpl. Andrew J. Tomlin	Fort Fisher	1865	USS *Wabash*
Sgt. Pinkerton R. Vaughn	Port Hudson	1863	USS *Mississippi*
	Korean Campaign 1871		
Cpl. Charles Brown			USS *Colorado*
Pvt. John Coleman			USS *Colorado*
Pvt. James Dougherty			USS *Carondelet*
Pvt. Michael McNamara			USS *Benicia*
Pvt. Michael Owens			USS *Colorado*
Pvt. Hugh Purvis			USS *Alaska*

NAME	PLACE	DATE	UNIT
	Interim 1872–1881		
Cpl. John Morris	France	1881	USS Lancaster
Cpl. James A. Stewart	France	1872	USS Plymouth
	Spanish American War 1898		
Pvt. Daniel Campbell	Cuba		USS Marblehead
Pvt. Oscar W. Field	Cuba		USS Nashville
Pvt. John Fitzgerald	Cuba		1st Marine Battalion
Pvt. Joseph J. Franklin	Cuba		USS Nashville
Sgt. Philip Gaughan	Cuba		USS Nashville
Pvt. Frank Hill	Cuba		USS Nashville
Pvt. Michael Kearney	Cuba		USS Nashville
Pvt. Hermann W. Kuchneister	Cuba		USS Marblehead
Pvt. Harry L. MacNeal	Cuba		USS Brooklyn
Pvt. James Meredith (name changed to Patrick F. Ford, Jr.)	Cuba		USS Brooklyn
Pvt. Pomeroy Parker	Cuba		USS Nashville
Sgt. John H. Quick	Cuba		1st Marine Battalion
Pvt. Joseph F. Scott	Cuba		USS Nashville
Pvt. Edward Sullivan	Cuba		USS Marblehead
Pvt. Walter S. West	Cuba		USS Marblehead
	Period of the Philippine Insurrection 1899–1902		
Capt. Hiram I. Bearss	Samar	1901	1st Regiment
Pvt. Howard M. Buckley	Luzon	1899	USS Helena

828

Sgt. Bruno A. Forsterer	Samoa	1899	USS *Philadelphia*
Sgt. Harry Harvey	Benictican	1900	1st Regiment
Pvt. Henry L. Hulbert	Samoa	1899	USS *Philadelphia*
Pvt. Joseph Leonard (enlisted as Joseph Melvin)	Luzon	1899	USS *Helena*
Sgt. Michael J. McNally	Samoa	1899	USS *Philadelphia*
Capt. David D. Porter	Samar	1901	Marine Barracks, Cavite
Cpl. Thomas F. Prendergast	Luzon	1899	USS *Helena*

Boxer Rebellion 1900

Sgt. John M. Adams (born George L. Day)	Tientsin	1st Regiment
Cpl. Harry C. Adriance	Tientsin	1st Regiment
Cpl. Edwin N. Appleton	Tientsin	USFS *Newark*
Pvt. Erwin J. Boydston	Peking	USS *Oregon*
Pvt. James Burnes	Tientsin	USFS *Newark*
Pvt. Albert R. Campbell	Tientsin	1st Regiment
Pvt. William L. Carr	Peking	USFS *Newark*
Pvt. James Cooney	Tientsin	1st Regiment
Cpl. John O. Dahlgren	Peking	USS *Oregon*
Pvt. Daniel J. Daly	Peking	USFS *Newark*
Pvt. Harry Fisher*	Peking	USS *Oregon*
Sgt. Alexander J. Foley	Tientsin	1st Regiment
Pvt. Charles R. Francis	Tientsin	1st Regiment

NAME	PLACE	DATE	UNIT
Pvt. Louis R. Gaiennie	Peking		USFS *Newark*
Pvt. Henry W. Heisch	Tientsin		USFS *Newark*
Pvt. William C. Horton	Peking		USS *Oregon*
Pvt. Martin Hunt	Peking		USS *Oregon*
Pvt. Thomas W. Kates	Tientsin		1st Regiment
Pvt. Clarence E. Mathias	Tientsin		1st Regiment
Pvt. Albert Moore	Peking		USS *Oregon*
Drummer John A. Murphy	Peking		USFS *Newark*
Pvt. William H. Murray (served under the name of Henry W. Davis)	Peking		USFS *Newark*
Pvt. Harry W. Orndoff	Relief Expedition		USFS *Newark*
Cpl. Reuben J. Phillips	Relief Expedition		USFS *Newark*
Pvt. Herbert I. Preston	Peking		USS *Oregon*
Pvt. David J. Scannell	Peking		USS *Oregon*
Pvt. France Silva	Peking		USFS *Newark*
Gunnery Sgt. Peter Stewart	Relief Expedition		USFS *Newark*
Sgt. Clarence E. Sutton	Tientsin		1st Regiment
Pvt. Oscar J. Upham	Peking		USS *Oregon*
Sgt. Edward A. Walker	Peking		USS *Oregon*
Pvt. Frank A. Young	Peking		USFS *Newark*
Pvt. William Zion	Peking		USFS *Newark*

Interim 1901

Sgt. John H. Helms	Montevideo		USS *Chicago*

Pvt. Louis F. Pfeifer (served as Louis F. Theis) — Pacific Ocean — USS *Petrel*

Vera Cruz 1914

Name	Unit
Maj. Randolph C. Berkeley	2d Advance Base Regiment
Maj. Smedley D. Butler	2d Advance Base Regiment
Maj. Albertus W. Catlin	3rd Regiment
Capt. Jesse F. Dyer	2d Advance Base Regiment
Capt. Eli T. Fryer	2d Advance Base Regiment
Capt. Walter N. Hill	2d Advance Base Regiment
Capt. John A. Hughes	2d Advance Base Regiment
Lt. Col. Wendell C. Neville	2d Regiment
Maj. George C. Reid	3rd Regiment

Haitian Campaign 1915

Name	Location	Unit
Maj. Smedley D. Butler	Fort Riviere	CO, detachments
Gunnery Sgt. Daniel J. Daly	Fort Dipite	2d Regiment
Pvt. Samuel Gross (real name: Samuel Marguiles)	Fort Riviere	USS *Connecticut*
Sgt. Ross L. Iams	Fort Riviere	USS *Connecticut*
1st Lt. Edward A. Ostermann	Fort Dipite	1st Brigade
Capt. William P. Upshur	Fort Dipite	2d Regiment

Dominican Republic 1916

Name	Location	Unit
Cpl. Joseph A. Glowin	Guayacanas	Artillery Battalion

NAME	PLACE	DATE	UNIT
1st Lt. Ernest C. Williams	San Francisco de Macoris		4th Regiment
1st Sgt. Roswell Winans	Guayacanas		4th Regiment
World War I 1918			
Sgt. Louis Cukela	Forest de Retz		5th Regiment
Gunnery Sgt. Ernest A. Janson (served under the name of Charles Hoffman)	Belleau Wood		5th Regiment
Pvt. John J. Kelly	Blanc Mont Ridge		6th Regiment
Sgt. Matej Kocak	Soissons		5th Regiment
Cpl. John H. Pruitt*	Blanc Mont Ridge		6th Regiment
Gunnery Sgt. Robert G. Robinson	Pittham, Belgium		Northern Bombing Group
Gunnery Sgt. Fred W. Stockham*	Belleau Wood		6th Regiment
2d Lt. Ralph Talbot	Pittham, Belgium		Northern Bombing Group
Haitian Campaign 1919			
Cpl. William R. Button	Grande Riviere		Constabulary Detachment
Sgt. Herman H. Hanneken	Grande Riviere		Constabulary Detachment
Interim 1921			
Pvt. Albert J. Smith	Pensacola, Florida		Marine Barracks
Second Nicaraguan Campaign 1928–1932			
1st Lt. Christian F. Schilt	Quilali	1928	Observation Squadron 7-M

World War II 1941–1945

Name	Location	Year	Unit
Pfc. Harold C. Agerholm*	Saipan	1944	10th Marines
Pfc. Richard B. Anderson*	Kwajalein	1944	23rd Marines
Maj. Kenneth D. Bailey*	Guadalcanal	1942	1st Raider Battalion
Sgt. John Basilone	Guadalcanal	1942	7th Marines
Lt. Col. Harold W. Bauer	Guadalcanal	1942	VMF-212
Cpl. Lewis K. Bausell*	Peleliu	1944	5th Marines
Cpl. Charles J. Berry*	Iwo Jima	1945	26th Marines
1st Lt. Alexander Bonneyman, Jr.*	Tarawa	1943	18th Marines
Staff Sgt. William J. Bordelon, Jr.*	Tarawa	1943	18th Marines
Maj. Gregory Boyington	Central Solomons	1943–44	VMF-214
Cpl. Richard E. Bush	Okinawa	1945	4th Marines
Pfc. William R. Caddy*	Iwo Jima	1945	26th Marines
1st Lt. George H. Cannon*	Midway	1941	6th Defense Battalion
Cpl. Anthony Casamento	Guadalcanal	1942	5th Marines
Lt. Col. Justice M. Chambers	Iwo Jima	1945	25th Marines
Sgt. Darrell S. Cole*	Iwo Jima	1945	23rd Marines
Maj. Henry A. Courtney*	Okinawa	1945	22d Marines
Cpl. Anthony P. Damato*	Eniwetok	1944	22d Marines
1st Lt. Jefferson J. De Blanc	Solomons	1943	VMF-112
Capt. Robert H. Dunlap	Iwo Jima	1945	26th Marines
Lt. Col. Aquilla J. Dyess*	Kwajalein	1944	24th Marines
Col. Merritt A. Edson	Guadalcanal	1942	1st Raider Battalion
Capt. Henry T. Elrod*	Wake Island	1941	VMF-211

NAME	DATE	PLACE	UNIT
Pfc. Harold C. Epperson*	1944	Saipan	6th Marines
Cpl. John P. Fardy*	1945	Okinawa	1st Marines
Capt. Richard E. Fleming*	1942	Midway	VMSB-241
Capt. Joseph J. Foss	1942	Guadalcanal	VMF-121
Pfc. William A. Foster*	1945	Okinawa	1st Marines
Maj. Robert E. Galer	1942	Solomons	VMF-224
Pvt. Harold Gonsalves	1945	Okinawa	15th Marines
Sgt. Ross F. Gray	1945	Iwo Jima	25th Marines
Pfc. Henry Gurke*	1943	Bougainville	3rd Raider Battalion
Pvt. Dale M. Hansen	1945	Okinawa	1st Marines
1st Lt. Robert M. Hanson	1943–44	Rabaul	VMF-215
Sgt. William G. Harrell	1945	Iwo Jima	28th Marines
Cpl. Louis J. Hauge, Jr.*	1945	Okinawa	1st Marines
1st Lt. William D. Hawkins*	1943	Tarawa	2d Marines
Pfc. Arthur J. Jackson	1944	Peleliu	7th Marines
Pfc. Douglas T. Jacobson	1945	Iwo Jima	23rd Marines
Platoon Sgt. Joseph R. Julian*	1945	Iwo Jima	27th Marines
Sgt. Elbert L. Kinser*	1945	Okinawa	1st Marines
Pfc. Richard E. Kraus*	1944	Peleliu	8th Amphibian Tractor Battalion
Pfc. James D. LaBelle*	1945	Iwo Jima	27th Marines
2d Lt. John Harold Leims	1945	Iwo Jima	9th Marines
Pfc. Jacklyn H. Lucas	1945	Iwo Jima	26th Marines
1st Lt. Jack Lummus*	1945	Iwo Jima	27th Marines
1st Lt. Harry L. Martin*	1945	Iwo Jima	5th Pioneer Battalion
Pfc. Leonard F. Mason*	1944	Guam	3rd Marines
Gunnery Sgt. Robert H. McCard*	1944	Saipan	4th Tank Battalion

Capt. Joseph J. McCarthy	Iwo Jima	1945	24th Marines
Pvt. Robert M. McTureous, Jr.*	Okinawa	1945	29th Marines
Pfc. John D. New*	Peleliu	1944	7th Marines
Sgt. Robert A. Owens*	Bougainville	1943	3rd Marines
Pvt. Joseph W. Ozbourn*	Tinian	1944	23rd Marines
Platoon Sgt. Mitchell Paige	Guadalcanal	1942	7th Marines
Pvt. Wesley Phelps*	Peleliu	1944	7th Marines
Pvt. George Phillips*	Iwo Jima	1945	28th Marines
Capt. Everett P. Pope	Peleliu	1944	1st Marines
1st Lt. John V. Power*	Kwajalein	1944	24th Marines
Pfc. Charles H. Roan*	Peleliu	1944	7th Marines
2d Lt. Carlton R. Rouh	Peleliu	1944	5th Marines
Pfc. Donald J. Ruhl*	Iwo Jima	1945	28th Marines
Pfc. Albert E. Schwab*	Okinawa	1945	5th Marines
Col. David M. Shoup	Tarawa	1943	2d Marines
Pvt. Franklin E. Sigler	Iwo Jima	1945	26th Marines
Pfc. Luther Skaggs, Jr.	Guam	1944	3rd Marines
Maj. John L. Smith	Solomons	1942	VMF-223
Pvt. Richard K. Sorenson	Kwajalein	1944	24th Marines
Cpl. Tony Stein*	Iwo Jima	1945	28th Marines
1st Lt. James E. Swett	Solomons	1943	VMF-221
Sgt. Herbert J. Thomas*	Bougainville	1943	3rd Marines
Sgt. Clyde Thomason*	Makin Island	1942	2d Raider Battalion
Sgt. Grant F. Timmerman*	Saipan	1944	2d Tank Battalion
Maj. Gen. Alexander A. Vandegrift	Solomons	1942	1st Marine Division
1st Lt. Kenneth A. Walsh	Solomons	1943	VMF-124
Gunnery Sgt. William G. Walsh*	Iwo Jima	1945	27th Marines

NAME	PLACE	DATE	UNIT
Pvt. Wilson D. Watson	Iwo Jima	1945	9th Marines
Cpl. Hershel W. Williams	Iwo Jima	1945	21st Marines
Capt. Louis H. Wilson, Jr.	Guam	1944	9th Marines
Pfc. Robert L. Wilson*	Tinian	1944	6th Marines
Pfc. Frank P. Witek*	Guam	1944	9th Marines

Korean War 1950–1953

NAME	PLACE	DATE	UNIT
Cpl. Charles G. Abrell*	Hill 1316	1951	1st Marines
Capt. William E. Barber	Toktong Pass	1950	7th Marines
Pfc. William B. Baugh*	Hell Fire Valley	1950	1st Marines
Pvt. Hector A. Cafferata, Jr.	Toktong Pass	1950	7th Marines
Cpl. David B. Champagne*	Tumae-ri Ridge	1952	7th Marines
Pfc. Stanley R. Christianson*	Seoul	1950	1st Marines
1st Lt. Henry A. Commiskey, Sr.	Yongdungpo	1950	1st Marines
Cpl. Jack A. Davenport*	Songnae-Dong	1951	5th Marines
Lt. Col. Raymond G. Davis	Toktong Pass	1950	7th Marines
Cpl. Duane E. Dewey	Panmunjom	1952	5th Marines
Pfc. Fernando L. Garcia*	Outpost Bruce	1952	5th Marines
Pfc. Edward Gomez*	Hill 749	1951	1st Marines
Staff Sgt. Ambrosio Guillen*	Hill 119	1953	7th Marines
Sgt. James E. Johnson*	Yudam-ni	1950	11th Marines
Pfc. John D. Kelly*	Tumae-ri Ridge	1952	7th Marines
Pfc. Jack W. Kelso*	Outpost Warsaw	1952	7th Marines
Staff Sgt. Robert S. Kennemore	Yudam-ni	1950	7th Marines
Pfc. Herbert A. Littleton*	Horseshoe Ridge	1951	7th Marines
1st Lt. Baldomero Lopez*	Inchon	1950	5th Marines

Sgt. Daniel P. Matthews*	Outpost Vegas	1953	7th Marines
Sgt. Frederick W. Mausert III*	Hill 673	1951	7th Marines
Pfc. Alford L. McLaughlin	Outpost Bruce	1952	5th Marines
1st Lt. Frank N. Mitchell*	Hansan-ni	1950	7th Marines
Pfc. Walter C. Monegan, Jr.*	Sosa-ri	1950	1st Marines
Pfc. Whitt L. Moreland*	Yanggu	1951	5th Marines
2d Lt. Raymond G. Murphy	Ungok Hill	1953	5th Marines
Maj. Reginald R. Myers	Hagaru	1950	1st Marines
Pfc. Eugene A. Obregon*	Seoul	1950	5th Marines
2d Lt. George H. O'Brien	The Hook	1952	7th Marines
Cpl. Lee H. Phillips	Sudong	1950	7th Marines
Sgt. James I. Poynter*	Sudong	1950	7th Marines
2d Lt. George H. Ramer*	Hill 680	1951	7th Marines
2d Lt. Robert D. Reem*	Funchilin Pass	1950	7th Marines
Staff Sgt. William E. Shuck, Jr.*	Outpost Yoke	1952	7th Marines
Pfc. Robert E. Simanek	Outpost Irene	1952	5th Marines
Capt. Carl L. Sitter	Hagaru	1950	1st Marines
2d Lt. Sherrod E. Skinner*	The Hook	1952	11th Marines
Staff Sgt. Archie Van Winkle	Sudong	1950	7th Marines
Cpl. Joseph Vittori*	Hill 749	1951	1st Marines
Staff Sgt. Lewis G. Watkins*	Outpost Frisco	1952	7th Marines
Tech. Sgt. Harold E. Wilson	Horseshoe Ridge	1951	1st Marines
Staff Sgt. William G. Windrich*	Yudam-ni	1950	5th Marines

Vietnam War 1965–1973

| Pfc. James Anderson, Jr.* | Cam Lo | 1967 | 3rd Marines |
| Lance Cpl. Richard A. Anderson* | Quang Tri Province | 1969 | 3rd Reconnaissance Battalion |

837

NAME	PLACE	DATE	UNIT
Pfc. Oscar P. Austin*	Near Da Nang	1969	7th Marines
Lance Cpl. Jedh C. Barker*	Con Thien	1967	4th Marines
1st Lt. Harvey C. Barnum, Jr.	Ky Phu	1965	9th Marines
2d Lt. John P. Bobo*	Quang Tri Province	1967	9th Marines
Pfc. Daniel D. Bruce*	Quang Nam Province	1969	5th Marines
Pfc. Robert C. Burke*	Le Nam	1968	27th Marines
Pfc. Bruce W. Carter*	Quang Tri Province	1969	3rd Marines
Pfc. Raymond M. Clausen		1970	HMM-263
Pfc. Ronald L. Coker*	Quang Tri Province	1969	3rd Marines
Staff Sgt. Peter S. Connor*	Quang Ngai Province	1966	3rd Marines
Col. Donald G. Cook*	Phouc Tuy Province	1964–67	Senior Marine Advisor, Republic of Vietnam
Lance Cpl. Thomas E. Creek*	Cam Lo	1969	9th Marines
Sgt. Rodney M. Davis*	Quang Nam Province	1967	5th Marines
Lance Cpl. Emilio A. De La Garza, Jr.*	Near Da Nang	1970	1st Marines
Pfc. Ralph E. Dias*		1969	7th Marines
Pfc. Douglas E. Dickey*	Gio Linh	1967	4th Marines
Sgt. Paul H. Foster*	Con Thien	1967	4th Marines
1st Lt. Wesley L. Fox	A Shau Valley	1969	9th Marines
Sgt. Alfredo Gonzalez*	Hue	1968	1st Marines
Capt. James A. Graham*	Quang Tin Province	1967	5th Marines
2d Lt. Terrance C. Graves*	Quang Tri Province	1968	3rd Reconnaissance Battalion
Staff Sgt. Jimmie E. Howard	Chu Lai	1966	1st Reconnaissance Battalion
Lance Cpl. James D. Howe*	Quang Nam Province	1970	7th Marines
Pfc. Robert H. Jenkins, Jr.*	Fire Support Base Argonne	1969	3rd Reconnaissance Battalion
Lance Cpl. Jose F. Jimenez*	Que Son Valley	1969	7th Marines
Pfc. Ralph H. Johnson*	Quan Duc Duc Valley	1968	1st Reconnaissance Battalion

838

Name	Location	Year	Unit
Lance Cpl. Miguel Keith*	Quang Ngai Province	1970	Combined Action Platoon 1-2-3
Staff Sgt. Allan J. Kellogg, Jr.	Quang Nam Province	1970	5th Marines
Capt. Howard V. Lee	Cam Lo	1966	4th Marines
Capt. James E. Livingston	Dai Do	1968	4th Marines
Pfc. Gary W. Martini*	Que Son Valley	1967	1st Marines
Cpl. Larry L. Maxam*	Cam Lo	1968	4th Marines
Staff Sgt. John J. McGinty III	Cam Lo	1966	4th Marines
Capt. Robert J. Modrzejewski	Cam Lo	1966	4th Marines
Cpl. William D. Morgan*	Quang Tri Province	1969	9th Marines
Pfc. Melvin E. Newlin*	Nong Son	1967	5th Marines
Lance Cpl. Thomas P. Noonan, Jr.*	A Shau Valley	1969	9th Marines
Cpl. Robert E. O'Malley	Van Tuong Peninsula	1965	3rd Marines
Lance Cpl. Joe C. Paul*	Chu Lai	1965	4th Marines
Cpl. William T. Perkins, Jr.*	Quang Tri	1967	3rd Marine Division (combat photographer)
Sgt. Lawrence D. Peters*	Quang Tin Province	1967	5th Marines
Pfc. Jimmy W. Phipps*	An Hoa	1969	1st Engineer Battalion
Lance Cpl. Richard A. Pittman	Near Demilitarized Zone	1966	5th Marines
Capt. Stephen W. Pless	Quang Ngai	1967	VMO-6
Lance Cpl. William R. Prom*	An Hoa	1969	3rd Marines
1st Lt. Frank S. Reasoner*	Da Nang	1965	3rd Reconnaissance Battalion
Sgt. Walter K. Singleton*	Gio Linh	1967	9th Marines
Cpl. Larry E. Smedley*	Quang Nam Province	1967	7th Marines
Staff Sgt. Karl G. Taylor, Sr.*	Near Da Nang	1968	26th Marines
Capt. M. Sando Vargas, Jr.	Dai Do	1968	4th Marines
Lance Cpl. Lester W. Weber*	Quang Nam Province	1968	7th Marines
Lance Cpl. Roy M. Wheat*	Quang Nam Province	1967	7th Marines

NAME	PLACE	DATE	UNIT
Pfc. Dewayne F. Williams*	Quang Nam Province	1968	1st Marines
Pfc. Alfred M. Wilson*	Quang Tri Province	1969	9th Marines
Lance Cpl. Kenneth L. Worley*	Quang Nam Province	1968	7th Marines

Primary source: Reference Information Pamphlet, History and Museums Division, USMC.

Source Notes

MCH—This designation, frequently used in the following documentation, means that the indicated source material is located in the archives of the History and Museums Division, Headquarters, U.S. Marine Corps.

Part I
The Early Years 1775–1902/pages 23–95

1 M. ALMY ALDRICH, *History of the United States Marine Corps* (Boston: Henry L. Shepard and Co., 1875), p. 33.

2 JOHN TREVETT, "Journal of John Trevett," *Rhode Island Historical Magazine*, vol. 7 (1887), p. 38. Original is in the Newport Historical Society, Newport, Rhode Island.

3 CHARLES OSCAR PAULLIN, *The Navy of the American Revolution* (Cleveland: Burrows Brothers Co., 1906), p. 36.

4 PAULLIN, *The Navy of the American Revolution*, p. 206; and Saltonstall Letters dated June 14 and 19, 1780, *Records and Papers of the New London County Historical Society*, Part IV, vol. 1 (New London, Connecticut, 1893).

5 ALBERT BUSHNELL HART, *American History Told by Contemporaries*, vol. 2: 1689–1783 (New York: Macmillan Co., 1896; reprint ed. New York: Macmillan Co., 1906), pp. 587–90.

6 GEORGE R. CLARK, et al., *A Short History of the United States Navy* (Philadelphia: J.B. Lippincott Co., 1910–30), p. 84.

7 *Biographical File on Franklin Wharton* (MCH).

8 DAVID PORTER, *Journal of a Cruise made to the Pacific Ocean by Captain David Porter in the United States Frigate Essex, in the Years 1812, 1813 and 1814* (Philadelphia: Bradford and Inskeep, 1815), p. 186.

9 THEODORE ROOSEVELT, *The Naval War of 1812*, 2 vols. (New York: G.P. Putnam's Sons, 1882), p. 28.

10 *1812 File* (MCH).

11 GRANT FOREMAN, *Indian Removal* (Norman: University of Oklahoma Press, 1932), pp. 166–76.

12 *Ibid.*, p. 176.

13 JOHN T. SPRAGUE, *The Origins, Progress, and Conclusion of the Florida War* (New York: D. Appleton and Co., 1847), p. 216.

14 *The Century*, April 1891, p. 923.

15 Letter dated 25 October 1847, *Biographical File of George H. Terrett* (MCH).

16 U.S. Congress. Senate. *Message of the President of the U.S. to the Two*

Houses of Congress at the Commencement of the Second Session of the Thirty-seventh Congress, S. Exec. Dec. 1, 1861, p. 792. Harris Report to Welles, November 23, 1861.

17 U.S. Congress. Senate. *Message of the President,* p. 793.

18 Report of Flag Officer William Mervine, *1861 File* (MCH).

19 *Diary of Oscar Smith, U.S. Marine Corps, Aboard Flagship Hartford, 1861–1862* (Library of Congress: Transcript with foreword by Carl Smith, dated 24 August 1937).

20 *Philippine Islands 1898–99 File, Philippine Islands Samar File, Biographical File on Littleton W.T. Waller* (MCH).

Part II
World War I 1914–1919/*pages 97–145*

1 FLOYD GIBBONS, *And They Thought We Wouldn't Fight* (New York: George H. Doran Co., 1918), p. 304.

2 JAMES G. HARBORD, *The American Army in France 1917–1919* (Boston: Little, Brown & Co., 1936), p. 290.

3 ROBERT B. ASPREY, *At Belleau Wood* (New York: G.P. Putnam's Sons, 1965), pp. 182–83.

4 Lecture, May 21, 1915, quoted in Jack Shulimson, "The First to Fight: Marine Corps Expansion, 1914–1918," *Prologue,* Spring 1976, p. 6.

5 JACK SHULIMSON, "The First to Fight, A Study of the Marine Corps Expansion to Meet the Exigencies of War during the Commandancy of George Barnett 1914–1918," undated manuscript (MCH), p. 17.

6 Eds. of American Heritage, narrative by S. L. A. Marshall, *The American Heritage History of World War I* (New York: American Heritage Publishing Co., 1964), p. 280.

7 *Ibid.*

8 HARBORD, *The American Army in France 1917–1919,* p. 283.

9 FREDERIC MAY WISE, as told to Meigs O. Frost, *A Marine Tells It to You,* (New York: J. H. Sears & Co., 1929), p. 204.

10 *Ibid.,* p. 202.

11 A. W. CATLIN with collaboration of Walter A. Dyer, *With the Help of God and a Few Marines* (Garden City, N.Y.: Doubleday, Page & Co., 1918, 1919), p. 103.

12 WISE, *A Marine Tells It to You,* p. 217.

13 *Ibid.,* p. 222.

14 ASPREY, *At Belleau Wood,* p. 251.

15 *Ibid.,* p. 258.

16 WISE, *A Marine Tells It to You,* pp. 233–34.

17 ASPREY, *At Belleau Wood,* p. 307.

18 HARBORD, *The American Army in France 1917–1919,* p. 298.

19 DON V. PARADIS, "Memoirs of Don V. Paradis, Former Gunnery Sergeant USMC," unpublished transcript of oral history report, 17 September 1973 (MCH), pp. 208–9.

20 GIBBONS, *And They Thought We Wouldn't Fight,* p. 299.

21 PARADIS, "Memoirs of Don V. Paradis," p. 87.

22 HARBORD, *The American Army in France 1917–1919*, p. 337.

23 *Ibid.*, p. 336.

24 General Orders No. 16, quoted in John A. LeJeune, *The Reminiscences of a Marine* (Philadelphia: Dorrance & Co., 1930), p. 284.

25 *Biographical File on Daniel J. Daly* (MCH).

26 HARBORD, *The American Army in France 1917–1919*, p. 452.

27 PARADIS, "Memoirs of Don V. Paradis," pp. 161–62.

28 LEJEUNE, *The Reminiscences of a Marine*, p. 402.

29 ROBERT SHERROD, *History of Marine Corps Aviation in World War II* (Washington, D.C.: Combat Forces Press, 1952), p. 17.

30 CLYDE H. METCALF, *A History of the United States Marine Corps* (New York: G. P. Putnam's Sons, 1939), p. 521.

31 Letter from Rheinbrohl, Germany, 14 December 1918, in Paradis, "Memoirs of Don V. Paradis," p. 224.

32 JOHN W. THOMASON, JR., *Fix Bayonets!* (New York: Charles Scribner's Sons, 1926), p. 232.

33 *Ibid.*, p. 239.

Part III
Imperialism in the Caribbean 1901–1934/*pages 147–203*

1 As told to Lowell Thomas, *Old Gimlet Eye: The Adventures of Smedley D. Butler* (New York: Farrar & Rinehart, 1933), p. 170.

2 DEXTER PERKINS, *The United States and the Caribbean* (Cambridge, Mass.: Harvard U. Press, 1947), p. 139.

3 *Ibid.*, pp. viii–ix.

4 GEORGE E. MOWRY, *The Era of Theodore Roosevelt and the Birth of Modern America 1900–1912* (New York: Harper & Row, 1958), p. 155.

5 THOMAS, *Old Gimlet Eye*, p. 168.

6 HOWARD F. CLINE, *The United States and Mexico* (Cambridge, Mass.: Harvard U. Press, 1953), p. 144.

7 CLYDE H. METCALF, *A History of the United States Marine Corps* (New York: G. P. Putnam's Sons, 1939), p. 413.

8 WILLIAM L. ROPER, "Air Action in Nicaragua," *Marine Corps Gazette*, November 1972, p. 54.

9 MERRITT A. EDSON, "The Coco Patrol," *Marine Corps Gazette*, November 1936, p. 41.

10 ROBERT L. DENIG, "Native Officer Corps, Guardia Nacional De Nicaragua," *Marine Corps Gazette*, November 1932, p. 77.

11 THOMAS, *Old Gimlet Eye*, p. 184.

12 *Ibid.*, p. 186.

13 *Ibid.*, p. 209.

14 JAMES H. McCROCKLIN, comp., *Garde d'Haiti 1915–1934* (Annapolis: U.S. Naval Institute, 1956), p. 74.

15 *Ibid.*, p. 79.

16 *Ibid.*, p. 141.

17 CARL KELSEY, "The American Intervention in Haiti," *Annals of the American Academy of Political and Social Science*, March 1922, p. 138.

18 McCrocklin, *Garde d'Haiti 1915–1934*, p. 154.
19 *Biographical File on Hiram I. Bearss* (MCH).
20 Metcalf, *A History of the United States Marine Corps*, p. 356.
21 Abraham F. Lowenthal, *The Dominican Intervention* (Cambridge, Mass.: Harvard U. Press, 1972), p. 10.
22 *The New York Times*, 1 June 1961.
23 Perkins, *The United States and the Caribbean*, p. 154.
24 Wayne A. Wiegand, "America's Dreyfus Affair?" *Biographical File on Charles H. Lauchheimer* (MCH).
25 *Biographical File on George Elliott* (MCH).
26 Kenneth J. Clifford, *Progress and Purpose: A Developmental History of the United States Marine Corps 1900–1970* (Washington, D.C.: USMC, 1973), p. 10.
27 Robert Debs Heinl, Jr., *Soldiers of the Sea* (Annapolis: U.S. Naval Institute, 1962), p. 155; Jack Shulimson and Graham A. Cosmas, "Teddy Roosevelt and the Corps' Sea-going Mission," *Marine Corps Gazette*, November 1981, pp. 54–61.
28 Dion Williams, "The Defense of Our New Naval Stations," *United States Naval Institute Proceedings*, June 1902, p. 185.
29 *Ibid.*, p. 187.

Part IV
Getting Ready 1919–1941 /pages 205–227

1 Benis M. Frank, "The Relief of General Barnett," *Records of the Columbia Historical Society of Washington, D.C.*, 1971–72, pp. 679–93; Merrill L. Bartlett, "Ouster of a Commandant," *U.S. Naval Institute Proceedings*, November 1980, pp. 62–65.
2 As told to Lowell Thomas, *Old Gimlet Eye: The Adventures of Smedley D. Butler* (New York: Farrar & Rinehart, Inc., 1933), p. 276.
3 O. Edmund Clubb, *20th Century China* (New York: Columbia U. Press, 1964), p. 52.
4 Robert Sherrod, *History of Marine Corps Aviation in World War II* (Washington, D.C.: Combat Forces Press, 1952), p. 28.
5 Clubb, *20th Century China*, p. 214.
6 Michael Blankfort, *The Big Yankee, The Life of Carlson of the Raiders* (Boston: Little, Brown & Co., 1947), p. 223.
7 Memorandum from Commandant dated 2 April 1924, *Biographical File on Earl H. Ellis* (MCH).
8 Waite W. Worden, "Lt Col. Earl Ellis," p. 3, *Biographical File on Earl H. Ellis* (MCH).
9 Holland M. Smith and Percy Finch, *Coral and Brass* (New York: Charles Scribner's Sons, 1948), pp. 64–65.
10 John L. Zimmerman, "The Marines' First Spy," *The Saturday Evening Post*, 23 November 1946, p. 100.
11 "Advanced Base Operations in Micronesia," quoted in Jeter A. Isely and Philip A. Crowl, *The U.S. Marines and Amphibious Warfare* (Princeton: Princeton U. Press, 1951), p. 27.

12 KENNETH J. CLIFFORD, *Progress and Purpose: A Developmental History of the United States Marine Corps 1900–1970* (Washington, D.C.: USMC, 1973), p. 30.

13 *Ibid.*

14 *Ibid.*, p. 36.

15 ISELY AND CROWL, *The U.S. Marines and Amphibious Warfare*, p. 4.

16 GEORGE CARROLL DYER, *The Amphibians Came to Conquer—The Story of Admiral Richmond Kelly Turner* (Washington D.C.: GPO, 1969?), p. 203.

17 ISELY AND CROWL, *The U.S. Marines and Amphibious Warfare*, p. 67.

Part V
World War II 1941–1949/*pages 229–425*

1 WALTER LORD, *Day of Infamy* (New York: Bantam Books, 1958), p. 121.

2 FRANK O. HOUGH, VERLE E. LUDWIG, HENRY I. SHAW, JR., *History of U.S. Marine Corps Operations in World War II*, vol. 1: *Pearl Harbor to Guadalcanal* (Arlington, Va.: Headquarters, USMC, undated), p. 70.

3 SAMUEL ELIOT MORISON, *History of United States Naval Operations*, vol. 3: *The Rising Sun in the Pacific 1931–April 1942* (Boston: Little, Brown & Co., 1958), p. 132.

4 *Ibid.*, p. 232.

5 *Ibid.*, p. 234.

6 *Ibid.*, p. 253.

7 HOUGH, LUDWIG, SHAW, JR., *Pearl Harbor to Guadalcanal*, p. 189.

8 *Ibid.*, pp. 188–89.

9 MORISON, *The Rising Sun in the Pacific*, p. 204.

10 S. E. SMITH, ed. and corres., *The United States Marine Corps in World War II* (New York: Random House, 1969), p. 101.

11 WILLIAM F. HOGABOOM, "Action Report: Bataan," *Marine Corps Gazette*, April 1946, pp. 25–33.

12 S. E. SMITH, *The United States Marine Corps in World War II*, p. 108.

13 ALEXANDER A. VANDEGRIFT as told to Robert B. Asprey, *Once a Marine* (New York: Norton & Co., 1964), p. 100.

14 SAMUEL B. GRIFFITH II, *The Battle for Guadalcanal* (Philadelphia: J. B. Lippincott Co., 1963), pp. 23–24.

15 VANDEGRIFT, *Once a Marine*, p. 122.

16 S. E. SMITH, *The United States Marine Corps in World War II*, p. 166; MCH files. Pfc. Ahrens was awarded the Navy Cross.

17 JETER A. ISELY AND PHILIP A. CROWL, *The U.S. Marines and Amphibious Warfare* (Princeton: Princeton U. Press, 1951), p. 129.

18 VANDEGRIFT, *Once a Marine*, p. 129.

19 HOUGH, LUDWIG, SHAW, JR., *Pearl Harbor to Guadalcanal*, p. 260; Samuel Eliot Morison, *History of United States Naval Operations in World War II*, vol. 5: *The Struggle for Guadalcanal August 1942–February 1943* (Boston: Little, Brown & Co., 1949), p. 17.

20 GEORGE CARROLL DYER, *The Amphibians Came to Conquer—The Story of Admiral Richmond Kelly Turner* (Washington, D.C.: GPO, 1969?), p. 358.

21 VANDEGRIFT, *Once a Marine*, p. 142.

22 MORISON, *The Struggle for Guadalcanal,* p. 73.
23 VANDEGRIFT, *Once a Marine,* p. 153.
24 *Biographical File on John Basilone* (MCH).
25 VANDEGRIFT, *Once a Marine,* p. 153.
26 HOUGH, LUDWIG, SHAW, JR., *Pearl Harbor to Guadalcanal,* p. 357.
27 MORISON, *The Struggle for Guadalcanal,* p. 287.
28 HOUGH, LUDWIG, SHAW, JR., *Pearl Harbor to Guadalcanal,* p. 372.
29 HENRY I. SHAW, JR., AND DOUGLAS T. KANE, *History of U.S. Marine Corps Operations in World War II,* vol. 2: *Isolation of Rabaul* (Arlington, Va.: Headquarters, USMC, 1963), p. 138.
30 SAMUEL ELIOT MORISON, *History of United States Naval Operations in World War II,* vol. 6: *Breaking the Bismarcks Barrier 22 July 1942–1 May 1944* (Boston: Little, Brown & Co., 1950), p. 224.
31 *Ibid.,* p. 370.
32 *Ibid.,* p. 378.
33 SHAW, JR., AND KANE, *Isolation of Rabaul,* p. 370.
34 S. E. SMITH, *The United States Marine Corps in World War II,* p. 490; Robert Leckie, *Strong Men Armed* (New York: Random House, 1962), p. 264.
35 ROBERT SHERROD, *Tarawa, The Story of a Battle* (New York: Sloan & Pearce, 1949), pp. 47, 108; Isely and Crowl, *The U.S. Marines and Amphibious Warfare,* p. 236.
36 SAMUEL ELIOT MORISON, *History of United States Naval Operations in World War II,* vol. 7: *Aleutians, Gilberts and Marshalls June 1942–April 1944* (Boston: Little, Brown & Co., 1951), p. 148.
37 HENRY I. SHAW, JR., BERNARD C. NALTY, EDWIN T. TURNBLADH, *History of U.S. Marine Corps Operations in World War II,* vol. 3: *Central Pacific Drive* (Arlington, Va.: Headquarters, USMC, 1966), p. 61.
38 *Ibid.,* p. 79.
39 ISELY AND CROWL, *The U.S. Marines and Amphibious Warfare,* pp. 251–52.
40 HOLLAND M. SMITH AND PERCY FINCH, *Coral and Brass* (New York: Charles Scribner's Sons, 1948), pp. 119–20, 142.
41 SHAW, JR., NALTY, TURNBLADH, *Central Pacific Drive,* p. 71.
42 SHERROD, *Tarawa, The Story of a Battle,* p. 35.
43 VANDEGRIFT, *Once a Marine,* p. 242.
44 ISELY AND CROWL, *The U.S. Marines and Amphibious Warfare,* pp. 255–56.
45 MORISON, *Aleutians, Gilberts and Marshalls,* p. 265.
46 *Ibid.,* p. 298.
47 SAMUEL ELIOT MORISON, *History of U.S. Naval Operations in World War II,* vol. 8: *New Guinea and the Marianas March 1944–August 1944* (Boston: Little, Brown & Co., 1953), p. 159.
48 H. M. SMITH AND FINCH, *Coral and Brass,* p. 161.
49 SHAW, JR., NALTY, TURNBLADH, *Central Pacific Drive,* pp. 240–41; Isely and Crowl, *The U.S. Marines and Amphibious Warfare,* p. 341.
50 SHAW, JR., NALTY, TURNBLADH, *Central Pacific Drive,* p. 295.
51 MORISON, *The Rising Sun in the Pacific,* p. vii.
52 *Ibid.,* p. 318.
53 SHAW, JR., NALTY, TURNBLADH, *Central Pacific Drive,* p. 313.

54 H. M. SMITH AND FINCH, *Coral and Brass*, p. 181.

55 *Ibid.*

56 ISELY AND CROWL, *The U.S. Marines and Amphibious Warfare*, pp. 346–47.

57 *Ibid.*, pp. 342–47; Shaw, Jr., Nalty, Turnbladh, *Central Pacific Drive*, pp. 302–20; H. M. Smith and Finch, *Coral and Brass*, pp. 176–88.

58 H. M. SMITH AND FINCH, *Coral and Brass*, pp. 196–97.

59 SHAW, JR., NALTY, TURNBLADH, *Central Pacific Drive*, p. 346.

60 H. M. SMITH AND FINCH, *Coral and Brass*, p. 189.

61 *Ibid.*, p. 210.

62 MICHAEL BLANKFORT, *The Big Yankee, The Life of Carlson of the Raiders* (Boston: Little Brown & Co., 1947), p. 337.

63 H. M. SMITH AND FINCH, *Coral and Brass*, p. 212.

64 SHAW, JR., NALTY, TURNBLADH, *Central Pacific Drive*, p. 392.

65 *Ibid.*, p. 448.

66 MORISON, *New Guinea and the Marianas*, p. 380.

67 Medal of Honor citation.

68 ISELY AND CROWL, *The U.S. Marines and Amphibious Warfare*, p. 376.

69 WILLIAM F. HALSEY AND J. BRYAN III, *Admiral Halsey's Story* (New York: McGraw-Hill Book Co., 1947), p. 199.

70 *Ibid.*, p. 195.

71 SAMUEL ELIOT MORISON, *History of United States Naval Operations in World War II*, vol. 12: *Leyte June 1944–January 1945* (Boston: Little, Brown & Co., 1958), p. 47.

72 GEORGE W. GARAND AND TRUMAN R. STROBRIDGE, *History of U.S. Marine Corps Operations in World War II*, vol. 4: *Western Pacific Operations* (Arlington, Va.: Headquarters, USMC, 1971), p. 285.

73 *The New York Times*, 22 September 1943, quoted in Robert Sherrod, *History of Marine Corps Aviation in World War II* (Washington, D.C.: Combat Forces Press, 1952), p. 264.

74 *Ibid.*, p. 265.

75 MORISON, *Leyte*, p. 6.

76 Letter by Chaplain Edgar E. Siskin in *Hebrew Union College Bulletin*, April 1945, pp. 7–8, quoted in Garand and Strobridge, *Western Pacific Operations*, p. 109.

77 *Ibid.*, p. 110.

78 GEORGE P. HUNT, *Coral Comes High* (New York: New American Library, 1957), p. 29.

79 *Ibid.*, pp. 72–73.

80 S. E. SMITH, *The United States Marine Corps in World War II*, p. 675, quoted from Russell G. Davis and Brent K. Ashabranner, *Marine at War* (Boston: Little, Brown & Co., 1961).

81 Medal of Honor citation; Garand and Strobridge, *Western Pacific Operations*, pp. 157–58.

82 *Ibid.*, p. 161.

83 S. E. SMITH, *The United States Marine Corps in World War II*, p. 680.

84 BURKE DAVIS, *Marine! The Life of Lt. Gen. Lewis B. (Chesty) Puller, USMC (Ret.)* (Boston: Little, Brown & Co., 1962), p. 226.

85 GARAND AND STROBRIDGE, *Western Pacific Operations*, p. 161.

86 SHERROD, *History of Marine Corps Aviation in World War II*, p. 325.
87 *Ibid.*, p. 303; Garand and Strobridge, *Western Pacific Operations*, p. 347.
88 RICHARD F. NEWCOMB, *Iwo Jima* (New York: Holt Rinehart & Winston, 1965), p. 46.
89 ISELY AND CROWL, *The U.S. Marines and Amphibious Warfare*, p. 485.
90 *Ibid.*, p. 487.
91 S. E. SMITH, *The United States Marine Corps in World War II*, p. 748.
92 H. M. SMITH AND FINCH, *Coral and Brass*, p. 270.
93 GARAND AND STROBRIDGE, *Western Pacific Operations*, p. 647; ALVIN M. JOSEPHY, JR., "Iwo Jima," *American Heritage*, June/July 1981, pp. 92–101.
94 Medal of Honor citation.
95 Medal of Honor citation.
96 GARAND AND STROBRIDGE, *Western Pacific Operations*, p. 681.
97 *Ibid.*, p. 710.
98 *Ibid.*, p. 712.
99 *The New York Times*, 26 February 1945, p. 1 quoted in *Ibid.*, p. 713.
100 ISELY AND CROWL, *The U.S. Marines and Amphibious Warfare*, p. 475.
101 H. M. SMITH AND FINCH, *Coral and Brass*, p. 245.
102 ISELY AND CROWL, *The U.S. Marines and Amphibious Warfare*, p. 558.
103 SAMUEL ELIOT MORISON, *History of United States Naval Operations in World War II*, vol. 14: *Victory in the Pacific 1945* (Boston: Little, Brown & Co., 1960), p. 217.
104 *Ibid.*, p. 172.
105 ERNIE PYLE, *Last Chapter* (New York: Henry Holt & Co., 1946), pp. 139–40.
106 Letter by Lt. M. H. Jaffe dated 14 April 1945.
107 VANDEGRIFT, *Once a Marine*, p. 291.
108 MORISON, *Victory in the Pacific*, p. 273.
109 Medal of Honor citation.
110 BENIS M. FRANK AND HENRY I. SHAW, JR., *History of U.S. Marine Operations in World War II*, vol. 5: *Victory and Occupation* (Arlington, Va.: Headquarters, USMC, 1968), p. 213.
111 Medal of Honor citation.
112 ISELY AND CROWL, *The U.S. Marines and Amphibious Warfare*, p. 575.
113 SHERROD, *History of Marine Corps Aviation in World War II*, p. 397.
114 BEVAN G. CASS, ed., *History of the Sixth Marine Division* (Washington, D.C.: Infantry Journal Press, 1948), p. 120.
115 Letter by Lt. M. H. Jaffe dated 17 June 1945.
116 ISELY AND CROWL, *The U.S. Marines and Amphibious Warfare*, p. 547.
117 CASS, *History of the Sixth Marine Division*, p. 157.
118 GEORGE MCMILLAN, *The Old Breed, A History of the First Marine Division in World War II* (Washington, D.C.: Infantry Journal Press, 1949), p. 413.
119 Quoted in Frank and Shaw, Jr., *Victory and Occupation*, p. 337.
120 Letter by Lt. M. H. Jaffe, 17 June 1945.
121 ROY E. APPLEMAN, et al., *Okinawa: The Last Battle* (Washington, D.C.: Historical Division, Department of the Army, 1948), pp. 384–86.
122 MCMILLAN, *The Old Breed*, pp. 423–24.

123 Quoted in Frank and Shaw, Jr., *Victory and Occupation*, p. 401.
124 JAMES S. SANTELLI, *A Brief History of the 4th Marines* (Arlington, Va.: Headquarters, USMC, 1970), p. 36.
125 ROBERT DEBS HEINL, JR., *Soldiers of the Sea* (Annapolis, Md.: U.S. Naval Institute, 1962), p. 519.
126 McMILLAN, *The Old Breed*, pp. 428–29.
127 FRANK AND SHAW, JR., *Victory and Occupation*, p. 564.
128 *Ibid.*, p. 572.
129 *Ibid.*, p. 573.
130 Quoted in O. Edmund Clubb, *20th Century China* (New York: Columbia U. Press, 1964), p. 263.
131 Quoted from *The North China Marine*, Tientsin, 28 September 1946, p. 1 in Frank and Shaw, Jr., *Victory and Occupation*, p. 618.
132 *Ibid.*, p. 625.
133 *Ibid.*, p. 633.
134 CLUBB, *20th Century China*, p. 290.
135 *Ibid.*, p. 295.
136 FRANK AND SHAW, JR., *Victory and Occupation*, p. 649.
137 HENRY I. SHAW, JR., AND RALPH W. DONNELLY, *Blacks in the Marine Corps* (Washington, D.C.: History and Museums Division, Headquarters, USMC, 1975), p. 1.
138 *Ibid.*
139 *Ibid.*, p. 3.
140 *Ibid.*, p. 35.
141 FRANK AND SHAW, JR., *Victory and Occupation*, pp. 446–47.
142 ISELY AND CROWL, *The U.S. Marines and Amphibious Warfare*, p. 12.

Part VI
The Korean War 1946–1953/*pages 427–589*

1 ALEXANDER A. VANDEGRIFT as told to Robert B. Asprey, *Once a Marine* (New York: Norton & Co., 1964), p. 295.
2 *Ibid.*, p. 308.
3 LYNN MONTROSS, HUBARD D. KUOKKA, NORMAN W. HICKS, *U.S. Marine Operations in Korea 1950–1953*, vol. 4: *The East-Central Front* (Arlington, Va.: Headquarters, USMC, 1962), p. 187.
4 HENRY I. SHAW, JR., AND RALPH W. DONNELLY, *Blacks in the Marine Corps* (Washington, D.C.: History and Museums Division, Headquarters, USMC, 1975), p. 59.
5 HARRY S TRUMAN, *Memoirs by Harry S Truman*, vol. 2: *Years of Trial and Hope* (Garden City, N.Y.: Doubleday & Co., 1956), p. 46.
6 October 25, 1945, quoted in Vandegrift, *Once a Marine*, p. 301.
7 *Ibid.*, p. 316.
8 *Ibid.*, p. 301.
9 *Ibid.*, p. 316.
10 WALTER MILLIS, ED., *The Forrestal Diaries* (New York: The Viking Press, 1951), p. 224.

11 Quoted in G. C. Thomas, R. D. Heinl, Jr., A. A. Ageton, *The Marine Officer's Guide* (Annapolis, Md.: U.S. Naval Institute, 1956), p. 70.

12 MERRITT A. EDSON, "Power-Hungry Men in Uniform," *Collier's*, 27 August 1949.

13 ROBERT S. ALLEN, "Too Much Brass," *Collier's*, 6 September 1947.

14 ROBERT LECKIE, *Conflict: The History of the Korean War, 1950–53* (New York: G. P. Putnam's Sons, 1962), p. 34; and Lynn Montross and Nicholas A. Canzona, *U.S. Marine Operations in Korea 1950–1953*, vol. 1: *The Pusan Perimeter* (Arlington, Va.: Headquarters, USMC, 1954), p. 14.

15 TRUMAN, *Years of Trial and Hope*, p. 329.

16 U.S. Department of State, *American Foreign Policy 1950–1955*, Basic Documents, vols. 1 & 2, July 1957, pp. 2317–18.

17 MALCOLM W. CAGLE AND FRANK A. MANSON, *The Sea War in Korea* (Annapolis, Md.: U.S. Naval Institute, 1957), p. 31.

18 ROY E. APPLEMAN, *South to the Naktong, North to the Yalu* (Washington, D.C.: Office of the Chief of Military History, Dept. of the Army, 1961), pp. 207–8.

19 ROBERT DEBS HEINL, JR., *Soldiers of the Sea* (Annapolis, Md.: U.S. Naval Institute, 1962), p. 539; and Lynn Montross and Nicholas A. Canzona, *U.S. Marine Operations in Korea 1950–1953, vol. 2: The Inchon-Seoul Operation* (Arlington, Va.: Headquarters, USMC, 1955), pp. 10–11.

20 ANDREW GEER, *The New Breed: The Story of the U.S. Marines in Korea* (New York: Harper & Bros., 1952), p. 56.

21 APPLEMAN, *South to the Naktong, North to the Yalu*, p. 308.

22 JAMES A. FIELD, JR., *History of United States Naval Operations Korea* (Washington, D.C.: GPO, 1962), p. 152.

23 R. L. MURRAY, "The First Naktong," *Marine Corps Gazette*, November 1965, pp. 84–85.

24 MONTROSS AND CANZONA, *The Pusan Perimeter*, p. 186.

25 *Ibid.*, pp. 203–4.

26 Escort carrier *Sicily* action report quoted in Cagle and Manson, *The Sea War in Korea*, p. 65.

27 APPLEMAN, *South to the Naktong, North to the Yalu*, p. 453.

28 MONTROSS AND CANZONA, *The Pusan Perimeter*, p. 236.

29 *Congressional Record*, 16 May 1952, pp. 5446–47, quoted in Heinl, Jr., *Soldiers of the Sea*, p. 547.

30 MONTROSS AND CANZONA, *The Pusan Perimeter*, p. 239.

31 WALTER KARIG, MALCOLM W. CAGLE, FRANK A. MANSON, *Battle Report: The War in Korea*, vol. 6 (New York: Rinehart & Co., 1952), p. 169.

32 FIELD, JR., *History of the United States Naval Operations Korea*, p. 179.

33 MONTROSS AND CANZONA, *The Inchon-Seoul Operation*, p. 90.

34 *Ibid.*, p. 92; Robert Debs Heinl, Jr., *Victory at High Tide: The Inchon-Seoul Campaign* (Philadelphia: J. B. Lippincott Co., 1968), p. 93.

35 Medal of Honor citation.

36 MONTROSS AND CANZONA, *The Inchon-Seoul Operation*, p. 161.

37 *Ibid.*, p. 214.

38 Interview with Lt. Gen. Robert H. Barrow, Headquarters, USMC, Arlington, Va., 27 May 1976.

39 MONTROSS AND CANZONA, *The Inchon-Seoul Operation*, p. 251.
40 APPLEMAN, *South to the Naktong, North to the Yalu*, p. 527.
41 HEINL, JR., *Victory at High Tide: The Inchon-Seoul Campaign*, pp. 212–13.
42 MONTROSS AND CANZONA, *The Inchon-Seoul Operation*, p. 247; Appleman, *South to the Naktong, North to the Yalu*, pp. 524–25; Geer, *The New Breed*, pp. 156–62.
43 APPLEMAN, *South to the Naktong, North to the Yalu*, p. 525.
44 MONTROSS AND CANZONA, *The Inchon-Seoul Operation*, pp. 256–57; Karig, Cagle, Manson, *Battle Report: The War in Korea*, vol. 6 pp. 258–59.
45 BURKE DAVIS, *Marine! The Life of Lt. Gen. Lewis B. (Chesty) Puller, USMC (Ret.)* (Boston: Little, Brown & Co., 1947), p. 272.
46 *Special Action Report*, night of 25–26 September 1950, from Supporting Arms Coordinator to Battalion Commander, 3rd Battalion, 1st Marines, 27 September 1950 (MCH).
47 MONTROSS AND CANZONA, *The Inchon-Seoul Operation*, p. 264.
48 NORMAN R. STANFORD, "Road Junction," *Marine Corps Gazette*, September 1951, p. 19.
49 MONTROSS AND CANZONA, *The Inchon-Seoul Operation*, pp. 297–98.
50 CAGLE AND MANSON, *The Sea War in Korea*, p. 75.
51 DEAN ACHESON, *Present at the Creation* (New York: W.W. Norton & Co., Inc., 1969), p. 447.
52 *Ibid.*, p. 451.
53 Joint Chiefs of Staff message 92801, 27 September 1950, quoted in Lynn Montross and Nicholas A. Canzona, *U.S. Marine Operations in Korea 1950–1953*, vol. 3: *The Chosin Reservoir Campaign* (Arlington, Va.: Headquarters, USMC, 1957), pp. 5–6.
54 U.S. Department of State, *American Foreign Policy 1950–1955*, pp. 2576–77.
55 ACHESON, *Present at the Creation*, p. 454.
56 Quoted in Appleman, *South to the Naktong, North to the Yalu*, p. 270.
57 ALLEN S. WHITING, *China Crosses the Yalu: The Decision to Enter the Korean War* (New York: The Macmillan Co., 1960), p. 118.
58 APPLEMAN, *South to the Naktong, North to the Yalu*, p. 757.
59 MONTROSS AND CANZONA, *The Chosin Reservoir Campaign*, p. 131.
60 APPLEMAN, *South to the Naktong, North to the Yalu*, p. 670.
61 MONTROSS AND CANZONA, *The Chosin Reservoir Campaign*, p. 39.
62 *Ibid.*, p. 67.
63 *Ibid.*, p. 98.
64 Medal of Honor citation; Geer, *The New Breed*, p. 233.
65 Medal of Honor citation; Geer, *The New Breed*, p. 234.
66 Medal of Honor citation; Phillips "Wound Card" on file MCH.
67 Medal of Honor citation; Montross and Canzona, *The Chosin Reservoir Campaign*, p. 119.
68 APPLEMAN, *South to the Naktong, North to the Yalu*, p. 772.
69 Quoted in Montross and Canzona, *The Chosin Reservoir Campaign*, p. 133.
70 APPLEMAN, *South to the Naktong, North to the Yalu*, pp. 772–73.
71 Medal of Honor citation; Geer, *The New Breed*, pp. 262–63.
72 Medal of Honor citation; Robert Leckie, *The March to Glory* (Cleveland: The World Publishing Co., 1960), p. 65.

73 Myers' Medal of Honor citation; Montross and Canzona, *The Chosin Reservoir Campaign*, pp. 216–18.

74 LECKIE, *The March to Glory*, p. 80.

75 Medal of Honor citation.

76 LECKIE, *The March to Glory*, p. 118.

77 Medal of Honor citation.

78 U.S. Department of State, *American Foreign Policy 1950–1955*, p. 2585.

79 MONTROSS AND CANZONA, *The Chosin Reservoir Campaign*, p. 255.

80 HEINL, JR., *Soldiers of the Sea*, p. 561.

81 Medal of Honor citation.

82 Medal of Honor citation.

83 Interview with Lt. Gen. Robert H. Barrow, Headquarters, USMC, Arlington, Va., 27 May 1976.

84 MONTROSS AND CANZONA, *The Chosin Reservoir Campaign*, p. 317; JOSEPH R. OWEN, "Chosin Reservoir Remembered," *Marine Corps Gazette*, December 1980, pp. 52–58.

85 Quoted in *ibid.*, p. 350; quoted in Ernest H. Giusti and Kenneth W. Condit, "Marine Air Covers the Breakout," *Marine Corps Gazette*, August 1952, p. 27.

86 *Time* (Pacific edition) 18 December 1950, pp. 18–19, quoted in Montross and Canzona, *The Chosin Reservoir Campaign*, p. 333.

87 *Newsweek*, 11 December 1950, p. 11, quoted in *ibid.*, p. 334.

88 *Time* (Pacific edition) 11 December 1950, p. 9, quoted in *ibid.*

89 *Ibid.*, p. 334 footnote.

90 Letter dated 4 December 1950 quoted in Davis, *Marine! The Life of Lt. Gen. Lewis B. (Chesty) Puller, USMC (Ret.)*, p. 312.

91 *Ibid.*, p. 325.

92 MacArthur letter dated 17 October 1956 quoted in Montross and Canzona, *The Chosin Reservoir Campaign*, p. 346.

93 TRUMAN, *Years of Trial and Hope*, p. 442.

94 *Ibid.*, p. 416.

95 ACHESON, *Present at the Creation*, p. 527.

96 LYNN MONTROSS, HUBARD D. KUOKKA, NORMAN W. HICKS, *U.S. Marine Operations in Korea 1950–1953*, vol. 4: *The East-Central Front* (Arlington, Va.: Headquarters, USMC, 1962), p. 150.

97 Medal of Honor citation.

98 Medal of Honor citation.

99 Medal of Honor citation.

100 MONTROSS, KUOKKA, HICKS, *The East-Central Front*, p. 186.

101 *Ibid.*, p. 190.

102 *Ibid.*, p. 193; Medal of Honor citation.

103 Quoted in Montross, Kuokka, Hicks, *The East-Central Front*, p. 199.

104 PAT MEID AND JAMES M. YINGLING, *U.S. Marine Operations in Korea 1950–1953*, vol. 5: *Operations in West Korea* (Washington, D.C.: Headquarters, USMC, 1972), p. 36; Medal of Honor citation.

105 *Ibid.*, p. 83; Medal of Honor citations.

106 *Ibid.*, pp. 91–92, Medal of Honor citation.

107 *Ibid.*, p. 95.

108 *Ibid.*, p. 93.
109 *Ibid.*, p. 127; Medal of Honor citation.
110 *Ibid.*, p. 138.
111 *Ibid.*, p. 147; Medal of Honor citation.
112 *Ibid.*, p. 163; Medal of Honor citation.
113 *Ibid.*, p. 168; Medal of Honor citation.
114 *Ibid.*, p. 206–7; Medal of Honor citations.
115 MORRIS R. WILLS as told to J. ROBERT MOSKIN, *Turncoat* (New York: Prentice-Hall, 1966, 1968), pp. 1–17.
116 Medal of Honor citation.
117 MEID AND YINGLING, *Operations in West Korea*, p. 287; Medal of Honor citation.
118 *Ibid.*, p. 294; Medal of Honor citation.
119 *Ibid.*, p. 296; Medal of Honor citation.
120 *Ibid.*, p. 311.
121 EUGENE KINKEAD, *In Every War But One* (New York: W. W. Norton & Co., 1959), p. 163.
122 MEID AND YINGLING, *Operations in West Korea*, p. 442.
123 KINKEAD, *In Every War But One*, pp. 163–64.
124 *Ibid.*, p. 16.
125 Quoted in Meid and Yingling, *Operations in West Korea*, p. 440.
126 *Ibid.*, p. 483.
127 *Ibid.*, p. 513.
128 CAGLE AND MANSON, *The Sea War in Korea*, p. 270.
129 MATTHEW B. RIDGWAY, *The War in Korea* (London: Barrie & Rockliff, 1967), p. 244.
130 MEID AND YINGLING, *Operations in West Korea*, p. 496.
131 *Ibid.*, p. 519.
132 S. L. A. MARSHALL, *Pork Chop Hill* (New York: William Morrow & Co., 1956), p. 211.

Part VII
Tumultuous Times 1953–1965/*pages 591–615*

1 WILLIAM BAGGARLEY McKEAN, *Ribbon Creek: The Marine Corps on Trial* (New York: The Dial Press, 1958), p. 266.
2 BURKE DAVIS, *Marine! The Life of Lt. Gen. Lewis B. (Chesty) Puller, USMC (Ret.)* (Boston: Little, Brown & Co., 1962), pp. 382–84.
3 J. ROBERT MOSKIN, "Revolution in the Marine Corps," *Look*, 28 May 1957, pp. 35–43.
4 JACK SHULIMSON, *Marines in Lebanon 1958* (Washington, D.C.: Historical Branch, Headquarters, USMC, 1966), p. 12.
5 Quoted in *ibid*, p. 14.
6 *Ibid.*, p. 36.
7 ROBERT McCLINTOCK, *The Meaning of Limited War* (Boston: Houghton Mifflin Co., 1967), p. 109.
8 Quoted in Shulimson, *Marines in Lebanon 1958*, p. 17.

9 ABRAHAM F. LOWENTHAL, *The Dominican Intervention* (Cambridge, Mass.: Harvard U. Press, 1972), p. 1.
10 *Ibid.*, p. 10.
11 JOHN BARTLOW MARTIN, *Overtaken by Events* (New York: Doubleday & Co., 1966), p. 40.
12 LOWENTHAL, *The Dominican Intervention*, p. 93.
13 Quoted in Eric F. Goldman, *The Tragedy of Lyndon Johnson* (New York: Alfred A. Knopf, 1969), p. 395.
14 R. McC. TOMPKINS, "Ubique," *Marine Corps Gazette*, September 1965, p. 37.
15 LOWENTHAL, *The Dominican Intervention*, p. 124.
16 RICHARD P. STEBBINS, *The United States in World Affairs 1966* (New York: Harper & Row for the Council on Foreign Relations, 1967), pp. 306, 314.
17 DAVID M. SHOUP, "The New American Militarism," *The Atlantic*, April 1969, p. 54.
18 MARTIN, *Overtaken by Events*, p. 705.
19 J. WILLIAM FULBRIGHT, *The Arrogance of Power* (New York: Vintage Books, Random House, 1966), p. 84.

Part VIII
The Vietnam War 1954–1975/*pages 617–693*

1 GEORGE McTURNAN KAHIN AND JOHN WILSON LEWIS, *The United States in Vietnam* (New York: The Dial Press, 1969), p. 31.
2 FRANCES FITZGERALD, *Fire in the Lake* (New York: Vintage Books, Random House, 1972), pp. 342–43.
3 *Ibid.*, p. 310.
4 KAHIN AND LEWIS, *The United States in Vietnam*, p. 175.
5 *The Marines in Vietnam 1954–1973, An Anthology and Annotated Bibliography* (Washington, D.C.: History and Museums Div., Headquarters, USMC, 1974), p. 38.
6 *Ibid.*, p. 43.
7 *Ibid.*, p. 53.
8 FITZGERALD, *Fire in the Lake*, p. 384.
9 LEWIS W. WALT, *Strange War, Strange Strategy* (New York: Funk & Wagnalls, 1970), pp. 125–30.
10 Medal of Honor citation; Walt, *Strange War, Strange Strategy*, pp. 161–63; Francis J. West, Jr., *Small Unit Action in Vietnam: Summer 1966* (Washington, D.C.: Historical Branch, USMC, 1967), pp. 15–30.
11 Medal of Honor citation; Walt, *Strange War, Strange Strategy*, pp. 157–59.
12 WEST, JR., *Small Unit Action in Vietnam: Summer 1966*, p. 119.
13 *The Marines in Vietnam 1954–1973*, p. 58.
14 Quoted in Bernard Fall, *Hell in a Very Small Place: The Siege of Dien Bien Phu* (Philadelphia: J. B. Lippincott Co., 1966), p. 28.
15 *The Marines in Vietnam 1954–1973*, p. 59.
16 FITZGERALD, *Fire in the Lake*, p. 449.
17 Document 118, 14 October 1966, *The Pentagon Papers*, as published by *The New York Times* (New York: Quadrangle Books, 1971), p. 555.

18 Interview with Lt. Gen. Lewis W. Walt, Da Nang, 1 February 1967.

19 *The Marines in Vietnam 1954–1973*, p. 65.

20 Medal of Honor citation.

21 *The Marines in Vietnam 1954–1973*, p. 71.

22 Medal of Honor citation; Walt, *Strange War, Strange Strategy*, pp. 147–49.

23 *The Marines in Vietnam 1954–1973*, p. 89.

24 EDWIN H. SIMMONS in *ibid.*, p. 96.

25 BERNARD C. NALTY, *Air Power and the Fight for Khe Sanh* (Washington, D.C.: Office of Air Force History, 1973), p. 21.

26 Medal of Honor citation.

27 *The Marines in Vietnam 1954–1973*, p. 102.

28 Quoted from speech of 19 October 1968 in *Nixon Speaks Out* (New York: Nixon-Agnew Campaign Committee, 1968), p. 231.

29 FITZGERALD, *Fire in the Lake*, p. 556.

30 Medal of Honor citations.

31 Medal of Honor citation.

32 Medal of Honor citation.

33 E. H. SIMMONS, *The United States Marines* (London: Leo Cooper, Ltd., 1974), p. 178.

34 HENRY I. SHAW, JR., AND RALPH W. DONNELLY, *Blacks in the Marine Corps* (Washington, D.C.: History and Museums Div., Headquarters, USMC, 1975), p. 72.

35 *Ibid.*, p. 73.

36 GARY D. SOLIS, *Marines and Military Law in Vietnam: Trial by Fire* (Washington, D.C.: History and Museums Div., Headquarters, USMC, 1989), p. 171.

37 EDWARD L. GREEN, "Equal Opportunity," *United States Naval Institute Proceedings*, June 1974, pp. 40–41.

38 *The New York Times*, 6 May 1975, p. 1; *Newsweek*, 21 April 1975, p. 33.

39 Department of Defense, *Table 1051: Number of Casualties Incurred by U.S. Military Personnel in Connection with the Conflict in Vietnam Cumulative from Jan. 1, 1961–Dec. 31, 1975* (15 January 1976).

40 JOHN M. COLLINS, senior specialist in national defense at the Library of Congress, "Ground Combat Operations," *Marine Corps Gazette*, March 1991, pp. 48–50.

41 DAVID M. SHOUP, "The New American Militarism," *The Atlantic*, April 1969, p. 55.

42 JAMES A. DONOVAN, *Militarism, U.S.A.*, with a foreword by David M. Shoup (New York: Charles Scribner's Sons, 1970), p. xi.

43 Interview with Chaplain Lester L. Westing, Jr., of Oakland, California, Da Nang, 1 February 1967.

44 Interviews with Cpl. Andre A. Williams, Vietnam, February 1967.

45 WALT, *Strange War, Strange Strategy*, p. 66.

Part IX
Starting the Third Century 1975–1989/*pages 695–766*

1 MARTIN BINKIN AND JEFFREY RECORD, *Where Does the Marine Corps Go from Here?* (Washington, D.C.: The Brookings Institution, 1976), p. 69.

2 Interview with Lt. Gen. Victor H. Krulak, Hawaii, 9 January 1967.
3 BINKIN AND RECORD, *Where Does the Marine Corps Go from Here?* p. 30.
4 THOMAS G. ROE, et al., *A History of Marine Corps Roles and Missions 1775–1962*, Marine Corps Historical Reference Series No. 30 (Washington, D.C.: Historical Branch, Headquarters, USMC, 1962), p. 10.
5 *Ibid.*, p. 8.
6 Gen. Clifton B. Cates quoted 1951 in *ibid.*, p. 25.
7 Statement by Gen. Louis H. Wilson on "Marine Corps Posture, Plans and Programs" before U.S. Senate Armed Services Committee, 2 February 1976.
8 J. ROBERT MOSKIN, "Our New Western Frontier," *Look*, 30 May 1967, pp. 36–46.
9 JAMES A. DONOVAN, *Militarism, U.S.A.*, with a foreword by David M. Shoup (New York: Charles Scribner's Sons, 1970), p. xii.
10 BINKIN AND RECORD, *Where Does the Marine Corps Go from Here?* p. 35.
11 All quotations by Gen. Louis H. Wilson in this chapter are from an interview at USMC Headquarters, Arlington, Va., 27 May 1976, unless other sources are cited.
12 W. R. BALL, "Brookings Defense Study," *Marine Corps Gazette*, March 1976, p. 7.
13 BINKIN AND RECORD, *Where Does the Marine Corps Go from Here?* p. 7.
14 Interview with Lt. Gen. Leslie E. Brown, USMC Headquarters, Arlington, Va., 28 May 1976.
15 DAVID M. SHOUP, "The New American Militarism," *The Atlantic*, April 1969, p. 55.
16 Transcript of Press Conference by Maj. Gen. Fred E. Haynes, Jr., Washington, D.C., 24 March 1976, p. 7.
17 *Ibid.*, p. 12.
18 *Report on Marine Corps Manpower Quality and Force Structure* (USMC, 1975), p. 4.
19 "Training the Marines," *The New York Times*, 14 April 1976, p. 36.
20 Interviews with Lt. Gen. Robert H. Barrow, USMC Headquarters, Arlington, Va., 28 May and 30 September 1976.
21 Unpublished paper by Lt. Gen. Robert H. Barrow.
22 Rescue Mission Report, August 1980, for Joint Chiefs of Staff (unclassified version).
23 *32d MAU After Action Report*, September–November 1982.
24 *Report of the Department of Defense Commission Beirut International Airport Terrorist Act, October 23, 1983*, 20 December 1983, p. 35.
25 BERNARD WEINRAUB, *The New York Times*, 30 September 1982, p. 1.
26 DREW MIDDLETON, "Shores of Beirut Airport," *The New York Times*, 27 July 1985.
27 BENIS M. FRANK, *Marines in Lebanon 1982–1984* (Washington, D.C.: Marine Corps Historical Center, 1987).
28 *24th MAU Situation Report No. 25*, 11 September 1983.
29 BERNARD GWERTZMAN, "Washington View," *The New York Times*, 20 September 1983, p. 1.
30 THOMAS L. FRIEDMAN, "America's Failure in Lebanon," *The New York Times Magazine*, 8 April 1984.

31 ERIC HAMMEL, *The Root* (New York: Harcourt Brace Jovanovich, 1985), p. 306.

32 FRANK, *Marines in Lebanon 1982–1984.*

33 *The Washington Post,* 21 December 1983, House subcommittee report (UPI), p. A23.

34 THOMAS L. FRIEDMAN, "America's Failure in Lebanon," *The New York Times Magazine,* 8 April 1984, p. 32.

35 *Navy Times,* 11 November 1983, p. 3.

36 *The New York Times,* 22 October 1983, p. A10.

37 RONALD H. SPECTOR, *U.S. Marines in Grenada 1983* (Washington, D.C.: History and Museums Division, Headquarters, U.S. Marine Corps, July 1984—not cleared for publication until August 1986, published 1987), p. 2.

38 PAUL X. KELLEY, Memorandum, 7 November 1983.

39 MICHAEL J. BYRON, "Fury from the Sea," *U.S. Naval Institute Proceedings Naval Review 1984,* pp. 119–31.

40 *Operational Overview, Jan–Mar 1984* (Quantico, Va.: Marine Corps Development and Education Command), p. 31.

41 Department of State, 21 January 1984.

42 *The New York Times,* 17 October 1985, p. 23.

43 *Time* magazine, 23 July 1984, p. 49.

44 *The Washington Post,* by Richard Harwood, 6 November 1983, p. 1.

45 All quotations by Gen. Paul X. Kelley as Commandant are from an interview at USMC Headquarters, Arlington, Va., 25 July 1985, unless other sources are cited.

46 Secretary of the Navy John F. Lehman, Jr., to the House Armed Services Committee, February 1982.

47 *Newsweek,* 25 June 1990, p. 31.

48 LAV Scout Press Release 14–90.

Part X
The Nineties 1990–/*pages 768–824*

1 *Newsweek,* 11 March 1991, p. 48.

2 TOM DELERY, "Away, the Boarding Party," *U.S. Naval Institute Proceedings,* May 1991, pp. 65–71.

3 *Newsweek,* 28 January 1991, pp. 54, 61.

4 *Newsweek,* 10 September 1990, p. 25.

5 All quotations by Gen. Alfred M. Gray, Jr., as Commandant are from an interview, 7 August 1991, unless other sources are cited.

6 *Newsweek,* 10 September 1990, p. 25.

7 Interview with Lt. Gen. Walter E. Boomer, *U.S. Naval Institute Proceedings,* November 1991, p. 48.

8 *Marine Corps Gazette,* January 1991, pp. 34–36.

9 ROBERT A. JONES, "Report on 6th Platoon," *Marine Corps Gazette,* June 1991, pp. 30–32.

10 *U.S. Naval Institute Proceedings,* May 1991, p. 92.

11 RONALD J. BROWN, "Operation Desert Sting," manuscript; *The New York Times,* 31 January 1991, p. A10; Associated Press article, 30 January 1991;

Marine Corps Gazette, July 1991, p. 65; interview with Col. John E. Rhodes, commanding officer, 13th MEU(SOC).

12 WALTER E. BOOMER, speech, Marine Corps Historical Foundation, Quantico, Virginia, 28 October 1991.

13 *The New York Times,* 31 January 1991, p. A12, statement by Gen. H. Norman Schwarzkopf.

14 *The New York Times,* 3 February 1991, p. 1.

15 *U.S. Naval Institute Proceedings,* May 1991, pp. 91, 93; *The New York Times,* 19 February 1991, p. A7; *The Washington Post,* 25 July 1991, interview with Gen. Carl E. Mundy, Jr.; *Newsweek,* 18 March 1991, p. 38; interview with General Gray.

16 *Brown Side Out,* I Marine Expeditionary Force, 27 March 1991.

17 ROBERT C. JENKS, "Charlie's 144 Marines deceived Saddam's Iraqi Corps," *Brown Side Out,* I Marine Expeditionary Force, 20 March 1991, pp. 1, 4–5.

18 GEORGE SPEAR, PAO, I MEF Press Release #085-91, 2 March 1991.

19 WALTER E. BOOMER, speech, Marine Corps Historical Foundation, Quantico, Virginia, 28 October 1991.

20 *The New York Times,* 17 February 1991, p. 18; *Newsweek,* 28 January 1991, pp. 28–29.

21 *Brown Side Out,* 27 March 1991.

22 WALTER E. BOOMER, "Persian Gulf Campaign: U.S. Marine Corps Operations, Command Brief," declassified from Secret, 22 June 1991, p. 25.

23 *Newsweek,* 18 March 1991, p. 39.

24 RONALD J. BROWN, "The Battle of the Emir's Farm," manuscript; JOHN H. ADMIRE, "The 3rd Marines in Desert Storm," *Marine Corps Gazette,* September 1991, pp. 67–71.

25 DALE B. COOPER, "Young Guns," *Leatherneck,* July 1991, pp. 41–42.

26 *The New York Times,* 28 February 1991, p. A8, press conference transcript.

27 *Ibid.; Leatherneck,* April 1991, p. 38.

28 WALTER E. BOOMER, speech, Marine Corps Historical Foundation, Quantico, Virginia, 28 October 1991.

29 *Marine Corps Gazette,* June 1991, p. 24.

30 RONALD J. BROWN, Marine Historian, Combined Task Force Provide Comfort, "Operation Provide Comfort: A Summary," manuscript.

31 T. W. PARKER, "Operation Sharp Edge," *U.S. Naval Institute Proceedings,* May 1991, pp. 102–106.

32 R. R. KEANE, "Night Mission to Mogadishu," *Leatherneck,* March 1991, p. 20; Ambassador JAMES J. BISHOP, "Escape from Mogadishu," *Foreign Service Journal,* March 1991, pp. 26–31.

33 Interview in *Seapower,* November 1991, pp. 14–15.

34 "Women Marines in the 1980s," Division of Public Affairs, Headquarters, USMC, revised 1983, p. al.

35 MARY V. STREMLOW, *A History of the Women Marines, 1946–1977* (MCH, 1986), p. 73.

36 *Ibid.,* p. 80.

37 Memo from Commanding Officer, Marine Security Guard Battalion, Quantico, Virginia, 20 September 1991.

38 STREMLOW, *A History of the Women Marines,* p. 99.

39 "Women Marines in the 1980s," p. 1.
40 *U.S. Naval Institute Proceedings*, May 1991, p. 139.
41 Letter dated March 20, 1991.
42 "Comments on the Contribution of Women," Memo from Command Element, I Marine Expeditionary Force, 30 March 1991, Manpower and Reserve Affairs Department, Headquarters, USMC.
43 Interview with Brig. Gen. Charles C. Krulak, *U.S. Naval Institute Proceedings*, November 1991, p. 57.
44 All quotations by Gen. Alfred M. Gray, Jr., as Commandant are from an interview, 7 August 1991, unless other sources are cited.
45 Interview in *The Washington Post*, 25 July 1991.
46 All quotations by Gen. Alfred M. Gray, Jr., as Commandant are from an interview, 7 August 1991, unless other sources are cited.
47 Interview in *Navy Times*, 8 January 1990, p. 25, quoted in *U.S. Naval Institute Proceedings*, May 1991, p. 135.
48 Interview in *Seapower*, November 1991, p. 9.
49 *Marine Corps Gazette*, August 1991, p. 72.
50 ALMAR 023/88, quoted in Edwin H. Simmons, Brig. Gen., "Memorandum from the Director: 'Amphibious' Becomes 'Expeditionary,' " *Fortitudine*, Spring–Summer 1988, pp. 3–7.
51 WILLIAM SHAKESPEARE, *King Henry V*, Act IV, Scene iii.

Bibliography

This is a functional bibliography intended primarily for the reader who wishes to explore more extensively any part of the United States Marine Corps' story. The research for this book has included many interviews, documents and correspondence in the files of the Marine Corps' History and Museums Division, monographs, professional and popular periodical articles and more than 300 books. Whenever any source is quoted directly, the reference will be found cited in the Source Notes. A review of the overall Marine Corps histories will be found in the bibliography for Part X.

Part I
The Early Years 1775–1902

In its bicentennial year, the United States Marine Corps published a superbly detailed account of the Continental Marines: *Marines in the Revolution* by Charles R. Smith (1975). Gardner W. Allen's *A Naval History of the American Revolution* (1913) is a classic, with extensive quotations from contemporary accounts. Oscar Paullin's *The Navy of the American Revolution* (1906) is invaluable. Readers with areas of special interest might turn to Samuel Eliot Morison's *John Paul Jones* (1959); Col. G.W.M. Grover's *Short History of the Royal Marines* (1948); William Stryker's *The Battles of Trenton and Princeton* (1898); and Alfred Hoyt Bill's *The Campaign of Princeton 1776–1777* (1948). Any serious investigator will want to look at *Naval Records of the American Revolution, 1775–1788*, edited by Charles Henry Lincoln, which is an annotated bibliography of the documents in the Library of Congress.

For the naval war with France there is probably no better source than *Our Naval War with France* by Gardner W. Allen (1909). The role of the Marines in the incident at Curaçao is well described in the unpublished article "Setting the Pattern: the Navy and Marine Corps at Curaçao, 1800" by the late Michael O'Quinlivan of the Historical Branch, USMC Headquarters.

The war with Tripoli is interpreted thoroughly in *The First Americans in North Africa* by Louis B. Wright and Julia H. Macleod (1945). Fletcher Pratt's *Preble's Boys: Commodore Preble and the Birth of American Sea Power* (1950) offers vivid portraits of the naval captains of the period. Marine Pvt. William Ray's firsthand account, *Horrors of Slavery: or The American Tars in Tripolitan Slavery*, was published originally in Troy, New York, in 1808 and reprinted in 1911 in *The Magazine of History*, extra number 14.

860

BIBLIOGRAPHY

The classic work about the War of 1812 is Theodore Roosevelt's *The Naval War of 1812* (1882). C.S. Forester's *The Age of Fighting Sail: The Story of the Naval War of 1812* (1956) makes exciting reading. To look further into special aspects of the war, the following are valuable: On the battle of Lake Champlain, the article "Commodore Macdonough at Plattsburg" by Rear Adm. A.T. Mahan in the *North American Review,* vol. 200, no. 705, August 1914. On the battle of Bladensburg, Edward D. Ingraham's *A Sketch of the Events Which Preceded the Capture of Washington* (1849); and the issues of the *National Intelligencer* published in Washington from August 23 through December 20, 1814. *The Dawn's Early Light* by Walter Lord (1972) effectively tells the story of the actions at Washington, Baltimore and New Orleans. For the battle of New Orleans see James Parton's *The Life of Andrew Jackson* (1860). For the cruise of *Essex,* the basic document is David Porter's fascinating *Journal of a Cruise Made to the Pacific Ocean* (1815). An interesting report of Gamble's experiences is an article by Marine Corps historian Edwin North McClellan entitled "John M. Gamble" and published in the *Thirty-fifth Annual Report of the Hawaiian Historical Society for the Year 1926.* Gamble's report to Porter was published in the *Niles Weekly Register* (Baltimore), vol. 9, December 23, 1815.

Very little has been written about the Second Seminole War. A useful source book on the war is *The Origin, Progress and Conclusion of the Florida War* by John T. Sprague (1847), which contains many official reports. Colonel Henderson's Florida journal has apparently been lost, but extracts are preserved in his biographical file at Marine Corps Headquarters. Marine Lieutenant Sprague's dramatic journal of his assignment to remove the Creeks to the West can be found in *Indian Removal* by Grant Foreman (1932), the most readable volume on this whole disgraceful episode.

There is no better account of the Wilkes expedition than Charles Wilkes' own five-volume *Narrative of the United States Exploring Expedition* (1845).

The most respected general account of the Mexican War is *The War with Mexico* by Justin Harvey Smith (1919). Any investigator of the Marine Corps' role will have to go to the Corps' archives, and especially the biographical files of Gillespie and Terrett; Gillespie's tale is usually told through Frémont's story. *Frémont-The West's Greatest Adventurer* by Allan Nevins (1928) is both calm and sympathetic. *Stephen Watts Kearny* by Dwight L. Clarke (1961) is a spirited, detailed pro-Kearny account. There are several interesting Frémont and Gillespie items in *The Century* magazine for March and April 1891.

For Scott's campaign and the Marine battalion's exploits leading to the Halls of Montezuma, *Captain Sam Grant* by Lloyd Lewis (1950) is the best-written book on the campaign. *Life and Correspondence of John A. Quitman* by J.F.H. Claiborne (1860) is of great value in following the Marines once they went into battle. *Decisive Battles of the U.S.A.* by J.F.C. Fuller (1942) includes a professional report of the fight for Chapultepec. And the proceedings of the court-martial of 1st Lt. John S. Devlin, USMC, entitled "The Marine Corps in Mexico," deals with the personal controversy that erupted between Lt. John G. Reynolds and Devlin over the events of September 13. Buried in it are many details of the Marines' climactic action.

In Mexico City, my research was greatly aided by Antonio Arriaga, Director of the National Museum of History, located in the castle on Chapultepec; by

Manuel Oropeza, Museum Curator, who familiarized me with the battlefields, and by Master Gunnery Sgt. Sterling McGinnis, USMC, then commander of the Marine Guard at the U.S. Embassy.

Although the Civil War has been an American passion, few accounts treat the Marine Corps' role in this conflict. Biographical and subject files in the Marine Corps' Historical Branch are essential sources. Bernard C. Nalty's mimeographed monograph *The United States Marines in the Civil War* (1958) is a thorough official summary. Jane Blakeney's *Heroes: U.S. Marine Corps 1861–1955* (1957) is uniquely valuable for citations of honors and decorations and has been used in this chapter and those that follow.

The classic account of the prewar incident at Harpers Ferry is *John Brown* by Oswald Garrison Villard (1910, 1929). Another useful study is *Thunder at Harper's Ferry* by Allan Keller (1958). Lee's report can be found in the Corps' Harpers Ferry file, and Israel Greene's letter is reprinted in the *Marine Corps Gazette* for September 1929. The *New York Weekly Tribune*, October 22 to December 3, 1859, contains full contemporary articles and comment.

Ralph W. Donnelly published *The History of the Confederate States Marine Corps* (1976), the most comprehensive work done on the subject. The Historical Branch also has a separate file on the Confederate marines.

There are no adequate accounts of the Marines' part in the first Battle of Bull Run. An important source is Official Records, Series 1, Vol. 2, Serial No. 2. Although they differ in details, three interesting secondary accounts are in *The Civil War* by Shelby Foote (1958); *Lee's Lieutenants* by Douglas Southall Freeman, volume one (1942), and *The Coming Fury* by Bruce Catton (1961).

The following sources are useful for readers interested in specific actions during the war: *How the Merrimac Won* by R.W. Daly (1957) and Bruce Catton's article on this battle in the *New York Times Magazine*, March 4, 1962. For the battle of New Orleans, *The Night the War Was Lost* by Charles L. Dufour (1960). Maj. Edwin North McClellan also wrote "The Capture of New Orleans" in the *Marine Corps Gazette* for December 1920. A firsthand account is the diary of an enlisted Marine, "Diary of Oscar Smith, U.S. Marine Corps, aboard Flagship *Hartford*, 1861–1862." A typescript, with a foreword dated August 24, 1937, by the author's son Carl, is in the Library of Congress. For Mobile Bay, see Charles Heywood's biographical file at Marine Corps Headquarters and *Harper's Magazine*, August 1891. Accounts of the sinking of *Governor* with Reynolds' battalion can be found in Senate Executive Document No. 1, 37th Congress, 2nd Session (1861).

The battle for Fort Fisher is reported in "The Federals and Fort Fisher" by Edwin H. Simmons in the *Marine Corps Gazette*, January and February 1951; "The Capture of Fort Fisher" by McClellan, in the *Marine Corps Gazette*, March 1920; "Fort Fisher and Wilmington Campaign" by James M. Merrill, *North Carolina Historical Review*, October 1958, and *The Naval History of the Civil War* by David D. Porter (1886). The story of Henry Wasmuth's heroism is told in *A Sailor's Log* by Robley D. Evans (1901).

Old Bruin, the biography of Commodore Matthew C. Perry by Samuel Eliot Morison (1967), ranges over the whole era from the War of 1812 through the expedition to Japan in 1853–4. There is no better source for Perry's expedition to Japan than the report compiled from notes and journals and authenticated by

BIBLIOGRAPHY

Perry himself: *Narrative of the Expedition of an American Squadron to the China Seas and Japan performed in the years 1852, 1853 and 1854* by Francis L. Hawks (1856). A basic account of the 1856 attack on the forts below Canton is in *Marine Corps Historical Reference Series Number 6* (revised 1962) entitled "The Barrier Forts" by Bernard C. Nalty. The attack on the Korean forts in 1871 is reported in M. Almy Aldrich's history of the Corps (1875) and in "Our First Korean War" by Capt. J. F. terHorst in the *Marine Corps Gazette*, December 1953.

The most useful document about the Marine Corps' part in the Spanish-American War is the mimeographed monograph No. 3 in the Marine Corps Historical Reference Series: *The United States Marines in the War with Spain* by Bernard C. Nalty. A second printing (November 1959) is available at the Marine Corps Historical Branch. Its notes contain a valuable bibliography.

The Correspondents' War by Charles H. Brown (1967) includes vivid eye-witness accounts of the Marines' engagements at Guantanamo Bay. My understanding of the topography at Guantanamo was increased by a visit to the Marine Corps base there on assignment for *Look* magazine.

Clyde H. Metcalf's history of the Corps (1939) contains considerable detail about the War with Spain. Among more general volumes are: *The Splendid Little War* by Frank Freidel (1958), a well-edited compilation of participants' accounts of the battles; Margaret Leech's *In the Days of McKinley* (1959); *The War with Spain* by Henry Cabot Lodge (1899), and *Remember the Maine* by Gregory Mason (1939).

The battles of Novaleta and the Sohoton Cliffs and Waller's march across Samar are best sighted in the Marine Corps biographical and subject files. A thorough account of Waller's adventure and court-martial is *The Ordeal of Samar* by Joseph L. Schott (1964). The U.S. military government of the Philippines is expertly examined in the unpublished Ph.D. thesis for the Harvard Graduate School of Public Administration, September 1948, "Between War and Peace" by the late Robert Neville Ginsburgh, Major General, U.S. Air Force.

Peter Fleming's *The Siege at Peking* (1959) is a fascinating account of the events in North China, with special orientation to the British viewpoint. Henry Leonard's report on the relief expedition is in the papers of the Military Historical Society of Massachusetts, Volume XIV, 1918. Pvt. James J. Sullivan's diary was published in the *Marine Corps Gazette* in November 1968.

As for the Marine Corps' part in the Boxer Rebellion, three accounts in the *United States Naval Institute Proceedings* are essential sources: an article by Capt. John T. Myers, USMC, "Military Operations and Defenses of the Siege of Peking" (September 1902); "The Seymour Relief Expedition" by Lt. Daniel W. Wurtsbaugh, USN (June 1902), and "Experiences During the Boxer Rebellion" by Capt. J. K. Taussig, USN (April 1927). The biographical files at Marine Corps Headquarters are also useful, particularly that of John Twiggs Myers.

Part II
World War I 1914–1919

Surprisingly, there is no superlative overall account of the Marines in World War I. Despite the fact that this experience introduced the Corps to modern warfare and was germinal to its modern role, information about the Marines during the nation's first effort at virtually total war must be retrieved from scattered sources. The only official account is a facsimile reprint (1968) of a monograph first published in 1920: *The United States Marine Corps in the World War* by Maj. Edwin N. McClellan, USMC. This 108-page account is a highly factual skeleton of names, dates and figures.

There is considerable reportage on the 4th Brigade in the exceptionally well-written *The American Heritage History of World War I* by S. L. A. Marshall (1964). *World War I* by Hanson W. Baldwin (1962) offers a brief, readable framework through which more detailed examinations can be fitted into perspective. *The American Army in France* by James G. Harbord (1936) details with care the period when the author commanded the Marine Brigade. And Clyde Metcalf's basic 1939 history of the Corps devotes many pages to World War I.

The battle for Belleau Wood, which stopped the Germans' 1918 offensive toward Paris and revolutionized Allied morale, has been treated in many versions, which often disagree on specific details. *At Belleau Wood* by former Marine Robert B. Asprey (1965) is the most extensive report and is sprinkled with accounts by participants. Anyone interested in that crucial battle will find this volume invaluable, as I did.

Decisive Battles of the U.S.A. by J.F.C. Fuller (1942) has a chapter on the Meuse-Argonne.

Activities at Vladivostok are presented in "American Marines in Siberia during the World War" by Major McClellan in the *Marine Corps Gazette* for June 1920.

The early days of Marine aviation are summarized in the *History of Marine Corps Aviation in World War II* by Robert Sherrod (1952, revised 1980). The official account is *Marine Corps Aviation: The Early Years 1912–1940* by Lt. Col. Edward C. Johnson (1977).

There is a variety of personal accounts of the war. Most valuable is *The Reminiscences of a Marine* by Maj. Gen. John A. Lejeune (1930), who commanded the 2d Division after Soissons for the duration. Capt. John W. Thomason, Jr.'s *Fix Bayonets!* (1926) is a vivid personal account that captures the flavor of life on the front. *And They Thought We Wouldn't Fight* by Floyd Gibbons (1918) deals effectively with Belleau Wood. *With The Help of God And A Few Marines* by A. W. Catlin and Walter A. Dyer (1918–19) is regrettably overwritten. *A Marine Tells It To You* by Frederic M. Wise and Meigs O. Frost (1929) is well written but not always accurate in detail. An unpublished oral-history transcript by former Gunnery Sgt. Don V. Paradis is available at the Marine Corps Historical Division. "The First To Fight: Marine Corps Expansion, 1914–18" by Jack Shulimson in *Prologue* (Spring 1976) tells authoritatively the story of the Corps' World War I expansion and its drive to fight in France. Of course, the files at the Marine Corps Historical Division contain much biographical and other essential information.

BIBLIOGRAPHY

Part III
Imperialism in the Caribbean 1901–1934

One of the better studies of the extension of United States influence and power southward into the Caribbean is *The United States and the Caribbean* by Dexter Perkins (1947). *The Era of Theodore Roosevelt and the Birth of Modern America 1900–1912* by George E. Mowry (1958) also treats the period during which the Marines first became deeply involved in the area.

For the specific Marine Corps interventions the following are recommended: *The United States Marines in Nicaragua* by Bernard C. Nalty (1958, revised 1961) is a superb photocopied Marine Corps report. *Garde d'Haiti 1915–1934* compiled by James H. McCrocklin (1965) is detailed but focuses primarily on the Garde rather than the Corps itself. *The United States and Mexico* by Howard F. Cline (1953) puts the 1914 invasion into the perspective of the Mexican revolution and of U.S.-Mexican relations. *Marines in the Dominican Republic 1916–1924* by Capt. Stephen M. Fuller and Graham A. Cosmas was published by the Marine Corps Historical Division in 1974. *The Dominican Intervention* by Abraham F. Lowenthal (1972) deals chiefly with the 1965 intervention but includes some background material on the earlier one. The Cuban situation is fully explained in Allan Reed Millett's *The Politics of Intervention, the Military Occupation of Cuba, 1906–1909* (1968).

Among the best personal accounts are: *Old Gimlet Eye, the Adventures of Smedley D. Butler* by Lowell Thomas (1933); *Reminiscences of a Marine* by John A. Lejeune (1930); *The Big Yankee, The Life of Carlson of the Raiders* by Michael Blankfort (1947); *Marine! The Life of Lt. Gen. Lewis B. (Chesty) Puller* by Burke Davis (1962), and *The White King of La Gonave* by Faustin Wirkus and Taney Dudley (1931). *—and a Few Marines* by Col. John W. Thomason, Jr., (1943), who also wrote *Fix Bayonets!* (1926) about World War I, re-creates the spirit of the Marines of his era. Merritt A. Edson's series of articles, "The Coco Patrol," in the *Marine Corps Gazette* (August and November 1936 and February 1937), is an excellent report on those expeditions and on guerrilla warfare. William A. Lee told his story to Tom Bartlett in a *Leatherneck* series called "The Iron Man" (July, August, September 1984). A more recent biography of Smedley D. Butler is *Maverick Marine* by Hans Schmidt (1987).

The basic source for the changes in the Marines' role during this period is the official *Progress and Purpose: A Developmental History of the U.S. Marine Corps 1900–1970* by Lt. Col. Kenneth J. Clifford (1973). Dion Williams' paper can be found in the *United States Naval Institute Proceedings*, June 1902. "The Lauchheimer Controversy: A Case of Group Political Pressure during the Taft Administration" by Wayne A. Wiegand was published in *Military Affairs* for April 1976. A modern appraisal of the prolonged turn-of-the-century controversy over the Marine Corps' mission will be found in "William Freeland Fullam's War with the Corps" by Lt. Col. John G. Miller, USMC, in the November 1975 issue of the *United States Naval Institute Proceedings*.

Part IV
Getting Ready 1919–1941

For the Marines in China, one of the best background studies is *20th Century China* by O. Edmund Clubb (1964). *A Brief History of the 4th Marines* by James S. Santelli (1970) is official and particularly valuable. Smedley Butler's autobiography is especially relevant here. And *The Big Yankee, The Life of Carlson of the Raiders* by Michael Blankfort (1947) is enthusiastic and detailed about Carlson's experiences with the Chinese Communists.

Several periodical sources are important: "Shanghai Emergency" by Maj. Richard B. Rothwell in the *Marine Corps Gazette* for November 1972; "China Marine" by Robert M. Leventhal in the same issue, and "Shanghai Duty 1937–1938," a picture portfolio with brief text in the *United States Naval Institute Proceedings* for November 1974. *The Walla Walla*, the intriguing newsweekly published by the Marines in Shanghai, is on file at the Marine Corps Historical Division.

The Marines' evolution toward amphibious assault is thoroughly reported in *Progress and Purpose: A Developmental History of the United States Marine Corps 1900–1970* by Lt. Col. Kenneth J. Clifford (1973). A superb analysis of the transition is contained in *The U.S. Marines and Amphibious Warfare* by Jeter A. Isley and Philip A. Crowl (1951). This study was sponsored by the Marine Corps, but the opinions are the authors' own. The most valuable official source is Volume I of the History of the U.S. Marine Corps Operations in World War II, *Pearl Harbor to Guadalcanal* by Lt. Col. Frank O. Hough, Maj. Verle E. Ludwig and Henry I. Shaw, Jr. The third volume of the epic history of the United States Naval Operations in World War II, *The Rising Sun in the Pacific 1931–April 1942* by Samuel Eliot Morison is magnificently readable. Robert Sherrod's *History of Marine Corps Aviation in World War II* has some material on the pre-war period.

Among the many personal accounts that touch on this crucial time are: *Once a Marine, The Memoirs of General A. A. Vandegrift* as told to Robert B. Asprey (1964); *Coral and Brass* by Gen. Holland M. Smith and Percy Finch (1948); and *The Amphibians Came To Conquer, The Story of Admiral Richmond Kelly Turner* by Vice Adm. George Carroll Dyer (1969). Lejeune's autobiography is not very helpful for his years as Commandant, and Butler's is, necessarily, on the periphery of the main thrust of amphibious developments.

Part V
World War II 1941–1949

The story of the Marine Corps in World War II has been told more fully than any other part of the Corps' history. Much of the telling has been superb. Although the source material available in the Historical Division at Marine Corps Headquarters is voluminous and essential, the reader wishing to pursue the story can well start with the published works. Although the source material available in the Historical Division at Marine Corps Headquarters is voluminous and essential, the reader wishing to pursue the story can well start with the published works.

Three overviews are basic: The five-volume *History of the U.S. Marine Corps Operations in World War II,* published by Marine Corps Headquarters, is the official history. Enormously detailed and for the most part clearly written, it is a comprehensive operational account of battles and units. Its chief limitations are that it tends to be impersonal and, of course, restrained in its criticism.

Almost equally useful is Samuel Eliot Morison's excellent fifteen-volume *History of United States Naval Operations in World War II.* Morison puts campaigns and battles into broader context. Although his main focus is on the Navy's engagements at sea, his work contains considerable material about the Marines' amphibious assaults, emphasizing again the inseparable relationship between the Navy and its Marine Corps.

Third, *The U.S. Marines and Amphibious Warfare* by Jeter A. Isely and Philip A. Crowl (1951) was sponsored by the Marine Corps; but the authors claim their conclusions as their own. It is a meaty, valuable analysis of the development and usage of amphibious warfare by the Marines.

The *History of Marine Corps Aviation in World War II* by Robert Sherrod (1952, revised 1980) is a highly readable study of a part of the Marine Corps' story too often neglected.

Blacks in the Marine Corps by Henry I. Shaw, Jr., and Ralph W. Donnelly (1975) is the Corps' own candid history of the black Americans who have been Marines and the Corps' evolving attitude toward them.

Among the more popular volumes telling the overall story of the Marines in World War II are *Strong Men Armed* by Robert Leckie (1962), an anecdotal account of Marines in combat; *The United States Marine Corps in World War II* edited by S. E. Smith (1969), an anthology of usually eyewitness accounts of Marine actions; and *The Big War* by Anton Myrer (1957), a novel that captures what it was like to be an enlisted Marine in this war.

Each of the six Marine divisions published a history of its own campaigns. The best is *The Old Breed* by George McMillan (1949). It tells not only the combat story but includes much on the periods that the Marines of the 1st Division spent in Australia and on Pavuvu. The *History of the Sixth Marine Division* edited by Bevan G. Cass (1948) also contains interesting details and biographies. The Corps' Historical Division has published as a monograph *Special Marine Corps Units of World War II* by Charles L. Updegraph, Jr. (1972).

There are many useful books on individual battles. *Into the Valley* by John Hersey (1943), a report of one patrol on Guadalcanal, and *Tarawa* by Robert Sherrod (1944) are classics. *The Battle for Guadalcanal* by Samuel B. Griffith (1963) is a professional's account, and *Guadalcanal* by Richard B. Frank (1990) is the definitive unofficial history. *Iwo Jima* by Richard F. Newcomb (1965) and *Iwo Jima: Legacy of Valor* by Bill D. Ross (1985) tell the story of the Marines' costliest battle. Ross' *Peleliu: Tragic Triumph* (1991) is the tale of their "forgotten battle." George P. Hunt's *Coral Comes High* (1946) is an exciting personal account by a rifle company commander on Peleliu. *Day of Infamy* by Walter Lord (1957) is a well-written account of the opening attack on Pearl Harbor.

Among the innumerable personal accounts of the war are the memoirs of Vandegrift and Holland Smith, Burke Davis' story of "Chesty" Puller, Michael Blankfort's book on Evans Carlson and George Dyer's two volumes on Richmond Kelly Turner—all referred to in the bibliography of Chapter 6. Others include

Admiral Halsey's Story by William F. Halsey and J. Bryan III (1947); *Baa Baa Black Sheep* by Gregory "Pappy" Boyington (1958); *Wake Island Command* by W. Scott Cunningham (1961); and *Flights of Passage, Reflections of a World War II Aviator* by Samuel Hynes (1988). William Manchester's *Goodbye Darkness: A Memoir of the Pacific War* (1980) deals especially with Okinawa. Richard Wheeler wrote *Iwo* (1980) and Robert Edward Lee produced *Victory at Guadalcanal* (1981). *Commander in Chief* by Eric Larrabee (1987) includes an in-depth chapter on Vandegrift.

The Marines' role in the opening of the war is presented in detail in three particularly useful accounts: In the Marine Corps Historical Division's Pearl Harbor file is the unpublished manuscript "Marine Barracks, Navy Yard, Pearl—December 1941" by Brig. Gen. Samuel R. Shaw (1972). In the Posts and Stations, Hawaii file is "The Japanese Attack of 7 December 1941 on the Marine Corps Air Station at Ewa, Oahu, Territory of Hawaii" by 2d Lt. Billie Hollingshead, USMCWR (1945). And in the *Marine Corps Gazette* for April 1946 is "Action Report: Bataan" by 1st Lt. William F. Hogaboom.

The story of John F. Kennedy's rescue of Marines at Choiseul is dramatically told in *PT-109: John F. Kennedy in World War Two* by Robert J. Donovan (1961) and *The Search for J.F.K.* by Joan and Clay Blair, Jr. (1976). The ambush at Anping is reported in detail in *The North China Marine*, August 3, 1946, published in Tientsin.

Part VI
The Korean War 1946–1953

Although the United Nations' military actions in Korea have been intensively reported, the causes, issues and implications of this pivotal conflict, in which the United States first engaged in major battle with a Communist power, have not yet received adequate comprehensive and objective attention. One searching for an understanding of the war's significance and the decision-making process must investigate a variety of often contradictory sources.

The following summary is limited to published sources available to most interested readers. As always, the files of the Marine Corps' Historical Division are indispensable.

For the problems discussed in Section One of this chapter during the period between World War II and Korea, the Washington battles over the unification of the armed services are dealt with in a number of studies. Most graphic are *The Forrestal Diaries* edited by Walter Millis (1951) and, from the Corps' point of view, *Once A Marine: The Memoirs of General A. A. Vandegrift* as told to Robert B. Asprey (1964).

Blacks in the Marine Corps by Henry I. Shaw, Jr., and Ralph W. Donnelly (1975) is a unique effort to filter out the participation of blacks in the Corps. *A History of the Women Marines, 1946–1977* by Col. Mary V. Stremlow was published by the Marine Corps History and Museums Division in 1986. The early and Korean development of helicopters by the Marine Corps is told in *Cavalry of the Sky* by Lynn Montross (1954).

The causes of the Korean war, the divergent views in Washington and Tokyo and finally the firing of MacArthur are portrayed in two intriguing personal accounts: the two-volume *Memoirs of Harry S Truman* (1955, 1956) and *Present at the Creation* by Dean Acheson (1969). Many of the documents involved will be found in the two-volume official *American Foreign Policy 1950–1955* (1957).

The crucial account of the Marines in the war is the official five-volume *U.S. Marine Operations in Korea* (1954–1972). This is thorough and interesting military history, despite the necessary detailing of the movement and activities of the various units involved. The story of the Marine air arm is relatively neglected in the earlier volumes but well covered in Volume V. An official account of interest is *Marines and Helicopters, 1946–1962* by Lt. Col. Eugene W. Rawlins (1976).

Allen S. Whiting expertly analyzes the Chinese entry into the war in *China Crosses the Yalu* (1960). *The Hidden History of the Korean War* by I. F. Stone (1952) discusses the political puzzles in a rather conspiratorial tone. *The Chinese People's Liberation Army* by Samuel B. Griffith II (1967) is highly professional and readable.

The overall military story of the war and the Marines' part in it are variously told in *Soldiers of the Sea* by Robert Debs Heinl, Jr., (1962); *Conflict* by Robert Leckie (1962); *The New Breed* by Andrew Geer (1952), and *The War in Korea* by Matthew B. Ridgway (1967). The former three authors were all Marines.

The early months of the war are effectively described in *South to the Naktong, North to the Yalu* by Roy E. Appleman (1960), the second volume of the official U.S. Army history of the war. The Navy's story is told by the *History of United States Naval Operations—Korea* by James A. Field, Jr., (1962); *The Sea War in Korea* by Malcolm W. Cagle and Frank A. Manson (1957), and *Battle Report, The War in Korea* by Walter Karig, Cagle and Manson (1952).

Two crucial Marine campaigns are related in enthusiastic detail in Heinl's *Victory at High Tide: The Inchon-Seoul Campaign* (1968) and Leckie's account of the Chosin Reservoir campaign, *The March to Glory* (1960). Eric Hammel wrote *Chosin: Heroic Ordeal of the Korean War* (1981). *This is War!* by David Douglas Duncan (1951) is a vivid eyewitness word-and-picture account of specific actions and the Marines in them by a superb combat photographer. Burke Davis' biography *Marine! The Life of Lt. Gen. Lewis B. (Chesty) Puller* (1962) continues with the Korean chapter of the career of this colorful Marine leader.

The record of Marine close air support is summarized in the series of articles by Kenneth W. Condit and Ernest H. Giusti in several issues of the *Marine Corps Gazette* in 1952.

For an understanding of the treatment and conduct of the American POWs see *In Every War But One* by Eugene Kinkead (1959) and *Turncoat* by the author (1968).

The Marine Corps Historical Division has also published *An Annotated Bibliography of the United States Marine Corps in the Korean War* by Michael O'Quinlivan and James S. Santelli (revised 1970).

My understanding of the topography of this war was improved by going over the Marines' battlefield from Inchon to Seoul and in some areas of western Korea while in South Korea on assignment for *Look* magazine.

Part VII
Tumultuous Times 1953–1965

A Marine's view of the Ribbon Creek tragedy and trial will be found in *Ribbon Creek: The Marine Corps on Trial* by William B. McKean (1958). *The U.S. Marine Corps in Crisis: Ribbon Creek and Recruit Training* by Keith Fleming (1990) is an independent account by a Marine Corps historian.

Details of the Lebanon landing are in Jack Shulimson's official monograph *Marines in Lebanon 1958* (1966) and in the appropriate chapter of *The Meaning of Limited War* by Robert McClintock (1967).

For more on the Dominican intervention of 1965 see "Ubique" by Maj. Gen. R. McC. Tompkins, a well-written account in the *Marine Corps Gazette*, September 1965; "Dominican Diary" by Capt. James A. Dare, USN, in the *United States Naval Institute Proceedings*, December 1965; *Overtaken by Events* by John Bartlow Martin (1966); *The Dominican Intervention* by Abraham F. Lowenthal (1972), and *The United States in World Affairs 1966* by Richard P. Stebbins (1967). Lt. Gen. Bruce Palmer, Jr., USA, commander of American forces in the intervention, told his version of the story in *Intervention in the Caribbean: The Dominican Crisis of 1965* (1989).

Part VIII
The Vietnam War 1954–1975

The Vietnam war was fought under unprecedented public exposure to mass-media coverage. Any account of the war must depend in large part on this voluminous and variegated reporting until time shapes the story into the perspective of history.

Research for this chapter was greatly aided by the author's three working trips to Vietnam during the war—two to South Vietnam (1967 and 1969) and one to North Vietnam (1970)—as the Foreign Editor of *Look* magazine. During the first two trips, he interviewed Ambassadors Henry Cabot Lodge and Ellsworth Bunker and Generals Abrams, Walt and Krulak, as well as many Marines and American and South Vietnamese officials. In Hanoi, he interviewed North Vietnamese leaders, under much more restricted conditions, for an article entitled "Report from Hanoi" (*Look*, December 29, 1970).

The Marine Corps' own report of its activities in Indochina during this war is being compiled in a series of monographs. The first volumes are *U.S. Marines in Vietnam 1954–1964* by Capt. Robert H. Whitlow (1977); *Marines in Vietnam, The Landing and the Buildup 1965* by Jack Shulimson and Maj. Charles M. Johnson (1978); *U.S. Marines in Vietnam, an Expanding War 1966* by Jack Shulimson (1982). Then came *U.S. Marines in Vietnam, Fighting the North Vietnamese 1967* by Maj. Gary L. Telfer, Lt. Col. Lane Rogers and V. Keith Fleming, Jr. (1984); *U.S. Marines in Vietnam 1970–1971, Vietnamization and Redeployment* by Graham A. Cosmas and Lt. Col. Terrence P. Murray (1986); *U.S. Marines in Vietnam, High Mobility and Standdown 1969* by Charles R. Smith (1988); and *U.S. Marines in Vietnam: The Bitter End 1973–1975* by Maj. George R. Dunham and Col. David A. Quinlan (1990).

A useful introduction is *The Marines in Vietnam 1954–1973*, published by the Corps' History and Museums Division in 1974 and revised in 1985. It contains reprints of thirteen professional articles from the *United States Naval Institute Proceedings, Naval Review* and *Marine Corps Gazette.* In addition to articles by Col. Victor J. Croizat, Lt. Col. Archie J. Clapp, Lt. Gen. Keith B. McCutcheon and others, the heart of this anthology is a series of four valuable articles on Marine Corps operations in Vietnam by Brig. Gen. Edwin H. Simmons, who served two tours in Vietnam and later as Director of Marine Corps History and Museums.

Other published sources dealing with the military side of the war begin with *Hell in a Very Small Place: The Siege of Dien Bien Phu* by Bernard B. Fall (1966). *Strange War, Strange Strategy* by Lewis W. Walt (1970) offers an excellent overview of the period during which Walt commanded III MAF. To understand what it was like for Marines to fight in Vietnam, one must read the vivid Marine Corps monograph *Small Unit Action in Vietnam: Summer 1966* by Capt. Francis J. West Jr. (1967). Its equal in visual terms is *War Without Heroes* by David Douglas Duncan (1970), whose photographs depict the tension, grime, pain and death of Marines in combat.

Tet! by Don Oberdorfer (1971) is an expert journalistic account of the 1968 attacks and their aftermath. The Marine Corps Historical Branch published *The Battle for Khe Sanh* by Capt. Moyers S. Shore II, an extensive monograph, in 1969. And the Office of Air Force History published *Air Power and The Fight for Khe Sanh* by Bernard C. Nalty (1973), a detailed report with emphasis on the contribution of air power and a reasonably balanced presentation of the "single manager" dispute. The controversial incident in Cam Ne is detailed in the Marine Corps' now-declassified file: Cam Ne Village, August 1965.

The evacuations of Phnom Penh and Saigon in 1975 are recounted in a *Marine Corps Gazette* series by Brig. Gen. Richard E. Carey and Maj. David A. Quinlan, in the issues of February through May 1976. The series was followed by an article on the Marines' Koh Tang-Mayaguez operation by Col. John M. Johnson, Jr.; Lt. Col. Randall W. Austin; and Major Quinlan. Roy Rowan's *The Four Days of Mayaguez* (1975) is a fine job of on-the-spot reporting by an experienced *Time-Life* editor; it focuses on the ship's crew, not the Marines involved in the incident. The Comptroller General of the United States published a report, *Seizure of the Mayaguez Part IV* in October 1976.

Dissenting views on the military aspects of this war are numerous. Three pertinent to Marines are: *The Winter Soldier Investigation* by the Vietnam Veterans Against the War (1972), which contains too many tales of Marine atrocities to be ignored; *The Betrayal* by Lt. Col. William R. Corson (1968), an angry report on the pacification program; and *Militarism, U.S.A.* by Col. James A. Donovan with a foreword by Gen. David M. Shoup (1970).

The political side of the war has been interpreted by many participants and observers. For the views of varied concerned individuals see the author's interviews in *Look* with Dean Rusk (September 6, 1966), Walt W. Rostow (December 12, 1967), Gunnar Myrdal (December 24, 1968), Arnold Toynbee (March 18, 1969) and Daniel Ellsberg (October 5, 1971).

Two of the best studies available so far are, from the perspective of Vietnam, *Fire in the Lake* by Frances FitzGerald (1972) and, from the perspective of Washington, *The Best and the Brightest* by David Halberstam (1972). *The Pen-*

tagon Papers, as published by *The New York Times* (1971), is indispensable for understanding the decision-making process through mid-1968. A readable academic analysis is *The United States in Vietnam* by George McTurnan Kahin and John Wilson Lewis (1969). *The Arrogance of Power* by J. William Fulbright (1966) effectively states the case against American involvement.

The inventory of books about the Vietnam war has increased over recent years. *Marines and Helicopters, 1962–1973* by Lt. Col. William R. Fails (1978); *Chaplains with Marines in Vietnam 1962–1971* by Commander Herbert L. Bergsma, CHC, U.S. Navy (1985); and *Marines and Military Law in Vietnam: Trial by Fire* by Lt. Col. Gary D. Solis (1989) are official accounts by the History and Museums Division, USMC. Solis' volume is remarkable for the candor with which he tells the story of the dark side of the Marines' Vietnam experience; the Marine Corps can be proud that it published this tale so honestly. Various views about the war and the Marines' part in it are expressed in *Fields of Fire* by James Webb (1978); *Rumor of War* by Philip Caputo (1977); *Dispatches* by Michael Herr (1977); and *Born on the Fourth of July* by Ron Kovic (1976).

More recent studies include *The Bridge at Dong Ha* by John Grider Miller (1989), which is the already-legendary story of Col. John Ripley; *Lima-6* by Col. Richard D. Camp, Jr., with Eric Hammel (1989); *The Combined Action Platoon: The U.S. Marines' Other War in Vietnam* by Michael E. Peterson (1989); *Valley of Decision: The Siege of Khe Sanh* by John Prados and Ray W. Stubbe (1991); and the moving *Fortunate Son* by Lewis B. Puller, Jr. (1991).

Part IX
Starting the Third Century 1975–1989

The post-Vietnam discussion of the Marine Corps' future is treated in "The Marines: Now and in the Future" by Brig. Gen. Simmons in the *United States Naval Institute Proceedings* of May 1975 and "To the Limit of Our Vision—And Back" by Gen. Robert E. Cushman, Jr., in the *Proceedings* of May 1974. The entire issue of the *Proceedings* for November 1975 was devoted to the Marine Corps. Most of Commandant Louis H. Wilson's statement before the Senate Armed Services Committee on Marine Corps Posture, Plans and Programs can be found in the *Marine Corps Gazette* for March 1976. The Haynes Board *Report on Marine Corps Manpower Quality and Force Structure* was published as a monograph by the Corps. "Missions and Force Structure" by William S. Lind appeared in the *Gazette* for December 1975. The Brookings Institution study by Martin Binkin and Jeffrey Record was published as *Where Does the Marine Corps Go from Here?* (1976). Brig. Gen. Simmons summarized the Corps' repeated efforts to maintain its existence in recent times in "The Marines: Survival and Accommodation," a chapter in *Evolution of the American Military Establishment Since World War II,* edited by Paul R. Schratz, A George C. Marshall Research Foundation Publication (1978).

Three sources are essential to an understanding of the Marines' mission and experience in Lebanon 1982 to 1984. The official account is *U.S. Marines in Lebanon 1982–1984* by Benis M. Frank (1987), published by the History and Museums Division, USMC. This volume, prepared with care and accuracy, is limited to the military activities that directly involved the Marines. Publication was delayed for political reasons beyond the control of Marine Corps historians. *Report of the Department of Defense Commission on Beirut 1983* is the official unclassified product of the so-called Long Commission and focuses primarily on the events of October 23, 1983, and the conditions surrounding it. The first unofficial account is *The Root: The Marines in Beirut August 1982–February 1984* by Eric Hammel (1985). This book is heavily dependent on interviews with Marines who survived the bombing of the Beirut barracks. Press reports on the Marines' Lebanon experience are numerous and often helpful.

The story of the invasion of Grenada by U.S. forces was kept under uniquely tight restraints. Press reporters were prevented from accompanying the Americans into battle and covering the invasion firsthand. Publication of no official account was permitted until long after the Presidential election of 1984. The official Marine Corps monograph, *U.S. Marines in Grenada 1983* by Maj. Ronald H. Spector (1987), was "scrubbed" and not even cleared for publication until August 1986. A basic, nonanalytical *Operations Overview* was issued to a limited Marine Corps audience for educational purposes by the Marine Corps Development and Education Command at Quantico, Virginia, in 1984. Major parts of the *Marine After Action Report* were embargoed. Fortunately, a few enterprising journalists tried to overcome the political cover-up and reported some of the most telling and controversial events of the hasty invasion.

Since then, several studies of the Grenada invasion have been published: *Grenada Documents: An Overview and Selection* by the Department of State and the Department of Defense (1984); *The Grenada Intervention: Analysis and Documentation* by William C. Gilmore (1984); *Grenada 1983* by Lee E. Russell and M. Albert Mendez (1985); and *Urgent Fury: The Battle for Grenada* by Maj. Mark Adkin (1989).

The Marines played a small role in the invasion of Panama in 1989; for better or worse, it was an Army show. The following sources are the most useful for the Marine Corps' Operation Just Cause. In the Panama file of the Marine Corps History and Museums Division are the Command Chronology of Events, 20–31 December 1989, which was declassified January 1, 1990; "Marines in Panama: 1989–1990," an unpublished research paper by Maj. Robert B. Neller; and a variety of other documents. Two good published accounts are "Attack on the DNTT Station" by Maj. Bron N. Madrigan (*Marine Corps Gazette*, April 1990) and "Marines Fight in Panama" by Tom Barlett (*Leatherneck*, February 1990). Danny J. Crawford presents an overview of the Marines' story on the Isthmus in "Corps Has Long History of Protecting American Interests in Panama" (*Marines*, March 1990).

Part X
The Nineties 1990–

Until now, the histories of the Marine Corps have all been written by Marines or former Marines. The 1875 *History of the United States Marine Corps* by M. Almy Aldrich was edited on the Corps' centennial from official reports and documents and a draft written by Capt. Richard S. Collum. It is most valuable for its Register of Officers 1798–1875. Collum himself wrote another version, *The History of the United States Marine Corps*, in 1890, which was updated in 1903.

Maj. Edwin N. McClellan compiled an extensive, unfinished history of the Corps' early years in the 1920s and 1930s. Never published, it can be found in mimeograph and microfilm form at the Marine Corps History Division and the New York Public Library. *One Hundred Eighty Landings of United States Marines 1800–1934* by Capt. Harry A. Ellsworth was mimeographed in 1934 and published as a Marine Corps monograph in 1974.

The first standard modern history, *A History of the United States Marine Corps* by Col. Clyde H. Metcalf (1939), is thorough but pedestrian. *The Compact History of the Marine Corps* by Lt. Cols. Philip N. Pierce and Frank O. Hough was published in 1960. Extremely readable though ardently partisan is Col. Robert D. Heinl, Jr.'s, excellent *Soldiers of the Sea* (1962). Capt. William [Bill] D. Parker wrote the official *A Concise History of the United States Marine Corps 1775–1969* (1970). The professional *The United States Marines* by Brig. Gen. Edwin H. Simmons was published in Great Britain in 1974 and in the United States in 1976, while Simmons was Director of Marine Corps History and Museums. Professor Allan R. Millett of Ohio State University and a reserve Marine officer wrote an institutional history of the Corps titled *Semper Fidelis: The History of the United States Marine Corps* (1980, revised 1991). The Marine Corps History and Museums Division has developed over a span of years a series of chronologically arranged pamphlets entitled *A Chronology of the United States Marine Corps* through June 1970.

The Corps' mission and development are usefully traced in two official monographs: *Progress and Purpose: A Developmental History of the U.S. Marine Corps 1900–1970* by Lt. Col. Kenneth J. Clifford (1973) and *A History of Marine Corps Roles and Missions 1775–1962* by Col. Thomas G. Roe, Maj. Ernest H. Giusti, Maj. John H. Johnstone and Benis M. Frank (1962).

Over the years, the Marine Corps has produced a host of monographs, unit histories and other historical reference pamphlets. Many of these are invaluable for those with special areas of interest. A complete list of these publications can be obtained from the History and Museums Division of Marine Corps Headquarters.

A reference book of inestimable value for anyone interested in the major awards won by individual Marines and much other Marine Corps lore is *Heroes: U.S. Marine Corps 1861–1955,* published by Jane Blakeney (1957). The Corps' History and Museums Division has also prepared and reproduced a Reference Information Pamphlet of all Marine Corps recipients of the Medal of Honor (1974). And the U.S. Government Printing Office has published for the U.S. Senate Committee on Veterans' Affairs *Medal of Honor Recipients 1863–1973* (1973). This work covers all the services and therefore includes the Navy corpsmen, chaplains and other personnel who served with the Marines.

Historians' detailed analysis of the Persian Gulf war of 1990–91 will develop methodically, but the most significant points are already clear. Understanding the war's impact and ramifications, of course, will require the perspective of time. The Marine Corps Historical and Museums Division has under way several volumes about the Corps' largest operation ever. They will be enhanced because Brig. Gen. Edwin H. Simmons, Director of Marine Corps History, sent historians to Desert Shield and Desert Storm. On the scene, Marine Reserve officers Col. Charles J. Quilter II and Lt. Cols. Ronald J. Brown, Charles H. Cureton,

Dennis P. Mroczkowski and Frank V. Sturgeon collected the story of the Persian Gulf war.

Several basic documents will be helpful to anyone looking more closely at these events. In the files of the Marine Corps Historical Center is a clarifying paper: "Persian Gulf Campaign: U.S. Marine Corps Operations, Command Brief" by Lt. Gen. Walter E. Boomer, Commanding General, U.S. Marine Forces, Central Command. (It was declassified from Secret 6/22/91.) Brig. Gen. Simmons authored two superb early interpretative chronologies of Desert Shield and Desert Storm in the May 1991 issue of the *U.S. Naval Institute Proceedings.* They are titled "Getting Marines to the Gulf" and "Getting the Job Done."

Other articles that focus on the Marines in the Gulf war include interviews with seven key Marine Corps generals of the war in the November 1991 issue of the *U.S. Naval Institute Proceedings;* "U.S. Marines in Operation Desert Storm" by Col. John R. Pope (*Marine Corps Gazette,* July 1991); and articles about the role of the 3rd Marines by their commander, Brig. Gen. John H. Admire, in the *Marine Corps Gazette,* August and September 1991. Sgt. Robert C. Jenks, the editor of *Brown Side Out,* the newspaper of the I Marine Expeditionary Force, wrote an expert and dramatic account of the small-unit recon action of C Company, 2d Light Armored Infantry Battalion in the March 20, 1991, issue. Lt. Col. Ronald J. Brown, Deputy Command Historian of I MEF during Desert Storm, wrote "The Battle of the Emir's Farm," a useful, unpublished article untangling the complexities of the Marines' largest fight. Commander Tom Delery, USN, wrote "Away, the Boarding Party" in the May 1991 issue of the *U.S. Naval Institute Proceedings.*

Three early books are *Thunder in the Desert: The Strategy and Tactics of the Persian Gulf War* by Maj. James Blackwell, USA, Ret. (1991); *In the Eye of the Storm* by Roger Cohen and Caludio Gatti (1991); and *Saddam Hussein and the Crisis in the Gulf* by Judith Miller and Laurie Mylroie (1990).

The Marines' efforts to rescue endangered civilians of many nations in Liberia and Somalia in 1990 and 1991 are described in the files of the Marine Corps Historical Center and in a few professional articles, especially: on Liberia, "Operation Sharp Edge" by Lt. Col. T. W. Parker in the May 1991 issue of the *U.S. Naval Institute Proceedings* and "Operation Sharp Edge" by Lt. Col. Glen R. Sachtleben in the November 1991 issue of the *Marine Corps Gazette;* on Somalia, "Night Mission to Mogadishu" by R. R. Keane in *Leatherneck,* March 1991, and "Escape from Mogadishu" by Ambassador James K. Bishop in the *Foreign Service Journal,* March 1991. The 1991 Bangladesh disaster relief operation is reported in "Operation Sea Angel" by Col. Donald R. Selvage in the November 1991 issue of the *Marine Corps Gazette.*

The best source on women in the Marine Corps is *A History of the Women Marines, 1946–1977* by Col. Mary V. Stremlow, published by the Marine Corps in 1986. It is clear and detailed but does not cover the important events of World Wars I and II or the more recent period, during which women Marines have continued to expand their role in the Corps.

A unique and useful book is the pocket-size field guide *Field Order of Battle Handbook,* published by the 11th Special Forces Group (Airborne), U.S. Army Reserve, Fort Meade, Maryland, May 1989.

Acknowledgments

During the many years since the 1956 Ribbon Creek tragedy first involved me in the U.S. Marine Corps' story, many people have helped me to know and understand the Corps, its past and its present, and to turn my ideas and manuscript into this book.

The accuracy of the facts and the validity of the opinions presented here are totally my own responsibility. Although Marine Corps historians have willingly and thoroughly read the entire manuscript for accuracy, any errors that remain are mine, not theirs.

I want to thank the Marine Corps itself and a great many Marines for the cooperation and helpfulness I received. They have opened their records and made themselves available for interviews unhesitatingly. No effort was ever made by Marines to limit my access to unclassified material, to hide the warts or to attempt to censor either facts or opinions. As I have discovered again and again in reporting and researching, those closest to a story are usually the most candid about it. This is certainly true of the Marine Corps leadership I have come to know over these years. And I have received the personal encouragement of a number of Commandants, most notably Generals Pate, Shoup, Greene, Wilson, Barrow, Kelley and Gray.

Since much of the early research was done during the years I worked for *Look* magazine, the book would never have been written without the support of William B. Arthur, the late Daniel D. Mich and the late Gardner Cowles, who published a magazine on which reporters were allowed to report precisely what they found. On *Look* also, photographer James Hansen made many trips with me around the globe, including visits to Vietnam, Korea and Cuba, and Robert Lerner photographed my first Marine Corps article in 1957.

At the McGraw-Hill Book Company, I want particularly to thank Frederic W. Hills, Mrs. Lou Ashworth, Tim McGinnis, Lisa Frost and the late Albert R. Leventhal for their good judgment and help. Lucia Staniels lent her professional skills to keeping this book alive when McGraw-Hill gave up all general book publishing.

For their special contributions, I want to thank George Buctel, who created the map section; Devorah Cohen, who did the extensive picture research; Stan Harvey, editing manager; art director Robert Mitchell; designer Jules Perlmutter; production supervisor Erna Helwig; and Doris Moskin, who shared the book's early years and prepared most of the initial source notes. Gail Russell Job and Vivien Lyons helped with skill and personal interest over many years. Benis M. Frank prepared the index.

I want to express particular appreciation to the late Phyllis Jackson, who persevered as my counselor and agent; to Don Congdon, who replaced her so ably and has allowed me to share his wisdom ever since 1977; to Robert L. Bernstein, who reinforced my original idea; to Mark, David and Nancy Moskin, who contributed in many caring ways; and to Lynn C. Goldberg, who has talked loving sense to me for the past decade.

For their help, encouragement and guidance in their fields of expertise, I would like to thank A. Doak Barnett, the late Bennett Cerf, the late Maj. Gen. Robert N. Ginsburgh, USAF, Martin Goldman, the late Henry Hillman, Donald W. Klein, Myrick Land, John and Janet Marqusee, the late Paula Mattlin,

ACKNOWLEDGMENTS

Gladys McPartland, Anton O. Myrer, the late Col. Donald R. Nugent, the late Michael O'Quinlivan, Brig. Gen. Hamilton D. South, Col. John H. Shotwell, the late Col. Richard S. Stark, and Woodrow Wirsig. Marcus Jaffe made available to me his letters as a young Marine in World War II, and David Douglas Duncan generously permitted me to include some of his magnificent pictures of Marines in combat.

Among the many Marine Corps historians who have helped with professionalism and enthusiasm, foremost has been Brig. Gen. Edwin H. Simmons, Director of Marine Corps History and Museums. I respect his professionalism and achievements as an historian and as a Marine. My appreciation also to Col. Herbert M. Hart, Henry I. Shaw, Jr., Col. F. Brooke Nihart, Lt. Col. Russell B. Tiffany and Dr. Graham A. Cosmas, Ralph W. Donnelly, Benis M. Frank, Roland P. Gill, Dr. Martin K. Gordon, Gabrielle M. Neufeld, Col. David A. Quinlan, Lt. Col. Lane Rogers, Jack Shulimson and Charles R. Smith.

For their help and guidance with this edition, I want to thank Marine historians Lt. Col. Ronald J. Brown, Lt. Col. Charles H. Cureton and Lt. Col. Dennis P. Mroczkowski, as well as Gen. Alfred M. Gray, Jr., Col. John H. Shotwell, Lt. Col. Eugene Brindle, Ann Ferrante, Robert V. Aquilina, Maj. Karen Heck, Col. John E. Rhodes and Gunnery Sgt. Paul Earle. With this and each earlier edition, Danny J. Crawford has been invaluably helpful. Cartographer George Ward made the maps on the Persian Gulf war. I am grateful to Little, Brown and Company for keeping this book updated and in print; and at Little, Brown, my thanks go especially to Catherine Crawford.

In addition to the library and archives of the Marine Corps Historical Division, research was done with the help of the National Archives, the Library of Congress, the New York Public Library, the Widener Library of Harvard University, the New York Society Library, the Newberry Library, the Chicago Public Library, the University of Chicago Library, the Harvard Club of New York City Library, the Scarsdale (New York) Public Library and the British Information Services Library in New York.

Index

878

895

About the Author

J. Robert Moskin is an award-winning historian and journalist. Formerly the Foreign Editor and member of the Editorial Board of *Look* Magazine, he has reported from around the world, including Moscow, Berlin, Warsaw, Jerusalem, Manila, Guantanamo, Seoul, Da Nang and Hanoi. He has written extensively about military and foreign affairs here and abroad. His reporting has received awards from the Overseas Press Club, the National Headliners Club, the Newspaper Guild of New York and the Sidney Hillman Foundation. A contributor to many magazines, he has written several books, including *Among Lions, The Battle for Jerusalem, June 5–7, 1967; Morality in America; Turncoat;* and *The Decline of the American Male* (co-author). He holds degrees in American history from Harvard and Columbia universities and during World War II served with the U.S. Army in the Southwest Pacific. Mr. Moskin has researched the four editions of this book over more than thirty years. In addition to studying thousands of documents in archives and libraries, he interviewed numerous Marines at Headquarters, from coast to coast and overseas. He has received the Distinguished Service Award of the Marine Corps Combat Correspondents Association for this work, which has also been placed on the Commandant's Reading List.